Bill 'Swampy' Marsh is an award-winning writer/performer of stories, songs and plays. He spent most of his youth in rural south-western New South Wales. Bill was forced to give up any idea he had of a 'career' as a cricketer when a stint at agricultural college was curtailed because of illness, and so began his hobby of writing. After backpacking through three continents and working in the wine industry, his writing hobby blossomed into a career.

His first collection of short stories, *Beckom (Pop. 64)*, was published in 1988; his second, *Old Yanconian Daze*, in 1995; and his third, *Looking for Dad*, in 1998. During 1999, Bill released *Australia*, a CD of his songs and stories. That was followed in 2002 by *A Drover's Wife* and *Glory, Glory—A Tribute to the Royal Flying Doctor Service* in 2008. He has written soundtrack songs and music for the television documentaries, *The Last Mail from Birdsville—The Story of Tom Kruse*, *Source to Sea—The Story of the Murray Riverboats* and the German travel documentaries *Traumzeit auf dem Stuart Highway*, *RFDS Clinic Flights (Tilpa & Marble Bar)* plus *RFDS Clinic Flights (Einsatz von Port Hedland nach Marble Bar)*.

Bill runs writing workshops in schools and communities and is a teacher of short story writing within the Adelaide Institute of TAFE's Professional Writing Unit. He has won and judged many nationwide short story writing and songwriting competitions and short film awards.

Bill is the author of the very successful series of 'Great Australian' stories including: *Great Australian CWA Stories* (2011), *New Great Australian Flying Doctor Stories* (2010), *The ABC Book of Great Aussie Stories for Young People* (2010), *Great Australian Stories - Outback Towns and Pubs* (2009), *More Great Australian Flying Doctor Stories* (2007), *Great Australian Railway Stories* (2005), *Great Australian Droving Stories* (2003), *Great Australian Shearing Stories* (2001) and *Great Australian Flying Doctor Stories* (1999). Bill's story of *Goldie* was published in 2008. *Swampy*, a revised edition of Bill's first three books, *Beckom (Pop. 64)*, *Old Yanconian Daze* and *Looking for Dad*, was published in 2012.

The Complete Book of Australian Flying Doctor Stories is a compilation of three of Bill's previous books: *Great Australian Flying Doctor Stories* (1999), *More Great Australian Flying Doctor Stories* (2007) and *New Great Australian Flying Doctor Stories* (2010).

More information about the author can be found at
www.billswampymarsh.com

THE COMPLETE BOOK OF
AUSTRALIAN
FLYING
DOCTOR
STORIES

THE COMPLETE BOOK OF
AUSTRALIAN
FLYING
DOCTOR
STORIES

BILL 'SWAMPY' MARSH

ABC
Books

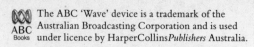 The ABC 'Wave' device is a trademark of the Australian Broadcasting Corporation and is used under licence by HarperCollins*Publishers* Australia.

First published in Australia in 2013
by HarperCollins*Publishers* Australia Pty Limited
ABN 36 009 913 517
harpercollins.com.au

This is a combined edition of three of Bill Marsh's previous books:
Great Australian Flying Doctor Stories (1999), *More Great Australian Flying Doctor Stories* (2007) (both first published by ABC Books for the Australian Broadcasting Corporation) and *New Great Australian Flying Doctor Stories* (2010).

HarperCollins*Publishers*
Level 13, 201 Elizabeth Street, Sydney NSW 2000, Australia
31 View Road, Glenfield, Auckland 0627, New Zealand
A 53, Sector 57, Noida, UP, India
77–85 Fulham Palace Road, London W6 8JB, United Kingdom
2 Bloor Street East, 20th floor, Toronto, Ontario M4W 1A8, Canada
10 East 53rd Street, New York NY 10022, USA

National Library of Australia Cataloguing-in-Publication data:

Marsh, Bill, 1950-
  The complete book of Australian Flying Doctor stories / Bill Marsh.
  978 0 7333 3214 2 (pbk.)
  978 1 7430 9926 1 (ebook)
  Royal Flying Doctor Service of Australia.
  Aeronautics in medicine—Australia.
  Country life—Australia—Anecdotes.
  Australia—Social life and customs.
362.1042570994

Cover design by Matt Stanton, HarperCollins Design Studio
Cover image: 'The Flying Doctor arrives by aeroplane' by Flynn, John, 1880–1951, National Library of Australia, an24721435
Author photo by Elizabeth Allnutt
Typeset in 10/14pt ITC Bookman Light by Kirby Jones
Printed and bound in Australia by Griffin Press
The papers used by HarperCollins in the manufacture of this book are a natural, recyclable product made from wood grown in sustainable plantation forests.
The fibre source and manufacturing processes meet recognised international environmental standards, and carry certification.

5 4 3 2 1   13 14 15 16

Contents

Book One
Great Australian Flying Doctor Stories

Special thanks to	2
Contributors	4
Foreword	5
A Cordial Invitation	7
A Day at the Races	13
A Mother's Love	18
A Piece o' Piss	20
A Stitch in Time	25
A Very Merry Christmas	28
An Egg a Day	30
And He Survived!	35
And the Winner is ...	38
And Then There Were Seven	41
As Full as a Boot	45
As Soft as Air	50
Born to Fly	54
Brainless	59
Break a Leg	62
Cried Duck	65
Dog's Dinner	67
Down the Pub ... Again	70
Fingers Off	72
From Bad to Worse	76
Great Break, Aye!	82
Gwen's Legacy	86
Handcuffed	88
Heaven	92
Kicking the Dust	94
Knickers	97
Love is ...	100
Mayday! Mayday!	102
Missing	105
Mission Impossible	108
Mud Happens	111
Night Eyes	116
No Thanks!	120
Off	123
Old Bill McDougall	127
Once Bitten, Twice Shy	132
One Shot	135
Pass the Hat	137
'Payback'	141
Peak Hour Traffic	147
Pepper Steak	150
Plonk	154
Rabbit	157
Richmond	161
Run and Catch	165
Skills and Teamwork	167
Snakes Alive!	170
Spot on Time	173
Squeaky the Stockman	176
Stowaway	180
The Pedal Radio Man	183
The Telegram	186
The Tooth Fairy	188
There's a Hole in the ... Drum	191
There's a Redback on the ...	195
Touch Wood	198
Train Hit by Man	201
We Built an Airport	206
Welcome to Kiwirrkurra	209
Where's Me Hat?	212
Whistle Up	215
Willing Hands	219
You Wouldn't Read About It	222

Book Two
More Great Australian Flying Doctor Stories

Acknowledgments	228	Over the Moon	403
Contributors	230	Porcupine	408
Introduction	231	Rabbit Flat	414
		Rissoles	418
My First Flight	237	Slim Dusty	420
A Committed Team	243	Slingshot	422
A Great Big Adventure	249	Small World, Large Bruise	424
A True Legend	261	Someone, Somewhere	430
A True Privilege	264	Statistics and Brief	
A Wife's Tale	267	History	435
Accident Prone	271	Sticks in the Mind	438
Amazing	276	Stories about the Flying	
Ashes	279	Doctor	442
Been Around, Done a Thing or		The Crook Cocky	444
Two	282	The Easter Bunny	448
Black 'n' Decker	286	The Flying Padre's Story	453
Blown Away	290	The Souvenir	461
Dirt to Dust	296	The Spirit of the Bush	465
Dobbed In	302	The Tangle with the Motor	
Emergency!	309	Bike	471
First Drive	311	Too Late	478
Gasping	316	Touched My Heart	483
Gone with the Wind	320	Tragedies	487
Got the Scours	326	Two in One	493
Hans from Germany	331	Two Lumps	498
Heroes out of Mere Mortals	335	Victorian Connections	502
How the Hell	342	Water, Water, Everywhere	
In the Footsteps of Flynn	350	But ...	508
In with the Luggage	354	Well Prepared	522
It's Alright Now	358	Where are You?	526
Just Day-to-Day Stuff	362	Wouldn't be Alive	530
Love is in the Air	367	Final Flight	538
Matchmakers	370		
Mystery Photograph	375		
Next to Buckley's	378		
Not a Happy Pilot	386		
Okay	390		
One Arm Point	394		
One Lucky Feller	398		

Book Three
New Great Australian Flying Doctor Stories

Contributors	550	One in a Trillion	722
		Pilatus PC 12	725
A Brief History	553	Preordained Destiny	729
A Short Little Story	569	Razor Blades and	
A Team Thing	572	Saucepans	736
Almost but not Quite	578	See Yer Later	740
Are You Sure?	582	Speared	742
Broken	585	Stroke	745
Burns	590	Stuck	749
Call the Doctor!	594	That's My Job	752
Camp Pie	597	The Normanton Bell	755
Captain 'Norty'	601	The 'Singing'	759
Coen	604	The Sweetest Sound	762
Dad	608	The Wrong People	765
Difficult Conditions	613	Things that Happened	769
Disappearing Flares	619	Through a Child's Eyes	777
Down the Lot	624	Too Close	779
Dr Clyde Fenton	628	Watch What You Say	783
From all Walks of Life	631	West of the Cooper	787
Gymkhanas	635	What If	791
Hats off	642	Glory, Glory—	
Heroes of the Outback	646	The Flying Doctor Song	796
I Was the Pilot	651	The RFDS Today	798
If Only	655	How You Can Help	800
In Double Quick Time	658		
In the ...	660		
In the Beginning	663		
In the Boot	668		
Injections	672		
Joe the Rainmaker	678		
Laura	685		
Lombadina	689		
Long Days, Great Times	693		
Looked like Hell	699		
Looking at the Stars	704		
Memories of Alice Springs	707		
News Flash	711		
Old Ways, New Ways	716		

GREAT AUSTRALIAN FLYING DOCTOR STORIES

Special thanks to

Lyn Shea for her ideas, support and enthusiasm

The Royal Flying Doctor Service and its
supportive staff

Ian Doyle, Broadcaster

Angela Faraj, Public Relations, RFDS (National)

The Broken Hill Outback Residencies Program

All those who so willingly shared their stories with me

To Margaret and James Holdsworth,
and Jarrod Bonnici

Contributors

Great Flying Doctor Stories is based on stories
told to Bill 'Swampy' Marsh by:

Joyce Anderson
Helen Austin
Bob Balmain
Joy Barton
Rosemary Chamberlain
Ben Dannecker
Maurie Denison
Ian Doyle
Jan Ende
Penny Ende
Brett Forrester
Anne Hindle
Campbell Holmes
Bob Irvine
Ray Jenner
Alf 'Bomber' Johnson
Verona Keen
Bill Legg
Geri Malone
Fred McKay
Marg McQuie
Lindsay Millar

Jack Mills
Mary Patricia Mitchell
Colin Munro
Liz Noonan-Ward
Fred Peter
Lorraine Rieck
Robert Ryan
Bruce Sanderson
Gabrielle Schaefer
Rob Seekamp
Chris Smith
Clyde Thomson
Audrey Tregoning
Penny Wilson
Maureen Woods
... and many others.

Foreword

Just after my last book came out I was having a cup of coffee with 'the lady down the road' (Lyn Shea). 'What're you going to write next?' she asked.

'I'm not sure,' I replied. 'Have you got any ideas?'

True to form, she had plenty, one of which was a collection of stories of the experiences people had with the Royal Flying Doctor Service.

And so began this book.

After receiving some funding from Arts SA I headed off to Broken Hill as part of a writer-in-residence program as well as to collect stories from a couple of friends of friends who worked out at the RFDS base. I was welcomed there, as I was at all the RFDS offices that I visited, with open arms and a swag of stories ready to be told.

'I'll knock this off in a couple of months,' I said.

But friends of friends have friends of their own and before long, whenever I mentioned that I was collecting Flying Doctor stories, someone would say, 'Oh, you've got to get in contact with so-and-so. They've got a great story to tell.' So I did, and after I collected their story they, in turn, would suggest someone else who had 'an even better story to tell'.

Then amongst all this story collecting I met a bloke, Ian Doyle, who was relieving on the ABC's Sunday morning radio program, Australia All Over, and he interviewed me about the project. The response was astounding. People rang from all over Australia, wanting to tell their story; unfortunately, more than there was space in this book for. I hope that, as time goes by, I get to meet many of the people I could only get to interview by telelphone.

The stories of the contributors' experiences with the Royal Flying Doctor Service and of their triumph against the odds have been an inspiration. So sit back, relax, and allow me to introduce you to some of Australia's unsung heroes and great characters ...

Bill 'Swampy' Marsh

A Cordial Invitation

I reckon it must have been back in about 1960 or
'61, whichever year it was that copped the worst of
the floods. There was this bloke, Harry, who was the
Head Stockman out on Durham Downs Station. A very
knowledgeable bushman he was too. Anyway, Harry
and his team of stockmen had been out mustering,
day in, day out, for three months straight, in woeful
conditions, so when they were given a week off they
decided to exercise their bushman's rite and go into
Noccundra to let off a little steam in at the pub there.

'Let's get the hell outa here,' Harry called to his
stockmen as they clambered up on top of the two-
wheeled camp trailer, cashed up and ready to go.

Now I don't know if you've ever seen one of these
camp trailers but they're massive bloody things, and
they have to be. Because when you're out mustering
for months on end they carry the whole kit-and-
caboodle—all the food, the cooking gear, the swags,
water, fuel, toolboxes, the lot. They're like a bloody
huge mobile kitchen cum garage, and they've got these
gigantic truck tyres on them, so huge that you'd almost
have to be Sir Edmund Hillary to climb up on the tray.

To complete the picture for you, this particular
camp trailer was pulled by a Deutz tractor which was
driven by the camp cook, an Afghan bloke who had
extremely dark skin, so dark, in fact, they reckoned
that the only thing you could see of him in the dead
of the night was the whites of his eyes. That's when

he wasn't sleeping, of course, or praying, which was something he did quite regularly, being the extremely devout Muslim that he was. This bloke's name was Frozella, Frozella the Afghan cook.

So off this mob of stockmen went through flooded creeks, rivers and tracks and, when Frozella finally pulled into Noccundra, Harry and his workmates went straight to the pub. And that's where they spent the entire week, in the pub, except for one very important trip which Harry made. That was to the local store to buy a bottle of raspberry cordial. The reason behind that was on their return journey they were going past an outstation on Durham Downs. And on this outstation there was a man and his wife and their three or four children and Harry had solemnly promised these youngsters that he'd bring them back a bottle of raspberry cordial, for a special treat.

As you might imagine, during that week in at the Noccundra pub, a lot of fun was had. A lot of alcohol was consumed too, which led to the usual number of stoushes. But no harm done. Anyway by the time they set off back to Durham Downs, Harry and his team were so knackered from their week's activities that not long after they'd crawled up on the camp trailer, to a man they'd fallen into a deep alcohol-induced sleep. And there, draped right up on top of the load, was Harry, snug and snoring under his military overcoat, and stuffed into one of the pockets of that coat was the precious bottle of raspberry cordial.

So there they were, in the dead of the night, a few hours out from Noccundra when they hit a bump. Off came Harry. Down from a great height he fell. And when he hit the ground he was not only knocked out cold from the impact but also the bottle burst and raspberry cordial went all over him. Now, none of the stockmen realised that their boss had disappeared. Neither did Frozella. He kept on chatting away to Allah while negotiating the tractor along the muddy tracks until he reached the boundary gate.

It was while he was at the gate that Frozella did a number count and discovered that Harry had gone missing. Now the little Afghan realised that his life wouldn't be worth living if he arrived back at Durham Downs minus his boss. So with the other blokes still fast asleep, he turned the camp trailer around and drove back in search of the Head Stockman. He'd travelled about twenty miles when there, illuminated by the mud-splattered glow of the tractor lights, Frozella saw Harry laying spread-eagled on the ground, covered in red gooey stuff.

So shocked at the scene was Frozella that he sat glued to the seat of the Deutz tractor. 'Oh Allah, oh Allah,' he prayed from the safe distance, hoping for a miracle and that suddenly Harry would arise and walk. But he didn't. Harry didn't even move a muscle. This caused Frozella to conclude that Allah had instigated the accident as a punishment for all his sins. Sins that kept multiplying in Frozella's brain the longer he looked down at Harry, lying prostrate in front of the tractor.

Then the panic really set in. Without bothering to check the body, Frozella turned the camp trailer around again and raced to Kihee Station. It was there that he told the station owner's wife, Mrs O'Shea, all about his sins, and how Allah had caused Harry to fall off the camp trailer, and about how the camp trailer had run over the Head Stockman.

'Oh Missus, blood everywhere,' Frozella kept mumbling. 'Blood everywhere.'

So Mrs O'Shea contacted the Flying Doctor.

The doctor in this case was the legendary Irishman Tim O'Leary. And Tim at that particular time was attending an extremely ill patient in at Thargomindah. So when Tim got word that the Head Stockman had been run over by a camp trailer, he organised for his patient to be flown back to the Charleville Hospital so that he could go straight out to Kihee Station and see to things there. The problem being, that because of all the flooding there was a lack of suitable transport in Thargomindah.

'I'll have a go at taking yer out in me little Hillman,' the husband of the nursing sister said.

'What we need is a tractor,' suggested Tim.

'It's the best I can do,' replied the bloke.

'Okay then,' Tim said, 'we'll give it a go.'

So they jumped into the little Hillman and set off on a nightmare journey through the mud and the slush. When they weren't getting bogged, they were pushing themselves out of bogs. And whenever they came to a swollen creek they placed a tarpaulin over the radiator so that the car's engine wouldn't stall, midstream, where the chances were that they'd be washed away, never to be seen again.

Now, while the Hillman was battling its way up the track, Jack O'Shea arrived home at Kihee Station homestead and listened to Frozella's story.

'Has anyone else seen to the bloke?' Jack asked, which of course they hadn't.

So Jack spat out a few choice words then drove off in search of Harry. A couple of hours later he came across him. There Harry was, much to Jack's amazement, sitting up beside a camp fire, attempting to dry his overcoat, the one that had been soaked in raspberry cordial.

'Good God man,' Jack said, 'yer supposed to be at death's door.'

'Yer must be jokin',' Harry replied. 'There's nothin' wrong with me that a couple of Bex and a good lie down couldn't fix.'

So Jack took Harry back to Kihee and Mrs O'Shea rang through to Nockatunga Station, where the little Hillman had just chugged up the drive.

'Look doctor,' Mrs O'Shea explained, 'Frozella's made a terrible mistake. In actual fact, the Head Stockman's got nothing more than a headache.'

After having just spent five and a half hours driving through hell and high water, in a tiny Hillman, then to be told that he'd been called out on a wild goose chase, well, it didn't go down too well with the irate Irish doctor.

'Let it be known, Mrs O'Shea,' Tim replied, 'that if ever this Frozella chap gets ill and I have to pick him up in an aeroplane, as sure as I stand here, drenched to the bone and caked in mud, I'm gonna toss him out and, what's more, from a great bloody height!'

Now news travels fast in the bush and when Frozella heard what Tim had said, he started believing that the sparing of the Head Stockman had just been a warning from Allah, and the greater punishment of being tossed out of a plane from a great height was awaiting him. Amazingly, the little Afghan didn't have a sick day for a number of years after that, not one. That was until the time he came down with pneumonia. Real crook he was. And even then he refused to see Tim O'Leary, the Flying Doctor.

'He's a gonna kill me, Missus. Allah has foretold it,' a delirious Frozella kept muttering to Mrs Corliss who was looking after him in at the Eromanga pub.

But eventually Frozella fell so ill that Mrs Corliss had to call Tim. And when he arrived in the plane, she pulled the doctor aside. 'Look, Tim,' she said, 'Frozella's locked himself in his room and refuses to let you see him.'

Now Tim had long ago forgotten the veiled threat that he'd made about tossing Frozella out of the plane from a great height. But Frozella hadn't. Not on your life. So much so that Tim had to force his way into Frozella's darkened hotel room. And when he did, the little Afghan wasn't anywhere to be seen.

Then, as Tim tells it, as he was about to leave the room he heard the faint mutter of prayers coming from under the bed. When he took a look, he saw the whites of two huge eyes, staring back at him, agape with fear.

A Day at the Races

The William Creek Races has to be the best kept secret in Australia. It's a real true-blue bush event. Seriously good fun with a dash of alcohol. What's more, it's a great fundraiser for the Royal Flying Doctor Service, held on the first weekend in April at Anna Creek Station, about eleven hours north of Adelaide.

The scene is, 'You bring your swags, we've got the nags.' That's because all the horses and camels are provided by Anna Creek Station. Along with the races it's a gymkhana affair. No bookies allowed. There's the Dick Nunn Memorial Cup, the William Creek Cup, plus all the gymkhana events—thread the needle, barrel races, and so on.

Community Service Groups, along with other volunteers, come from all over to donate their time and energy into helping put the weekend on. Ten dollars a day allows you to eat as much as you can. And when I say 'as much as you can', I mean it that way. Because if you can get it down your throat without choking, then you can eat as much as you like.

Because, I tell you what, some of that beef's bloody tough. Again, it's all donated and mainly from the next-door neighbour's property, I might add. It's cheaper that way. Why donate your own when it's just as easy to donate the bloke-next-door's? But that's the way it is out there. Things are tight. So tight, in fact, rumour has it that the only thing a local will give you is a handshake and a homing pigeon. But, mind you, they're pretty amazing when it comes to the Royal Flying Doctor Service. That's a different matter.

The big day is the Sunday. Before then, the horses and camels are put up for auction and everyone spends up big trying to buy something that might win one of the fifteen to twenty events for the day. Up for grabs are prizes and ribbons. The owners of the winning horse or camel are supposed to keep the prizes and the jockeys the ribbons but it usually happens the other way around. The jockeys in this case are mostly station people, jackaroos and jillaroos, or anyone who can sling a leg over a horse or camel.

And these young riders don't hold back. Not on your life. They go as hard as they can, so hard in fact that they sometimes get injured. So you're up there raising money for the Royal Flying Doctor Service and you have to get the Royal Flying Doctor Service to fly up to collect these people. The airstrip's graded, flares set up, kerosene tins alight, so the plane can land at night and take someone who's injured back to Port Augusta.

I remember the time in particular when one young stockman came a real cropper. The horse shied just past the finishing post. Down come this bloke. Thump. He hit the ground like a bucket of spuds and just laid there. Motionless he was. For about five or ten minutes he didn't move a muscle and things looked real crook.

'Where's the doctor?' the cry went up.

Being a Royal Flying Doctor Service event there were plenty of doctors about but they'd all had a beer or two or three by that stage and the last thing they wanted was to face headlines reading 'Drunken Doctor Attends to Injured Rider'. So all these doctors gathered around the injured stockman. Cumulatively, well over a couple of hundred years of medical expertise was then proffered. 'Don't move him,' said one. 'Get a stretcher,' suggested someone else. 'Check his pulse,' came a voice. 'Is his windpipe clear?' another asked. 'At least get an umbrella over the bloke or he'll fry in this heat,' suggested yet another doctor. 'We'll have to get the RFDS up,' said another. 'Good idea,' half agreed. 'I don't know so much,' the other half said. 'There must be something we can do.'

It was while this verbal medical consultation was taking place that the young stockman's workmate, a big bloke he was, staggered out of the bar. 'Where's me mate Clancy?' he asked, to which someone pointed over to the gaggle of doctors standing around a prostrate figure.

So this bloke came in search of his mate. He walked over, pushed the medicos aside, took a look at his mate, and shouted 'Get off yer big fat arse, Clancy, yer nothin' but a lazy bastard.' But still Clancy didn't move. So this bloke gave him a swift boot in the bum. Thwack. In response, Clancy gave a couple of twists, woke up, got to his feet, dusted himself off, then he and his mate staggered back to the bar, arm in arm, leaving the gathering of doctors to marvel at the effectiveness of simple bush medical treatment.

Then there's the story about Phantom and his Pommie bride, Alison Tucker. How that came about was that Alison had been hitch-hiking around Australia when she ended up at the William Creek pub. Don't ask me why. It could have been fate because it was there that Phantom, the manager of Hamilton Station, caught her eye, wooed her, won her, and six months later they got married at the finish post during the William Creek Races.

A big ado that was, the full ceremony, the whole shooting match. Father Tony Redden from Coober Pedy got special permission to carry out the wedding. The William Creek Race organising committee programmed the event between the fourteenth and fifteenth race or something. Everyone was invited to attend.

Phantom called on his two best mates to be his best men, so you wouldn't reckon that there were too many secrets there. They'd all been knocking around together for years. Anyhow, when the moment arrived the three of them appeared at the top of the straight like gunslingers, dressed in black Stetsons, full black tails, waistcoats, fob watches, new RM Williams boots and cigars, the lot. It looked like something out of Gunfight at the OK Corral, especially when the wind picked up from the south-east.

As these blokes strode down the straight, everyone fell silent. You could even hear the pig sizzling away on a spit out the back. It'd been donated, a wedding gift, no doubt one of the bloke-next-door's pigs. Then as the male wedding party neared the finish post the bride and her bridesmaids arrived on the track in a Peugeot driven by the then head of the Flying Doctor Service from Port Augusta, Vin O'Brien. It was daubed with ribbons. Immaculate, it was.

Alison, who'd dressed in the William Creek pub, stepped from the Peugeot, out into the dirt, dust and flies. She looked stunning: an absolute peachy English bride, wearing a full-length wedding outfit with a parasol to boot.

Seeing as Phantom was a pretty popular bloke around the area, the ceremony had been organised to go over the loudspeaker system. So when Phantom and his mates reached the bride and bridesmaids, Father Tony stepped to the microphone and began the ceremony. Everything was going well until the Father got to the part where he read out their names ... 'Do you Mark Spears take Alison Tucker to be your lawfully wedded wife?' he said.

At that point the service ground to a halt. There was a gasp from the outer audience. Phantom went a bright red. The bride went white with shock.

The wind dropped. The flies ceased flying. The bridesmaids turned to each other with questioning looks. The bride did the same at her bridesmaids. The bridesmaids looked questioningly at Phantom's best men. They gave a shrug. They didn't have a clue. Then everyone turned to the groom.

In his embarrassed state, Phantom leaned over to the Father. 'Excuse me, Father,' he said, 'but no one around here knows me by that name.'

'Not even the bride?' enquired Father Tony.

'Nope. Especially not the bride.'

Then Father Tony, always the professional, took up from where he left off and he said ... 'Mark Spears, who'll be from here on known as Phantom, do you take Alison Tucker as your lawfully wedded wife?'

'Yep,' said Phantom.

'Yep, I do,' said Alison.

Then, apart from the odd smirk or two from his mates and a bit of ribbing from the outer, the remainder of the ceremony went off like a dream.

A Mother's Love

Like I said, in the days before the Royal Flying Doctor Service was set up here in Tasmania, back in about 1960, basically the only aircraft that were available for evacuations from the Bass Strait islands and other remote areas were aircraft owned by the state's two major Aero Clubs. Those clubs were the Tasmanian Aero Club, which was based at Launceston, and the Aero Club of Southern Tasmania, based at Hobart.

Now I wasn't ever a commercial pilot and I've never flown for the Flying Doctor Service, as such. I was just a private pilot who flew out of our local Launceston club back in those early days. The aircraft we were using at the time was the single-engine Auster J5 Autocar, which was a small four-seater fabric aircraft.

But the most heart-wrenching trip I ever made was after a couple of children had been severely burnt, out on one of the islands. These kids got inside a car and were playing with matches or whatever. There they were, mucking about, when the vehicle exploded in flames, leaving them trapped inside. So we got the call during the night and I think it might've been Reg Munro, our Chief Flying Instructor, who flew out and brought the children back to the Launceston Hospital.

Anyway, the following day I went over to the island to pick up the children's mother. Now just before I took off I heard that one of the kids had died. The problem was that, when I picked the mother up, it was obvious that she hadn't yet been informed about the death. To remind you, I was just doing the job as a private pilot through the Aero Club so it wasn't really up to me to inform her that her son had just passed away.

But, God, I felt for that poor woman.

I reckon that there'd be nothing worse than to lose one of your own children, especially one as young as that little feller was. So there I was flying this woman back to Launceston, knowing that her child had just died, and knowing that she hadn't yet been told about the death. And there she was sitting in the plane with me, full of a mother's concern, full of a mother's hope, full of a mother's love.

A Piece o' Piss

I wasn't working at the time so the only company I had at home, apart from the kids that is, was a little transistor radio. Now in saying that, there wasn't much to listen to around Broome in those days, other than Radio Australia. So what I used to do was to tune into the Royal Flying Doctor base and listen to all the telegrams, and the gossip, and in particular to the medical schedules.

The reason why I kept such a close ear out for the medical schedules was that my husband, Tony, was the Flying Doctor, and by listening in on the tranny I was able to find out when, and if, Tony was coming home. Now that might sound like a strange way of going about things but quite often he got so caught up in what he was doing that he didn't have the time to give me a ring. I mean, he might go out to a station to attend some emergency or other during the morning and end up in Perth later that night, and what's more have to stay there for a couple of days or more. You just didn't know what was going to happen. But that's how the life of a Flying Doctor was, and we adjusted to it.

A prime example was the time the RFDS pilot Jan Ende flew over from the Derby base with the Flight Sister, Rhonda, to pick up Tony and go out on routine clinics around the area. They'd had a very quiet morning and Jan was flying the plane back to Broome to drop Tony off before heading back to Derby. Anyway, I was listening in on my tranny when I heard an emergency call come through. A major car accident had occurred between Fitzroy Crossing and Halls Creek.

As it turned out, what had happened was that two elderly couples were travelling in opposite directions, one coming from Darwin, the other going to Darwin. There were four or five people involved altogether. I can't remember exactly. The road wasn't in the best of conditions, which was something that I knew for a fact because Tony and I had recently travelled over that stretch and we'd smashed the cross member of our vehicle. That's how rough it was. It was dirt, of course, corrugated, with lots of potholes and bulldust.

Anyway, one of the cars had been stuck behind a road train for a fair distance. Then when they reached the only straight stretch between Fitzroy Crossing and Halls Creek the driver thought, 'Well, it's now or never.' He put his headlights on, pulled out to overtake the road train and, wham, drove straight into an oncoming car.

Of course, with so much dust about, the truck driver didn't even notice what had happened and he continued on his way. It was only when a couple of blokes from the Department of Main Roads came along that the accident was discovered. Now, luckily, there was a radio in the Main Roads vehicle and that's when the Flying Doctor base at Derby was alerted.

So there I was, sitting in Broome listening to this drama unfolding over my tranny. I could hear the base talking. I could hear Jan and Tony in the plane. The manager from Christmas Creek Station had also arrived at the scene and I could hear him talking. They were all in contact.

It was a chilling experience, I can tell you. But the thing that I was most concerned about was just how Jan thought he was going to put the plane down on that rough and relatively short stretch of road. What's more, the plane he was flying was a Queen Air, and a Queen Air needed about 3000 feet of straight strip to land and take off.

So I was getting quite worried listening to all this drama. Terribly worried, to be honest. So much so that it eventually got the better of me, and that's when I rang Jan's wife, Penny, who was a flight nurse sister back at the base, to see how she was bearing up.

'Well,' she said, as cool as a cucumber, 'there's nothing I can do about it. The best we can do is just hope.'

By that stage, some details had been radioed through about the condition of the accident victims and Jan flew the Queen Air on to Broome so that Tony could pick up whatever medical supplies he thought might be required. Meanwhile, the manager from Christmas Creek Station and the Main Roads people had blocked the ends of the straight section of road and, as vehicles were forced to stop, they got the people out to help knock down ant hills and clear the stones off the road in preparation for the plane to land.

So Tony picked up the medical supplies from Broome and they flew out to the accident scene. When they arrived Jan did a low pass-over, to check the situation out. Things didn't look good. One of the vehicles had its engine smashed back into the driver's compartment. The other wasn't much better off. What's more, the road looked a bit iffy for landing on account of both its condition and its lack of length.

Anyway, even though Jan had to negotiate some short shrubbery on his way in, he still managed to put the plane down safely. Then Tony and Rhonda set to and attended the injured. And they did a wonderful job. They really did. Especially given the conditions—the heat, the dust, the flies—and taking into account that a couple of hours had passed since the accident had occurred. And under all those external pressures they didn't miss a diagnosis: fractured hips and fractured ribs, dislocations, punctured lungs, the lot. Of course, that's excluding the usual head and body injuries and so forth that go with such a horrific collision. What's more, all the accident victims survived.

But there was still one major hurdle to overcome. With so many people being injured, there was no possible way that they could fly everyone out in the Queen Air. Now, as luck would have it, the Army was conducting manoeuvres in the area and they had a Pilatus aircraft. Now the Pilatus is just a small thing so it could only evacuate two of the injured, three at a pinch. But it had one great advantage over the Queen Air in that it was a short landing/take-off plane which made it ideal for those sorts of conditions.

By the time the Pilatus arrived, about half an hour later, Tony and Rhonda had all the patients organised and ready to be flown out. Then, lo and behold, who should jump off the army plane, none other than one of Tony's old mates from his medical student days. But this was no time for grand reunions, not on your life. It was a quick handshake, a hello, then they got stuck into loading the patients into both the planes.

Now, as I said, the Pilatus was a short landing/take-off aircraft so it got out with no problem at all.

Now came the scary bit. The Queen Air had needed every inch of the road-strip to land and, with the extra weight of the patients, things looked grim. As Jan prepared for take-off he calculated that he needed to reach a speed of at least 90 knots just to get the thing off the ground.

'Here we go,' Jan said to Tony.

Then he gunned it, and they went thundering down the road. The trouble was that by the time he got to 70 knots they were rapidly running out of straight road.

'Jan,' Tony asked, 'do you reckon we'll make it?'

'A piece o' piss,' replied Jan.

But Tony reckoned that Jan wasn't looking anywhere near as confident as he sounded. He'd gone a fearful whitish-grey colour. His face had set like concrete. He was sweating profusely, and his eyes had taken on a fixed glassy stare.

'Go, you bastard, go!' Jan called, and gunned that Queen Air like it'd never been gunned before.

At 75 knots Tony knew that they were done for. At 85 knots they'd run out of road. That's when Tony ducked for cover. Then as Jan attempted to lift the plane off the ground there came the horrible crunching sound of the propellers cutting the low shrubbery to shreds.

The next Tony knew, they were in the air.

'There,' called Jan. 'I told you so. A piece o' piss.'

A Stitch in Time

We were up at Mintabie one time, Mintabie being a small opal-mining town in the far north of South Australia. Anyway, we'd just finished doing a clinic there and we were about to pile into the car to go out to the airstrip when this ute came hurtling down the road.

'Oh, my God, something terrible's happened,' I mumbled.

'Obviously some disaster or other,' replied the doctor.

Anyway, somewhere among a cloud of dust and spitting gravel the ute skidded to a halt beside us, and out from the ute jumped this bloke. He was in a blind panic, we could see that, and he starts calling, 'You've gotta help me, doc. There's been a huge fight, an' Igor's had his chest cut open. There's blood an' guts everywhere.'

'Okay,' said the doctor. 'So where's Igor?'

'I brung him along,' this bloke replied, rushing around to the back of his vehicle. 'Here he is, right here in the back o' me ute.'

So we grabbed our medical gear and shot around to where the bloke was standing and there was Igor, all sprawled out on the floor, blood everywhere, his guts hanging out, just like the bloke had said.

'Oh, my God!' I gasped.

But it wasn't so much the sight of the blood and guts that made me gasp. What really did it was the mere sight of Igor himself. Because Igor turned out to be a dog. What's more, he wasn't your normal sort of average household mutt. Not on your life. Igor was absolutely huge, massive even, and without a doubt he was most surely the ugliest thing that'd ever been born into the dog kingdom.

And not only was Igor abnormally huge and abnormally ugly, he was also abnormally angry, more angry than I've ever seen a dog be angry. Even with his intestines spilling out all over the back floor of the ute, Igor still had enough anger in him to snap off your hand in one bite. No beg pardons. And that would've been no problem at all because he had teeth on him like walrus tusks which, in a subliminal flash, made me wonder just how big and angry the other dog might have been and just how ugly it might have looked, as well. That's the dog that caused so much damage to Igor, I'm talking about.

'But Igor's a dog,' I protested.

'Igor's more than a bloody dog,' the bloke replied. 'He's me bloody best mate. Got a heart o' gold, he has.'

'But we're from the Flying Doctor Service,' I said. 'We're not vets. We don't work on animals.'

'Fer Christ's sake,' spat the bloke, 'if'n yer can stitch up a bloody person, surely yer can stitch up a bloody dog.'

Now there was no way that I wanted to get within cooee of the brute, 'heart o' gold' or not. I'm not too keen on those sorts of dogs at the best of times and I made my feelings felt. But I could see that there was a flicker in the doctor's eye and I could see that he was of a different mind and, what's more, that at that very moment he was thinking along the lines of having a go at sewing Igor back together.

'Let's have a go,' he said.

There. I was right.

So, among much fear and trepidation we got the bloke to hold Igor still and I stuck a drip into him and gave him an anaesthetic. Then, when he was knocked out, away we went.

I tell you it was one of the quickest operations in the history of canine-kind. A electric sewing machine couldn't have done the job any faster. In a flash we'd stuffed Igor's stomach back up where it was supposed to go and the doctor was busy doing a frantic stitch-up job.

Then, just as the last stitch was completed and tied off, Igor started to come to. That was made obvious because he gave a guttural growl which shook the ute right down to its bald tyres.

'Let's get out of here,' I called.

So we did. We were in that car and out of there like greased lightning.

A Very Merry Christmas

One year, just before Christmas, a small bush town hospital got in contact with us. They said they had an extremely ill patient and could we fly down and transport the person back for treatment.

'It's an emergency,' they said, so we headed down there straight away.

Unfortunately, by the time we arrived, landed and drove to the hospital, the patient had died. We were about to turn around and go back out to the airport to return to base when we were confronted by some members of the hospital staff.

'Could you take the body with you, please?' they asked.

This seemed to be a strange request, and we said so. Usually, if someone dies in one of these small towns that has a hospital, and that person's going to be buried there, in the local cemetery, they go straight into the morgue awaiting the funeral.

'Is the morgue full or something?' we asked.

'Yes, in a sort of a fashion,' came their reply.

We thought this was a little odd so we asked what they meant by their morgue being full 'in a sort of a fashion'. Either it was too full to store the body or it wasn't. Fashion had nothing to do with it. And if it was full, what kind of disaster had occurred in the town? What's more, why hadn't the Royal Flying Doctor Service been notified about it?

'What's happened then?' we asked, thinking the worst. 'A plague? A bus accident, perhaps? Shootings?'

'Something like that,' they said.

'Well?' we asked.

'Well, what?' they replied.

'Well, what sort of disaster's happened that's caused the morgue to be too full to put the body in it and why haven't we been informed?'

'Look, fellers, where's your good will?' they pleaded. 'It's almost Christmas and it'd help relieve the town of a potentially disastrous situation if you just took the body back with you and we could arrange to pick it up, say, in the New Year.'

This intrigued us even more so we decided to investigate. And it was only then that the extent of the potentially disastrous situation was revealed. The staff were right. There was no possible way that the body could have fitted into the hospital morgue. Not on your life. It was chock-a-block full of the town's supply of Christmas beer.

An Egg a Day

Back in April 1988 I was involved in the Great Camel Race, which was a fundraising event for the Royal Flying Doctor Service. A big ado it was, too. It took two years of planning and involved almost a hundred locally bred camels and a couple of hundred people, some from all parts of the world. To take part each competitor and their support crew had to be totally self-contained food-wise, drink-wise, medical wise and otherwise, in the race on camel-back from Uluru through the desert and over to the Gold Coast. The total distance of the journey was 3329 kilometres.

There were seven of us in our team from Coonawarra in south-east South Australia, comprising the competitor and his six support crew. Originally, I went as the first-aider but before long I landed the job of truck driver as well.

Pretty organised we were too. We even took along four White Leghorn chooks—May, Colleen, Penny and Sally—who helped us out egg-wise. On our trip up to Uluru to meet with the other competitors, after we'd set up camp each night we let the chooks out to stretch their legs and have a scratch around. To start with we used to tie string onto their little ankles which, in turn, was tied to our folding chairs so that they wouldn't get away. And they were fine with that. Friendly little things, they were. They really fitted in.

Then on one particular night, I forget where we were exactly, but there was this one-eyed dog from the caravan park where we were staying. And while we were having tea we could see this dog under the truck, slinking along on his belly, eyeing the chooks off with his one eye, thinking that here was an easy feed in the offing.

'Someone's gonna have to keep a close eye on those chooks,' the cook said, half as a play on words and half seriously because, as I said, the dog only had one eye. Do you get it?

So I guess that's when it was decided that my responsibilities as first-aider and truck driver were to be expanded to include the all-important job of—Chief Chook Minder.

This added responsibility was something I didn't mind at all. As I said, the chooks were friendly little things and we'd sort of hit it off right away. What's more, as it turned out, being Chief Chook Minder fitted in well with my other jobs. See, I had a fair amount of time on my hands, because being the truck driver, what I did was to drive ahead down the track for about 10 kilometres, then wait for our competitor, Chatter Box the camel, and the remainder of the support crew to catch up.

So each time I stopped, I'd let the chooks out of their cage which was on the back of the truck and they'd wander around and have a bit of freedom, like. Still I felt sorry for the poor things, being attached to something solid, so over time I weaned them off the camp chair by tying a wee rock on the end of the string so that they couldn't run too far. Then when it looked like they were comfortable with that, I got brave and took off the rocks, which meant that they just had the strings attached to their legs. Then finally I got very brave and pissed the strings off and they were fine. They'd stick close by me, no problems at all.

As I said, I had a fair amount of time up my sleeve so, after I'd sorted out the chooks and got them settled, I'd sit back and read a book or something until everyone arrived. Then, by the time the competitor got off Chatter Box I'd have his chair ready and he'd sit down and I'd change his socks and give him something to drink. After I made sure that he was okay, he'd walk for a while because with Chatter Box being the smallest camel in the race we'd worked out that if the poor thing was to last the distance our competitor had to walk at least two-thirds of the total journey.

After everyone had left, I'd pack things up and call out, 'Hey, Penny, Colleen, May, Sally,' and the chooks would come scampering over and I'd pick them up, put them back in their cage, and off we'd go again.

They became more than animals, more than pets even. They were more like companions really because they got very attached to me, Sally in particular. At night, when we were sitting round the camp fire, if she was looking for somewhere to roost she'd perch herself on my head. That'd cause Penny, Colleen and May to get jealous and they'd come over and snuggle in beside me, a bit like the way that little children do. Thinking about it now, they kept me sane in many ways. Chooks are very faithful animals, you know, those ones especially.

Anyway, one time the chooks and I were sitting in the truck up in the channel country, about 250 kilometres out of Boulia, waiting for our rider to catch up. Boulia, if you don't know, is about 300 kilometres south of Mount Isa, on the Burke River. There I was, deeply engrossed in my book. I should've known that something was wrong because the chooks weren't keen on scratching around outside that time. Instead, they'd gone real quiet and were snuggling into me like they wanted protection. So there we were, sitting in the truck, and all of a sudden a massive drop of rain hit the windscreen.

'Wow,' I said.

I was so excited. But the chooks weren't. They started cackling and carrying on. The next thing I heard was a yell from behind the truck and when I turned around there was our rider in a real panic. He hopped off Chatter Box, ran over, and jumped into the truck with me and the chooks.

What happened next was unbelievable. I've never seen rain like it. It just poured and poured, and it continued pouring and pouring for a couple of days, non-stop, until we were stuck, true and proper. The mud was so deep that it was up to the top of the wheels of the trail bike we'd brought along with us. We couldn't go forward, couldn't go back. We were stuck, with the rain still pelting down. And believe it or not, that's the only time the chooks went off the lay. Right up until the rain came they each produced an egg a day like they knew that they had an important job to do as well.

But the rain upset them. It upset the rest of us too, mind you. I got ill. The race was called off for a while due to the conditions. Yet, true to form, after the wet, those hens took up laying again.

When we finally got to the Gold Coast there was a rumour going around that they were going to knock the chooks on the head and kill them, like. But I wasn't going to be in that, no way.

'Over my dead body,' I said.

So in the end Penny, Colleen, May and Sally were taken back to their old farm in Coonawarra where they had lots of space to scratch around in. That's where they spent their well-earned retirement, no doubt telling their chickens and their grand-chickens all about their epic journey from Uluru to the Gold Coast, and the big rain that came and caused them to stop laying. And I also hope that they mentioned me in passing too, just like I do them when I tell the story, because it's amazing just how attached you can get to chooks, those ones in particular. I still miss them. They had such loving personalities.

And He Survived!

Gee, it was pretty rudimentary back in those days. Basically, the only aircraft that were available for emergency evacuations in and around Tasmania were those that were owned by the local Aero Clubs. The main one that we used at Launceston was a single-engine Auster J5 Autocar, which was a tiny four-seater, fabric aircraft. And I tell you what, things could get pretty hairy at times, especially if the evacuation was done at night.

For example, just say a call came through in the middle of the night from one of the islands out in Bass Strait. Take Flinders Island, for instance. When that happened, the Aero Club would respond and the Chief Flying Instructor, a chap called Reg Munro, would come out and hop into the little Auster. Mind you, this aeroplane had no landing lights, no navigation lights, no instrument lights, no radio. All he had for navigational aid was a magnetic compass and a torch. In actual fact, knowing Reg, he probably took two torches along, just in case the battery went flat in the first one.

So off he'd go. Now if it was a really nice, clear, moonlit night then Reg might go direct from Launceston to Flinders Island. But that would've been a very rare occurrence. More often than not it was a bit murky so he'd have to rely on getting his bearings from the various lighthouses and townships along the way.

First, he tracked down the Tamar River to the lighthouse at Low Head. Then he headed along the north-east coast over Bridport and over a few of the other small settlements along that way where he could position himself from their streetlights. From there he tracked to Swan Island which is off the north-east tip of Tasmania.

When he came across the Swan Island lighthouse Reg turned north and headed to the lighthouse on Goose Island which was just to the west of Cape Barren Island. So he tracked to that, then just kept flying north until he reached Flinders Island. By the time he got to Flinders Island, they'd have arranged some cars along the airstrip and he landed the Auster using their vehicles' headlights as a guide. Then, once he'd landed, he'd load the patient, then fly back to Launceston taking the same route.

Now the particular incident that I'd like to tell you about wasn't a night-time evacuation, thank God, but it was just one of the many that got us thinking along the lines of 'Gee, we'd better get a bit more coordinated than this.' And that's when we first went about getting the Royal Flying Doctor Service set up here in Tasmania, which was around 1960.

What happened in this case was that a call came through that a chap from Flinders Island had received serious spinal injuries after he'd been involved in either a tractor or a bulldozer accident, I'm not certain which. Now the locals knew about the Auster's limitations so they made it very clear to us that the patient was a big man. 'A very big chap, indeed,' they said. And why they made that point was because they were only too well aware of our awkward stretcher-loading technique.

Normally, what we did to get the patient into the Auster was to first strap the person tight onto the old stretcher to minimise their movement. Then we'd open the door, tip the stretcher up sideways, and sort of wriggle it inside. When that manoeuvre had been completed we'd then have to slide the stretcher forward as far as it could go until the patient's head ended up on the floor underneath the instrument panel and their feet were facing aft. That left one seat for the pilot and one seat alongside the patient, in the back of the aircraft, for an attendant.

Anyway, with this particular chap being so big, and because of the nature of his injuries, there was no way we could strap him onto the stretcher and load him through the door by tipping him sideways and wriggling him about, and so forth. That was completely out of the question.

So Reg took an engineer along with him, a chap who worked at the Aero Club at the time. Now the aircraft had a sort of turtledeck back window, if you can imagine that, where the wing is elevated and you can look straight out through the back, through the window. When they landed at Flinders Island the engineer set to and unscrewed the window, which they then removed from the aeroplane. With that done they strapped the patient onto the stretcher and eased him in through the opening and into the plane. Once the chap was settled, the engineer then screwed the window back into position. When that was completed they flew back to Launceston where they had to reverse the procedure to take the patient out.

And he survived!

And the Winner is ...

I remember back when I was working for Telecom up in the north-west of New South Wales, one time. They held this Charity Ball at a place called White Cliffs, and this ball was the culmination of some pretty vigorous fundraising activities in aid of the Royal Flying Doctor Service.

Now you know how a Charity Ball works, don't you? That's when the participants, usually young beauties, have spent a while raising money for a certain charity and they hold a ball to crown the Queen, the Queen being the person who'd raised the most money. Well, this ball was exactly like that except it was called a Golden Granny Ball. So instead of young beauties, these finalists were the more elderly, or should I say more mature, type of women. And what's more, they'd come from places like Tibooburra and Wilcannia and even maybe Cobar and Wentworth. Well, these grannies had completed their fundraising activities and arrived with their hubbies and other family members for the big Charity Ball in the White Cliffs Town Hall.

It was your pretty standard sort of bush show. Everyone was done up to the nines at that early stage of the night. It was a BYO affair, like. You know what that means, don't you—Bring Your Own food and grog. And I specifically mention the grog at this point because the pub hadn't set up a bar in the hall, as you might naturally assume it might. No, the publican was a lot smarter than that. His line of thinking was that when the blokes had run out of grog in the hall, they'd not only wander over to the pub to buy more supplies but they'd have a couple of swifties while they were out of sight of prying eyes—in particular, the prying eyes of their spouses. Now you can't tell me that that wasn't a stroke of economic genius, especially knowing some of those blokes, as I did.

Anyway, other than the naming of the Golden Granny there were also a number of raffles held to raise money for the Flying Doctor Service. The first prize was actually provided by the publican, and consisted of a week's free grog, food and accommodation at the White Cliffs pub. There was only one stipulation, and that was that the offer had to be taken up within the next three months, before tourist season or whatever began.

Now this was a pretty sought-after prize, especially among the blokes, if for nothing else than the free food and accommodation that you'd need after spending a day drinking the free grog. The offer of free food was viewed by most as an optional extra in this case. I don't know how many books of tickets they sold but there was a fair few because I saw them being snapped up left, right and centre.

Then just before they had the crowning of the Golden Granny they drew the big raffle. You could have heard a pin drop in that hall. I saw blokes with their fingers crossed. I saw blokes with their fingers and legs crossed. I saw blokes with their fingers, legs and everything else crossed. You'd have thought that a million dollar lottery was about to take place by the looks on some of those faces.

So the judge stepped up, dug his hand in the barrel, pulled out a ticket and said, 'And the winner is ... blue, number twenty-six.'

And you wouldn't read about it. The bloke who'd bought the winning ticket had just been banned from the pub for six months. When this matter of technicality was drawn to the attention of the judges they got the publican over from the pub and had a confab with him. God knows why this bloke had been banned. Maybe it was for creating some drunken disturbance or other. I don't know. But for whatever reason it was, it must've been pretty bad because the publican was adamant that the offer had to be taken up within the next three months. The upshot of it all was that the winner was deemed ineligible to take up his prize and a redraw took place.

And, boy, wasn't the chap nice and dirty about it.

And Then There Were Seven

The Code One Emergency came through from Papunya, the second largest Aboriginal community in central Australia. So we hopped on the plane and flew out there. There was a doctor with us that time who'd had a lot of paediatric experience.

When we landed, the police were waiting at the airstrip. They stuck us in the back of their paddy wagon and we were rushed into the Papunya Community Clinic where we were taken in to see a sixteen-year-old girl. Two community nurses were there along with the girl's grandmother and mother. Lots of other women were gathered in and around the clinic and also a mob of kids were outside wanting to know what was happening.

The young girl was going through a difficult labour. She'd been fully dilated for a couple of hours and by the time we arrived she was getting exhausted. The contractions weren't as strong as they had been and the baby wasn't being pushed out.

It's dicey in a situation like that, going into a place where the community nurses are familiar with everyone and are held in such high standing. You sort of get the feeling that you're imposing in some way so you don't want to tread on any toes and stuff up the delicate balance of the community's social structure. You're also careful about what you say and how you say it or else you might come across as being overly pushy which could get people's backs up.

'Oh,' I said, hinting at helpfulness, 'maybe she should go to the toilet.'

'We've tried that,' came the reply.

'Then maybe she wants to walk around,' I suggested.

'No. She's tried that too.'

We weren't getting anywhere and neither was the girl. The baby had to get out some way and, no doubt, it was getting tired as well. Then after a bit of a discussion we decided to take the girl back to Alice Springs where she could have a caesarean section.

So we got the girl up and walked her over to the clinic car, a Toyota four-wheel drive, 'troop carriers' or 'troopies' they're called. They love them out there. They're ideal vehicles because there's so much room in them. You can easily fit a stretcher in the back if necessary. But in this case the girl got in the front along with the grandmother who was coming back with us, to keep her company. We hopped in the back and then we were returned to the airstrip. Then just as the young girl was being helped up the stairs into the plane I said to the doctor, 'Oh, I'll get the obstetric kit out just in case.'

There were two pilots in the plane that day, our senior Royal Flying Doctor Service pilot and one who was on a Mission Aviator's Scholarship. They're a separate group of pilots who work for the Mission Aviation Fellowship and they do a lot of community runs in the mail plane, picking things up and dropping things off to the remote communities. The MAF were getting a new aircraft, one of the Pilatus planes, so their pilot had come along as part of his training.

Anyway, because of all the control and instrument checks and so forth, it takes about five or ten minutes for the plane to get ready for take-off. And during that time one of the jobs that the pilot has to do is to call flight control and notify them of the POB which registers the number of people who are on board the aircraft. While the pilot was doing all that the girl had four or five contractions and it became pretty obvious that she was going to have the baby much sooner rather than later.

After we'd taken off, the girl had a couple more strong contractions. We were up about 15 000 feet at that stage. I remember that the grandmother was in one seat, the doctor was in a seat, there was a crib on the back stretcher, the girl was on the other stretcher, and I was in another seat with the headphones on.

'Oh,' I said to the pilot, 'I think we're going to have a baby so I'll take the headset off for a while.'

Then just as I did, the girl gave a much stronger push so I thought that I'd better have a look, which I did, and I could see about a 20 cent size of the baby's head being pushed up.

'We might move grandmother to the front seat so we have more room,' I said, thinking that by five pushes this baby would be out.

Then the doctor said, 'If you deliver the baby, I'll look after it.' Like I said, she'd had a lot of paediatric experience.

'Okay,' I replied.

So I got grandma out of the way pretty quick smart and grabbed the obstetrics gear and got the clamps and the oxygen ready. And then the baby was born. I delivered the baby. A little baby girl. It was amazing. And after I rugged up this beautiful little baby girl, I put the headset back on.

'We've just had an addition,' I announced to the pilot. 'You'll have to amend the POB.'

'Wow,' he said, 'I've been with the RFDS for seven years now and this is the first time I've ever had to amend the POB.'

Then he notified flight control. 'Flight control. Amended POB. We now have seven POB.'

Even the air traffic controller, a normally dry, quiet and emotionless voice over the airways, as they all seem to be, well, he came back on and he was also really excited. 'Yeah,' he said. 'Congratulations.'

So the baby was born and everything was fine. There was hardly any mess at all. But it was such a thrill to do it and what's more to be able to say that we'd done it in midair. It was just amazing. There we were, up at 15 000 feet. We were all so excited, the young girl, the doctor, me, the two pilots and, of course, grandma. Grandma was over the moon.

As Full as a Boot

No doubt you've heard of the term 'as full as a boot'. Well, here's a story that'll take some beating. It's about a Padre who went one better.

It happened back in the Christmas of 1937 when, after a stint of work on a station up in the middle of Cape York, a stockman, a real gentlemanly cove he was, came down to Normanton to celebrate. Now this type of celebration was, and still is, a bush ritual. After a group of stockmen have been out living and working in cattle camps for months on end, as soon as the mustering season is over they take a break and head straight for civilisation, and in particular to the nearest watering hole, there to celebrate.

Anyway, along with his mates, this chap arrived at the National Hotel in Normanton determined to enjoy himself. And as occasionally happens in these situations, he got a bit carried away. Well, more than just a bit, really. He overcelebrated to such an extent that when he decided to go to bed, he encountered great difficulty in climbing the two flights of stairs leading to his second-storey room. But patience is a virtue and he awkwardly edged his way upwards, step by precarious step, much to the admiration and encouragement of his mates.

Given the condition this feller was in, he did a sterling job. That is until he was about to take the final step in that almost 'Hillarian' climb to the summit. As he turned to wave to the cheering crowd below, a minor mishap of judgment occurred and, lo and behold, back down the stairs he came, thump ... thump ... thump, until he reached the bottom and there he stayed, unconscious and injured.

After the unfortunate accident, the publican got in touch with the Australian Inland Mission at Cloncurry —the AIM being the organisation that pioneered the Royal Flying Doctor Service—saying that the chap was in real trouble at the foot of the stairs.

'Looks like the poor bloke's injured his noggin and broke his shoulder bone,' the publican explained.

Now this was the first real 'Flying Doctor' trip that the particular Padre in question had gone out on. Normally he was a patrol parson with the Presbyterian Church who, in turn, ran the Australian Inland Mission. And it was his job to cover the area from Birdsville to Normanton and beyond by road, that's if you could describe some of the bush tracks that he travelled over as being roads. In actual fact, he virtually lived in his truck, covering hundreds of miles each year, christening bush children, installing pedal wireless sets, and so forth. John Flynn used to travel with him quite a bit.

Anyway, as this clergyman prepared to get on the plane, the doctor picked up on his apprehension.

'Padre,' the doctor said, 'don't worry. This is just a plain evacuation. We'll go out there, collect this feller, and bring him straight back to Cloncurry. All will be hunky-dory.'

With those words of assurance, they clambered into the small Fox Moth 83 Ambulance aeroplane. After turning the propeller, the pilot jumped into the outside cockpit and prepared for take-off.

Now the Fox Moth 83 was by no means an aeroplane designed for passenger comfort. It only had enough room for two seats, a stretcher and the doctor. What's more, it was held together with little more than wood, cloth, string and wire. So they set off at top speed, which was about 80 miles an hour, in the old money; about a four-hour trip it was.

When they arrived in Normanton they headed straight for the National Hotel, fully expecting to find this chap still laying at the bottom of the stairs. But nothing was going to get in the way of this stockman's big occasion. This was his big night. It was his ritual and nothing was going to curtail his celebrations, not even head injuries, nor concussion, nor shoulder injuries. Nothing! Somehow he'd gained his second wind and had managed to find his way back to the bar.

Now this chap proved to be a big man of around 15 stone, if not more. Quite a 'bush gentleman' he was, in his own sort of way, and one who could tell cattle-camp yarns by the dozen, which he seemed more intent on doing at the time than returning to Cloncurry to get his injuries seen to. But in the end four mates got him into a truck and they drove him out to the airstrip.

But getting this chap out there was only part of the fun. Like I said, he was a solid lump of a man and it took some wangling to get him into the Fox Moth and fixed up in one of the seats in the cabin. When that was done, the doctor clambered in, followed by the clergyman who sat beside the stockman. The pilot spun the propeller, the plane sparked into action, then he jumped into the outside cockpit and they prepared for take-off.

'Just keep an eye on the patient, Padre,' the doctor said, and they took off, heading back to Cloncurry.

As I said, it was a good four-hour trip, longer when there's an extra 15 stone on board. There they were, halfway to Cloncurry, and they were flying over Donor's Hill when the big stockman made it known that he'd received the urgent call of nature. His exact words won't be quoted. All I'll say is that the stockman used his own particular style of vernacular to get his point across in a crystal clear manner. The rest is up to your own imagination.

Naturally, the Fox Moth 83 didn't have the facilities to cater for such an exotic exercise. But that wasn't going to inhibit the stockman. As enterprising as he was, he took off one of his riding boots. Out it come, and he proceeded to fill the boot. Then after the stockman had filled the boot, he stood it up on the floor next to the Padre. Now if that didn't give our good clergyman a shock, worse was to follow. The stockman then removed the other boot, the left one it might have been, and proceeded to fill that one up as well, or nearly up.

'Ah, there, that's better,' he sighed and calmly stood it up beside the other one, right next to the Padre's seat.

So there was the Padre, watching these two boots jiggle precariously about on the floor of the vibrating aeroplane, when the voice of the pilot crackled through the speaking tube from the outside cockpit. 'Hold on tight, fellers,' he said, 'we're going to strike some rough turbulence over these Cloncurry hills.'

That really threw the Padre into panic. He took a look at the stockman. Then he took a look at the jiggling boots. Then he took a second look at the stockman. But the stockman didn't seem too perturbed about the matter so the clergyman was forced to take things into his own hands, so to speak, and as they flew through the turbulence over the Cloncurry hills, he steadied both boots to keep them from spilling all over the place.

They finally landed in Cloncurry where the ambulance was waiting. As soon as they came to a stop, four husky men helped lift the bulky, injured patient out of the plane and into the ambulance.

'See you later, Padre,' the doctor said as he jumped in the back of the ambulance, and off they dashed to the hospital, leaving the Padre behind.

So there he was, this Padre, standing out on the airstrip, wondering how he was going to get home when it suddenly dawned upon him that he was still hanging on to these two filled stockman's boots.

He must have looked a rare sight because the pilot appeared not long after, and didn't he have a chuckle. 'Well,' he laughed, 'I've heard of the saying "as full as a boot"—but, Padre, I reckon you might have gone one better there!'

As Soft as Air

It was just one of those nights that you really didn't need to go out flying in, especially if you were a pilot like I was. The weather was bloody abominable. It was the middle of the wet season. Thunderstorms were everywhere.

But around nine o'clock there was a call from Balgo Hills Mission, which is out across the desert, halfway between Alice Springs and Derby. Believe it or not, a chap by the name of Father Hevern ran the mission, a terrific guy he was. Anyway, they had a patient who was deteriorating rapidly.

So the doctor called me. 'Look,' he said, 'will you go?'

'Yes,' I said. 'Of course I will.'

And so I set off with the doctor and a nursing sister. Like I said, the night was exactly as predicted. The weather was foul; thunderstorms were everywhere.

It might sound a bit rudimentary but, although radar was available at that time, we were nowhere near getting it in the Queen Air that I was piloting. So I adopted my usual technique of flying under those types of conditions and I navigated by the intensity of the lightning. That meant getting my belly down in the weeds, as the flying term goes, down to about 3000 feet, under the base of the cumulonimbus which were around 5000 to 6000 thousand feet. Then I'd wait for a bolt of lightning. That wouldn't take long.

When the lightning struck, it'd burn a photo imprint or impression on the back of my retina which gave me a bloody good idea of what was up ahead. So I just took the line from the lightning and flew in that direction until I hit another lightning strike, then on to another, and another, and so forth, and I kept on steering around the columns of rain where the most severe turbulence was.

As I said, it's called navigating by the intensity of the lightning, and it works. Mind you, we took a bit of a bloody hammering at times but it was the safest way to go.

On this particular night we wound our way through the thunderstorms, the down drafts and severe turbulence for nearly two hours. It was a pretty horrendous ride for everyone concerned. Not even the doctor or the nurse had much to say to me. Either they were too scared, or they were sick, or they just figured out that I had a few other things on my mind, which of course I did.

See, other than negotiating the foul weather there was also another problem I had to be wary of out in that area. It's what's called 'jump-up' country, a flat mesatype landscape where high steep-sided rock plateaus just jump up in front of you. Balgo Hills Mission is a typical example. Balgo sits on top of a rocky plateau. It's quite impressive really. The only thing is that if you undershoot you'll fly straight into the side of a cliff.

So I got close to Balgo. But I still couldn't see it. They'd radioed and said they'd have the basketball court lights on but I couldn't even find them. Then as luck would have it, when I flew over where I thought the place should've been, I caught a glimpse of the mission down through some broken cloud. So I did a circuit, came back round, and lined myself up on final approach.

Now, on final approach, a pilot's technique is to look at the end of the runway and if the lights are getting further apart it means that you're getting too high and if they start to join together then you're obviously getting too low. And it was pretty important that I got the approach right this night because, as I said, if I didn't I could well fly smack-bang into a cliff face.

I set myself up on final approach all right. There was some pretty severe turbulence. The windscreen wipers were belting away, and I was sitting there glued to the lights along the runway. Then as I prepared to land I noticed that the runway appeared to be getting shorter, and I'm thinking, 'What am I seeing here?'

So I tried to analyse what my brain was telling me and, while that was going on, the runway's getting progressively shorter and shorter and more and more lights are disappearing up ahead of me. Suddenly, only about half of the lights were visible. Then less than half.

'To hell with this,' I thought. 'I've come this far, I've got to land.'

So I thumped the aeroplane across the threshold, banged it on the runway and as I did, the remaining runway lights completely disappeared. I couldn't see a thing. Not a thing.

Then it struck me. What was happening was that a thunderstorm was sweeping in and a torrential wall of water was working its way down the runway. By the time we were rolling to a stop, the runway lights on either side of the wings had vanished. You couldn't see them. That's how heavy this sheet of rain was.

You couldn't have heard yourself scream inside the aeroplane from the intensity of the rain.

So we just sat there in the middle of the airstrip waiting for a slight break in the downpour and I called the doctor up and I put it to him. 'In view of the intense nature of this trip,' I shouted, 'if there'll be no dramatic improvement by transporting the patient back to Derby tonight, we should look very closely at overnighting here in Balgo and seeing how the weather is tomorrow morning.'

Well, that was duly noted. Then when there came a bit of a break in the rain, I managed to turn the aeroplane around and taxi back to the holding area where the doctor and the nurse disembarked and were rushed off to attend to the patient. After they'd gone, I did the things that I had to do then waited until someone came back and transported me into the mission.

So there I was, as it happened, in a little room at Balgo Hills Mission. The very same establishment that was run by Father Hevern. I suppose, in retrospect, it must've been a small dining room or something. I was totally by myself. By this time, it was around eleven o'clock at night. And I was sitting there reflecting about how narrow the margins of error got on the way out, and contemplating the horrors of a return flight to Derby that very same night, when I received this premonition—a spiritual experience, you could even describe it as.

A nun quietly opened the door behind me. As soft as air, she walked around and looked straight into my eyes. Then, without saying a word, she placed a bottle of Queen Ann whisky and one glass in front of me, walked out and closed the door behind her.

Born to Fly

Jim, the base director from Derby, phoned one night and said, 'Listen, Jan, we've got a bad one up at Kalumburu Aboriginal Mission.'

'What's up?' I asked.

'A guy's been run through by a bull's horn and pinned against a fence post.'

'Oh, gee, Jim,' I replied. 'Penny and I have got to go to Kalumburu at six tomorrow morning to do a clinic. Can't the patient wait?'

'No,' he said. 'The patient's dying.'

'Okay,' I said. 'We're on the way.'

Mind you, as well as being the Royal Flying Doctor Service's flight nurse, I was also married to Jan and six months pregnant with Dan at the time. Anyway, we rushed out to the airport and jumped into the Beechcraft Queen Air. By that time it was about nine at night.

The weather itself wasn't bad, but it was the middle of the dry season. That's when all the burning off takes place and, to make matters worse, the prevailing easterlies had brought in a mass of smoke and dust across the Northern Territory. So once I was at cruise level, I could hardly see the ground. Still, it was something that I knew I'd encounter. I'd actually mentioned it to Jim during the call—the possible complete lack of horizontal visibility due to the low-lying smoke, especially when I came in to land.

'Don't worry about that,' Jim had said. 'I'll get them to turn on the lights of the basketball court.'

As you might imagine, with the whole of the outback being dotted by fires, the lights of one basketball court weren't going to make a scrap of difference. What's more, it's bloody uncanny the way those fires seem to run in lines just like streets lights do. You'd swear black and blue that there was a town or a settlement down below. So all I really had to rely on was my previous flying experience throughout the area.

I hadn't mentioned my concerns to Jim, though. 'Thanks, Jim,' was all I'd said at the time because my mind was already mulling over another problem that I was afraid we'd run into. And I'd been right. Not long after we took off, we lost HF radio contact because the Asian radio stations were jamming the airways. They'd blown us right out of the air. For all intents and purposes we'd disappeared off the edge of the planet. No base. No bugger-all.

Still, I kept on track and heading until we eventually found Kalumburu. Now most people who fly in there will tell you that Kalumburu's a pretty risky place to negotiate because it's shaped like a dish surrounded by hills. At night some of the pilots get quite edgy about it. So we flew over the top and I caught a sighting of the mission down through the smoke. But, because of the prevailing conditions, there was no bloody way in the world that the horizontal visibility was going to permit us to see it at a low-landing level. It was like an extremely thick fog down there.

But, as luck would have it, there was some moon this night so I went back, right up over the Bonaparte Gulf, and let down over the water, down to about 500 feet. Then I followed the moon path up a creek that led to the threshold of the runway. Right opposite the threshold of the runway I knew there was a bend in the creek. So I flew up there with the moon behind me, turned left at the bend and figured that the runway was dead ahead.

While Jan was doing that I'm sitting there knowing what's ahead. And I know that at the other end of the airstrip there's a great big mountain, a massive pointed lump of rock. As I said, I'm about six months pregnant at this time and I've got my hands tucked underneath my safety belt so that I can't touch anything because I'm getting particularly anxious and I'm starting to climb backwards up the seat. I don't know if you've ever climbed backwards like that, but it's quite unnerving because what you're trying to do, in effect, is to remove yourself as far as possible from the point of contact.

Throughout all this, Jan's still driving on with his eyes glued into the white smoke-filled air. He's nice and cool and collected. He's a particularly calm sort of pilot, just a natural. And I'm saying to him, 'Put the lights on, Jan. Put the lights on. I want to be able to see what's going on up ahead.' This is through the thick smoke, like. So Jan finally said, 'Oh, all right.' And he put the lights on and it's like a total nothing, nothing but a blanket of thick white. You can't see a bloody thing. At this point I'm terrified.

'All right,' I shouted. 'Turn the bloody lights off.'

So I did. I turned the lights off. By this time I reckon that I'm lined up for the runway. I just had to be because

I got the turn of the creek right. The gear's down by this stage, half flap out. I still couldn't see a bloody thing. A total white-out, like Penny said. So I just keep flying the heading. 'Fly it. Fly it,' I'm saying to myself.

Then, like a flash, right before my very eyes, the first of the runway lights come into sight. Bang, the wheels hit the ground, just like that. We'd landed. We were down. We were on the runway.

So we picked up this wretched guy, the one who'd been run through by the bull's horn.

And he wasn't too bloody happy either, I can tell you. So we loaded him on board. By this stage, just about every bloody air radio station in the country is calling for us. 'Foxtrot. Delta Victor. Foxtrot. Delta Victor. Do you read me?'

It's now two hours out and nobody's heard 'boo' from us and they can't contact Kalumburu Mission anyway because the radio is out and there were no telephones in those days.

When we took off again I climbed out of Kalumburu and took the Queen Air to the highest bloody altitude it could get to, in an attempt to clear up the airways and get some range into the signal. I even tried to raise somebody on the higher VHF frequency instead of the more usual HF. There I was, calling, calling and calling, and still no bastard wanted to know me.

While Jan's doing all that, he's having some oxygen so that he can keep flying without too many problems and I'm giving the patient oxygen to keep him going. Then I'm giving me and the baby-to-be some oxygen.

Jan eventually got us out of there and back home where we delivered the patient safely. But even now

Jan and I reckon that it was because of the excitement and the rush of adrenaline going through my body on that particular night, it's why our son, Dan, was born wanting to fly; which was something that he went on to do. He became a pilot, just like Jan. What's more, he still flies, right up to this very day.

Brainless

You meet some drongos in this game. You really do. Just take the feller who wanted to go from Adelaide to Cairns. He glanced at the map. 'Ah yes,' he said, 'the shortest way is straight up the Birdsville Track.'

So he set out in the middle of summer in his four-cylinder rust-bucket. He had no spare petrol. No spare water. One baldy spare tyre. No supplies. Nothing. Anyway, he got up towards the north of South Australia and the car broke down.

'Bugger,' he said, and sat there wondering what to do.

Then somewhere he remembered hearing that if you break down in the outback, rule number one is to wait with your car. So he waited ... for the first day, the second day, the third day. By this stage he was getting a bit thirsty. And during the intercourse of these thirsty feelings he looked out over the flat shimmering landscape, and the deeper he looked into the shimmering the more it looked like there was a lake out there, away in the distance.

'There's a stroke of good luck,' he said, and hopped out of his car and set off, walking towards the lake.

The strange thing was, though, the further he walked towards the lake, the further the lake moved away from him. So at the end of the fourth day he concluded that the lake must have been one of those optical illusion things, and he decided that he'd better go back to his car.

He was surely blessed because it was a miracle that he found his vehicle. Still and all, by that stage he was absolutely perishing. It then struck him that the only water he was likely to find in a place like this was the stuff in the radiator. So he tapped the radiator. Now the radiator had anti-freeze in it, and what he didn't know was that anti-freeze contains ethylene glycol. And one of the side effects of drinking ethylene glycol is that it could well cause brain damage.

Anyway, not too much later a car came along and took him into Birdsville where he went straight to the pub and commenced oral rehydration. At that stage the Flying Doctor Service was called and we flew out to Birdsville where we gave him some intravenous rehydration. To give you some idea as to how severely dehydrated this feller was, he was given three litres of fluid intravenously to get just one millilitre of urine out of him.

Later on, in Charleville Hospital, when he asked if there were any side effects caused by drinking radiator water, I explained that unfortunately the radiator had anti-freeze in it and that anti-freeze contains ethylene glycol.

'And what's the problem with that?' he asked.

'The main side effect,' I said, 'is that it could well damage the brain.'

'Gawd,' he said, with a worried look, 'what do yer reckon the chances of me getting brain damage might be?'

I must say that it was a struggle to keep a straight face. I mean, you'd have to be brainless in the first place to attempt to drive across one of the most unforgiving parts of Australia, in the middle of summer, in a vehicle that wasn't in any fit condition to do so, without spare petrol, water or food.

So I said to the chap, 'It's my opinion,' I said, 'that in your particular case, there'd be Buckley's chance of brain damage occurring.'

'Who the hell's Buckley?' he replied.

Break a Leg

Now I might get these couple of blokes into strife here if I mention their real names, so let's call the pilot 'Jack' and the doctor 'Don'. Anyway, the pilot who's Jack in this story was the same bloke who taught me to fly. There's a hint. And the doctor is also well known, especially around these parts. There's another hint. But I'd better not mention their true names, like I said, just in case.

One night Don got an urgent call to go out to a seismic camp where a chap had reportedly been bitten by a snake. These seismic people were doing the survey work in preparation for oil rigs to move in. There were about thirty or so men in this particular camp.

Jack was a spot-on navigator, one of the best I've ever seen. So he stoked up the Navaho and they flew to Quilpy. That way may sound like the long way of going about it, but it's a far surer way of finding someone out in the never-never than to fly to a known point then bear another heading. It shortens the distance and lessens the error.

So out they flew in the dead of night to find this camp, and when they came across it these seismic blokes were as disorganised as buggery. They were still running around trying to light up the bloody airstrip. So Jack circled the Navaho around for a while until he could get a good sighting of the runway. Then, lo and behold, just as they were about to touch down one of the idiots aimed a spotlight fair in Jack's eyes, blinding him.

'The plane musta landed itself,' Jack has since told me.

Anyway, they landed safely, and when they taxied back to these seismic blokes they discovered that the whole mob of them were as drunk as skunks.

'Which one of youse is the one that's been bitten by the snake?' Don asked.

I don't know if these blokes were just playing funny-buggers or not but they were so under the weather that they reckoned they'd forgotten which one of them had been bitten. Now this sort of antic didn't go down too well with either Jack or Don, no way, not even when these idiots grabbed a chap and stripped him off and started looking for a snake bite.

'Listen,' said Don, 'if you buggers aren't sick in the head now you certainly will be tomorrow.'

And, boy, didn't he gave them a fair sort of rev. He told them that while he was out here buggerising around there could be an horrific accident somewhere else, a life and death situation, where he was badly needed. And this is what I impress upon people, station people as well. Don't go calling the Flying Doctor out for a sore toe or a bloody broken thumb or something like that, especially if you can get the patient out in a light aircraft or motor car yourself. The Flying Doctor Service is there for emergency life-threatening complaints. They're not a bloody flying hospital factory. So, anyway, as you might imagine, both Jack and Don were pretty riled up about this pack of idiots.

Well, Jack was telling me that when he taxied down the other end of the strip to take off, he saw red. So when he turned around, he opened both taps up on the Navaho. And as she gathered speed, there were all these blokes still drinking and skylarking about on the airstrip, right in the middle of his take-off path.

'Bugger it,' he said to Don. 'I'll teach these blokes a lesson.'

So he lined them up with the plane and aimed the headlights straight at them. Blinded them just like they'd done to him. They couldn't see a damn thing. All they could hear was the drone of the Navaho bearing down upon them at a great rate of knots.

Jack reckons that he's never seen the like of it. There was this mob of drunken seismic blokes, all pushing each other out of the way, hitting the deck, tripping over themselves and diving for cover, left, right and centre, screaming and yelling.

Then as the Navaho roared over the top of them Don yelled out, 'Break a leg, you bastards, break a leg.' Then they flew off into the night.

Cried Duck

I'm not sure if you should publish this but, just in case you do, I'll change the people's names in an attempt to protect the guilty.

My pilot, Joe, and I used to fly around the outback for the Royal Flying Doctor Service in a Dragon DH 84 plane. There wasn't much to the old Dragons really, seeing that they were made out of little more than wood, rag and string. Still, being built that light gave them one great advantage—and this did happen occasionally. If ever you needed to come in for a crash landing, you could put the plane down between a couple of trees that were close together. Now that'd wipe the wings off but, more importantly, you'd come to a fairly soft and safe halt.

But perhaps something of a more realistic concern was that, if you blew an exhaust gasket in one of the engines, the chances were that it'd catch fire. See, the Dragon had two engines, each with its own separate fuel tank. So if you blew a gasket in one of them, to save going up in flames, what you had to do was to throttle the offending engine right back which, in turn, caused you to lose ground speed. Mind you, it also put a big strain on the working engine and used up a lot of fuel in its tank as well.

Anyway, whenever Joe and I flew across the bottom of the Simpson Desert, we'd track along the Cooper Creek. The reason for that being, given the right season and with enough water about, more often than not there'd be large numbers of ducks along the creek.

So Joe and I would keep an eager eye out and wherever we saw a promising place I'd call up Ted, the radio operator, back at the base.

'Look, Ted,' I'd say, 'I think we've blown an exhaust gasket in the starboard engine and we'll have to put down and take a look at it.'

'Okay,' Ted'd say. 'Please give your location just in case you need us to send someone out to get you.'

Which I'd do. Joe would land on a suitable claypan. Then we'd take a quick look at the exhaust gasket, find that there was nothing wrong, radio Ted back and tell him that we're okay and we'll only be delayed for a while, then go and shoot some ducks for dinner.

Anyway, this particular day we were heading across the Simpson Desert at about 5000 feet. That's about as high as you could get a Dragon to fly in hot weather, and we had a forequarter of beef on board which we'd picked up along the way, legally mind you. And, lo and behold, we blew an exhaust gasket, in real life.

So Joe throttled the engine back and sagged the Dragon down to about 500 feet. Then to lighten the load we chucked the bloody forequarter of beef out and hung the plane in at between 400 and 500 hundred feet.

'Things don't look too good,' Joe said.

'Okay,' I said. So I called up the base on the radio. 'Ted, we're in a lot of strife out here,' I said. 'We've blown an exhaust gasket and we might have to put down.'

'What did you say?' he asked.

I said, 'We've blown an exhaust gasket and we might have to put down.'

'Oh righto,' he replied, all excited, 'so it's duck for dinner again, is it?'

Then he went off the air.

Dog's Dinner

A few years ago there was this feller out on a station who'd somehow got his hand caught in a piece of machinery and had lopped off one of his fingers. Amputated it, like.

So we got the call from this feller; pretty laid back about the accident he was. Like most bushies, real laid back. 'Just lost me finger, doc,' he said. 'What do yer reckon I should do about it?'

'Look,' said the doctor, 'just put a bandage around the stump to stop the bleeding. When that's done get your finger, the missing one, wrap it in a tea towel which is packed with ice and we'll see if we can attach it when we get out there.'

'Ah, doc,' replied the feller, 'me finger's pretty well, yer know, stuffed as far as I can see. It don't look too good at all.'

'Yeah, that may well be the case,' said the doctor. 'But, still and all, grab the finger, put it in a tea towel packed with ice and when we get out there we'll have a good look at it. Right?'

When we landed at the station where the feller lived, way out it was, he sauntered over to the plane. One hand was bandaged up around the stump and he's got a tea towel in his other hand. Both the bandage and the tea towel were soaked through with blood. A real mess, it was.

So we got out of the plane. 'G'day,' we said. 'How yer doing?'

And he said, 'Oh, not real flash.'

Then we asked if we could have a look in the tea towel, just to see how bad the severed finger was.

'Okay,' he said.

As I said, this feller had one hand covered in bandage and he was carrying the tea towel containing the severed finger in the other hand, making things a little awkward for him. Most of the ice had melted, which made it even worse. So when he went to pass over the bloodied tea towel it slipped out of his hand. Before we could catch it ... plop, it came to land on the dusty ground.

Now, that wasn't too bad. But with it being a station there were stacks of working dogs around the place. And all these dogs were kelpie-blue heeler crosses and they all looked the same and they all hung around in packs of about ten or twelve, gathered around the place.

What you've got to realise at this point is that on these stations they keep their working dogs fairly lean. They don't like to overfeed them. That way they've got more stamina when it comes to mustering the sheep or cattle. Now these dogs can smell a free feed from about a kilometre away, and there was a pack of these kelpie-blue heeler crosses hanging around nearby.

Anyway, just as we were about to lean over and pick up the bloodied tea towel containing the mangled finger, one of the dogs shot out from the pack and started ripping into it, tearing it to shreds. We attempted to take the tea towel from the dog but, in a frenzy of hunger, it let us know in no uncertain terms that there was no way it was going to give it up. It was in no mood to have a free feed taken away from it.

In a flash the dog had munched the tea towel to shreds, then it scampered back into the safety of the pack. So we searched for the severed finger among the shredded tea towel but couldn't find it, which left us to assume that the dog had swallowed it. The problem was, with a pack of ten or twelve of these dogs looking exactly the same, we had no hope of working out which one had just eaten this poor guy's finger. Neither did he. He took a look at the tea towel strewn across the ground, then a look at the pack of dogs.

'Beats me which one it was,' he said with a shrug of his shoulders.

'What can we do now?' we were thinking. 'Don't panic. Okay, we can knock these dogs out, open them up one by one. Then, when we find the finger, we can assess the situation and take it from there.'

But the feller must have read our minds. He gave the remnants of the tea towel a bit of a kick with his riding boot and said, 'Ah, fellers, take me word fer it. The finger was pretty much stuffed anyways. What's more, there's no bloody way yer gonna cut open any of my dogs just to look fer me missing finger. I got nine of the buggers left, anyways.'

Down the Pub ... Again

Mate, my story concerns my sister and my brother-in-law. They've since been divorced, but when all this went down they weren't getting along real well. What's more, my brother-in-law was spending a hell of a lot of time in the various pubs around the place. He had a forestry business, a forestry business where he was a logger. But at this particular time the weather had been too rough for logging out in the forest so he'd taken his team into Cairns, where they were working in a shed.

Then one day around lunchtime my brother-in-law decided to go off, up into the forest, and check out the site where they'd been logging, just to get some idea of how long it'd be before they could get back out there, like. Now the particular camp he wanted to visit was about 140 miles north of Cairns, out on the Cooktown road, way back in the forest.

Anyway, as was normal with my brother-in-law, he jumped into his vehicle and off he went without telling anyone. And when he got up there, down came the rain like you wouldn't believe and a flash flood locked him in.

'Bugger,' he said, 'I'll be stuck up here for days now.'

Then he started thinking that if he didn't turn up at home or at work for a few days everyone might start thinking the worst. The only problem was that he couldn't get in touch with anyone because he didn't have a radio or anything with him. So he went down to the State Forestry Camp where there was a communications unit. The only trouble was that when he got there, the place was all shut up. So, with no one about, he thought they wouldn't mind if he broke into the State Forestry building, just to get the message through, like. So he did that. He broke in and got on the two-way radio.

As it turned out, the only people he could get hold of was the Royal Flying Doctor Service. So he explained things to the woman there and asked if she wouldn't mind giving his wife a ring, just to let her know that he was stuck in the forest and wouldn't be able to get home for three or four days. The woman who took the message at the Flying Doctor base said that that was fine and, when she'd finished talking to my brother-in-law, she called my sister.

'This is the Flying Doctor Service here,' she said. 'Your husband's just been in touch and he wanted us to let you know that he won't be able to get home for a few days because he's been rained in, up in the forest.'

As I said, around this particular time my sister and my brother-in-law weren't seeing eye to eye and, what's more, he'd been spending a lot of time out on the town drinking and carrying on. So my sister thought that this was just another one of her husband's elaborate excuses and he'd talked some floozy of a barmaid into ringing through with the message.

Anyway, when the woman from the Flying Doctor Service had finished explaining my brother-in-law's situation, my sister replied in a very curt fashion, 'Oh, yes, and tell me, dear, just what hotel are you calling from?'

Fingers Off

There were only about sixty people living in Coober Pedy back when my pilot, Vic, and I flew there in the little Dragon DH 84. The main reason for that was they had no water. They didn't have water over in Andamooka either. Dry old places they were, and pretty wild too, I might add.

I remember the first time we went to Coober Pedy I did thirty-two tooth extractions in the one day. Bloody hard they were too. Some of those people out that way were as tough as nails. You'd have to be, just to live there. I tell you, I had a hell of a bad case of wrist drop the following day. Mind you, there wasn't even a proper dental chair. In those days all the tooth-pulling and so forth was carried out on a wooden box or a kitchen chair.

Then, after this day of tooth-pulling, Vic and I were getting ready to fly out to Andamooka and there was this chap who was an opal buyer at Coober Pedy. He's dead now. Funny bugger he was. A big chap. Anyhow, he asked if he could come along to Andamooka with us. The only problem that I could see was that we had an Aboriginal chap on board who had open TB, infectious TB. So I explained the situation to the opal buyer and he was still willing to come along.

'Yeah, that's all right by me,' he said.

Then I looked at Vic. 'Oh, yeah, suppose so,' was Vic's response.

Our first port of call on the way to Andamooka was

a place called Coward Springs which is near the foot of Lake Eyre. Now the population of Coward Springs was focused around the publican and the station master. But, as they say, wherever there's a station master there's sure to be a railway station and I wanted to get this chap with the TB organised on a train so that he could go down to a decent hospital and receive the right treatment.

The problem with landing the Dragon at Coward Springs was that the town didn't have a proper airstrip. So Vic flew over the place and, to his surprise, he saw what he reckoned was a nice stretch of black gravel, perfectly situated alongside the railway line. 'What luck,' Vic said. So he put the Dragon down. And, by put down, I mean put down. Once we hit the ground we came to a shuddering halt in about 18 inches of bulldust which had a thin layer of gravel on top.

Anyway, after I got the Aboriginal chap organised to go on the train, we wandered over to the pub for a couple of beers. It was a hot day. When we came back I said to Vic, 'Well, Vic, any idea how we're going to get the Dragon out of this bulldust and up in the air?'

The only thing that Vic could come up with was to run the plane up and down the strip a few times in an attempt to blow as much of the bulldust out of the way with the propellers as he could. It seemed to be a reasonable idea to me even though it'd create a bit of a dust storm in town. But the publican and the station master were pretty used to dust storms, living in a place like Coward Springs. So we explained what we were going to do to the opal buyer and he seemed to be okay with it as well.

'Yeah, that's all right by me,' he said.

So all was set.

'Youse blokes get in the plane, anyway,' Vic said to the opal buyer and me. 'You never know, if we get up enough airspeed I might have a go at taking off.'

Now take-off speed in the Dragon was about 70 miles an hour. The old plane travelled at about 80 or 90 miles an hour flat out, I think. So we tore up and down the strip a couple of times and moved some of the bulldust. By that stage, the best Vic had got the plane up to was about 60 miles an hour. The opal buyer was sitting in front of me in one of the canvas seats. Then, on the next go, Vic got the plane up to about 65 miles an hour.

'There's a chance we might have a go at this,' he shouted, 'so youse blokes make sure that you're well strapped in, just in case.'

By this stage we'd been there kicking up the dust for almost an hour, using up valuable fuel, and the opal buyer was getting a bit toey. So Vic gave the old Dragon all he had, which still wasn't quite enough. The tail was up but, instead of hauling off and coming back to have another go at blowing more bulldust out of the way, Vic tried to pull the aeroplane off the ground.

I could see from where I was sitting that we were heading directly towards a creek with some low, dead bushes in it. The opal buyer by this time had gone white with fear. But I could guess what Vic was up to— just the other side of the creek there was a claypan and his idea was to hurdle the creek and hit the claypan where he could get the Dragon up to speed for a decent take-off.

At that point I was in contact with the radio operator back at the base, a chap called Frank Basden. There I was talking away to Frank through the small microphone radio. It was one of those radios where you had to press a button when you were talking. So I've got my finger on the button and I'm saying to Frank, 'We're just taking off from Coward Springs, Frank. I'll call you when we're in the air' when all of a sudden up jumps this opal buyer, out of his seat.

That was the last thing we needed, especially as we were about to hurdle the bushes in the creek. See, the Dragon's a very light aircraft. It's only made out of wood, canvas and string and you have to have it very well balanced, particularly on take-off, or it'd upset everything, the pilot and all. So I grabbed the opal buyer by the shoulder and dragged him back down into his seat and didn't I give him a serve or two. 'Sit down, you stupid so-and-so,' I said, and then proceeded to call him all the names under the sun.

So that was fine. We got over the creek, hit the claypan, picked up speed, went about 80 yards, got off the deck and up we went, into the sky. When we arrived in Andamooka we said cheerio to the opal buyer and I went about my business.

By the time we got back to base, the incident with the opal buyer was almost forgotten. Then a few weeks later I received a letter from the Postmaster General's Department which was in charge of the Department of Civil Aviation in Adelaide. What'd apparently happened was that, while I was giving the opal buyer a mouthful, I still had my finger down on the button of the radio microphone. At that point in time the Department of Civil Aviation was monitoring our radio frequency and, boy, they certainly sent a very terse notice concerning my use of obscene language over the national radio network.

From Bad to Worse

It was a terrible day to start with, a December day, and over 40° even at that early stage of the morning. What's more, the feeling was that things weren't going to get much better because all the dogs had gone under shade and there was no way they looked like they were keen on moving. It was only us of the human kind that went about our business, preparing to face the day.

And face it we did. At 9.30 am the Mount Isa Royal Flying Doctor Service received an emergency radio call from a vehicle that was bogged in bulldust about 8 kilometres south of Prospect Station. 'Where the hell's that?' I hear you ask. Well, for those who are interested, Prospect Station is about 350 kilometres north-east of Mount Isa, 150 kilometres south of Normanton and 250 kilometres north-west of Julia Creek. In other words, it's out there in the middle of nowhere.

But back to the story: what had happened was an elderly lady was driving along with two young teenagers in a Holden station wagon and they'd left the road, gone into a creek and run smack-bang into a tree. The kids were okay but the woman had suffered head injuries. Apparently, the station wagon wasn't too badly off but, when the teenagers had attempted to reverse it out of the creek, the vehicle got bogged in the bulldust.

Now I don't know if you've been bogged in bulldust or not but I can tell you that it's worse than being bogged in mud. So, there they were, stuck up to the axles. They couldn't go forward. They couldn't go backwards. So they called for help.

On this type of flight we usually carry a Flight Nurse with us but on this occasion, with three people being stuck out there, it was decided that only the doctor and I should go along. So, with me being the pilot, I fired up the Beechcraft Queen Air and we headed out to Prospect Station which was about an hour and a half's flying time away.

When we reached our destination, we circled low over the homestead only to find that it'd been abandoned. The upshot of that was if we landed at Prospect there'd be no one to drive us out to the accident scene. And as the doctor stated, 'There's no way that I'm going to carry a stretcher for eight kilometres. Not under these conditions. It could well be the end of us.'

Still, I did a couple of dummy runs over the airstrip just in case. It was littered with ant hills so Prospect Station was out of the question, anyway. Our next best option was Esmeralda Station which was about 30 or 40 kilometres east of Prospect. More to the point, it was further away from the accident scene but, with little choice, we flew on.

When we arrived at Esmeralda Station there didn't look like there was much life in the homestead either. Still, the airstrip was in a much better condition so I put the Queen Air down and we waited in the hope that someone would come out and pick us up. Which didn't happen. So we wandered through the low scrub and sweltering heat, up and over the maze of dirt tracks and hills until we finally came upon the homestead.

'Is anybody there?' we called.

Not a sound. Esmeralda homestead had also been deserted.

So there we were, about 50 kilometres from the accident scene, with no transport. What's more, because of all the scrub, there was no way we could have flown back and landed any nearer to the bogged vehicle. So we hunted through the homestead and the outbuildings and there we stumbled across an old Toyota LandCruiser.

Now it was obvious that the vehicle hadn't been used for some time. For starters, it was about thirty years old. It was covered in a thick coating of dust. It was rusted. The tyres were perished. But, to our surprise, the keys had been left in the ignition. So we gave it a go and after a bit of pushing and shoving and mucking about we managed to get the old Toyota started. The only problem was that we didn't have a clue how much fuel was in the vehicle because none of the gauges worked.

With no fuel tanks in sight, that left us with a big worry, a big worry indeed.

'Will we chance it or won't we?' was the sixty-four million dollar question.

'Well, we've come this far, and it is an emergency,' echoed the answer.

So we decided to give it a shot.

As I said, there was a maze of tracks around the place, all going off in different directions. No signs, of course. What's more, because of the terrain, hilly and low gidgee scrub, we couldn't see for any great distance to get a decent bearing. Anyway, we followed something that resembled a once well-used track and somehow we ended up out on the main dirt road. Don't ask me how. I wouldn't have a clue. But we did.

There we were, driving down the road, hoping to hell that the Toyota wouldn't run out of fuel, when we saw the two young teenagers walking towards us through the shimmering mirage. They'd seen our plane fly over and they'd decided to head in the direction of where they thought it'd landed. By that stage these kids had trekked about 8 kilometres in the searing heat, and they were terribly dehydrated. Terribly dehydrated.

So we picked them up, got some water into them, then we drove them back to their bogged vehicle. By now, a good hour or so had passed since we'd headed out in the old Toyota. When we got there, the elderly woman wasn't the best. Being as large as she was didn't help much either. It certainly hadn't been her day. Along with the head injuries, she was now suffering from severe dehydration to boot.

Anyway, the doctor got stuck in and started to sort the woman out. So there I was hanging around with nothing better to do than mull over the accumulation of the day's disasters. And it got me thinking, which was a big mistake, but that's what happens when I've got nothing better to do. Now, it was obvious that siphoning the petrol out of the Holden station wagon and putting it in the Toyota wouldn't work because the car ran on petrol and the Toyota ran on diesel. So that was out. But what could I do to save the situation? And the more I racked my brain, the more I started to formulate the idea that, if I dug the car out of the bulldust, all our troubles would be over and we wouldn't have to worry about running out of fuel in the Toyota.

So I grabbed a shovel and started to dig the car out. Now that was one of the most stupid things that a bloke could attempt to do, especially in 40° plus heat. As I said, even the dogs back in Mount Isa had crawled under the shade so that the sun wouldn't fry their brains. There I was, digging the wheels out, when I started to go all woozy.

'Oops,' I mumbled, and down I went like a sack of potatoes.

Well, that certainly put the doctor into a spin. He now not only had a dehydrated woman with head injuries plus two dehydrated teenagers on his hands, he also had a pilot who'd collapsed from heatstroke. And, what's more, without a pilot he knew that he couldn't go anywhere. He was well and truly stuck. So the doctor then had to turn around and rehydrate me.

Anyway, to cut a long story short, when I was feeling a little better we bundled everyone into the Toyota, got it going again, then headed back to Esmeralda Station. Now that was no real problem. But finding the airstrip from the homestead proved to be a different matter. Not only did we have the worry of not knowing how much fuel was left in the Toyota, we were all suffering from heatstroke to varying degrees. The old woman, in particular, was feeling it something terrible. What's more, the thermometer was still rising rapidly and we seemed to have lost our way among the myriad of tracks.

Then I started thinking again, which, as I said, was the worst thing I could possibly do. But it just seemed that, along every step of the way, things had gone from bad to worse to worser, if there's such a word. And I must admit, it was at that particular point in time that I started to have very grave doubts about any of us getting out of there alive.

So there we were, driving aimlessly through the rugged terrain, when the Toyota spluttered over a rise. And there she was, the aeroplane, the Queen Air—my Queen Air—sitting on the airstrip, waiting patiently for us.

God, she was the most beautiful sight I've ever seen in my life.

Great Break, Aye!

The life of a Flying Doctor is certainly a pretty demanding affair, I can tell you. And if it isn't these days, it certainly was when my husband, Tony, was working in the far north of Western Australia.

After we'd been back in Derby for twelve months, I distinctly remember us sitting down and working out that Tony hadn't had a single day's break and, mind you, that included the weekends. While we were living there he was responsible for the routine hospital work, the surgery, the clinics, the lot. And, because the dramas had no time schedule, rarely a night went by when he wasn't called out of bed. What's more, apart from annual holidays, we could only recall him having three days off in the past three years.

'Enough is enough,' I said. 'For one, you need a break. For two, we both need a break to spend some quality time together.'

So we decided to pack up the three kids and spend a nice, relaxing weekend as far away from it all as possible. To that end, the place we chose was the Australian Inland Mission Hospital out at Fitzroy Crossing.

After Tony had organised things on the work front to cover for his absence, the day finally arrived. Early one Saturday morning we loaded the kids into the car and drove the 300 or so kilometres across to Fitzroy Crossing.

Finally, we arrived. And what a relief. A whole weekend together lay ahead. What's more, the girls from the Inland Mission were so excited to see us. They'd even gone to the trouble of planning a big barbecue for the Saturday evening and had invited a few of the station people to come along, especially to meet the doctor and his family.

Anyway, we were just settling into our accommodation when Halls Creek sent through an emergency radio call to the Derby base, informing them that a seven-year-old kiddie had accidentally shot a six-year-old in the chest. Of course, the Derby Hospital was without its doctor-surgeon, wasn't it, and not being able to deal with such an extreme case on their own, they got in touch with Tony.

The next thing I knew, the Queen Air aircraft had been dispatched from Derby and was on its way to pick up Tony at Fitzroy Crossing and take him to Halls Creek—which duly happened. Then at Halls Creek they picked up the gunshot victim and flew the child back to Derby Hospital. Tony remained there in surgery for most of the Saturday afternoon and into the night until he was confident that the child was out of danger and was on the road to recovery.

'Bugger it,' he said, 'I'm still going to have this weekend away with the family.'

So he asked the matron at the Derby Hospital if he could borrow her car for a couple of days. This she agreed to and, at nine o'clock that night, Tony left Derby and drove the 300 or so kilometres back to Fitzroy Crossing to be greeted by a dinner of cold remains from the barbecue that'd been held in his, absent, honour.

Anyway, we finally wandered off to bed sometime later that night or, more than likely, early the following morning. By that stage, Tony was so exhausted he had trouble getting to sleep. But, not to worry, this was our weekend away from it all and we could take it easy and sleep in.

At seven o'clock on Sunday morning, Wyndham Hospital contacted Derby Hospital, who in turn rang Tony to inform him there'd been a very bad car accident involving three teenagers. One person had been killed and two were badly injured, one of whom had sustained severe head injuries. Tony was needed to do surgery.

However, during the three-way phone link-up between Wyndham Hospital, Derby Hospital and Tony at Fitzroy Crossing, an electrical storm hit and contact between the two hospitals was lost. It couldn't have happened at a worse moment. I mean, there they were, right in the middle of discussing blood groups and trying to organise whatever equipment Tony might need so that the hospital staff could get everything ready for when he arrived in Wyndham.

Anyway, the plane left the Derby base at nine o'clock that morning and picked Tony up at Fitzroy Crossing, for the second time. I think they had a theatre sister and an anaesthetist on board on that trip as well, but I'm not sure. Off they flew to Wyndham where Tony remained in surgery all that day and well into the evening.

Tony eventually stabilised one of the lads enough for him to be sent down to Perth for further treatment. But the patient with the severe head injuries was a different matter. There were real problems there and it was deemed too dangerous to evacuate him to Perth along with his mate. So Tony stayed in Wyndham for the next three days monitoring the lad and helping him through that critical post-op period.

And, all this time, there I was in Fitzroy Crossing with the three kids and two cars, our own and the one that Tony had borrowed from the matron. Now, I don't know how they got the matron's car back to Derby. All I can remember is muttering a million times over, 'Great break, aye!' as I drove our car back home, across that 300 or so kilometres of damn road.

Gwen's Legacy

My friend Gwen had to go down to Adelaide in the Flying Doctor aeroplane a few years back. And on her way down she saw these little teddy bears in the plane. They were dear things, about 14 or 15 inches tall, all hand-knitted, with embroidered eyes and noses, and all of that.

'Oh,' she said to the nursing sister, 'they're just so cute. What are they for?'

'Well,' the nurse explained, 'they're what we call trauma teddies. If a child gets upset we give them a teddy to keep and explain that the teddy's got the same injuries that they have.'

The Nursing Sister also happened to mention that the Royal Flying Doctor Service was in desperate need for people to make the trauma teddies, on a voluntary basis. So Gwen said, 'Right, you're on. As soon as I get back home, I'll go to the Probus Club and the Senior Citizens and the CWA [Country Women's Association] and I'll get people knitting.'

But, as it turned out, when Gwen got down to Adelaide she was diagnosed with terminal cancer so, when she arrived back home, she came to me. 'Audrey,' she said, 'I've made this promise to the Flying Doctor Service that I can't fulfil.'

Then she asked if I could start the trauma teddies off in the Riverland, which I was pleased to do. I went to the various community groups and explained how Gwen wanted the trauma teddies to continue and I asked if anybody else could pick up the basket because I was too tied up with other things. So a lady from the Lutheran Church took it on. And she's done a great job because now lots of groups in the Riverland are knitting trauma teddies, getting them ready to go down to be labelled for the Flying Doctor Service and their support services.

Anyway, I just mentioned that story because, even though Gwen's been dead for about three years now, her original promise has been more than fulfilled and no doubt those trauma teddies have helped many children and will continue to do so for a long, long time to come.

Handcuffed

To my knowledge Dr Clyde Fenton was one of the rare 'true' Flying Doctors in as much as he was both an accomplished pilot as well as being a very good, and greatly admired, doctor. And when I say 'an accomplished pilot' I say that with a touch of mirth, as my story will reveal, because while Clyde was a bit of a character, a real larrikin so to speak, he was also quite naughty at times, the daredevil type. Still, he did a tremendous amount of good up in the Northern Territory which was probably why he was able to get away with so much.

When I first ran into Clyde, which was immediately after the war, Darwin was still under military control. And in those days, my late husband, Fred, an ex-RAAF Squadron Leader, had been appointed as the Regional Director of Civil Aviation. This was a posting that made him instrumental in assisting in the re-establishment of overseas air services, both in and out of Australia.

Anyhow, Clyde and Fred didn't see eye to eye on many issues. For starters, Clyde didn't have too much respect for public servants. His favourite description of their livelihood was that of a 'dog-eat-dog' existence. So, when the new Department of Civil Aviation went about restructuring Air Traffic Control, Clyde dug his heels in. Though he still kept on flying, he steadfastly refused to obtain the appropriate pilot's licence.

It was then that the Department of Civil Aviation

sent a directive, via my husband, insisting that Clyde obtain this certain category of licence in accordance with the type of planes he was flying. Of course, Clyde, being Clyde, was of the mind that having already been a pilot during the war a licence issued by the DCA wasn't worth a fig.

'A complete load of administrative rubbish' was how he described the situation.

So dear old Clyde completely disregarded the directive and continued on his unflappable way. Naturally, this type of behaviour riled the DCA. Yet they were caught between the devil and the deep blue sea because the only pilots who they could legally stop from flying were the ones who had been licensed under their own organisation and, of course, Clyde had refused to get that particular licence.

Now a lot of people admired Clyde for this particular stance. They saw him as someone who wasn't afraid to buck the system, a kind of Wild West maverick, a rough diamond.

But the DCA didn't see it that way. Yes, Clyde was a delightful feller and he was a proven pilot. No one could argue with that, what with his war record and all, but things were changing in Darwin. With so many people coming into Australia so soon after the war, the authorities just couldn't have these self-willed pilots out there doing their own thing.

For example, imagine the turmoil it might cause if a Constellation came in to land and there was Clyde doing a couple of loop-d-loops around the airstrip, which, I might add, was something that he'd been known to do. Another of his tricks was to put the wind up everyone by flying low over the open-air picture show at night or over people who were having a quiet picnic on the beach.

Now this might have been a great lark for Clyde, but the DCA demanded order in the skies. So the Melbourne Headquarters became increasingly impatient with Clyde and they said to Fred, 'You've got to get him licensed.'

So Fred followed it up and this is where my story comes in.

One evening everyone was gathered in the Darwin Club and the big talk of the moment was how Clyde had refused, yet again, to get his licence. There they all were, Clyde included. Now Clyde liked a few drinks and after a while he saw Fred talking to the local sergeant of police. 'Watch this,' he said to his group of mates and he came over to Fred and the sergeant.

'Righto,' Clyde said, holding out his hands. 'Here I am, you might as well handcuff me now and drag me off to prison.'

Then, as was usual with Clyde, he put on a big song and dance about the whole affair. Anyway, this skylarking about started to get up the nose of the sergeant and he said to Fred, 'I'll fix him.' Quick as a flash the police officer took out his handcuffs and snapped them on Clyde's wrists.

Well, this was a great joke, especially to Clyde. He started wandering about the club, holding his glass in his handcuffed hands, amid much laughter and carry-on.

'Look what they've done to me,' Clyde announced to all and sundry. 'They've finally arrested me.'

Oh, it was a real talking point.

Anyway, as the story goes, the sergeant got sick of all this carry-on and went home. So when Clyde had

had enough of the handcuffs and couldn't find the sergeant, he came over to Fred. 'Righto, Fred,' he said, 'the joke's over. You can take these things off now.'

'Sorry, Clyde, no can do,' Fred said. 'The sergeant's gone home and he's taken the keys with him.'

'But you can't leave me like this,' Clyde retorted.

Now Fred wasn't beyond having a bit of a joke himself. So he said to Clyde, 'Well, Clyde, the only thing that I can suggest is I take you down to the police station and you can wait there until the sergeant comes back on duty.'

'When'll that be?' asked Clyde.

'I think he's gone to Alice Springs for a couple of days,' Fred said in a matter-of-fact way.

Well, Fred reckoned that you should've seen the look on Clyde Fenton's face. The wind had really been taken out of his sails at that comment.

Heaven

I was stationed in Derby, living by myself at the time. There I was, a guy in his twenties with no commitments at all.

My wife-to-be was a community nursing sister over in Wyndham, and every week she drove down to the stations around the Halls Creek area, giving immunisations and that type of thing. Then every second Thursday, in order to link in with her previous clinic trips, I flew up there to pick up her and a doctor, and we did the follow-up air trips.

The standard procedure on those mornings was to get out of bed at about three o'clock. It'd be as black as the insides of a pig. I'd have a cup of tea, then drive to the airport, open up the hangar, push the Queen Air out, put the car in the hangar, and close the doors. Then I'd climb into this aeroplane, an aeroplane, mind you, that someone had just about given me free rein to fly. It was virtually mine. And I'd fire this monster up, stoke up all the radios, call up on the HF frequency and talk to Perth or Port Hedland, whichever one was on duty.

'Perth (Port Headland), this is Foxtrot, Delta Victor, taxiing, Derby for Wyndham.'

And they'd come back sounding surprised, as they always did, thinking 'Who in their right mind would get out of bed at bloody three o'clock in the morning to go flying?'

Me.

So I'd taxi out, do all my run-ups and cockpit checks, then thunder down the runway, focusing on the instruments. As soon as I left the runway lights it was pitch black. Apart from the faint reflective light inside the windscreen, it was just a puddle of ink outside. Under those conditions there's no horizon. No visual reference. No bugger-all. I'd just focus on and fly the instruments.

Up I'd go. I'd turn left and climb towards 7500 feet. When I hit 7000 feet I'd engage the auto-pilot. Then I could relax. I was free.

There I was in this magnificent aeroplane at four o'clock in the morning, nobody within a million miles of me for all it mattered. And I'd sit back and look out the window at billions and billions and billions of stars. Each and every one of them was mine. I was in heaven, and heading to Wyndham for the six o'clock pick-up of the doctor and the nursing sister.

Kicking the Dust

Well, it's all just been pretty predictable stuff really. The evacuations that we've had to make out of here have gone off pretty much without a hitch. By 'here' I'm meaning Mount Vernon Station which is north of Meekatharra, in the central east of Western Australia.

Anyway, it's always amazed me how the Flying Doctor has been able to get in and out in quick-smart time. They're pretty efficient, you know, the lot of them— the doctors, the nurses, the pilots. We haven't even had any high-flaunting dramas about aeroplanes getting bogged in the bulldust or the mud like they have at other places. Still and all, there was one time I remember when the Flying Doctor plane was delayed from leaving our place, and that was for a bit of an odd sort of reason really, so I'll tell you about that one if you like.

As I said, the Flying Doctor plane has been able to get in and out in no time at all apart from this occasion when a young lad, a jackaroo he was, came off his horse and got his foot caught in the stirrup. Gee, he was in a mess. The poor kid had been dragged along the ground for a fair way and, among all that, the horse had trampled over him. I tell you, he was a pretty bruised and battered young man.

Anyway, we sent out an emergency for the Flying Doctor. When the plane arrived, on board was a doctor, a pilot and a nursing sister. So they settled the young stockman down and had just loaded him onto the plane when the nursing sister decided that she'd better go to the toilet before they flew back to the Meekatharra base.

'Sure,' I said and directed her off to the nearest loo, an outside construction it was. 'You go down this way and that, and it's just around the corner, over there, in that direction.'

Now one of the peculiarities of this particular toilet was that it had a metal door. So, when the sun shone on it, the metal expanded. Of course, we knew this and whenever we used the toilet we kept the door slightly open. But the nursing sister didn't, and with all the kerfuffle over the young stockman it completely slipped my mind to tell her. To make matters worse, this was a warm day, a very warm day indeed.

So off she went and the doctor completed what was necessary for the young stockman while the pilot did his pre-take-off checks. Some time passed and the nursing sister still hadn't returned. So there we were, standing around, trying to fill in the time with idle chat. And we waited and we waited until eventually we'd just about exhausted every avenue of conversation from the price of beef right through to the current climatic conditions ... and still she hadn't appeared.

By this stage, the patient was looking quite distressed, the poor kid. What's more, the doctor seemed pretty anxious and the pilot was gazing at his watch then up at the skies then back at his watch again. So there we were, hovering around the plane kicking the dust with our boots, trying to think of what to talk about next, which we couldn't because all the while we were wondering what the hell was going on with the nursing sister.

Anyway, all this tension proved too much for my

husband. 'Oh gee,' he blurted, 'I don't know, perhaps she isn't feeling too well.'

With this comment, the men turned to me. Being a female I put two and two together and came up with the obvious—that they weren't too comfortable about knocking on a toilet door to find out what a woman's problem might be.

'I'd better go and check on her, then,' I said.

'Good idea,' they chorused.

So I went over to the toilet and tapped on the door. 'Excuse me,' I said, 'but are you okay in there?'

'I'm in big trouble,' came the plaintive reply.

'What's up?' I asked, thinking the worst.

'The door's stuck and I can't get out.'

So I had a go at opening the thing and it was stuck, all right, stuck good and proper. What's more, it wouldn't budge no matter how hard I tried. Then I had to call the men around to have a go. God it was funny. If you can imagine the scene, there we were out in the middle of nowhere with these three men huffing and puffing and pushing and pulling at the door of the toilet which in turn was causing the complete structure to sway back and forward, and there was this poor woman stuck inside thinking that all her nightmares had come at once.

But they eventually managed to free it.

'One, two, three,' they called and gave an almighty pull.

The toilet door flung open and out stepped one very embarrassed nursing sister—as red as a beetroot, she was.

'Well,' she snapped, 'shall we go then?' And she strode off in the direction of the plane.

Knickers

I first became aware of the Royal Flying Doctor Service through a chap called Dr Clyde Fenton. That was back during the war, like, when Clyde was the Commanding Officer of No 6 Communications Unit, out at Batchelor, which was about 60 miles south of Darwin.

At that time, Clyde was working solely as a pilot, not as a doctor. What's more, he had an excellent reputation as a pilot, one which was only surpassed by his dubious reputation of being a bit of a rogue, especially where the establishment was concerned. Clyde simply refused to obey their rules. In actual fact he didn't obey much at all. He was pretty much a law unto his own. Still and all, I must say that, in my experience, I found him to be an extremely likeable and fair Commanding Officer.

But as well as being a pilot and a rogue and, no doubt, a good medical man, Clyde was also a well-versed story-teller.

There's one story that sticks out in my mind, just for starters. This incident happened when he was a Flying Doctor, back before the war. It involved either a Tiger Moth or a Fox Moth, I can't remember exactly. But it doesn't matter because both aircraft were two-seaters. Now what I mean by the planes being two-seaters is that, in both the Tiger Moth and the Fox Moth, the pilot sat in the back seat and the passenger sat directly in front of him, in the front seat. And to make matters more difficult there was no direct means of communication between one and the other.

Anyway, one day, Clyde got a message to go out to pick up Mrs so-and-so from some station property. Miles away, it was. This Mrs so-and-so was due to have a baby and they were keen to get her into the maternity ward so that they could keep an eye on things. So Clyde jumped into his plane and off he flew. But when he arrived, he checked this woman over and came to the conclusion that there was no real rush over the matter. In his medical opinion, she had another week or perhaps even two weeks up her sleeve.

But to save himself another long trip out to the property and back, Clyde decided to take the woman back into the hospital anyway. So he positioned her in the front seat. He made sure that she was comfortable, then double-checked that she was okay. 'Are you sure that you're okay?' he asked. 'Yes,' she replied. Then he took off to return to the base. They'd been in the air for about half an hour when Clyde noticed that the woman seemed to be in some sort of discomfort.

'She can't be,' he muttered to himself.

But the further on they flew, the more this woman's discomfort seemed to increase, and before long, there she was, twisting this way and that. Now the more that this woman wriggled about, the more Clyde began thinking that his previous diagnosis might've been a week or two off the mark. It'd happened to doctors before. You couldn't always be right. Nothing's 100 per cent certain. Perhaps the stress and vibration of the flight was bringing the baby on prematurely. But it was only when the situation reached desperation point and the woman attempted to lift herself out of the seat that Clyde's concern turned to panic.

'Hell,' he said, 'the baby's coming.'

So Clyde was left with no other option than to put the plane down, and put it down mighty quick, or there could be big trouble. Now it isn't the easiest thing in the world to put a plane down in the middle of nowhere, especially when that 'middle of nowhere' happens to be nothing but desert and scrub. So he searched around the area and the first piece of half reasonable land he came across, he took the bit between the teeth and went for it.

Now, as you might well imagine, landing a plane in those sorts of geographical conditions was a precarious exercise at the best of times. But with a woman on board who was on the verge of giving birth, Clyde was fully aware that any sudden bumps or violent shaking may well get the birthing process rolling before he could attend to the situation.

But as luck and good flying skills would have it, Clyde managed to make a reasonably smooth landing. Then as soon as the plane came to a halt he shouted, 'Keep calm. Keep calm. Breathe nice and deep. First, I'll get you out of the plane and we can take things from there.'

Then he grabbed his medical bag, jumped out and raced around to tend to the woman. It was at that point that Clyde happened to notice a strange, sheepish look on the woman's face. Now this particular facial expression caused him to do a double take.

'You are about to have the baby, aren't you?' he said.

'No,' whispered the woman.

'Then why all the discomfort in the passenger's seat?' he asked.

'Me undies got all knotted up,' she replied.

Love is ...

Remember back in the 1970s when they had those little logos—'Love is ... something-or-other'? For example, 'Love is ... not having to say you're sorry'. Well, there's a saying around here that goes 'Love is ... not pressing charges', and that stems from the time when we had an emergency flight to a town where there'd been a domestic dispute.

What had happened was that this feller and his de facto wife had come home after a session on the grog, they'd had a blue and, amongst the turmoil, she'd picked up a large kitchen knife and knifed him in the chest. Down he went like a sack of potatoes with the knife sticking out of him and blood gushing everywhere. When the woman realised what she'd done, she panicked, rang the ambulance, and before they arrived she nicked off out bush.

As you might imagine, it was quite a mess and the victim wasn't in the best of conditions. That's when we got the call to fly out and pick him up.

Anyway, they brought this feller out to the airport so that we could load him straight onto the plane. There were a couple of policemen in tow, just in case. At that point the feller was conscious and still had the large kitchen knife embedded in his chest. Then, as we started to wheel him out to the plane, his de facto appeared out of nowhere. She'd seen us come in to land, realised what was going on, and had rushed out to the airport. But just as she started to run towards the plane, she was grabbed by the two police officers.

If you can imagine the scene, there we are, loading this critically injured feller onto the plane. And there's this woman being restrained by two policemen. And with the tears flowing down her face, she starts sobbing out at the top of her voice, 'I'm sorry, darlin'. I didn't mean ta do it!'

And this feller, there he is with the knife sticking out of his chest. Well, he struggles to raise himself and he starts calling back at the woman, 'That's all right, sweetheart. I forgive yer!'

Then she replies, 'I love yer, darlin', honest I do!'

'I love yer too,' the feller calls out. 'And don't worry about a thing, sweetheart,' he says, 'I'm not pressing charges!'

Mayday! Mayday!

It was, um, 19 October, actually. I was about nine months pregnant at the time and still working in Derby as a flight nursing sister. Not that there was much flying for me. I'd been thrown off the aeroplane because I was bigger than most by that stage with my bub being due fairly soon. Anyway, my husband, Jan, had gone off flying the aeroplane, doing a clinic circuit with a doctor and a nurse, and I was back at the base doing a radio session.

You know about the radio sessions, don't you? Well, I used to go on air and ask if anybody wanted drugs or medications for their station's medical chest and, if so, I'd organise for them to be sent out. Also, sometimes people just wanted to ask general questions about health and so forth so that they wouldn't make idiots of themselves when the doctor came on line. In other words, I did a lot of trouble shooting.

So there I was chatting on to people and I got the strong feeling that Jan was listening in from the aeroplane because he often used to count the times that I said 'um' over the radio. As you might have gathered, um, it's a little habit of mine, though I'm getting better. Anyway, Jan used to count my 'ums' and he'd give me a bit of backchat. It was just a fun thing, really.

So I'd just finished my part over the radio and the doctor came in and sat down and said, 'Good morning. And what're the stations for medicals today?'

Just at that point, Jan came over the radio. 'Mayday! Mayday!' he called.

'Oh, shit,' I blurted out, because I'm sort of a vocal person.

'What on earth did he say?' the doctor asked.

'Mayday,' I said. Then I asked Jan, 'What's your problem?'

'My wing's on fire,' came the reply.

Apparently, Jan had left Tableland Station with the doctor, the nurse and some patients on board, and they were heading down to Lansdowne Station, in the north-east of Western Australia. So there he was, flying along at about 3500 feet, when he looked out the window and the whole top of the left wing was going black and buckling. What's more, the aeroplane was trailing a plume of black oily smoke.

That's when he called through with the mayday.

'Okay, Jan. That's okay,' I kept saying as he explained the situation and gave his location, in case they went down. When he'd finished giving me the details, he said, 'I'm going to the other frequency. Over and out.'

'Okay,' I said, 'anything else I can do?'

'No,' he replied and radio contact ceased.

Just then, one of our doctors who'd overheard our conversation came rushing in and said, 'What's he done to my aeroplane?'

'Oh, he's just had a bit of an accident,' I replied, in a manner that came over as, perhaps, far too casual.

Now my being so calm took everyone aback because they imagined the instant panic that they'd go into if they knew that it was their spouse stuck up there, at 3500 feet, in an aeroplane that was on fire.

But it didn't happen to me. Even though I knew that things must've reached an extremely critical stage for Jan to have put through the mayday call, it was almost like I had a premonition that everything was going to be okay. There was nothing to worry about. Jan was in control. Jan would save the day.

Much to everyone's complete amazement, after Jan had gone off air I carried on with our medical schedules, 'scheds' as they're called. And the doctor carried on with me. So I just kept right on going and finished off the scheds, and when they were done we went back to find out what Jan was up to.

As it turned out, after the mayday call, Jan had shut the left engine down in case it was contributing to the problem. But unbeknown to him at the time, the fuel tank had ruptured in the left wing and the wiring loom had set fire to it. So not only was the wing on fire but by that stage it'd burnt the flap controls out, leaving him with full flap condition on one side and none on the other. It's called an asymmetric flap condition.

Then after he shut the engine down, he dropped the landing gear in case the fire raged through into the undercarriage as well. By that time things were starting to get pretty interesting from a flying point of view. But Jan being Jan, he somehow managed to wrestle the burning aeroplane onto the ground at Lansdowne Station. When it rolled to a stop he got everybody outside to safety. With that done he went back and grabbed the fire extinguisher from inside and managed to put the fire out.

So, my premonition had been right, after all. Jan had, um, saved the, um, day, thankfully.

Missing

During 1955 to '56 I was working on Troughton Island which is just off the far north coast of Western Australia, out in the Timor Sea. The island itself was quite small, only about three-quarters of a mile long and half a mile wide. A year and a bit I was there, employed at a government high-frequency direction-finding station, keeping track of shipping movements in the area.

In early February '56, I got a toothache; pretty bad it was, so we flagged down a passing ship which took me to the mainland, to Wyndham in fact. There I went to see the local doctor in the hopes that he'd be able to extract the tooth.

'Not my cup o' tea,' he reckoned.

This doctor was an Australian Rugby Union international. As strong as a bull, he was. But when it came to pulling teeth, especially without the aid of anaesthetic, he went to water.

'Well, you've got to have a go,' I said. 'The pain's killing me.'

So he did.

But no matter how hard he tried, he couldn't remove the tooth. As a last resort, he suggested that we go down to the local drinking establishment and have a few whiskies. The object there was to induce an anaesthetic effect on me and for him to gain some much needed Dutch courage. So we did that, and when we came back he had another go at the tooth.

That didn't work either so we headed off down to the local watering hole again for a top-up.

We did this a few times, back and forward, back and forward, but still the tooth wouldn't budge. By this time neither of us could walk a straight line.

'Best I can do is to get yer to Darwin,' he slurred, and added that there was a plane passing through in a couple of days.

So I cadged a lift on that plane. Bugger of a trip it was, with the thing landing at every station and halfway house between Wyndham and Darwin, dropping off grog and supplies. Mostly grog, I might add. It was pretty wild out there in those days. And on every landing, the station people were sympathetic to my problem and plied me with a top-up of 'anaesthetic'.

By the time we landed at Darwin airport I was anaesthetised to every inch of my body, except where it mattered—to the aching tooth. My cheek had puffed up like a balloon. When I finally saw the dentist he took one look, put his hand in my mouth, gave the tooth the gentlest of tweaks and ... out it came, just like magic.

It was while I was in Darwin that the Flying Doctor Service over in Derby got a call from an outlying property. The station manager's baby was very sick so they flew out there. The weather was atrocious. Anyway, they arrived safely at the station, picked up the sick child and the mother, and took off again to return to base.

On their way back, they went missing.

A search was mounted and a plane with direction-finding equipment on board was flown from Perth up to Darwin. Somehow the news had spread that I was in town so they contacted me to go out in a search aircraft. My job was to pick up the automatic distress signal which the pilot would've set off the moment that he knew he was in strife. If we heard the signal then we could pinpoint where the plane was and go in and get the survivors. To help us in our mission all transmitting stations throughout Australia which ran on that particular frequency were shut down for an hour or so.

So we set off and flew over the search area. Extremely rugged country it was. Up and down we went, this way and that. But I never heard a sound.

Then later that month, the wreckage of the plane was discovered in the King Leopold Ranges, out from Derby. They'd flown straight into a cliff face. All five people on board had been killed.

Mission Impossible

They say that you can't do the impossible. And I'd have to go along with that. If something's impossible to do, then it's impossible to do it. You can't do it. It's impossible. Full stop. But I'll give you a tongue twister. I reckon that the Flying Doctor Service has gone as close to doing the impossible as it's possible to do, and on quite a few occasions, too, I might add.

Why, just a year or so ago there was this young geophysicist chap. He and his survey crew were correcting boundaries by satellite, out in the Tirara Desert, beyond the Simpson Desert, in probably one of the most isolated parts of Australia.

One morning, around 8 o'clock, this young chap left the camp to go out and do some survey work. There he was in his Land Rover, driving through the bush, when he came upon a desert taipan. Now these things are the most venomous snakes in Australia, even more so than the Cape York taipan, and they're pretty deadly. So what he did was he ran over this blinking five-foot-long snake. The trouble was that he made a slight error of judgment and ran over the tail section of the snake and not the body as he'd intended.

He must have had his elbow resting out the window at the time because this snake bounded up like lightning ... Zap ... and latched onto him. There he was driving along with the fangs of this desert taipan embedded in his arm. The more he tried to shake the thing off the tighter it latched on, and the tighter it latched on the more poison it pumped into him. Eventually, he shook the snake off and he got on his Traeger radio and called up his camp.

'I've just been bitten by a hell of a snake,' he exclaimed.

'Well, you'd better get back here quick and we'll start to get things happening at this end,' his mate replied.

So his mate called the Flying Doctor Service in Broken Hill.

'What sort of snake's he been bitten by?' the doctor asked.

Now that was something no one knew at the time, not even the lad, but to be on the safe side the doctor said that they'd fly up there immediately and bring along as many vials of antivenene as he could find. So, after they sorted out where the nearest airstrip was, the mate got on to Santos in the Moomba gasfields who said they'd send up a helicopter, post haste, to transport the lad from the camp to the airstrip.

So the Flying Doctor plane, a Super King Air, arrived at the designated outback airstrip, a map reference of about 30 miles from where the boys were camped. Not long after, the helicopter arrived with the young chap aboard. By this stage the lad was almost unconscious. It was touch and go so the doctor pumped some antivenene into him. Then they whipped him into the aircraft where the doctor gave him another shot which he apparently had a severe reaction to.

They took off from this dirt airstrip which was, as I said, out in one of the most remote parts of Australia, and in just under an hour they had the young feller in intensive care in the Royal Adelaide Hospital.

Now that's as close to achieving the impossible as you can get, I reckon. What's more, the lad lived and is now back on the job. He should have died but he didn't. It was just one of those miracles of survival, one that even surprised the young chap. When he woke up two days later, the first thing he said was, 'Tell Mum I'm still alive!'

Mud Happens

Just the day to go out wearing my new Rossi boots instead of my normal old nurse's shoes. Just the day to wear a good pair of pants instead of shorts. But it was cold, and we were heading out to a cattle station just north of Alice Springs where I knew that it'd be much colder.

An old station owner had been driving along in the manner that old farmers do when his ute hit a bump. Up he went, and when he came down again, he smashed his chest on the steering wheel.

'He might'a cracked some ribs, I reckon,' a young jackaroo had told us over the radio.

It'd been raining so we asked the jackaroo if he knew what condition the airstrip was in. 'Just hang on a tick,' he said. There was some shouting in the background before the jackaroo came back on. 'The old bloke says yer won't have any trouble at all,' he said. 'Reckons it's as good as gold, as good as gold.'

Still, the pilot waited for a strip report to confirm that it was okay and then off we went, out to pick up this old man, just the pilot and myself. There wasn't a doctor on that trip. There was no real need, really. It was a simple evacuation. In and out, and back to Alice Springs.

The clouds were quite heavy so we stayed low. Then when we arrived, the pilot flew over the runway just to double-check its condition. Everything seemed okay, just like the old bloke had said, 'as good as gold'. The young jackaroo was down there waiting with the man. A young jillaroo was also there. So we landed and loaded the old boy onto the plane. About eighty he was. As deaf as a post. A cantankerous old bugger to boot.

'What're yer doin'?' he asked.

'I'm checking your blood pressure,' I said.

'Me what?'

'Your blood pressure,' I shouted.

Everything was 'What's that?' or 'What're yer doing?' Then I'd have to repeat myself before he understood. It was just that he didn't hear properly.

Anyway, it was about 10.30 in the morning when we got the old bugger settled in the plane. We said goodbye to the young jackaroo and the jillaroo, who turned out to be brother and sister. Over from Queensland they were. One had been there a week, the other for about three months.

So the pilot taxied to the end of the strip to prepare for take-off, which was the end from where we'd landed. As he was sweeping the plane around in a wide arc, we came to an abrupt halt. There was this sinking feeling, and down we went into a well-disguised, grassy bog.

Now, bogging an aeroplane is one of the worst things that can happen to a pilot. It's something they're never likely to live down, a stigma that stays with them for the remainder of their days. And our pilot was well aware of the fact. But what made it all the more painful in this case was that he'd been given a strip report that assured him everything was okay. So, there he was, up the front, slapping the dashboard and swearing to the heavens.

So I let the pilot be. When he'd settled down we got out and inspected the situation. It didn't look good. We were in deep. Mud was halfway up the front wheel and also the right-hand side wheel.

'What's wrong?' the old farmer called from inside the plane.

'We're bogged,' I shouted.

'We're what?'

'We're bogged!'

'Could've told you it were soft up this end.'

The pilot and I raised our eyebrows to the heavens and, without saying a word, we agreed to leave the old chap inside while we had a go at lifting the plane out of the bog. So, with the two young kids helping us, we pushed. We pulled. We shoved. We dragged. But the plane wouldn't budge. So I opened the door of the aircraft to see how the old bloke was going.

'What's goin' on out there?' came a familiar voice.

'We're still bogged,' I called back.

While the brother and sister went back to the homestead to get another four-wheel-drive vehicle, the pilot called our mechanics in Alice Springs to find out where to tie the towropes so that the undercarriage wouldn't get damaged as we were pulling the plane out. Then the kids arrived back, loaded to the hilt with more towropes, bog-mesh, shovels, fence posts and chains. So we dug around the wheels, hooked up the towropes to the four-wheel drives and we pulled. Snap went the towropes.

'Bugger,' I said, then looked down at my mud-soaked Rossi boots and long pants. 'Double bugger.'

But we didn't give up. We dug out more mud, retied the towropes, laid down the bog-mesh, hooked up the vehicles and pulled again. This time—Whoosh—the wheels went straight through the bog-mesh and deeper into the mud. So we dug some more, then tried putting chains under the wheels for traction. That didn't work either. It seemed like nothing was going to work.

For a fleeting moment we even considered sitting the old bugger outside on a chair and getting him to help out with a few directions and suggestions. But that was for only a fleeting moment.

'Used ta be a swamp down this end, it did,' he shouted, 'but we filled it in ta make the airstrip.'

'I thought you said it was as good as gold,' I said.

'What?' he called.

'I said, I thought that you told us that the strip was as good as gold!'

So we dug some more and we tried packing timber around the wheels, and still the plane wouldn't budge. By this stage the pilot was about ready to give up.

'Come on,' I said, 'just a little bit longer, just keep trying.'

The other option was to borrow the front-end loader from Utopia, an Aboriginal community about 30 kilometres away. Utopia, by the way, is the place where Aboriginal dot painting first began. But, from where we were, Utopia was a good hour or so's drive, over and back, which would've meant that we'd have to stay the night out there in the company of you-know-who.

So, desperate measures had to be taken. And they were. I straddled the cockpit and opened the window so that I could hear, then I tried to steer with my feet in an attempt to keep the nose wheel straight. But that didn't work either. So we grabbed some metal fence posts, 'star-droppers' they're called, and we laid them sideways under the wheels in the hope they might act like a little ramp. And it worked, and we finally managed to pull the plane out. Over four hours it'd taken. But we'd done it. We were out.

'What's goin' on now?'

'We're out of the bog.'

'We're what?'

'We're out of the bog!'

'Let's have a cup o' tea and some biscuits, then,' he said.

So we did. Apart from my wrecked Rossis and pants, things could've been worse. We were just lucky that the cranky old bugger's injuries weren't more serious than they were. But the person who I really felt sorry for was the pilot. He knew he was going to be in for a hell of a ribbing when we got back to Alice Springs. And he was.

The moment we arrived, the engineers appeared on the scene. 'We weren't worried, Penny,' they said. 'We knew a country girl like you would get him out o' trouble.'

Night Eyes

One day we got a call from this chap who was up in the Flinders Ranges, in the north of South Australia. He said that he'd been following a car along a dirt road when it'd overturned, leaving two ladies stuck inside with bad injuries. A third woman, who was also hurt, had been able to free herself from the vehicle. When we asked the bloke his whereabouts, he gave his location as being near a certain airstrip in the national park.

'We'll meet you there, then,' we said.

'No worries,' he replied. 'I'll stay with the ladies until I see your plane coming in then I'll drive straight out and pick you up.'

'Okay,' we said, 'we'll be there ASAP.'

Now, attempting to land a plane in the Flinders Ranges is a difficult task at the best of times, especially in the national park. Firstly, it's quite mountainous in places and, secondly, the airstrips are extremely short. But the pilot was willing to give it a go just as long as we could get out of there before dark. Getting out before dark was the least of our problems. We had plenty of daylight hours up our sleeve. What's more, with the accident occurring near the airstrip as the bloke had said, things were set for a speedy evacuation.

So we flew to the airstrip that the chap had mentioned but when we landed no one came out to meet us. We waited for a while. Then we waited for a little while longer, and still he hadn't turned up. Eventually, we radioed through and found out that the chap had mistakenly given us the name of the wrong airstrip and the accident had occurred about 30 or 40 kilometres down the road.

'Here we are,' said the doctor, 'stuck in the middle of nowhere with no visible means of road transport and the accident victims are stuck in their car down the track'—which just about summed the situation up, really.

We were scratching our heads, considering our minimal options, when a cloud of dust came around the corner. And out of that cloud of dust appeared a small tourist bus. At the sight of the bus we ran over and blocked the road to make sure that it'd stop.

Now when the bus driver pulled up you'd swear that a couple of those tourists thought it was a hold-up because video recorders and cameras disappeared from view and their eyes glazed over with fear. I don't know what they were thinking. Maybe they thought that we were the Kelly gang in disguise or something and I was Ned Kelly in drag, all dressed up in a nurse's uniform for the occasion. I don't know. What's more, we didn't take the time to check. We were too busy telling our tale of woe to the driver and asking if he could drive us down to pick up the injured people.

'That's fine,' he said. 'Anything to be of help.'

Then he told the tourists that they had to get out of the bus, which was something that a few of them didn't look too keen on doing, I might add.

'No, no. No robbery,' he said, trying to allay their fears. 'No, no. No hijack. Everything fine-and-dandy.'

When the last of the tourists was evicted, we loaded our medical gear into the small bus and jumped aboard. Then the driver took off, leaving the pilot behind to attempt to explain to the tourists why they'd been dumped in the middle of the uninhabitable wilds of Australia, as they saw it.

When we arrived at the scene of the accident we finally met up with the bloke who'd given us the name of the wrong airstrip and together with the bus driver we all managed to get the two ladies out of the car. Once we'd stabilised them we placed them in the bus and started to head back to the airstrip.

Now, because of the extent of the injuries and the poor condition of the road we were only able to travel at a snail's pace and that left us in a very tricky situation. Along with all the other cock-ups during the day, the sun had already set and darkness was falling at a rate of knots. By the time we arrived back at the airstrip it was pitch black. But the pilot hadn't been hanging around idly discussing the pros and cons of bushranging to the tourists. Not on your life.

When we'd flown in, he'd noticed that the national parks people were doing some roadworks further down the track, and after we'd left he'd rounded up a couple of graders and a few other vehicles. So as we were loading the injured ladies onto the plane, they positioned the vehicles along each side of the airstrip, ready to turn their lights on so we could see where to take off. What's more, when they'd run out of vehicles they filled up all the tin cans they could find with kerosene or diesel and used them as flares to help light the strip.

Now that in itself was an amazing piece of resourcefulness but the rescue still relied on the pilot's ability to fly us out of there. As I said, it was quite mountainous, the airstrip was extremely short, and by this time it was pitch dark, around 9 or 10 pm. Then, as we were taxiing down the runway, another problem popped up. And when I say 'popped up', I mean popped up. With it being a national park, a million and one kangaroos appeared out of the bush to see what all the hoo-ha was about.

With the doctor in the back of the plane attending to the accident victims, I was up front alongside the pilot. As we picked up speed down the runway the noise of the engines spooked the kangaroos. In blind panic they started hopping all over the airstrip, left, right and centre.

I sat there, frozen with fright as the pilot threaded the plane through the startled kangaroos then made a sharp ascent up through the mountains and into the sky.

'Wow,' I gasped in astonishment at the pilot's skill. 'I must say that that was an amazing piece of flying.' Then I heard his faltering voice ask, 'Is it safe to open my eyes now?'

No Thanks!

He was only a young lad, a jackaroo at Innamincka Station. Pretty new to the game he was. Anyway, he went into Innamincka and got stuck into the grog. Then on his way back out he came across a snake. Being young and stupid and, more to the point, pissed to the eyeballs, he tried to be smart and pick the thing up. The obvious happened—he got bitten. That's when we got the call.

'Look,' said the manager from Innamincka Station, 'I don't know how much of this is bullshit or not but we've got a kid here who's as drunk as a skunk and saying that he's just been bitten by a snake.'

We took the call like it was a life and death situation— which in actual fact it proved to be. An inland taipan it was, one of the most venomous snakes you're likely to find. Trouble being, time was against us. In cases like that, the sooner the initial treatment is carried out the better chance the patient has of survival. As it stood, it would have taken the Flying Doctor Service too long to fly from Broken Hill down to Innamincka then get a lift out to the station to give that treatment. So, with me being at Moomba, in the gasfields, Santos offered to helicopter me out there straight away to have a look at this kid.

It was a woeful night. The wind was blowing a gale by the time the pilot and I set off. Then just as the lights of Innamincka Station come into view, all hell broke loose. The helicopter suddenly went into free fall. It was like being at the top floor in a lift and the wires snapping. The air vanished from under us. The rotor blades were still whirling. There was nothing the pilot could do. Down we came from an awful height. Crunch! We hit the ground and bounced a couple of times before the helicopter flipped over on its top with the blades still spinning. There was screeching, groaning, sparks. Then they ground to a stop. Silence.

The pilot and I sat in our seats, upside down. It took a while to register that we were still alive.

'Are you all right?' the pilot finally asked.

'I think so,' I replied.

'Guess we'd better get out of here, then,' he said.

'Guess so,' I replied.

So he undid his safety belt and fell to the top of the bubble of the helicopter. I followed and down I came, right on top of him. Poor bloke. Cracked his ribs or something. I can't remember now. But, miraculously, they were the only injuries either of us received apart from general bruising and things.

As we were sorting ourselves out, the strong smell of fuel started to fill the cab. I had visions of the helicopter exploding in a massive fireball like they do in those American movies. The pilot must have seen the same films. 'Let's get out of here,' he called, and we scampered from the wreckage and took to the bush.

Thankfully, the station manager had been waiting outside the homestead for us to arrive in the helicopter. He'd seen the lights come over the hill, then disappear. Thinking the worst he jumped into his ute and came looking for us. The pilot and I must have been running on adrenaline because the manager reckoned he found us about 4 kilometres from the upturned helicopter.

The odd thing was, though, when we arrived back

at the homestead all those years of nurse's training took over. To this day I can't remember having one thought pass through my mind about how battered and bruised I was or just how close to death we'd come. My total focus was on the patient.

Things weren't looking too good for the lad, though. He'd passed out, which only clouded the issue. How much of his comatose state owed itself to drunkenness and how much to the snake bite was difficult to tell. I stabilised him the best I could and made sure that the Flying Doctor Service at Broken Hill were on their way down to pick him up. Then we drove the kid into Innamincka. With it being night, the locals came out to help light flares along the airstrip so that the plane could land. Trouble was, the strong winds kept blowing all the flares out.

Anyway, the RFDS pilot circled a few times, summing up the situation. It was just too risky to attempt to land without flares to light up the strip and they decided to fly on to Moomba, hijack the ambulance, and come out and meet us halfway. So with the lad still out to it from the effects of the alcohol and the snake bite we headed off to meet them. Down the track a way the ambulance came into view. I can tell you, it was one of the most welcoming sights of my life.

'Thank God you're here,' I said.

So we stacked the lad into the ambulance and the doctor took over. The lad was taken back to Moomba then flown to Broken Hill. His life was saved. He recovered okay. The odd thing was, though, and I'm just not on about myself here, a lot of people put their lives at risk or volunteered their time and effort to save that lad, and not even one word of thanks. Never.

Off

It's not like being a normal doctor, working as we do, away out here. You haven't got the luxury of being able to sit down face to face with a patient to make a learned diagnosis. What's more, more often than not the initial contact is carried out through a third party. So you have to be a bit of a mind reader as well as having a good grounding in the bush lingo.

Imagine, for example, a new doctor, fresh to the Flying Doctor Service with hardly any experience of bush people at all. Some bloke's taken ill, way out on a remote station somewhere. Normally, those types of males feel awkward about talking to a doctor about their problems, let alone anyone else, so the wife's the initial contact.

'Hello, Doctor, me hubby's taken crook,' she might say.

'What do you mean, crook? How crook is he?' the doctor would ask.

'Darl, the doctor wants to know how crook yer are,' she says, asking her hubby.

'Tell him I'm as crook as a dog,' comes the chap's voice.

'Doctor, he reckons he's real crook.'

'Can you give me some idea as to where he's feeling crook?'

'Darl,' she asks, 'the doctor wants to know where yer feeling crook?'

'Christ, woman, I'm feeling crook all over.'

'Doctor,' she says, 'Hubby reckons he's feeling crook all over.'

'Well,' says the doctor, 'before I can prescribe treatment, we've got to isolate the problem area, okay? So let's start from the top. Is he crook in the head?'

'Darl, the doctor wants to know if yer crook in the head.'

'What sort o' bloody question's that?' echoes the gruff voice. 'Course I'm not bloody crook in the head, woman. I'm as sane as the next bloke. Sounds to me like he's the one who's crook in the head, not me.'

'No, Doctor, he's not crook in the head.'

'Well, is he crook in the abdomen?'

'In the what?' she asks.

'The abdomen. The stomach.'

'Oh, you mean the guts!' she says. 'Darl, are yer crook in the guts?'

'Too bloody right I'm crook in the guts! That's the bloody reason I'm calling the idiot.'

'Yes, Doctor, he's crook in the guts.'

'Has he got nausea?'

'Nausea? What's nausea?'

'Has he been vomiting?' says the doctor.

'What?'

'Has he been spewing?'

'No, I don't think he's been spewing. Darl, yer haven't been spewing again, have yer? No doctor, he hasn't been spewing.'

'Well, has he opened his bowels today?'

'What do yer mean by "opened his bowels"?'

'Has he had a crap?'

'Darl, have yer done number twos yet, today?'

A loud call of 'No!' is heard in the background.

'No, Doctor, he hasn't done one of those.'

'Well, has he voided?'

'What's that?'

'Has he urinated?'

'Urinated? What's that?' she asks.

'For God's sake, has he had a piss?'

'No need to get angry, Doctor,' comes the reply. 'Darl, the doctor wants to know if yer done a number one today.'

'Tell him to mind his own bloody business!'

'He's not sure, Doctor.'

And so the conversation continues until the doctor eventually eliminates the possibilities and homes in on the problem.

But sometimes, of course, it gets more serious than that, a lot more serious. Like the time we were doing a clinic out at Thargomindah and the emergency beacon was activated on the HF radio. A station feller was calling from about three-quarters of an hour's flying time away, saying that there'd been an accident.

As it turned out, a motor cyclist was on his honeymoon and he'd been riding along with his wife in the side car. They'd come to the end of the bitumen section and hit the gravel. He'd lost control, veered off over the table drain, and his leg got caught between the motor bike and a mulga tree. His wife was okay but he wasn't. As I heard it over the radio, the station feller said that the motor cyclist had his leg broken.

To piece the situation together, I began with a few questions. Firstly, how did he know the leg was broken, to which I received the sharp reply of 'Yer'd have to be blind not to see that it's broken, Doc.' So that established that. Then I asked which leg was it, right leg or left leg? Was it broken above the knee or below the knee? 'Above the knee,' I was told. Then I asked if it was bleeding.

'Yes,' the station feller said, 'it's bleeding quite badly.'

So I questioned him about the bleeding. Was it seeping from the breakage point or was the blood spurting out?

'It's spurting out,' came the reply.

'How far?' I asked.

'Oh, only about four or five yards,' he said.

Well, that told me something. I imagined the situation again. A motor cyclist, still alive, thankfully, but in deep shock. The accident. The bike. The tree. A leg which had been broken. The spurting blood. It must surely have been a severed artery. That was the first problem we had to sort out. So, I told the station feller to apply pressure to the bleeding spot and try to contain the bleeding.

So we activated the plane and off we flew. We were met at the airstrip in a ute and driven to the scene of the accident. It was only as we drove up to the motor cyclist that the whole story was revealed. The mental picture I'd drawn was complete, apart from one major discrepancy. The station feller forgot to inform me of one very important fact about the broken leg. The leg wasn't just broken, it'd been broken completely ... off. And there was the motor cyclist, sitting under the tree, and propped up beside him was his severed leg.

Old Bill McDougall

Old Bill McDougall lived in a dilapidated caravan at White Dam, about 10 kilometres out of the small opal-mining town of Andamooka, in central South Australia. And alongside the caravan he built a tin shed which became widely known as, amongst other things, the 'Ettamogah Pub'. The reasoning behind that was the place looked in worse condition than the cartoon of its namesake.

Anyway, Old Bill and his Ettamogah Pub gained quite a reputation. They became a tourist spot. People from all over used to go out there just to visit. And, as a lot of these travellers were going around Australia, they'd 'borrowed' road signs and the like to specially deliver to Old Bill. So signs like 'A new McDonald's restaurant is about to be built here' or 'Black Fella's River' or 'Beware of Crocodiles' sprang up around the place. Quite a sight it was too.

Any time from 6 am through to midnight, if anyone dropped by, Old Bill was there to welcome them, dressed as he always was in his long Royal Flying Doctor T-shirt, shorts and a pair of ripple-soled desert boots without laces. And he'd greet everyone by calling them either 'sonny' or 'lass' or 'girlie'. It didn't matter who you were or if you were twenty or a hundred, a pauper or royalty, it was still the same, 'sonny', 'lass' or 'girlie'.

Of course, the moment you arrived you'd be handed a schooner glass of port. It didn't cost anything. Nothing. It was for free. But Old Bill was a crafty bugger. There was a catch. And the catch was that you had to pay to play that board game, the one they have in pubs where the board's had lots of holes drilled into it which have been filled with pieces of rolled paper, and on those pieces of paper there's prizes written. In Bill's case the prizes were souvenirs of the Royal Flying Doctor Service.

When we flew up there to do clinic, Old Bill was invariably booked in for a consultation. Then while the doctor was checking him over, out would come a couple of thousand dollars or so.

'Here, sonny,' he'd say, handing the stash over to the doctor. 'Look after this.'

It was all cash. No receipts. So we can't exactly tell just how much Old Bill raised over the years but it had to be in the hundreds of thousands of dollars, and that was for both the Flying Doctor Service along with the Andamooka Hospital.

They say that Old Bill started his working life as a engineer with the Merchant Navy. When he got out of that, he wanted to go to a place where he didn't have to look at water. Sick of the stuff, he was. Andamooka was the perfect spot and he became very much a creature of his adopted environment. Loved it out there, he did. Why, I remember the day that Old Bill and I were philosophising about life over a few ports.

'Bill,' I said, 'have you ever thought about where you're going to go and what you're going to do when you eventually decide to chuck all this in and retire?'

'Don't yer worry, sonny, I got it all sorted out,' he said. 'First, I'm gonna stay right here, as far away from water as possible.' Then he stopped talking and looked lovingly out over the dry, dusty landscape. There wasn't a blade of grass in sight, not a one. Then he said, 'And as fer somethin' t' do, I reckon I might start up one of them lawn mowin' rounds. I reckon that should keep me more than busy enough.'

That was Old Bill. He had the vision to look beyond the normal plus the wit and cunning to go with it. Like the time he came up with the idea of raffling his caravan as a fundraising venture. He did that for about fourteen years on the trot. Year after year the raffle tickets came out. Mind you, it was the last thing that anyone wanted to win. That caravan was a total wreck. But still, everyone bought tickets. Snapped them up they did. The people didn't mind. They joined in the fun. The reason being, they knew that every cent was going into the Flying Doctor Service.

Another incident that comes to mind was when he was awarded the OAM (Order of Australia Medal). The 'Old Aussie Mug', he called it.

'Well, sonny,' Old Bill would say, bursting with pride. 'I'm officially an Old Aussie Mug.'

There was a slight hitch with that, though. Old Bill kicked up a bit of a stink when he was told that he had to come down to Adelaide to receive the award. He hated the city. He loathed the city, almost as much as he loathed water. He wanted the Governor to go up to Andamooka to hand over the OAM. At least, then, they could both sit back and indulge in a port or two in a more relaxed environment.

'Cause I tell yer what,' he grumbled, 'I'm not too keen on all that pomp and ceremony they go on with at those sort o' shows.'

Anyway, we finally talked him round and he accepted his fate on the assurance that we'd look after him while he was in Adelaide. That was okay. So, when the time came, we went down to the Adelaide airport to meet him. When the plane landed, off steps Old Bill all decked out in his T-shirt, shorts and desert boots.

'Where's your suitcase?' we asked.

'What suitcase?' he replied. 'I travel light.'

'You can't rock up at Government House dressed like you've just wandered in off the opal fields,' we said.

'Why not?' he reckoned.

Anyway, Jeff Cole, who was the General Manager of John Martin's at that stage, as well as being on the South Australian Tourist Board, rushed him off to Johnnies and decked Old Bill out with a suit and tie, shoes and socks, jocks, the lot. He even had his hair cut and his beard was trimmed. I tell you, he looked an absolute picture of sartorial splendour by the time we dropped him off at Government House.

A few of us had arranged to meet him back at the Grosvener Hotel after the ceremony. Eventually Old Bill arrived looking like a million dollars. We were about to shout him a couple of drinks but when we looked round he'd disappeared. Nobody could find him. Then ten minutes later he appeared with a grin from ear to ear. There he was—he's got his old T-shirt on, his desert boots, his shorts and he's as happy as a pig in shit.

'Okay, sonny, your shout,' he announced.

That suit never again saw the light of day.

I tell you, he was a real character was Old Bill. Then later, of course, he got real crook. There were numerous things wrong by that stage, all the results of his free-and-easy lifestyle. I remember the day that we flew him out of Andamooka to bring him down to hospital in Adelaide. The poor old bloke knew that it was his last flight. He knew he was dying. As we were loading him onto the plane, he leaned over and slipped a heap of money to Margo Duke, his great friend from the Andamooka Post Office.

'This is fer me wake, girlie,' he said.

And some wake it was too, I can tell you.

So that's Old Bill, like I said, a real character. He's been dead now for near on eight years. But he certainly hasn't been forgotten because on every Easter Saturday people from all over set off on the 10 kilometres' walk from Andamooka out to Old Bill's place at White Dam. On the day, they raise $6000 to $8000 for the Royal Flying Doctor Service. Then when they arrive at the Ettamogah Pub site everyone gathers around and they have a few drinks and a barbecue, all in memory of Old Bill McDougall.

Once Bitten, Twice Shy

I reckon it must have been about four, or half-past four, on a Sunday morning. I was still in bed for some unknown reason. Anyway, the telephone rang. It was Big Joe McCraddok, the police sergeant from Birdsville. Mind you, I've changed names and locations here to protect the guilty.

'Come quick. Come quick,' Joe called.

'Why, Joe?' I replied. 'What's the matter?'

'Roota Kozlowski's been bit b' a snake,' he said. 'Roota Kozlowski's been bit b' a snake.'

Now you'd be able to imagine the sort of character Roota Kozlowski was, just from his nickname, but maybe you haven't heard about Big Joe McCraddok. He's quite famous around these parts. A real true-blue bush character. They did an article on him in one of those monthly magazines, a while back. The locals really gave him a stirring about that, especially the way he was posing outside the pub, in his uniform and all. Anyway, that's the media for you. Because, believe me, Big Joe's nothing like that. He's as male as they come; a real man's man, through and through.

'What symptoms has Roota got?' I asked.

'I don't know,' Joe said. 'He's still about half an hour out of town but he's on his way in so, if you come now, you'll be here just that much quicker.'

That sent me into a spin. I mean, Joe of all people knows that it takes time to organise the plane and everything, and there he was expecting me to be in Birdsville at a moment's notice.

'Look, Joe, you'll have to give Roota first aid yourself,' I said. 'I won't be able to get there within half an hour, you know that.'

'Oh,' came the disappointed reply. 'Must I?'

'You've done it plenty of times before,' I said. 'All you've got to do is to apply pressure immobilisation on him the moment he arrives in town.'

There was dead silence.

'Where's he been bitten?' I asked.

The dead silence continued.

'Joe, are you there?' I said. 'Where's Roota been bitten?'

'Look, Doc, I can't speak too loud 'cause I'm ringing from the pub. There's a few of the blokes here and all they know is that Roota's been bit b' a snake, but I haven't told them exactly where.'

'But I've got to know exactly where he's been bitten, Joe,' I said, avoiding the question as to what he was doing in the pub with 'a few of the blokes' at that hour of the morning. 'Joe, can you hear me?'

'On the penis,' came the whisper.

Well, that certainly got me thinking. I mean, Roota's Roota and the many and varied stories of his sexual exploits were known far and wide, but how in the hell a bloke could've got himself bitten in that spot defied imagination.

'On the what?' I asked.

'You heard me. Roota's been bit on the penis,' came the answer, fractionally louder.

Well, that was clear enough. It also explained Big Joe's apprehension about having to give first aid. You could just imagine the comments from the blokes in the pub as they watched Joe apply pressure immobilisation to Roota Kozlowski, especially with it being in that particular region. And so soon after the magazine article and all. Joe'd never live it down.

'Look, Joe,' I said, 'I know what's going through your mind, mate, but you've got to forget all that rubbish. The point is, if you don't give the treatment, Roota could well die. Do I make myself very clear, Joe?'

Silence.

'So, Joe,' I continued, 'as soon as Roota arrives, get him to whip down his pants, then apply pressure immobilisation. And what's more, hold onto it until I get there, right.'

Silence.

'Do you hear me, Joe!'

'Okay,' came the reluctant reply.

As the story goes, Roota pulled into town not too much later, very groggy from the snake bite. He blundered into the pub and saw Joe over by the bar with a few of the blokes, all of them looking extremely downcast.

'Have yer spoken to the doctor?' Roota asked.

'Yes,' Joe mumbled.

'What did he say?'

'Well, Roota,' Joe said, 'doc reckons yer gonna die.'

One Shot

This happened in a place called Boulia, which is 140 nautical miles south of Mount Isa, in the Diamantina channel country. And as in many of those places out that way, they've got very wide main streets. That's because, in the olden days, they needed a hell of a lot of room to turn the bullock wagons around. Later, of course, they came in handy if there was some emergency or other and you needed to land your aeroplane in the town.

Boulia was such a place.

To paint the scene, it's big sky country, not many trees, dead flat. You can see forever, and, as evening nears, it takes a long time for the sun to go down. It seems to just hang there, inching its way down to the horizon. Then all of a sudden, poof, and it's gone. There's very little twilight under those conditions.

Anyway, it's late afternoon in Boulia and there's this guy and his wife, or de facto, who'd had a few too many drinks in the pub and they have this doozey of an argument, a real donnybrook. 'F'n this and f'n' that.' All the accusations, the incriminations, the whole works. The upshot of all this is that this woman storms out of the pub. 'I'll give yer a lesson yer'll never forget, yer bloody so-and-so,' she says.

'Yeah, yeah,' the bloke slurs in a smart-arse manner. 'Yer wouldn't have the guts.'

But little did he know that she's on her way home to get the .22 rifle. So she grabs the gun and comes back and waits on the diagonal corner about 150 yards down-sun from the pub.

Eventually, the bloke wanders out. And remember how I was saying that it takes a long time for the sun to set? Well, there he is, with the sun at his back, and he can see this woman with the gun as clear as day. Conversely, she can't see him too well because the sun's shining straight into her eyes. But she knows it's him. She knows it's the guy. And it's her full intention to shoot in the general area of the guy, just to put the wind up him, like, to give him the lesson that she said she'd give him.

So he starts to move towards her, holding his hands up, and she lifts the gun to her shoulder and takes aim. No doubt she's still a bit pissed, like. So then she pulls the trigger. Bang. One shot. Straight through the guy's head.

Soon after, we get the call in Mount Isa. Now the doctor reckons that most gunshots turn out to be fatal. 'Look,' he says, as we rush out to the aeroplane, 'if he dies, it then becomes a police matter and it's no longer got anything to do with us.'

But the report comes through from the nurse at Boulia that this guy is still alive. So there we are— I've done all the checks. The engines are warming up. Everything's just right. And I'm just about to open it up and head down the runway when the doctor gets a call through on the HF long-range radio.

'Hang on,' he says.

So I stop.

'He's gone.'

So I kill the take-off.

Pass the Hat

One of the first fundraising appeals for what was then known as the Australian Inland Mission happened back in November 1928. It was on that date that old Jock McNamara passed his hat around the front bar of Mrs Palmer's pub in McKinlay. And, what's more, he made a few quid too, or so I heard.

At the time old Jock owned Squirrel Hills Station which was situated halfway between McKinlay and Boulia, out in the north-west of Queensland. One day he and his son-in-law, Tom Lucas, were out mustering cattle in the Selwyn Ranges. Now, for those who don't know, the Selwyn Ranges consists of some very rugged and mountainous country, most of which is impassable by vehicle. Anyway, old Jock was climbing through a particularly rough patch on his horse when all of a sudden the rubble gave way. The horse reared. Up it went, it lost its balance, toppled over backwards and thud down it came smack-bang on old Jock, squashing him and breaking his pelvis among other things. Very badly injured he was. Couldn't move.

Now this happened before pedal radios existed. Alf Traeger came up with the first of his radios a year later, in 1929, so there was no way that Tom could call for help, not from out in the middle of the Selwyn Ranges, that's for sure. What's more, there were no telephones out that way either.

So Tom dragged old Jock under the shade of a tree.

'Here, Pop,' he said, 'here's some water and a bit of food. I'll go and see if I can get some help.'

And that's where Tom left old Jock, propped up under a tree, out there in the Selwyn Ranges, with some water and food and a gun to keep the dingoes at bay. Then Tom rode for ten hours straight until he came across a mustering camp. Mind you, that was still out in the middle of nowhere, but when he told the head stockman about old Jock's accident the bloke offered to drive him into McKinlay, which was where the nearest telephone was.

When they finally arrived, Tom went straight to the McKinlay Post Office where he rang through to the Australian Inland Mission in at Cloncurry and gave them the details of the accident and the general location of where he'd left old Jock.

'We'll be there as soon as we can,' the AIM Flying Doctor said.

Now the actual plane that was used for the evacuation was imported by Hudson Fysh of the then Queensland and Northern Territory Aerial Service, later to be known as Qantas. That happened back in 1924. It was a De Havilland DH 50, a single-engined four-seater biplane where the pilot sat in an outside cockpit. John Flynn had leased the DH 50 for two shillings per mile, plus a pilot, a chap called Arthur Affleck, and two engineers. There's a big model of this very same aeroplane in Cloncurry, if you're ever up that way.

Anyway, that aside, having now alerted the Flying Doctor, Tom jumped back into the truck and they drove to a nearby station where they organised an old iron bedstead to be used as a stretcher. Then along with a couple of volunteers they headed back out to old

Jock. When they'd driven as far as they could into the Selwyn Ranges, they grabbed the bedstead and set off by foot.

By this time Arthur Affleck, the pilot, had landed the small plane on an open patch of country, still many miles from the accident scene. But it was as close as he could get with the De Havilland. Now the doctor on that trip was a Kenyan chap by the name of Dr K St Vincent Welch. He was the world's first Flying Doctor, meaning that he was the first doctor employed by the Australian Inland Mission. Anyway, Dr Welch grabbed his gear and along with Arthur he started to walk in the direction of where old Jock was supposed to be.

While Dr Welch and Arthur were on their way, Tom and his helpers had reached old Jock. As you might well imagine, after having been stuck out there for almost two days the old feller's condition had deteriorated somewhat, but he was still alive and that was the main thing. So they laid him out on the bedstead, latched onto an end each and they set off, back out of the Selwyn Ranges.

Tom Lucas and his crew travelled for what was left of that day and into the night until, as luck would have it, they stumbled across Dr Welch and Arthur. 'Dr Welch, I presume,' Tom remarked. Mind you, he didn't really say that. I just added it in because it sounded appropriate. Anyway, when the doctor saw the agony that poor old Jock was in he gave him an injection of morphine right on the spot. Then, as they headed back to the plane, to save all the time they could Dr Welch kept administering injections as they walked along.

Finally, they got old Jock into the De Havilland. Now the nearest hospital was at Cloncurry but unfortunately at that particular time there was an epidemic of some sort going through there and so they decided to fly him to the Winton Hospital.

Anyway, to cut a long story short, old Jock McNamara must have been a terribly tough sort of chap because he made a remarkable recovery and, three months later, in November 1928, he came back home to Squirrel Hills Station. Of course, by this time the news of his accident and his miraculous survival had spread near and far. It'd been written up in all the papers as well.

But one of the first things that old Jock did on his return was to go into the local pub, Mrs Palmer's pub it was, right there in McKinlay, and after everyone had welcomed him back he took his hat off and passed it around the front bar.

'Dig deep, fellers, it's for Flynn's Inland Mission,' he said. 'Saved me life, they did. Who knows, it could be yours next.'

'Payback'

I was already really, really tired after having just arrived home off night shift from another flight. Then the call came through. 'We've got a Code One emergency out at Nyrippi,' they said. 'A guy's unconscious with a GCS of three.'

Now a GCS, or Glasgow Coma Score, is the way that head injuries are rated and, among other things, is gauged on your best verbal response, eyes opening, and your best motor response. If there's nothing wrong then your score is usually fifteen. If it's under nine you've got a serious head injury. Having a three wasn't a good sign really; more like a life and death situation, with the odds stacked towards death.

Mark, the doctor, Peter, the pilot, and I flew out on that trip to Nyrippi. A sixteen-year-old guy had been cracked over the back of the head by a person wielding a firestick. Apparently the week before the young kid had caused some sort of trouble. This was his 'payback'.

We got out there in about an hour which was pretty good considering that we had to drive out to the airport and pack some special equipment into the plane. Peter also had to do all his flight checks and so forth before take-off. Anyway, when we landed at Nyrippi the community officer was waiting to pick us up. So I grabbed whatever gear I thought we'd need and threw it into the back of his ute on top of his welding gear and bits and pieces of cars and other scrap. Then we headed into the community.

John was the community nurse on duty that night. I think it was his first week at Nyrippi, if not the first night he'd spent by himself out at the community. And he'd done a fantastic job. When the young guy had first come in he'd put a plastic stiff-neck collar on him to keep his neck in alignment. He'd put a drip in, got the oxygen on him, checked his blood pressure, and then rang the Flying Doctor Service in Alice Springs.

By the time he got back from calling us, the young guy had stopped breathing, and that's when John started bagging him. So he must have been bagging the patient for at least an hour. By 'bagging' I mean physically squeezing oxygen into his lungs through a mask, virtually breathing for him.

It was amazing. In a hospital, you bag someone for ten minutes and your hands are aching beyond belief. Ten minutes and, like I said, John had been at it for at least an hour. It's heat of the moment stuff. It's all full-on. And John was the only one bagging. There may have been a health worker somewhere but when it's their own family they tend not to want to be hands-on.

What's more, fifteen or so of the family were in the same room watching every move John made, which must've added to the pressure. There were also a few extra police there by that time. They'd driven over from another community because they knew there could be some serious trouble brewing.

So we got into the clinic and Mark said, 'Okay, what's going on?'

'This is the situation,' John said, then explained the medical details and what'd happened.

Then Mark took over which gave John the chance to stand back for a while and catch up with things.

Of course, the first thing that Mark requested was mannitol, which is a drug that releases the fluid off the brain. Silly me, of all things to leave back in the plane, I'd left the mannitol. But, luckily, just a few weeks beforehand I'd shown Peter, our pilot, where everything was packed, just in case. So he was able to go back out and grab the drug from the bottom of the cupboard. While Peter was doing that I was getting ready for Mark to intubate by checking the patient's blood pressure and his pupils, and putting up another bag of fluid.

And so we got the young guy intubated, which is sticking a tube in his throat to clear the windpipe. We continued to bag him, though. He was still unconscious. While we were moving him onto a spinal board for the trip back out to the airstrip we got Peter, the jack-of-all-trades, to do the bagging. When that was done, Mark explained the situation to the family.

'Look,' he said, 'he's had a big head injury and he'll probably have to go to the theatre and have an operation.'

After Mark had finished talking, a faint wailing started to rise up from among the women in the room. And as that gathered momentum everyone outside began joining in. This wailing, I don't know if you've ever experienced it, but it's the most haunting sound you're ever likely to hear. It's filled with such pain and sadness that the hairs on the back of your neck go stiff. And there they all were, watching everything that we were doing and wailing at the same time. Louder and louder, all around us.

So we loaded the young guy into the back of the Toyota four-wheel-drive 'troopie' and I hopped in with him. The grandmother and the auntie also hopped in and the two of them kept up this wailing all the way out to the airstrip. Meantime this guy's blood pressure was really low and I was thinking, 'What sort of situation are we in? No one would ever believe this.' And you think, 'If only people could see what it's like, to be out here in the middle of nowhere, with these poor women wailing and their young boy fighting for his life.' It's so scary. It's weird. It's surreal. People just don't believe that you have those sorts of experiences.

By the time we reached the airstrip, about sixty people had gathered from the community. There they were, all just wanting to touch the young guy because they thought that it was probably the last time they'd see him alive. By then the wailing had built up to be a whirlwind. It was like a wall of sound. And it just went on and on and on, spinning around us.

Eventually, the police stepped in and gave us a hand to get the patient onto the plane. One of the family members, a cousin it was, came along to keep the guy company. By that stage Peter was quite distressed. He'd never seen or heard anything like it. It really got to him.

Anyway, we got the young guy onto the plane and as we were flying back to Alice Springs his heart suddenly faltered. It went into an odd sort of rhythm. And that's when you realise that you're all by yourself. There's no one you can turn to and ask 'What do you reckon about this?' because you're just up there in black vastness. You can't even fax anything to anyone.

It makes you realise just how isolated you are in a situation like that, when you're thousands of feet up in the sky. No one's there to help you. Even when you're being trained in a hospital, they say that if a patient has a cardiac arrest then there'll always be someone to do the airways, someone to do the chest compressions, someone to do the drugs, someone to write it all down and someone else will be there to do this, that and the other. But there we were, just Mark and I, a doctor and a nurse, doing everything we could, and there was this poor young guy, deteriorating further and further.

Still, we managed to get a request through for an anaesthetist to meet us at the airport. Then as soon as we'd landed and got the patient into the ambulance the anaesthetist came and took one look at him. 'Go!' he shouted to the driver. 'This patient needs lots of people focusing on him.'

So the ambos and doctor drove into the hospital with lights and sirens blaring. By that time the young guy was having a cardiac arrest. In the plane I'd noticed that he had a big lump on his temple. It'd sort of swelled up. Like, there was no blood coming from his ears. There was no obvious bleeding from his head. It was all internal.

After the ambos had left, I went back out to clean up the plane. Though he hadn't bled externally, he'd still lost a lot of bloody frothy sputum and there was a mess on the floor. So I cleaned that up. Then I cleaned the equipment. Then I restocked the plane so that it was ready to go again, just in case something else happened.

I must've spent an hour or so cleaning and checking things. By that time it was four in the morning. As I said at the beginning, I was already really tired from a night shift, before the call from Nyrippi came through. But in those sorts of situations your brain doesn't stop and you're always thinking, 'Could I have done something better? Is there something that I didn't see?' Always analysing things.

So on my way home I decided to go into the hospital and that's when I was told that the young guy had passed away.

All the staff were good about it, reassuring me that I'd done everything I could. He'd had an autopsy and it was found that his skull was cracked right across, from one ear right through to the other.

'There's nothing more you could've done,' I was told. 'Even if he was in the neurology unit he still would've died because he'd had such huge internal bleeds.'

But it still upset me. I was also tired beyond belief. But I just wanted to go outside and sit by myself. Just to take my breath. I needed to be alone for a while. So I went outside and I was sitting there, about half-past four in the morning. Everything was quiet, dead quiet. I was tossing things around in my head when a wind blew up from a distance and I swear that it brought with it that haunting sound of people wailing.

Peak Hour Traffic

Bush people are different, you know.

There's two types in our area, out from Broken Hill. First, you've got the sheep people. They're pretty urban sorts because they come to town a fair bit. Then there's the other breed, that's the cattle people. They live right out in the harsh country.

The cattle people don't get to see civilisation too much, maybe once or twice a year, sometimes even less. They're the ones you see around town with the big hats on. Slow movers they are, and they talk in single syllables. 'Yeah. G'day. How, yer, goin'? All, right.' That's because, out there, there's not many people for them to mix with, except for their own types. But that's their lifestyle and they reckon it's wonderful, and you can't knock them for that. They probably think that our lifestyle's pretty weird, and you couldn't blame them for that either, especially with all the goings-on you read about in the paper and see on the box.

But it's the isolation that makes the cattle people so unique.

There was an old bloke. His name was Joe. And old Joe was one of the cattle people types. He had been most of his life. He's gone now, God rest his soul. And what you've got to understand here is that there's a lot of these old fellers, just like Joe, who live out on these stations. They don't own the stations, like. They don't even manage the stations. Yet they've lived on the properties for most of their lives, helping out here and there, doing odd jobs, mostly as jackaroos. And a lot of them never get married but they become like family so, when they retire, they just go on living on these stations in a caravan or something.

Anyway, old Joe was a real bushie, retired he was, and he developed a medical problem which we had to keep an eye on. But when we suggested that he move into Broken Hill he dug his heels in.

'There's no way I'm gonna live in a place with street lights,' he complained, and you could tell by the steely look in his eye that he meant every word of it.

So the next best thing we could come up with was for him to move into Tilpa where we flew in regularly to do clinics. Tilpa was the ideal place. There definitely weren't any traffic lights there. Dead quiet it was. It had a population of about eleven, if you can imagine that—just a pub, post office, petrol bowser, that sort of town. But Tilpa had a caravan park, in a manner of speaking. Pretty basic it was. Nothing like the ones you see in the tourist brochures. What's more, it didn't need to be too flash either because you'd be lucky to get one or two tourists coming through every month or so, and that was in peak season.

So old Joe agreed to come in off the station so we could keep an eye on him. Which he did, and he instantly laid claim to being the only permanent resident in the Tilpa caravan park.

As I said, having the problem that he did, whenever we were up there we'd go and visit him in his caravan.

'How yer doing, Joe?' we'd ask.

'Yeah, okay,' he'd say in that real slow bushie drawl of his which didn't give us a ghost of an idea as to how he was really feeling.

Then one day we flew into Tilpa and we noticed that his caravan had gone. It wasn't there any more. So we asked the nurse, 'Where's old Joe?'

'Oh, he's shifted,' she said.

She told us that he'd moved out of town, down the road a bit. So we shanghaied a four-wheel drive and we drove out of town about 10 kilometres and there's old Joe's caravan, parked well off the road, away out in the scrub. So we knocked on the door of the caravan.

'G'day, Joe. How yer doin'?' we asked.

'Oh, okay,' he drawled.

Then we asked him how his health was, and about his problem, and all that sort of stuff.

'Yeah, okay,' he said, which was a fair bit for Joe, even at the best of times.

Then I asked, 'Joe, how come you've moved out of the Tilpa caravan park? What're you doing way out here, in the middle of nowhere?'

'Ah, it was the bloody traffic,' he grumbled. 'The bloody traffic in Tilpa was drivin' me bloody balmy.'

Pepper Steak

It's a few years ago now but when I was a Flight Nurse there was one property in particular that we were never too keen on visiting. It was only a smallish place, an outstation, right on the edge of the Simpson Desert.

We didn't drive out there of course, we flew. But on the mornings that we did, we had to be up at the crack of dawn, ready to take off at 6 am, to get to the outstation by 8 am and begin our clinic or whatever. And, as was the routine, when we reached any of these stations we'd circle the homestead a couple of times just to let the people know that we'd arrived and then they'd drive down to the airstrip to pick us up.

Anyhow, on this particular occasion we did just that. We circled the place a couple of times then we landed. The only trouble was—no one came to meet us. No one, that is, apart from the flies. And when I mean flies, I don't mean just the odd couple of hundred. There were swarms of them. Sticky things they were, too.

So there we were, Llew, the doctor, and I, hanging around in the stinking heat, swamped by these flies, when finally an old EJ Holden station wagon drove up.

'Jump in,' the driver said.

'Where?' Llew asked.

Now this may have sounded like a silly question but for starters there was no back seat in the vehicle. And, what's more, apart from the space where the driver sat, the rest of the station wagon was stacked to the hilt with big pats of cow dung, all at various stages of being dried. Now, when these cow pats were thrown onto a camp fire they might have worked miracles in keeping the mosquitoes at bay, but to the flies they acted like a super magnet. If, as I said, we were swamped by flies when we stood beside the airstrip, we were drowned by the blessed things as we stood beside the vehicle.

With no help in the offing, Llew and I started reorganising these cow pats in an attempt to make some room for ourselves. When that proved to be impossible, we ended up having to perch ourselves on top of this dung the best we could manage. So there was Llew, hanging on for grim life to his doctor's bag full of sterilised gear. There was me, squashed in next to him, dressed in my freshly washed and ironed atomic-blue nurse's uniform. And not only was the inside of the station wagon a sea of flies but I could well imagine a dark cloud of the things trailing the vehicle as we drove through the dust and up to the homestead.

Then, lo and behold, when we got in the homestead we were tossed a piece of hessian to hang off the verandah for our shade. And so began our clinic, the full medicals, the lot, among the flies and the heat, and in the most basic of hygienic conditions.

While we were checking people over, I could smell kerosene and I remember saying to Llew, 'God, Llew, can you smell that kero?' He just screwed up his nose at the stench and went back to the job at hand.

Not long after that a woman came out and started to set up a fire to cook lunch just a few metres away from where Llew and I were working. I was going to say something to her but I thought better of it. I guess I must have been staring at the massive pieces of pepper steak that were laid out on a plate because she turned around to me and said, 'Would youse people like somethin' ta eat?'

Now the strong smell of kerosene was getting to me so I didn't have much of an appetite. But you have to be very careful not to offend some of these people so I said, 'Yes, just a small piece, please. It looks like very nice pepper steak you've got there.'

'Nothing for me,' said Llew, who was a bit more forthright on the matter.

Anyway, the woman didn't say anything so I continued helping Llew and she got up and disappeared into the homestead. When she came back she was carrying a tin can and in that tin can was some sickly greenish stuff which, to my horror, turned out to be fat. I couldn't stand to look but when she threw the fat into the pan the smell of the bubbling, burning mixture, along with the strong stench of the kerosene, got my stomach in a spin.

'Just a small piece,' I called. 'A very, very small piece.'

But again the woman didn't say anything so I started to walk over to make sure that she'd heard what I'd said. That's when she went to pick up the steak. And that's when it struck me that the pepper bits on the steak weren't pepper bits at all but, in actual fact, all this while the meat had been smothered in flies. Because, as she picked up the meat and threw it into the pan, the flies took to wing. In saying that, I must add that there were a good many who were a bit slow on the uptake and they ended up in the frying pan along with the meat and the bubbling greenish fat.

Llew must have seen my reaction because he came to my rescue like a shot and made the excuse that we couldn't stay for lunch because he just remembered we had an emergency to attend to. So we wrapped up the clinic quick smart and were taken back down to the airstrip in the station wagon which was still stacked to the hilt with cow pats. But we weren't so concerned this time. It was just such a relief to be getting out of there. When Llew and I were dropped off, we said goodbye, loaded the plane and were out of there like a bolt of lightning. Just as well we did, too, because that wasn't the end of the saga.

Later that night the news came through that there'd been a fire out at the homestead. As luck had it, there were no injuries. But, apparently, what I'd been smelling during the day was the kerosene fridge leaking. Then, after we'd left, the fridge blew up and the homestead was burnt down, leaving just the roof and the supports, and no doubt the flies.

Plonk

Now this all happened many years ago, so I can't be 100 per cent sure of all the facts. But I was doing an adult education course back in the 1950s and there was this journalist-cum-playwright chap who came to our campus to give us a talk about his travels through central Australia. That would've been some sort of feat back in those days, especially considering that he was driving a small Morris. There weren't any bitumen roads, dirt tracks more like it, nothing but corrugations and dust. It must have been horrendous.

Still and all, as fascinating as it was, especially the way he told it, full of adventure: all about sleeping out under the stars in Central Mount Stuart and the time the Morris got bogged in fine bulldust, apparently, the only way that he could get the car out was to slide something solid under each of its rear wheels so that he could gain the traction he needed to drive out of the bog. So he hunted around the place and found a strip of corrugated iron which was wide enough to fit under just one of the back wheels. And it was then that he said he realised that he wasn't the only person who'd been stuck in the same spot because painted on that thin strip of corrugated iron were the words 'Now find the other piece.'

Another time he was camping around the site where some blacks had been massacred by whites, back in the 1800s, and to keep his fire stoked up he was absent-mindedly tossing sticks onto it. One stick that he picked up felt different. It was almost smooth, so he had a closer look and discovered that it was half a boomerang. When he later had it checked out he was told that it'd been scraped by shells, so he kept it as a talisman.

But out of all his stories, the one that's stayed in my mind for all these years was told to him by one of the Flying Doctors on his travels. A pretty gruesome story it was, too. It was about a couple of old chaps who'd gone out mining and one of them committed suicide.

Maybe the chap who killed himself had rushed away from some place or other because he'd been let down in love or something, or perhaps he'd done all his dough on their mining venture and they hadn't found a brass razoo. I don't know. That was never fully explained. Anyway, this chap and his mate were apparently tossing down the plonk, the wine like, and the drunker this particular chap got the more depressed he became, until eventually he got a right dose of the miseries.

Anyway, the long and short of it was that he grabbed a knife and ran it across his throat. So his mate got in touch with the Flying Doctor. Frantic he was.

'Oh, God,' he called, 'yer gotta come 'n' see me mate. He's just cut 'is throat. And the blood. You should see the blood. It's terrible. There's blood everywhere.'

And in response the Flying Doctor said, 'Look, keep calm. Get a needle and some cotton and sew it up.'

'But I haven't got a needle and cotton,' called the chap's mate.

'Well,' said the doctor, 'get a bag needle and string.'

'Haven't got that neither,' came the reply. 'Oh, my God, the blood,' the chap kept saying. 'Oh, my God, the blood.'

The poor chap who'd slit his own throat died not long after and, as the story was told to us, the Flying Doctor had to go out to verify the death. So the doctor said to the chap's mate, 'Look, have the grave dug, ready for when I arrive.'

'Okay,' said the chap, 'I'll get a grave ready.'

Anyway, by the time the Flying Doctor got there the other chap had sobered up and had dug the grave. Stone cold sober he was by that time. So the Flying Doctor verified the death. Then, just as they were about to toss the dead chap into the grave, his mate asked in an embarrassed manner, 'Do yer mind if I ask yer something?' he said.

'No,' replied the doctor, 'go ahead.'

'Well,' said the chap, 'I used ta be a butcher, see, and I know all 'bout the interiors of animals. And fer the life of me I've always wondered about the insides o' people, so I was wondering if there was any chance yer could show me some o' the parts.'

'Okay,' said the doctor. He must have been keen to brush up on his surgical skills because he took out a knife and away he went. 'This bit here is the liver.' (Plonk, and into the grave it went.) 'This is the heart.' (Plonk, into the grave it went.) 'And this is the stomach.' (Plonk, into the grave it went.) And so forth and so on until they'd disposed of the body.

And that's the story. Now, as I said, I don't know whether it was exactly true or not, but I can remember that journalist-cum-playwright chap telling us that story to this very day. And each time he said the words 'Plonk, and into the grave it went', you could see all the students' jaws drop that little bit further, mine included.

Rabbit

I heard you on the radio, reading some stories about the Flying Doctor Service, and it reminded me of the time that Mum and Dad were coming over to our place for dinner. It was Dad's birthday and I wanted to cook something special. I'm a pretty good cook, you see, or that's what most people say. But, apart from that, it's something that I really enjoy doing, you know, experimenting with this and that, trying different recipes, different tastes and flavours.

Anyway, I was having a chat to Mum on the phone, discussing plans for the night, and she asked what I was going to cook. I said that I'd planned to start off with some basic nibblies, followed by an antipasto platter, then a seafood soup, and for main course I was going to cook some rabbit.

'Rabbit!' Mum interrupted. 'You're not cooking rabbit, are you?'

'Well, yes,' I replied. 'I've got a really nice recipe for rabbit that an old Italian chap's given me.'

'I don't want any,' she snorted, and then came one of her deathly silences, the ones that she gives when she's digging in her heels about anything.

'Why, Mum?' I asked. 'What's wrong with rabbit?'

Then she told me that when she was a teenager at boarding school, over in Perth, one of her girlfriends invited her to spend the school holidays out on her family's station property. I'm not exactly sure where the station was, but it was away out bush somewhere, south-east of Perth, I think. It was quite a remote place, anyway.

At that stage of her life Mum hadn't been too far from the city and, for the past couple of years, everything that she'd heard from this girl about her parents' station property conjured up images of a romantic life in the outback. There was the freedom of living out in the wide open spaces, the fresh air, the beautiful sunsets, the millions of stars at night, of being able to ride horses from dawn to dusk.

When Mum checked to see if it was okay with Gran and Pop, they were fine about it.

'Go, girl,' Pop said. 'It'll be a great experience.'

So she did.

But, unfortunately for Mum, the experience turned out to be anything but romantic. Quite the opposite really—more like a nightmare. After spending three days cooped up in a sooty old train, when they eventually arrived at the station property Mum found the sparseness of the area to be overwhelming, daunting—frightening even. The air was hot and dusty. Instead of looking in wonder at the millions and millions of stars, she spent the nights swatting millions and millions of mosquitoes. Where her friend stood in awe of beautiful sunsets, Mum was only relieved to know that she'd survived yet another day among the flies. Yes, they did ride horses but, after the first morning, Mum reckoned her behind was so sore that she doubted if she'd ever be able to walk again.

But perhaps what was worst of all was the complete lack of fresh fruit and vegetables. What's more, there wasn't a shop or a green-grocer within cooee.

'Oh,' Mum's girlfriend said, 'we get a delivery of fresh food every couple of months.'

Mum must have looked extremely disappointed at that remark because her friend was quick to add, 'Don't worry, Margaret, the next delivery's due in a couple of days' time.'

The mere thought of sinking her teeth into a nice, crisp apple was the only thing that kept Mum going. So she suffered through the lack of fresh vegetables and fruit. She suffered through the desolation. She suffered through the heat and the dust. She suffered through the flies and the mosquitoes. She even attempted to get back on a horse, but she fell off.

Then, the day before the delivery of fresh food was due, the storm clouds rolled in, the sky opened and down came the rain. Mum reckoned that she's never seen the likes of it, still to this day. What's more, the rain didn't look like stopping. It kept bucketing down. And with the soil out that way being sand and clay, or whatever, the water just built up and up. The creeks burst their banks and they got flooded in so bad not even a horse could get in or out.

To start with there was still a little food remaining. But, after a week, things were getting pretty desperate. Then the week after that they were in real trouble. That's where the rabbits came in. They'd been flushed out of their warrens and had scrambled onto the only piece of available land they could find, which was around the station homestead.

Poor Mum. If one of her major gripes was the inferior quality of the food, by the third week her staple diet consisted of not much more than dried bread, black tea and rabbit, rabbit, rabbit and more rabbit.

Mum reckons that they had boiled rabbit, roasted rabbit, minced rabbit, fried rabbit, rabbit portions, fricassee of rabbit, rabbit stew. They had rabbit every-which-way, day in, day out, and still the water didn't look like receding.

'Without a word of a lie,' Mum said, 'there were so many rabbits that you could sit on the back doorstep and just about shoot the blessed things with your eyes shut.'

So there they were, out in the middle of nowhere, surrounded by a sea of water, facing the choice of either starving or eating more rabbit. Mum said that it even reached the stage where starving looked like being the better of the two options.

Then one morning as Mum and her friend were lying around in bed, thinking about making a move, they heard a plane fly overhead, really low it was.

'It's the Flying Doctor,' the girl's father shouted from the kitchen.

They were up in a flash and everyone raced out onto the verandah. And it was, too. It was the Flying Doctor plane. Mum thought that it might have been a DC3 or something like that. It was one of those bigger planes, anyway. When the aeroplane did a second fly-over, they threw out a hessian bag stacked full of food.

Mum reckons that she still remembers the meal they had that day. Though it wasn't the nice, fresh, crisp apple that she'd longed for, there was still milk, tinned meat, tinned vegetables, fresh bread and jam.

Everything except rabbit.

Richmond

I'm living in a shed these days. That's where I am now, away out in the bush near Sarina, outside of Mackay. That's in Queensland if you don't know. But it wasn't always like that. I haven't always lived in a shed. Not on your life. I used to own houses, trucks, the lot, but the Public Trust got stuck into me. Took the lot, they did. That was after a semi-trailer cracked my upper jaw and my lower jaw and many other unidentified bones in my skull, along with my collarbone to boot.

That all happened a few years back and now I can't talk properly either, as you might have guessed. It's not only affected my voice. It's gotten to my memory as well so my memory's not quite the same either. Like, I don't know how old I am these days. That's because I used to work the years out by which truck I had at the time. Just like a calendar those trucks were. I used to be a truckie, see, but a semi-trailer got me so I'm nothing now. Then the Public Trust got to me after that and they took everything I owned, the trucks, my two houses, seven acres of freehold land, family heirlooms, two Rayburn slow combustion stoves, my water tanker, pumps, hoses, two caravans, a mobile workshop, the lot. They got everything. I've got all the paperwork here to prove it, if you want to see it.

What's more, they were hoping that I'd die too, but I haven't died yet and I won't for a long time to come, either. You can tell them that as well. I took them through the Supreme Court in the end, and I got them too. It's the principle of the matter that counts. The case might've cost thousands but I got the $110 they owed me. I've got the receipts right here, somewhere. You can have a look at those as well if you like. But that's the Public Trust for you. That's why I live right out here in the shed near Sarina. They can't get me here. You can tell them that too, in your book, if you like.

Anyway, that's got nothing to do with the Flying Doctor Service, has it? But I was just telling you how things are and who to watch out for. That's why I do most of my business by phone, though I write lots of letters about this and that. My mother was born right beside the Combo Waterhole, out past Winton. Winton's the place that Banjo Paterson made famous with that song 'Waltzing Matilda'. There were no doctors out there then. I was born out near Richmond, about 307 miles into the sunset from Townsville.

Anyhow, it might've been somewhere between the mid 1940s and the early '50s, I can't remember exactly. It could've even been before that, maybe. My memory's not the same since the Public Trust got stuck into me. But back then we owned two stations, Rowena and Rolling Downs.

Anyway, it was when I was living in Richmond. I was only a kid then and in those days the main street didn't have 240 volts installed. Some people had their own charging plant but that wasn't everybody. But, also, Richmond had a real wide street, dirt it was, no one out there knew what bitumen was back then. Anyhow, because there wasn't 240 volts there were no electricity poles or anything, no obstructions in the street, and more than once the planes used to land in the main street. Goldring Street it was. I remember that.

I also remember the time that this feller came looking for a woman. He wasn't with the Flying Doctor Service or anything. The plane was called the 'Silver City'. Gee, I remember that too. And he landed just out of town and I led him up Goldring Street. Then when he got to the main intersection he got out of his plane and wandered off to use the telephone. He left the engines going and all. So, anyway, there I was looking after the plane for the chap and the police arrived. I tell you what, they weren't too happy about it either because the propellers were kicking up a mini dust storm.

'Stay away from those propellers, young feller,' the police warned me. 'We don't want to have to collect the pieces of a curious kid who's got chopped into mince by those blades.'

Then there was another time, the one that the Flying Doctor was involved in. There was a woman. I can't remember her name now. My memory's not the same since the Public Trust got to me. Anyway, this woman was pregnant and it was the wet season and you couldn't drive anywhere because the roads were all mud. Mud was everywhere.

So there was this woman who was pregnant, like I said, and it was an emergency, so the Flying Doctor landed and they came down Goldring Street. I don't know if the police blocked the road or not. Still, there weren't many people there, anyway, not in Richmond at that time there wasn't. But the plane landed. It was either a DH 86 or a DH 84. It wouldn't have been a Goonie Bird, that's what a DC3 was called. Not many people know that. But I don't think Goonies were around back then. But I'm not real sure. Not since.

Anyway, the Flying Doctor came in and he landed in Goldring Street to pick up this lady, the one who was in the family way. I'm not even sure if she was married or not. I can't remember seeing her wearing a ring. I wasn't looking at that. The Flying Doctor might've had a nurse with him but I'm not sure about that either.

In those days one end of the street sloped down and the other was on a bit of a hill, an up-slope, like. That was called Bore Hill. Naturally, being called Bore Hill, you could get free showers there too, day and night, anytime you like—right out of the bore. Good water it was, too. Not like some of the stuff you get, real brackish.

At any rate, I can't be certain if it actually happened right there on the street or just as they got the woman into the plane but there was a hell of a commotion and I couldn't see any more. People were running everywhere, so I asked someone what was going on. 'Hey,' I said, 'what's going on?' And the person told me that the woman had produced a baby.

Then as the plane zoomed up Bore Hill and took off on its way to Cloncurry, apparently she produced another one. So she had twins, like. Anyway, I don't remember what their names were but I reckon that the woman might've called one of them Richmond or something.

Run and Catch

You've got to remember that at that stage my wife, Penny, and I were in our mid to late twenties. We were totally invincible. Nothing could happen to us. We'd go out and do anything. It really didn't matter. It was just one of those things. It was a job that you just had to do because people needed you. So you went and did it. And of course with the RFDS pilot and nursing sister living together, as a team we were simply brilliant. The phone would ring and I'd elbow Penny in the side and say, 'Come on, we've got to go.'

Like the night we went to pick up that guy out of Wyndham. They phoned around midnight. 'We've got a bad one here,' they said. So I gave Penny a nudge and we were out of bed in a shot and into the plane in about twenty minutes. I fired the monster up, then we went like a bat out of hell for Wyndham.

What had happened was that there's this very beautiful little place at Wyndham called The Grotto. It's a waterhole set in steep granite walls and cliffs rising to about 100 feet high. It's completely sheltered, and it's always running with crystal clear water which is gorgeously cool even in the middle of the hottest day. Everybody used to go swimming there.

Anyway, these people got full of booze and wandered out there at night. Then this guy decided that he'd take the easy way down so he dived off the top of the cliff. The only drawback was that he landed in about two inches of water.

Honestly, it was like picking up a bag of jelly. It was terrible. Shocking. We never did much of what they call 'stabilising' in those days. It was all 'run and catch' where we picked the patients up and flew them to a hospital as quick as we could. And this guy had broken everything that it was possible to break.

Then when we got him on board the aeroplane, they said, 'Look, you're going to have to take him to Perth.'

'Bullshit,' I said, 'he'll never make it to Perth. Call Darwin and tell them we're coming.'

'No, you can't go to Darwin,' they argued. 'Darwin won't accept you.'

'Pig's arse, they won't,' I said. 'Just tell 'em we're coming.'

So I took off and headed straight to Darwin and we put down on the airstrip just as dawn was breaking. Thankfully an ambulance was there to meet us. As we unloaded this guy I said to Penny, 'Well, Pen, we'll never see him again.'

Three months later he walked off a Fokker Friendship back in Wyndham. Absolutely, bloody unbelievable.

Skills and Teamwork

Being a doctor, a lot of the stories that I have are of a medical or technical nature. They're not real humorous so I'm not sure that they'll have much appeal. I'd just like to say that if anything exemplifies what the Royal Flying Doctor Service is about, it's skills and teamwork. No one along the line of operations is either more or less important than the other. It doesn't matter if you're a doctor, a nurse, pilot, radio technician, engineer-mechanic or whatever, we've all got our own particular skills. We've all got to pull our weight. If one link in that chain falters, so does the whole operation.

I'll give you an example just to demonstrate what I mean. We had a call one day that there'd been a motor vehicle accident out on the Ivanhoe to Hay road, about 80 plane-kilometres from Ivanhoe. The police who were at the scene informed us that there were two very critically injured people and one who was not so bad.

The problem was that there weren't any airstrips nearby so we either had to motor the injured out or we had to get in there somehow and land on the road.

Now, there's certain criteria for landing on a road. Firstly, it has to be declared an emergency and has to be approved by the Aviation Safety Authority. Then there must be a straight stretch of road of at least two kilometres. It must be more than amply wide enough. All the guard posts have to be knocked down. No culverts. The camber of the road must be such that it won't affect the safety of the plane's landing. The road must be blocked at either end by the police. Also the wind has to be in the right direction, that's as well as the usual landing conditions.

Normally, we only take one crew in the plane, along with the pilot. A crew consists of a nurse and a doctor. But in this case the injuries were such that we decided to take two crews. That made a total of five people, including the pilot.

Then as we were about to land we were informed that one of the victims had just died. This caused us to have a rethink about the situation, taking into account the high risk involved in landing on a road at the best of times. But there was still one patient down there who was in a critical condition so we decided to go ahead.

When we landed, and very successfully I might add, it struck me just how skilful the pilot was. It was an impressive feat. He'd just taken a King Air plane worth $4 to $5 million, weighing 5 tons or so, with five of us on board, and landed the thing dead square at 180 kilometres per hour on a bush road. What's more, I noticed later that he had only about 18 inches (that's 30 centimetres) to spare on each side of the plane's wheels to the verge of the road.

That's what I mean about skills. Amazing.

Still and all, in that particular case things didn't turn out well. The remaining critically injured patient unfortunately died while we were attempting to resuscitate him. We were able to fix up the not-so-injured person without too much problem. In that patient's case, time wasn't such a vital factor. So the police took us all into Ivanhoe, leaving the pilot free to take off with an empty plane—because of the safety factor once again.

So, as I said, the Royal Flying Doctor Service is all about working as a team where everyone uses their own particular skills to the best of their abilities.

Everyone relies on each other and, even then, you can have all the skills, expertise and teamwork in the world but time's against you. It's especially sad when there's young children involved.

That's a real tragedy, a tragedy beyond words.

Snakes Alive!

There was one poor feller who lived out near Lake
Stewart, up in the far north-western corner of New
South Wales.

Anyway, it was a very hot night. The moon was
full. As bright as a street lamp, it was. This feller
and his wife were sleeping outside in the hopes of
catching any breeze that might happen to drift by.
During the night he rolled over, and that's when he
felt something scratch his back, razor sharp it was.
Initially, he thought it was the cat but, when he
turned over to shoo the thing away, he made out the
deadly form of a snake slithering off in the direction
of the chooks' coop. So he dashed inside, got his
shotgun, charged back outside, and started firing
into the chooks' coop in an attempt to kill the snake
before it got away.

Of course, all this noise woke his wife. When she
saw her husband blasting away into the chooks' coop,
with her precious hens flying left, right and centre,
and him calling out, 'I'll get yer, yer dirty bastard!',
she drew the conclusion that the poor bloke had finally
cracked. He hadn't been himself lately. What with the
extreme isolation, the extreme heat, the extremely full
moon, and the extremities of their current economic
concerns—all these things had eventually caused him
to go off his rocker.

So there was this chap's wife telling him off, yelling
at him to stop slaughtering her chooks, and him still

blasting away, mumbling something about how he was trying to kill a snake that'd just bitten him.

'Well, where's the snake then?' she shouted.

He stopped firing and when the dust had settled they peered through the moonlight. No sign of a snake. So he showed her his back. The wife took a look and saw a couple of deep scratch marks.

'You've been scratched by the cat,' she said.

'It were a snake,' he replied.

'A cat,' she said.

'A snake,' he replied.

This went on for a while, with his wife arguing that he'd been scratched by the cat which, in turn, had caused him to lose his marbles and shoot up her chooks, and him declaring that he was in full control of his marbles and that a snake had bitten him and, what's more, he'd seen it slither into the chooks' coop which was why he was shooting in that direction.

With both of them finally agreeing to disagree, he put in a call to the Flying Doctor. The doctor advised that the best thing for him to do was to drive into Tibooburra and get the nurse to have a look. 'Okay,' he said and he headed off to Tibooburra, leaving his wife behind to tally up the dead in her chooks' coop.

But his troubles didn't stop there. By the time the chap got to Tibooburra the snake venom had started to take effect. So when the nurse was disturbed at some ungodly hour by a bloke with a very slurry voice banging on her door, she assumed that he was drunk. It'd happened before. Blokes getting a skinful and knocking on her door. Usually, they weren't too much of a problem. All she had to do was tell them to get lost and they'd wander off, most of the time not knowing what they'd done in the sober light of day.

But this drunk was different. No matter how many times she told him to get lost, he still wouldn't budge from her door. Then when the chap started ranting and raving about how he needed to see the nurse because his wife didn't understand him, she rang the police.

So before the chap knew it, he was being apprehended.

'Yer got it all wrong. I've been bit b' a snake,' he protested groggily.

'That's the best one I've heard in a long time,' replied the policeman.

While all this kerfuffle was going on, the doctor had been attempting to get through to let the nurse know that the chap coming in from Lake Stewart had a suspected snake bite, and could she keep him under close observation. The problem was that the nurse didn't hear the call. It was only after the chap had been carted off that the doctor made contact. Yet, even then, the nurse didn't twig. In fact, during the conversation she complained to the doctor about the hell of a night she was having. How it was as hot as Hades and then, just as she had finally got to sleep, some drunk started banging on her door and she'd had to call the police to come and cart him off.

Anyway, the chap went from bad to worse during the night which caused everyone to reassess his situation and he was flown to hospital the next day.

Nearly died, he did.

Spot on Time

It turned out to be the most wonderful experience. But it certainly didn't start that way, especially with a neighbour's wife ringing me one night, from out past Rawlinna, saying that her husband had come a cropper off his motor bike.

'Well,' she said, when I asked about the extent of his injuries, 'fer starters, all his head's scalped back, like.'

This didn't sound too promising for the bloke, not at all. What's more, I surmised that the chap had received multiple head injuries, which proved to be right. The thing was that, as a nurse, I could only do so much. For him to get the proper treatment for the injuries he'd sustained we had to get him into a hospital, and as soon as possible.

Timing was always going to be the critical factor as to whether he lived or died. So I got in touch with the Flying Doctor at Kalgoorlie and asked them to fly out to Haig immediately—Haig was the closest airstrip to the chap's homestead, out along the railway track. The problem then was that it'd take me at least two hours to drive out to the property along the railway service road, then bring the patient back to Haig to meet the plane. Mind you, out along the Nullarbor the service roads are terrible travelling at the best of times.

But luck was with me. The Road Master at Rawlinna stepped in and offered his help. And that's what saved the bloke's life. See, the Road Master had a Toyota Hilux which, as well as having normal tyres for road use, had also been specially fitted with steel wheels so that it could run on railway tracks. So he put the Toyota up on the hydraulics gismo, which was situated under the vehicle, and jacked it down on the railway track.

Just before we headed off I asked my hubby to gather everyone together and go out to Haig and light the airstrip with little kerosene lanterns—'flares' we call them—so the plane could see where to land.

The next thing I knew we were hurtling along the railway track at 100 kilometres an hour with the Road Master fiddling around, getting things ready to place the injured chap in.

'Look, no hands,' he said as a sort of joke. He must have seen the shock on my face because he was quick to add, 'Don't worry. It's so flat out here that, from when you first see a train's light until it reaches you, well, you can allow a couple of hours at least.'

Anyway, that particular problem didn't arise because within twenty minutes we were as close to the injured bloke's homestead as we could get by rail. So the Road Master lifted the Toyota off the track and onto its normal tyres ready to drive the couple of kilometres to the homestead.

When we got there the bloke was a real mess, worse than what I'd first imagined. Things were touch and go. I patched him up the best I could and we put him in the back of the Hilux before we transported him back across country to the railway line. That was the roughest part of his journey. Once we were there the Road Master put his vehicle back on the railway track and we headed off the 30 or so kilometres to Haig.

I must say that I was deeply concerned for the life of the accident victim. But just as we were about to take the Toyota off the track at Haig, a bright light appeared in the sky, out to the north. I forget who was helping me in the back of the vehicle, but I remember saying, 'God, what're those lights?' Then it dawned on me. 'Oh hell,' I said, 'it's the plane. It's just coming in to land!'

So we dropped the wheels again and drove straight out to the airstrip. I tell you, with all the turmoil of that particular night, the arrival of the plane couldn't have been more spot-on. It was like we'd rehearsed it a million times over. Then when the doctor got out of the plane, a female it was, she must have been pretty new to the game, well, she reckoned that the scene looked like something out of the television show 'The Flying Doctors'. There it was, about half-past eleven, twelve at night, and there were all the neighbours who'd come along to help light up the airstrip with flares.

So they flew the bloke straight out to Perth where they fixed him up. And though he had a really bad time of it, with long-term memory loss and whatnot, he's as good as gold now. No problems. He's got two more kids and, what's more, he's back on the job, riding that bloody great big motor bike of his, the same one that bucked him off.

Squeaky the Stockman

It was a hot, still Sunday in Nappa Merrie when Squeaky the stockman and his mates began maintenance work on an old Southern Cross windmill.

As usual, Squeaky somehow managed to draw the short straw and was given the job of climbing to the top of the windmill to oil the blades, grease the bearings, and so forth. There he was, working away, when a gust of wind came out of nowhere. The blades of the windmill suddenly spun into motion and Squeaky was knocked clean off the top platform. Down he fell in a flail of arms and legs.

For those who don't know, it's a good distance from the top of a windmill down to ground level. In this case, the only thing in the way was a water delivery pipe, about a yard or so off the ground.

The rest is history.

Some say that the pipe saved the wily stockman's life. But at what pains? I ask. Because a split second before impact Squeaky inexplicably parted his legs. Crunch! There he sat, motionless, astride that pipe, a loose leg dangling either side, his mouth rendered ajar, his eyes almost popped out of their sockets.

His workmates rushed to his side. 'How are yer, Squeaky?' they asked. 'Are yer all right, mate?'

But Squeaky didn't say a word. He tried to, mind you, but it was like there was an obstruction in his throat, somewhere just below his Adam's apple, stuck in his oesophagus.

'Ouch,' said his mates as they gently extricated him off the water delivery pipe. After they placed him on the ground, carefully, they called the Flying Doctor.

'Ouch.'

I don't know if you know or not, but Nappa Merrie's over in south-west Queensland so it took a while to fly out there. Then just as they'd settled Squeaky into the Nomad aircraft, another call came across the radio. This time a bloke down at Moomba had put a chunk of wood through his leg while chopping a log for the barbecue.

This left the doctor in an awkward situation. On one hand there was the bloke at Moomba who was in desperate need of help. On the other, there was Squeaky. Now Squeaky was a single bloke, a bit on the shy side with women like, but still and all there was the chance that he might want to settle down and raise a family some day. If so, an emergency operation might have to be carried out. Time was of the utmost importance and Moomba's in the north-east of South Australia, well out of the way.

'Well, Squeaky,' the doctor said, 'it's up to you, mate. Are you well enough to make the trip to Moomba before we head back to Broken Hill?'

At that point the wily stockman gave a sort of half-throatal gurgle which the doctor took to mean that he was okay to do the trip to Moomba.

'Brave decision,' the doctor said, before loading Squeaky up with pethidine, just in case the pain caught up with him somewhere along the way.

So they arrived in Moomba and picked up the bloke with the chunk of wood through his leg. The doctor gave the Moomba chap a shot of pethidine, plus an extra shot to Squeaky, just in case. As they were about to take off, lo and behold, another call came through. This one was from my wife who'd contacted them to say that I'd scalded my arm and was in need of emergency treatment.

Now the bloke with the lump of wood through his leg was no real problem. He could wait. But Squeaky ... Squeaky was a different matter.

'Well, Squeaky,' the doctor said, 'it's up to you, mate. Do you reckon you're well enough for another diversion before we head off back to Broken Hill?'

Squeaky gave another half-throatal gurgle, which the doctor took as an assurance that he was okay to do the trip from Moomba over to our property, just south of Broken Hill, before heading to the hospital.

'Brave decision,' the doctor said, then loaded Squeaky up with another dose of pethidine, just in case.

The doctor radioed ahead explaining the situation and asked if I could be ready to board the aeroplane as soon as it landed. So my wife drove me to the airstrip and the moment the plane cut its engines I jumped aboard. But when the pilot attempted to boot the engine of the Nomad, it was as dead as a doornail. He tried again. Same result. Dead silence. All we could hear was Squeaky letting go with one of his gurgles.

'We'll have to call out another plane,' said the pilot. 'The Nomad's buggered.'

So my wife drove us back to the homestead to escape the heat until the reserve plane arrived. There the doctor pumped some more pethidine into us all, just to tide us over.

Now perhaps it was because of the pethidine, I don't know, but soon after, Squeaky began to lighten up. Not that he could talk, mind you, but his throatal gurgles began to rise in pitch. So much so that by the time the reserve plane landed, Squeaky was sounding like he'd had a triple overdose of helium.

'Squeaky, yer getting squeakier and squeakier,' the pilot remarked.

Now I know it wasn't much of a joke. I guess you had to be there at the time, but it was enough to get Squeaky, me and the bloke with the lump of wood through his leg giggling like little kids, which was something we continued to do right up to the time we arrived at Broken Hill Hospital.

I don't know what happened to Squeaky the stockman after that. We sort of lost contact. He went one way and I went the other. So whether or not his family jewels needed rectifying, I don't know. But that was a fair while ago now and he still comes to mind occasionally—oddly enough, when I think about him I can't help but wince a little.

Stowaway

There was an accident in the middle of the night. A car had turned over with two people in it, a husband and wife. The husband was dead. The wife, who was the passenger in the vehicle, was still alive but in an extremely critical condition.

It was touch and go.

We flew to the nearest town immediately. As I said, it was in the middle of the night so they had to line the runway with flares. It was a bit hairy there for a while but we landed and the ambulance drove out to meet us. We loaded the woman into the plane. Then the problem arose as to what we'd do with the husband's body.

We looked blankly at each other for a while until the ambulance feller asked if we'd be able to take it back in the plane with us. Of course we could see the logic of the request. Taking the body back home with us was the most practical and economically feasible thing to do. The funeral was to be held there so it'd save another trip out. But, naturally enough, our doctor wasn't keen on having the body in the aeroplane in full view of the wife.

'She's critically ill and extremely distressed,' he reasoned. 'If she saw her dead husband it could be a turning point and she could give up hope and go the same way.'

The only thing that we could come up with, to get around the problem, was to stow the body in the rear luggage locker of the Nomad aircraft. The problem was, the luggage locker wasn't large enough to take the body lying down. So we got the ambulance feller to give us a hand to get the husband's body into such a position that it'd fit inside the locker. In this case, we were forced to squash him up into a crouched kneeling position. After we got the husband safely stowed away in the luggage locker, we then took off to the nearest city where the wife could receive emergency treatment.

I'd say it took us about an hour and a half to get to the city. Turbulence was minimal, which was lucky. It's distressing enough to go through a rough patch inside the plane itself where the air pressure is equalised and you've got safety belts on to minimise the bumpy ride. But there's no such luxury in the luggage locker, and the last thing we wanted was to have the body thumping around in the back.

Things went quite smoothly. When we'd landed, the ambulance was waiting and the woman was rushed to hospital where she eventually went on to make a full recovery. But we were left with a problem out at the airport. With the wife now not in the plane, it would have been far better to have had the husband's body in with us for the return trip. We all agreed on that. But it was a busy airport and, if anyone saw us dragging a body out of the rear luggage locker of a Nomad aircraft, a few questions might be asked, questions that we weren't too keen on answering, considering the delicate situation.

Eventually, we decided to leave the body where it was, just in case. So we departed the airport to fly back to our base. That trip took us about another hour and twenty minutes, and once again we were relieved by the lack of turbulence.

Anyway, we arrived back home quite exhausted from all our travels, only to be confronted by the undertaker. Now the undertaker was a very pedantic man, as most undertakers seem to be. Everything had to be just right. There he was, the coffin at the ready, all organised for the body to be placed in, nice and snug and neat. Apparently, he'd been waiting for a fair while so he wasn't in the best of moods to start with but worse was to follow. See, the rear luggage locker of the Nomad isn't heated so the temperature during the flight got down below minus 2°. Not only that but a few hours had gone by since the chap had died.

'Show me to the body,' the undertaker said in his dry, formal manner.

So we did. We flung open the rear luggage locker and there was the body in its crouched position, frozen stiff and locked solid with rigor mortis.

The Pedal Radio Man

Alf Traeger's known as many things—'the Pedal Radio Man' just for starters. He's also been described as the person who gave a voice to the bush and in doing so connected the more remote areas to the Royal Flying Doctor Service. There's no doubting that Alf was a bloody magnificent technician, I'll vouch for that. The only trouble was that he was the type of chap who wouldn't let anything be. He was always fiddling with the radios, trying to improve them, and that's what drove us up the wall.

After the 5 watt pedal radio was established in the bush, Alf started working on a couple of modifications. The thing with all those radios—and there were a couple of hundred or so in the network back in 1950 to '51—was that someone had to service them, right. Frank Basden, the radio operator at the Broken Hill base, did some, as did Alf himself, which caused us all the headaches.

But those chaps like Alf and Frank weren't travelling around anywhere near as much as we were. So each time Vic Cover, the RFDS pilot, and I used to do the rounds of the stations we also did a bit of servicing on these radios, when the need arose. Vic knew a lot more about them than I did. But the thing that we came up against very smartly was that if Alf had had his hands on them after they'd been installed, the circuit diagram on the inside of the sets never matched the wiring because he'd gone and changed things about.

Anyway, the ones that we couldn't fix on the spot we used to cart back to Frank Basden who, as I said, was the radio operator at the Broken Hill base, and Frank would have a go at fixing them. By this stage Frank had been with the Flying Doctor Service for about twenty-five or thirty years and he knew Alf Traeger very well. Frank was an interesting feller too. He's dead now, unfortunately. A very knowledgeable chap, he was. He had to have been to be able to follow Alf's so-called 'modifications'. Anyway, apart from fixing these radios on the base, Frank also gave advice over the air if someone out on a station was having problems.

When Vic and I told Frank about the fun and games that we were having with the radios Alf Traeger had fiddled around with, he just laughed.

'You reckon that Alf drives you blokes bloody balmy,' he said. 'I'll tell you a little story. Do you know the bloke who was at Pincally Station, the one with the droll sort of voice?'

'Yes,' Vic and I said.

'Well, he got on the radio about the same sort of problem that you're having with the circuit diagram. "Ah," he said, in that voice of his, "are you that bloody Frank Basden bloke?"

'"Yes, I'm Frank Basden," I said.

'"Well, Frank," he said, "I've got a bit o' bloody trouble here with the 44-metre frequency, 'n' the 78's not all that bloody good neither."'

At that time there were three available frequencies, the 44, the 78 and the 148. The 148 didn't carry very well with those little radio sets and we had to rely upon people relaying the messages which, of course, they did, and everybody within range used to tune in and listen in to the message. That's why the 148 was ideal for the 'Galah Sessions' where all the ladies used to get on and talk to each other. Worked perfectly for that. What's more, the whole network used to come alive as soon as the doctor got on the air.

'Then the chap from Pincally says, "Frank, I had a go with the bloody screwdriver last night and I think me radio's buggered."

'"What did you do?" I asked.

'"Well, I took the bloody guts outa the middle'a the thing to see if there were anything wrong and everything looked like it were hooked up proper."

'"What do you mean, Pincally," I said, "by saying that you took the guts out of the radio?"

'"Well, I undid that big round piece, you know, the bloody one that's got all them little contacts on the outsides because it wasn't turnin' around, 'n' I thought that it might'a been the trouble but it wasn't 'n' now the whole thing's in bloody pieces 'n' I don't know what to bloody do."

'"Oh, God," I said. "You shouldn't have done that, Pincally, definitely not without the proper authority and advice."

'"Well, I got that, okay," said the chap. "I rang up that Alf Traeger bloke the other day and he said, 'Well, have a go at fixing it yerself, 'n' if you can't you'd better get in touch with that bloody Frank Basden bloke. He'll know what to do.'"

The Telegram

After I left school back in 1950 I spent a hell of a lot of time in the pastoral area out in the west of New South Wales. And around that time the Royal Flying Doctor Service incorporated an on-line radio service through its base in Broken Hill.

This particular service was greatly appreciated by the station people because they didn't get into town much and it gave them the chance to place orders for food or machinery parts or whatever. In actual fact, I reckon that about 90 per cent of station business was carried out that way, back in those days.

Now, aligned to this on-line radio service, the Flying Doctor base also ran what us station hands called 'Galah Sessions'. And these Galah Sessions were in part set up so that, after the business was concluded, the station women could have a good chat to each other and catch up on all the gossip and stuff. But also, there was some time set aside for urgent telegrams to be read over the air.

Anyway, most of us out on these stations used to listen in on the Galah Sessions whenever we could and then to the telegrams as they came through. Everyone used to do it. It was a bit of a lark. What's more, it sort of brightened up our day, hearing the gossip from different parts—who'd had a baby, who was crook, who'd died, who was getting married, and so forth. And also, you never knew when an urgent message might come through for yourself from family or whoever.

Anyway, at this particular time I was working out on the White Cliffs road at Koonawarra Station, just doing ordinary stock work and the like. And we were sitting around one morning listening to these telegrams being read out when we heard what I reckoned to be the daddy of the lot.

Apparently things weren't going too well for one particular family down in Tasmania and there was this telegram which was read over the air to a station hand out at Naryilco Station, in south-west Queensland. I forget the poor chap's name but, anyway, the message said it all and, what's more, with the minimum of words.

It read: DEAR (whatever his name was)
FATHER DEAD—TOM IN JAIL—
SEND TEN QUID.
LOVE
MOTHER

The Tooth Fairy

This is one of Fred McKay's stories. It isn't mine so you'll have to check the details with him.

It happened back in the late 1930s, long before John Flynn died and Fred took over. Fred and Meg had recently been married and they were visiting a cattle station out in the Barkly Tablelands, just over the Queensland border, into the Northern Territory. Anyway, the station's storekeeper-cum-bookkeeper had an abscessed molar, very painful it was.

'Meg'll sort it out,' Fred offered, brimming with confidence in his new wife.

Now, even though she'd completed a two-week crash course in 'tooth extraction' at the Brisbane Dental Hospital before they'd set out, Meg didn't quite share Fred's enthusiasm in her ability. She was new to this rugged bush lifestyle. As you might imagine, it was a big change for someone who was virtually a city girl and she was still trying to find her feet among the dust, the flies, the heat, the cold, the camping out, the cattle, the bore water, the stockmen. Still, she tentatively agreed to give it a go.

But whatever minimal confidence she had completely vanished when Meg arrived at the store. The storekeeper looked a formidable customer indeed. He was a huge man, a mountain in comparison to the 'dental-dummy' that Meg had trained on back in Brisbane. To make matters worse, when the news had spread that a woman was going to have a go at extracting the storekeeper's molar, a crowd of sceptical stockman had gathered, all eager to watch the event unfold.

Until that point in time, Meg had hardly ever pulled a tooth, let alone done it in front of a crowd as rough and as doubting as this mob was. Still, she couldn't turn back now. She'd volunteered her services and she'd have to see it through to the end, whatever that end may be. So she sat the chap down on an old box outside the station store. She gave him an injection and then set to with the pliers or whatever.

Now you might be able to imagine some of the remarks coming from the stockmen when it became obvious that the harder Meg pulled on the molar, the more it seemed that it wasn't going to budge. And the more the molar wouldn't budge, the more anxious the storekeeper became about allowing a woman to attempt to extract his tooth. But if there was one golden rule that Meg had learned in at the Brisbane Dental Hospital, it was 'Once you've got a good grip, never let go.'

So she didn't.

She latched onto that molar and she pulled with every ounce of strength she could muster. Even when the storekeeper started to gargle a protest, Meg straddled him and still hung on and pulled. And when he struggled to free himself from off the old box, Meg clambered up on the box and still hung on and pulled. Then, as the storekeeper attempted to walk away, Meg gave an almighty twist and yank and ... out came the tooth.

Well, this brought the house down, so to speak. As Meg stood there in complete triumph displaying the molar, the gathering of stockmen exploded into cheers, whistles and applause. But the person that was most stunned was the beefy storekeeper himself. He gazed down upon Meg in complete wonderment and, with the tears pouring down his cheeks and the blood running down his chin, he called out, 'What a woman!'

There's a Hole in the ... Drum

My father was a pretty tough sort; a roo shooter, on and off, for most of his life, he was.

But back in the days that this incident happened we were living in very isolated conditions, about 60 miles out of Mingah Springs Station, which is about 150 miles north of Meekatharra, in central Western Australia. It was in either the October or November, I'm not sure which, but it was stinking hot and in the middle of a drought, which wasn't unusual way out there.

Anyway, Dad had spent a trying day out building stockyards and it was late in the afternoon when he finally came in. Then just before tea he remembered that he still had to organise some meat for the dogs, so he grabbed his .22 rifle and headed off to kill a kangaroo.

He must have been awfully tired because after he'd shot a roo and sorted it out for the animals, he came back in, put the gun away, had his tea and went straight to bed. Then, early the next morning when he grabbed the gun again, it went off and the bullet went into his stomach, right through his kidneys, and came out his back.

When my mother saw the mess that my father was in, she went into a real tizz. To make things worse, Mum couldn't drive and she was afraid that Dad was going to die before she could organise some help. Anyhow, we did have an old two-way radio. It was one of those ones that ran with the aid of a 12-volt battery. The only trouble was, when Mum went to call for help she discovered that the battery on the radio had gone flat.

Now, to recharge the battery you had to go through a bit of a rigmarole. See, my father had set up an alternator to an old push-bike. And the idea was, when you hooked the flat battery to the alternator and peddled flat out, it'd recharge the thing.

So Mum hooked the battery up to the alternator, jumped on the bike and went like a bat out of hell. Mind you, this was all happening while my father was still sprawled out inside. Then, when the battery was finally recharged, mother took it back inside, wired it up to the radio and started calling the Flying Doctor for help. As I said, she was in a real tizz and with the shock of having to cope with my father being shot, then having to recharge the battery in the growing morning heat, it was all too much. In the middle of explaining the situation to the doctor, she fainted.

Down she went, leaving Dad to struggle over to the radio and complete the call.

As I said, Mum couldn't drive and we lived in a very isolated area. But as luck would have it there was a gentleman, Val Sorenson, who owned Mingah Springs Station as well as Briah Station, and he just happened to be visiting Mingah at the time and overheard the call on his radio. Then Mr Sorenson came on the line and offered to come up to our place and pick up my father, then take him back to Mingah which had the closest airstrip to where we lived.

'Yes, please,' my father said.

So Mr Sorenson jumped into his old open-top jeep and drove the 60 miles up to our place. That trip took a fair amount of time because there wasn't really a proper road between Mingah and our place. In actual fact, it was more like a bush track, and a pretty rough one at that. It wasn't even graded or anything.

When Mr Sorenson arrived a couple of hours later, he loaded Dad and Mum and my little sister into the jeep and they headed back towards Mingah. As I said, it was a hot October or November day and the journey was over a rugged track so Mr Sorenson had to take it extremely slowly. Yet throughout that whole journey Dad remained conscious and kept reassuring everyone that he'd be okay. Like I said, he was a pretty tough sort, especially keeping in mind that almost ten hours was to pass from the time my father had been shot until the time that Mr Sorenson finally arrived back at Mingah Springs Station.

Anyway, while they were making their way back down the track the pilot from the Flying Doctor Service arrived at Mingah in his Cessna; or it might have been an Auster, I'm not sure which. All I know is that it was a small plane and there wasn't a doctor on board. But with all the confusion over the radio, with the flat battery and my mother fainting, then my father having to take over in his delirious state, and Mr Sorenson coming in and offering his help, the message hadn't come across very clear at all. So when the Flying Doctor pilot arrived, he fully expected to find my father there ready to be flown straight off to hospital where a doctor was waiting. But of course he wasn't anywhere to be seen.

The pilot then tried to radio through to clear up the situation but he couldn't raise an answer. So he waited for a couple more hours and when it looked like no one was going to turn up he decided that the best thing to do was to fly back to Meekatharra and take things from there. The only problem was that he didn't have enough fuel to get back to the base so he hunted around the place until he found an empty 4-gallon drum. He then took the drum and walked the distance over to where the fuel tank was.

But after the pilot filled the drum he discovered there was a hole in the thing and he had to struggle back to the plane with the filled drum while attempting to cover the leak with his finger. It was those extra crucial minutes of delay that saved my father's life because, when the pilot finally reached the airstrip, he drained the fuel into the plane, jumped in and was about to take off ... and that's when Mr Sorenson's jeep came into sight.

There's a Redback on the ...

Back in the early 1970s I went to the Northern Territory as a very young and naive school teacher and took up a position on Brunette Downs Station which was then owned by King Ranch, Australia. I was teaching Aboriginal kids there, which was a steep learning curve because, coming from where I did, I soon realised that I had a lot to learn about the Aboriginal culture. But I really enjoyed it, and I still think that we could all learn a lot from the Aboriginal people, particularly as far as caring for family goes.

Anyway, I was in the schoolroom one day and I felt this thing on my neck. 'It must be a fly,' I thought, so I tried to wave it away, like you do. But still the thing didn't move so I gave it a slap. Then when I squashed it, it felt like someone had placed some burning tongs on my neck. When I took a look at the thing, I realised that I'd been bitten by a redback spider.

It was almost lunchtime so I said to the kids, 'Oh look, you can go out for lunch a bit early today.' When they'd gone I went up to the clinic to see the nursing sister. A funny person she was.

'I've just been bitten on the neck by a redback spider,' I said, and she gave me a vacant sort of look.

'Are they poisonous?' she asked.

'Yes,' I said, astounded that she didn't know anything about spider bites.

'Oh,' she replied, 'then I'd better get in touch with the Flying Doctor Service to see what we can do about it.'

'Thanks for all your help,' I said, with a hint of sarcasm.

So I went into my room where I had a first-aid book from teachers' college, ancient as it was, and I had a look in that. It said that if you're bitten by a spider the first thing to do is to put a tourniquet on. That seemed a bit ridiculous, especially with me having been bitten on the neck. But by that time I was feeling sick and I was starting to get a fever as well, so I went to bed which, as it turned out, was the best thing to do.

In the meantime, the nurse had been on the radio and explained my situation to the doctor. She was told to treat it like shock and keep a watch for any symptoms. Now what you've got to realise here is that, when anyone's talking over the radio, anyone else can listen in. And they do, quite a lot. So unbeknown to me, my being bitten on the neck by the wretched spider was broadcast throughout the Northern Territory.

Then a couple of months later I went up to this race meeting at Borroloola, which is on the Gulf of Carpentaria, on the McArthur River. That was a hoot. It's also quite an extraordinary place, mind you. My education continued non-stop while I was up there. Anyway, there was this guy from Mallapunyah Station. A sort of a legend around the area, he was. Well, he came up to me.

'Oh, gee,' he said, in his real droll bush voice, 'so you're the teacher from Brunette Downs, are yer? The one that got bit on the neck b' the redback spider?'

'Yes,' I said, 'that was me. Why?'

And he just stood there, ogling at me, eyeing me up and down from tip to toe. Then finally he shook his head from side to side.

'Jeez,' he said, 'I would 'a liked to 'a been that redback spider.'

Touch Wood

I was a band master at the time and had been sent down to Esperance to get the local brass band started. Anyway there was this vacant brick residence out on a farm, a lovely place it was, and the owners wanted someone living in it, to keep it tidy and so forth. I needed some accommodation so I moved in.

Then I had a heart attack. So they drove me into Esperance Hospital where they got in touch with the Queen Elizabeth Medical Centre in Perth. And the people in Perth said, 'Look, we haven't got any beds just at the moment. You'd better try and keep him alive down there until we can sort something out.'

So I stayed in Esperance Hospital for half a day with the doctors pumping things into me and so forth. Then the message finally came through that there was a bed available in Perth, which was a great relief, I can tell you. But of course, the problem then arose as to how to get me to the Queen Elizabeth Medical Centre post haste. Anyway, to cut a long story short, the hospital got in touch with the Flying Doctor Service out at Kalgoorlie who were at that very moment getting ready to fly to Perth with a couple of chaps who'd almost killed each other in a pub brawl.

Now the idea of travelling in the confines of a small aeroplane along with two blokes who'd tried to murder each other didn't fill me with too much excitement, I can tell you. So I expressed my concerns.

'Don't worry,' I was told, 'these blokes are so well sedated that they wouldn't harm a fly.'

'Okay then,' I said. 'Count me in.'

So the plane came down to Esperance to pick me up and when it arrived there were these two blokes laid out on the floor, on stretchers. And they were sedated all right, sedated to the eyeballs with alcohol. The plane stank like a brewery. It almost made me crook. Just how on earth they could have inflicted the injuries on each other that they did was beyond the realms of comprehension. But there they lay, completely out to it, both of them severely cut about with glass, 'sedated' to the eyeballs.

Anyway, with the plane being diverted to Esperance at such short notice, the nurse had only enough time to make some quick preparations to accommodate me after they'd taken off. As I said, these two blokes were as full as boots and there was no way that she could get them to budge off the floor. So the next best thing she could do was to set up a little box at the back of the plane, way down the tail end where the fuselage came down in a slope. And that's where I sat, hunched over with my chest almost on my lap, my stomach turning cartwheels from the smell of alcohol, while being hooked up to all sorts of drips and things.

If you think that particular situation sounded uncomfortable, worse was to follow.

'Look,' said the nurse when we were halfway to Perth. 'Look at all that lovely lightning out there. Isn't it exciting!'

'It might look exciting to you,' I replied, swallowing deep.

The next thing, there we were in the middle of a violent thunderstorm and, of course, being down at the rear of the plane was the worst position to be. We were being thrown all about the place. The nurse was stumbling around, struggling to keep all my drips and stuff in. By this stage, not only was my stomach turning over ten to the dozen but a pain started to rise in my chest—not a violent pain, mind you. Still it was just enough to start me thinking, 'You could be in big trouble here, mate.' And throughout this calamitous event, there were these two blokes stretched out on the floor, completely oblivious to the thunderstorm, if not to life itself.

'The only way to travel,' the nurse said at one point, with a nod in the direction of the drunks and, by the way I was feeling, she might have been right, too.

Thanks to both the pilot and the nurse we worked our way through the storms and arrived safely in Perth. When we landed there was an ambulance waiting which whipped me into the Queen Elizabeth Medical Centre, where I was placed straight on some machinery.

They did the open-heart surgery a day or two later. That was a while back now and I'm still here today and, touch wood, I still will be tomorrow and for a good while to come yet.

Train Hit by Man

Now Barton's an interesting place. Ever heard of it? Not many have. It's a small railway siding out in the Nullarbor, at the start of the world's longest straight stretch of track, leading from there to eternity, then further on to Kalgoorlie. There's bugger-all there these days apart from millions of flies and a fluctuating population of between one and six, and that's counting the stray horses and camels. Even for the most imaginative of real estate agents, the best that could be said about Barton is that it's 'nestled comfortably among endlessly rolling red sandhills'. Beyond that you'd be scratching for compliments.

Back a few years ago when the railways scaled down, there was an old German bloke by the name of Ziggie, a railway worker of some sort, a fettler maybe. Anyway, with all the kerfuffle Ziggie decided to retire after thirty years on the job. But instead of retiring to the Big Smoke of Port Augusta like the rest of the workers out that way did, he thought, 'Vell, bugger it. I've no family, novere to go. Zo as-t long as-t zee Tea and Sugar Train still delivers vater and supplies, I'll stay in zee Barton.'

The trouble was that he'd been left with no place to live. So for the next couple of years he wandered up and down the track with a wheelbarrow picking up the sleepers which had been cast aside during track maintenance. And out of those he built a huge three-roomed bunker, complete with a patio where he could sit and sip on his Milo and watch the sun set over the endlessly rolling red sandhills.

Now you may think that the mention of him sipping on Milo, instead of a gin and tonic or a cold beer or something of a more refreshing nature, was a slip of the tongue. But it wasn't. Old Ziggie drank nothing but Milo. In actual fact, his staple diet was Milo, oranges, potatoes and, as the strong rumour had it, canned dog food. Yep, you heard it right ... canned dog food. Canned dog food, Milo, oranges and potatoes for breakfast, dinner and tea, and a good brand too, mind you.

So Ziggie settled down to life at Barton along with his seven dogs. And he's had a good many more than seven dogs in his time because he keeps a collection of their skulls. If you go to Ziggie's place, the one made out of discarded railway sleepers, there they are, all these dog skulls lined up, along with the empty cans of dog food and the empty Milo tins which he uses as an antenna for his short-wave radio.

But other than being the collector of dog skulls and a connoisseur of fine dog food, oranges, potatoes and Milo, old Ziggie just happens to be one of the best informed individuals that you're ever likely to meet. As you might imagine, there's not too much for him to do out at Barton except to listen to his short-wave radio, which he does day in, day out. Ziggie knows more about the goings-on of the world than anyone I know. What's more, he has an opinion on any subject and if he doesn't he'll soon make one up.

So life's a pretty solitary affair out at Barton which, in turn, causes the Bartonites to get mighty suspicious when a blow-in lobs into town. Not that many do, mind you. Maybe one or two each decade or so. But just enough for the locals, including Ziggie, to have formed the solid impression that the rest of the world is inhabited by ... weirdos.

And so it was that one of the locals wandered out at the crack of dawn one day and discovered that some bloke, a blow-in type, had appeared from God-knows-where in the middle of the night and had been bowled over by the Tea and Sugar Train as it was pulling into the siding. The evidence was right there for all to see. There was this complete stranger, sprawled under the front of the train, out to the world, comatose in fact, with his head split open, stinking of grog and looking on death's door.

'Typical of these blow-ins, aye,' someone muttered, to which there was total agreement.

Of course, the train driver was upset. But as he said, 'How the hell could I have bowled someone over when the train only travels at snail's pace?' And there were those that saw his point of view. See, it's been rumoured that the driver of the Tea and Sugar Train wasn't given a timetable upon departure from Port Augusta. Instead, he was handed a calendar because it really didn't matter when he arrived in Kalgoorlie, just as long as he did, at some stage of the year.

Naturally, not long after Ziggie had appeared on the scene he'd come up with a theory about the accident. He reckoned that the train hadn't hit the blow-in, but that the reverse had occurred. In fact, upon closer inspection, Ziggie deduced that the bloke had been so pissed when he'd staggered out of the sandhills and into Barton at some ungodly hour of the night that he'd walked headlong into the stationary train. Crack!

Split his head open and down he'd gone like a sack of spuds, right under the front wheels, and hadn't moved a muscle since.

After much discussion the Flying Doctor from over in Port Augusta was called. And while the blow-in lay prostrate under the train, the discussion raged as to whatever reason the bloke might have had to be wandering around the desert in the middle of the night. And so the discussion continued right up until the locals saw the plane land. Then they put a hold on things while a ute was sent out to pick up the doctor and the nurse.

It was during the brief respite that Ziggie organised the making of a bush stretcher. The reasoning behind that was to save precious time so the blow-in could be placed into the back of the ute as soon as the doctor had checked him over. So they slung a bit of canvas around a couple of bits of gidgee then rolled the unconscious bloke onto the stretcher.

When the doctor arrived he went through the full medical procedure. 'This bloke's in an extremely critical condition,' he concluded. 'So, fellers, when you pick up the stretcher take it nice and easy.'

Now, constructing a house out of railway sleepers may have been one of old Ziggie's fortes but making a stretcher out of a strip of canvas and a couple of bits of gidgee apparently wasn't. Because, when they lifted the stretcher, the canvas gave way and the blow-in went straight through and hit his head on the railway track with an almighty thud.

'Holy Jesus,' someone said, 'we've killed him fer sure.'

But almost before those words had been spoken, the blow-in miraculously snapped back into consciousness.

What's more, to everyone's surprise, particularly the doctor's, the bloke sat bolt upright. He took one look at the menagerie of faces gawking down at him, then a quick glance out at the endlessly rolling red sandhills.

'Where the bloody hell am I?' he squawked.

'Barton,' came the reply, to which the blow-in got up, shook his head and staggered off down the track, leaving the doctor mystified and locals only more reassured at the weirdness of humankind in the outside world. This, of course, included Ziggie, who wandered back home to tuck into a nice hearty breakfast.

We Built an Airport

It all started when the old airstrip out at Pete May's place was forced to close over winter. For those who don't know, and I guess that there'd be many, Pete May's place is near Elliston which is on the Eyre Peninsula, in the Great Australian Bight. So, anyway, with the airstrip being out of action, it meant that the Flying Doctor couldn't fly in if there were any medical emergencies or if there'd been a serious accident.

We reckoned that it just wasn't good enough. So some people went to Council and complained. They reckoned, and quite rightly too, that either the old airstrip should be upgraded or an all-weather strip be built on a new location. Council agreed in principle but they said that everything was in limbo just at the moment because they were awaiting the outcome of current grant applications to the state and Commonwealth governments. So, when the various governments reckoned they didn't have any money for airstrips and the like, the ratepayers made such a big song and dance about it that a public meeting was called.

An engineer chap came to the meeting with the recommendation that the new airstrip should be placed over the Elliston Swamp which was within half a kilometre from the front door of the hospital. But, without funding, Council said they couldn't afford to go ahead. It was then that the people offered to volunteer their services, vehicles and equipment, on the proviso that Council was prepared to foot the bill for the fuel and maintenance on the vehicles and equipment plus lend us some Council labour.

With Council agreeing to that proposal, the first step was to remove the hills. Blasting started around the end of October. That was a mammoth task in itself, one which caused Council to snaffle every stick of explosive held by all the other councils throughout the Eyre Peninsula.

When the majority of the blasting had been completed we got an expert to come down from Coober Pedy to remove what was left. But because we didn't have the money to pay the bloke, the owners of the motel offered him free accommodation while the pub provided his meals. Another chap came in after that with a stone picker and broke up the rubble.

Then nothing much happened over Christmas, with the harvest in full swing. But straight after harvest the Airport Committee approached various people and community groups in the area seeking their help and support.

Now Elliston's only got a population of just under 300, with around 800 in the district, but within two weeks vehicles and machinery appeared on site. There were about six double-axle tipper-trucks and several smaller single-axles. There were bulldozers, graders, tractors, the whole works. Some started digging out the quarry while others were working on the sandhill. The sandhill itself ran virtually halfway along the proposed airstrip. But when the job was finished it'd been flattened into the runway and was mixed in with over 100 000 tons of fill from the quarry.

All the community got involved: farmers, townspeople, storekeepers, even the surfers. We worked rosters and shifts. Those that had to stay in their shops or businesses donated food or helped with morning tea. Anyone who hadn't brought any lunch along could get a free one at the local cafe.

Luckily there was no need for the Flying Doctor during the four weeks that the bulk of the work was done. Still and all, babies were born during that time. I'm not sure now if it was one or two. But something's for certain—with everyone working flat out I don't reckon that many would've been conceived.

Then after the job was completed there were two openings. The first was a political affair after some money had miraculously appeared out of government coffers to pay for the lighting and sealing of the airstrip. Not that we didn't appreciate it, mind you, but that opening was a fizzer in comparison to the second one.

The second opening was the real one. It was the one for the people. There was a true carnival atmosphere. Aircraft came from all over. There were fly-bys, lolly drops, parachutists, games and free gifts. We were just so proud of what we'd done that we had a special car sticker made up which read: WE BUILT AN AIRPORT.

Welcome to Kiwirrkurra

We've got a lot of Aboriginal people up here. They're great, the kids especially. They're so friendly and inquisitive. You get a lot of pleasure out of working with them. I love it.

Why just the other day I went over the Western Australian border to a place called Kiwirrkurra. We were picking up a woman who'd actually had a baby that morning and the baby was a little bit small so we were going to transport them both back to Alice Springs where we could keep a closer eye on things.

Anyway, we arrived a bit early.

Now I don't know if you've ever been out that way but the airstrips are just red dirt with spinifex growing along the side and a few sandhills around the place. And usually they have a little lean-to which is the 'airport terminal', so to speak, and this one had a little corrugated-iron lean-to. A real classic it is, all done up in the Aboriginal colours, with a sign which read:

WELCOME TO KIWIRRKURRA AIRPORT
900 FEET ABOVE SEA LEVEL
360 NAUTICAL MILES TO ALICE SPRINGS

I'd always wanted to get a photograph of the Kiwirrkurra 'airport terminal', so on this occasion I'd brought my camera along. So I took the photo. The next thing, the four-wheel-drive police vehicle turns up and there's about twenty kids in the back, on the top, all over the place, and they jump off and run over with their huge welcoming smiles.

'Hullo, hullo, hullo,' they're all saying.

'Oh, I've got my camera here,' I said. 'Do you mind if I take some photos of you all?'

Then they all push in front of the camera, and there's these twenty kids calling out, 'Just one of me only. Just one of me only.'

I didn't have that much film but I took a few photos anyway. Then I saw that one of the kids has a tattoo on his arm, you know, one of those lick-on tattoos.

'What've you got there?' I asked.

So he shows me. Then all of the kids lift up their shirts and they've got these tattoos stuck all over their stomachs and up their arms. Everywhere they were.

'Oh,' I said, to one of the kids, 'can someone take a photo with just me and you mob in it?'

'I'll take the photo. I'll take the photo,' said the oldest one.

Then he grabs the camera and starts clicking away taking lots of photos. And all the kids want to be in on it. One jumps on one of my hips, another jumps on the other hip, and another kid stands behind me with her hands on my head. And they pack in tight around me. So there I am posing with these kids who are laughing and carrying on and I can feel something moving through my hair.

'Oh yeah,' I'm thinking. 'No worries, it's just that the kid behind me's playing with my hair.'

So we finished the photograph and I looked around at this kid, the one who'd had her hands on my head, and I noticed that she's not only got the most beautiful smile that you're ever likely to see but she's also got a half-melted Mars Bar dangling from her fingers.

Where's Me Hat?

We were flying out to Tibooburra to do a clinic one day when we received an urgent request to divert to Noocundra, in south-western Queensland. Someone had been severely burnt. The odd thing was, though, the chap who put through the call couldn't stop laughing. Naturally, we thought that it mustn't have been too serious, and we said so. But the chap, the one who was laughing, was adamant that the victim was badly burnt and, yes, it was anything but a laughing matter, which he was, if that makes any sense.

As the story unfolded, it'd been a stifling hot day in Noocundra and a few of the locals were in the pub attempting to escape the heat. The problem was that a large tiger snake was thinking along similar lines. It appeared in the pub and had a look around. But when it saw the accumulated gathering, it decided that it didn't like the company and headed off to the next best place it could think of, that being the outside toilet, one of those long-drop types. So out of the pub the tiger snake slithered, down the track a bit, into the outside toilet, and disappeared down the long-drop where it was nice and cool.

Now this chap saw where the snake had gone and he came up with the bright idea of incinerating it. He downed his drink, put on his hat, went and got a gallon of petrol, wandered back through the pub, down the track a bit, into the outside toilet, and tossed the fuel down the long-drop where the snake was. The problem was, after he'd tossed the petrol down the long-drop, he searched through all his pockets and couldn't find his matches. So he wandered back inside the pub.

'Anyone seen me matches?' he asked.

As I said, it was a very hot, still day in Noocundra, stinking hot, in actual fact. So after he found his matches, he thought that he may as well have another drink before he went back outside and sorted out the snake. Meantime the petrol fumes were rising up from out of the long-drop and, with there not being a breath of a breeze to disperse them, the toilet soon became nothing short of a gigantic powder keg.

After the chap had downed his drink, he grabbed his matches and put his hat back on. 'I'll be back in a tick,' he said. Then he wandered outside, down the track a bit, in the direction of the toilet. Without having a clue as to what he was in for, he walked into the toilet and took out a match.

'Goodbye, snake,' he said, and struck the match over the long-drop.

There are those from the outlying districts who go so far as to say that they felt the reverberations of the ensuing explosion. I don't know about that, but one thing's for sure, it certainly put the wind up the blokes who were hanging around the bar of the Noocundra pub. Such was the instantaneous impact of the blast that they didn't even have the time to down their drinks before they hit the floor. Mind you, that's only a rumour because, knowing some of the chaps out that way, no matter what the emergency they always finish their drinks before taking any action, even if it's a reflex action.

Still, you've got to feel sorry for the chap who went up in the sheet of flames. Critically burnt he was. Left standing over what had once been the pub's long-drop toilet with his clothes smouldering away. Stank to high heaven he did. It affected the chap's hearing too. Deaf as a post he was for a good while. And the shock, poor bloke. Even by the time we got there he was still as dazed as a stunned mullet.

As for his hat, it's never been found.

Whistle Up

A few years ago there were quite a lot of people moving into the pastoral country, out here near Meekatharra, in the central west of Western Australia. Anyway, being new to the area, they weren't familiar with the particular system we had if we wanted to activate an emergency call in at the Royal Flying Doctor base. Mind you, this is well before we had the modern transceivers. Back then, the emergency system was activated by a specially designed whistle. To give you some idea of this whistle, it was about three to four inches long and V-shaped, as in a Winston Churchill victory sign, so that you could blow down each side in turns, one long side, the other shorter.

So say, for example, there was an emergency. What you did was to press the button on the microphone which was attached to the radio then blow one side of the whistle for about ten seconds, then the other side for about six seconds, and that would activate the Flying Doctor emergency call in at Meekatharra.

Of course, it wasn't the perfect system. It definitely had its problems—it was rather difficult to activate the call signal in summer when you were competing against thunderstorms, or if you were one of the older folk or maybe a heavy smoker where you easily ran out of puff. And also, believe it or not, you had to develop a certain technique because when you changed from blowing down the long side to blowing down the short side you only had about a one second gap between blows otherwise it wouldn't work.

Anyway, the bloke who was the base operator in Meekatharra around this time decided that we should set a Sunday morning aside so that everyone could have a practice at blowing their whistles over the radio. Now this was a great idea because it not only gave a chance for the newcomers to get familiar with the system but it also provided the opportunity for those of us who'd lived in the area for a long time to brush up on our whistle-blowing skills.

So on this particular Sunday morning the base operator had us all raring to go. He got us on line then went through the rollcall to make sure that everyone was okay and that they had their special whistles nice and handy, which they did. After that was settled he began to go through the people one by one and listen to them blow their whistles, one long, one short. Quite a few people were successful, others had trouble. That was because they hadn't used the whistles before, or they ran out of wind or, in some cases, the whistles hadn't been used for so long that wasps or whatever had built little mud nests inside which prevented the whistles from working properly.

Anyway, the base operator got to this old feller called Harry. Now Harry had been in the bush for quite a long time and the base operator said, 'Okay, Harry, now blow the long side of your whistle.' So Harry blew into his whistle and the sound it made came over our radios, nice and clear.

'Well done, Harry,' the base operator said, 'now blow the short side.'

Then Harry blew his whistle again and, oddly enough, it gave off the exact same sound. So the base operator asked Harry if he was sure that he'd blown down the other side of the whistle. Well, I can tell you that Harry sounded more than slightly put out by this remark. 'I most certainly did,' he snapped. 'I blew down one side of the whistle, then I blew down the other side of the whistle.'

That seemed clear enough, so the base operator then asked Harry just how long ago it'd been since he'd last used his whistle. Harry replied by saying that he couldn't really recall the exact date but it was definitely the year when a certain bush footy team took out the grand final.

'Well, okay then,' the base operator said, 'take your whistle and give it a good wash in some soapy water, then shake it dry, and I'll come back to you later and we'll give it another go.'

So off went Harry to wash his whistle and the base operator went on to listen to some other station owners blow their whistles, one long, one short. Then finally he returned to Harry. And when Harry blew his whistle, lo and behold, the shrill came across sounding exactly the same again, both the long side and the short side.

'Look, Harry, there's only the one tone coming through,' the base operator said. 'There must be something stuck down your whistle, maybe some mud, or wasps, or something like that. So how's about you go and get a little bit of wire and have a poke around inside.'

'Okay,' said Harry.

So away went Harry and when he got back on the air about five minutes later he tried his whistle again.

There was no change. The result was the same. Still only one tone came through on both the long side and the short side.

The base operator by this stage was getting quite perplexed over the matter so he said to Harry, 'I can't understand what's going on here, Harry. There's definitely only one tone coming through. Are you dead sure that you're using the right whistle?'

'Of course I am,' replied Harry, 'it's the very same whistle I used when I was umpiring that grand final I told you about.'

Willing Hands

It was a Sunday. I was working an afternoon shift when we were called to a car accident at De Rose Hill, which is a cattle station just over the border into South Australia. Normally, Port Augusta would have taken it but for some reason they didn't have an aircraft available. That's why we went. We always help each other out. It's good like that.

From the information we received, a young tourist couple had rolled their car a few times and ended up crashing into a fence. The girl wasn't too bad, she only had a broken ankle, so after the accident she'd dragged the male occupant out of the passenger's seat and had laid him on the side of the road. Then while she was waiting for someone to come along she shielded the guy from the heat by holding a tarp over him.

But the guy was the big worry. We were told that he didn't have any body movement from his shoulders down.

Now De Rose Hill is a difficult place to land the twin-engine aircraft because the airstrip's very short and it almost banks out onto the highway. So to gain every metre we could, we had to hit the airstrip as near to the road as possible. That meant while Pete, the pilot, kept his eyes glued on the strip ahead, I had my eyes peeled on the highway.

'Pete,' I'm saying, 'watch out for the road train on the left there.'

Anyway, we missed the road train, landed safely and checked the couple out. There hadn't been anyone medical there until the ambulance arrived, that's apart from some volunteers, of course, and they'd done a really good job. They'd put the guy on spinal boards and all.

Other than having broken her ankle, the girl was extremely distressed, so we gave her some sedatives then attended to the guy. The fifth vertebra in his neck, the C5, had actually gone over and severed his spinal cord. The C5 is above the C4. Christopher Reeves damaged a C4; you know him, don't you, the bloke who acted as Superman? That's why he lost his breathing capability and was placed on a life support machine. Luckily, this guy wasn't quite that bad. At least he could talk.

So we put drips and different things into the guy to get him as comfortable as possible. Now, he was a very tall man, extremely tall in fact, which made me even more thankful that there were so many willing hands there when it came to getting him onto a spinal mattress and into the aircraft. One old station chap even shaded the injured guy's face with his big bush hat. It was amazing just how helpful everyone was.

Now the way that the aircraft's set up is that there's a seat on the right-hand side, then room enough for two stretchers to go down the other side. But with the guy being so tall, we had to drag the spinal mattress up to the end of the aircraft and put his head on the seat so that we could fit the stretcher in with the girl on it. Then when she was settled we dragged the guy back down and put pillows and other bedding under his feet.

So finally we got the couple settled on board. 'Thanks,' we said to all the helpers. As I said before, they were fantastic. If it wasn't for them, we'd have been in big trouble. Anyway, we said cheerio to everyone, got into the aircraft and Pete started making his take-off preparations. Then just as we were about to taxi up the runway, a mob of cows came out of nowhere and wandered onto the airstrip.

By this time the ambulance people and our willing helpers had jumped into their vehicles and were on their way back to Marla or wherever, leaving no one behind to disperse the cows. So we taxied up and down a couple of times in an attempt to scare the cattle away. The only trouble was that by the time we reached one end of the runway, the cows had already wandered back onto the strip, down the other end.

We did have a telephone in the plane but that only worked within a certain radius of a few places and De Rose Hill wasn't within the radius of anywhere. So we had to go about it the long way.

What we did was we got in touch with the tower in Adelaide, who got in touch with the Adelaide Ambulance Service, who got in touch with the Ambulance Service in Marla, who got in touch with the ambulance that was returning from the accident scene, via a satellite phone, and they turned around and came back to shoo the cows off the airstrip, so that we could take off.

You Wouldn't Read About It

A good while ago they were filming that television show called 'The Flying Doctors' up here in Broken Hill. I mean, it's all over now but at the time they were aiming to shoot twenty episodes. The problem—or so I found out—was that they only had thirteen or so stories written. Now I reckoned that I had a great one to tell so I tried to get in contact with the girl who was involved in this particular incident, in the hopes that we could get together and collaborate on a script. The long and short of it was that I couldn't find her. Still can't. So perhaps if she ever gets to read this story she might like to get in touch. You never know.

Anyway, to go back a step or two, or three, before this particular incident occurred I used to work up at the mines in Broken Hill. That was until the day I received the old DCM. You know what that is, don't you? It's short for 'Don't Come Monday'. So, with a fair amount of time on my hands and nothing better to do, I hooked up with an operation driving a small tourist bus around the area.

Then one time we'd just made it into the tiny opal-mining town of White Cliffs before it bucketed down. I'd never seen anything like it. What's more, it left me with a big problem. See, I had some tourists on board who had to get back to Broken Hill by a certain day and there was no way that the type of bus I was driving could make it through in those sorts of wet and muddy conditions. Anyhow, as luck had it, I managed to organise their return with another carrier and I stayed behind with the bus.

So there I was the next day, stuck in the White Cliffs pub, waiting for the road to dry out. And with nothing much else to do, I filled in my day sipping on a beer, playing some darts, then having a game of pool, then some more darts, some more beer, a bit more pool, darts, pool, beer, and so on and so forth, until I wandered off to bed with the old wobbly boot.

It must have been about one in the morning when I was woken by the sounds of people running all around the place. Well, that certainly shook off the wobbly boot, I can tell you. Lights going on and off, cars taking off outside, shouting, the works. 'Christ,' I thought, 'the pub's on fire.' So I threw on some clothes and decided to get out of there quick smart.

The funny thing was though, as I was making my way outside it suddenly struck me that amid this confusion there wasn't even a whiff of smoke. So I pulled one chap over and asked him what all the kerfuffle was about. 'What the hell's going on?' I said. And this bloke told me there was a young girl who lived up the track at a station property, well, she'd been on a dialysis machine for a good while and the Flinders Hospital in Adelaide had just rung through to say that they'd found her a donor.

'But,' this chap added with a grim face, 'we've got to get her to Adelaide by 7 am, or else.'

Mind you, by this time it was just after 1 am in the White Cliffs pub which is way up in the north-west of New South Wales. What's more, the roads were almost impassable and they had less than six hours to transport the girl from the station property into White

Cliffs and then fly her down to Adelaide, a distance of about 700 kilometres.

But none of that seemed to deter these people, the publican in particular. He was the nerve centre of the whole evacuation. He had all the radios and stuff and he was frantically organising things. The Flying Doctor at Broken Hill had been notified and was on the way up. One group of locals had gone to meet the father as he brought the girl into town through the floods. Another group had gone out to clean up the airstrip after the downpour and to set up the flares and get rid of the kangaroos.

To my eye they seemed to have a good enough handle on things so I wandered back to bed. Then in the morning I asked how the evacuation had turned out and I was told that they'd met the father out on the track, the plane had landed okay, they'd gotten the girl to Adelaide in time, and it looked like the operation in at Flinders Hospital was a success.

So that was that.

Then some time later, down the track a bit, I was taking a group of tourists around the Royal Flying Doctor Service base at Broken Hill. I was telling these people this story, about how they got the girl out of White Cliffs and into Flinders Hospital under some very extreme conditions and time constraints. There I was telling this story and one of the staff from the base pulled me aside.

'Guess what,' he said.

'What?' I replied.

'I was the pilot who flew that young girl down to Adelaide,' he said.

Well, that was one piece of coincidence.

Strangely enough, another happened about three years after that particular event. I'd left the small tourist operation by that stage and was working in the Adult Literacy Program in Broken Hill. Anyway, I got a call from a woman who said her granddaughter was staying with her and she was having a bit of trouble with her writing. So I got together with this girl, a nice kid she was, and as always with these cases I made the comment, 'So, you've missed a little bit of school along the way, have you?'

'Yes,' she replied. 'I was on a dialysis machine for a while when I was living out on a sheep station.'

Well, that girl turned out to be the exact same girl who was picked up when I was stuck in White Cliffs all those years ago. You wouldn't read about it, would you?

MORE GREAT AUSTRALIAN FLYING DOCTOR STORIES

Acknowledgments

In memory of previous contributors and supporters: Gordon Beetham, Chris Cochrane, Joe Daley, John Dohle, Slim Dusty, Doc Gregory, Pro Hart, Bill Hay, Don Ketteringham, Mrs Luscombe, Pep Manthorpe, Clive McAdam, Neil McTaggart, Jack Pitman, Les Rourke, Mavis St Clair and John 'Spanner' Spencer.

Special thanks to: HG Nelson, Todd Abbott and the crew at Summer All Over 2006, Angie Nelson (Program Director, ABC Local Radio), Perth contacts Jan and Penny Ende, RFDS—Gerri Christie (Vic), Sally Orr (Brisbane), Monique Ryan (NSW), John Tobin (SA), Stephen Penberthy (Qld), Lisa Van Oyen (Kalgoorlie), Cheryl Russ (Derby), Clyde Thomson, Barbara Ellis, Robin Taylor and Becky Blair (Broken Hill), Luke Fitzgerald (ABC Rural Radio, Port Pirie), Brian Tonkin (Broken Hill City Library).

Thanks to: Kerrie Tuckwell and Bill Rawson (Media Monitors).

For 'the lady down the road'—Lyn Shea—with many, many thanks.

Contributors

More Great Australian Flying Doctor Stories is based
on stories told to Bill 'Swampy' Marsh by:

Rhonda Anstee
Laurel Anthony
Rod and Gail Baker
Bob Balmain
Peter Berry
Reverend John C Blair
Colin Bornholm
Etheen Burnett
Donna Cattanach
Jane Clemson
Ruth Cook
Graham Cowell
Dave Crommelin
Jack Cunningham
Heather Curtin
Phil and Sue Darby
Rick Davies
Bill Day
Jan and Penny Ende
Lionel Ferris
Norton Gill
Jack Goldsmith
Alex Hargans
Judy Heindorff
Hans Henschel
Bill Howlett
Micky Hunter
Wayne and Robina Jeffs
Ruth Ko
John Lynch
Lady Ena Macpherson
Susan Markwell
Rod McClure
Neil McDougall
Michael McInerney

David McInnes
Noel McIntyre
Anne McLennan
Norm Meehan
Laurie and Coral Nicholls
Barry O'Connor
Emily Pankhurst
Stephen Penberthy
Fred Peter
Peter Phillips
Jacqui Plowman
Graeme Purvis
Kitty Powell
Charlie Rayner
Sharon Reddicliffe
Cheryl Russ
Monique Ryan
Chris Smith
'Myf' Spencer-Smith
Graham Townsend
Kim Tyrie
Esther Veldstra
Dr Rob Visser
Nick Watling
Margaret Wheatley
Graham Winterflood
... plus many, many more.

Introduction

The early 1970s was a time of turmoil, not only for this country but also for many of us who lived here. The Vietnam War was coming to an end, the political climate was heading for a huge shift and a large section of my generation felt a sense of loss of 'self' and 'self-identity'. Along with many others, I felt that Australia had little to offer so I decided to travel the world with my then girlfriend. We sought solace amid the tumult of India. We visited a war-torn Kashmir, climbed to the heights of Nepal. We lived on a Greek island. We worked through a freezing winter in London. We drove through Europe, crammed up, along with two Australian friends and all our gear in what must've been the smallest Fiat ever manufactured. We travelled in the bilge of a Portuguese immigrant ship down the coast of Africa. We lived and worked amid the Apartheid regime of South Africa and drove through troubled Rhodesia (Zimbabwe) to view the well patrolled Victoria Falls. In many ways those couple of years were my life's education and I came to realise just how lucky we really are in this country and what huge potential we have.

I remember the day of our return: we were picked up from Fremantle docks by some people we'd never met before and, as the sun set on that warm night, we were welcomed into their house. Neighbours arrived from far and wide, the barbecue was lit, the outside beer fridge received a hammering and—for what seemed the first time in ages—I felt completely comfortable among people. What's more, they understood my humour—those one-liners, those small turns of phrase that we Australians, and virtually only we, can fully understand. Then as we all stood around an old upright piano singing out of tune, it suddenly struck me that I was home, and just what a precious place this 'home' is. As I said in the Introduction to *Great Australian Railway Stories*:

> ... after returning from that two-year trip
> overseas, Shirley and I travelled on the Indian
> Pacific from Perth, across the Nullarbor Plain,
> where just outside the window lay so many
> of the answers to the questions I'd spent the
> previous couple of years wandering around the
> world trying to sort out.

Since then, I've tried to write and collect as many Australian stories and songs as I can in the hope of saving them before they disappear. Because these are 'our' stories; the ones that belong to all of us; the ones that 'glue' us together as a reminder of who we are; the ones that this nation was built on regardless of colour, race or creed. To that end they should be taught in our schools, sung about in songs, shown in our cinemas, performed on our stages. Yes, we must remain open and learn from others—and we have a lot to learn— but if we allow our stories, songs, films and plays to be overshadowed by those from different countries then we'll be the lesser for it. We'll lose that all important sense of 'self'.

So, after many of life's twists and turns, I began my series of 'Great' books, which includes my first collection of *Great Flying Doctor Stories* plus *Great Australian Shearing Stories*, *Great Australian Droving Stories*, *Great Australian Railway Stories* and now *More Great Australian Flying Doctor Stories*.

Before beginning each book I try and contact as many of my previous contributors and supporters as possible, just to see if they have a yarn to tell or perhaps they might know of someone who has. Sadly, many of those great, old and not so old characters have passed on. I have given those people a mention under 'In memory of'.

Still and all, the support continued and *More Great Australian Flying Doctor Stories* grew out of the efforts of many, many, like-minded people. It's impossible for me to get to all the little far-out places to meet and interview people, so it was with much appreciation that HG Nelson and his Summer All Over team found the time for an interview on ABC National and Local Radio to help get the word out there that I was looking for stories. The response to that interview was nothing short of fantastic. Also, many thanks for the support I've received from everyone in the Royal Flying Doctor Service (RFDS), especially to those wonderful people in Broken Hill who always give so freely of their time, encouragement and expertise. In addition, I'd like to thank those who helped so much when I was in Derby, where I was lucky enough to travel into the beautiful Kimberley area of Western Australia.

On a more personal level I'd like to thank my partner Margaret Worth for her continuing support, encouragement, patience and understanding, David Hansford, my musical mate—who can fix anything from a light bulb to a laptop, and has had to do so on many occasions—and Stuart Neal and his staff at ABC Books. Since my first publication, back in 1988, David and Christine Harris have given me a $50 emergency fund to take on each of my travels—'just in case'—and eight books later they're still doing it ... and it still gets spent along the way through one debacle or another. I'd like to thank my family: my dear little mum who, as I write, is a 'healthy' ninety-three years of age, my 'big' sister, Barbara, who doesn't want her age published, and my second 'biggest' sister, Margaret, who was such a support with transcribing my poorly recorded interviews. That also goes for Ian Bourne and Shannon Lore Blackman. I have two mates who are doing it a bit tough at the moment and I'd like to mention them, Shaw Hendry and Gerd Janssen. Their courage is inspirational.

My next venture is going to be 'Great Australian Stories from Little Outback Towns'. If you have a quirky, interesting, funny, sad, entertaining or dramatic story concerning an outback town with a population of less than two hundred, please feel free to contact me via my web site—www.billswampymarsh.com—before the cut-off date of July 2008.

Please don't send in any written material as all the stories in my books are adapted from recorded interviews.

I'm sure you'll enjoy this second book of great Flying Doctor stories as much as I have enjoyed collecting and writing them. The Royal Flying Doctor Service is an organisation quite unique to us and our environment. It was born out of Reverend John Flynn's dream to create a 'Mantle of Safety' for all remote and outback people. There're some great characters in here, some extremely humorous moments and there're some frighteningly dramatic ones—ones that had me on the edge of my seat as I was listening to them being told.

In conclusion, I'd like to acknowledge the staff of the RFDS. As one of my contributors said:

> On a daily basis they put their lives on the line
> for people who are complete strangers to them.
> They don't care who these people are, or what
> their nationality is, or what religion they are.
> And it doesn't matter ... how those very same
> people probably wouldn't take a similar risk for
> them. In fact, they wouldn't even realise the risk.
> What's more, the RFDS do it for free.

So I'm sure you'll appreciate that it wouldn't be possible to run an organisation which has 41 aircraft, 71 doctors, 115 nurses, one dentist plus a dedicated support staff without the public's help. If you wish to make a donation to the Royal Flying Doctor Service, you can call 1300 669 569 or 1800 467 435.

My First Flight

I did my General Nurses' Training in Brisbane, then went to Sydney to do my Mid (Midwifery Training) before coming back to Queensland to do Child Health. In those days they used to say that you had to have your 'Mid' and your Child Health if you wanted to work in the bush. And I wanted to work in the bush. I'm from the country, anyway. I come from Mareeba, in far north Queensland.

After I'd done my General and Midwifery Training I went to Thursday Island, which is just above the tip of Cape York. I was there getting experience in Midwifery and filling in time before I could do my Child Health in Brisbane. Then after completing my three certificates I went to the Northern Territory and worked in the Darwin Hospital for two years—this was before Cyclone Tracy.

I then left Darwin in 1974 and went to work in the Gulf of Carpentaria, in the Normanton Hospital. This hospital was serviced by a doctor from the Royal Flying Doctor Service on a weekly basis. I gathered lots of skills and a fair bit of experience while I was there and I think that this was where I got the idea of becoming a nurse with the RFDS. By then I'd also put a little money away so I decided to go overseas for a year, not working, just travelling around. And, as you do, when I came back home from my travels I had no money left. So, I looked in the paper and I saw that the RFDS in Western Australia was looking for a flight nurse, in

Derby, up in the Kimberley. In those days Western Australia used to snap up all the nurses they could. So I applied for the job and they wrote back to say that the position had already been filled but they could offer me some Relief Community Health Work, out of Derby, and when a flying position became available I'd be given first option.

'Good,' I thought, 'that's what I'll do.' So, I flew to Perth where I had three weeks' orientation—two weeks with Community Health and then a week out at Jandakot for the Air Medical part of it. After that I came to Derby to do Relief Community Health Work. And I remember that I wasn't all that long in Derby when they came to me and said, 'Here's a four-wheel drive vehicle. Go south to La Grange Aboriginal Mission. The nurse there has been by herself for three months and she needs a break.'

'Okay,' I replied, 'but where's La Grange Mission?'

'South of Broome,' they said.

Anyway, even though I'd never driven a four-wheel drive vehicle in my life before, they put me in this huge thing and said, 'You'll find the place easy enough. Just head south and turn left at the Roebuck Roadhouse, then right when you get to La Grange. There's no bitumen. It's all dirt. A distance of well over 300 kilometres.'

And, oddly enough, I found the place.

Of course, I was a little petrified at first but I got through it okay. I just ran the clinic down there for about ten days and the RFDS would fly in and do a doctor's clinic every week. Then after my relief at La Grange I came back to Derby and I did other small stints out at places like Looma, which is another

Aboriginal community about 100 kilometres south of Derby.

But I'll always remember my first RFDS flight. At that stage I was still doing Relief Community Health Work but I was very keen because I really wanted to get in the air as a flight nurse. Anyhow, I was living next door to the normal flight nurse. Even though she was just about to leave she hadn't quite resigned as yet. And in those days, in Derby, there were only two flight nurses, one plane and one pilot and the nurses used to have alternate weekends on and the person who worked on the weekend had the Monday and Tuesday off. Also, with there being just the one pilot, he'd always use up his flying hours pretty quickly and when that happened the RFDS would charter a plane, if they thought it necessary.

Anyhow, this weekend the flight nurse who was on call wasn't feeling well, or so she told me, and she got asked to go out on this two-and-a-half-hour flight, down to Balgo Aboriginal Community [Mission], to pick up an Aboriginal lady who was in labour. So then the nurse asked me if I'd like to go in her place and, of course, me being all green, I immediately said, 'Oh yes, I'll go.'

'Thanks,' she said. 'Our pilot's out of hours so it's going to be a charter flight.'

'That's fine by me,' I said.

Anyhow, the charter turned out to be the local pest controller who had a little one-propeller Cessna. He used to fly around the communities spraying for ants and termites and things like that. And I clearly remember that on the side of his little Cessna he had a sign that read 'Phantom Sprayer' along with a photo of the Phantom character, from the comic books.

When I saw that, my first thought was, 'Dear me, this looks a bit odd for a RFDS retrieval.'

But it was still okay, just another part of the adventure. So then I worked out that, with this Aboriginal lady being in labour and with it being a two-and-a-half-hour flight out there to Balgo then two and a half hours back to Derby, I really needed for her to be able to lie down in the aeroplane. My main concern was that if she had the baby while we were in the air, I wanted to be sure she could deliver safely and wasn't going to haemorrhage or whatever.

With all that in mind I rang the pilot and asked him, 'Can you take the seats out of the plane? You know, the back seats, because this lady will probably need to lie down.'

And his reply was, 'Gees, I wouldn't have a clue how to do that. I've never taken the seats out before.'

But in those days in Derby we had MMA (McRobinson Miller Airways) who I knew had an engineer. MMA had an Otter, which is a type of aircraft that they used to fly across to Koolan Island and back. But the thing was, they had an engineer who looked after all their aeroplanes so I said to the Phantom Sprayer, 'Look, how about we get the MMA guys to see if they can take the seats out?'

'Well,' he said, 'that'd be really good if we could.'

So, eventually he got the MMA guys to take the seats out and we put a mattress inside the little Cessna and then we loaded in all the emergency equipment and so forth. This was back in 1976 when we didn't have any telephone so it was all radio contact through the RFDS base. So there I was, out at the airport, all keen to go on this flight and we set off and because

I'm as keen as anything I'm sitting up there and I'm checking a map to see where we're going.

Actually, at one stage, I thought I was looking at the map upside down. 'Oh, where are we now?' I said to the pilot, you know, wanting to get a bearing of where we were on the map.

'Well,' he said, and he pointed out the window, 'in about ten minutes, out on that side of the aircraft, you'll see Christmas Creek.'

On the map, Christmas Creek was about halfway between Balgo and Derby. 'Oh, okay,' I said. 'Good.'

Anyhow, there I am, I'm peering out the window in the direction of where he said I'd see Christmas Creek. And after about another ten minutes had gone by and still nothing had appeared, I'm thinking, 'Well, surely we're going to get there sometime soon.'

Then fifteen minutes went by and I'm thinking, 'Hey, what's going on here?'

So I said to the Phantom Sprayer, 'Where's this Christmas Creek you said we were going to pass?'

'Hang on,' he said, and he gazes up over his dashboard and he's looking over here and he's looking over there—like he's pretty lost—then he says, 'Oh, there it is, over there.'

So then he turns the plane and heads in the direction that we should be going. And I tell you, that didn't inspire confidence, not one little bit.

But we eventually found Balgo, much to my relief. At that stage I think it was the Saint John of God nuns who actually worked at the clinic out there, at Balgo Mission. So, we landed and a vehicle came out to meet the plane and they said, 'Oh Sister, come into the hospital quick, we're having an emergency.'

Of course, my first thought was, 'Well, there's got to be trouble with the baby.'

But, as it turned out, when we got in there everything was fine and the Aboriginal lady had just delivered her baby. Then, in those days, even though the baby was perfectly okay, as was the mother, you still had to bring them back. So we fixed her up and we got her in the plane and she had a comfortable ride back to Derby on the mattress.

And that was my introduction to flying with the Royal Flying Doctor Service, all the way with the Phantom Sprayer, and I'm thinking, 'Oh well, hopefully, if I ever do this again I'll go with a RFDS pilot so at least I'll have a proper aeroplane to fly around in.'

But still, I wasn't all that daunted. I just so much wanted to be a flight nurse. Then not long after that first flight, the flight nurse who'd been 'sick' on that particular day, well, she resigned and I got the position.

So I was really pleased about that. I mean, I guess it's no big deal, really. There's no great fanfare where you get presented with wings or anything. It's just that my title then became Community Nurse with Flying Duties and that's because we were going out doing clinics, mostly. Oh, there was a bit of emergency work, retrievals from accidents and that, but mainly it was clinic flights. And all that happened not long after I first came to live in the Kimberley, back in 1976, and, except for holidays, I haven't been away since. So it's a sum total of thirty years now, that I've been living in Derby.

A Committed Team

I guess I should clear something up first. Initially it was John Flynn's idea to provide a Mantle of Safety, as he called it, for those living in outback and remote areas. To do that he established the Australian Inland Mission (AIM), which was part of the Presbyterian Church, and that organisation set up outback hospitals and sent out trained nurses and Patrol Padres, of which my father, Fred McKay, was one.

So, the AIM, as it became known, was instrumental in opening up a lot of the outback hospitals, which were staffed by trained nurses, who were recruited and sent out for two-year stints. Then the Flying Doctor Service was, in a way, established to work in conjunction with those services that the AIM and other outback-care organisations had set up. And those nurses relied on the Flying Doctor Service very heavily. Like the Flying Doctor would come and conduct medical clinics and everyone would turn up to see the doctor and, of course, the RFDS was available for emergency services like evacuations and so forth, as well. And, of course, that's developed on a very big scale now. So the AIM and the RFDS were both instigated by Flynn and, even though they were run as two separate organisations, they were inextricably linked.

John Flynn's title was Superintendent of the Australian Inland Mission and, though I was too young to remember him personally, I would've met him when I was an infant. Then, when he died at the end of 1951, Dad was appointed to take over. We were actually living in Brisbane at that stage so we shifted to Sydney, where the AIM's Head Office was, and we moved into a home that had been provided by them for the Superintendent.

We'd been in Sydney for about a year and, I guess, things within the AIM were getting a bit rocky. There were financial difficulties and there were also problems within the Board. That's no real secret there because it's all been well documented. Of course, being only seven or something, I was too young to be aware of what was going on. But, apparently, it was getting to the point where the future of the Australian Inland Mission was in doubt so, when they were having difficulties getting staff at the Bush Mother's Hostel in Adelaide House, out at Alice Springs, Mum (Meg McKay) offered her services as Matron. And she offered to do that for gratis.

So, really, we'd just got established at school in Sydney and were beginning to make friends and then we were, sort of, uprooted to go out to live in Alice Springs. Adelaide House had originally been a hospital but then, when they built a new hospital in Alice Springs, the AIM took over Adelaide House and John Flynn redesigned it with the wide verandahs and the natural air-conditioning system that uses the soil temperature underneath the building. That was quite revolutionary back then. So Adelaide House became what was called the Bush Mother's Hostel and that was the place where mothers could come into Alice Springs before they had their babies at the local hospital. Then they could also convalesce there afterwards, before going back to their properties.

So, that was how we ended up in Alice Springs. I mean, we all thought it was a big adventure but, of course, Alice Springs wasn't the town it is now. There were only about two or three thousand people living there back then and we lived in a small, square upstairs room in Adelaide House, which is in the main street, Todd Street.

At that stage there were three of us kids in the family: my brother, my elder sister and myself. So when Mum and Dad were there, it got pretty crammed at times with the five of us, all living together at the top of the building where we also had to deal with the extreme heat in the summer and the bitter cold of the winter. But, of course, Dad was still going backwards and forwards to Sydney. So it was basically just the four of us upstairs, with the outback ladies living downstairs and the other staff members. Jean Flynn was there for the first few months also.

But then, when they started building the John Flynn Church, on the vacant block next door, my father more or less returned to supervise that. So we watched the church being built, which was quite amazing because it also showed a lot of the Flying Doctor story. Out the front there's the two wings, which symbolise a Flying Doctor plane. I mean, they really did an amazing job in designing and incorporating the entire story of John Flynn's life and achievements into that building. So Dad was involved with the building of the church and I remember we had the architect staying with us a lot of the time, and what a very eccentric and funny man he was, too.

So we had two years in Alice Springs before we returned to Sydney. Then the following year, in 1956, the AIM started up a home in Adelaide at the seaside suburb of Grange, where outback children could come and stay while they were receiving specialist medical treatment. Once again, my mother offered her services as matron and my brother and I went to live with her in Adelaide, while my elder sister, who was doing her Leaving Certificate, stayed in Sydney.

I remember that as a difficult and emotional year for everybody because the family was, sort of, split in two. Dad was off everywhere, but mostly based in Sydney. Mum, my brother and I were in Adelaide and my eldest sister was boarding with the neighbours in Sydney. Then somewhere in amongst all that my youngest sister was born. So I got another sister, and then at the end of 1956 we returned to Sydney and we were based in Sydney from then on.

But Mum and Dad, they were a real team, and a very committed team. Mum wasn't nursing after we came back from Adelaide but, instead, she was going around and speaking to a lot of women's groups and other organisations. The term they gave it was 'Deputation Work'. It was more or less publicising the work of the AIM in conjunction with the Royal Flying Doctor Service and, I guess, seeking donations and support and manpower and just keeping the work in the minds of, mainly, the church people. So she was quite busy with her speaking engagements and whatnot.

And Dad, well, as Superintendent of the Australian Inland Mission, he spent a lot of time travelling around to the various outposts visiting the nursing staff and the various developments that were happening. Later on he'd do a lot of flying—some of it with the RFDS—but in the earlier days he still drove. Sometimes he'd be away for anything up to a month or six weeks. So, we saw little of him and there were even Christmases when we never thought he'd make it back home.

I recall one particular Christmas when he was driving his truck, an International. We were living in the Sydney suburb of Northbridge then and from our front windows we could look out over the gully and see the traffic approaching. And I remember all us kids, full of excitement and anticipation, sitting at the windows watching and waiting for him to come home for Christmas.

So, yes, they were a very committed couple, especially to the work they were doing, and I think my father sort of missed out on the family a lot. But at every opportunity they'd try and make up for it. I mean, we never felt deprived or unloved or anything like that. It was just the area of service they were involved in. And of course, being kids we didn't fully realise that we had to share our parents with a lot of other people and a very big space of country. So, yes, I guess we felt that we didn't have them around enough. And also, with Dad not being there that much, it must've been hard for my mother. But when we did have time together, they both made a special effort. Holiday times were very memorable. Oh, we did some really wonderful things together as a family then.

Then, of course, they passed away pretty close to each other. We'd all grown up and had left home by then. But Dad passed away quite suddenly in 2000. It was unexpected. Our mother's health had been deteriorating for some time but, after Dad died, she sort of really went downhill. I think it was because they were such a team that, without him, she felt she really had very little more to offer. So she lost a lot of her sparkle, then she passed away in 2003.

A Great Big Adventure

Well, for a lot of years I'd been wanting to do a big trip because my grandfather had Clydesdales all his life. He did all the roads around Victoria, up around Kerang and that area. That was his lifetime job, and I sort of grew up with the horses there, and I thought, 'Well, I'm gonna do something one day.' And I started thinking about it and I thought, 'Oh well, while I'm doing it, it'd be good to do something helpful for somebody.'

Then, probably about ten years beforehand, I'd had a hernia after doing the Border Dash out on the Nullarbor. I was in a bit of a bad way there for a while and the RFDS flew out to the Nullarbor Roadhouse and they picked me up and they took me to Adelaide. Then they picked me up and flew me back again.

Now, with the Border Dash, I guess that I should explain that every year over on the Nullarbor they had, and still do have, I think, an event that they call the Border Dash. It's also a fundraiser for the Royal Flying Doctor Service. It started off as just a bit of an argument one night in the pub at Border Village when they reckoned one bloke couldn't run the 12 kilometres from Border Village Roadhouse in South Australia, to Eucla Roadhouse, which is in Western Australia. So he ran it. Then the next year they said, 'Oh well, you know, we might make this a yearly thing.'

So it became known as the Border Dash and, back when I got my hernia, it used to be a very friendly run. You know, you'd have a support vehicle driving along beside you and there'd be a stubby of beer passing hands, here and there. It was all very social, nice and casual. And Eucla's a little township and there're a few married women there and they'd come along and be pushing their kids in prams and all that and the women from the roadhouse staff, they'd join in, and so while most people ran, some people walked.

But everybody who went on the Border Dash had a sponsor and whatever amount they were sponsored for, it all went to the Royal Flying Doctor Service. Of course, it's all grown since then. Nowadays, they get professional runners from Adelaide, Perth and all sorts out there. Oh, they get big heaps of people. It's just before football season and a lot of the footy teams use it as a training run, plus it's also a bit of a bonding weekend for them.

Anyhow, about four days after I did the Border Run, I come down with this hernia. So when I started thinking about doing this big trip, I started thinking about how the RFDS helped me out back then and I thought, 'Why can't I do it for them? They probably saved my life out there.' So I said, 'Yeah, I will. I'll do it for the RFDS.'

So I went and saw the Flying Doctor people here in Rockhampton and I told them that I wanted to do a trip from Rocky, which is about 700 kilometres north of Brisbane, all the way down to Ceduna, which is out on the west coast of South Australia. And they gave me the addresses of who I should contact about it all and I wrote away and I told them what I was going to do and they sent me big heaps of pencils and stickers and stuff like that.

That's how it sort of first got going. Then I had to send away and get a letter that made it all legal for me to raise money for the RFDS. And I went to the Commonwealth Bank and opened a special account and they gave me a pay-in book, with all the details, so that each time I got to a town I'd bank what I'd picked up along the road. That's where most of the money ended up coming from: people stopping along the road to have a yarn and to take a photo, then they'd put $2 or $5 or $10 in the Royal Flying Doctor Service collection tin I carried with me. Rotary Clubs along the way helped out as well.

While I was getting all that organised, I did a lot of test runs. You know, I'd go out for three or four days testing things. I had a covered wagon and one of me mates set up one of them things that the sun shines on—a solar panel—and that charged the battery I had on the side of the wagon. I ran lights and a little caravan fridge off that. Actually, this mate first set it up with a generator that he had running off the rear axle, but I couldn't keep the belts on it so we gave that away and we finished up settling for this solar panel. So that was good. It worked out well. And I just had a piece of flat timber going from one side of the wagon to the other and bunked down in there, in the swag. But a lot of nights it turned out to be so beautiful that I just threw the swag down by the camp fire. Fantastic.

So when everything was organised, I set out in the wagon from Rocky with two Clydesdales, Big Mac and Bill, and my little dog, Minnie, a fox terrier. And all along the way people helped with water and horse feed and a bit of food. It was really unbelievable, especially through outback New South Wales. There was an eight-year drought going on and nobody out there had anything. Oh, it was a terrible, terrible drought.

You know how the little bit of moisture runs off the edge of the road of a night, and so there's the tiny pickings there? Well, the drought was so bad that the kangaroos were coming into the edge of the road just to get what was left of that. And they were so weak from lack of food that they couldn't move. They didn't even bother to take any notice of me when I come along, and the horses didn't worry them either. And you'd see a vehicle go past and the driver would toot the horn to warn the roos and half of them would fall over dead. That's true. There was just no feed, no nothing. It was that bad, it was.

And a lot of the stations out there, they were still going, but they just had managers on them. You know, there's thousands and thousands of acres or whatever and these managers, all they did was go around the boundary fences. They had no stock or anything. I guess the properties were all owned by Sydney lawyers and doctors or what have you: probably tax dodgers or something. I don't know. But these people had nothing out there, you know, and they did everything in their power to help me. Absolutely everything.

Because what you've got to realise here is that there wasn't just Minnie and me. The horses needed food and they needed water every night. Like a Clydesdale will drink 75 litres a day. You know, I did carry water but just emergency water and the New South Wales Pastoral Protection Board supervisors helped with water drops along the way. But, oh, I would've never have been able to do it without the station owners or the station managers, that's for sure.

Well, there was one woman, she heard that I was coming through and she drove all the way out to the main road with some water and food for the horses, then she picked me up, took me back to her place where I had a shower and what-have-you and I had a beautiful tea with her and then she drove me all the way back to camp. And that was a 210-kilometre round trip she did. That was the sort of thing that was happening.

And a lot of these people I'd never even met before. Some I didn't even get to meet. Like, I'd just be driving along and there'd be a 44-gallon drum of water and a couple of bales of hay, sitting on the side of the road, with a sign on it saying, 'For the Royal Flying Doctor Service horse-drawn wagon trip.' And I didn't even have a clue who left these things.

Then, at one stage, I got bogged. That was near G4 Station, between Walgett and Brewarrina, in the central north of New South Wales. It's all black soil through there and we got this rain and the horses were slipping this way and that and the wheels on the wagon were sliding all over the place. Then the trailer wheels got clogged, and the horses just couldn't handle it. So we just could not move.

Anyway, I walked the horses into G4 Station and the people there came back out with a big four-wheel-drive tractor and towed the trailer in. Then we were there for about eight or ten days, waiting for everything to dry out enough to get out of the place. But they looked after us really well. They killed a sheep for us and everything. And those people had nothing, neither.

Then sometimes the news would get out that I was coming along and people would kill a sheep and they'd cut up half a side and put it in little bags for me. And here I am with a little caravan fridge, you know. The freezer was flat out holding six mutton chops and here they are hitting me with about thirty or more chops.

And another funny thing; everybody wanted to give me eggs: and you can't say 'No' because they just won't take 'No' for an answer. Anyway, this particular day I had about six dozen eggs with me and this elderly couple pulled up. They were pensioners who were just touring around in their little caravan on holidays. So when they pulled up I asked them if they'd like to have a dozen eggs.

'Oh, lovely. Oh, lovely,' they said.

Anyway, there I am talking to the elderly lady and the old bloke's walking around and around and around the wagon. And he's looking under it here and over it there and all through it and then, after he'd searched all the wagon over, he comes back and he says, 'Where do yer keep yer chooks?'

And, oh, I had to laugh because he was thinking it was like in the olden days when they always had a cage of chooks underneath the wagon. That's what he was looking for. Yeah, 'Where do yer keep yer chooks?' he asked, and I didn't even need to have any chooks because everyone was giving me all these eggs.

So, there was quite a few funny little things like that that happened. Another one was with two English girls. They were probably in their early twenties or something. They were travelling around Australia and they stopped for a chat because they'd never seen anything like a horse-drawn wagon in their lives before, and one of them asked if she could travel with me for three or four days.

I said, 'Yeah, that'll be fine.'

Then the other one says, 'No, you can't travel with him because we've got to get to such and such a place at such and such a time.'

Well I thought that was a bit rich, you know, but then there was nearly a blue. Oh yes, I thought there was going to be an all-out brawl between the two of them so I said, 'What about I make a compromise?' I said, 'I'll get the fire going and put the billy on and you can have tea with me then you can head off.'

'Oh, that'd be lovely,' they said.

So anyway, after tea they nuzzled off and away they went.

But I must say that I did have a couple of run-ins. See, I went through Bourke and followed the Darling River down to Wilcannia, then along the road to Broken Hill and down the Barrier Highway into South Australia. But Walgett, Brewarrina and Wilcannia, they were terrible. It's a shame. The police at Bourke weren't going to let me go through to Wilcannia. Apparently, not long beforehand two young couples had been driving along and they were forced out of their cars, then they were beaten up and the cars were hijacked and taken for joy-rides. So they were wary of me going down that way, because of the trouble. But I said, 'Well, what am I going to do? I've got no other way to go, you know.'

So, I went on and when I got to Wilcannia there was an old Aboriginal bloke, a full-blood. He used to be a drover, and when he saw me coming past, oh, he run out and he waved me down and I probably spent a good hour and a half there with him while he was going on about the old droving days. Oh, he was showing me all his old photos and all that. And oh, it was fantastic. I enjoyed every minute of it.

Then a couple of hundred yards further down the road the kids started pinching gear. They'd just walk along beside the wagon and they'd grab something then they'd take off. And most of the time they were grabbing lumps of harness and stuff like that; stuff I needed, that was of no good to them. But they'd just take it anyway. It was really just a pain in the butt. That's what it was. And there was nothing I could do about it. But they're funny, kids, aye. It's sad, that's all you can say.

But you get all types, don't you, both black and white, because further down along the highway, over near Peterborough in South Australia, these two white blokes pulled up in a ute. One was a decent sort of a bloke, but the other one, I think he was on something already. Anyway, the decent bloke was talking to me and, just out of the blue, the other one said, 'So, where's yer drugs?'

'There's no drugs on this trip, mate,' I said. 'I don't believe in that sort of stuff.'

'Bullshit,' he said. 'Yer'd have ter be on drugs ter be doin' somethin' as mad as this.' Then he said, 'Anyway, I'm gonna have a look.'

'No, yer not, mate,' I said. 'You just don't walk into people's houses and do those sort of things.'

Anyway, I had a knife that one of me mates gave me, back here in Rocky. He'd made it out of a saw blade, so the blade was probably about 12 or 13 inches long, you know. I was using it for any dead kangaroos I came across; like cutting the roo meat for Minnie and what have you. Well, I had it behind the seat so I just pulled it out and started cleaning my fingernails with it. And this bloke, well, he did a bit of a double take when he saw the knife. So while he was goggling at me I said, 'I haven't got any drugs here, mate. I don't believe in 'em so I wouldn't have 'em here in the first place.'

Anyway, he went, 'Eh, we'll bloody see about that. We'll be back.'

They took off then and I was a bit concerned that they might come back, but they didn't.

But Minnie loved the journey. She was a little girl— elderly—but she just absolutely loved it. I thought I lost her one time. Did I tell you about that? Well, there was quite a few pig shooters of a night through some of those outback places in New South Wales. Anyway the sound of their guns must've frightened her and she took off. And, oh, I never had a clue where she was. I couldn't find her anywhere. There I was yelling out and yelling out and wandering around the place. But, no, nothing.

Anyway, I hung about till around ten o'clock the next morning before I left. And I was just about to hop into the wagon and drive off and here she comes. She's in a real lather and there was blood all over her feet. Red raw, they were. God knows how far she ran that night. But it was good to have her back, I can tell you, because she was great company and, as I said, she just loved the trip.

Then I guess the highlight of the great big adventure was my sixtieth birthday at the Tilpa pub. That was unreal, that was. How it came about was that, well, the night before I was camped at a station property out of Tilpa and the people there, oh, they were fantastic. I've still got all their names and everything but they were having a barbecue there for their grandson's birthday. He was eight years old or something. Anyway, I was talking to the little feller and I just happened to say, 'You and I are nearly twins.'

And he said, 'Why?'

I said, 'Because it's your birthday today and it's my birthday tomorrow.'

Well, he got a bit of a giggle out of that. So, anyway, the elderly lady there—she must've been the grandmother—when she brought the birthday cake out she had two candles on it: one for the little feller and one for me. And it was a really lovely night: with a good feed and what-have-you, plus a few yarns. Then the next morning I headed off and I got into Tilpa and I set up camp, probably about 300 or 400 yards from the hotel. Then after I'd done that I thought I'd go over and see if they served a counter tea and, if they did, I'll shout myself a meal for me sixtieth birthday. So I went over to the pub and the publican there, he said, 'Have yer set up camp for the night?'

'Yeah.'

'Well, do yer reckon yer'd know your way there and back?' he said.

Of course, all this had me sort of intrigued, so I said, 'Yeah, why's that?'

And he said, 'Because yer probably mightn't be able to walk back to camp tonight.'

'Why?' I said.

He said, 'Because I believe it's yer sixtieth birthday.'

Well, within half an hour, I reckon there would've been, oh, I don't know, about sixty people came and went, you know. At any one time there was probably thirty people there, in the pub. And there were only about six people who actually lived in Tilpa. There was the publican and he had a barmaid and then there was a couple over at the little store. Well, that was about it. So there might've only been about four people, I guess, that lived in Tilpa. So, all these other people, I don't know where they come from. But I reckon there was a good number of ringers and fencers and shearers and all that amongst them so they must've come from off properties or something.

Now I think what must've happened was that the elderly woman where I stayed the night before— the grandmother—she must've rung the publican. And things travel fast in little places like that. But I never saw a penny go over the bar all night so I think the publican and this elderly lady must've paid for everything. I don't really know. And the next morning the publican handed over something like $400, which was good money. And then, when I opened me little camping fridge that night, they'd also snuck a couple of fresh bunny rabbits in there. So that was Tilpa, yeah at the Tilpa pub.

And so I finally made it to Ceduna. I left Rockhampton on 9 April 2001 and finished up in Ceduna on 26 October 2001 and I travelled a distance of 3200 kilometres. Seven months it took me, and I raised a total of $4511 for the Flying Doctor Service.

But that's just what the typical Aussie is, isn't it: a giver. And since then I've been back and I've seen a lot of the people who looked after me and here they were, doing the same thing again. I mean, they weren't giving me donations but they were making me stay overnight and they were feeding me and all the rest of it. So it truly is an amazing country with some amazing people living in it. And what truly amazed me was how the isolation out there in the outback doesn't really isolate people, it brings them together, and the Royal Flying Doctor Service is a great part of that.

A True Legend

This is an interesting story about a feller, a true legend, who was a pilot with the Royal Flying Doctor Service for I-don't-know-how-long. His name's Phil Darby.

At the time this particular incident happened I was Chief Pilot with the RFDS here in Cairns, in far north Queensland, and also their Senior Checking and Training Pilot. So, in that capacity, I quite often found myself out at different RFDS bases for a couple of weeks either checking and training pilots or doing relief work while one of our pilots went on holidays or something.

In this case it was one of my very early trips down to Charleville, in south-western Queensland, and while I was relatively new to that area Phil had previously been the pilot down there for—oh, for heaven's sake, I don't know—maybe ten years or more. Actually, Phil worked with the RFDS when it first opened down at Charleville so by then he'd had a chance to solidly cement his persona within the township and the surrounding countryside.

Anyway, by this stage, Phil had been posted over to Cairns and I was relieving out at Charleville and while I was there we were called out to this property— Thylungra—which was then owned by CSR (Colonial Sugar Refining Company). It was also the place where they had a polocrosse weekend, you know, the polo they play on horseback. But Thylungra was run on behalf of CSR by a manager chappie whose surname was Green. Anyhow, this chappie's wife fell ill and we were called to go out there. So the doctor and I and a Nursing Sister, we climbed into—I'm not sure if it was a Queen Air or we took the King Air that time—but anyway, off we went out to this property.

When we landed, there was the truck waiting at the airstrip so we pulled up and we all got out of the aeroplane and the manager bloke, Green, was there with his wife, and she was looking very grey, indeed. She was not well at all. So the doctor went to have a closer look at the wife. Anyway, the manager, this chappie, Green, I could see that he was sort of eyeing me up and down in an extremely suspicious manner. And he was rolling a durry—a roll-your-own cigarette— in the fashion that they can only do in the outback. You know how they roll the durry, sort of nonchalantly while they're deep in thought about something or other, and in this particular case I had the strong feeling that it was me he was thinking about.

'Well,' I said to myself, 'this feller obviously doesn't know who or what I am.' So I went up to introduce myself. 'G'day,' I said, 'my name's Nick Watling. I'm flying the aeroplane today.'

'Oh yeah,' he said, in a half-interested sort of way. 'So where's Phil?'

'Well,' I said, 'Phil's been posted. Phil and I are at the same base in Cairns these days.'

'Oh,' he grunted, sounding none too pleased with this turn of events.

Then he left it at that, but you could see that what I'd said wasn't really sinking through to this feller, Green. So there he is, he's still rolling his durry and he's deep in thought then he looks at me and says, 'But Phil's the pilot for Queensland, isn't he?'

And I thought what a brilliant job of PR Phil had done during the years he was out there, in the Charleville area. Because this feller, Green, he just could not possibly imagine that anyone else other than Phil Darby flew aeroplanes for the RFDS. And the fact that Phil had gone to Cairns, you know, 800 nautical miles to the north-east, didn't affect a thing. If anybody was flying out to pick up anybody's wife or anyone who was sick or injured, the pilot had to be Phil. Nobody else would do, and so who was this strange bugger by the name of Watling, and what right did he have to be out there flying 'Phil's aeroplane'? And that's the way it felt to me.

So that was Phil Darby, a wonderful feller, a brilliant bloke who was tremendously valued and loved as both a man and a pilot, particularly throughout the Charleville area, where they virtually looked upon him as a god. Oh, he'd give you the shirt off his back, Phil would, he was that generous. And if you ever wanted someone to fill in anywhere, there'd always be Phil. He'd be the first to put up his hand, every time.

But, on the other hand, if you wanted someone to obey the rules to the strict letter of the law, well then, perhaps not Phil. Of course, being Chief Pilot, I was responsible to the Civil Aviation Authority for the running of the place and Phil had to be reined in on occasions. So we had our moments together. But, in saying that, Phil went through his many, many years flying for the RFDS without having one accident relating to that sort of approach to life. In fact, I'd reckon that Phil could land the aeroplane on a postage stamp, in the middle of the night, you know, and there's not too many that could do that.

A True Privilege

Well, I suppose, something that pops straight into mind was my first lesson in cultural safety. To be more accurate, I guess I should say that it was a real lesson in how to work appropriately with an Aboriginal patient.

There was one old fella, he was into his seventies and it was the first time he'd ever been in an aeroplane. The only trouble was that I didn't speak his language and he didn't speak English so we had this real communication problem right from the start.

Anyhow, we got him into the aeroplane and I'm trying to tell him to put his seat belt on, but he couldn't understand what I was on about. So then thinking I was being helpful, I went over to show him how it was done. And, well, didn't he take exception to that. He got angry at me for trying to interfere with him. Obviously he didn't know what was going on because he got stuck into me. Oh yeah, he was hitting out at me and everything. Then finally I worked out how he must've been seeing the situation, from his point of view, what with it being his first time in an aeroplane and then, to make matters worse, here was this white woman pushing and pulling him around.

'That's okay. Now I understand,' I said and I got one of the other patients to explain to him what he had to do, and he was alright after that.

Then I had another old patient who was incredibly incontinent in the aircraft, so then we had an overflow problem, out onto the floor, didn't we. And at the altitude we were flying, it was so cold that the urine froze. At the time I was unaware of what had happened, that was until I went to stand up and I felt this crack, crack, cracking. That's funny, I thought, and when I looked down I saw that my shoes were stuck to the floor of the aeroplane.

And there was another old fella who obviously didn't understand the principals of aircraft safety because he decided to light a fire on the floor of the aeroplane. Oh, he just got cold so he started pulling old bits of rubbish and stuff out of his pockets and then he tried to light it with a match. Yeah, on the floor of the aeroplane, as we were flying along, because he was cold.

Of course, when we saw that we freaked out. 'No, no, you can't do that!'

'But I'm cold,' he said.

'I'll turn the heater up! I'll get you a blanket! I'll do anything, but don't light a fire on the floor of the aeroplane!'

So, yeah, I must say, it's a true privilege sometimes with these Aboriginal people, particularly with the real old traditional people, to see them when they're having a first-time-in-their-life experience. I remember when I took one old fella from here, in Alice Springs, down to Adelaide. Oh, he was a lovely man. I'd say he'd also have to be well into his seventies and, anyhow, he'd never seen the ocean before.

At first, I found it really hard to believe. But then, when I thought about it, I realised that he wouldn't even have come across an ocean on television or anything because he'd never even seen a television before, either. Maybe he'd seen a dam. I guess he'd seen a creek and probably a river, but it was obvious that he couldn't grasp the concept of what an ocean actually was. But you just think that everybody knows, don't you? We just sort of take it for granted.

Anyhow, I pointed out the window of the aeroplane and I said to him, 'Out there, that's the ocean.' And he gazed down upon that huge, vast expanse of water, spreading all the way out over the horizon, and he was so shocked. He just couldn't believe there could be so much water anywhere. Even the word 'ocean' was strange to him.

'Ocean?' he kept asking. 'What is ocean?'

I said, 'Water. Karpi.' Because karpi is the word for water in their language.

So he stared back out the window of the plane for a while, then he looked back at me and he said, 'No, no, not karpi. Too much for karpi.'

A Wife's Tale

I met my husband, Phil, in Cairns. He'd previously been a pilot with the RFDS out in south-western Queensland, at Charleville, and had come to fly with them in Cairns. That was around 1974. At that time I was working for the Queensland Education Department as a teacher at the School of the Air in Cairns, and, in a way, we shared the HF radio because the School of the Air was in the same building as the RFDS.

It proved a very suitable accommodation for both organisations because the RFDS did medical calls before school started of a morning, then we took over. But just because School of the Air was using the radio, that wasn't to stop anyone from out bush, who had an emergency, to cut in and call on the same frequency. When that happened, someone from the School of the Air would go and get someone from the Flying Doctor side of things. So, yes, it worked quite well, really.

Back then, at the Cairns base of the RFDS, I think they only had two pilots, two doctors and two nursing sisters. So staff wasn't all that plentiful and it was just in Phil's nature to be ready to go at a moment's notice. That's just the sort of person he was. So, you know, it was like he lived his life waiting on his next call. Of course, they didn't have mobile phones or anything back then. They just had, like, a little beeper that they attached to their belt and when that went off it meant you had to ring up the base and see what was going on.

Virtually, he was on call seven days a week, twenty-four hours a day; so your life was pretty governed by the beeper, and that placed huge restrictions on where we could go.

I can remember a time in the late 1970s when the other pilot went on holidays and that left Phil to hold the fort for about two weeks. And, as what usually happens, you know, that coincided with a very busy time and he was working for forty-eight hours straight or something. I mean, they just wouldn't allow those sorts of things to happen nowadays. In fact, I think it'd be illegal, even if it were in special circumstances.

But I suppose a lot of the flights Phil did perhaps mightn't have had that great twist in the tale for them to be good reading. Oh, I'm sure he made a lasting impression on the people or the patients who he flew out for and brought back to hospital or whatever. But I doubt he'd remember most of them because being a pilot for the RFDS was his job, and that was that.

Like, I was thinking the other day of an American lady who lived at an outstation of Wandovale, west of Charters Towers. She was a mum of five and an aeronautical engineer by profession who'd married an Australian stockman. I was quite friendly with them because I taught the kids through School of the Air. At one stage she purchased an ultralight aircraft and during clinic flights out there she and Phil used to talk flying.

But bringing up a family is tough at any time, let along doing it in a remote area like that where things can become even more difficult. Because, one day, in just a few unsupervised moments her second littlest child poured a whole packet of Rinso over the face of the littlest one—a babe who was probably only eight months old or something. Phil then got the call to say that a child was suffocating.

And that was really dramatic for the mother, as you might well be able to imagine, and Phil flew out there for that child and it all ended up happily ever after. But there were no difficulties with the weather or in landing the aeroplane on the dirt airstrip and there were no problems with the people getting the child to the airstrip or any of that stuff. You know, in a movie they'd make it much more dramatic. But in real life it was just a part of Phil's job, so to speak.

And I'll tell you a funny one. Phil hadn't been feeling too well with the flu one weekend and he was called to fly to Cooktown to pick up a lady who'd miscarried early in her pregnancy. No one was accompanying him so he asked me if I'd like to go along for the ride, which I did. It was a beautiful clear day and we arrived in Cooktown after a stunning flight up the coast. Being the only other person on board, after we landed I let down the door of the Queen Air and the young lady and her partner made their way over to the plane. Of course, they mistook me for a nursing sister and so the patient handed over a rather large specimen jar—it was bigger than a coffee bottle—that must've contained the miscarried material.

I'm a bit more hard-hearted now but, back then, blood didn't really grab me. So I was a bit taken aback, but I tried to take it in my stride. Anyhow, we flew the patient back to Cairns where an ambulance took her to hospital. But then, later on, and this is the funny bit, Phil told me that there was a further side to the story. Apparently, Phil had met the partner of the lady who'd had the miscarriage at a clinic, in another town, the year before and he'd shared with Phil the fact that he was organising a vasectomy for himself. Yes, a vasectomy. And that was always a bit of a joke between Phil and myself because it was obvious that this lass was, unfortunately, caught out in one way or another. So I guess if any story had a twist to it that one would have.

Accident Prone

This story goes back to about March '65, up at Bulloo Downs Station, and it's about an old Aboriginal mate of mine, a chap by the name of Rex Athol Yarnold. Oh, and there was also Lenny Brock—'Brockie' as we called him. We were all mates. I think the way we all first got caught up together was with this bloody speedway driving, you know. We were all speedway drivers. Anyhow, this story hasn't got anything to do with that except that that's where Rex, Brockie and me first teamed up, speedway driving.

But Rex and I had already been up to Bulloo Downs the previous year—that'd be in '64—to do a bit of shooting for a week or two and in the end it bloody flooded and the water went all grey so they put some lime in it and, the next day, we were drinking it. So there you go, the lime cleared it all up.

Bulloo Downs? It's in the far south-western corner of Queensland, tucked in there, near the New South Wales and South Australian borders. If you ever want to get there, you go up to Hungerford and, when you leave the Hungerford pub, you turn west and you run along the fence for 64 miles and you open and shut about ten gates and eventually you'll come to the Bulloo Downs boundary. From there you go off to the homestead where Bill Rinke lived. Bill was, like, the manager up there or some bloody thing, you know. Any rate, that's where the Flying Doctor had to come and pick up Rex.

So, as I said, Rex and me, we'd been up there to Bulloo Downs to do some shooting back when it flooded in '64 and then Brockie come with us when we went again in '65. Brockie was a speedway driver, too.

How we got to know about Bulloo Downs was that Rex had some relatives living up that way who were working rabbits. They were a couple of Aboriginal ladies by the name of Gene and Maude Glover and they had about a dozen kids or more, you know, from different relatives and that, all living there on Bulloo Downs. I reckon that both Gene and Maude would've been in their fifties at the time, and by working rabbits I mean they had all the rabbit traps and all the gear and they were trapping for Sydney Rabbit Supply. A chap called Pat Wade was running Sydney Rabbit Supply back then and he worked out of the Haymarket, in Sydney, and Pat was paying Gene and Maude.

But anyway, all over Bulloo Downs they had these chillas. A chilla is what you put the dead rabbits in so that they don't go off in the heat. And these chillas had a motor on them that you had to start so that the rabbits would be kept cold. Well, one day, when Rex, Brockie and me was up there, this bloody chilla was playing up so Rex goes over to see if he can get the bloody thing going. The only trouble was that when he tried to, his fingers went through the pulley thing that was attached to the motor of the chilla and it took the tops of his fingers off, on his left hand. Three fingers, just down to the first knuckle. Yeah, just up the top, up there, yeah, so he lost them.

So we took Rex up to the homestead where that Bill Rinke lived and they got in touch with the Flying Doctor Service, you know. Then the Flying Doctor flew out and they decided to take Rex back into Broken Hill with them so that they could sort out his fingers. So off they went and it looked like Rex was all okay then because they said they were taking him straight to Broken Hill.

That's the last I saw of Rex for a while but later on, when I caught up with him in Sydney, he was telling me that while they were flying him back to Broken Hill they got a call that someone else out that way was in trouble. I don't exactly remember what the problem was but I think some bloke's back went on him or something, you know, and so they decided to stop off to get this rooster. But when they landed, the ground was too soft and the plane got bogged and it wouldn't budge. So then the pilot told Rex that if he wanted to get to Broken Hill, he'd better get out and push the bloody plane to help get it going again.

So Rex says, 'Here I am, a bloody patient, who's lost me fingers, and I'm out there on the wing of this aeroplane pushing the bloody thing along so we can take off.'

Then, when it got going, he had to jump back into the aeroplane real quick before it took off without him, you know. Anyway, in the end, he finished up in Broken Hill, and they'd have a record of it there about how Rex lost the tops of his fingers.

So that's the story about Rex and the Flying Doctor. But, oh, Rex was always in some sort of strife or other. There's something else that's interesting, if you want to hear it. This didn't have anything to do with the Flying Doctor because this was later on. But see, Rex and me, we had a bit of a falling out there for a little over ten years when he was living down at Ardlethan, in the south-west of New South Wales. So for ten odd years I didn't speak to him. Then right out of the blue, one time he come up to see me. I'm not exactly sure when it was right now but I remember it was just before Light Fingers won the Melbourne Cup. By then Rex'd already had a bloody stroke and he was telling me all about it, how he was stuck in a wheelchair for about four months and, oh, he reckoned he was dirty on the world and crooked on all the people in the hospital and then, one day, he just thought, 'Oh, I'd better get over this.'

So he decided to get up out of that wheelchair and get on his way again. Oh, he was still a bit gimped up, like. You know, he just had a gimp on the leg and the arm, but he was mobile.

Anyhow, when Rex come up to see me that time, just before Light Fingers won the Cup, he had these bloody clippings from the local newspaper, down Ardlethan way, and it was all about him having a big run-in with a train. So he showed me these clippings and he said to me, 'Barry,' he said, 'I was just driving along in the station wagon, mindin' me own business, and I looked up and there's this bloody train there, right in front of me, and by then it was too late to stop so I just drove straight into it.'

And when he drove into the train he reckoned he hit it so hard that he got pushed right from the front seat of his station wagon and he finished up stuck against the back window, you know, of the station wagon. And he reckoned that when they came to have a look at him, he could hear them saying, 'He's dead. He's dead.' And Rex's all squashed up at the back window, thinking to himself, 'I don't bloody think so.'

So yeah, he walked away from that one, and soon after that he come up and he showed me the bloody things all about it in the paper. So yeah, he was pretty accident prone. Well, the whole lot of the Yarnold family was really, even his son, Henry. See, old Rex had a bit of a problem with Henry and Henry was up the Cross, in Sydney, one night and I don't know what was going on in his bloody head but he jumped off a four-storey building. The only thing was that instead of landing on the pavement like he planned, he landed in this bush. So he got up and walked away, and there was a chap there who had a camera and he won an award for taking photos of it, you know. So yeah, they were a pretty accident prone family but they always seemed to survive, somehow.

Any rate, after Rex come up and seen me that time with the paper clippings of him having a prang with the train, not long after, he went back home to Ardlethan and he dropped dead from a heart attack. That was on 2 January, the year after Light Fingers won the Melbourne Cup.

Amazing

In about 1958 I was working at Alice Springs Hospital. Back then the RFDS didn't have their own specialised nursing staff so, if there was a call out, the Matron would come along and just grab whoever she could from the hospital's nursing staff. I actually worked in the Maternity Ward for white women, but it didn't matter what ward you worked in, you might even be lying in your bed—it could even be on your day off—and the Matron might come around and say, 'Hoy, Kitty, we've had a call from the Flying Doctor Service. Get on the plane, you're going out to wherever it was.' And you just had to jump to it, grab whatever medical supplies you thought you might need and get out to the airport as quick as possible to fly out to wherever, help stabilise them and then bring them back into Alice Springs.

Anyway, this time the Matron came along and she said that I had to go out to, I think it was, Areyonga Aboriginal Community. 'There's a demented lubra out there who needs to be collected and brought back into Alice Springs,' she said.

Areyonga's south-west of Alice Springs and, as it turned out, she wasn't demented at all, just depressed. But anyway, off I go and I must've been a bit demented myself because I forgot to take any restraints or anything. All I grabbed was 10cc of a sedative called paraldehyde, just in case.

Now, back then the Flying Doctor Service was using Connellan Airlines. Like, Eddie Connellan was quite a famous person and he owned an airline, and the RFDS chartered his planes for their flights. So we get out to Areyonga Aboriginal Community and the manager there met us at the airstrip and he said to the young pilot, 'The Community vehicle's broken down. Can you taxi the plane up to wherever this woman was.'

That was something you couldn't really do, you know, just drive the plane off the airstrip and down a dirt track. But anyway, the young pilot did. Then there was some sort of delay while we waited for them to get the Aboriginal woman ready. Anyway, the manager was very interested in planes so, while we were passing the time, the pilot took him for a bit of a flip around, which I'm sure he wasn't supposed to do either. But he did, anyway.

By the time they got back from their joy-flight the woman was ready and they carried her the short distance from the settlement to the plane, on a litter, which is like a type of stretcher. So, we load this Aboriginal lady, the one that was supposed to be demented, onto the plane. She was only quite young and, as I said, I think she was more depressed than demented because after she got in the plane she was as quiet as a mouse and didn't say anything.

So off we fly. Now, a lot of the pilots that used to go up to Alice Springs to work for Connellan's were young pilots who went up there to clock up their flight hours. Many were relatively new to the job so a lot of them weren't all that experienced. Anyway, we're flying along and this pilot somehow got lost and he turned around to me and said, 'Do you know where we are?'

I took a look outside and couldn't see any landmarks that I recognised. It was all the same, sort of, looking desert. 'No, I don't know where we are,' I told him.

'Oh,' he said.

Anyway, I wasn't too worried because that happened, at times, out in the middle of nowhere, and you'd just fly along looking for a road or the railway line and, when you found it, you took your directions from that. So there I was, looking out the window, hoping to see a road or something, when I happened to say to this young Aboriginal lass, I said, 'Do you know where we are?'

As I said, she hadn't said boo up till this stage, but she lifted her head, took a quick look out the window and she said, 'Jay Creek'.

That's all she said, Jay Creek. And she was right. She was spot on. We were at Jay Creek, and she was the only one who knew where we were. And I thought, 'How ironic was that.' Because, you know, she'd never been in an aeroplane before. So she'd never looked down on the land from that height so how could she just glance out the window and pinpoint exactly where we were? Amazing, isn't it?

Ashes

This happened back in 1975 and there's no humour in this story because it was a fairly tragic event. At the time we were shearing up at Winning Station, which is about 150 miles north of Carnarvon, just inland from the central Western Australian coast. And the shearers' cook there, what he did with all his scraps and fat and bones and rubbish and things was, he used to burn them outside the shearers' quarters.

Anyhow, we were there for quite a few weeks and so there was just a heap of white ash. You know, if you looked at it, you wouldn't even know it was hot. But one of the shearers was there with his wife and two little kids and well, you know, we'd finished work that day and it was just on dark and one of the little kids—about two years old, he was—he didn't have any shoes on or anything and the next thing we heard him screaming.

So we rushed around and there he was, this little kid, standing in the middle of all this hot ash. I guess he'd run across it and got stuck, so panic set in and he just stood there, right in the middle of it, screaming and screaming. Actually, he was very lucky that he didn't fall over in the fire or anything because it was just red hot coals; well, just all white hot coals really, and you couldn't see them.

Anyway, myself and another chap, we ran over and we pulled him out of it. But all his feet were badly burnt. They were more or less cooked, really. Oh, he was in such agony the poor little feller. So we rushed around to the neighbouring station with this little kid and they gave him some pain-killers from the Flying Doctor medical kit that they always kept at the homestead. And they also had an airstrip. It was only a dirt one but it was still a usable strip. By this time it was about seven or eight o'clock in the evening and we got on to the Flying Doctor on the two-way radio. No, actually, I think it might've even been a pedal radio back in those days. But it was the Carnarvon base we got in touch with.

We told them what had happened and that it was an emergency and they said they'd fly straight out. Then, at the airstrip, being just dirt, there were no lights or anything and we had to get all the cars we could muster so that the Flying Doctor pilot could find out where to land by just using the car lights as his guide. So we had the cars lined up and down each side of the runway and then we had a couple up at the far end so that the pilot could see where to stop. I'd say there must've been about twenty cars. From memory they had them on low beam and the pilot, sort of, flew into the lights. I think it was a twin-engine Beechcraft Baron or something like that. As I said, it was just a dirt strip, and it was in the dark and still this chap landed the RFDS plane perfectly, just by using the car lights as a guide. I tell you, you've got to marvel at those chaps.

Anyway, he had the doctor on board with him so the doctor treated the little boy on the plane and they flew him back into Carnarvon, then down to Princess Margaret Hospital in Perth. But unfortunately, one of the little boy's feet finished up like a club foot and he lost the toes on both his feet. And, you know, even now, I can still see that little kid standing in that hot ash, just screaming and screaming.

So it's not a happy story, like I said, but still, it was a great thing that the Flying Doctor was able to fly out and get him because otherwise, I wouldn't even want to contemplate what the end result for that little boy might've been.

Been Around, Done a Thing or Two

I'm seventy years old actually, and I've retired. I was in the car game for forty-five years but, oh, back a while now, I had a bit of a heart turn and I was in Chinchilla Hospital. Chinchilla's west of Brisbane, between Dalby and Roma. Anyway, after four days, the Flying Doctors came out and they flew me to Brisbane. So really, I just wanted to say an extra thank you to the Royal Flying Doctor Service, you know, not only for how they helped me but, for all us bush people, especially those that live out in the real remote areas. They'd be done without them.

So that's all I was going to say and then I was going to tell you a little story about my dad. Dad used to be a drover. Out through the west of Queensland he was commonly known as 'Flash Jack McIntyre'. You might've heard of him. I used to go out droving with him too, right out Charleville way, all around throughout that district: Tambo, Augathella, Cunnamulla, Eulo and all them places. One of my brothers also used to be out that way. He was a Senior Sergeant of Police: Neil McIntyre.

But long before he joined the police force, Neil and my other brother, Duncan, and myself—my name's Noel—we all done a stint or three out the west, droving with Dad and other fellers. It was an experience, I can tell you. As a matter of fact, do you know Howard Hobbs? From memory he's the Local Member for Maranoa. Well, we used to do a lot of droving for his father. I think his name was also Howard Hobbs, and they lived at Tambo.

Oh, there's stacks of stories I could tell. It just goes on and on. But see, if someone asked me to go camping today, I'd say, 'No thank you, very much.' Because, you know, when you were out droving, it was a tough old life. You hardly saw anyone and you didn't eat very well and you only had a wash every time you got to a creek or a bore drain. Don't get me wrong, it was good experience but it certainly made me realise the good things in life.

Anyhow, see, Dad was out droving one time and, back in those days, the telephone lines they had were only bush telephone lines. You know, they were just a length of old wire cable that ran between properties and properties, and they were only strung up loosely between one old rickety wooden pole to another or, if they could find a tree, it was hung from one tree to another tree, that sort of thing; pretty rough. Anyhow, Dad used to hang a leading-line between the horse he was riding and the pack-saddle horse. So he was going along, nice and steady, when a telephone line got caught in the pack-saddle and the packhorse shied and it threw the pack-saddle back and it hit Dad fair on the mouth. Then, as Dad got hit, he flinched and his spurs dug into his horse and it leaped and bolted off. And that's how Dad ended up in Charleville Hospital, where he had quite a lot of stitches in his mouth and all that.

Now, what you've got to understand is that this was fifty odd years ago and, back then, there were lots of people who were living out in those real remote places who'd never even been into a big town. Like, they were born in the bush and that's where they stayed for the whole of their lives, out in the bush.

Anyhow, the nursing people in at the Charleville Hospital were telling Dad about this old-timer who'd worked out on a remote station property. He'd never been out of the bush so he'd most certainly never seen a town as big as Charleville, which meant it was a dead cert that he'd never been in a hospital before. Anyhow, he'd been pretty badly bunged up. I'm not real sure just why now. It might've even been a riding accident or something. But the thing was that it happened away out in one of the real remote areas and the Flying Doctors had to go out and bring him back into Charleville for treatment.

Well, this old-timer arrived at Charleville Hospital—as I said he was pretty bunged up—and the nurses said, 'We're going to have to take you for X-rays.'

Now, of course, this old-timer didn't have a clue what an X-ray was so he started to get real worried. 'Will it hurt?' he asked.

'No,' they said, 'You won't even know you've had one.'

But that didn't seem to ease this old-timer's worries. For starters, he was a bit suspicious about putting all his trust in these strange, city-type people. To his liking they talked too fast and, anyway, you'd have to be mad to want to live in a big place like Charleville. So he was really nervy. Then by the time they got him into a wheelchair, he was even more nervy. He'd never been in one of those neither. As they were wheeling him down the corridor, he was so bad that he was sweating.

By the time they pressed the button for the lift he was in a real panic. Then, while they were standing around, waiting for the lift to come, they noticed that the old-timer's knuckles had gone white from gripping so hard onto the wheelchair.

'It'll all be over very soon, sir,' they said, trying to reassure the old-timer.

So the lift arrived and they rolled this old feller into the lift and they pressed the button to take the lift to the second floor of the hospital, which was where the X-ray Department was. Then just as they wheeled him out of the lift on the second floor, the old-timer let go a big sigh.

'Are you alright, Mr so-and-so?' they asked.

'Well, you were right,' he replied. 'Isn't it bloody marvellous how they do X-rays, eh? That didn't even hurt a bit.'

And Dad was laughing his head off about this because, you know, Dad had lived. He'd been down to Brisbane and all those places, where they've got lifts and escalators and all that. So he'd been around, done a thing or two, as they say. But, you know, back fifty years or so a lot of those old-timers away out in the backblocks of Queensland, they'd never seen a lift, and there was this old-timer, who'd never been out of the bush, well, he thought that the lift was an X-ray machine, didn't he.

Black 'n' Decker

My name's Micky Hunter. I'm from out at Hillston, in the central west of New South Wales, just west of Griffith. I'm part Italian, part Aboriginal so, mate, that's why I tell everyone I'm from the 'Wog-Abo Tribe'. But I worked a long time as a stockman-ringer, all over the place, and a lot of that ringer stuff is what I'm writing in a book. I'm calling it 'Not Another Bloody Book' and it's stories of the incidents and the old fellers I met along me life and stuff like that.

Have you heard of Sir Sidney Kidman? Well, mate, Sir Sid is my top, number one, best Aussie. His fairness and everything is just one great thing about him and another is that the man never swore or drank or smoked cigarettes. But, yeah, I did all that. I still do but I don't drink now, but I did all that stuff. So there you go. But with my book, I've been working on it for a long while now, and talking to people all about it, and yeah, it's a good idea but I can't find a structure at all, you know.

Anyhow, here's a Flying Doctor story that's going to be in my book. It's probably one of the best of them really because it's fair dinkum. It really happened. Because, just between you and me, there's a lot of make-believe stories in my book so there's a few in there that are a bit 'stretchy', if you catch my drift. But this one's a true one, and it's about how a Flying Doctor helped a young ringer when his horse went over on him up in the Normanton area, in the north-west of Queensland.

What happened was that there was different mobs of us ringers, all over the place, mustering up there in the claypan country, and it happened around one of the mustering yards. I couldn't tell you the name of the property offhand because it was a long time ago now, mate, back in the mid-60s, before the boys went to 'Nam (Vietnam). Anyhow, we'd been mustering, yeah, and in our mob there was fifteen of us ringers and there was four or five thousand cattle.

See, with the mustering, you bring the cattle into the yard and you do various different things with them. Most of them was scrubbers that, you know, you hadn't seen for eighteen months or two years or something like that. So we'd brand them, de-horn them and de-knacker them. There was just five of us blokes who were in our contract team and the other ten we employed was mostly good Aboriginal fellas from around the country. Up there we sort of knew everyone around the place. It's a brotherhood, you know, all us ringers are, yeah.

Anyhow, our boss brought the plane down and he said he'd just heard over the radio that there'd been an accident over with another mustering team, a couple of hundred kilometres away. Now you know how you sort out strays? Well some men do it with vehicles and it's like a game, you know, they bellow and holler and they get the cattle extremely excited so when one takes off, one of the 'Yahoo-ringers' goes and chases it on a horse. And a boy was chasing some strays, like I said, and his horse went over on him and he was squashed by his beast.

So then we was listening to all what was going on over the boss's aeroplane radio. A young doctor was already there with the injured boy. He might've already been in the area doing clinics or something, so he touched down there pretty quick to check the boy out. Then he reported into Head Office, you know, because he didn't know what to do and he wanted to talk to an expert doctor.

Now, I'm not sure where he rung into but it might've been Cloncurry or one of them bigger Flying Doctor bases. And we could hear them talking through the airwaves to each other, so we could hear all what was going on, yeah, and it wasn't too good. From what the young doctor was telling the expert doctor, the young ringer, who'd got trampled on, well, he had real bad head injuries so there was a lot of pressure on the brain and it looked like he was going to die.

Well, the expert told the young doctor that the first thing he had to do was to try and relieve the pressure on the ringer's head. But then the young doctor said that he didn't know how to do that. Maybe he was either a young first-timer or maybe he hadn't done a lot, I don't know. Anyway, the expert doctor asked the young doctor if there was one of them home electric drills handy. You know, one of them Black 'n' Decker-type drills, the same as we was all using in the workshops. So it was one of those, and the expert doctor wanted a steel bit put into it. Yeah, a steel bit.

So they found an electric drill and the young doctor got someone to put the drill bit into the drill because he didn't know how to do that neither. Then after they done that, the expert started telling the young doctor how to operate on this young ringer: like, where to drill a hole in the boy's head to relieve the pressure.

And we could hear it all because, see, we was all standing around the boss's plane listening to the outcome of this young ringer being squashed by the horse. And we even heard the sound of the drill, because there was a big whirring sound when he first started it up and then, when the drill was going into the boy's head, the whirring sound slowed right down. And he done it. The young doctor done it. He drilled into this boy's head. I don't know what come out of the head, whether it was blood or whatever it was, but the young doctor relieved the pressure alright because this young fella, they flew him out in an emergency plane and apparently everything turned out alright. So there you go.

Blown Away

In 1990 my wife and I and a small group of friends made plans to travel down the Canning Stock Route. There were four cars, three Land Rovers of varying vintages and us, with our Hilux. For my wife and I it was literally the start of five months travelling, which was fantastic. Actually, it was brilliant.

One of the blokes who was probably the key to putting the trip together was my mate, Murray. Murray's no longer with us I'm afraid but, to give you some idea as to what sort of character he was, some years ago Murray decided to tackle the Simpson Desert. And where everyone else drives it—and Murray had already driven it about five times—this time he decided to walk it. Yes, walk it. So he put together a bunch of people with camels and followed the route of Madigan the explorer across the Simpson.

One of the other guys who went with us on the Canning trip was a feller called Vic Jaeger. Vic's Member Number One of the Victorian Land Rover Owners' Club and what Vic doesn't know about four-wheel drives and travelling, probably isn't worth knowing. Now, Murray was the best mechanic I knew and he told me that Vic was the best mechanic he'd ever known. That's how good Vic was, so he was a handy sort of person to have along on a trip like that.

Anyway, my wife and I stayed back in Melbourne a little longer than the others because they wanted to take their time in getting to our rendezvous point of Halls Creek. Then my wife and I sprinted from Melbourne to Halls Creek, doing the trip in five days, which included having to fix a car problem along the way. When we got to Halls Creek we ended up waiting for three days before Murray, Vic and the others arrived. They got there a bit late.

Then we all headed off from Halls Creek and instead of going down the usual way, we thought we'd go off the main stock route. The track, if you could even describe it as that, proved to have been so little travelled that, when we got to one particular spot, a 20-foot tall sand dune had literally covered the track. There were no wheel tracks over it, either. Nothing. That's how much out of the way we were at that point. I'd even go as far as to say that it was the most remote place I'd ever been in, in my whole life.

So, it took a bit of work for us to get our vehicles up and over this dune. Then, when we eventually got over, you wouldn't believe it, there, just on the other side of the dune, waiting to come up, was a feller in a Nissan Patrol, with his wife and two kids. Now we didn't expect to see anyone away out there, let alone a feller driving by himself with his wife and kids.

Given that we were in such a desolate place and we were there with four beautifully equipped cars, our instant thought was, 'This feller must be nuts to be out here by himself.'

But as it happened, that wasn't actually the case because the feller told us that he and his family had left his travelling companions that morning, after there'd been an accident and the RFDS had come to the rescue. Apparently this feller, his family and another couple and their children had been travelling together. They'd stopped overnight on a claypan, a bit further back down the track, and a little nine-year-old girl from the other family climbed the only tree out on this claypan. Then, as little girls sometimes do, she fell out of the tree and, unfortunately, when she landed she suffered a fracture of one thigh. So it was a fairly serious situation that they then found themselves in.

Luckily, they were well equipped with both their vehicles having radios and so forth. So they got on to the Royal Flying Doctor Service and the RFDS gave them directions to a disused airstrip, which was relatively close to where the young girl had fallen out of the tree. Then, after they'd arrived at the strip, the RFDS had asked them to call back and give them an estimate of the condition of the strip so they could get some idea as to the possibilities of landing an aeroplane.

So they did just that. These two families drove out to the disused strip and had a look and, as anyone would do in an emergency like that, they called the RFDS back and told them that the strip would be safe enough for an aeroplane to land on. After they'd made the call, the two families then proceeded to get stuck in and clear the shrubbery and what-have-you off the strip, the best they could. When that was completed, they set up a smudge fire so that the pilot could gauge the wind direction when he came in to land. Then they waited.

While all this was going on, the RFDS pilot had taken off from Derby—I think it was Derby—in a King Air, with a doctor and nurse on board. And when they arrived, the pilot did a series of low overflights to check the condition of the strip for himself, before deciding whether it was safe to land or not. He then deemed it an emergency and he put the King Air down on this disused, freshly cleared strip. That, in itself, was an extraordinary effort because the King Air is a heavy plane and, what's more, it needs about 800 metres to take off, which was another concern they were yet to face.

Anyway, all went well and the injured girl was picked up and was, at the time we met the feller, on her way to a hospital in Perth in the King Air and her parents had parted from the family in the Nissan Patrol to head off for the closest town, which was Newman. From there, their plan was to fly down to Perth and meet up with their daughter.

So that was what the feller in his Nissan Patrol told us, when we met at the dune.

But when I got to thinking about it all, I was just blown away by the logistics of that particular RFDS operation, on many counts. Firstly, the pilot, when he arrived at that roughly cleared airstrip, way out in the middle of nowhere, he had to make an instant assessment of its condition, and he had to get it absolutely right. If he got it wrong, it'd spell disaster for everyone. Of course, he'd be fully aware that these people would've told him that this airstrip was safe enough to put the aeroplane down, even if it wasn't, because their assessment was that of desperate parents with a badly injured child. They'd just want somebody there who could save their child. Secondly, the pilot would know that the decision he was about to make was not only about the life of a little girl but that he was also responsible for $6 million worth of aeroplane along with the lives of the doctor and the nurse he's got on board.

Also, of course, the doctor and the nurse have to place their absolute faith in the pilot's assessment of the situation. Even if they're terrified about what he's about to do, all they can do is sit there. If you talk to some of the nurses, and I have asked this question, 'Don't you get scared when you go out on some of these tricky retrievals?'

They'll tell you that, 'Yeah, there are times when we're terrified, but we have complete confidence in the judgment of the pilots and the decisions they make.'

So there was all that to be taken into consideration before they even landed the King Air. But then, what also astounded me, in that situation, was the absolute remoteness of where the retrieval had taken place. We'd travelled south for a week, without seeing a soul, to reach that 20-foot dune along the Canning Stock Route and the other two families had travelled north for a week, without seeing anyone. Just to give you some idea, the closest town was Newman, which was a good three or four days' drive away—I repeat days—and when you have a little girl with a fractured femur, any sort of delay in getting treatment might mean she could suffer permanent damage or lose a leg or, possibly, even die.

And it was only thanks to the professionalism and the courage of the RFDS crew that, on the same day this little girl fell out of the tree, they flew out there and plucked her out of the most isolated place I'd ever been in my life and had delivered her to a major hospital in Perth. So quite possibly a little girl's life was saved. Well, her leg was saved and that's the next most important thing.

Now, this's going to sound terribly naive, I know, but for me, the pilots, the doctors and the nurses of the Royal Flying Doctor Service are my heroes because at any given time they display that same courage and competence as they did in that situation with the little girl. On a daily basis they put their lives on the line for people who are complete strangers to them. They don't care who these people are, or what their nationality is, or what religion they are. And it doesn't matter to those pilots, doctors and nurses how those very same people probably wouldn't take a similar risk for them. In fact, they wouldn't even realise the risk. What's more, the RFDS do it for free. How good is that?

Dirt to Dust

Right back in 1928, when the Flying Doctor Service first started in Cloncurry, Qantas used to supply planes for them. Then in about 1957, Qantas handed it over to TAA. So I became the third TAA pilot in Alice Springs, and that was in about 1965.

By that stage I was familiar with flying around in the dust because, prior to joining TAA, I'd flown light aircraft all over northern Australia. Then when I joined TAA, they based me in Charleville and I was flying DC3s down to Birdsville every Sunday night. That's when Birdsville was a scheduled service. We'd go as far as Adelaide one week, and Broken Hill the next week. I remember we also used to overnight in Windorah, where we'd stay at the local pub. Oh, we had some great times there until we inadvertently drove a Land Rover through the front fence of the pub. After that the publican wouldn't let us stay there. She wouldn't have a bar of us.

But that's another story, though it was ironical that about two years after going through the fence we had an engine failure out at Windorah and the plane needed an engine change. That meant we had to stay overnight so, naturally, I thought that the pub would be the place to go and get a room. And as soon as I walked in the front door, the woman who owned the pub, she took one look at me and she shouted, 'Hey, you, I told you before, get out and stay out!'

So that was that, and I had to find somewhere else to stay.

But anyway, because I was used to flying in the dirt and the dust, out around Birdsville and all those places, TAA management rang me up one day and said, 'How would you like to go to Alice Springs?'

'Okay,' I said and so I went to Alice Springs.

And there was certainly plenty of dust out that way because there was an eight-year drought going on. Even the gum trees were dying. That's true. You'd drive in from the airstrip, into Alice Springs, and there'd be no undergrowth at all, and even the big gum trees along the Todd River were dying.

Mine was supposed to be a two-year posting but I enjoyed myself so much, and I got on so well with everyone, that they left me there for three years roughly, up until 1968. It was during that time that I was seconded into the Royal Flying Doctor Service.

In Alice Springs, in those days, the Flying Doctor Service only ran the radio base, that's all, and the Commonwealth Government used to foot the bill for the doctor, the nursing sisters, the pilot and the aircraft. Then, as time went by, and the RFDS gradually started buying their own aircraft and using their own pilots, TAA bowed out of that operation.

But back in the mid-60s, they didn't have any of the fancy aircraft they have today. In Alice Springs, the plane we used was a twin-engine De Havilland Dove. The Dove was the first civil aircraft built by the Poms after World War II and, for its time—1946—it was a remarkable aircraft. It had two 370 supercharged Gipsy Queen motors with fully feathering props, pneumatic undercarriage, flaps and brakes. It had a fuel system that came out, many years later, in the DC9, that you could operate manually or by booster pumps which, for its day, was an excellent system. We could put eight hours' fuel on, which gave us enormous range for a light aircraft of that era. They even had engine fire bottles, which was unheard of in light aircraft, back then. Plus the Dove was the only IFR (Instrument Flight Rules) aircraft in Alice Springs and I was the only instrument-rated pilot. So, naturally I got every dirty trip. And over the three years I was in the Alice I'd say I transported around fifteen hundred patients and conducted near on two thousand medical clinics in small towns, Aboriginal communities and out on cattle properties. In fact, my area extended north to Newcastle Waters, west to the Western Australian border, east to the Queensland border and south over the South Australian border. To give you some idea just how vast the landmass was, someone once got a map and they superimposed England, Scotland and Wales into the area we—the Alice Springs RFDS—covered.

But, with the dust, as I said, there was an eight-year drought going on, and when I arrived in the Alice, they were keeping sand off the station homesteads and stockyards with bulldozers. All the grass and all the herbage had gone. There was nothing left but drifting sand and dirt. It was so bad that the blowing sand used to bury the runway markers, even in Alice Springs.

Now here's a very strange phenomena. I remember, one morning, I taxied out and there was unlimited visibility. It was as clear as a bell. I did an engine run and everything was right to go. Then, just as I was about to take off, I looked up and, to my amazement, the dust was rising up out of the ground, vertically. I repeat, vertically.

It was unbelievable. I'd never seen anything like that before I went to Alice Springs and I've never seen it since leaving Alice Springs. There was no wind. It was dead still, and this dust cloud just rose up, out of the ground. And I've got no solid explanation as to why that would've happened. I can only guess that, as the sun warmed up the earth, it created a vertical current which lifted the dust up. So from having unlimited visibility, by the time I took off, I only, probably, had less than 300 metres visibility. And that all happened within ten minutes.

Another time I was coming back into Alice Springs after I'd been on routine medical visits, right out near the Western Australian border. It was about a half hour before dark and when I was nearing Ayers Rock there was unlimited visibility. But my sixth sense kept saying, 'There's something wrong here.'

We weren't in any dust or anything. There was no wind. I just had this feeling, you know, that conditions just seemed right for the dust to come.

Well, I had two doctors and two nursing sisters with me and one of the doctors was sitting in the cockpit, so I said, 'Do you mind if we stay at Ayers Rock. I don't like the weather very much.'

'What's wrong with it?' he said.

'I don't know,' I said. 'I've just got a feeling that there's some dust coming up.'

So I called up Alice Springs: 'What's your latest forecast regarding dust?'

'There's no dust to mention,' they said. 'It's fine. It's beaut. Unlimited visibility.'

Now you've got to remember that, in those days, the only radio aids and runway lights were in Alice

Springs, Oodnadatta and Tennant Creek and, by that stage, we were still about 300 miles from Alice Springs. So we were due to arrive some forty-five minutes after last light. As it was, we could land at Ayers Rock and we had accommodation there. So we could stay there if we needed to, but Alice Springs said, 'No, it's fine in Alice Springs. You'll have no problems at all. It's beaut.'

We still had a cattle station to visit. That was our last chance to stop. But I still had the inkling that something wasn't quite right so, while we were at the cattle station, I called Alice again and I said, 'Are you sure there's no dust there?'

'Unlimited visibility,' they said.

'Okay,' I said, but I still wasn't convinced.

Anyhow, if I really needed an alternative I still had enough fuel to continue on to Tennant Creek. So we flew out and then, when I was about 30 miles out of Alice, I called up again and they said, 'Sorry, visibility's now down to zero in dust.'

'Well, thanks a million.'

Anyhow, I decided to do one instrument approach at Alice Springs, then divert to Tennant, if need be. And when I got down to minimum flying level I could just make out the lead-in lights. So I followed them in and, plonk, we landed safely on the ground. But honestly, the dust was so thick that I had trouble finding the taxiway to the hangers. And my wife was coming out to pick me up and, when she arrived, she said, 'Oh, that dust's terrible. I had to keep stopping the car on my way out because I couldn't see anything on the road.'

And that dust had come from nothing.

Then another time, see, we had to be checked every six months for our instrument rating renewal and, anyway, the bloke came up to check me and we flew out over the South Australian border to Ernabella Mission. Ernabella was, I suppose, about 250 nautical miles away. And it was a dusty trip; a very, very dusty trip.

Anyway, I finally found my way to Ernabella Mission and when we got on the ground, the bloke who was supposed to be checking me, he said, 'Well, I haven't seen anything since we left Alice Springs so it's got me absolutely rooted just how you found your way out here.' He said, 'I couldn't understand why you kept going. I was expecting you to turn around and go back to Alice Springs.'

Now I didn't tell him but, you know, because we were flying out in these areas all the time, you could just about find your way through anything. And what I'd done was, I knew that you'd have all the red of the soil and then there'd be the white of the salt lake, and just the other side of the salt lake there was a road that ran down to Ernabella.

So I just came down through all the red dust and, when I could just make out the white of the salt lake, I knew, exactly, where I had to turn right and follow the road to Ernabella. But I didn't tell him that because you don't give away your trade secrets, do you? And he said, 'Well, I'm rooted. I didn't see a thing the whole trip.'

And that just about covers some of the experiences I've had flying with dust and dust storms.

Dobbed In

Two things before we start. First, about the medical chests that all the station properties, and so forth, have. The Royal Flying Doctor Service provides those free of charge and there's about eight hundred of them throughout Western Australia and they're worth about $1200 each. Oh, I think that some of the bigger mining companies might pay for theirs.

A while ago I remember there was a doctor here in Derby, and he used to say, 'You could wait for up to five hours in a big city hospital to see an emergency doctor. Whereas, if you're in the bush, thanks to the Royal Flying Doctor Service, you can talk to a doctor within a minute on the radio or on a telephone. You've got over $1000 worth of free drugs at your disposal and, within two hours, an aeroplane, which has all the equipment you're ever going to need, will be there to pick you up. And it's free of charge, not only in this state, but anywhere throughout Australia.'

The only people the RFDS actually charge for their services are workers' compo cases and overseas insurance travellers. But the thing is, after the Flying Doctor Service gets you there, to wherever you're going, you do have to find your own way home. The RFDS doesn't bring you back. And when that happens you have the PAT (Patient Assisted Travel) Scheme to help you. I think there's a PAT Scheme in every state, though most probably it goes under a different name. Now I'm not sure, but I don't think you even have to pay for that service. You just go to the PAT clerk at the hospital and they'll organise everything for you.

The second thing I'd like to mention is just how strong the CWA (Country Women's Association) is here in Western Australia. We do a lot more than make scones and cakes and stuff and sell them at small street stalls, along with the occasional raffle ticket or two. Yes, we still do those types of things but we're also an extremely strong political lobby group. So much so that, these days, the government either run or they bow when they see the CWA coming. For example, it was through our efforts that the first remedial teacher and the School of the Air teachers were provided with a car. We also lobbied strongly for the Flying Doctor Service to employ their own doctors instead of using hospital doctors. By employing their own doctors you have greater continuity of service by properly trained people who are familiar with all facets of RFDS procedure. And that only happened five years ago, up here in Derby. So that's the strength of the CWA.

Now as for stories, most of what I remember happened during the Royal Flying Doctor radio sessions. How it all worked was that, just like in other states, we also had the infamous 'Galah Sessions' where everyone could get on the radio and chat with their neighbours and all that. They went from midday to one o'clock every day. The 'Galah Sessions' were really strong up here until about 20 years ago, which was when the telephones came through the Kimberley.

Prior to the arrival of the telephones, everything was organised through the RFDS radio. Not only were there the usual emergency calls and the medical sessions with the doctor but you also organised all your P and C meetings, all your CWA meetings, your Ag Department meetings over the RFDS radio. Plus, you ordered your cattle trucks, ordered your food through the RFDS radio system and, of course, everyone within cooee who was able to listened in.

How the day panned out was: there was a morning medical session at seven o'clock with a doctor on the other end of the radio. So if you were crook you told the doctor—along with the rest of the Kimberley—what was wrong with you or your family and, hopefully, the doctor could help treat you. If the doctor couldn't help you, it was more than likely that someone might chip in with some suggestions.

Then there were eight o'clock, eleven o'clock and three o'clock sessions where the telegrams were read out over the radio. These arrived from the post office and were read out from the RFDS base. Also, if you needed to send a message, you called in to the base on your radio and that message was then phoned through to the post office where it was sent out as a telegram.

And, of course, the School of the Air also shared radio facilities with the RFDS. In fact, Port Hedland School of the Air still have their offices combined with the RFDS. And that service was just wonderful for our kids when we were out on Gibb River Station.

But the School of the Air sessions were hilarious, mainly because the teachers couldn't see what merry-hell the kids were getting up to. I remember that twice a year all us parents who were home tutors and their kids, and the governesses and teachers would get together and attend a seminar-meeting at the Broome Camp School. And at this camp us parents used to perform skits for the teachers, just to show them what the kids got up to behind the scenes, and you'd get these new teachers watching our performances and they'd go, 'Oh my God, is that what really goes on?'

One skit we did was about a session that was called 'M and M' (Music and Mayhem). 'M and M' was held early in the morning and was designed for the kids to have some exercise. So you'd have your child sitting beside you and you'd go on the air and the teacher would tell the kid what exercise they were supposed to do, then they'd say, 'Okay, Johnny, are you jumping around there?'

And Johnny would be just sitting there looking completely bored with it all, and the teacher would say, 'Okay, then, how did you go, Johnny?'

And little Johnny would put on this huge act like he's completely exhausted and he'd huff and puff into the radio, 'Really well, Miss. That exercise was a tough one.'

Another skit we did was about when they'd send out Christmas recipes which showed the kids how to make like, you know, those milk-ball things made with apricot and coconut and all that stuff. So we'd act out how the kids would be mixing up all this squishy stuff and we'd have the 'teacher' pretend to come on the air and ask, 'Now, how are you doing out there, Jenny?'

Then we'd have the person who's playing the part of poor little Jenny, well, she'd be up to her elbows in this gooey stuff and, all of a sudden, she's expected to pick up a microphone, and say, 'I'm fine. Things are going real well, Miss.'

Of course, with the School of the Air sessions, you'd also get a very clear insight as to what was going on at all the other properties. We had one lady out on a station near Halls Creek. They were just starting up back then so things were pretty rough. You could imagine, at that early stage, they just had a shed and not much else to live in. But this lady was a real character and her boys were just so full-on, if you know what I mean. And one day this little boy who was in my daughter's class, you could hear him sounding really upset, so the teacher asked, 'Are you alright, Donald?'

'Sniff ... Sniff ... Yeah ... Sniff ... I guess so.'

'Are you sure you're alright?'

'Sniff ... Sniff ...' Then he bursts out crying, 'Wahhhh ... Wahhhh ... Mum's just hit me!'

Of course, all this is going out over the airwaves. Then another time his mother had obviously gone off to do something else and he was stuck with his school work and he got upset, so the teacher asked, 'Are you alright, Donald?'

And then you hear this little whimper, 'I need my mum.'

Oh, he was a real little character, he was. But she was too, you know. Like, the teacher would say, 'Okay, Donald, you've finished your painting now. Put it down and maybe you should put a rock on it to hold it there until it dries.'

Then you'd hear the mother shouting in the background, 'Bloody hell. Nick off down the bloody creek and get a bloody rock to hold this bloody painting down.'

And the creek's like 200 yards away or something. So you could imagine everyone who's listening in is rolling around with laughter while all this stuff's going on.

Then—and this happened quite a few times—you'd hear this great big bang coming out over the radio and the teacher would come on air and ask some kid or other, 'What's going on there?'

'Oh, it's alright Miss, we just shot a snake in the corridor.'

And all those wonderful bits and pieces would be broadcast out over the Kimberley. There was another little boy. One day he's dreaming away. You know, boys can be terrible that way, and the teacher couldn't get his attention so she said, 'Are you alright, Andrew? What's going on there?'

'Oh, I'm just watchin' all the boys [Aboriginal stockmen]. They're outside there, sittin' 'round, havin' a beer and a smoko.'

'And is that more interesting than doing your school work?'

'Oh yeah, you bet!'

So you couldn't get away with anything. One of the big ones was when one of the kids told the teacher, 'Dad's not here today. He'll be back tomorra.'

'Oh, where'd he go?'

'He's just gone over to get a killer.'

A 'killer', of course, is an animal you kill for your own meat. And, I mean, it's a well-known rural joke that if you ever wanted to find out what your own beef tasted like, you just went over to your neighbour's place and had dinner there. So here's this kid broadcasting to everyone in the Kimberley that his dad wouldn't be back until tomorrow because he was on his way over to the cattle station next door to knock off one of his neighbour's cattle. So the kids were always dobbing you in, in one way or another, and the RFDS provided the radio.

Another one, and I'll make this the last little story;

it's about a woman out at one of the stations who really got dobbed in. One time, the teacher wanted to speak to her so she said to the kid, 'Can I talk to your mum, please?'

'Mum can't come. She's busy,' the kid replied.

'But I need to talk to her. Could you go and get her, please.'

'Mum can't come.'

'Look,' the teacher said, starting to get really frustrated with the kid, 'I really need to talk to your mum.'

'Mum can't come.'

'And just why can't she come?'

Then the kid gathers up enough courage to shout back at the teacher, 'She can't come because ... SHE'S SITTING ON THE TOILET!'

Emergency!

Just a quick story and you may have already heard it. It's not my story. It was told by a well-known doctor-surgeon who used to be here in Dubbo, in central New South Wales. The doctor's name was Bob North. I think that's what his name was, anyway. Anyhow, Bob told this one at his farewell presentation, type of thing, about four years ago, when he was leaving or retiring or whatever he was doing.

Bob reckoned he was on duty in at Dubbo Hospital, one time, and there was this other doctor, a much younger feller, who'd just arrived from Sydney. I'd say he'd only been in Dubbo for a very short time. As far as I know he was straight out of university. The thing is, he was new at the job so he was pretty inexperienced as far as the more practical matters of doctoring go.

Anyhow, Bob was working flat out in surgery, performing some extremely delicate operation. It was something very critical so he was very focused and very busy and this young doctor comes racing into the surgery. 'There's an emergency,' he says. 'We've just taken a telephone call from the Flying Doctor base and they want a doctor to fly up to Lightning Ridge with them, immediately.'

'What's the problem?' Bob asked while still focusing on the job at hand.

'Well, they say that there's a bloke up there who's fallen down one of the mine shafts.'

'Doesn't sound too good,' Bob replied.

'No,' said the young doctor, 'apparently he's been stuck down the mine shaft for about a week, with nothing to eat, and he's only been keeping himself alive by drinking his own urine.'

Anyway, Bob said, 'Well, son, as you can see, I'm flat out, so you'll have to go up to Lightning Ridge with the RFDS by yourself and see to the feller.'

Of course, this really threw the new doctor into a flap. Being just out of university this was something very different than what he'd ever been taught.

'Well,' the young doctor said, looking to Bob for some wise and worldly advice, 'what do I do when I get there? How do I go about treating him? What's the procedure?'

'Well, son,' Bob said, still concentrating on his patient, 'the first thing yer gonna have to try and do is to get the feller off the piss.'

First Drive

My first flight for the RFDS was as a freelance 'driver' out of Cairns. I describe myself as a driver because, basically, that's all a pilot is. The only difference between us and a bus driver is that we've got wings. Anyhow, that was back on 13 November 1982 and because all the aircraft were already busy, we did that flight in a non-RFDS aircraft, but with an RFDS doctor.

In fact, I've just got the old log book out and, before that first flight with the RFDS, already on that day, I'd been from Darwin to Groote Eylandt, Karumba and on to Cairns in a Shrike Commander. But what happened back in those days was that there was an operator out of Cairns called Outback Air, who was owned by Richard Murray-Prior, and Richard used to be the casual pilot for the Flying Doctor Service. So Richard must've been unavailable on this occasion because his wife, Ilma, rang around looking for somebody to fly an aeroplane and she got me and asked if I could go out somewhere with a doctor to evacuate someone.

It was dark by then and, as I said, I'd already been around the place a bit already so I said, 'Well, Ilma, I'm not long home from Darwin. But if you can't get anybody else just give me a call back.'

Of course, by my saying that, she had me then, didn't she? In actual fact, a few years later, when I was employed full-time with the RFDS, Ilma worked for us as a manager of the RFDS Visitors' Centre, here in Cairns, and I happened to ask her one day, 'Ilma,' I said, 'away back then, in '82, did you really ring around and look for anyone else to go out on that evacuation?'

And her reply was along the lines of, 'Don't be silly, of course I didn't.'

Anyway, it didn't take Ilma long to get back in touch with me to say that she's rung around all over the place—which, of course, she hadn't—and that she couldn't find anyone else.

So I said, 'Yes, okay, I'll do the trip.' And then I was told that the place I had to go out to was a small town called Mount Surprise, which is south-west of Cairns, east of Georgetown.

It was all quite an odd experience for me really because, for starters, I'd never been to Mount Surprise before and secondly, I'd never flown in the aeroplane I was going out in: a Piper Aztec. I mean, I was endorsed on it, but I'd never been in this particular one before so, as far as that goes, it was a strange aeroplane to me. Then the doctor that came out with me was a feller by the name of Russell Findlay and along with his medical gear Russell also had a book which gave the details of where the Mount Surprise airstrip was and so forth.

Then we were on our way out there and when I looked at the book Russell had brought along, it placed the aerodrome—this is from memory because it's going back a while now—but it placed the aerodrome something like about 20 miles west from Mount Surprise.

And I said to Russell, 'Gee, it sounds pretty strange for them to have an airstrip that far out of such a little town like Mount Surprise.'

'Oh well,' he said, 'that's what the book says.'

Anyway I was still a bit concerned about it so I checked in with Townsville Flight Service to see if they could verify where the airstrip actually was and they said, 'No, we can't tell you, but Phil Darby will probably know where it is.'

Phil was a very experienced pilot with the Royal Flying Doctor Service. He'd been everywhere and knew the area like the back of his hand. Anyhow, Phil was coming back from Weipa and the bloke in Townsville said, 'We'll have a talk to Phil.'

So, when Phil got into range they explained how we were on the way out to Mount Surprise but the information in the Aerodrome Book seemed a bit odd because it positioned the strip as being well west of the town.

'Yeah, that's where it'd be,' Phil told them. 'That'd be right.'

'Oh, okay then,' I said and that was that.

But luckily enough, Phil must've had a bit of a think about it and decided, 'Hang on, I don't know so much about that.' So he looked it up in his aeroplane and he got back in radio contact and he said, 'The book you've got is wrong. The strip's actually closer to town.'

Then he asked if I'd ever been there.

'Well, no,' I said, 'I didn't even know that Mount Surprise existed until someone rang me up tonight.'

And he said, 'Well there's a big hill right next to the strip, be wary of that.'

'Thanks for the warning,' I replied.

Now, I'd flown a bit at night, of course, but when you're coming out of Cairns and those sort of bigger towns where there's plenty of lights around them it's fine, but, with a little place like Mount Surprise you know it's going to be quite a black spot. Anyway, they had flares out and so we found the place alright and I remember—and it still happens to this day—next to the hill you get what we call a katabatic wind, which is where the air cools down and rushes down the hill. So you get quite a wind off it and when you're going in to land there's quite a bit of drift. Still, we negotiated that and we landed okay and the doctor said, 'Do you want to come into town with me to see this patient?'

'No thanks,' I told him, 'I'd prefer to have a look around here.'

So the doctor went into town while I stayed out at the airstrip. But when my eyes started to get used to the dark and I got my bearings, I could see this hill right next to the strip. Anyway, I had a bit of a look around for future reference, just in case I came back again. Then before too much longer they returned with the patient. As it turned out it was a female school teacher who'd taken an overdose of drugs, so we loaded her up and tied her into the seat and we prepared to leave.

Now, you've got to take off at a certain speed so that, if you have an engine failure, you can still keep flying. And I remember that I got a little bit slow when we lifted off. And it's all in the mind, because it's very hard, you know, to lower the nose when you don't know the area and you don't know exactly where the hill is out there. Anyhow we made it. But I can remember still holding onto the aeroplane until we got to about 7000 feet and once we got to 7000 feet I put the auto-pilot on. But gosh, it was as dark as hell. I'd never had that experience before. It was certainly a real eye-opener for me.

So we arrived back at Cairns without any trouble and, yeah, the teacher would've survived okay. But whether she stayed off drugs is another thing. Who knows. I mean, I've since discovered that there's a lot of sad cases out there; people who just don't look after themselves.

Anyway, that was my first flight, 'driving' for the Flying Doctor Service. I'm now full-time with the RFDS here at the Cairns base and then, sometimes, I'll relieve drivers out at the RFDS bases in places like Mount Isa and Charleville.

But I learned a lot from that first flight, because there's nothing worse than going out to some place where you've never been before, especially at night, and you don't know what obstacles there are, you know, if there's towers about or there's hills around the place. So it certainly got me going. And because of that experience, what I try to do now is that, on the days I go out to some of these more remote towns and properties, I take as many digital photographs of the area as I can and I put them on a disk and keep them in the hangar. Then, when a new driver comes along, someone who's unfamiliar with these areas, I can say, 'Before you go out there, have a look at these because they'll give you a bit of an idea as to the lay of the land.'

Gasping

Yeah, the RFDS did actually come out for me once. At the time my husband, Pad, and I were working at Mount House Station, up the Gibb River Road, here in the Kimberley. It was during the wet season and the Station Manager was away on holidays so there were only four of us in residence. Anyhow, all of a sudden my lips went blue and I began to really gasp for air. It was smoko time and everyone was sitting in the kitchen and I walked up to Pad and I said, 'Pad, I can't breathe.'

And he took one look at me and went, 'Oh, you're not doing too well at all, are you?'

The Flying Doctor Service radio was down at the Station Manager's homestead so they took me down there and they did the emergency button thing on the radio to get in contact with Derby. You know what that is, don't you? It's when you press the emergency button and a light in at the RFDS base comes on to let them know there's an emergency.

Anyhow, by this stage I'm lying on my back. The girl who was with us, she was good. She'd rolled up a towel and put it behind my neck, you know, to support my neck and open up my airways. But even then I was still really gasping because I just couldn't get any air. Probably a little bit of panic had set in as well, which mightn't have helped things.

So, they answered the emergency in at the Derby RFDS base and they ask what's wrong and Pad gets on the radio and says, 'My wife can't breathe!'

Then they start asking him all these questions. 'Does she suffer from asthma?'

'No.'

'Has she done this?'

'No.'

'Has she done that?'

'Do you have any idea why she's not breathing?'

'No.'

'Is she pregnant?'

Pad had to think about that one. 'I don't think so,' he said. 'Not that I know of, anyway.'

Then he asks me. 'You're not pregnant, are you?'

'No,' I gasped.

'No, she says she's not pregnant,' Pad replied. 'She's just lying here, gasping. You know, like, what else can I say?'

And I'm thinking, 'Oh my God!' Because I'm getting pretty frightened by now. Like I'd tried very hard to lie there and relax and just think of something else but when your husband's on the phone calling out, 'She's lying here gasping!' well, it's a bit hard to relax.

Anyway, they said, 'well, okay, we'd better come out then.'

And they did have to divert their flight. Apparently they were going to Fitzroy Crossing or somewhere, and it wasn't an emergency, and Mount House Station wasn't all that far out of their way, which was fortunate. So it was a relief to hear them say that they were actually going to come out.

Still and all, they weren't able to arrive for about an hour so I just laid there on the floor trying to relax. Then about half an hour after we'd made the call to the Flying Doctor my breathing started to come good again, and my lips weren't quite as blue. But then I came out in this most hideous rash, mainly around my collar, round my socks, around the tops of my jeans. It was burning unbelievably and I started getting these great big welts.

When that happened we immediately figured out what was wrong. See, I must've walked under an itchy caterpillar nest and all the dust had fallen out onto my clothing. You know the little hairy caterpillars? It's their defence mechanism, you know, so that things won't touch them. Well, all their hair creates a dust that accumulates in their nest and if you get it on your clothes it rubs into your skin and you get this god-awful rash. So that's what happened. It was the itchy caterpillar.

Anyhow, once the rash came out, Pad was fine then. He started to relax when he realised what had happened. But, of course, the rash didn't come out until after I'd almost drawn my last breath, did it? Well, it certainly felt that way. I honestly thought I was going to stop breathing.

So then Pad stuck me under a nice cold shower and that got rid of most of the itchiness. But I was still having a bit of trouble breathing so, with the Flying Doctor already on his way, we went out to meet him. And that was a fair drive because the RFDS registered airstrip was about a 30-kilometre drive around the other side of the mountain. It's a big long, wide strip. So then I had to endure being bounced around in the front of the car.

Anyway, when we got there, we waited for another half an hour until they arrived and we were able to tell them that it was probably the itchy caterpillar that'd caused the reaction.

'That's unusual,' the doctor said, 'because normally it's the rash that hits you straight away and not the struggling for breath.'

He likened it to me having an enormous asthma attack and, had they known, they would've been able to tell Pad to give me a spoonful of liquid Ventolin that was in the RFDS medical kit in the homestead. And that would've reduced the reaction. Anyhow, they gave me some antihistamine shots to get rid of the welts and that and then they were off again. But they were really good about it. You know, they were glad to see I was alive. But, oh gee, it knocked me around for a few days, and I certainly did appreciate them coming out.

Gone with the Wind

It was around the beginning of 1969. The Flying Doctor base was about three or four miles out of Broken Hill, on the Wilcannia road, and they had an auditorium there where they used to show a promotional film, for the tourists, about the RFDS and what they did.

Now, the actual RFDS doctor, at that particular time, was Dr Graham Ambrose and the pilot was Vic Cover, or just 'Cove' as he was known amongst his friends and enemies. I knew both of them very well. Cove had a reputation as an incredible pilot, plus he was a bit of a larrikin, to boot. He had a weekender out at Menindee, along Sunset Strip. I went to a couple of his New Year's Eve parties there and they were events to remember, that's if you could, of course. Cove was well-known in the district and, as I said, a terrific pilot. Graham Ambrose was a young doctor, forty-ish, and a nice bloke. We were in Rotary together. He was President and I was Vice-President, and quite often he'd be away on Flying Doctor visits and so forth and I'd step in for him on Rotary nights.

Anyway, Graham said to me one day, 'Fred,' he said, 'the Stuyvesant cigarette company are keen to improve their corporate image so they want to make a film along the lines of a day in the life of the Flying Doctor.' He said, 'Fred, would you be willing to act as a patient?'

I'd done a bit of local repertory so I said, 'Yes, of course, I'll only be too willing to play the part of a patient.'

Well, out come this film crew from Sydney. Now I don't know whether it was because I'd built my expectations up too high or not but, I must say, I was a little surprised that there were only three in the film crew. Still, there you go. There was the director, who was quite well-known back in those days because he'd made a bit of a name for himself introducing 'This Day Tonight' or 'Today Tonight'; you know, one of those television news-type shows in Sydney. He was a corker bloke and so was his crew. There was a cameraman. Now, the cameraman had recently broken his right leg, I think it was, in a motor bike accident and was in plaster from heel to hip. So he had a bit of trouble getting around. Then there was the sound man who had this big recording box and a microphone set up.

It was planned that we'd meet out at the RFDS base at a certain time and we'd fly out to Mooleulooloo Station to shoot the first part of this film. Anyhow, who should suddenly appear in Broken Hill, none other than some heavy in the Flying Doctor Service. He was either a Group Captain or a Chief Pilot or a Chief something-or-other. Now, whether he arrived in town on purpose or just by accident, I don't know. But he rocked up and, sort of, invited himself to come along with us.

So at the allotted time we all met up out at the RFDS base. The plane we were flying in was an old Drover. I think it was made by De Havilland. The Drover was originally a two-engined aeroplane that'd just been recommissioned and had a third engine put in it so that it now flew higher, faster and had shorter take-offs; something like that.

Anyway, before we even got to the stage of taking-off there was a brief debate between this Group Captain, or whatever he was, and Cove. The Group Captain wanted to fly the plane and Cove dug his heels in. 'No,' Cove said, 'I'm responsible for the aeroplane so I'm gonna fly the damn thing and that's all there is to it.'

So there was already some friction between this Group Captain feller and Cove. Anyway, Cove wouldn't budge on the matter and eventually the Group Captain gave in and Cove flew us out to Mooleulooloo Station, which was about 70 or 80 miles north-west of Broken Hill, over the border, into South Australia. I reckon the Treloars had the place back then and probably still do.

Now, there was no script or anything. It was only while we were flying along that this director feller and Graham had a bit of a discussion, along with a few interruptions by the Group Captain. It came down to my problem being either a heart attack or a burst duodenum ulcer. So that was going to be my part, because I'm going to have to have something very dramatic that's going to cause an emergency call to the Flying Doctor. Anyway, they settled on a burst duodenum ulcer because they thought it best that a cigarette company, like Peter Stuyvesant, wasn't associated with a heart attack. Then they decided that I might be doing some welding on the front of a trailer and that's when I'd have this burst duodenum ulcer and it'd hurt very much and I'd fall down on the ground and roll around in agony and they'd call the Flying Doctor.

Anyway, we landed at Mooleulooloo Station and, first, they set me up in a room where I'm pretending to talk to a mate over the radio. This was all supposed to be taking place during one of the infamous 'Galah Sessions'. We were talking about stock prices or oil prices, or what have you, then I said, 'Look mate, I've gotta get off the air now because I've gotta go and weld this trailer up before we head off into town.' And I get up and out I go, outside. Cut. They were my major lines in the film.

Meantime, while they're doing all this filming, not only is Cove having continuing problems with the Group Captain, but the cameraman's also having trouble with him. Unfortunately the Group Captain somehow just happened to have brought his little camera along and each time they're about to do some filming, he's forever tapping the cameraman on the shoulder, checking the light reading or some such, and telling him where he's going wrong. So the Group Captain fancies himself with the camera as well as being an expert pilot.

So to the next scene and I'm welding this trailer. Well, I've never welded before, but I've got this mask on and I'm making lots of sparks and all of a sudden I'm hit by this burst duodenum ulcer. I fall down and I start rolling around on the ground in agony—gyrating and contortionising—because I'm supposed to be in such a bad way. Cove reckoned that Burt Lancaster couldn't have done it better.

Then it must've been the lady of the house who called the Flying Doctor because the next scene is where they're carting me out to the plane, which is conveniently parked nearby. I'm on a stretcher, Cove's in front and Graham's at the back. The Group Captain's offering advice. Now, I don't know if you've ever seen the old Drover but the aeroplane door's about six feet off the ground. So when they get to lifting me up into the plane, there's a problem in getting the stretcher so high up and then getting it in line with the door. You could liken the situation to a couple of heavy weight-lifters, where they have to lift the weight up to the waist then do a jig and push it right up and over their heads. But Cove and Graham were struggling and I was stuck there on the stretcher, halfway between a clean and jerk and a snatch and lift.

Anyway the director said, 'Hang on, we'll fix this.'

So, with a bit of mastery of filming, they managed to get one end of the stretcher balanced just inside the plane door. Then, while Cove's holding it up, with his arms outstretched, they cut the filming so that I can crawl out of the stretcher and lay down in the plane before they get the action going again. So that fixed that problem.

Then behind Mooleulooloo Station there's this monstrous hill—it's a tiny Ayers Rock—and they decide to go up there to film the Drover while it's taking off, then as it's landing. The only trouble is that the cameraman's got his flipping leg wrapped in plaster. Anyhow, he declined the offer of the Group Captain to take over the filming and, with a lot of effort, the cameraman stumbles up the top of this hill. When he's settled, the director gives a wave of his arms to start filming and Cove takes off, does a couple of circuits, then he lands again. Cut. That shot's completed.

Anyway, after a quick lunch, we're on the plane and we're flying back to Broken Hill, over the border, into New South Wales. There we were, we're flying sedately at about 3000 feet, with the Group Captain keeping an eagle eye on Cove, just to make sure he's doing everything right when, all of a sudden, the plane rears up in the air and points skyward. It's vertical. And

Vic's got the stick back like we're in big trouble. Oh, it was gut retching. Then just as suddenly, the nose drops and down we come again, then we flatten out again.

'Christ, what was that?' the Group Captain shouts.

And Vic says in that slow laconic voice of his, 'Oh, didn't you see it? We just flew over the border fence.'

So Cove got him in the end and the Group Captain shut up after that.

Anyhow, after we arrived back in Broken Hill we went up into Graham's house where they'd set up a little room to double as a single hospital ward, with all these electrical things around the place. So I'm lying in bed with all these ECG things stuck on me, left, right and centre, because I'm still supposed to be in bad shape. Graham's all professional in his white coat and he's got his stethoscope and he's telling me that I'm going to be alright, thanks to the Royal Flying Doctor Service getting out to Mooleulooloo Station, just in the nick of time, and that no permanent damage has been done, and I'm going to be safe. I'll live.

'Good,' I say. 'Thanks very much.'

And really, that was pretty much it. But I tell you, when the film come out, it wasn't actually too bad, even if I do say so myself. It went for about twenty minutes and, as Cove says, 'They ended up playing that film in the RFDS auditorium, three times a day, seven days a week, for about ten straight years.' And when you come to think of it, that's a pretty long run for a film, maybe even longer than *Gone with the Wind*.

Got the Scours

My father, Charlie Shultz, owned Humbert River Station, which was 32 miles west of Victoria River Downs Station, in the central west of the Northern Territory. Humbert River runs into the Wickham River, which Vic River Downs was on, and that ran into the Victoria River. My father sold the property in about 1972, and I grew up there and left when I was about twenty-five.

I'd surmise that, around the end of 1945, there was still no Flying Doctor Service in Wyndham because when I was a baby I was quite ill and my mother had to take me on the mail plane from Vic River Downs Station and I ended up in the Derby Hospital for a couple of weeks. We didn't have an airstrip at Humbert River and Vic River Downs had a big landing strip. Back in those days, the mail run came out from Wyndham to the bigger stations like Vic River Downs, then back to Halls Creek and on to Derby. That's why I ended up over in Derby rather than going to Katherine where they also had a larger hospital.

Humbert River was virtually at a dead end and during the wet season we had to ride on horseback the 32 miles to Vic River Downs to get our mail. Usually we'd head off early in the morning with a couple of changes of horses, along with a couple of packhorses, and you'd go over one day and come back the next. I mean, you didn't go over every week, you'd only do that once a month or something. In the dry season we could drive over but even then it took two and a half hours just to get there, which might give you some idea as to just how bad the road was.

Then we only got in food supplies once a year. Those supplies would come up by boat to Wyndham and we'd pick them up in about August or September. My mother was the cook. We had about thirty to forty Aboriginals in all and of those only about ten actually worked for us and the others were their family members; you know, the older people and young children who also stayed on our property and were kept by my family. That was in the days when a lot of the half-caste children were being taken away from their Aboriginal mothers and my parents took on about four part-Aboriginal children and schooled them on the station so that they weren't taken away. In fact, later on, my parents took on some more.

So, it must've been later in the 1940s before the Flying Doctor Service started coming out. Then we got a radio in about 1952, maybe '53, which was linked into the Royal Flying Doctor Service network out of Wyndham. And, oh, it was just like having a lifeline, you know, for all sorts of things. As you might imagine we were quite isolated and they were something that you were really in touch with.

I remember the RFDS radio contact sessions. The first one was at eight o'clock in the morning, which would've only been 6.30 am in Western Australia. The doctor would be at the hospital, on a direct line, and he'd come on air and say they were open for medical appointments. First, he'd ask if there were any emergencies and they'd be dealt with while everyone else waited their turn to have their questions answered.

Now, with the Wyndham RFDS base, the furthest easterly cattle station that they broadcast to was south of Katherine, in the Top End of the Northern Territory, just near Mataranka. Then the furthest south would've been, perhaps, Inverway Station, which is virtually on the Northern Territory–Western Australian border plus, of course, there were a lot of places in Western Australia.

We actually had a normal 12-volt car-battery operated wireless—it was a Traeger. All the two-way radios in the outback were Traeger. And we all had a different call sign. So you'd give your call sign and say who you were and tell them if the patient was a female or male and what their age was and so forth. Then you told them whatever was wrong or, you know, that somebody had fallen off a horse and what their injuries were.

After listening to all the information the doctor then had to try and judge what to do. If the patient was critical they'd fly out and get them and if they weren't critical, the doctor would prescribe some treatment or medication from the cattle station's medical chest. Really, it must've been pretty hard to work out what medications they should take, especially if the person at the calling end wasn't trained or even educated in any medical sort of way.

All the medications came from the Royal Flying Doctor medical chest. It was quite big, probably about 4 foot wide by about 2 foot 6 high and 2 foot 6 deep. On the inside of the lid there was a plan to let you know what medicines, or what-have-you, all the trays in the chest contained. Originally the trays were named by their medical terminologies but because people didn't understand the medical names of the drugs they later numbered them, which made it much easier. If you could imagine, it was like ordering a Chinese meal where the numbers related to a specific medication. And when you ran out of anything you just wrote away and asked them to send you the refills.

Now, I don't think the RFDS medical chest was absolutely free. I think, back then, it was heavily subsidised because I do remember we paid a certain amount to be on the radio network and, obviously, we paid for telegrams and such. Then I have a vague memory of the medical chest rental being on the bill at the end of the year.

As far as the medications went, one of the favourite items in the medical chest most certainly would've been the sulphanilamide powder. This must've been before antibiotic or penicillin powders came out and the sulphanilamide powder was sprinkled like a talcum powder on open wounds and things like that. Of course, being in that sort of country, a lot of it was also used on the horses, which I don't think the Royal Flying Doctor Service would've been too happy about. We got it in big packets, like in 2-kilogram bags. You know, we didn't waste it, but my father certainly used it on horses. It was very good, actually.

Then there was the Golden Eye ointment, which was also very good. I think it was another sulphur-based ointment, and that was used for all sorts of eye infections. The flies were really bad and the Aboriginal people always had sore eyes. You know, you'd try to teach them to chase the flies out of their eyes but you were still always using the eye ointment. Actually, the

Golden Eye ointment seemed to fix most things, so, once again, it was also used on the horses.

But that was just the way it was and, of course, everybody listened in on these sessions so everybody knew everybody else's intimate business. I mean, the men in particular seemed extremely embarrassed if they had to get on the radio and talk about medical problems; you know, especially if they were talking about their wife. But that wasn't unusual because the men out there were far more comfortable describing what was wrong with a cow or a horse than they were with a female. I can remember one funny occasion when the wife of one of the pastoralists was ill. She had a bad case of diarrhoea and her husband came on the radio and said to the doctor, 'The wife's crook.'

And there was a lady doctor up from Perth, filling in for the usual male doctor in Wyndham. Anyhow, it was obvious that the pastoralist felt very awkward talking to a woman about what his wife's problem was because he was humming and haring a lot and not quite getting to the point. But the female doctor kept probing him in an attempt to get a clear and proper understanding of just what he was on about. Anyway, in the end it all got a bit too much for the pastoralist and he blurted out to the female doctor, 'For heaven's sake woman, don't you understand? My wife, she's got the scours.'

Hans from Germany

You must know, it is ten years ago that Germany founded the fan club of the Flying Doctors from the Australian television series. It was translated into the German language and many Germans liked the actors of this series, and so they founded a fan club. I am a member of this fan club, too.

My name is Dr Hans Henschel. In Australia they know me as 'Hans from Germany'. That is my name in Australia. I am a paediatrician in Germany; a doctor for babies and kids and youth to eighteen and I have a big practice. We are three paediatricians in this practice. I am the senior doctor. Two paediatricians must always be in the practice. This is our agreement so that the door of my practice is always open for the sick children. Parents can always find an open door. And, you know, I am a workaholic. I work Sunday, Saturday, seven days a week. I work, work, work, and then I think, I must come to Australia.

But I have always loved Australia. I don't know where that comes from—perhaps from the heart—but when I was much younger I was always very interested in Australia. In my life before I think I was an Australian, perhaps I could even have been an Aboriginal, I don't know. But it's a long time that I'm very interested in Australia.

I come here the first time in the year of 2001 and I see this country. Spectacular! I was infected. We say in Germany, we are infected with this country. I love, very much, the outback, the nature, the animals, the sunrises and sunsets; it's fantastic. To dream in the outback and to feel it, that is very great for me. And when I see the country the first time, I come to Alice Springs and I visit the Flying Doctor base there. This is my first real contact to the Flying Doctor. And then I realise, because of my profession as a doctor, there is much more in Australia than the country, the nature, the animals, the plants and all those things. There's also a very important health service. The Royal Flying Doctor Service, it exists, already, over more than seventy-eight years. John Flynn founded it and it is very important for the people who live and work in the outback, and for the people who are travelling there. And in the outback there are travelling much more Germans and if there becomes health problems the Flying Doctor helps, and it costs no money.

And this is why I founded, in Germany, the association to support the Royal Flying Doctor Service. I am President and I am the founder of this association and I guide this association, because I thought I should do much more to support the RFDS. And I knew many people in Germany who would give much more money if only they could use it as a tax deduction, and the fan club cannot do that. And so I founded this association. It's incorporated, so if they give a donation they can claim it on their tax return. We have a President—that's me—and we have an Assistant President, who is a doctor of law and he has done the statutes, and we have a cashier. You can find all about it at the website. But it is not so important for me to have much members because the most money we get in Germany, we get not from the members, we get from the people we speak to and tell them all about the organisation of the RFDS and what it is doing. Then, of course, many pharmacy factories and other factories also donate their money. But it's very important for me to get money to support the Flying Doctors.

So it is two years, nearly three years, since we have become an association. And now, I come to Australia two or three times every year, for four or five weeks each of those times, and I travel all over Australia and I visit as many of the Flying Doctor bases that I can to give them the money. This time we handed over more than $52 000, cash, to the Royal Flying Doctor Service bases, all over.

But, oh, I love Australia. So many, many Germans do. My fascination will be, Australia is a country where I can breathe. I like to be free in the outback, to feel the nature, to see the sky, to see the landscape, to see the sunsets and the sunrises. You cannot do these things in Germany. You can only do that in Australia. And if I will be in a town or a city for some days or weeks, I then must go back to the outback, to see the wideness again.

When I come back from my trips to Australia I see many people standing in the airport who are very sad to leave this nice country. If you go out of the aircraft at Frankfurt, a busy town, people don't look nice and much stress will be there in them. I'm sad to leave too, but it's just a little sad now because I know I will work very, very hard when I get back and then I can tell, 'Now, I must fly back to Australia.' So I am not so sad.

But after coming back from Australia, I will come back to my practice with much more inside power and I am happy once again to be in my practice. And all these emotions I bring with me from Australia help me, and I can work ever much harder with that power. But after some weeks or some months, I know I must come back to Australia to refresh my motivation. So I'll be back here again after three or four months, and with some more money to give to the Flying Doctors.

Heroes out of Mere Mortals

When I was reading through the first book, *Great Flying Doctor Stories*, I came across one that was titled 'Peak Hour Traffic' and I thought, You know, hang on a tick, I've been writing history books about Tilpa for the past twenty-five years or so and I've never heard this story before.

So I rang the RFDS base at Broken Hill and I was speaking to the lady there and she told me I should go back to the source and see if I could clear up whether the old character named as 'Joe', who featured in the story, well, maybe he was someone else and things have been changed around so as not to incriminate the guilty, so to speak. Because, for the life of me, the name Joe just does not ring a bell, that is, of course, unless his real name's been changed, just in case, and it's actually old Clem who the story's about.

And also I was thinking about how it says in the story that this character Joe lived in the caravan park when there's never really been a caravan park in Tilpa. Oh yes, there's accommodation rooms at the hotel, and Carol and Bernie Williams, who own the Tilpa Trading Post—the store—they now have a couple of cabins and sites for caravans. But they didn't have them back then, when the story took place, and they're certainly not situated next to the pub. They're next to the building where the first Flying Doctor clinics were held. Actually, the funny thing about Tilpa is that what now is the store was originally the hotel and what's now the pub used to be the store. So they've sort of swapped functions.

But my line of thinking is that, if that story about the old feller in the book was about Clem, well, I can understand that because Clem was a very private sort of a bloke, just like the Joe character. What's more, Clem would also be the sort of bloke that, if two cars drove past his caravan on the one day, yeah, he'd say that the traffic was getting too much for him.

So I reckon that it might be about old Clem and I know a fair bit about him because Clem was a bit of an institution around here. I say was because he's dead now. He was also a Tobruk Rat. Originally he came from, I think it was, out Tibooburra way or Broken Hill, maybe. From recollection, a couple of his sisters used to live in Broken Hill, where they taught piano.

But Clem was a fencing contractor in the Tilpa district for, I'd say, about forty years and, oh, wasn't he a perfectionist, especially when it came to fencing. The words 'It's just about right' weren't in his vocabulary. If the fence wasn't absolutely perfect, he'd go and pull it out again and put it back in at his own expense and in his own time. He was that sort of a bloke was Clem. Then when his working days were behind him he moved into a caravan over on the opposite side of the Darling River, across from the hotel, and it's quite possible that, as the story in the book said, when the Flying Doctor came up here to run their clinics they kept an eye on him.

I'll just tell you a little story about Clem that'll give you some idea as to what a sort of tough and independent character he was. On one occasion, he wasn't too well, he was crook, and he realised that he needed to visit a doctor. So rather than ringing up someone he knew at the hotel or anyone locally and asking them if they could give him a lift he literally walked over to the edge of the road and hitched a ride the 150 miles or so, all the way to Cobar to see a doctor.

And that's where he died. He died in Cobar. And he'd expressed a wish that, if he did die out this way, he wanted to be buried in the Tilpa cemetery. Then, well, one thing led to another and because the Tilpa cemetery was actually situated on private ground and the people who owned the property didn't want him buried there, Clem ended up having to be buried in Cobar, which is something we were all sorry about. So, basically, that was Clem.

Now, as for Flying Doctor stories, I could tell you a few of those because my family have been involved with the medical clinic here in Tilpa since it first came into being, back on 18 September 1969. My mother had been a Matron with the Red Cross in the Second World War so, being a trained nurse, she took on the role of, well, not quite district nurse but at least clinic coordinator, when the RFDS clinic first came into existence in Tilpa.

And that, in itself, is another story, because how my mother got out here to Tilpa was that, well, she married a local of course, and that local was my father. But there's a funny little story about that, too, because my mother and my father first met in my mother's grandmother's house in Wilcannia. That was on the Wednesday before my mother's aunt was to marry Dad's uncle, the following Saturday. At that time Dad, whose name was Roy McInerney, was only sixteen years old—I think he acted as the best man for his uncle—and Mum was only nine years old. And to her dying day, Mum swore that the moment she saw this young sixteen-year-old, Roy McInerney, she said, 'That's the man I'm going to marry. He's the one for me.'

But Dad was never one to do anything in a hurry because, you see, it was twenty-six or so years later, when he was forty-three, that they got married. So there'd been a whole lot of life going on and a whole lot of water under the bridge, between times. So that's how Mum got to Tilpa and when she got there she took on the clinic coordinator's role and she did that right up until I got married in 1973. After Mum finished, one of the other ladies in the district, Pat Luffman, she took on the role for a few years, until she and her husband retired to Cobar. Then, carrying on the family tradition, my wife, Jill, she took on the job as clinic coordinator and she's been doing it ever since. And on the few occasions we've been away over the last couple of years our daughter's taken it on. So you could say that it's been in the family for three generations.

But as to some stories about the Tilpa clinic, I can remember one of the very, very early ones. This was after the days when they had a punt going over the Darling River, at Tilpa, and we used to hold the monthly RFDS clinics in a couple of rooms in a house that had previously been the old Puntman's Cottage. One room was for the doctor and the other room was for the dentist, and the verandah acted as a waiting room, sort of thing. So everybody would line up on the verandah.

The Puntman's Cottage was owned by the local postmaster, Fred Davidson. Fred lived and had his post office in a separate building in Tilpa and had, for some reason or other, also acquired the old Puntman's Cottage, which then became known as Fred's Flats or The Villa Davo. And it was just lucky that he did because years later the building came in handy when the post office building burnt down and the 'office' was shifted to the 'Flats'.

But in those earlier days, with the dentist, all his drilling equipment was powered off a 12-volt battery and, as well as me being the official driver to get Mum into the clinic, it was also my responsibility to make sure I brought along a fully charged 12-volt battery. The only trouble with that was, as the clinic wore on, the power in the battery tended to wear down. So if you happened to be the last one in the queue, it was a case of the drill going at a slow woo ... woo ... woo. And it's not very funny to start to get a filling with a very, very slow drill. In actual fact, there's been a couple of cases where they had to send out an SOS for someone to pull a battery out of a vehicle somewhere and use that before the old battery went flat and the drilling equipment stopped completely. So the trick was that, if you had to have any fillings, you tried to make sure you got there nice and early.

I can remember one clinic in particular when Ted Eslake was the dentist. Actually, I think that Ted first started with the Royal Flying Doctor Service in Broken Hill, as a dentist, and later on he became the Director for the south-eastern section of the RFDS. It's a bit like Clyde Thomson, how he used to be the Chief Pilot with the RFDS at Broken Hill and now he's the CEO there. Anyway, I can remember this particular RFDS clinic when Ted was the dentist. And you must remember that this was an afternoon clinic because they'd already been to Louth or Wanaaring or White Cliffs or somewhere before they flew into Tilpa. But when they got there Ted had twenty-one patients to deal with and the last three, would you believe it, were all extractions.

So, by the time Ted gets to them, the sun's slowly going down, down, down and the RFDS pilot's watching the sun get lower and lower and lower and, of course, he's getting very, very toey because we only had an outback dirt airstrip at Tilpa so there was no lighting or flares or anything back then. Anyhow, it's getting very late and the sun's setting and the pilot's getting extremely worried about all this so, in the end, to save time Ted lined these three blokes up—the ones that needed the extractions—and it was like working on a production line. It was a jab ... 'A needle for you.' And jab ... 'A needle for you.' And jab ... 'A needle for you.'

When he'd finished doing that he waited for the shortest possible time then he came back to the first feller and asked, 'Is it numb yet?'

'Yeah, I think so.'

'Good.' And so it was yank and out come the tooth. 'Here's a wad of cotton wool. Chew on it.'

Then he went to the next feller, 'Is it numb yet?'

'Yeah, I think so.' So out come that feller's tooth and, 'Here's a wad of cotton wool. Chew on it.'

Then the same thing to the third one. 'And here's some cotton wool. Chew on it.'

So there's the three fellers, still sitting there like stunned mullets, munching on these huge wads of cotton wool, and Ted calls out to the pilot, 'Okay then, let's chuck all this stuff into the car and go out and get on the plane.'

And I've got a sneaking suspicion that they took off only about half a minute after last light. And so that would've been back in about 1970, because by November 1971 we had a new Community Centre in Tilpa, which had a separate room for the doctor. Unfortunately, though, the dentist was not so lucky because he had to work in a corner of the main room.

But that old area we had for the dentist, I tell you what, it made heroes out of mere mortals, because the only thing they had around the dental chair, to screen it off, was a bit of a curtain sort of thing. That's all there was between you and the audience. So everybody knew if you were whimpering or not. Oh absolutely, if you screamed, everybody in the district of Tilpa knew all about it.

Naturally, things have changed over the years. We've now got a three-roomed demountable building for the RFDS doctor and whatever nurses arrive. And the dentist, she's now got her own room off the end of the hall. Mind you, she's still using the same old dentist's chair that Ted Eslake used away back then. So it's a pretty well-worn dentist's chair and a lot of us can still recall a life-changing event occurring while we sat in that chair, getting our teeth pulled or drilled or what-have-you. Of course, that's the few of us that remain living in the district and who can still remember back that far.

And what's more, the Flying Doctor people have tried a few times to get that old dentist's chair back and put it in their museum at Broken Hill, and every time they try, we've said, 'Not on yer life. That's part of Tilpa's history, that is.'

How the Hell

I'm afraid I don't talk about it too much because I still get a bit emotional about the whole thing. But it was 1966, about this time actually, February, bad dust storms. Terrible dust storms. You see, there was a big drought throughout central Australia at that time. I don't know how long it actually went on for but I was told that there were seven-year-old kids living out there that had never seen rain. Then when it broke, later in '66, I happened to be in Alice Springs and when the rains came, almost everyone in the whole town went down to the Todd River, just to look at the water going past.

I was only new to the Northern Territory. I was only a young feller out there with my best mate, Ken McEwen. We'd done everything together ever since we were little school kids. Anyhow, I'd never seen a dust storm in my life and I don't think Ken had either, and when we first arrived in the Territory it'd been so dry that there was hardly a scrap of vegetation anywhere and the little that there was looked like it just wanted to blow away. So on a regular basis we'd get these huge dust storms. I remember when I was in Alice—and I filmed it happening—it was as clear as anything, then, in the distance, you could see this mountain of dust and it rolled in like a massive cloud from the west and engulfed everybody and everything.

And when the dust started coming through town it got so dark that the street lights automatically came on and you could see all the street lights and the car lights turn blue. And that's true because, apparently, the silica in the sand turns the lights blue. Then sometimes the wind stops and it's deathly still but the dust is so fine that it just hangs up there in the air, like it's suspended. Oh, it's real eerie, I can tell you.

So anyway, we had quite a few terrible dust storms the particular year it happened. At the time I was working for a Canadian company called ODE (Oil Drilling Exploration). ODE was doing a lot of contract well-drilling, out in central Australia, for oil and gas. They contracted for companies like X Oil and French Petroleum. I think they were also involved with Shell because Shell was also drilling madly all over the place in search of oil, even over in western Queensland.

How it all worked was that there was another company, Austral Geophysics, and they'd go ahead of us and do some preliminary drilling then get all the relevant information up on maps. Then Austral would go to X Oil or French Petroleum or whoever owned the leases, show them the maps, and the oil companies would decide where they wanted to drill and they'd come to ODE and say, 'Righto. Put down five holes for us over in this particular area.'

Then we'd charge them whatever-it-was per foot and we'd bring the rig in, put it up, drill the hole, have a look, finish the hole, knock it down, pull the drill rig down, put in what we called a 'Christmas tree' and then we'd move off to the next place to drill another hole. A Christmas tree was a structure that sealed off the drill hole for safety because of the gas. Oh, there were all these painted valves on it and illuminated safety signs bolted to the chain wire fence that surrounded it. They stood out like dog's balls in the desert, that's why they were called Christmas trees.

That was forty years ago and I was out there for most of that year, working all around the place. We drilled all around what they called the Mereenie Fields. The tourists now call it the Mereenie Loop Road. I remember one Easter, for a bit of a break, we went out to what was then known as Ayers Rock. And at Ayers Rock, back then, there was only the caretaker's hut, a bit of a rough caravan park and an old motel that was built from fibrolite. And over that particular Easter there was only the four of us and three other tourists. That's all there was. Now, today, I believe there's well over a thousand people who actually live there, and that's just the people who are looking after the place. So there wasn't much there, back in 1966, believe me.

Anyhow, when we were drilling we worked seven days a week and as far as the structure of the team went, we had three shifts going and on each shift we'd have two Roughnecks, a Motorman, a Derrickman and a Driller. So in all, I'd say we'd probably have anywhere up to twenty blokes living out on the actual rig site, and you'd work your way up through the game. You'd go from a Roughneck to a Motorman—that's the feller who looks after all the engines you drill with—to a Derrickman, to the Driller and then you'd become Tool Pusher.

The actual accident happened to the bloke who was the Tool Pusher. He was like the boss of the oil rig, the head man while we were out there in the desert. I don't know why they called him a Tool Pusher because he certainly didn't push any tools. We were the ones that done all the big tool work. And this particular Tool

Pusher, he was a nice bloke who, I must say, was very good to work for, yet he was also very strict.

Anyhow, as you might gather, living and working out in such remote places there wasn't much to do with any spare time we had. So, yeah, for a bit of play, when we had a bit of time off we'd just grab the old Land Rover and we'd go out shooting donkeys or camels, and sometimes the Tool Pusher would come along as well. The donkeys and camels weren't for eating, just for sport. Oh, they were everywhere. When we'd fly in and fly out you'd see herds of up to four hundred of them, all over the place.

But anyhow, on this particular day I was working a shift and some of the other blokes went out shooting and the Tool Pusher went with them. And while they were out there, driving about, they hit a sand dune and over they went. But when the Land Rover rolled over the Tool Pusher's head got jerked out the window and it got squashed in between the top part of the door and the sand. Really, he was lucky that it was sand or otherwise he'd have been killed instantly. Still, he was very badly injured. He was unconscious. He couldn't move or anything.

Anyway, one of the blokes walked back to camp and grabbed the old Bedford truck—an old pole truck. So they took that out and brought the Tool Pusher back and put him into one of the air-conditioned dongas, which is a portable room, a bit like a little transportable. And they got him into a bed and, naturally, he was covered in blood and sand and everything.

In the meanwhile, a dust storm had been hanging around for a bit and it was starting to build.

We had another bloke out there who was second-in-charge of the rig, a Canadian bloke. He was a driller. From memory, I think he had a bit of first-aid experience. So the driller, he got one of the blokes to call in to the Flying Doctor base at Alice Springs and the doctor there sort of instructed us how to dress the Tool Pusher's injuries and clean him up a bit by using what we had in our first-aid kit.

The Tool Pusher was still unconscious, at this stage. In fact, he really wasn't very good at all and he was getting worse, as was the dust storm. So things weren't looking real flash.

Then, with the Flying Doctor Service, I believe what happens in an emergency situation like that is that the doctor makes all the immediate medical decisions and the pilot has to decide if it's safe enough to fly. They work as a team. We had an airstrip there, of course, so the driller spoke to them and he said, 'Look, this feller's not real good. We can't move him at all and, to be honest, he's not going to last a 300- or 400-kilometre drive, over a dirt road, all the way into Alice Springs. He's just not going to make it.'

And while all this's going on, outside the dust storm's getting worse and worse. So the pilot asked what the conditions were like out our way—which, by then, were pretty horrible—and then he had a discussion with the doctor along the lines of, 'Well, do we fly through a dust storm like this and risk all our lives—the lives of the doctor, the pilot and a nurse—for the sake of, perhaps, saving just the one life?'

It was a tough call but, in the end, they decided that it was best to hold out until the next day when they'd check on the condition of both the Tool Pusher and the dust storm before making any final decision. But by the following day the condition of both the Tool Pusher and the dust storm had gotten worse. In fact, the Tool Pusher was fading.

In the meantime there was an Aboriginal settlement about 150 kilometres away from where we were, called Areyonga. It's one of the furtherest settlements on the western side of Alice Springs, right out towards Kings Canyon. And someone from over there, at Areyonga, made an emergency call into the Alice Springs RFDS to say that they had a lady out there who was going through a tough time having a baby and she was in need of urgent help. So the people from the RFDS got together and sort of said, 'Well, we've got an emergency at Areyonga and we've got another one over at the drilling site. But the dust storm's still very bad so, what do we do, do we head off or not?'

Anyway they made their decision to go, and they flew off and, first, they went over to Areyonga to pick up the lady who was having trouble with the baby, then they set off over our way. By this stage the Tool Pusher was slipping away.

It was day time, but because of this big dust storm it was terribly dark. You could hardly see your hand, right in front of your face. Of course, they didn't even have radar or anything like that in their aeroplanes back then so it was obvious that the pilot was going to have great difficulty just trying to find us, let alone attempting to land the thing. Also, our strip had no lighting. All it had was a bloody wind sock and there was no way he'd be able to see the wind sock through all this dust. The only way we could be of any help was to get all our vehicles and put them down on the end of the strip, with their lights on, so that when, and if, the pilot found us he'd be able to use the vehicle lights as some sort of guide when attempting to put the plane down.

We knew he was coming in from the west, from Areyonga, and I think our strip ran north and south. So we did that, we lined up all our vehicles, with their lights on and, like I mentioned about when the dust came through Alice Springs that time, the dust here was so heavy that all the lights on the vehicles turned blue because of the silica.

With the pilot not being able to see anything, the best he could do was to try and keep in two-way radio contact with our people on the ground. And so we were in our vehicles and some of us would flicker the lights on and off and we'd also grabbed a couple of spotlights that we used for roo shooting, and we shone those up into this blanket of dust, in the vague hope that the pilot might see them and get some direction.

So we waited, with the Tool Pusher hanging on by a thread, as we flickered our vehicle lights and shone the roo spotlights up into the dust. And then we heard him. At first, you could hear this very dull sort of droning and, as the aeroplane got closer, the louder the droning got. And we were just sitting there saying, 'How the hell is he ever going to get down through this dust?'

But then, he appeared. Somehow he come out of the browny-black sky. And I tell you, if ever there was a mob of grown men—and tough ones at that—go to water, that was it. At the first sight of that Flying Doctor's aeroplane breaking through the dust storm the emotion got to us all and we were jumping up and down like little kids and we were cheering. Oh, there were tears—the lot—because, see, we knew straight away that our work mate was going to be saved, you know. Anyhow, down, down, down he come and he landed on that strip and he taxied up to us and there was a frantic rush to put the Tool Pusher in the plane, and away they went.

Now I'm not exactly too sure what happened with the Tool Pusher after that, but he did live, and that's the main thing. I never saw him again but I believe he eventually came good. And I also don't know what happened to the lady who was having a difficult time with the baby. But, I mean, they might well have saved two or even three lives on that one day, and through that terrible dust storm.

So yes, the old Flying Doctor, aye. As I said, it still gets to me. But anyway, perhaps that might give you a real insight into what the RFDS do and how they go about their work. And taking into consideration, of course, that forty years ago they didn't have the sophisticated planes and equipment that they have now. In fact, I think it was one of those old three-engine Drover aeroplanes he was flying that day. So the expertise of those pilots was unbelievable because, how the hell he came through that huge dust storm, I just would not have a clue.

In the Footsteps of Flynn

I suppose I could almost talk under water, but have you heard about 'In the Footsteps of Flynn', with Fred McKay? I think that's a beautiful story because it really depicts, you know, the greatness of Fred McKay and, in particular, the modesty of the man.

To start with, I'll just have to go back a bit in time. Fred McKay told me this yarn himself. Well, it's not really a yarn, it's a true story, and I remember the day that he told it to me, up in Queensland, Fred was born in Mackay, in northern Queensland, and when he was a youngster he became very, very ill. I think he was probably around the age of nine or ten. Anyhow, when he told me this story he couldn't remember just what the exact illness was but apparently he was in and out of consciousness so, naturally, his family was desperately worried about him. But Fred clearly remembered, at one particular stage, opening his eyes and seeing his mother sitting on the end of his bed, looking desperately worried. Of course, she was unaware that her young son was observing her. And Fred said that he watched his mother as she looked to the heavens and in simple prayer she said, 'Lord, if you make my little boy well, I'll make him a minister.'

And, you know, Fred went on to become one of the most celebrated ministers in the land, I suppose. And that's right, it's true, because when Fred told me that story he chuckled and he said, 'Stephen, my destiny was already carved out for me from such a very young age.'

Anyway, throughout Fred's ministerial training, John Flynn recognised the incredible qualities that Fred possessed and every time they'd meet, Flynn would always try and talk Fred into becoming one of his Outback Padres. Actually, it's my own thought now that, even at that early stage, John Flynn was looking down the track for a successor and he had Fred in mind. Back then, John Flynn's title would've been the Very Reverend John Flynn because he was the Superintendent of the Australian Inland Mission, an organisation that was inextricably linked to the beginnings of the Flying Doctor Service by Flynn's unerring drive to create both a medical and spiritual Mantle of Safety for all remote and outback peoples, regardless of colour or creed.

But still, Fred didn't want anything to do with it. He wasn't going to be talked into anything by anyone. He was quite tunnel-visioned about the matter and he'd already planned that, after he became ordained here, in Australia, he was going to head off to Edinburgh, in Scotland, where he'd continue his theological studies. Still, John Flynn was determined never to give up, so he persisted, and every time they met he'd come up and try and convince Fred that his true calling was right here in Australia as an Outback Padre with the Australian Inland Mission.

Then Fred's first church was a Presbyterian church at Southport, on the Gold Coast, in south-eastern Queensland. By then he'd met the love of his life, a nurse, named Meg. Because Fred was just ordained, I suppose his correct title would've been Reverend Fred McKay. But Fred loved the water and, on this particular day, after he'd finished his sermon he went home and put his togs on and went down for a swim, and it was while he was there that he looked to the far end of the beach and he saw quite an unusual figure coming towards him. I say unusual because it would've been quite a sight for Southport beach to see a tall, thin man wearing a three piece, pin-striped suit, with a hat on, walking along the sand. And as the figure got closer, Fred realised that it was John Flynn.

Naturally, Fred's first thoughts were, 'Here we go again. He's come to try and talk me into becoming an Outback Padre.' And that's exactly what John Flynn was about to do because he'd come back this one more time to try to convince Fred that he should join 'Flynn's Mob', as they were called. So they greeted one another and they sat down on the beach and John Flynn started his convincing.

Then, you know how, when you sit on a beach, you unconsciously play with the sand. You just pick it up in your hand and you let it run through your fingers. Well, there they were, sitting there on the beach and John Flynn realised that they were both running sand through their fingers. So Flynn stopped the conversation and he said to Fred, 'Fred,' he said, 'the sands of Birdsville are much finer than the sands of Southport.'

And that's what changed the life and the destiny of Fred McKay. That's what started his great career. Fred told me later, he said, 'Look, Stephen, I don't know whether it was divine intervention or what but, at that precise moment, I knew exactly where my destiny lay.'

So that's when Fred McKay agreed to join John Flynn's Australian Inland Mission. But then immediately after agreeing to become an Outback

Padre, Fred had a sudden pang of anxiety and in his anxious state he said to Flynn, 'Look, what am I going to say to these people in the bush when I go out there?'

And John Flynn simply said, 'Nothing. Just go and listen to them and you'll get your calling from there.'

That satisfied Fred and so they stood and they shook hands on it and then they started walking off the beach. And when they walked off the beach, John Flynn was slightly ahead of Fred and Fred clearly remembered trying to step into the indentations left on the beach by John Flynn's footsteps—and what giant footsteps they were. So right up until just prior to Fred's death, which was a couple of weeks shy of his ninety-third birthday, Fred remained a very prolific public speaker who spoke about the tremendous work of both the Australian Inland Mission and the Flying Doctor Service. And that's the reason why Fred's talks were always titled 'In the Footsteps of Flynn'.

In with the Luggage

Just by the way of background, I'm the Director of Aviation and also the Chief Pilot of the Queensland Section of the RFDS, and I've been here for about seven years. This revolves around an event that happened some years ago. So let me just tell you the story as I'd tell it if we were sitting around having a beer.

It was some years ago, three or four, I can't remember exactly, and, as a Senior Manager, I don't fly all that often though I do try and fly occasionally, just to let the troops know that the 'old man'—that is me—can still do it.

Anyhow, I was flying a Super King Air aeroplane and it was the second job that we had for the night. The first job was a close one. I think it was Goondiwindi, in the south-east of Queensland. Then the second job was to pick up an old chap out at Cunnamulla, which is further out west.

When we left Brisbane it was a typical wet winter's night, very, very cold, and it was also a typically wet winter's night in south-western Queensland, and also very, very cold. Then to compound matters, while flying out there, at all levels there was a strong westerly. From the fuel-burn point of view for the Super King Air aeroplane, in the mid-20000 feet levels, where I would've liked to have been, the wind was about 120 knots on the nose. Even down in the mid-teens, where I was flying, it was still about 70 or 80 knots on the nose.

So it took an awful long time to get out to Cunnamulla and the fuel flow was high because turbines are more thirsty at low level. Anyhow, we eventually got there—by we, I mean myself and the flight nurse—and I remember I had to make an instrument approach because there was rain and a fair bit of cross wind. But we landed safely. By this time it was about two o'clock in the morning and, as you might imagine on a night such as that, I wasn't at all too pleased with the world.

Then we always kept about half a dozen fuel drums in a shed at the airport at Cunnamulla and something about Cunnamulla is that you've always got to brave the brown snakes. The only saving grace to all this is the fact that the Shire out there is very, very supportive of the RFDS and their employees always gave you a bit of a hand to roll some fuel drums out, even if it was two o'clock on a cold, wet and windy winter's morning. So I wasn't bitten by a brown snake. I survived that and, after quite a deal of time, the ambulance came back with our flight nurse and, from memory, there was also a nursing sister—or perhaps it was a young doctor—from the Cunnamulla Hospital. They had with them this old chap who'd had what you and I would euphemistically call a cardiac event.

Now, quite often in the more remote parts of Queensland, particularly within that older generational group, you encounter people who have never been in an aeroplane before. It happens a lot, especially out in those places, and this old bloke was no exception because it was patently obvious that he'd never flown before. So the old chap's there, looking a bit anxious about the whole thing, and he's on the stretcher and he's all hooked up with these things that are beeping and carrying on. At that stage my flight nurse and the nursing sister, or whoever it was, from the Cunnamulla Hospital, were about 20 or 30 feet away doing the hand-over process.

I was preparing to load the old chap and I had the left-hand wing locker of the King Air open. Now the wing locker is the luggage compartment or an equipment compartment at the back of the left-hand engine. It's exactly like the boot in a motor car and it's where we keep our loading equipment and all sorts of things, like spare stretchers and that. Well, I had this wing locker, or luggage compartment, propped open with a stay, similar to the stay you use on the bonnet of your car.

So this old chap, he wasn't in real good shape so he was pretty short of breath. But as I was preparing to load him, he beckoned with his gnarled finger for me to lean down to where I could listen to him. It was fairly windy, and he was obviously quite concerned about something so I put my ear as close as I could to his face and he sort of pointed towards the luggage compartment and he whispered to me, 'You're not gonna put me in there are yer?'

And I was quick enough, even at two o'clock in the morning, to see the humour in this. In fact, it was the only thing that had made me smile all night. So I called out to our flight nurse, 'Nurse, if Mr so-and-so is well behaved and he promises not to put his arms or his legs out the windows, do you reckon we could let him travel inside the aeroplane with us?'

Now, for a start, you can't put your arms or your legs out of the window of a pressurised aeroplane.

But she was a smart girl, the flight nurse, and she also still had her wits about her, even at two o'clock in the morning, so she replied, 'Well, just as long as he behaves himself, I suppose we can make an exception, just this once, and put him inside with us.'

And this feller, oh, he was so very, very grateful, even privileged, that we'd allowed him to fly inside the aircraft with us. And we didn't tell him any different so then we loaded him into the King Air and I closed the wing locker and off we went. Then other than that wonderful slice of humour, I suppose the only other good thing about that long, cold and wet winter's night was that by going very high and taking advantage of the 120 knots of tail wind we got the old chap into Brisbane in pretty much record time, where he'd get better care for his cardiac event.

So that was the silver lining to the otherwise dismal cloud. It's an interesting story, and a true story. I can't remember the names, and I suppose I could reconstruct the date if I went back through my log books. But it was just one of those events in life that I always have a wry smile about.

It's Alright Now

It was about ten years ago this August, I suppose. We were living south of Broken Hill, on a property only about 15 kilometres out of Menindee. Do you know where the Menindee Lakes are? Well, we were there. I was actually out in the paddock cutting wood with a chainsaw and my wife, Margaret, she said something to me so I put the chainsaw down and I came inside and left it for a while.

Now, I didn't have much fuel left in the can, hardly any at all. There was only fumes in it really, but I didn't put the lid on it properly and I had leather-soled boots. Then after we loaded some wood, I went to pick the can up and the static electricity went from my fingers to the top of the can. And you know, as static electricity does, it just went zap and it blew the fumes up.

Then of course, when it exploded, flames blew up the length of my cotton shirt. The only trouble was, I'd been wearing the shirt beforehand, when I'd done some cleaning with kerosene, and I think there must've been some kero still on it because, next, the shirt caught alight. Then it went from bad to worse because it was a fairly new shirt and it was one of those that only do up to halfway down the front. You know what I mean; it didn't have buttons right the way down. So then, when the shirt got on fire, there were flames everywhere and we—the wife, Margaret, and I—we just couldn't get it off, over my head, and my wife had leather gloves on and all.

I even tried rolling around on the ground but that didn't work either because the flames, they just seemed to be following me around. We got the shirt off in the finish but, you know, I'd been burnt pretty well by then. My chest was all burnt and my hands were burnt, and my face and under my face and my ears and my head, that sort of thing, down as far as my waist. Luckily I wasn't burnt any lower than the waist.

Then once we got the shirt off, Margaret called on the UHF and somebody came on and she got them to ring the Flying Doctor Service. So then she got me back home and the ambulance came out and they took me to the Menindee Hospital. Then the Flying Doctors came out from Broken Hill and landed at Menindee and they took me down to Adelaide, and I ended up in the Royal Adelaide Hospital. And that's about the last I remembered about it for about fourteen days or something like that.

But I don't know what degree of burns they were. All I know is that some of the burns on my chest were pretty deep because, when I was in hospital, they kept on prodding around at me and I said, 'Well, that can't be burnt too bad because I can't feel it.'

'That's the problem,' the doctor said. 'It's burnt so deep that all the nerves are burnt, too.'

So they must've been pretty bad and then I got the infections and that didn't help much, either. I suppose I was there, in the Royal Adelaide, for about a couple of months before I come out again. So the burns were bad enough but then that infection wasn't too good either because the pain from the infections was worse than the burns.

But since then I've had about another fourteen operations; you know, patching parts up and more skin grafts and things like that. But no, it's alright now. I'm alive, that's one thing about it. The worst part is the hands, you know, because I've got to wear gloves all the time.

So that was one episode when the Flying Doctors took me down to Adelaide. The other one was with the motor bike accident and the lip. That was in October, not the same year though, more recent, it was. But this time I was out mustering sheep and I hit a stump in the grass and, when I did, the stump kind of catapult me into a tree. And although I always wear a helmet, I didn't have a full-face helmet on so when I hit the tree, my face come down and hit the handlebars and it just ripped the skin from, oh, from the right-hand corner of my mouth and it just took the skin back, top to bottom, right down under my chin and right back to the teeth and gums.

Anyway, I knew I was in a bit of a mess so I picked myself up and got back on the bike. But then I had the thought, 'Well, I've been out here nearly all day mustering these sheep so it'd be a waste of a lot of time and effort if I just let them go again.'

So I went and put the sheep in the yard first. Then after I'd done that, I rode the 15 kilometres back home again. And when I come in the back door, before she even seen me I said to Margaret, the wife, 'Don't panic.' I said, 'I just took a bit of skin off.'

And Margaret turned around and just took one look at me and she was nearly sick. Oh, there was blood everywhere and there were flies all stuck to it and everything by then. So Margaret rang the RFDS and we drove to Broken Hill and the Flying Doctors flew me to Adelaide, and when I got into the Royal Adelaide Hospital they stitched all that up. I think I had about a hundred and forty something stitches in my face, and in the gum. I didn't lose any teeth or anything but they had to sew the bottom of the gum, on the inside of the lip, first. Actually, I think they did more inside sewing than anywhere else, really, and then they finally sewed up the outside. Anyway, when the surgeon come back in and seen me the next morning, he said, 'You certainly made a bloody mess of it, didn't you?'

But, you know, it didn't feel too good there for a while but it's alright now. It's a bit numb, but it's not too bad. It's going along alright. But that was only a little episode, that one.

Just Day-to-Day Stuff

Well, I don't know if I've got any sort of real 'feel good' Flying Doctor stories because most of it was just day-to-day stuff, really. Stuff that goes on all the time. I was a pilot with the service for about twenty-seven or thirty years in South Australia. I was at Port Augusta for about fifteen years after the RFDS took over the air-ambulance side of things up there, then I came down to Adelaide and flew out of there.

Back then, Port Augusta was considered as a place where the, so called, traditional Royal Flying Doctor Service work happened; you know, stuff like going out on clinic runs and that. It was a fair time ago now, so, when I started, it was pretty basic, well, very basic, actually. The hot ship of the day was a Beechcraft Baron. Then they went on to the Chieftains and the Navajos, which served us well for many years. They were beautiful planes but they weren't pressurised. So then it was time to move on to pressurised planes, which improved the comfort levels for the crew and, of course, the patients who would arrive in a much better state. It's just progress so you simply go along with it. Nowadays, I don't think people wouldn't even get in a Beechcraft Baron.

With the flying side of things, I'd say that, mostly, it was more difficult back then than what it is now. Nowadays the aeroplanes have heaps better instrumentation and navigation equipment. So while we were still doing the same things, now you don't have to work at it too much. I mean, we didn't even have radars or altimeters and GPS (Global Positioning System) wasn't even thought of. So, basically, it was watch and compass stuff; just time and distance, really.

It's like a seeing eye dog, now. You just look at the GPS and you know exactly where you are. Yeah, we had a few nav (navigation) aids around the place, to get some sort of cross-reference, but out in the backblocks there's nothing much there so you really had to work at it, especially during the night. So to find some of those more remote places we relied on a decent amount of good luck, a bit of good management and a hell of a lot of local knowledge. You know, sometimes you'd be flying out in the middle of a dark night and if you saw a light you'd say, 'Oh well, that must be it.'

From Port Augusta we'd regularly do clinic runs up to Oodnadatta and Marree. We used to do Tarcoola and Cook and all the other settlements out along the Transcontinental Railway Line, right out to the Western Australian border. Nowadays just about all of those little settlements are closed down. Then I think they still go out to Maralinga and Hope Valley Aboriginal Settlement and Yalata Community, of course. Coober Pedy was always there. Mintabie, they still go there, and the other opal fields like Andamooka.

But we also used to do a lot more station people back then too, as far as clinics went. We'd go to all the station homesteads up the Birdsville Track and those places. We'd even overnight at Birdsville, sometimes. They just had RAD phones—radio telephones—in those days. The RAD phones were the only real means of communication, actually. That's what they had the medical sessions and the famous 'Galah Sessions' on. All that came through Port Augusta. They had the main transceiver there, at Port Augusta, for all of South Australia. But now they've got telephones or satellite phones or whatever.

So that was the basic day-to-day stuff and then, of course, you'd occasionally get called out on emergency retrievals. They could happen any time of the day or night though, for some odd reason, most of the worst ones seemed to happen at night. The retrievals were always the urgent missions, like road accidents, and so we'd have the entire crew plus all the retrieval gear on board.

But they were pretty full-on and, as I said, a lot of it was road accidents. You'd see some tragic circumstances, say, where you'd have the father down the back of the aircraft on the stretcher and you're trying to fit the mum and the kids in as well and you'd try and screen them from what they might see as far as the father's condition went. We never used to like to do it but sometimes we'd have to put some of the family members up the front, in the cockpit. But we only did that when it was really necessary, like when one of the family members down the back had died and so you were trying to keep the others well away from view.

Over my time we had a couple of major accidents. I don't remember what year it was, but there was a big bus smash up north, between Coober Pedy and Mount Willoughby. That was a major smash where we actually landed on Mount Willoughby Station airstrip, which was right next door to the accident site. I don't know how many fatalities there were but it was like a war zone. The doctor at the time was a New Zealander and he just sort of lined everyone up and, basically, we crammed as many of the injured as we could into the aeroplane and flew them back to Coober Pedy. Then we spent the next few days ferrying people from Coober Pedy back to Port Augusta Hospital or down to the Royal Adelaide Hospital, depending on their severity.

Then in later years there was another big bus accident up near William Creek; same type of thing, you know, it was a rollover. School kids, I think they were, on an excursion from New South Wales, somewhere. The bus ended up upside down. The only people that were there before us were the ambulance officers from Coober Pedy. They'd driven straight out as soon as they got the news and they reckoned there were kids just thrown all over the ground.

I was in Adelaide at the time. We had King Airs then and it was one of the worst nights as far as the weather went. We were flying the retrieval teams up to Coober Pedy and there were thunderstorms all over the place. It was horrific. Just getting to Coober Pedy was terrible. I was up flying around the 29 000 feet mark, trying to dodge the thunderstorms all the way. For that one we also had planes coming in from Broken Hill to help out as well and they were experiencing the same weather problems.

Then, once we got to Coober Pedy—we used Coober Pedy as our base—once we landed there, we went up by road to the accident site to help pull out the most severely injured. Then it was just a mad scramble to get them back into Coober Pedy Hospital. And again, we spent the next few days ferrying kids from Coober Pedy back to Port Augusta Hospital or down to the Royal Adelaide Hospital, depending on how bad they were.

So yeah, that was a bit of a long night, too. But as I said, most of the time it was pretty much just day-to-day stuff.

Love is in the Air

This happened in 1965 or '66. My maiden name back then was Astbury. I was nineteen at the time and I was at Rottnest Island, holidaying with my friend, Jan, and I fell off a push bike. How the actual accident occurred was that we were out bike riding and, do you know Rottnest Island? Well, there's one hill on it and we were up the top of the hill and I said to Jan, 'Let's just freewheel down to the bottom.'

Famous last words because I came off my bike, didn't I, and oh, I was in a terrible mess. Amongst other things I smashed down on my face and cut right across my lip. Then I put my head down into my lap and when they got me to the Nursing Post on the island I was bleeding like mad and the Nursing Sister thought that maybe I was haemorrhaging and there were all sort of things the matter with me. But actually, it was mainly just my face and my shoulder and my knees. But it was scary. And being nineteen, that's the stage of your life when you think you're just so gorgeous.

This all happened towards the evening. So the nursing sister decided to call the Flying Doctor. Then there was a bit more drama because, with it becoming dark, they didn't have electric lights on the runway so they had to light flares along the side. From memory they were just like lighted sticks in 44-gallon drums or something like that, placed along the runway. I'm afraid my memory of all that isn't too clear because I was in shock and I was bleeding from my face and

I was all mushed up. I just remembered these flares. Anyway, the Flying Doctor arrived in the dark and, when I eventually got on board, I said to the pilot, 'Look, do you mind if I take a friend?'

'Okay,' he said.

Well, Jan was my age. She was blonde, vivacious and quite gorgeous looking. So I'm lying in the back of the plane—there I am 'dying'—and in the front of the plane all I can hear is this chat, chat, chat, chat. Like, I didn't know just who Jan was talking with but it was certainly a male. I can't actually remember anyone else being up there other than a pilot and Jan. I can't even remember if there was anyone else in the back of the plane with me. All I could remember was that Jan was chatting to this chap all the way to Perth.

So it would've only taken about ten or fifteen minutes to fly from Rottnest Island to Perth. It's not very far. You can actually see Rottnest from Fremantle. So I arrived in Perth and they took me to Royal Perth Hospital in an ambulance and I was there for a week to ten days having operations on my face and all that. Oh, I had skin grafts and all sorts of things. I really mushed up my face, badly. I remember my auntie coming in to visit me and she took one look and she burst into tears. 'Oh Laurel,' she said, 'why couldn't you have broken your legs or something, instead of smashing up your face?'

But anyway, I healed and they sent me home to recuperate at my parents' farm at Harrismith, which is south-east of Perth, near Wickepin, in the wheat-belt. So there I was, recuperating at my parents' farm and, the next thing, well, Mum got this telephone call from a male person who said he was from the Royal Flying

Doctor Service and he was ringing just to enquire how I was getting on. Mum said that he sounded very caring. You know, 'How's your daughter? She was in a bad way and we got her across to Perth and we got her to hospital ...' Blah, blah, blah.

'Oh,' I thought, 'that's pretty amazing. He's being so very nice, you know, ringing to see how I was after my accident.'

So Mum explained to him that I had to have skin grafts and I had to have stitches here, there and everywhere.

'Oh, that's good,' he said. 'I'm glad she's recovering. And by the way,' he said, 'the lass that accompanied her over, she was very nice, too.'

Then he asked Mum if he could possibly have the name, address and/or phone number of 'the beautiful-looking girl who accompanied me over from the Rottnest Island'. So there was an another reason for him ringing. There was a bit of hocky-docky romance going on in the plane that he probably wanted to follow up on.

But Mum being the old fashioned lady she was said, 'Oh no, I don't think I could give you that. It just wouldn't be right.'

And as far as I know, nothing else happened. So that was forty years ago. I've still got scars, but I healed fine. You know, it was just one of life's little accidents.

Matchmakers

HG Nelson: HG Nelson with you on 'Summer All Over'. We have Jacqui from Yandina on the line. Jacqui, how are you this morning? Now, you've got some connection with the Flying Doctor Service.

Yes, well, back years and years ago I used to live with my then husband, John, and my two baby boys, in the south-west of Queensland at a place called Yaraka, which is unheard of. Yaraka's at the end of the railway line that goes out from Rockhampton then down past Blackall. And once a month the Flying Doctor people used to fly out from Charleville to run medical clinics in each little area around the place and, when they came down our way, sometimes they'd stay overnight with us.

So I think this was probably in the late '60s, when I was in my mid-twenties, and we were all reading the *Peanuts* comic books. Do you remember those? Well, we kind of thought that the Snoopy character from the *Peanuts* comics would look good on the nose-cone of the Flying Doctor aeroplane. You know, the drawing where Snoopy's doing his 'Red Baron' act and he's sitting in a plane with his flying goggles on and a scarf blowing out behind him.

Anyhow, we teed it up with the RFDS pilot and doctor that the next time they were going to come out to Yaraka on a clinic run we'd have the paint and brushes all ready. Of course, we didn't know if it'd be approved by Tim O'Leary, who was the Head of the Flying Doctor network back then, but we decided to do it anyway. And if Tim asked any questions when they got back to Charleville, then the pilot and the doctor would tell him that they didn't have a clue how the painting got there, nor who did it.

So on the day, as soon as we heard the plane buzzing overhead we whooped out to the airstrip and, while my two little boys were looking on, we painted Snoopy on the nose-cone. The actual plane was named the 'Allan Vickers'—Allan being one of the original doctors who worked with John Flynn. After he retired, I think he actually died while he was coming back from England on a boat and they buried him at the Cape of Good Hope.

Anyhow, so we did this paint job on the nose-cone of the aeroplane and when Tim O'Leary saw it he thought it looked great and so it stayed on, and everybody loved it. After that, each time the 'Allan Vickers' was serviced, the engineers painted an extra whisker on Snoopy. So I reckon he might've got a bit hairy before that particular RFDS plane was replaced. Then, when they finally did replace it with a new plane, they even got a sign writer to paint a new Snoopy on the nose-cone of that one as well. And they've had new planes since and I gather that Snoopy's still on there. He's become, more or less, the mascot for the Charleville Flying Doctor Service.

HG: So if you see a Flying Doctor plane with the Snoopy character from *Peanuts* drawn on the nose-cone, now you know the story of how it got there.

371

Then, of course, the Flying Doctor Service had an awful lot to do with my ex-husband and I getting engaged. Both Tim O'Leary and Allan Vickers were incorrigible romantics who seemed to want everybody in the same miserable state of marriage because both of them were always trying to match-make people.

HG: Well, that's an aspect of the Flying Doctor Service I didn't know about. So it's not only a medical service?

No, they did all sorts of things. They'd find you a partner whether you wanted one or not. I remember with John, my husband-to-be, though I didn't know it at the time ...

HG: Tell me more.

Well, this was long before the Snoopy episode because I was working out at Dalby, which is west of Brisbane, and John had a property with his brother out at Yaraka. We'd met a couple of times, that's all, and we used to write to each other occasionally, but just as friends. I mean, it was a bit far to pop down to Yaraka from Dalby just for a dinner. Anyhow, one time, John wanted to survey a boundary track because he was thinking of taking a tank-sinking plant out to the edge of his property. Mind you, these were pretty big properties. So he set off and, as you do in the country, you always have a gun in the vehicle with you.

Anyway, John was on his way out when he met up with Jimmy Davies, 100 miles from nowhere. Jimmy was an old 'dogger', meaning that he made a living out of the bounty money he earned from shooting wild dogs, dingos in particular. So they started having a chat, out in the middle of this nowhere, and Jimmy asked John, 'What're doing out here?'

So John explained how he was thinking of taking a tank-sinking plant out and he just wanted to survey the area.

'I may as well come along with yer, then,' said Jimmy.

So they both jumped into John's vehicle and while they were driving out they saw a dingo and John grabbed his rifle and took a pot shot at it. The only trouble was that he had some faulty ammo in his rifle and the gun blew up in his face, damaging his right eye. So then Jimmy had to drive John home and when they got there they called the RFDS. Anyhow, both Tim O'Leary and Allan Vickers came out in the plane and by the time they finished patching John up and got him settled, it was too dark to take off, so they decided to stay the night then fly John to hospital the next morning.

As I said, John and I had only met a couple of times before and while we did write the occasional letter, there was really nothing in it. Now the accident must've occurred on a Melbourne Cup day or close thereafter because I'd won some money in a sweep so, feeling a little flush with money, I decided to ring John on impulse, that particular night. Then when I rang up to have this chat with John, the phone was answered by someone who had an Irish accent. It was Tim O'Leary and so he told me about the shooting accident and he mentioned that they were going to take John to Brisbane the next day. So a couple of days later I rang around and found the hospital where John was and I went down to visit him.

Then, when Allan Vickers found out that I'd been to visit John, he suggested to the doctor—the eye specialist—that the best thing for John to do, in his current situation, was to spend a weekend in the country to recuperate; perhaps even a short trip to some place like Dalby, even. It was all a set-up, of course, so John then caught a bus out to Dalby and he arrived on my doorstep. I didn't know he was coming or anything. In actual fact, I was doing the ironing and I heard this knock ... knock on the door and when I opened it, there was John.

'I'm here,' he said.

And ten days later we were engaged.

HG: Well, that's an insight into the Flying Doctor Service that I didn't know about. Not only can they analyse mystery photographs, as John in Ingleburn is about to inform us, or solve crossword clues as I suggested they might, but they also match-make as well as fix a myriad of ailments such as broken arms and bung eyes ... and all at the same time.

Mystery Photograph

HG Nelson: And now we have John from
Ingleburn on the air. So what's your Flying
Doctor story, John?

Thanks HG, I've got one that I thought was a bit interesting. I've flown over Australia quite a number of times and, I mean, it's brilliant, absolutely brilliant. I've taken shots of Lake McKenzie. I've taken shots from across the centre. Actually, one time I was coming back home and I spotted the Birdsville Track. I knew what it was straight away because I'd been out through there quite a few times, you know, and it's just fascinating to see the beauty of this land. You know, the colour, it's just brilliant.

But back in '98 I was flying over to Europe with Singapore Airlines and we were about 10000 metres high. Anyway, I'd had a couple of scotches and, as we were passing over Alice Springs in the Northern Territory, I thought I'd take a photograph out of the plane window. Anyway, we weren't on the right angle for me to get a shot of the Alice and, naturally, I couldn't get the bloke—the pilot—to turn around so I took a shot out of the left-hand side of the plane.

Anyway, I didn't think much of it and when I got back home a few months later, I got the film developed and there was something there, on the ground, and I just couldn't work out what it was. It sort of resembled an airstrip, but I knew that there wasn't one there—

well, there wasn't supposed to be one there. Anyhow, I was stumped so I had a bit of a think about it and my reckoning was that the Royal Flying Doctor Service were always in the air around the Territory and, if anyone knew what this thing was, they would. So just on the off-chance, I sent the photo to the Flying Doctor base in Alice Springs and in the letter I asked them if they could help me identify it. And anyway, an RFDS pilot, I think it was, he wrote back and said, 'Yeah, as soon as I seen it, I knew what it was.' And it turned out to be the Jindalee BEA 'over the horizon radar transmitter', which is just north of Alice Springs.

> HG: Isn't that interesting? So you're telling me that the Flying Doctor Service, in its spare time, answers questions from people flying across Australia. Absolutely fantastic.

So, yes, they're a great service, and that was an aspect of their work that I was completely unaware of. Well, I didn't know, I just thought, well, who else could help me identify this shot—this photograph—and then straight away I thought of the Flying Doctor Service. I mean, they're in the air all the time up that way, so I reckoned that if anyone knew, they might.

> HG: Well, that's a terrific call there from John in Ingleburn and, obviously, about how the Flying Doctor Service solved the mystery of his photograph.
> You know, they're better than the *Encyclopaedia Britannica.* Say if you got stumped on a crossword

puzzle question. For example the clue is,
'Monkey'—three letters. You've already got the P
and you can't work it out or you just completely
can't think of anything, well, just ring the Flying
Doctor Service and they'll solve all your crossword
puzzle problems as well. Oh, they can do anything.
I mean, I'd love to think that if people had
barbecuing problems, you know, like how to clean
barbecues, all they had to do was to contact the
Flying Doctor Service. And they're also very good if
you need to know how to get stains off carpet or off
sheets, for that matter, or, let's face it, if you have
any sheep crutching problems, well, all you have
to do is get in touch with the Royal Flying Doctor
Service and they'd be able to help you.

Next to Buckley's

This happened many years ago, when I was working up bush, at the Moomba gas and oil fields. Moomba's in the far north-east of South Australia so it's usually a desolate, dry country, as you might be able to imagine. But at this particular time there'd been a lot of rain and it'd caused flooding all through the north-east, and there was this guy who'd always dreamed of doing a walking trek from Innamincka, north-west through the Sturt Stony Desert and up to Birdsville, which is just over the border into Queensland. He was a very experienced bushman and he'd done all his research and all that sort of stuff, so he was well prepared. Then he decided to take a younger mate along with him, an English feller, who was a very inexperienced bushman. So they decided to do this walk.

Now, it was the middle of winter and by then the weather was okay: bitterly cold at night, mind you, but the days were okay, and not too hot. As I said the experienced bushman had done his homework, right. They had a radio with them, plus all the maps and they had backpacks and a cart to carry their supplies. They'd even organised rendezvous points along the way, where they'd meet people and pick up fresh supplies.

So they set off from Innamincka and they'd been walking for a couple of days. But what happens up in those regions is that, when you get big rains, a lot of water comes down all the little creeks and what-have-you, and they overflow and then you get these huge floodplain areas—like surface water spreading out everywhere. Now all this surface water doesn't appear on a map because it's rarely there. So they were walking along and they came to this big lake, over a floodplain, which wasn't on the map. They then had to make a decision: what do we do? Do we take a couple of extra days to go around it or do we try and wade across?

As a trial, they walked out a couple of hundred yards and it was only, you know, a foot deep or something like that. 'Well, it can't be too deep,' they said, and they decided to walk across this lake.

But there must've been a washaway or a creek that they didn't know about or wasn't on the map, right? So they were wading along, carrying all their gear—the experienced feller was strapped to the supply-cart— and suddenly they went from water that was about a foot deep to water that was right over their heads. They both went under and because they had lots of gear strapped onto them, they sunk like rocks.

Now, somehow the inexperienced Englishman managed to struggle to the surface. Then, when he got to safety he realised that his mate, the experienced bushman, wasn't there. So he went looking for him and some time later he found him, but unfortunately he'd drowned.

Anyhow, the Englishman's first thought was, 'I'd better get this guy back to the shore.'

So he unstrapped all of the dead feller's gear, and he left his own gear there and he started dragging his dead mate all the way back through this stretch of water. Eventually, he got the body to dry ground but then, when he went back to retrieve his gear, it was gone. Everything. He couldn't find it. So there he was, trapped out in the middle of nowhere, with nothing but the clothes he's wearing, which were, basically, just a pair of shorts and a T-shirt. That's all. He'd even taken his shoes off to swim. So now he's thinking, 'Well, what do I do now? How do I get myself out of this mess? I've never been in the outback before. I don't know how to navigate. I don't even know where I am. I don't have any maps. Nothing. I'm going to die.'

Then he remembered that two days previously they'd crossed something that resembled a road, so he thought, 'If I can get back to the road I might be able to find someone or track someone down.'

Obviously, he couldn't take his dead mate with him so he had to leave the body there and he starts backtracking. There's plenty of water because there's lots of waterholes, you know, but he hasn't got any food. Not a crumb. Nothing. So for two days he walks back the way they'd come and eventually he stumbles across this road, right. But, unbeknown to the Englishman, the road wasn't a real road, it was what's known as a shot line, okay? Now, what a shot line is: with oil and gas mining they sort of bulldoze these tracks like grid lines so that when they fly over them, they can use them for survey lines, you see? Vehicles don't drive up and down them, they're basically put in and abandoned, right? But this guy thought it was a road. But it's not—it's a shot line.

So he thinks, 'Good, I've got to this road but now, what do I do? Do I sit here and wait for a car to come along or do I keep moving?'

Well, he sat and waited for a while and there was no sight of a car so he decides it'd be better to keep moving. But then he was faced with another problem: do I turn right and walk and see what I can find or do I turn left and walk and see what I find?

Now, what you've got to realise, this's out in the Sturt Stony Desert and the nearest town is Innamincka, and that's like 100 kilometres away. What's more, the guy's got no idea where he is; not even a clue. But he decides, for whatever reason, he doesn't really know: I'll turn left and walk down the road a bit and see how I go.

So he turns left and starts walking down this shot line, which really isn't a road. Then about 100 yards further on he walks over a rise and sitting there, in the middle of all this nowhere, is a wrecked telephone booth.

Now, what had happened was, about fifteen years before the Englishman arrived on the spot, there'd been a little camp there that they'd used when they were grading the shot lines, and maybe drilling a couple of holes or something like that. So years ago there'd been a small camp there, you know, with five or ten guys, living in caravans for about four or five weeks before they moved on. And back then, what sometimes happened was that, with these little camps, they never used radios for communication. They only had one of those old wind-up telephones, right, and they'd just plonk it in the middle of a camp, stick a bit of a telephone box around it and they'd run maybe 20 or 30 miles of telephone cable, above ground and, when they happened to come across another telephone cable, they'd just cut into that, alright. Then, when they abandoned the camp, they'd pick up the telephone box, wind the cable up and move on to the next site and set it all up again. But for some inexplicable reason, on this one and only occasion, they'd up and left and they'd abandoned this telephone and the wires.

So, you know, this guy sees this telephone box like it's an apparition. But it's been exposed to the elements for donkey's ages; the doors are hanging off, there's no windows, the old Bakelite receiver's all cracked, wires are hanging off it and, you know, there's a dirt floor. So the Englishman thinks, 'Well, in for a penny, in for a pound.' And he jumps into this telephone box, picks up the receiver, he winds the handle and, all of a sudden, out of the deadness comes this voice. 'Hello Santos, Moomba Coms, can I help you?'

Now, for some strange reason this telephone box was not only still there but it'd never been disconnected, as well. And this guy just couldn't believe his luck, right? He's out in the middle of nowhere and finds a telephone box and an old wind-up receiver and he gets straight through to Santos Communications at Moomba. So the Englishman told his tale of woe to the communications guy. Then the Coms guy said, 'Look, okay, but do you have any idea where you are because we can't track you on this telephone line. We didn't even know it existed.'

'I've got no idea,' the Englishman said. But he tried giving him a basic outline, you know, like, 'We were walking between Innamincka and Birdsville and then two days later this accident happened and I backtracked for a couple of days and I came across this road and I turned left and I think I headed south, but I'm not quite sure.'

So the guy at Moomba said, 'Alright, well, tell you what, stay on the line, I've got a couple of old blokes who were out on the surveying camps years ago. They might remember the area so perhaps they can give us a rough idea of, maybe, where you might be.'

In actual fact the Coms guy didn't hold out much hope. But anyway, he rings up a couple of old blokes and they come in and get the story. They don't hold out too much hope either but they get out their old surveying maps—the ones they'd had stored away at the back of their wardrobes for the past twenty years or so—and they blow the dust off them and lay them out on the table. So there's these two old crusty miners, you know, looking at these maps and going like, 'Gawd, it could be this camp.' 'No it couldn't be that one but I remember this camp. That could be the one.' And between them they, sort of, figured out, 'Well, he might be somewhere in this region here but, you know, then he could be somewhere else. But if we were going to have a stab in the dark, here's as good a place as any to start looking.'

And that's when they got the Flying Doctor Service involved. As I said, I was working up there at the time. So they called me over and they said, 'Well, look, we've got a guy. He's out bush somewhere and he's found an old telephone and he's on the line and we're going to try and find him.'

So we got the helicopter pilot in for a briefing and these crusty old miners said, 'I reckon we should do a grid search, starting from here and just see how we go.'

'That's fine by me,' the chopper pilot said. 'We'll start at that point and just work our way back in a criss-cross pattern.'

And well, what you've got to realise is that the lost Englishman could've been at any one of about a hundred and fifty possible old camp sites, okay? Anyway, off we all go in the chopper and this Englishman's still on the phone talking to Moomba Coms and he looks out of the broken down old telephone box and he sees this helicopter away in the distance, and we could see the phone box and we could see him waving and we're thinking, 'Oh God, this is unbelievable. It's a miracle. We've found him.'

Now, from him making the telephone call to us finding him would've only taken, probably, an hour. Mind you, he'd already been wandering around out there for a couple of days without adequate clothing and, of course, no food. But as luck would have it, that was the first point in our search pattern. So we landed the chopper and the pilot, he switches the engine off and he walks over to this English guy, who's still standing there with the phone in his hand, wondering if what he's seeing is really real or not, and the pilot says to him, 'Excuse me, were you the guy who phoned for a taxi?'

And this guy couldn't believe it. Well, neither could we. All the cards had fallen his way. He told me later that he thought it was sort of a religious experience. Like, I know his mate died and all that sort of stuff but he said, 'I've never believed in God but gees, I do now because, you know, there I was out in the desert with next to Buckley's of getting found and all of a sudden an ancient telephone box appears that somehow gets me through to Moomba Coms and then a helicopter arrives out of nowhere to pick me up.'

Anyway, before we went back and retrieved his mate's body we flew the Englishman back to Moomba and, amazingly, he wasn't too badly exposed. His feet were really blistered and he had a bit of sunburn. But, you know, in the scheme of things, he wasn't too bad, though he did keep saying how hungry he was, which you could understand. So when we arrived back at Moomba, of course, all his clothes were shredded and as we walked into the Health Centre I threw him a pair of overalls and said, 'Look mate, just put these on and we'll go and get you something to eat.'

And he went, 'Oh great because, like, I'm really hungry, you know.'

Well, he threw the overalls on and I took him over to the Moomba mess hall. Now, the Moomba mess hall is this great big, gigantic dining room, which can cater for about four hundred workers, right, and the food's phenomenal. You can get just about anything. You know, this is around lunchtime and there's salads and sandwiches and four different sorts of hot meals and there's an ice-cream machine there, and desserts. It's like a huge buffet at a hotel. So we go into this mess room and this guy, well, here he is, an hour and a half earlier he thought he was going to die from starvation and now he walks into this food fest.

'Can I have anything I want?' he said.

I said, 'Go for it mate, you're the one that hasn't eaten for days.'

So he grabbed a plate and he piled it full of T-bone steaks, right. And I've never seen a guy go through three T-bone steaks so quick in my life. He just wolfed them down. And he'd just finished this enormous meal, right, and he turned to me and he said, 'Oh, cripes, I've just forgotten. I'm a vegetarian. I haven't eaten meat in ten years.' Then he added, 'But I tell you what, that was the best meal I've ever had in my life.'

Not a Happy Pilot

I suppose you could say that I actually started with the Flying Doctor Service back in 1987 when I was working with the Division of Child Health out at Charleville, in south-western Queensland. At that stage the nurses from Child Health were seconded across to the RFDS as flight nurses. From Charleville I moved back to Innisfail, in far northern Queensland, which is where I was born. And then in 1991 the structure changed within the Division of Child Health and we were employed by the RFDS. So since '91 I've been a Senior Flight Nurse, here in Cairns.

The area we cover is, well, we go right up to Torres Strait, then west out to Georgetown, and down south to just north-west of Townsville. So it's a fair area. And the daily structure, if there is a structure—and that's the beauty of the job because there isn't much of a structure—is that in the Cairns, Charleville and Mount Isa RFDS bases we help the doctor run the general clinics as well as on-call work. So we'll be on a four-week roster doing clinic work and also, because we've all got child health experience as well, we go out and set up a 'Well Baby Clinic'—that's like a child health clinic. You know how, when you're in the city, you go and take your baby in to be weighed and to get advice and all that sort of stuff, well, that's what we do on the Well Baby Clinic.

The other thing is that, when you're on your four-week roster, you're on day call or night call so you have to stay in town and you, virtually, wait—just in case there's an emergency or whatever. Basically, it's a twelve-hour shift and so you know when you're going to work but, if there's an emergency, you don't quite know when you're going to come home from work. That's about the only catch, really.

But there's many, many happy stories. I suppose delivering a baby while you're in the air and then having to tell the pilot we've got an extra one on board still gives me a thrill. But that's nothing out of the ordinary, really. It just happens. But I was thinking about some other types of stories and I remembered once when I was working out of the Charleville base. This doesn't have anything to do with the delivering of babies. I guess it's really more just a comedy of errors, which, in turn, caused Bill McConnell not to be a happy pilot on this particular occasion.

Bill was an old and wise and very experienced pilot who'd been flying around out in the bush for years. Anyway, a seismic crew was out there in the outback somewhere looking for oil and they radioed through one night to say that one of them had been bitten by a snake and they thought he was going to die. So it was an emergency.

On this occasion there was Bill, a doctor and myself who headed out to this place to evacuate the bloke. Now, because we didn't normally go there—it was an airstrip that Bill didn't really know too well—he wanted everything prepared for our arrival. To that end, Bill gave them instructions about lighting flares along the strip to help guide him down and he also asked for a small fire to be lit so that, when he saw the white smoke, he could judge wind direction, which would help with his landing the aeroplane.

As I said, it was night, but when we got out to where Bill thought the strip was, there's nothing there. No flares. No fire. Nothing. So we're circling round and round, trying to figure out what's going on. What was even more baffling was that Bill had also prearranged a channel to talk to these seismic blokes on and now we'd lost complete contact with them on the radio. So we're flying round and round and round until finally another voice comes over our radio and says, 'Well, they had a bit of an accident on their way out to the airstrip. They run into a tree and their radio's out.'

Nobody had been hurt in the accident, thankfully, and we were told that they'd soon be out at the airstrip waiting for us.

'Okay, then,' we said. So we flew around for a while longer and then, 'Yes, there's the strip and they're there but the flares are pretty dull and I can't see any white smoke.'

Anyhow, being an emergency, Bill decided to go ahead and land anyway. Then on final approach we realised that, instead of lighting a small fire to produce a thin wisp of white smoke, they'd basically built this huge bonfire and stacked it with old rubber tyres. So, instead of white smoke, there's this huge plume of black smoke blowing right across the strip, which, of course, made Bill's job of landing the aeroplane extremely difficult because he could hardly see the airstrip at all.

But as I said, it was an emergency so with Bill muttering curses at the seismic blokes' stupidity, he decided to continue with the landing. Down we came on final with me up the front, trying to help poor Bill negotiate his way through all this black smoke. Then just as we are about to put down, one of the seismic blokes decides that he'd better take a memento of the occasion. So we're only about 10 or 15 foot off the ground when—Flash!—Bill's just about night-blinded by the flashlight of a camera. That was immediately followed by some very colourful and derogatory language coming from our pilot punctuated with, 'Just hang on!'

Considering all the circumstances of a strange strip, the darkness of both the night and the smoke, plus being blinded by flashlight, Bill did a great landing. Though, by now, he's not in a very cheery mood at all. So he gets out to have a bit of a go at these blokes and it was a Kiwi who'd been bitten. And I hate snakes. Anyhow, these blokes came over and they hand me a jar. 'Here it is,' they said.

'Here it is, what?' I replied.

'Here's the snake that bit him.'

And I just tossed the jar over to Bill, screamed with fright and ran back to hide in the aircraft. When Bill took a look at the snake he grunted, 'It's a child's python. That won't kill yer. It's non-venomous. It wouldn't kill a fly.' Then he walked off shaking his head at all the unnecessary trouble they'd put us through. I can tell you, he was not a happy pilot at all.

So, with me hiding in the aircraft and Bill having walked off, the doctor was left to manage the situation by himself. Anyhow, we ended up evacuating the bloke. I think, being a Kiwi and there not being any snakes in New Zealand, he was a bit traumatised just by being bitten by one anyway.

Okay

I guess these two stories are about communication in its different forms. The first one is, perhaps, more rightly about miscommunication. It's about a young bloke who was a ringer cum jackeroo at Nappa Merrie Station. Nappa Merrie's out in the channel country, over on the south-western Queensland, north-eastern South Australian border. The Cooper runs through the property. That's where the Burke and Wills monument is and The Dig Tree.

Anyway, history aside, this young feller had been on a holiday to Brisbane where he'd befriended a young woman. He was obviously very serious about her because, after he came back to Nappa Merrie, he then made up his mind to return to Brisbane, with the express purpose of meeting the young girl's father and discussing future plans with regard to marriage or whatever. The only trouble was that, when they met, the young woman's father wasn't at all impressed with the young lad. What's more he told him in no uncertain terms that the only way the romance had any chance to continue was, as he said, 'over my dead body'.

The young ringer had then returned to Nappa Merrie in quite a distraught state. Then, one night, when he was feeling particularly lonely, he gave the girl a ring. But, as luck would have it, the young girl's father answered the telephone and was rather blunt with the ringer. In fact, he told the young lad something along the lines of: Go away and slash his wrist. Which, of course, the young ringer did. He did exactly that.

It was at that stage I received the call to say the young ringer had cut his wrists and I advised them what to do to try and arrest the haemorrhage, until I got down there. We flew out from Charleville and, when I got down there to Nappa Merrie and went to the small room where the young ringer was, it looked like he'd done a pretty good job of it. There was blood all over the place.

To begin with, I resuscitated him. Next up, I had to examine the wound to see what sort of damage he'd done to himself. And it was while I was doing the examination that I felt a strange sensation running up my legs, and when I looked down I discovered that the floor was covered with meat ants. Now, I don't know what attracted them, whether it was the smell of the blood, or what, but these meat ants had decided to crawl up my legs, which was not very comfortable, I can tell you. Anyway, I then had to get rid of them before I could fix the feller up.

Well, the young ringer survived, though I don't know what happened to him after that, though I don't presume his romance with the young woman from Brisbane went any further.

The second story, and perhaps a more humorous one, also deals with communication; though, more rightly, this time you could describe it as non-communication.

I was called to a motor bike accident about a couple of hundred kilometres west of Thargomindah, again in south-western Queensland. This feller, he was a middle-aged Japanese bloke and he was riding a big motor bike. I can't remember what sort of bike it was, nor what size, but it was a big bike.

Anyhow, he'd had this accident and, of course, he couldn't speak any English, and me, in my ignorance, couldn't speak any Japanese. What's more we didn't have access to telephone or radio, to get an interpreter or anything like that. Not out there. But I soon found out that we did seem to have one word in common, and that was the word 'okay'. We both knew the meaning of 'okay'. Well, I presumed he understood the term 'okay' because as I was diagnosing him, I'd do something and ask him, 'Okay?'

To which he'd reply with an, 'Okay.'

Anyway, this Japanese bloke had suffered, amongst other things, a fractured pelvis. In fact, his pelvis was in quite bad shape. So having diagnosed him and resuscitated him there were then certain procedures I had to perform before he was considered fit enough to be loaded on the Pilatus PC 12 and be flown back to the hospital. And these were quite invasive sorts of procedures. In fact, they were not the sort you'd expect to have to do, out in the middle of the bush, including, amongst other things, the insertion of a tube into his bladder plus a physical rectal examination.

Of course, everything was done with an 'okay'. And everything was going 'okay' until we came to the rectal examination. Then as I began my examination I looked at him and asked, 'Okay?'

To which he sort of winced a little, but still replied, 'Okay.' Though, this time I noted that his 'okay' was not spoken in a very convincing manner.

Anyway, he got the appropriate treatment whether he liked it or not. Then we got him into the plane and we took him to Toowoomba, where he began his pathway to recovery, before being sent home to Japan.

But now, thinking back, I'm not sure just how much he actually understood about the procedures I did on him, nor why I had to do them. So I have the feeling that, by the time he'd returned to Japan, he was convinced that these rough Australian doctors were anything but okay.

One Arm Point

At the time of this story, my wife, Gail, and I we were teachers up at One Arm Point. Mind you, we're still with the Eduction Department. I'm now a District Director in Geraldton and a lot of the area that I'm responsible for goes into the outback from Geraldton. So I have a large spread of responsibility. Gail is now a school principal. So we've moved on in thirty years, but we still have a strong link with the north-west of Western Australia.

Now, One Arm Point is an Aboriginal community about 200 to 240 kilometres north of Broome, on the Dampier Peninsula. The Aboriginals there—the Bardi people—had once lived on Sunday Island, which is probably about 10 to 15 kilometres off the mainland. But then, for a number of reasons, their community on Sunday Island folded so they moved into Derby.

But the tribe really suffered in Derby from drink and unemployment and eventually, after quite a number of years, some of the Elders decided that they'd like to return to their land. Now, setting up a community back on Sunday Island was impractical. That was out of the question, so they got a lease on the mainland as close as possible to Sunday Island, which is where One Arm Point is now. On a map, it's at the tip of the point that goes north-eastish from Broome, as well as north-westish from Derby. Cape Leveque is just near by. That's where there's a lighthouse.

So in 1975 Gail and I were asked by the Superintendent for the Kimberley to go to One Arm Point and open the school, which we did. By that stage, the Aboriginal community had only been going for a year or two and we were the first teachers to go there. We were young. I'd been teaching for seven years and Gail had been teaching for six. So we were pretty inexperienced really, and we were certainly inexperienced as far as Aboriginal communities and Aboriginal people were concerned. But we said, 'Yes.' And we bought ourselves a Nissan four-wheel drive and headed off.

When we arrived we had no house and there was no school to teach in. We taught under a tree and we lived in a caravan. I must say that it was quite a cultural shock really, but for all that it was to prove to be a wonderful experience.

Anyway, we'd only been at One Arm Point for two or three weeks when a cyclone came through. And that was another experience, I can tell you. Oh, there was a lot of rain and a lot of wind, that sort of thing. It knocked down a lot of trees and it really put the road in terrible condition. We had the only four-wheel drive vehicle at the community and were the only ones who could get through when the road was that bad. Then, at about two or three o'clock one morning, there came this bang ... bang ... bang on the side of our caravan and, when we opened the door, a white guy, Brian Carter—he's married to an Aboriginal person there— said, 'Would you mind taking one of the young women to Lombadina, she's in labour.'

Now, because One Arm Point was so new, it had no medical facilities. Oh, there was a very short airstrip there, but it couldn't take the Flying Doctor aircraft, certainly not at night time. So basically, there was nothing at One Arm Point while Lombadina—the Catholic Mission about 30 to 40 kilometres south—had a serviceable airstrip, plus it had lay missionaries, and that included a nurse.

So Gail and I got ourselves dressed and we jumped into the Nissan and headed off around to the camp where this young woman was in labour. We pulled up there and her mother and her mother-in-law and a couple of other people carried her out on a mattress and put her in the back of our vehicle. She didn't look too well, at all. Then the mother and mother-in-law got in the back with her and we headed off to Lombadina. It was still dark. Thankfully, the high winds had passed by then, but there was still a fair bit of rain around and the road was, as I said, in a terrible condition.

Anyway, we'd been driving for, I don't know, about fifteen minutes or so, when we heard a lot of cries from the young lady in the back. And all of a sudden, one of the older women lent over and said, 'The baby's come. The baby's come. Will you stop? Can you get me a razor blade?'

Well, you know, we didn't have a razor blade lying around in the vehicle, but Gail hunted around and she did find a pair of scissors in the glove box. So they used this pair of scissors to cut the baby's umbilical cord then they said, 'Oh, can you give us some string?'

Well, we didn't have any string either, nor fishing line. I mean, we just weren't prepared for an event like this. But anyway, we did have some old carpet in the back of the Nissan so we pulled a thread out of the carpet and they used that to tie the baby's cord. So then we continued on to Lombadina, with the newly born baby, the mum and the two new grandmothers, all in the back.

We eventually arrived in Lombadina Mission at about sun-up and we got the lay missionary out of bed. She was a lovely girl. She came out and took the mother and baby inside, into their clinic there, and tended to her. At the same time she got on the radio and called the Flying Doctor who gave us an estimated time of the plane's arrival at about seven o'clock in the morning. We then headed out to the Lombadina airstrip, again using our vehicle as the ambulance, and the RFDS plane landed and they took the baby and the mum. After the plane had taken off, the grandparents returned to One Arm Point with us.

But the baby was tiny. I think it only weighed about 2 pounds. It was quite premature. Now unfortunately, I can't provide you with a happy ending because, I don't know if it had anything to do with the baby being so premature or whether the cyclone had anything to do with it or not but we found out that the baby died about a week later. So yes, it didn't make it. But that was the story.

One Lucky Feller

I'm a doctor at the RFDS base here in Kalgoorlie and I have two experiences that you may want to hear about. The first one: I can't remember the exact details, but the guy was a Driller's Assistant for an exploration outfit. He was with a small team of men who, I think, were drilling for gold. Anyhow, they were doing some drilling just over 200 kilometres south-west of Kalgoorlie. If you can imagine, they were in line roughly between Norseman and a place called Lake Johnston. So they were west of Norseman, and it was about four hours' drive, on an unborn track, from where they were working to the nearest airstrip at Lake Johnston.

Now, from what I remember, the phone call came into the Kalgoorlie RFDS base at around three o'clock of an afternoon, in November 2004. The first-aider from the drilling company rang to say that they'd just heard about an accident that'd happened about four hours out bush from where the company was. It was all a bit scratchy and second-hand but, from what I could gather, apparently these guys were out drilling and the drill rig struck a tree and a tree branch fell down on this twenty-six-year-old guy and pinned him under it. The first-aider said that they had a lot of gear out there so they were quite confident they could get the tree off the guy but, due to the injuries he'd sustained, they didn't know if they could get him out to the nearest airstrip at Lake Johnston.

Eventually we got in communication with the accident site and when I spoke to them it sounded like the guy had some pretty serious injuries. He had a very nasty open-fractured leg, abdominal injuries and probably some chest injuries, as well as possible spinal injuries.

The next set of problems we faced were, first, how we could get to him and, second, if we got there, how to get him out. One option was to get the exploration company people to drive an ambulance out to the guy, pick him up, do their best and bring him down to Lake Johnston where we could fly in to meet them. But, as the first-aider had said, they weren't sure that, with his injuries, he'd survive the four-hour, four-wheel-drive trek from the accident site to Lake Johnston, over some pretty rough ground.

The only other option was for us to fly down to Lake Johnston, hop into a four-wheel drive and go out to meet him, assess his injuries and then, somehow, take it from there. That was all guesswork and, of course, that again meant he'd still eventually have to be transported the four hours over some pretty rugged ground to Lake Johnston.

Anyway, we eventually decided to fly out to Lake Johnston while the mines people headed off in an ambulance to try and get to the accident site.

Now, yet another problem was the available light. Naturally it's far better for a rescue operation like that to happen in the daylight, but we were rapidly running out of daylight. And the guys from the exploration company reckoned it'd take them at least six hours to get out to the accident site, pick the guy up, then drive him over to Lake Johnston in the dark. They'd then, of course, have to put out kerosene flares or set up car headlights for us to land.

So we were in an extremely difficult situation, with this guy's life in the balance and daylight running out. But then, just as we were in the process of packing our aircraft, we heard a flight of Navy helicopters coming into Kalgoorlie. As it turned out they were on their way from Perth, back to Nowra, in New South Wales, and were stopping overnight to refuel. So after they landed, I went over and had a talk to one of their commanding officers and within about twenty minutes they'd received permission to help us out. So we loaded up a Navy Seahawk helicopter and they flew myself and the Flight Nurse straight out to the accident.

It probably took us just under an hour to fly down there and we landed in a clearing right next to where the accident had happened. The ambulance had just arrived by then and they already had the guy on a stretcher and had given him a little bit of pain relief. So we took over and stabilised him, loaded him onto the helicopter and flew him back to Kalgoorlie in the Navy helicopter. Then from Kalgoorlie we put him into a RFDS fixed-wing aircraft, the Pilatus PC 12, and took him through to one of the trauma centres in Perth.

And he survived. Mind you, he ended up with quite a lot of injuries, including spine injuries, and he spent quite a time in hospital but he survived and now he's okay. So he was one very lucky feller.

The other incident happened quite recently, and he was a lucky feller, too. We do clinic flights out of Kalgoorlie to the remote stations and roadhouses, and one of these stations is Madura Plains Station, which is just north of the Eyre Highway. I'd actually been there the day before to run a clinic and we were on our way back along the Transcontinental Railway Line. I think we were at Cocklebiddy, which is a roadhouse along the way, and we got a call from the manager at Madura Plains Station to say that they'd been mustering and a jackeroo had failed to call in on the radio. So they went looking for him in the mustering plane and they eventually spotted him, lying on the ground next to his motor bike, and it looked like he was unconscious.

Then about a quarter of an hour later some of the other musterers were directed to him by the mustering plane and they rang to confirm that, 'Yeah, this guy's come off his motor bike. He's hit his head and appears to be unconscious and it looks like he's been fitting.'

Luckily we were only about half an hour away in the clinic plane so, yeah, they wanted us to come and get him. Now, when we do clinics, we only use a small charter plane. We can't carry patients with us. We just carry all the basic medical gear for the more minor medical first-aid treatments and pain relief and things like that. But the Flying Doctor plane, the Pilatus PC 12, you know, it's fitted out like an ambulance, with all the proper aero-medical outfit. So the RFDS in Kalgoorlie decided to send that out as well.

Anyway, the pilot and I, we landed at Madura Plains Station in the clinic plane and we jumped in a four-wheel drive and then it was probably a pretty good fifty-minute drive out to the scene of the accident. When we arrived there we stabilised the injured jackeroo and we packed him up, put him in the back of the ute, and by the time we got him back to the airstrip at Madura Plains Station—which took about two and a half hours in total—the PC 12 had arrived with a doctor and nurse on board and they took over and flew him to Kalgoorlie Hospital. So he was one lucky feller, too.

Over the Moon

My story goes back to January 1959, when I was a nineteen-year-older, fresh out of teachers' college in Perth and I took up my first appointment in the little school at Coonana. For those that don't know, and I guess there'd be many, Coonana's a small railway siding township out along the Transcontinental Railway Line, approximately a couple of hundred miles east of Kalgoorlie, in Western Australia.

Up until that stage in Coonana, if you had a medical emergency and needed to get to Kalgoorlie, the only thing you could do was to catch the Fast Goods train. The passenger train wouldn't stop, only the Fast Goods train would stop. There were a number of drawbacks with that, the main one being that the Fast Goods only came through occasionally and even then it took four hours to get into Kalgoorlie; so, for a critically injured person, that could well be too late.

Anyhow I was just getting settled there and I was fossicking around trying to sort out what was what, when I uncovered a metal box. I guess it would've been about 2 feet by 2 feet and when you opened it up it created more compartments. I soon found out that it was an old Royal Flying Doctor Service medical chest, and that there were all sorts of medicines in it, which were all out of date. Then also, just sitting there was this unusable old wireless.

So, I got in contact with the RFDS people and they came out and they set the wireless up so that we could now use it and they replaced the medicine chest with a complete batch of new medicines. I got the job of being their contact so if someone was crook I'd ring the Flying Doctor base in Kalgoorlie and explain what was wrong with the sick person and they'd tell me the number of the medicine to take out of the box and I'd dispense it.

Now, when I first arrived at Coonana, most of the people who were out there were refugees from countries like Germany, Italy, Yugoslavia and whatever European countries. In fact, no one spoke much English, apart from me, which made things a little bit difficult at times, especially with teaching. But I got the idea that now we had an operational wireless I could use it as a teaching aid for the twenty or so children who hadn't heard much spoken English. So in the mornings, when the chat sessions were on, I'd get the kids involved. Our call sign was '8 BAKER TARE' and the kids used to get on the radio and they'd call through and chat and we also sent telegrams and received messages from people out along the trans-line. And that worked very well indeed.

Then one day a Commonwealth Railways bulldozer—or grader—came through Coonana. The driver was out there cleaning up the edges of the track and so, when I was talking to him, I said, 'Hey, what'd be the chances of you putting an airstrip in here?'

And typical, he didn't consult anybody, all he said was, 'Yeah, okay, I'll give it a go.'

So he got stuck into it and he graded an airstrip out the back of the school. Then after he'd finished I got all the kids together and in an emu fashion we walked up and back the thing, at least twenty times, to pick up any sticks, glass, tin or anything else that could cause a problem with respect to the aeroplane's landing. So now we were in the situation that, if there was an emergency, the RFDS plane could be in and out from Kalgoorlie well within an hour and a half, which was a far cry from an irregular four-hour train trip.

When I told the Flying Doctor people that we now had an operational airstrip they put us on their monthly clinic run. And you can just imagine the huge excitement of the twenty or so kids when the first plane landed. Because, even though they didn't grade the strip, they felt that they were virtually responsible for establishing it. Oh, they were over the moon.

The RFDS held their clinics in my office where the mothers or whoever came in to see the Flying Doctor. The other thing was that, with the clinic, the pregnant women out there could now have the opportunity to be checked by a doctor.

Also, another thing, once we'd established the airstrip, other planes, like crop dusters and people like that, started to use Coonana as a stepping stone to other places out along the trans-line: say, from Kalgoorlie to Coonana, then Coonana to Rawlinna and so forth. And of course, that was absolutely wonderful for the kids because even though some of them had seen aeroplanes in Europe, they could now get close to them and see inside of them, and they just loved that.

I was also entrusted by the RFDS people to collect the 10 shillings per year levy off all the people out there. Now, I don't know if you've got it over in South Australia, but in Western Australia, if you pay 'x' amount per year to St John's Ambulance then you get free use of the ambulance, if you ever need it. But if you don't pay that then, if you need to use an ambulance, you have to pay the full price per kilometerage. Well that was the same with the Royal Flying Doctor Service. If you paid the ten shillings per year you could be carted to wherever for free. So if you had to be flown from Coonana to Kalgoorlie then from Kalgoorlie on to Perth, it was all free, apart from the ten shillings per annum, of course.

And that caused some hardship because, it's got to be remembered that the people out there at Coonana, in those days, did not see much money because, even though there were a couple of Australian families living there by then, the vast majority were still the refugees coming out from Europe. And those refugees were heavily in debt to the Commonwealth Railways because when they first arrived they had nothing but the job.

So the Commonwealth Railways supplied them with furniture, clothing, bedding, their food, and when they got their pay, not only did the Taxation Department take their bit out but the Commonwealth Railways took their slug as well. So they'd get their pay envelope and it'd state that they now only owed the Commonwealth Railways another £540, or whatever it was. For many, the only cash they got was Child Endowment and that's what they used when it came to paying their levy to cover themselves for the Flying Doctor.

So yes, they were very difficult times for many of those people, and I remember one family saying, 'No, we just can't afford it and, anyway, we don't use the Flying Doctor Service.'

But Murphy's law: guess which family had to use the Flying Doctor. It was them.

Anyway, that was the establishment of the RFDS in Coonana. As I said, it started with the discovery of an outdated medical chest and a disused wireless, sitting idle in the school house. And of course, when they were sorted out it opened up communications for the children. Then the opportunity came along with the arrival of the grader and the kids helping prepare the airstrip so they had a great feeling of ownership and pride in being involved, as well. Add to that John Flynn's ideology of placing a Mantle of Safety over the people in the bush, plus the huge contribution by the Royal Flying Doctor Service, and that's what happened in that small community. And to those people at Coonana, it was absolutely unreal.

Porcupine

I was born on 3 October 1950 and I got into strife on the Christmas morning of 1951, so I was too young to remember what actually happened. But I've heard all about it, of course, and I've still got the scars on my lungs. We were at Canopus Station, which is between Renmark and Burra, in South Australia. Later on, Dad sold Canopus to a bloke called Bill Snell, then Bill sold it to the South Australian Government and it was absorbed into a massive national park, the Danggali Conservation Park.

But right from the time I was born, I had an incredible bond with my father. Incredible! Oh, as a kid, I used to go everywhere with him. I was like his shadow. Anyhow, that Christmas morning, when I was about thirteen or fourteen months old, my dad was cleaning out the bath with power kerosene. Power kero was what we used to get rid of the greasy marks and stuff that had built up from the old dam water we washed in. And the kerosene was in this container—a tin—but he left it on the floor when he went off to do something else. Then I crawled along and, next thing, Mum heard the sound of an empty tin hit the ground and, when I started coughing and going on, she realised that her little boy had helped himself to the kerosene.

I don't know how much I drank but it was enough to be absorbed into my lungs, which started the coughing. Then, after that I became unconscious fairly quickly. But my father thought it was all his fault and he got really upset and he started to panic and he wanted to put me in the car and head straight off for Renmark. I think Renmark was something like 56 miles from Canopus, but it was just a dirt and sand track in those days, with fifty gates or something that had to be opened and shut along the way. So you know what a trip like that would've been like for a very sick little boy.

Anyhow, Mum said we weren't going anywhere. She reckoned I'd die if I was moved. So then they settled me down the best they could and they waited for the Flying Doctor to come on air. See, at a certain time of the morning the Flying Doctor Service kept the channel clear and if anybody had any issues they'd be able to get on the communications radio and talk to the doctor. But, because it was Christmas Day, it just happened to be the only time of the year that the Flying Doctor base wasn't open for their usual morning doctor's session.

I think the Canopus call sign in those days was something like 'ABS 6-CANOPUS' and you'd get on the radio and say, 'ABS 6-CANOPUS calling Broken Hill, calling Flying Doctor.'

So that's what they did, and they just kept calling and calling but they couldn't raise anyone at the Flying Doctor base in Broken Hill. To make things even more difficult we didn't have any 240-volt electricity coming into the house. All we had was 32-volt power and the radio for the Flying Doctor; it ran on a 12-volt battery. And of course, with all this continual calling and calling, our transceiver used a lot of power which, in turn, kept old Butch Batty busy, running batteries backwards and forwards from the outside generator room and swapping them over.

Just to give a bit of background: Butch was a real identity of the district. He was a former clown who was working with Dad in those days. He used to call Dad 'The Engineer'. But poor old Butch was an alcoholic and every now and again when we'd have to take him into town to see the doctor or get his glasses fixed or something he'd get on the grog, then he'd come back out home and dry out.

Mum said that, on one particular occasion, they went to get Butch from the pub and when they got him outside there was a little feller—a young kid—selling newspapers and Butch just put his hand in his pocket, dug out what was left of his money and gave it all to the kid.

And Mum said, 'Oh Butch,' she said, 'what'd you do that for? That's all the money you've got left.'

'Missus,' he said, 'the poor little feller was battlin'.'

See, old Butch reckoned that he didn't need the money back in the bush so he just gave it all to the boy. Anyway, that's just a bit about Butch, and when I was unconscious after drinking the kero, he spent all his time swapping the batteries over so that we could stay on the transceiver calling Broken Hill. Actually, it was my mum who was on the radio, doing all the calling because, apparently, my father was nursing me. So things were pretty desperate.

Now, I'm not too sure how it works, though I think whenever you made an emergency call into the Flying Doctor's base it used to light up an instrument panel. But it wasn't until after the doctor had had his Christmas lunch and come back out to the base that he saw the emergency light was on. So he jumped straight on the radio and said, 'Where's the station calling the Flying Doctor?'

And Mum was back in a flash, saying it was her and, as I said, there was my dear old dad, the man I had this incredible bond with, at his wit's end, cradling me in his arms. *This is interesting. As I just mentioned that, the emotion's all just rushed up in me. Sorry about that.* So, yeah, well, and, well, then Mum hooked into the doctor and the doctor told her what to do. I don't know exactly what the instructions were but he told her what particular medications to give to me from out of our Flying Doctor's medical chest. And he also confirmed that, you know, my mother had done the right thing by me and to just continue to nurse me through it gently and, along with the medication, I'd be okay; I'd survive, which I did. And to this day I've still got scars on my left lung and whenever I have an X-ray I've always got to explain to the people that I got a scarred lung from that particular experience with the kero.

So I mean, they didn't have to fly me out or anything but there were plenty of times when the Flying Doctor did fly out to Canopus. In those days, when I was growing up, the doctor was Dr Huxtable and Vic Cover was the pilot. I've got photos of the family and all of us standing by the Flying Doctor's plane because Mum and Dad used to put on so many different fundraisers, especially after my stuff happened. I've even got cuttings from the newspaper in at Renmark where, you know, they wrote that Canopus Station raised something like £2500 for the Royal Flying Doctor Service.

For the fundraisers, Dad and Mum ran a woolshed dance every year plus a cricket match. I remember when we'd get up early and Dad would drive us into Renmark to get the ice and lots of ice-cream for the kids, which was in those big old canvas bags. And he'd bring home a heap of kegs of beer for the adults and they'd set up the kegs under a shady thing they called a bow shed. Basically, a bow shed was just a few sticks with some green mallee laid over the top of it, and that was the pub. And for the cricket match, Dad actually poured a concrete wicket out in the middle of the airstrip and, to this very day, I reckon I could just about walk you out to it, blindfolded.

Also, I remember how Mum used to get cardboard tea packets and she'd cut them straight through the middle with a sharp knife and pour the tea out into another container. All year long she'd save these empty tea packet halves. Then before we had a fundraiser she'd cover them all with leftover Christmas paper or whatever coloured paper she could get—or we'd both do it, me and her—and she'd make little handles and attach them to the boxes, then she'd fill them with homemade lollies, coconut rough and all that stuff, and all the kids that came along would get a couple of packets of lollies. Everything was free. I didn't see any money changing hands so they must've paid through the gate or something to raise the amounts of money they did.

Now, I've just remembered another story I was told. It was when Mum was pregnant with me. The airstrip was just off the side of the house and, anyhow, on one occasion the Flying Doctor flew out to Canopus Station to give my elders, Andy, Wally and Marion, smallpox injections or something like that. So they landed and then the crew came over to the house and the nurse said, 'Okay, who's gonna be first?'

And my brother Wally, who was always the cheeky one, he raced forward, looking real tough, and he said, 'Oh, me, me, me, I'll be first.'

'Okay,' the nurse said, 'pull down your pants.'

Then the nurse got the needle out and started to get it ready for the injection. But when Wally saw the size of the needle, oh, he was off like a shot and he bolted through the scrub and they chased him everywhere, trying to catch him. But he was too quick and they all got tired, so then they decided that they'd get him later on, when he turned up back home again.

Anyhow, Andy was the eldest bloke so he got his needle, then Marion got hers. But young Wally was a pretty wise young feller and he hid out in the bush until he saw the Flying Doctor plane take off before he decided to come back home again. I must add at this juncture that Wally could also make up a pretty good story when the need arose because, when he eventually turned up later in the afternoon, he snuck in home, pretending he had a sore bottom and he announced, 'I've already had my needle so I don't need another one.'

'How's that?' everyone asked.

And Wally replied, 'I went and sat on a porcupine!'

Rabbit Flat

In 1975 and '76 I worked for a charter company who contracted to the Royal Flying Doctor Service in Alice Springs. We had a Beechcraft Baron. Anyway, I was wondering if you've heard the story about Rabbit Flat? It was in all the newspapers and magazines, as well as being on television and radio.

Of course, you know where Rabbit Flat is, don't you? Well, it's in the Northern Territory, out on the Tanami Track, on the way to Halls Creek, roughly 600 kilometres north-west from Alice Springs and about 150 kilometres from the Western Australian border. If you can imagine, it's typical Tanami desert, flattish country, just spinifex. So there's not a lot out there apart from this roadhouse on the Tanami Track at a place called Rabbit Flat. It's actually privately owned by a couple called Bruce and Jackie Farrands and, at the time this occurred, Jackie was pregnant and was about six weeks away from giving birth. Actually, I can give you the precise date: it was 6 August 1975.

Anyhow, the night before—on the fifth—I got a phone call from my boss asking me to take off in the Beechcraft Baron early the following morning to arrive over Rabbit Flat just on first light. Apparently, the Flying Doctor Service base had received a radio message via either Perth or Darwin or somewhere and it looked like Jackie had gone into labour. Bruce couldn't get in direct contact with the RFDS at Alice Springs, himself, because of the poor atmospheric conditions. Then just after the message had arrived the conditions turned so bad that radio contact was cut completely and they couldn't get any more information about Jackie.

So we took off before sunrise and we flew out to Rabbit Flat. There was just myself and a nursing sister, Maureen Eason. I can't remember exactly but it took us something like an hour and a half, flying out to the north-west, and we arrived just after first light at Rabbit Flat. We circled over the roadhouse to let Bruce know we'd arrived then, when we landed, he came out in his vehicle to pick us up.

The first thing Maureen said to Bruce was something along the lines of, 'Has anything happened yet? Is Jackie okay?'

'Oh sure,' said Bruce. 'She's already given birth.'

Maureen was quite surprised at that news so she said, 'Oh, so how's Jackie and how's the baby?'

'Well,' Bruce replied, 'the first baby's fine.' Then he said, 'And so is the second one.'

So there were two of the little buggers. Twins; both boys.

And no one knew. Not even Jackie's doctor knew that she was expecting twins. Anyway, the babies were fine. Bruce had them wrapped up in cotton wool, in a washing basket. So Bruce and I, we sat down and had a cuppa tea while Maureen attended to Jackie and got her ready to be transported back into Alice Springs. We'd taken a humidicrib with us so Maureen put the baby boys in the humidicrib and we put Jackie on the stretcher, in the Beechcraft. Then just before we hopped into the aircraft, Bruce said to me, 'Oh, this'll be good publicity for Rabbit Flat, eh.'

'Oh yeah, okay,' I said, and I took off.

Well, it was a bit strange for Bruce to say something like that, you know, about wanting publicity for Rabbit Flat, because he was such a quiet sort of bloke; a bit of a loner, really. Well, you'd have to be to even contemplate going out there to live in a place like Rabbit Flat, in the first place, would you?

But anyway, on the way back into Alice Springs I began thinking that he really must be keen on seeking some sort of publicity. So after I landed and my services were no longer required, I raced over and there was a phone in the corner of our hangar, and I rang the local ABC Radio in Alice Springs. A male voice answered the phone—I don't know who it was—and I said, 'Do you want a good story?'

He said, 'Yeah.'

'Well,' I said, 'the population of Rabbit Flat doubled last night.'

Now, the last thing I expected was to be quoted verbatim. But the next thing I know, it actually started hitting the headlines as a human interest story. I'm pretty sure it was on the front page of *The Australian*. If you go back and look at 7 August 1975 you'd probably find it in the paper, there somewhere. It even made the *Women's Weekly*, and I think it probably went into *Pix* or *Post* and most of those popular magazines at the time.

So it was a big story and it even went international because people in England even started ringing up Bruce. It was also actually written up in some publication or other over in England. Oh, Bruce had phone calls from everywhere, all over the world. So then it became a bit of a stampede out to Rabbit Flat, there for a while. But it got a bit too much for Bruce because he was left out there to deal with it all by himself until Jackie and the babies, Daniel and Glen, were ready to go back home.

Then, I think it was 'A Big Country', well, they went out there and did a television program on Bruce and Jackie and their lives in Rabbit Flat. In fact, just recently, 'A Big Country' approached Bruce again because they were re-running some of their old stories and I think they wanted to do something along the lines of 'A Big Country: Twenty Years On'. So they rang Bruce about doing a follow-up program. But Bruce's a bit shy of publicity these days. In fact, he's not real keen on it at all. He reckons he had enough back in '75 to last him a lifetime.

Rissoles

I reckon I might've been about one of the first recipients of the Flying Doctor Service. This was in 1929, back in the depression era when no one had two pennies to rub together. Things were pretty tough and Dad was out in the bush with the railways, so my mum took work anywhere she could to get some money. Anyhow, she got this job, working as a domestic on a cattle station called Davenport Downs. Davenport Downs is on the Diamantina River, in the channel country, in south-western Queensland.

I was only about two or something so I can't remember exactly what happened but, apparently, there was a black gin—an Aboriginal woman—who was working in the kitchen as one of my mother's helpers. Anyhow, this gin was doing some mincing; mincing up leftovers to make rissoles. And so, yeah, she sat me up on the table where she was doing this mincing and she must've turned away or something because I stuck my hand in the top of the mincing machine and it took me finger off, right down to the first joint. It was the first finger—the index finger—of the right hand. Yep, right down to the knuckle. So she must've still been turning the mincer and she didn't see me stick my hand in the thing. I mean, I was only two or something so I lost the top of my finger in the mincer.

Now, there would've only been the old peddle-type radio back then and I presume that's how they got in contact with the Flying Doctor. So they came out to pick me up in what would've been, back in those days, an old canvas plane; an old biplane, an Avian or something like that. I think the Avians were about the first ones the Flying Doctor Service used. There's one up at the Museum in Longreach. I'm going to Longreach sometime this year because I want to find out for sure what exactly happened, you know, whether my name or my mother's name is on their records out there.

Anyhow, the Flying Doctor came out and they flew me and my mother from Davenport Downs back into Boulia Hospital. And, as they did in those days, they just took what was left of the minced up joint-bone out, pulled the skin back over it and then they sewed the fingernail back on. So I've got a nail on my knuckle, yeah, but I don't know where they got that from. Perhaps they fished it out of the rissole mince.

Then when we got back, the black gin had taken off somewhere. I don't think she'd ever seen an aeroplane before so when she saw the Flying Doctor plane come and take me away she probably thought she'd killed me and I was being taken off into the spirit world by this strange thing that flew in the sky.

Anyway, that's my story. As I said, I was only about two at the time and I've still got the fingernail growing out of the knuckle of the index finger on my right hand and, no, I don't know what happened with the rissoles.

Slim Dusty

I suppose you've heard of Slim Dusty the singer? He's dead now but back in 1985 I published a book called *Slim Dusty Around Australia*. Basically, it was a collection of photographs, with only about two pages of writing, and it was about his concert days and all that sort of thing.

I'm not really into music, but I was just a fan, that's all. And how it all come about was that I was working in the Public Service and in my spare time I'd travel around with Slim and take lots of photographs. Like, I'd go behind the scenes. And I'd go into towns where he'd been and go to the local newspapers and, you know, I'd go to some of his record store appearances on the day he was to sign autographs and I'd attend some of the awards that he got, even the ones he received outside the music industry.

Anyhow, over time the collection gradually built up. So, in the end, I sorted them all out and put it together and I included about two hundred and fifty photos in the book, which was about one hundred pages long, and then I had a thousand copies printed and, really, the rest is history. They've all gone now, but that was my little mark on history.

Then in the 1980s, after I left the Public Service, I did some volunteer mission work up in the Kimberley region, up in the far north of Western Australia. I did a year in Derby, about four years at Lombadina Aboriginal Mission, another year up in the Kalumburu

Aboriginal Mission, then another year in what was originally known as Port Keats, which is now the Wadeye Aboriginal Community.

When I was in Derby I ran the School Hostel, on the outskirts of town, there. See, the church had a boarding hostel for the little Aboriginal school kids who lived up that Gibb River Road. And they'd come into Derby for the school terms and they'd board at the School Hostel and go down to either Derby Primary School or to the Catholic Primary School. Our job was to look after them and feed them and clothe them and provide recreational activities for them and things like that and then, on their school holidays, they'd take off and go back to their communities.

Then one Sunday night, when I was in Derby, I was listening to the local ABC Radio's 'Country Music' program and they were having an appeal to raise money for the Royal Flying Doctor Service. And I knew that Slim was a great supporter of the Flying Doctor Service. I think he even sung a song about it and I'm certain that he did a couple of concerts over in Charleville, where he donated part of the proceeds to the RFDS.

Anyhow, I still had a copy of the book with me so I rang up the radio station and asked if they wanted to auction a book. And when I explained what the book was about, well, the ABC got really rapt in it, you know, because everybody up there loved Slim Dusty and they played him all the time. Anyhow they agreed to auction it over the radio, amongst all the listeners, and, I mean, I was only selling it for about $10 a copy and I think they ended up auctioning it for somewhere between $250 and $300.

So that was my small contribution to the RFDS.

Slingshot

Did you ever run into people by the name of Clarrie and Emily Pankhurst? Clarrie only passed away eighteen months or so ago, but he was the last of the Boss Drovers. I mean, this feller could be on the road for anything from six to eight months with fifteen hundred head of cattle from Wave Hill, which is in the west of the Northern Territory, over to Camooweal, just inside the Queensland–Northern Territory border, then all the way down south of Mount Isa, to be trucked from Dajarra. Camooweal was where they used to keep all their horses and that. So it was an amazing life some of these fellers had, wasn't it?

Actually, a book's been written for Clarrie and his wife, Emily. It's called *The Boss Drover*, and it's a great read. To tell you the truth, I know a lot about it because we lived across from the Pankhursts at Mount Isa, and me and my brother, we both went out with Clarrie, you know. So we know the guy first-hand. None of it's fiction so if you give any credit to anybody for this story, I'd rather it be credited to Clarrie and his wife, Emily, formally of Mount Isa, because that's where they used to live when they weren't droving.

Now, I want to get this as close as possible; so this was in 1956. Clarrie and his ringers were yarding up some cattle out on a station property, well out into the Northern Territory, near Newcastle Waters, and this young feller come off his horse and broke his leg. It didn't happen near the homestead because they were out a way. The young feller, he had a few rib injuries as well, but mainly the leg was badly broken and, well, they had to call the Flying Doctor to come in from Alice Springs. But all around the particular area where they were at the time, where the accident occurred, there was a lot of scrub so there wasn't much room for a plane to land.

Anyhow, the pilot got the plane down alright, but because the airstrip was so short and because of all this scrub, plus they now had this young injured feller on board, the pilot needed a much longer run-up to get the aeroplane back in the air. So what they did was, they got three ringers to hang on to each of the wings and two ringers to hang on to the tail—that's eight of them—and these ringers just dug in their heels while the pilot built up the revs on the plane. And they held on for as long as they could and then the pilot gave them a signal out the side of the plane and he just took off like a slingshot. Vroom, off he went and he just made it over the scrub. He wouldn't have made it without them doing that, and they got the feller to hospital alright.

But, Clarrie and Emily, they were both wonderful people. And, you know, these sorts of things come because people are ingenious in times of trouble. It's sort of like thinking outside the square. But as tough a life that those people had—and yes, Clarrie was a hard man at times, but he was always fair and honest—you know, once you got to know him well, he was a real friend and so was his wife, Emily.

Small World, Large Bruise

In the late 1970s I transferred out to Mootwingee Historic Site as a ranger and, basically, we—myself and the senior ranger—looked after the Historic Site and around the National Park district. Mootwingee's in the far west of New South Wales about a hundred and something kilometres north-east of Broken Hill, as the crow flies.

Mootwingee's known as a Historic Site because that was one of the classifications the National Parks used at the time. It was only a relatively small area and like the Kurnell area at Botany Bay was called Captain Cook's Landing Place Historic Site. It was, in fact, part of the Sydney Metropolitan District, which included Sydney Harbour National Park, which was later called Botany Bay National Park or something similar. So, it's just one of the classifications they had; you know, you had National Park, Nature Reserve, and Historic Site, and each was established under the National Parks and Wildlife Act.

But the Mootwingee Historic Site was very popular with visitors, especially in the cooler months. And during those cooler months one of the local tour operators used to bus visitors—tourists—out from Broken Hill on a day trip to the Historic Site. So, upon their arrival, first, they'd come into the Visitors' Centre and have a look around at the displays and then they'd get back into the bus again and go down to a picnic area, where they'd have something to eat and they could go on a couple of designated walks and what-have-you.

Anyhow, on this particular day the bus arrived and the bus driver brought the tourists in and they spent their normal twenty minutes or so looking around the Visitors' Centre, which basically had displays of Aboriginal relics and fauna and flora of the area. Of course, we also used to sell a book on the Historic Site plus other New South Wales National Parks publications. Then after they'd gone through the Visitors' Centre their bus took them down to the picnic area. The walk they were doing that day was the walk up and around the dam and past Snake Cave.

Snake Cave was one of the most significant parts of the Historic Site. It was a very large overhang, with a huge painting of a snake on it. I'd say that it'd be a good 20 or 30 feet long. I'm not up with what's happening now but, at one stage, I recall that they actually stopped people from going to Snake Cave unless it was by prearranged guided tours. So it's a fairly significant site.

Now, basically, the bus driver used to leave the tourists free to go around the walks and he'd stay at the picnic area and have a rest or sort out lunch or whatever. But then, on this particular day, about half an hour after they'd left the Visitors' Centre, the bus driver returned to the office and said that one of the elderly ladies had fallen over and she appeared to have broken her leg.

That's when he added, 'And she's a very large lady.'

Anyway, my house was behind the Visitors' Centre and there was a fairly large garage there also. So I went and got the Stokes Litter from the garage. I'm sure you're familiar with what a Stokes Litter is: it's a light aluminium-framed stretcher, where the patient actually lies into it, as opposed to a conventional stretcher where the patient lies on top of it. Basically, it's designed for search and rescue. The idea is that, when you're taking someone over rugged terrain or winching them up a cliff, they don't fall off the thing.

At that time I had a Volvo station wagon, so I decided to drive that down to the picnic area because the alternative was to take the Toyota four-wheel drive tray top and I didn't think that'd be really appropriate for transporting an elderly lady around the place in. The Senior Ranger was also there, so he and the bus driver and I headed back down to the picnic area in the Volvo and we set off on foot with the Stokes Litter.

As it turned out, the bus driver had given us a very adequate description because, when we arrived at the scene of the accident, I could see a very large lady lying on the ground. She must've been 18 stone. Her arms were probably as big as my legs and she was obviously in a great deal of pain and had a very swollen ankle.

So we enlisted the help of a few of the male tourists to lift this lady into the Stokes Litter and we started the slow trip back to the picnic area. I can't remember exactly how long it took but, once we got back to the picnic area, I put the rear seat of the Volvo down and we slid her into the back, ambulance style. Then we drove the injured woman straight down to my house where I thought she'd be more comfortable.

There was a Flying Doctor radio in my house, as well as in the office, so we placed her on the lounge-room floor, as I'd intended, and got on to the radio. Now, on the Flying Doctor radio there's a little emergency button and when you press that, it emits a high-pitched sound which alerts the nearest RFDS base that somebody needs a doctor urgently.

So literally, within thirty seconds, there's a doctor on the other end. And what happens is, you press a button and a doctor comes on and says, 'Broken Hill Flying Doctor Service' to the caller who's on the emergency button. Then you identify yourself. So I identified Mootwingee and the doctor then asked what the problem was and I explained that we had an elderly lady with what appeared to be a broken ankle.

Then we went through the consultation process where the doctor asked a series of questions and established that the woman was in quite a great deal of pain. In such circumstances it was usual for them to prescribe a pethidine injection. If you know the system with the Flying Doctor kits, they're a large metal chest with a whole lot of numbered medicines and bandages in there, plus syringes and whatever. So on instruction from the doctor I removed one of the syringes and an ampoule of pethidine. I then proceeded to prepare the syringe by putting the appropriate amount of pethidine in it, then pressing lightly on it to ensure that there was no air in the syringe.

So there we were, with the lady on the floor and the Senior Ranger and I with this syringe. Now, I'd never given an injection before and, as it turned out, the Senior Ranger hadn't either. But because he was the more senior officer, well, he got the job, didn't he? In this case, with the patient being a rather large lady, we were instructed by the Flying Doctor that we were to give the injection into the arm.

Anyway, he went ahead and administered the pethidine which, after a short while, took effect as it obviously made the patient more comfortable. Because it was best not to move the injured woman, we kept her on the Stokes Litter all the time. Mind you, she filled it pretty well. But she seemed reasonably comfortable in it and we didn't want to disturb her, especially after the pethidine kicked in.

In the meantime, the doctor had informed us that he was sending out a plane to pick her up. Now, because the airstrip was only about, at most, 800 metres from the house, we waited until we heard the plane buzzing around. Then, when it was circling, ready to land, we picked up the Stokes Litter and we bundled the lady back into the Volvo and I drove her down to the airstrip. The RFDS were using a Nomad aircraft at that stage. They had a doctor, a nurse and the pilot and, basically, they took charge as soon as they arrived. The woman was taken out of the Stokes Litter, put onto the plane's stretcher, then into the plane where they secured her, and off they went to Broken Hill.

Then a few days later my wife, Robina, and I went to Broken Hill to do our shopping and, while we were there, we decided to call in and see how the patient was faring. We went into the hospital and found her in one of the wards. She had plaster on what, she informed us, was a triple fracture of her ankle.

And that's when I asked her, 'So, how's the ankle?'

'It's not the worst bit,' she joked.

Then she showed me her arm and, oh God, I could not believe that such a small needle could give such a large bruise. This bruise was a good 4 inches by 3 inches. It was huge. I mean, with someone who's overweight, yes, they do tend to bruise easily, I know, but this one was the biggest, blackest bruise I've ever seen. I just couldn't believe it.

But she was fine about it. She was in good spirits and was quite happy and she thanked us for all we'd done and we had a chat for a while. And though I didn't find out until some time later, it turned out that the lady was related to a counterpart of mine, one of the rangers in the Blue Mountains. Small world, isn't it?

Someone, Somewhere

I'm constantly reminded of the diverse types of people that we, in the Royal Flying Doctor Service, serve. And in doing so, it's important that we respect and embrace those differing cultures. Of course, with so many of the Aboriginal people being 'out there', obviously, they are a large percentage of our clientele both in their traditional areas, where they're more nomadic, as well as in communities or towns where they're less so.

I remember when I went to Port Augusta for a Consumer Network Group meeting. That's when we get together with our constituents to sort out how the RFDS can better serve their needs. And the majority of the people who attend those meetings are the station people, mostly white. Anyhow, it was the night before the meeting, so the few of us who were already in town were having a meal and there was music coming from the next room, a larger dining area that'd been partitioned off. So I opened the door and there was this Aboriginal group. Up front were a couple of people playing guitars and singing and another bloke was on the drums. As it turned out they were taking part in an Aboriginal workshop about Native Land Titles.

Anyway I introduced myself. 'G'day,' I said, 'I'm John Lynch, CEO of the South Australian Division of the Royal Flying Doctor Service.' Then I told them just how much I was enjoying their music.

'Do you sing?' they asked.

'Oh yeah,' I said, 'I sing, alright.'

Well, I can't sing, but I reckon I can. So anyway we did a couple of John Williamson and Kenny Rogers numbers together, then we sat down and we swapped a few yarns. And gees we had a good time. Then the next day they invited us into their morning tea, which was outstanding.

And that's what we need to do. We need to share the cultures. That was John Flynn's ideology: for each and every one of us within this greater organisation to serve the people who live out in the harshness, no matter what their colour or creed, in as much as nobody should be without access to health services, which was born out of the Jimmy Darcy story.

Now, are you aware of the Jimmy Darcy story? Well, it was big news back during the First World War when a young stockman by the name of Jimmy Darcy was working on a station property, up the Kimberley area of Western Australia, and he fell from his horse and was severely injured.

In those days there was no medical help available up in the Kimberleys. There wasn't even a doctor. No radio. Nothing! So their best bet was to try and get Jimmy to Halls Creek, which was about 80 kilometres away, where they knew that the local postmaster, a feller by the name of Tuckett, had at least done a first-aid course. So they loaded Jimmy into a buggy and took him along a rough bush track to Halls Creek. When they got there, Jimmy was in such a bad state all that Tuckett could do was to give him a shot of morphine to try and relieve the severe pain.

Tuckett then decided to Morse code over 3650 kilometres of telegraph wire to Perth to get help. Then, from the post office in Perth the doctor diagnosed Jimmy's injuries and concluded that it was a life or death situation and he needed immediate surgery. And, what's more, because poor old Tuckett had completed a basic first-aid course, he was the unfortunate soul to be given the job.

So then, for the next seven hours the doctor's instructions were relayed by Morse code all the way from Perth to Halls Creek while Tuckett operated on Jimmy with the use of just a penknife and razor blades. The only antiseptic that was available was Condy's Crystals. The only form of anaesthetic was morphine, and that just relieved some of the pain. Anyhow, the operation proved to be a success but, unfortunately, complications set in so then the doctor decided to come up from Perth.

Now, it took six days by a cattle boat for the doctor to reach Derby. Then it was a day and a half by car out to Fitzroy Crossing, followed by a further thirty-six hours—including breakdowns—in a smaller car to get within 50 kilometres of Halls Creek. They then had to travel the rest of the way by horse and sulky, only to find that Jimmy Darcy had died just the day before the doctor arrived.

That tragedy made newspaper headlines all over Australia and it really brought it home to John Flynn that, if there'd been medical services in the bush, Jimmy may well have survived. And I'm getting right off the track here, but also, at that time, when aeroplanes were first being used in the First World War, a feller named Clifford Peel pointed out to Flynn that with the use of aircraft it was now possible for patients to be transported by aeroplane. Then, of course, add to that the communications expertise of Alf Traeger and so this wonderful organisation was born.

Since then, of course, we've developed and become more advanced, and more sophisticated. We've even expanded to include capital city inter-hospital transfer and organ harvesting. But we should always acknowledge the traditional owners of this land as well. We should acknowledge the courage and commitment of the people that've been prepared to go out and explore and develop the harshness of our outback, and who provide us with the wealth. And that's something we must never lose sight of.

Then at the same time we should also acknowledge our own people, those who work within the RFDS. I see it as a privilege that's been bestowed upon us to be able to carry the mantle of serving what we've created. Because it doesn't matter what time of the day or night it is, or what the weather's like—unless, of course, it's absolutely foul and it's impossible to get out there— there's a courage and commitment from our staff to deliver services, above and beyond the call of duty.

And it's not only the lifesaving adventures that should be noted. It's also the day-to-day occurrences: the simple things. We had a community health nurse who's now working in either Canada or Alaska where she drives sled dogs to do medical clinics. When she was with us at our Port Augusta base, every morning she'd go to the bakery and buy fresh bread to take to whatever clinic outpost she was heading to that day. She'd also take some daily newspapers so that the people out there could read up-to-date news, which was a real rarity, and sometimes she'd even take out icy poles or some such for the kids. And you know, that had nothing to do with her nurse's training. None of that was in her brief. She just cared enough.

So I reckon we're lucky to be part of this great organisation. To tell you the truth, I've got to pinch myself sometimes in the knowledge that I've been chosen, or that I'm privileged enough to work within the RFDS. Because I reckon that every one of us— all our staff—when we wake up we know that, at the very least, during the course of that particular day somebody within our organisation will make a difference to someone, somewhere. That's our lot, and I love it.

Statistics and Brief History

Queensland The first base of the Flying Doctor Service was established in Cloncurry, in north-western Queensland, in 1928.

Victoria The Victorian Section was formed on 9 November 1934 and was the first of the Sections of the Australian Inland Aerial Medical Service. Because there was no need for Flying Doctor services in Victoria this section went outside its state borders and took over the responsibility of providing medical services in the vast and remote north-west of Western Australia, in the East and West Kimberley. The section's first base at Wyndham became operational in 1935.

New South Wales The New South Wales Section was formed in 1936. Its Broken Hill base, in the far west of the state, was initially jointly operated by the South Australian and New South Wales Sections and became operational in 1937. It later became known as the South Eastern Section.

Central Formerly known as the South Australian and Northern Territory Sections, this section was formed in 1936 and has since been changed to Central Operations and is administered from South Australia. Initially it operated (from 1937) out of Broken Hill, jointly with the New South Wales Section.

This arrangement continued until the Central Section opened its own Flying Doctor base at Alice Springs in 1939.

Eastern Goldfields Although the Eastern Goldfields Section was officially established in 1937, in the Kalgoorlie area, the 'Goldfields Flying Doctor Service' provided a medical service for people in the outback as far back as the early 1930s.

Western Australia The Western Australian Section was officially registered on 14 June 1936. However, a provisional Section Committee had already purchased a De Havilland Fox Moth Aircraft in 1935. The section's first base at Port Hedland became operative on 10 October 1935, and the first medical flight was made on the opening day.

Tasmania Although emergency medical flights were operated in Tasmania going back as far as the 1930s, the Tasmanian Section of the Flying Doctor Service was the last section to be formed, in 1960.

RFDS GROWTH STATISTICS

	1928	1948	1968	1988	2005
Number of Aircraft *	1		19	34	50
Number of Doctors	1			27	115
Number of Nurses				41	117
Patients Attended	225		43562	102554	234783
Healthcare Clinics			332	3734	11239
Aerial Evacuations			3072	11259	33339
Number of Landings	50		2959	24379	57857

	1928	1948	1968	1988	2005
Telehealth			21 163	24 748	73 694
Kilometres Flown Per Year		320 461	1 863 611	7 392 128	19 524 359
Bases	1	8	14	16	20
Staff (F/T + P/T)				261	639

* In 1928 the aircraft was leased from Qantas. Up until the late 1950s/early 1960s many of the aircraft used by the RFDS were chartered rather than purchased.

Sticks in the Mind

Well, all up, I was flying for forty-five years, and the last eighteen of those were with the Royal Flying Doctor Service. It was a marvellous time really, as well as a great way to finish one's flying career and, I must say, the RFDS were a great crowd to work for. They were just wonderful people. And it goes without saying that the people in the outback were marvellous as well; a hardy variety of Homo sapiens. Then, of course, we also had great aeroplanes to fly, particularly the turbo prop ones. And what tremendous machines they were.

As far as stories go ... let me think: well, there's one that I've quoted before. Actually, it might've even appeared in a Flying Doctor publication at some stage of the game, but it's one that really sticks in the mind. It happened before we received our first King Air, so it was back while we were still flying the Queen Airs, which probably made it about 1983.

Anyway, we got an emergency call one night to go to a place called Cape Flattery. Cape Flattery's in far north Queensland, about 120 nautical miles up the coast from Cairns. It's where they have a big silica sand mine. In those days they used to bring the larger vessels in as close as they could to the little bay area behind the hill, then they'd take the silica sand out on smaller barges, called lighters, and load it up onto the larger ships with cranes and so forth.

But one vessel that came in on this particular day had a lot of Korean seamen on board and one of the unhappy fellers managed to get his hand and arm caught in a winch, which, I must add, is not something to be recommended. Actually, it might be more accurately described as exquisitely painful. So they called on us to go up there to get him. 'This feller, he's in a real bad way,' they said. 'His arm's shockingly damaged and he's bleeding badly.'

Of course, the weather had to be bad, didn't it? You know, it's Murphy's law. You could put your money on it every time. I went with a nursing sister, Stone was her surname. So we took off in the Queen Air from Cairns, with this not-very-promising forecast, and as we got closer to Cape Flattery nothing improved. In fact, it got worse. When we arrived, the place was nothing but cloud and rain.

Now, Cape Flattery was just a sandy surface airstrip that ran sort of north-west/south-east, with a bunch of kerosene flares along each side to provide the light. There were no navigation aids there and by now it was about eight o'clock at night and, being night time, of course, that made it even worse. So I was faced with the immediate decision of: What do I do?

Anyhow, we went down to what they call 'the lowest safe altitude'. That's as low as you can go in cloud and still have a nice clear buffer from any of the surrounding high terrain. And, oh dear, it wasn't looking too good at all.

We had the radar on, which I had in weather mode just in case there were any storms amongst all this stuff, which, luckily, there weren't. It was mostly rain from stratiform cloud. So I turned the radar into mapping mode and picked up the coastline and the area around Cape Flattery and very quickly devised a circuit and an approach to the airfield, using the radar on the aeroplane. This particular action was not approved, of course, not at all. But under the circumstances, considering the condition of the bloke, I figured that the risk was worth taking. It was a calculated risk, put it that way.

Of course, I had escape clauses all the way along. There was absolutely no point in compounding the tragedy by ending up with a crashed aeroplane and two dead crew members: myself and Nursing Sister Stone. In a case like that, the final analysis, of course, doesn't help the patient at all.

So anyway, I worked out this circuit diagram and, by using the radar, I was able to track myself down to a downwind leg and a base leg and line myself up into where the radar indicated the runway should've been. So I started letting some flap down, and the gear extended, and in I came on a fairly low powered setting. So what you're doing is that you're bringing the speed back to—I forget what it was in the Queen Air—but it'd probably be approaching about 100 to 110 knots.

We didn't have a radar altimeter on board so we were just using the pressure altimeter. I'd already made the decision that, when we got to the 300 feet indicated, then if I didn't have visual siting it'd have to be, 'Well, sorry mate we've done our best. We'll just have to put on the power, pull the gear up, pull the flap up and go home.'

But would you believe, I was just about to say, 'Well that's it' when lo and behold these dim runway lights appeared from these kerosene flares. So I plonked the Queen Air down, and I must say that it wasn't the most gentlemanly of arrivals. But that didn't matter. It was still pouring with rain and we sloshed our way down the strip. Then we turned around and taxied back up again and, I can tell you, there was a tremendously grateful group of people there, waiting for us, with this very, very sick Korean feller.

So we took him back to Cairns and they saved his arm, which was tremendous because, I mean, I'm no doctor but I'm guessing that if we hadn't been able to fly him out when we did, at an absolute minimum, he would've most certainly lost his arm, or else he probably would've been dead by the morning.

Stories about the Flying Doctor

Howdie,

I did my best to get some stories on the Flying Doctor. I have this letter from Etheen Burnett who was round in the Gulf Country but being well into her eighties and has had bad health for the last six months. Even so she has typed out these two stories in the hopes that you may be able to use them in your book if it be at all possible.

I have had no experience re: the Flying Doctor Service but I saw plenty of planes flying over me when I was droving out of the Gulf Country straight after the war, but never had to call them.

With the good roads and most of the places having their own planes now and of course with big four-wheel-drive vehicles, I think all that may relieve the pressure on the Flying Doctor Service. But, I know that the Flying Doctor will always be there, picking up the pieces if called upon.

Regards

Jack

* * *

Etheen's Letter

I remember one day my niece and I, returning from the stock camp, were told the Flying Doctor was due to land to see a patient from a neighbouring station.

We quickly drove out to the airstrip about three miles away to make sure there were no cattle on it. As we drove along it we noticed the plane landing on one end so we quickly drove off into thick grass on the side. My niece was standing on the running board and I had one arm on the door above the glass window.

No one noticed an ant hill in the long grass which we duly hit. What a jolt! My niece fell off the running board skinning her shin badly. My arm was cut by the glass and both of us were bleeding profusely when the doctor got out of the plane. The patient whom he had come to see with a broken arm was there and on alighting the doctor looked at us and asked which one is the patient? Of course we thought we would be okay but after three days my niece developed blood poisoning and had to be taken away by the Flying Doctor. She and I still have the scars of that accident.

* * *

When Dr Tim O'Leary was Flying Doctor in Mount Isa he was very particular about treating patients with dysentery, especially children. He insisted only fluids and no solids whatsoever. One child he was treating did not seem to be improving so he flew out to see him. While examining him the child vomited and brought up fruit cake. Can you image what our Irish Doctor said!

The Crook Cocky

Yeah, just a little story here, HG. Back in 1984 I was doing a bit of an outback adventure and I ended up in a little whistlestop town called Kajabbi, which is out near Mount Isa, sort of in the Cloncurry area, in north-western Queensland. And I stayed there for a few days in the local pub. Now, when I say a township, basically, there was just a pub. That's all. There was nothing much else there, at Kajabbi, though I believe that, at one time, it was a rather large place but, over the years, it'd declined to the state of it being, more or less, just the hotel.

But the story is: I was in the bar at about eleven o'clock one mid-week morning. There were about four people in the bar and all the talk was around the doctor coming to town. And I was quite amazed. I thought, 'Well, what would a doctor be doing out here?' In my mind, of course, I was conjuring up ideas of a buckboard arriving and a doctor jumping out with an old medical bag—that type of thing.

Anyway, about twenty minutes later I heard the sound of an aircraft. It circled around overhead a few times and, along with everybody else, I went outside and, with drinks in hand, we all watched the aeroplane land on an airstrip, which was just in behind the hotel.

When I say 'everybody else' I mean the whole four people that were in the bar.

Then about five or six minutes later a doctor came in and, by that time, a few more people had drifted into the pub. Now I believe that there was just the doctor, on his own, because I didn't see a pilot. So I assume he was piloting the aircraft himself. But anyway, by now I'd pieced it together that this was the Flying Doctor who'd come to visit and that the pub was a regular stop for him; meaning that he came, like, once a fortnight or whatever, stopped off and all the people who wanted to see him would drop in at the pub for a medical consultation.

Anyway, the doctor disappeared out to a back room, followed by one guy, and when the guy returned I noticed that he had a new dressing on his hand. After him, a couple of other people went out to the back room for a while before returning to the bar. Then about ten minutes later the doctor, himself, came out into the bar and I saw a feller go over and talk to him. And this feller looked like he was of some sort of Indian extraction.

Now, I couldn't actually hear what the conversation was about but it seemed quite intense because this Indian feller was nodding to the doctor in a very concerned fashion. Then, after a while, the Indian guy turned and he nodded to his wife and she went outside and, when she came back into the bar, she was carrying a cockatoo in a cage. It was a golden-crested, well, a silver- or sulphur-crested cockatoo. To explain, the lady, herself, I think she might've been of South Sea Islander extraction, with blonde hair. As I said, the husband looked like he was Indian. I found out later that he was Fijian Indian and, apparently, he and his wife had lived there, in Kajabbi, for many years.

So I'm sort of taking this all in and by now I'm thinking: 'Surely the doctor's not going to look at the cockatoo', you know?

But anyway, the cockatoo came out of its cage and it got on this Islander lady's shoulder and I watched as the doctor went over and lifted its wings. Then after he'd taken a good look underneath each of the wings he lifted its comb up and took a check around its head area. Now, I was absolutely amazed that this aircraft had flown into this little country town and here was the Flying Doctor actually diagnosing a cockatoo.

HG: Oh, they can do anything, the Flying Doctor Service.

But I was just spellbound, HG. I just couldn't believe it was happening. The whole scenario was just absolutely crazy. But anyway, after he'd checked over the cockatoo, the doctor spoke to the South Sea Islander woman for about four or five minutes then she thanked him very much for his expert advice. Then she popped the bird back into the cage and placed the cage on the bar.

The next thing I see is the hotel owner talking with the woman who had the cockatoo and out came a plastic bag and they put some crushed ice in the plastic bag and then they flattened it out, sealed the end off, put a few pegs on it, and sat the cockatoo's cage on top of this bag of ice. So I assume that the Flying Doctor had diagnosed that the cockatoo was suffering from heat stress and, believe me, it was very hot.

Then the doctor, well, he grabbed his gear and he disappeared out the back door. And I was amazed that everyone sort of automatically got up and, with drinks in hand, they wandered outside, to the back of the pub, and they watched as the Flying Doctor gunned the aeroplane up and down the airstrip and away he went out into the wide blue yonder.

But that always stuck in my mind. To think, well, you know, here in the middle of nowhere, which it was because Kajabbi is a long way outback, was the Flying Doctor arriving, not only to look after the local people—you know, to put a dressing on a guy who'd obviously hurt himself plus, probably, talk to a few other people—but also he gave service to this lady's, obviously, much-loved cockatoo, which, I may add, thanks to the Flying Doctor, is most possibly still alive and well at Kajabbi today.

The Easter Bunny

In total I worked with the Royal Flying Doctor Service for nine years. That was at both their Broken Hill and Dubbo bases. For much of that time I was employed as an emergency flight nurse and well, in the end, I more or less left because I got married and we moved over here to Walgett, in the central north of New South Wales. That's the only reason why I finished up. But I really loved my time with the RFDS, and I actually kept a diary through the years I was working for them so I've looked up a few stories, if you're interested. I guess they're both about determination of spirit, but in very different ways. What's more, both incidents happened up at Tibooburra, in the far north-western corner of New South Wales.

Well first: one time we got a phone call from a very distressed husband up at Tibooburra. He told us that he'd delivered their last nine babies, all by himself, and there'd been no problems. That's right, nine! And he'd delivered every one of them. But now he said that he was having a bit of trouble delivering their tenth baby. His wife had been in labour for quite a while and, to make matters worse, she didn't want any medical help. In actual fact, she was adamant that there be no medical intervention. No doctors. Nothing. She wanted all home births—just natural— and that was that. No argument. So there he was, this distraught husband, hiding in the next room, out of earshot from his wife, whispering to us over the phone, 'The baby just won't come. What to do?'

From what he was telling us, we surmised it was probably a breech birth because it wasn't coming down well at all. Anyhow, we had a clinic plane in the area so we sent that out and, you know, they arrive and they went in to see how the wife was going and she gets very upset, particularly with her husband, because he'd gone against her wishes and he's asked us to come in to help her. In fact, she's downright angry with him. She was still in labour at that stage and had been for a good twenty-four hours or so, which was very unusual for a tenth child. They should come, probably, within about an hour.

So they tried to settle her down and talk her into coming back down to Broken Hill with them to have the baby in the hospital there. Anyhow, much against her wishes, they eventually managed to coax her on the aircraft and I was in radio contact, waiting at the other end for them in Broken Hill.

There was little change during the flight but then, just as the clinic plane was coming into Broken Hill, they told me over the radio that they thought the baby was coming. So I was telling them what to do and where to find the delivery packs on the aircraft. Still and all, she hadn't had the baby by the time they landed so I got straight onto the aircraft and helped the woman out into the waiting ambulance. Even at that stage she was still complaining about our intervention.

Then, just as we were going over the bridge on our way to the Broken Hill Hospital, we delivered a breech baby in the back of the ambulance. So, we ended up with a hell of a mess and I virtually finished cleaning up the baby and the woman in the ambulance bay of the Broken Hill Hospital.

Now, once the placenta is delivered the mother, more or less, stops bleeding and she can stay fairly comfortable. Anyhow, after I'd cleaned everything up, I turned around to the woman and I said, 'Look, how about we just take you into the hospital and get you checked out?'

But the attitude of the woman hadn't changed one little bit. 'No, no,' she said, 'it's alright.' And she packed the placenta up and she wrapped the baby up and she wandered off to get a taxi downtown so that she could catch the next bus straight back to Tibooburra.

I tell you, it's amazing some of the mums you come across. She was a tough one, alright. And this was her tenth child. But I did feel for her poor husband. I imagine he would've been in the bad books for quite a while, after she got home.

So that was one incident, and the second one was ... well, actually, you do have to laugh at times, don't you? As I said, it's another one about the strength of spirit but in a very different and funny sort of way.

This happened around Easter time and we got a call from the bemused nurses up at Tibooburra saying that they'd just been out in the ambulance and picked up a man who'd been wandering down the Barrier Highway in quite a distressed state. Now, it was extremely hot at the time and, as it turned out, this man was schizophrenic and he'd either broken out, or got out, of a Psychiatric Hospital near Morisset, which is just south of Newcastle, on the central coast of New South Wales. How on earth he found his way out to Tibooburra, I couldn't tell you. I wouldn't have a clue.

Anyhow, he'd told the nurses at Tibooburra that the reason why he was in the area was that he was off to pick pears. Now, mind you, we are talking about the far north-western corner of New South Wales and, as you might imagine, the nearest pear orchard could've been anywhere up to 1000 or so kilometres away. So I think he was in the wrong place.

But, that's not all. What really got the nurses going was that this poor man was not only off to pick pears but he'd also somehow got it in his head that he was the Easter Bunny. So when they found him, he was walking down the road stark naked, apart from wearing his underpants on his head and, for added effect, he'd stuck a carrot up where he shouldn't have— up his rectum. But the nurses said that he wasn't violent or anything because, apparently, when they went out to get him, they simply stopped and asked him if he'd like to hop in the back of the ambulance and in he hopped, no problem at all.

Anyhow, first of all, we found out where this man's father was and contacted him because we thought he might be worried about his missing son. But when we got on to his father and explained the circumstances all he said was, 'Yes, he does that kind of thing, quite a bit. You should've seen what he did last Christmas.'

So then, we flew out to get him and we took him back to Sydney and, again, he got in the plane, no problems at all. But, oh, he was totally off the planet. He had no idea where he was or who he was, other than believing he'd come out to Tibooburra to pick pears and that he was the Easter Bunny. And, what's more, there was no way he was going to let us take his underpants off his head or take the carrot out of his rectum. In his mind, he was the Easter Bunny and that was it. So he stayed that way the whole trip back to Sydney. But you'd think it'd be uncomfortable, wouldn't you, particularly with the carrot.

The Flying Padre's Story

You may well ask, What connection does an American have with the Australian Royal Flying Doctor Service? Well, to begin with my wife, Becky, is one of several Americans who have worked for the RFDS. She's currently the Tourist Facility Supervisor at the Broken Hill base. The Museum there also identifies Reverend Dr John Flynn's ethos of a Mantle of Safety to serve the people of the outback. That not only includes pilots, doctors and nurses, but also ministers on patrol. Over the years these Padres have travelled by everything from camel, bicycle, motor bike, and automobile—as Flynn's successor, Reverend Fred McKay, did in an old International truck. Then there have been a few more fortunate ones, like myself, who fly an aeroplane. I'm known as a Flying Padre. I can reach a destination in hours where, in earlier days, it could've taken days or even weeks.

I'm the seventh Flying Padre, with the Uniting Church's Far-West Ministry—currently in its fortieth year. I am currently flying our third aircraft, a 1974 high-wing, single-engine Cessna 182, which is a great aeroplane for remote airstrips and extreme conditions.

But before I tell my story, just a bit of background. I'm originally from Cedar Rapids, Iowa, USA, which is where you'll find industries such as Quaker Oatmeal and Collins Radio. My first love was aviation but, at the age of eighteen, when I took my physical for the 'draft'

I was told, 'Sorry, you measure 203 centimetres. We can't take you for the Air Force or any of the services because you're just too tall.'

Then, when I got on the bus to return back home, I remember very clearly asking myself, 'So what else do you want to do with your life?' And an internal voice—and I suppose it had greater dimensions—replied, 'Well, I've always liked church. I'll go into church work.' It wasn't an angry voice but more of an 'Okay, God, you win, take me' kind of thing. So that was the way I decided to go.

Then Becky and I met at university, after she'd returned from a Brazilian high school exchange. She saw me singing in a musical group for their orientation week. Then in the second week I met her at a church coffee house. It was love at first sight. That night, I walked her home, and I've been walking her home ever since. We married in 1969.

Becky was also aware of my passion for aviation. My first posting, following seminary, was to a small village up near the Canadian border. There was a little airport and flight instructor in Milan, New Hampshire. So when Becky got a job as a State Social Worker, it was just a case of, 'Hey, we've got a little money. Go get your flying lessons.' Six hours of lessons later I flew my solo and I finished my licence in quick time.

But we soon learnt that hot summers were short, usually only a week or two, and the long, dark nights of winter could last for months. It could reach 40° below zero (Fahrenheit!) and it seemed like shovelling snow was everyone's hobby. I could tell you about the time I tried to keep the Volkswagen's engine oil warm overnight. I was advised to plug in a light bulb by the engine, then put a blanket over it. Not only was the oil warmed but, a couple of hours later, the blanket and the car caught fire. The good news is that, conveniently, there was snow everywhere and we saved the car by throwing snow on the engine compartment. I could also tell you about the nails in that house becoming so cold in the dead of winter that they'd contract and pop like pistols being fired at close range. Ministry can be so exciting!

So, it was a difficult two years for us. The highlight was my learning to fly and organising a successful 1974 air show. Four groups benefited: our own Methodist parish, an orphanage in South Carolina, the Catholic church down the road, and Father Tony Gendusa, a flying priest in Rabaul, PNG (Papua New Guinea).

However, before another New Hampshire winter came Becky and I would move to Melbourne, Australia, where we thawed, retrained and tested ourselves in many ways. I had accepted a hospital chaplaincy internship at the Austin Hospital, Heidelberg. After eighteen months, I happily moved on to teach at St Leonard's College, in East Brighton. Becky worked at Trans-Australia Airlines.

After two and a half years living in Australia we moved back to the States, to Atlanta, Georgia, where our son, Matt, was born. Then when my residency in Pastoral Counselling was finished, I became the Director of the Atlanta District Counselling Service. It gave me eight years of building skills, which would come in very handy later. We left 'Hotlanta' for central New Hampshire for seven more years of good pastoral town and rural country work before I ended up serving as a Church Pastor near Boston, Massachusetts.

Boston was a tough placement especially when you see churches losing their vision and wearing down their memberships. You could liken it to when someone you love loses their way. So, for a break, we came over to Australia for holidays. We were at Narromine, in central New South Wales, visiting the parents of an Australian friend who was studying in Boston, and I remember as we drove past the local airport, on the way to the Dubbo Zoo, our friend's father asked, 'What's your hobby?' And I told him that I truly loved flying and church work.

'Well,' he replied, 'you know, we've got a Flying Padre position open in Broken Hill.'

And I asked three questions: 'What's a Flying Padre?', 'Who broke Broken Hill?' and 'Where do I apply?' Then it took eight months or so but everything got resolved and we started work in Broken Hill on 1 May 2002. And though tragedies do happen, the job's a delight; the people have been absolutely wonderful. Here in the outback, I don't have to shovel snow, and I haven't set fire to my automobile ... not yet, anyway.

Now, to my story: I was minding my business one cold and blustery Sunday in, gosh, I think it was back in September 2003, when the news first reported that Mrs Luscombe had gone missing. She was a Broken Hill resident who suffered from dementia. She lived alone, on the south side, near the Broken Hill Airport, where a carer, a neighbour and some relatives kept an eye on her.

Every day she'd walk part of the perimeter of the airport with her dog, Dazzie, a blue heeler cross, and occasionally a neighbour's dog would join them. But when Mrs Luscombe hadn't shown up by dark a neighbour became concerned, even more so when the neighbour's dog returned home alone. Basically, all Mrs Luscombe was wearing for weather protection that day was a light jacket. So the police were called, the relatives were notified and a full-blown ground search was organised that Sunday evening.

Becky's office, at the RFDS base, was just a stone's throw from the search headquarters at the airport. So, with still no sign of Mrs Luscombe by Monday morning, after dropping Becky off at work, I stopped in and—as a New South Wales Regional Police Chaplain—I offered to fly my Cessna in an aerial search. I was well aware that people had previously gone missing into the vast surrounding desert, never to be seen again. It was an urgent situation.

Because of Mrs Luscombe's condition, she wore a signal-emitting necklace that sent out a beep, beep, beep to a tuned receiver. One of the relatives said that they had put fresh batteries in the necklace. We only hoped that she was still wearing it. So I got into my Cessna with a couple of SES (State Emergency Service) people who had a radio and an antenna receiver system to track the necklace. We took off and spiralled south and north from the airport, thinking that Mrs Luscombe and Dazzie, the dog, were more likely to head toward town rather than going out in the bush. But, after two and a half hours without a response from our receiver I thought, 'Well, surely they'll find her in their wide-cast ground search.'

But, you know, the ground search continued on Tuesday then on the Wednesday and still without any sign of her. By Friday morning the weather had warmed up and I got a Police Search Director's call saying, 'Look, we're going to have to shut down the search but, for the sake of the family, would you mind taking just one more aerial run?'

I was happy to do that. They double-checked the radio equipment to make sure everything was working properly. It was another very windy day and I wanted to go slowly to do a visual search as well. I started my increasing spirals and then laps on the southern side at about 700 feet above the ground. Then we were about 10 or 12 miles south of Broken Hill when Josh, the chap who had the signal meter said, 'Turn left!' So I did and he called out, 'Mark it.'

Then, Leslie, the SES volunteer in the back of the Cessna, marked the latitude and longitude from her hand-held GPS (Global Positioning System). We did this four times, from different directions, measuring the numbers each time. Below us were two water-filled dams and a couple of powerlines. Being windy I wanted to avoid getting fried on the wires, but I got down as low as possible and when I saw something of colour in the water, my first thought was, 'Gee, I hope that's not her.'

At this stage, because we were just tracking a piece of jewellery that might've popped off as she'd walked along, we couldn't positively confirm if we'd found Mrs Luscombe or not. When we landed back at the search base we marked out the spot on a map and handed copies to the ground searchers. Then I waited on the ground for another ten minutes before I overflew the motor bike searchers and others and I circled the exact spot to give them direction. And that's where they located Mrs Luscombe, lying near the dam.

By the time I landed back at the airport I still hadn't heard the actual outcome. But as I was tying the Cessna down, one of the ground staff, who was nicknamed 'Flies', came over and his voice broke as he said, 'They found her ... and she's alive!'

I was then informed that Mrs Luscombe had been found lying in a roughly dug hole, dehydrated, sunburnt and semi-conscious, though still communicative. But because of the rough terrain, the SES people had to get a four-wheel-drive vehicle in there to retrieve her. From there she was driven with as much care as possible to a waiting ambulance, before going on to hospital. So we all felt pretty good and when I returned to the search headquarters, the extremely anxious family was now shedding tears of relief and happiness.

So that's how Mrs Luscombe was found. I believe she's now living in Adelaide with family, and has had extra years of life, care and love. And with the Uniting Church Flying Patrol celebrating its fortieth year, what a memory that particular event is for me. And to think that it's the same satisfaction felt, almost daily, by the Flying Doctors' staff. I just wish everyone could be a part of such an experience.

But, of course, Dazzie, the dog, was the real hero. Apparently, it was he who'd led Mrs Luscombe to water. Then, when a hole was dug, that faithful dog had laid on top of her to keep her warm enough to avoid freezing.

Now, don't quote me on this. But I heard a story sometime later that one of the family came to visit Mrs Luscombe and because she was a victim of dementia, naturally, they didn't want to scold her for what had happened. But quite understandably, the family member said to her, 'You know, you really gave us a fright.'

And in a moment of clarity, I understand Mrs Luscombe's response was, 'Well, you know, I didn't have such a good week either.'

The Souvenir

In 1958 I was working up on the west coast of the Cape York Peninsula at a place called Rutland Plains Station, which is about 180 mile north of Normanton. The property, itself, was about 1500 or 1600 square mile, and it bordered on an Aboriginal settlement, up on the Mitchell River, called Kowanyama.

Now, I did two long droving trips that year, of about five weeks each, taking bullocks from Kowanyama, down the Mungana Stock Route to the railhead at Mungana. Anyhow, just before the last trip we were mustering up some eight hundred bullocks and the Head Stockman from Rutland, well, he came to me on the quiet and he said, 'Now, Goldie, I could use a feller like you, so there's a job here after yer've delivered this mob, if you'd like it.'

Good. That was fine by me but then, during the droving trip, one of my molars—I forget now if it was a pre-molar or a back molar, but, anyway—it started aching. And I tell you what, if you've got a toothache while you're out droving and you just can't go to sleep, you generally end up doing a night watch for someone else, you know. But anyway, after we had the bullocks trucked at Mungana, I came back to Rutland to work there and, at that stage, the molar wasn't quite as bad.

But then, after about another three months, this toothache came back and it began getting worse and worse until, eventually, an abscess grew on it and I had a huge swollen jaw. And, you know, with all the pain, you try everything from putting tobacco in the thing or if you drink enough brandy or whisky that deadens it sometimes, and cloves, they're good, too.

At that time we were at a mustering camp on Rutland Plains Station named One Mile, which was about 15 mile from the homestead. It was called the One Mile because it was 1 mile from the Kowanyama boundary. So the Station Manager from Rutland said that my best chance would be for me to catch up with the Flying Doctor at the Kowanyama Aboriginal settlement, on his next monthly clinic visit.

'Okay,' I mumbled. 'Good.' Then he told me to ride into Rutland homestead on such and such day and he'd drive me the 20-odd miles over to the settlement to meet the Flying Doctor.

Well, the day finally arrived and I rode into the homestead and the manager drove me over. It was dark when we got to Kowanyama and the doctor, Tim O'Leary, his name was, well, he had all these Murries—that's what they called the local Aborigines— he had them all lined up, giving them injections, checking them over and so forth, doing a clinic. Now, Tim was a great character and a very well known and liked doctor with the Royal Flying Doctor Service, and after he'd finished treating all the Murries, I remember the manager saying to him, 'Tim, I've got a white stockman here, Jack Goldsmith, aged twenty-four and he's got a jaw like a lumpy jaw bullock.' Lumpy jaw's a disease that bullocks get.

'So you're Jack Goldsmith?' Tim O'Leary said.

And I said, 'Hello, so what have you heard?'

Then he gave a sort of grin. 'Oh, only rumours,' he said, 'just rumours.' Then, he said, 'Okay, let's have a look at this tooth.' And after he had a bit of a poke around he said, 'I shouldn't even attempt to pull that molar. It's got an abscess on it and a bad one at that.'

'Well,' I said, 'I'm not leaving here until it's out.' And I tell you, I wasn't going to budge an inch until that molar was gone.

Anyhow, he says, 'Okay then, I'll give it a go. Sit on that box.' And there was this box alongside a post in the building; just a wooden box, you know, about 70 pound or 50 pound, in weight. It's what they used to put butter into.

'Take your belt off,' Tim said.

Now, I didn't know what he was on about but I took me belt off, anyway, and I gave it to him. Then he got the belt and he tied my head to the post, by the forehead, so I couldn't move. So he strapped my head to the post, and then he started to work on the tooth, with just a huge pair of pliers, under the light of a dull globe, hanging down from the ceiling. And he pushed and he pulled and he yanked it this way and that way. I doubt if he even used anaesthetic and, if he did, it didn't do nothing to ease the pain. By this stage I was starting to feel pretty faint with it all, I can tell you. But the molar wouldn't budge.

Now, there was some Murries still there and they were watching all these goings on, and all with a bit of a smirk on their dials. But I had to put on a brave face, see, because I had a big rep up in that country because I used to mill a lot; you know, scrap around and brawl and fight and all that. So all these Murries reckoned I was real tough, except I wasn't, especially when Tim really started getting stuck into me with the pliers. Oh, he was huffing and puffing and pulling this way and that until I could feel the crunching sound of my molar and jaw. Now, I don't know if you can go numb with pain, but I reckon that I did. And then I started sweating all over and going from pale to paler and all this while these Murries were looking at me like they were enjoying every moment of it.

Anyhow, Tim eventually got it out. And I tell you what, I can still remember it. There he was, Dr Tim O'Leary, standing there with this huge, bloodied tooth in his pliers, holding it up to the dull light and saying, 'No wonder it was so difficult to get out. Look,' he said, 'the roots are crossed.'

And apparently, when the roots are crossed, half of your jaw comes out with the molar. So there Tim was, looking very proud of himself, and he turned to me and he said, 'And what's more, that's only the second tooth I've ever pulled.'

'Well then, keep it fer a souvenir,' I replied, half jokingly.

So that was one of my experiences with the RFDS, and that was with Dr Tim O'Leary, back in 1958. And for the life of me, I don't know where that molar ended up. I never saw it again after that, so I reckon he might've taken my word and kept it as a souvenir, aye.

The Spirit of the Bush

My name is Esther and I am the first female pilot of the Royal Flying Doctor Service within the Central Division. That is only the Central Division because, as you might be aware, the RFDS already, I believe, has had a female pilot over in Western Australia, somewhere, and also there has been another female pilot up in Queensland. I was just reading the book again the other day and the Queensland pilot, her name was Beth Garrett. Her husband initially worked for the RFDS in Queensland and he died, and years later, I think it must've been in the late 1960s, she started flying there. So she was one of the real pioneering women doing it.

But for me: how did I get to become a pilot for the RFDS? Well, it is a long story. I was three months old, initially, when I first came to Australia from Holland with my parents, and we lived here till I was the age of four. Then we lived for two years back in Holland and then we went to the United Arab Emirates for a few years and to Nigeria, to Holland a bit again then back to Australia. And the last time when we just landed here in Australia, in 1989, in July, I literally come off the plane and we drove from the airport to where Dad had a home in Sydney and I just looked around and I thought, 'I'm home. This is it. Australia is my home.'

But my parents, they left again after another four-year stint in this country and, of course, I stayed and it took me in total six years to get my permanent residency, and I got stuck here, and I have no regrets at all. I love it.

Then in 1996, after I got my pilot's licence in Bankstown, Sydney, I went looking for the 'famous first flying job'. I had planned to look as far as Sydney to Dubbo but I ended up in Darwin, and the further I got into the outback the more I loved it. So yeah, that was it. I was hooked with the outback.

But to get a job with the RFDS, it was just through a lot of experience in different areas of flying and general aviation. I've worked in the Northern Territory in places like Arnhem Land, Darwin, Kununurra. I've done night freight from the big cities like Sydney to Brisbane and Melbourne and I was also based in Queensland doing what they call bank runs. That's where all the documentation from the bank is needed to be back to their State office, or their head office, at the end of each day. So from the smaller towns, all over Australia, you've got all these aeroplanes that leave at six in the morning and they deliver, not just bank documents but also overnight freight. Then at four in the afternoon they backtrack their steps before they return to the main city again. And that happens all over Australia.

Over that time, already, I'd applied to all the Flying Doctor bases, Australia-wide, and one day the Chief Pilot from the Central Division in Adelaide was nice enough to call me up and say, 'You have an interview.'

So here I am at the Royal Flying Doctor base, at Port Augusta, at the top of Spencer Gulf, in South Australia. I've been here now for about eight months and the Central Division covers anywhere from Adelaide to Tennant Creek, in central Northern Territory, and from over near the Western Australian border which, I think, Cook is the nearest place, then over to about Mildura, which is into north-western Victoria. I think, off the top of my head, it is something like 840000 square kilometres. But of course, we have a Flying Doctor's base in Alice Springs and another base in Adelaide, so we only do the area south-east of the Riverland if Adelaide is busy doing other stuff and we only go up to Alice Springs sometimes, because they always cover their own area.

The plane I fly is a Pilatus PC 12. They are our newer aeroplanes. It has a single-engine turbo prop so they're a cheaper plane to operate than our previous plane, the King Air, which has a twin turbo prop. The PC 12s have a shorter land and take-off than our King Airs do, so they have become a great success. And I think that the South Australian Section of the RFDS has got the highest flight time of PC 12s anywhere in the world. But they're very expensive, up around $5 or $6 million, all fitted out. That's why we were doing some fundraising at a rodeo last night. Every little bit helps.

But I was very accepted as a female pilot. It has been great. In the first few weeks I was working in Port Augusta one of my first night shifts I was on, I was sent to Peterborough, which is about 150 kilometres south-east of Port Augusta. As we do at Peterborough, the lights need to be put on by an airport manager. The Airport Manager at this time was Norm. So the Coms (Communications) people here in Port Augusta contacted Norm saying when we are expected to be in to Peterborough and he would go out and turn on the lights. And apparently the Coms people, when they were talking to Norm, they were saying about 'she' and 'her' in regards to the pilot. So by the time I got there, Norm just came up to the door straight away and said, 'How fantastic.' He said, 'You are the first female pilot I am meeting.'

That was so nice and a few weeks later there was an article in the *Peterborough Times* about, you know, the first female pilot working here, and Norm was such a gentleman that he actually made a copy of it and sent it to the base here in Port Augusta. So that was just a really lovely reception and a good thing to remember. But it was very funny that, often in the beginning, people would come up to me and start talking about the patient as if I am supposed to be the flight nurse. Of course, by now, I think most people are used to me being the pilot.

But the outback people are the most wonderful, and their support for the Royal Flying Doctor Service is just absolutely fantastic. I was saying that I was at a rodeo just last night and the RFDS had a little tent there and they were being supported by the people. Wherever you are, it's just amazing. You know, it makes me almost always so proud to be part of it because I can be just going on a four-wheel-drive trip on my own and you meet some people and they say, 'Oh, where do you live and what do you do?'

And I say, 'I live in Port Augusta and I am a pilot with the RFDS.'

Well, the people just look at you and they go, 'Oh, that must be such a fantastic job, working for the RFDS.'

And anybody, whether they are German or Japanese or Australian people they all have heard about it. It's like there's some sort of invisible communication out there, in the outback, and that was what John Flynn was fascinated about too. Even though, of course, nowadays, you do have different means of communication, the attitude in the bush is still just amazing.

I remember when I came from Broken Hill to Port Augusta for the first-time interview and I came through the mountains from Wilmington, and the mountains were nice and green and as soon as we got over the mountains everything was that yellow dead colour. Then 5 kilometres further on you see the power station and then there's Port Augusta, and I loved it just so much that I said, 'If things would change, or anything like that, I might just buy a little farm here, up in the hills near Wilmington.'

And I was just talking to the organiser last night, at the rodeo, about it and she asked me, 'Why would you like a little farm?'

'It's always been my dream,' I said, 'to have a little farm with a few horses, you know.'

And she said, 'Oh well, if you get any horses, you don't need to buy a farm. I've got 2000 acres. You can just put them up there.'

You know, where else in the world would someone just offer land like that to another person? It's as if it was, 'Oh, don't worry about it. Take some of mine.'

So I said, 'You must be joking. I could not do this.'

She said, 'No, I mean it.' She said, 'If you have a horse and you want to put it somewhere, give me a call and you can put it up on my land.'

It was like the most normal thing ever, you know. And where would you come across anything like that? I think only in Australia, in the bush. It's the spirit of the bush. It was just so simple an offer, but so very nice.

The Tangle with the Motor Bike

I'd actually moved from Adelaide to Western Australia. Then my ex-boyfriend had a friend who was a real estate agent in Katherine and, this real estate agent, she needed someone to look after a station property that she was selling in Arnhem Land. So yeah, we decided to do that and so we flew up there, out to Mountain Valley Station, up in the Top End of the Northern Territory.

But at Mountain Valley I was doing little bits of everything and I didn't like that too much. I even ended up being the cook and I didn't really enjoy cooking. I wanted to find some place where I could get involved with the mustering and everything, so I ended up going down to Mittiebah Station to work there. Mittiebah's in the Barkly Tablelands area of the Northern Territory. It's about 1.8 million acres, so I got to do some mustering and stuff like that, and no cooking.

Out at Mittiebah they had composite cattle; it's like Brahman and Shorthorn Cross and then they second cross with something else. It's basically just a whole lot of different types of cattle that are bred to get what they want as far as beef quality and temperament and stuff goes. And, also, we were trialling a different sort of technique where we don't try and stress the cattle out too much. It's like low-stress cattle-handling. Because if you get them all agitated they'll get stressed out and start to lose condition, and that's the last thing you want. So we weren't allowed to use dogs or stockwhips or any poles or anything like that and we weren't even supposed to make too much noise in the yards or anything.

Actually, I haven't learned all that much about it yet, because of my accident. But we're doing a course this year where you learn to use pressure release and make the cattle work off you. Pressure release is when, say, the cattle are all in a mob, in the corner, and you want them to go through the gate. Well, you've just got to walk in on them and once they start moving, you back off and they'll go through the gate. Of course, if you educate the cattle they're a lot easier to handle and they sort of know what to do and so they work off you. We still use horses and motor bikes and stuff, but the horses are easy on them and, though the motor bikes make a bit of noise, I don't think they stress them out too much, either.

But about the accident—the tangle with the motor bike—that happened on 12 December 2005. I was riding a Honda XR 250 at the time and I was mustering some cattle with my Overseer, Mike. Anyway, Mike and I, we'd sort of done one back bit of the paddock and we were pushing the cattle—the bulls—up along the fence line. They'd settled pretty well, so Mike decided to leave me with that lot and go and get the next mob of cattle from the other side of the paddock. Then, yeah, we were going to meet at a fenced-in bit called 'the cooler', where we could hold them on water. Probably they call it the cooler because that's where the water is and the cattle can cool down there. It's certainly not a meat cooler.

So, I was pushing these bulls along, then I left the fence line and I took the bike out around the mob a bit and, while I was doing that, I hit a hole. But because I was only going very slow I decided to give the bike a few revs to jump it out of the hole but, when I did, the bike stalled. So then I put my leg down to try and hold the motor bike upright but, because I was in the hole, the bike rolled back and I lost balance and it fell on me. At first I didn't realise what had happened because my initial thought was, 'Oh, I've gotta get the bike off me.'

But then, when I tried lifting the bike, I noticed that my jeans were ripped up around the area of my inner-left thigh. So I had a look and, yeah, there was the clutch lever stuck right into my leg.

Anyhow, I still had to try and lift the bike up and pull the clutch leaver out of my thigh. And I was really worried about doing that because I thought that when I pulled it out there might be a great spurt of blood or something because, maybe, I'd cut the main artery that's there. So that was the first thing I thought of, the blood spurting out, and I sort of freaked out a bit about that.

But anyway, yeah, I eventually pulled the clutch leaver out of my thigh and no blood spurted out. That was good because it meant that the main artery wasn't broken. Perhaps it was only just sort of punctured or something. The cut, or the gash, in my thigh was about 7 centimetres by 4 centimetres. That's what the doctor told me later, anyway. And yeah, there wasn't much blood at all, so I was really lucky with that.

But, just to be safe, I ripped the sleeve off my shirt and I tied it around my leg to act like a tourniquet. I was thinking that that was what I was supposed to do, though I found out later it's what you're not supposed to do at all. But I didn't know that at the time, so I tied the ripped shirt sleeve around my leg and then my idea was to get back on the motor bike and ride home, back to the station. The only trouble was that, when I tried to stand up, I couldn't put any weight on my leg, so then I was stuck out there.

As I said, I was still off the fence line, but I did manage to get over there and put my helmet on the fence, like on a picket, because I thought that was the only way they'd find me, by seeing the helmet on the fence. And then I just went back and crawled under a native berry bush because I knew that when Mark reached the cooler with his cattle and saw that I hadn't arrived yet, he'd realise there was something wrong.

So, I just waited there in the shade of the berry bush and, naturally, Mark came back along the fence line looking for me and when he found the cattle but not me, he really got a bit worried. So he kept on coming along the fence line and it was just as well that I'd put the helmet on the fence because, when Mark got there, he didn't see me, but he saw the helmet. So he stopped there and had a bit of a look around and, yeah, that's when he found me.

But when he asked me what was wrong, I didn't want to freak him out too much, so I just said, 'Oh, I've just cut myself and I can't stand the bike up.'

'That's okay,' he said, 'I'll stand the bike up.'

Then I said, 'Oh, and when we get back, I might have to go to town, though.'

'Why?' he said.

And I pulled my jeans over a bit so he could have a look and he goes, 'Oh fuck, Myf.' And he nearly vomited. He said, like, 'Don't worry about the bike, you stay there and I'll go and get help.'

Then he rode back to the station and he got the bore runner, which is the dude that checks all the bores on the station, and the bore runner came to get me in one of his bore utes, and he also brought along a big bottle of water, thank goodness. Then, because the bore ute's got a big 900 litre diesel tank on the back and there's not much room, the bore runner, he got me in the front of his ute. It's got like a bench seat and so I sort of lent against him and stuck my leg out the window for the trip back.

Yeah, so then the bore runner, he took me back to the station and he put me on the table in the kitchen and everyone started coming in to have a good look, while they were having a cup of tea. But the cook there, Kay, she had some sort of nursing training so she took over then. The first thing she decided to do was to cut my jeans off and I was a bit freaked out about that because I don't wear undies when I work. It's more comfortable, that way. And so I was freaking out, like, because there's a couple of guys in the kitchen and I'm, like, whispering, 'Hey, Kay, I don't wear undies.'

So Kay got everyone to leave the kitchen and then she cut my jeans off to see just what damage had been done. While she was doing that the others had been on the phone, calling the Flying Doctor and all that sort of thing to find out what they needed to do. Apparently the doctor told them that I was meant to have morphine, which I didn't have. I didn't want it anyway, because I wasn't in that much pain. Well, I didn't really have that much time to think about the pain and so, maybe, that's why it didn't hurt just then. So yeah, Kay just tried to dress the wound as best she could and they said that the RFDS were going to send a plane out to get me.

But then there was some sort of complication about flying out to pick me up—and I can't quite remember what it was—but our airstrip was just a graded strip and, maybe, there was something wrong with it, like it'd rained the day before and it was too wet to land an aeroplane on it or something. So they decided to drive me over to the station next door, to Alexandria Station, where they had a really big, all-purpose airstrip. The same company owned both Mittiebah and Alexandria Stations. So we jumped in the car and it was about an hour's drive over there, I think.

Anyway, the RFDS arrived at Alexandria Station and they picked me up and then, while they were flying me over to Mount Isa, they had a close look at the leg and, yeah, there was still heaps of dirt and stuff in the hole in my thigh so they just sort of redressed it and then put a drip in me, just for liquid.

Oh, and they also asked me if I wanted some morphine, but I said, 'No, I'm okay', because I didn't really have any pain until I was nearly at Mount Isa, and that's when it really hit. Still, I wasn't really keen on that sort of thing. But anyway they said, 'Well, it's better to get the morphine into you now, before the pain gets worse, otherwise it takes too much morphine to get it back down again.'

So they gave me 1 millilitre of morphine then and, when that didn't do anything, they gave me another 2 millilitres.

Yeah, so then I arrived at Mount Isa and they took me by ambulance from the airport to the hospital. I think the accident happened at about one o'clock in the afternoon and I left Alexandria Station just after four o'clock, maybe, and we got into Mount Isa at about six at night. I can't really be sure about that because I didn't have a watch or anything, but that's what I told the hospital people, anyway.

Then the next day, they cleaned out the wound in surgery. I don't know too much about what happened there because they knocked me out, thank goodness. But apparently they had to, like, really open the wound up to get into it, to scrub all the dirt and rubbish out of the hole in my thigh. And after they'd done all that, they packed the hole back up with seaweed. I really don't know what the significance of the seaweed was but I think it was to help with the healing somehow. Then five days later I went back into surgery and they took out the seaweed and stitched it all up. But then the terrible heat up there, in Mount Isa, got to it, which made it worse there for a while.

Yeah, so I had twelve stitches along the top there, inside my left thigh. And the accident happened on 12 December 2005, only about a week before I was supposed to leave Mittiebah Station, which was a bit unfortunate. But, yeah, that's about it. So there you go. Cool!

Too Late

When you go out to live in a place like Wittenoom, up in the north of Western Australia, you soon realise that you're a long way from anywhere. Like, it's not the sort of place where you can just get up and wander down the street to go and visit the doctor; though I think at one time, they used to have a doctor come over from Tom Price once every so often and—in the hope that he'd keep up the service—everyone in town would front up and pretend that they had something wrong with them. But when that ended, then the Royal Flying Doctor Service virtually took over the medical side of things.

The first dealings that I had with the RFDS was through my brother. He was running tours of the gorges, out from Wittenoom, and every day the Flying Doctor base at Port Hedland would call, just to check that everything was okay. My brother had two vehicles so, if he was out on tour, at a certain given time the Flying Doctor base would call me and I'd just answer, 'Whisky ... go ... go' or whatever. I just can't remember what my call signal was now. But that was my first experience.

Then I became a member of the Wittenoom St John's Ambulance. We had a pretty old ambulance and there were just a few locals and we'd get called out if there was an accident or whatever. Like, at one time, a man was riding a motor bike up the gorge, with his girlfriend as a pillion. They were from the caravan park. He was sixty-six and she was sixty-four, I think. Anyway, a kangaroo jumped out and hit him. Bang, over they went and he broke his tibia and fibula.

Luckily, both the girlfriend and the motor bike weren't too badly damaged so the girlfriend rode into town, in the moonlight. She wasn't a small lady either, and she went to the power house, where the generators were, and the guy there called us. So out we went in the old ambulance to find this bikie. Anyhow, we patched him up the best we could and got him back to town then we called the Flying Doctor to fly out and pick him up. So that was one occasion.

But even I had to use the Flying Doctor. See, we'd had a lot of rain and the creeks were flooded right near the town so I drove out for a swim with the dog. Anyway, when I got out of the car, I felt this sting on my leg. At first I didn't take much notice, but went I hopped in the water, all my hands and feet started burning. I knew something was wrong then, so I hopped back in the car and drove straight back to town. By the time I got back home I was in a real mess. As it turned out, I'd been bitten by a marsh fly. I think that's what they're called ... or maybe it's a march fly. They're like big blow flies that come around after the rain and, as I found out, I'm extremely allergic to their bite.

So I raced inside and called the Flying Doctor. We had a RFDS medical chest in town; you know, one of those huge boxes that contain all the various medications and so forth, which, mind you, you were supposed to check regularly, just to make sure nothing was out of date. Anyhow, the doctor said to get some

Phenergan: that's an antihistamine. So the girl that had the medical chest, I called her and she brought some Phenergan over and gave it to me.

'There you go, that should fix it,' she said.

But it didn't because the itch—the irritation—didn't go away, at all. Then she took a look at the Phenergan and said, 'Oh, this's only a child's dosage and, what's more, it's out of date.'

So then I had to call the doctor back again and he was very upset. 'Well,' he said, 'is there anyone there that can give you an adrenaline injection?'

Now, I had a small amount of medical knowledge, enough to give myself an injection, but my partner at the time, he said that he'd give it a go, which is typical of males ... trying to be the hero. So I sorted out the injection for him and handed it over.

'What do I do now?' he asked.

Typical. And so I just held my leg up and said, 'Put it in there.'

So he gave me an adrenaline injection and that settled everything down. Then the next day—and you won't believe this—I'm sitting in my lounge room and another marsh fly landed on my arm and it bit me. And, oh, the side of my mouth, my tongue, everything was swelling up and I had to call the Flying Doctor straight away, again. So I had another adrenaline injection then and I had to have another one the next day because the reaction to that bite was far worse the second time around.

And that's what I mean: you know, if I was in, virtually, any other town I'd just go down to the local pharmacy and tell them that I needed adrenaline and ask them to keep it in stock at all times—and there'd be no problems. So it's in situations like that when you realise that you're a long way from anywhere.

Then, another time, we had a man. I won't mention his name, but he was a local, in his sixties, and he'd previously had an operation for throat cancer. He'd had his voice box removed so that when he spoke he had to hold a cloth over this hole in his throat. Anyway, we didn't know it then but they'd apparently given him all the treatment they could and they'd said, 'Well, sorry, but that's the best we can do for you.'

So it was January and, you know, up there in the north, you get stinking hot temperatures. We had visitors from Austria, as well as my daughter from Sydney, all staying at my place at that time. We'd all had a few drinks when I got a call from the partner of the bloke who had throat cancer, to say that he'd collapsed and there was blood everywhere.

It was in the middle of the night by that stage and when we went down to their place we found out that the woman had been sleeping at one end of the house and her partner was sleeping up the other. Apparently, he'd woken up when he knew that something terrible had gone wrong and he was stumbling about, trying to find his way out to the woman, and he'd collapsed in the kitchen, near the fridge. What'd happened was that the veins had burst in his throat where the cancer was, so there was blood all over the walls where he was trying to find the light switches. It was dreadful. So we called the Flying Doctor straight away.

In those days the RFDS was still flying into Wittenoom and we had lights and everything at the airstrip. So some people went out there in the old ambulance and turned the lights on and waited for the plane to arrive and bring the doctor back in. The bloke had stopped bleeding by then so we got him back into bed.

Anyhow, when they brought the doctor back from the airstrip, the first thing he said was, 'Why didn't you clean him up?'

'Well,' I replied, 'we weren't game to touch him because there's just blood everywhere.'

And so we loaded him into the ambulance and we all went back out to the airstrip and we helped to get him on the plane. I can tell you, I breathed a real sigh of relief when I saw that Flying Doctor's aircraft begin to taxi down the airstrip to get ready for take-off. I had the man's partner beside me. I was trying to comfort her. But then, all of a sudden, the plane stopped and it turned around and it came back to where we were.

Apparently, as they were getting ready to take off, the woman's partner had started bleeding again. The doctor said that that's the way people with throat cancer go in the end. The blood vessels in their throat burst and you can't do anything about it, so the doctor had said, 'No, this isn't going to work. We're too late.'

So they came back and they got her this time and they took her off with them to the hospital at Port Hedland. Then I thought that, with all the heat, you can't just leave it so I went back to their house and I tried to clean up all the blood. That was about two or three o'clock in the morning, and he died in Port Hedland. So the doctor knew that he wouldn't last the night. Then someone drove up there, to Hedland, the next day and they brought the woman home. But at least she was with him when he died.

Touched My Heart

Talking from the viewpoint of an ex-RFDS pilot, I guess you always remember the times that touched your heart or touched you emotionally or whatever. One very poignant story in that vein was a call we got in at our Port Hedland base to go to Geraldton, which is on the coast, about 300 or 400 kilometres north of Perth. And understand that in Western Australia we've got RFDS bases in Jandakot, which is in Perth, then there's Kalgoorlie, Port Hedland, Meekatharra and Derby. And I think there might've even still been a base at Carnarvon back when this happened because then they closed Carnarvon down in the early to mid '90s.

But yes, we were called in to pick up this young sixteen-year-old girl who'd been riding her push-bike in a storm and she turned in front of a car and got hit. She was declared brain dead but they had her on life support just to keep her body alive, and our job was to pick her up in Geraldton then take her down to Perth where they were going to harvest her organs.

But the thing was that the girl's parents came down in the aeroplane with us. And I could only imagine just how difficult it must've been for those parents, to have this happen to their gorgeous daughter and, you know, she didn't look marked at all. She was just beautiful and, of course, being only sixteen it had been the parents' call to allow her body to be made available for the harvesting of organs.

The thing is, I've got daughters as well and I just couldn't help thinking if I would've been able to make that same decision. You know, whether or not to donate their organs, especially at a time like that. Because how on earth, as a parent, could you work your way through a logical process to reach such a clear decision when it's all compounded with the trauma of the accident and everything else?

Then, what's more, once that decision had been made, they chose to come along with us and sit in the aeroplane beside their daughter, who, as I said, was on life support. Oh, they were just so brave, strong and wonderful. I just so admired them. My heart went out to them, having to sit in that aeroplane for the hour or so's flight time, looking at their beautiful, unmarked, young daughter and knowing that it'll be the last time they'll ever see her.

So, that's one that really touched my heart and, I guess, another one I'll remember forever is when I was with the check and training captain. That's when you go out on a normal call and the check and training captain comes along to have a look at what you're doing and how well you're doing it. Then after the flight's over, you sit down together and you're given a précis of your performance. You know, if there's anything that could've been done better or worse or whether it was all fantastic.

Anyway, I was working at Port Hedland at that time and we actually got called out to Geraldton to pick someone up. Along with the check and training captain, we had a doctor and a nurse with us. You understand that not all flights normally have a doctor on board, but we happened to have one on that particular day.

Now, I can't remember what that particular Geraldton retrieval was for, but, while we were there, we got an emergency call to say that there was a lady at Carnarvon who was bleeding internally. Apparently she'd been in hospital there for a while and they hadn't had any success stemming the bleeding. And so they'd used up their supply of blood and it was imperative that someone get her down to Perth quickly, where there were more blood supplies.

So we shot up to Carnarvon straight away. When we landed at Carnarvon, the doctor and the nurse went into the hospital to try and stabilise the patient enough to bring her out to the airstrip. Anyway, they did that and they brought her out to the Carnarvon Airport. The story was that she'd given birth to a baby two weeks beforehand and she had post-partum bleeding. See, when the afterbirth comes away, the patient normally stops bleeding. But this woman didn't stop bleeding. She was thirty-four years old and this was her ninth child.

We'd already been in contact with the medical authorities in Perth to make them fully aware of the urgency of the situation. To that end, they were going to meet us, with the blood supplies and a full medical team, as soon as we landed at Jandakot Airport.

Now, when they put the woman in the aeroplane and I sat in the pilot's seat, the stretcher was sort of close behind me, to my right. And as we were about to take off, this poor woman reached her arm back and grabbed my hand and she said to me, 'I'm scared.'

And like you'd naturally do, I replied, 'It'll be okay. Everything'll be alright. We're on our way. We'll have help for you in less than an hour.'

Anyway, we wasted no time in getting going and on our way down to Jandakot we got all sorts of special flight clearances through military controlled airspace and so on. So we went the most direct and quickest route possible and, what's more, I had the throttle to the wall, so to speak. Also, as we got nearer, they even cleared the air traffic in the Jandakot zone.

Then, just one or two minutes from Jandakot, the doctor said, 'She's died.'

Still, we went straight in and landed and I taxied very quickly to where the medical team was waiting. I pulled up and before the engines had even stopped, people were in the aeroplane trying to revive her. And they tried to get her going again for about forty minutes. But they just weren't successful. She was dead. They just weren't successful.

And I'll remember that for as long as I live. That was a real toughie. It was just so sad. But, you know, I'm sure that every pilot and every doctor and every nurse has got a similar story or two to tell. So, I guess, the thing you've got to keep reminding yourself is that our success rate is a hell of a lot higher than our failure rate.

Tragedies

It must be stressed that tragedies do happen, and over my twenty or so years of flying for the RFDS there are two that immediately come to mind. Perhaps the saddest event in which I ever had to be involved was an accident that occurred at King Junction Station, which is west of Cairns, on the Mitchell River. It was January, in the middle of the wet season. And for some strange reason, even though the wet season's the time when people aren't as busy on their property as they normally might be, it always seems that, if anything wrong is going to happen, it always happens in the 'wet'.

Anyway, Ray Piggott had a high-winged, single-engine Cessna 182 in which he'd been out inspecting the property. Two of his children, a boy and a girl, heard his plane returning home and so they decided to go down on their little motor bike to greet him. The boy was on the front of the bike, the girl on the back.

It was just on sunset and Ray was landing into the east, which meant that the sun was directly behind him. He was on final approach when the children arrived at the airstrip. But because they were looking into the sun's rays, of course, they were blinded to the approaching aeroplane. Then, just as Ray was about to touch down, the children rode across the airstrip about 100 metres in front of him. By the time Ray saw his children, it was too late.

There was nothing he could do. It was a one in a million chance and he collided with the bike. Though they missed the prop and the wing, the tail of the plane knocked the children from their motor bike. As it turned out, the young son, who was on the front, was only slightly injured but the daughter was badly knocked about.

The RFDS was called and I flew out at once in the Queen Air with a doctor and a flight nurse. It was dark when we arrived at King Junction. I'm not sure if it was raining, but I remember it was still very wet. Anyhow, they'd organised for some cars to light the airstrip and all went well with the night landing. The doctor attended the patients and reported that the daughter was in a dangerous condition; critical, in fact.

So we loaded both of the children onto the plane, ready for the trip back to Cairns. All looked well for a quick evacuation but then, on taxiing for take-off, we struck a spring, which had caused a soft patch to form on the airstrip. Of course, in the dark it's impossible to see such a thing. Anyway, we got bogged.

Fortunately the Flying Padre, Reverend Tony Hall-Matthews, had flown in that afternoon after he'd heard about the accident. And so, when they saw we were bogged, Tony drove up to our aircraft. We told him that we were well and truly stuck. One main wheel and part of the nose wheel were bogged so it was going to be some time before we dug ourselves out.

With the young girl being in such a critical condition, it was imperative that she reach specialist medical help as soon as humanly possible, so I asked Tony, 'Would you be able to fly the girl back into Cairns?'

Tony had never done anything like this before but his immediate reply was, 'Yes' and he was only too happy to declare it a mercy flight in the hopes of saving the daughter's life. So then we were able to transfer Ray's daughter and her mother on to Tony's aircraft, and I think the Nursing Sister as well, and they flew off to Cairns.

It then took us a couple of hours to dig the much heavier Queen Air out of the bog. Well, we ended up virtually lifting and pulling it out with a tractor, then Ray drove the tractor down the strip so that I could follow him and not get bogged again. Remember, of course, all this was going on in the dark. But then once all that was done we flew the young boy to Cairns.

Unfortunately, the next day we were advised that the daughter had died of her injuries in Cairns Base Hospital. But during an emergency situation like that, of course, you're always so busy that there's little time to stop and think. However, afterwards, I spent quite some time contemplating the terrible impact the accident had on that family, especially for Ray, being the father and pilot of the aircraft that hit the children, and also, of course, the poor mother who had lost a child in such tragic circumstances.

Another event that had a profound effect on me was the death of the Cape York grazier Fred Shepherd. I knew both Fred and his wife, Ruth, very well. They were good people and had been great mates all their lives. They worked hard together and they worked well together. Then late one afternoon we had a call to go to Marina Plains Station, north of Cairns, near Princess Charlotte Bay.

Again, it was the wet season. Fred and Ruth had been out contract mustering for the manager of the property, Louis Komsich. Fred was thrown from the horse and the horse had rolled on him. Things didn't look too good at all and we got there as quickly as we could. From memory, I think it was about an hour and a half flying time from Cairns to Marina Plains, maybe not even quite that.

Anyway, it was after sunset when we arrived for the evacuation. There were no hills and I knew the area very well. I also knew the airstrip well so I felt that, with it being such a delicate emotional situation for those on the ground, I could land safely enough without giving them the extra burden of having to put out flares to light the airstrip.

We landed safely and the only people present were Fred's wife, Ruth, and Louis Komsich was also there. Louis was very upset at what had happened and Ruth, though she exhibited a practical side, was extremely distraught. With darkness closing in, the doctor immediately attended to Fred and suggested that, even though there was little hope of Fred surviving, we should get him away from there as soon as possible.

At that point I felt it hardly appropriate of me to ask a woman—especially someone's wife, who'd just witnessed such a terrible accident—to go and put out flares so that I could take off. It'd only be more upsetting for both Ruth and Louis, plus it'd waste precious time. So knowing the area as well as I did, I decided I'd take off by using just my landing lights.

Having made that decision, we next had to solve the issue of a mob of cattle and some horses roaming on the airstrip, and I did ask Louis to drive a car down to clear the area. When that was done my landing lights proved sufficient light to guide me down the strip and I took off without any problems, leaving Ruth and Louis behind. Unfortunately, on our way to Cairns the doctor confirmed that Fred had died of his horrific injuries. This was extremely upsetting to me because, as I said, I knew the Shepherds very well. But at least I knew I'd done everything in my power to give them the best possible help.

Then about a week or so later the DCA (Department of Civil Aviation) called me in. Apparently, the doctor who was on board with me—and I won't mention names—had written a report to them saying that he was frightened about my taking off without the extra guidance of flares. This was deemed to be a dangerous manoeuvre by the DCA and I hadn't met department requirements.

I strongly disagreed because I never did anything that I didn't know I was capable of doing. I didn't take any risks. It might've seemed that way in a written report to someone like the DCA, but because of my extensive experience in charter work and many years of flying in the bush, what I'd done was a perfectly safe manoeuvre for someone like me. In the worst case, if I'd had an engine failure or anything like that after take-off, it wouldn't have been any problem in turning around on one engine and get on to final approach again and land with the landing lights. So basically, it didn't worry me one scrap.

Anyhow, I was called to Brisbane. I walked into the room. There were two people there from the DCA and they started to question my 'irresponsible behaviour'. So I explained that the reason I hadn't asked for flares to be put out was that for me to have had those people to go running around and organising flares would've been even more upsetting in the situation, especially for Ruth. Plus, of course, it would've been wasting more precious time. Then to finish off I simply stated to them, 'Well,' I said, 'taking all that into consideration, what decisions would you have made under those same circumstances? You've got an extremely upset man. Plus, you've got a distraught wife with a dying husband. So what do you expect me to do; just sit there and do nothing?'

Well, they didn't have an answer to that. They were silent for some time then they sort of, almost, congratulated me and said, 'Well, Mr Darby, we won't be going any further with this so you won't hear from us again.'

And I think from then on they had a much deeper understanding and a much more tolerant attitude towards that which was reported to them as having been 'irresponsible behaviour'.

Two in One

Now, I've had a couple of story ideas about my time as a pilot with the RFDS and one incident occurred with my Flight Nurse, Penny, who was by then my wife—still is, of course.

We were living up at Derby, in the north-east of Western Australia, and, well, we started our clinic circuit at 6.30 on the morning of 31 December, when we took off in the Queen Air aeroplane from the Derby RFDS base and went to Fitzroy Crossing. That's about a fifty-minute flight. We did a few hours clinic work there at Fitzroy, then we went on to do the clinic at Halls Creek.

It was late afternoon by the time we'd finished at Halls Creek. Then on our way back home to Derby we were asked to divert back to Fitzroy Crossing to pick up a patient. So we did that, we returned to Fitzroy, picked up the patient and then flew back home to Derby. This was now New Year's Eve.

Anyhow, we were invited over to our next-door neighbour's place for a champagne and chicken dinner, to celebrate the coming New Year. It'd been a bit of a day for Penny and I and so we were both really looking forward to that. So we got home, had a shower and we were just about to get dressed when the phone rang. It was the Derby base and they said, 'Look, Jan, sorry, but the patient you picked up from Fitzroy Crossing has deteriorated and we really need to get them to Perth.'

So it was goodbye to the chicken and champagne. Instead, we threw on some gear, rushed back out to the airport, loaded the patient, strapped ourselves in the Queen Air again and we took off at about 8.30 that night. Things were going pretty well until around Mount Newman, where we hit line after line of thunderstorms. At the time I remember using the descriptive expression that the lightning was 'hitting the ground like a picket fence'.

But the outside action was almost overshadowed by the turmoil going on in the back of the aeroplane. Being subjected to such severe turbulence the rear end of the plane was virtually fish-tailing as we were flying along. Of course, that didn't help things much at all because before long the doctor who we had on board with us soon became all but unconscious through airsickness, which left Penny as the only person still 'standing'. So there she was, being tossed around, desperately trying to keep the patient's neck immobilised by placing sandbags around the head to support the foam neck brace.

It was just after midnight when we landed in Meekatharra en route to Perth and it already felt like we'd been to hell and back, so to speak. But much to our relief, the Flying Doctor crew at the Meekatharra base very kindly came out to greet us with a cup of coffee and best wishes for the New Year. No, it wasn't chicken and champagne, but still it was greatly appreciated. In fact, that particular cup of coffee was absolutely bloody marvellous.

We then refuelled at Meekatharra before we took off and we headed on and arrived in Perth, to deliver our patient, just before dawn on New Year's Day. But by the time we landed, I estimated that Penny and I had been on duty for something like nineteen continuous hours, which is something that you'd never be allowed to do these days of far more strict regulations. And to the best of my knowledge, the patient survived and—you could say for effect that—the doctor who'd been so airsick on the journey took a little longer to get over the experience.

And that story—and it's a true one at that—could well be called, something along the lines of, 'Talk About Tour of Duty' or 'Happy New Year.'

So that was one story. Now, the other one you could possibly title something like, 'Did you feel the pain?'

That came about after we'd been out to Balgo Hills Mission for a routine medical clinic. Balgo's away out into the Tanami Desert area of Western Australia, over near the Northern Territory border. Again, I was flying the Queen Air and we were returning to Derby. Anyhow, we'd climbed to cruising altitude and we were about halfway home when Derby Flight Service Unit called and asked me to call the Flying Doctor on their discreet frequency, at the RFDS base in Derby. I did that and on came our base director who said, 'Jan, we've got a bad one back at Lake Gregory. It's an injured stockman. Have you got enough fuel to go back?'

'Yes, Jim,' I said, 'I've enough fuel for that.'

'Goodo,' he said, 'can you give us an ETA [estimated time of arrival]?'

So I gave Jim an ETA and I turned the Queen Air around and headed to Lake Gregory to pick up this seriously injured stockie.

For those that don't know, Lake Gregory's right out in that rotten bulldust country. You know the stuff I mean? It's very soft and dirty, sandy soil. Terrible stuff. Anyhow, we duly landed and we got the stretcher poles and the canvas and we set off in a flat-bed truck, across country to where this injured stockie was. On the way out we were told that a horse had thrown him, then it'd rolled on him, then it'd got up and tap-danced all over him, before galloping off into the bush. In the process the horse had pushed the poor old bugger half underground into this bulldust and, from their description, it seemed that the horse had broken practically every bone in his body.

By the time we arrived, the stockie was still lying there, sunken into this bulldust, and he was not looking too well, at all. In fact, the only sign of life was that he had a tiny, wee, thin roll-your-own weed drooping from his lips, from which rose the occasional wisp of smoke. So, no, things didn't seem too good.

But I must say, he looked like a tough old bugger. If I had to give a description of him, I'd liken him to a piece of old mulga. You know those old wizened mulga trees that've been stripped bare of leaves, where the wood's gone all grey and it's as hard as an old railway line? He was like that; the classic old stockman, as tough as you can make them.

Anyhow, as they were trying to gently slip the canvas under him, to lift him up out of the bulldust, I could see that the old feller was obviously in very great pain. And so, I guess, to give the poor old bastard a little bit of moral encouragement, I leaned across and gently said to him, 'How're you goin' mate?'

And I'll never forget it; he looked up at me with his watery, fading eyes, the excruciating pain etched into every crease of his weather-beaten face, and he took another tiny breath on his weed and he wheezed, 'Not too good, mate.'

Oh shit, the poor bastard. I just about wept at the situation. But he did survive. We put him on the back of the truck and drove him back to the Queen Air and we flew him to Derby Hospital and, eventually, he walked out of town and most probably went back to doing the only thing he knew how to do, stock work and riding horses.

Two Lumps

After I'd finished my Midwifery I went over to Western Australia with a girlfriend. We worked at Derby and we went out to Fitzroy Crossing and also to Halls Creek, sometimes. So that's when I really started to admire the work that the girls were doing in the Australian Inland Mission. The AIM, as it was known, was part of John Flynn's vision of a Mantle of Safety, which not only included the Royal Flying Doctor Service but also linked into the on-ground health and spiritual services.

Then, when I came home from Western Australia, I contacted the AIM and I finished up working at Cape York, up on the tip of the Cape York Peninsula, for two years. I was a bit wet behind the ears when I first went up there, but it was an amazing adventure for a young woman, and a very educational one as well. And when you're stuck out there, in such an isolated place like that, and you strike a real tough problem well, I can tell you, the sound of that Flying Doctor Service King Air aeroplane coming in to land, you know, it was music for the soul.

So that's where this story takes place: up at Cape York, on a big Aboriginal reserve.

I was the nursing sister at the little hospital there that was run by the Australian Inland Mission. That also included a hostel for school children. Basically, a lot of the work I was doing was what the average mother would do at home: you know, cleaning up cuts and scratches and things like that. Still, you had to keep a pretty close eye on things because you couldn't, say, give the Aborigines the whole course of antibiotics at once because they'd either take them all at once or share them around with everyone else. So you had to have them come back a couple of times a day to take their antibiotics.

And I must say, most of it wasn't too stressful. But, of course, you had to be able to cope with whatever came in and having that doctor on the end of the radio, when you really needed help, was a godsend. At the Mission, we had a scheduled chat with the Flying Doctor from the Cairns RFDS base, once or twice a day, on the radio. How it worked was that the doctor conducted a medical session and, if you had a problem, you discussed it over the radio with him and he worked out what he thought was wrong, then advised you as to what medication to take out of the RFDS medical chest. Of course, something that was very important was that, when you were talking to the doctor, you had to be anatomically correct or else it could well lead to a wrong diagnosis.

At that time, David Cook was the main doctor for the RFDS at Cairns. I'm not exactly sure just how many other doctors there were, but whenever one of them went on holidays or whatever, Drr Tim O'Leary used to take over. I think by then, Tim had been elevated to being an administrative person. But he still much preferred getting out and about rather than sitting in an office.

Tim was an excellent doctor and had my utmost admiration as a diagnostician. He was also a real character, so, when he was on the radio, everybody used to listen in because of his great entertainment value. Mind you, those very same people secretly dreaded being the person on the receiving end of some of Tim's wit.

And that leads into this story.

It was around Christmas time—the wet season—so there was a lot of humidity around and a bit of thunder activity. All this was playing havoc with radio communications and, when that happened, you had to have somebody relay the messages on, because the radio signals weren't strong enough to get through to Cairns. So I was actually relaying messages and a call came through from the CSIRO research station at Somerset, which was just a little south of Cape York. It was from this young feller who was working up there for a few months. He'd been out in the field and he'd developed a problem so he'd radioed in for a diagnosis from, as it just so happened, Dr Tim O'Leary.

As usual, when you first got on the radio, you gave the doctor your personal details like your name, age, sex and so forth. Of course, I'm relaying messages backwards and forwards over the radio and, of course, all those who could were glued to their radios as well, because they knew that when Tim was on the line, there'd be some good entertainment.

So this young feller gave Tim all his personal details, then Tim asked, 'And what seems to be the problem, son?'

'I felt a pain between my legs, Doctor, so I put my hand down the front of my trousers and I discovered two large lumps, Doctor.'

'So, you've got two lumps between your legs, son.'

'Yes, Doctor.'

'Are you sure that there's two of them, son?'

There was a brief silence followed by the young feller saying, 'Yes, Doctor, I'm sure that there's two lumps between my legs.'

And Tim, being the wily old Irishman that he was, replied, 'And how old did you say you were, son?'

'Twenty-three, Doctor.'

And Tim's voice comes back over the radio with a poorly disguised laugh, 'Well, son,' he said, 'all I can say is that if you've got to be twenty-three years old and you've only just found out that you've got two lumps between your legs then you have my very deepest sympathy.'

And you know, there was dead silence—a pregnant pause, you could say—much to the embarrassment of this young feller. Then after everybody had settled down, questions and answers flew backwards and forwards and, in fact, as it turned out, this young chap had an infected wound on his foot, which, in turn, had caused the swelling of the glands in his groin. So that's what I mean about having to be anatomically correct when you were talking to the Flying Doctor, Tim O'Leary in particular.

Victorian Connections

Just because you live in a state like Victoria, with its small land area and very little outback, it's no reason to assume that you don't have the need for the Royal Flying Doctor Service, and I'll tell you why.

It was New Year's Eve 1994, very early, at about two o'clock in the morning when we got the telephone call from my youngest son, Ian, who lived in Western Australia, to say that my other son, Neil, had had this accident on Rottnest Island.

It's quite a long story really, but Neil was on Rottnest holidaying with his family. In fact, I'd spoken with him just the day before, on his mobile, and he was saying just what a great time they were all having. But Neil's wife had gone back to the mainland to keep an appointment that day and Neil had stayed there, on Rottnest, with their children. Neil, his wife and their children had a cabin, and some, practically, life-long friends were also there, staying in another cabin, with their children. Neil had spent that day with his close friends and all the children had been playing games and what-not. Then by night, all the children were tired so they went to bed in Neil's friend's cabin and, as Neil rode off on a bicycle to go back to his own cabin, they said, 'We'll meet you on the beach tomorrow.'

On Rottnest Island they only have push-bikes. There's no motor traffic on the island apart from the official stuff like a few buses and what-have-you. So that's what Neil was riding, a push-bike.

It was a downhill ride from Neil's friend's cabin and we simply don't know what happened. Neil could've hit a quokka (small wallaby), because they move around at night, or maybe the front wheel could've gone into a hole, because the place wasn't lit. Well, it is lit now, but it wasn't then. The police also ruled out foul play because his wallet and everything was still in his pocket when he was found.

So, we don't actually know what caused Neil to have the accident, but he went straight over the handlebars and fell on his head. The bike wasn't even damaged. This was before helmets were compulsory. After that they did make helmets compulsory. But he fell on his head, which rendered him unconscious, and the strange thing was, there wasn't even a mark on him, so he wasn't injured in any other way.

Luckily, a nursing sister and her husband were walking back from the town and that's when they found Neil, lying unconscious. Of course, they didn't know at that time if it could've been the result of foul play. But if they hadn't found Neil he might well have laid there until daylight and he could've died. The nursing sister could tell that there was a real problem, so she got her husband to ride back into town, on Neil's bike, to get help from the police and a doctor, which he did, and also an ambulance drove out to as near as they could, to pick up Neil.

Rather than wait until morning, the Flying Doctor was called and they took Neil straight to Jandakot Airport. Then, I suppose, he was transported by ambulance from there to Sir Charles Gairdner Hospital, where he was put on life support. And that's when we got the call.

Anyhow, my eldest son, who was with me at the time, he and I flew from Victoria to Western Australia on the first plane we could get, and my two daughters followed on a later flight.

But the brain injury was too great. Neil was kept alive until we all arrived, but he never regained consciousness. Then two days later, after all the various tests were done, he was pronounced brain dead. By that time the whole family was there. But one thing that I am thankful for is that, if it wasn't for the Flying Doctor Service, Neil would never have reached the hospital alive and we would have never have reached his side in time.

Neil had just turned forty, the previous October, and I'd been over for his birthday party and he was as fit as a fiddle; a fine physical specimen. But people were not all that conscious of organ donation back then. It wasn't publicised as it is now, so I asked, 'Did Neil sign his licence as an organ donor?'

And the answer was, 'No.'

I said, 'Well, I feel that he should be an organ donor.'

And there were a couple of ums and ahs.

I said, 'He's going to be cremated, isn't he? What good is his body going to be? You're not going to preserve it, if it's cremated.'

Of course, the organ donor people were there at the hospital, as were Neil's doctors, and Neil's doctors said, 'We want you to understand that we're always here for the patient and we don't have any connection with the organ donor people, so it must be your decision.'

Then we found out that Neil also had an unusual blood group and I said to the doctor, 'How's that possible? My husband and I had perfectly ordinary blood groups and I know that Neil's my son and I know my husband was his father.'

'Well,' the doctor said, 'that's quite possible. It's not unusual.'

So finally the family came around to my way of thinking as regards to organ donation. And there was, in fact, a heart patient—a family man—with that same blood group, who was waiting and then there were two kidney people, and Neil's bone tissue was also used. But they don't take any organs that aren't being waited for. His liver wasn't taken. The only organs that were required at the time were the ones they took.

And that was all made possible because of the speed with which Neil had been transferred to Perth by the Flying Doctor Service—that his organs were then available to be donated to people awaiting transplants. That, at least, gives us some comfort. And, oddly enough, Neil's organs were flown back to the eastern states; back to where he was born. So that was a strange one. But it was quite a remarkable thing and I do believe it helps the healing process—it really does— to know that the body is being used, and is made possible, to save someone else's life.

In actual fact, I had a wonderful letter sent through the organ donor people. You don't have any direct contact with the people who have received organs, but this lovely letter arrived and it said that this particular person—I don't even know if it was a man or a woman—was looking at two legs, of the same length, for the first time in their life. And after a little more rehabilitation they were hoping to walk perfectly normally, for the first time in their life. And that was such a wonderful letter to receive. What's more, Neil's two children have grown up into the most delightful people, extremely well adjusted, and we all keep in close touch.

So that was one story. Now, there's a second part to our close Victorian connection with the RFDS and it was that our granddaughter, Melissa—the daughter of my oldest son—was living on the central coast of Western Australia, at Carnarvon. Her husband was actually teaching there and, in 2001, six years after Neil's accident, Melissa was riding a friend's horse and the horse slipped. It came down with her on it, and her leg was crushed under the horse. The only way Melissa could get back for help was to get back up on the horse, which she managed to do with great difficulty.

As it turned out, Melissa's leg was very badly broken and it needed a lot of work on it, as did her ankle. A rod was put in and all sorts of things, so she was literally screwed up. But the thing was, she kept on being terribly sick. I mean really, really sick and the doctors said, 'Well, you don't get sick with a broken leg.'

An ultrasound proved that Melissa, unbeknown to herself, was six weeks pregnant, which was why she was being so sick. So then they stopped all her treatment immediately because, being pregnant, she couldn't have any more X-rays.

But it's 900 kilometres from where she was at Carnarvon to the Royal Perth Hospital and the Royal Flying Doctor Service flew her up and down on numerous occasions and, as you'll know, they never charge. They were quite wonderful, and she flew up and down with her leg in plaster for a lot of the time she was pregnant.

Actually, she spent a lot of time on those crutches because her leg was so crooked she couldn't walk properly. She had a terrible time. But now, I've got a beautiful great-grandson. I go to Western Australia as often as possible, especially for birthdays, Christmas and weddings. And that's just one of my great-grandchildren. I've got another three in Melbourne.

And so that's why I, for one, Lady Ena Macpherson, am such a staunch supporter of the RFDS.

Water, Water, Everywhere But ...

Lionel: It was in about 2000 when all this happened. If we did the trip now we'd go later because I remember it was wintertime and it was freezing in the mornings and it was very wet. So I think it must've been around April or maybe a little bit earlier when we first set off from Nhill. There was just the three of us: Bill Day, Rex Bunge and myself—Lionel Ferris—and we only took one vehicle. The idea was to get up to Halls Creek, in the Kimberley region of Western Australia, then do the Canning Stock Route, which was something we'd talked about for quite a while.

Now, I'm just trying to think which way we went to get to Halls Creek because we were nearly a fortnight getting onto the stock route and another fortnight coming down. A lot of people go the other way, but we didn't. We started at the northern end and came back in the opposite direction, if you get what I mean. But Bill Day's got a fair account of it in his diary so you'd better let him fill in the gaps.

Bill: Well, before we start, you've sort of really got to know Lionel to appreciate what he's all about. He's a feller that consistently down-plays things. He's unassuming to the extreme. In other words, what anybody else thinks is an important story, he just brushes it off as if it's an everyday occurrence, or at least he tries to. Then he's also got one of those really dry, wry senses of humour. Like he used to be a helper on some of our outback tours and, on those trips, one of the first things we'd do was to get everyone together and let them introduce themselves by telling something about their life, and Lionel used to always rock them by saying that he left school at the age of thirteen because, by then, he was old enough to realise that it was severely interfering with his education.

So that's Lionel, and he's got lots of sayings like that. But he's a wizard musician—he can just about play anything—and yeah, he's probably told you he's a bachelor. And he's a collector and, believe me, if Noah kept two of everything, I reckon Lionel's gone one step better because I'd say he's got just about three of everything, and in all sorts of conditions. You just really need to meet him one day.

But yeah, that trip was quite an experience for him, I'm sure.

Okay, so we headed off from Nhill in western Victoria. There was only the one vehicle and three of us: myself, another chap by the name of Rex Bunge and Lionel. We went up through the Gawler Ranges, across the Stuart Highway, over the Oodnadatta Track to Oodnadatta, right up through Dalhousie Springs, then out to Andado Station. Andado's Molly Clarke's station. It's an extremely remote property out on the north-western edge of the Simpson Desert. Old Molly's the owner of the place. She's a bit over eighty now and she still lives out there. Then, from Andado we went back into Alice Springs for supplies and spent a couple of days there, then we crossed the Tanami Desert to Wolfe Creek, up to Halls Creek.

At Halls Creek we refuelled and so forth before we started off down the Canning Stock Route, and we were probably about four or five wells down when we heard that the stock route had been closed due to the wet weather. And boy-o-boy, was it wet. But we just kept plugging on because we'd heard that some people were still coming the other way. I mean, it wasn't totally impassable or anything like that and we weren't chopping the hell out of the place because most of the rain was down the bottom end, which we still had to get to, of course.

Then, not far from the bottom end, Lionel first started to show signs of getting, you know, something wrong with him. Yeah, just a bit of stress. And then, when he finally sort of said that he couldn't pass any urine I thought, 'Hello, we've got troubles here' because basically he had urine retention.

Lionel: Of course, had I known I was going to have all the trouble, well, I wouldn't have gone out into such an isolated area in the first place. But everything seemed to be working fine. Then as we went down the stock route I started having just a bit of trouble with my prostate. At first I didn't say anything because I thought it might spoil things for everyone. But then, on the last part of the journey down the Canning, we were actually camping on the station property and that's where it came on.

Still, I wasn't too bad for a while. You know, I'd go for a walk about every hour or so and that seemed to keep me going. But before too long I had to walk more often and then it got to the stage where I couldn't really walk at all and I just had to lay there. I couldn't drink or eat anything either, not that I felt like it, anyway, mind you. But I had no idea you could get so crook with something as simple as that.

So then, it sort of knocked me for six really, and that's when Bill and Rex decided they'd better get help. The trouble was, of course, we were still a long way from anywhere and so the first thing we had to think about was whether we'd go back or continue on. Anyway, I wasn't too keen on retracing our steps so we opted to go on.

Bill: It was in the evening when Lionel sort of realised he had trouble. Then the next morning I got on the RFDS radio to the Flying Doctor base at Meekatharra and they advised us to go to Wiluna where there was a doctor and a hospital.

So that's where we headed and because of the state of the track we did it with great difficulty. I tell you, I've never seen water running up hill, but it very nearly was, and it was still raining. Anyhow, we basically travelled non-stop to Wiluna and we got Lionel to the doctor there and they fitted a catheter to him, which relieved him greatly. And then, after the doctor removed the catheter, we thought, 'Alright, well, he'll be okay now.'

Still and all, the doctor suggested that we stay in Wiluna for two or three days just to keep an eye on things, which we did. Well, because of the wet conditions nobody was allowed out of town anyway so we had to stay there. In fact, it was so bad that the town had run out of fuel because no one could get in to supply them, and we were about the only ones that had any.

Lionel: Well, they finally got me to Wiluna and I went to see the doctor and he fitted me with a catheter until he thought he had me right. And I thought I was right, also. Everything seemed to be working as it should.

Bill: Lionel was quite convinced that he was fine by then, too. And after the doctor had given him the okay, we went to the coppers and they said, 'Righto, well, you're the only ones in town who's got fuel—if you want to go, you can.'

By then the track was okay, so we took off and headed south and we stayed at Leonora overnight. It was still raining but Lionel seemed to be going well so we said, 'Righto, we'll start out going home along the Anne Beadell Highway.'

So we told the coppers at Leonora where we were going and they said, 'Well, okay, but there's already been somebody stuck out there so, you know, be careful and let us know when you get through.'

'Okay,' we said and so we went out east of Leonora to a little mining village—I can't think of the name of the place now. Then about a day and a half later Lionel's problem returned, only, this time, it was far more serious. Anyhow, Rex and I had a bit of a talk about the whole thing and we decided that we really had an emergency situation on our hands. So we called up the RFDS again and I'm not exactly sure which base station we got in contact with. Kalgoorlie would've been the closest place but it mightn't have necessarily been the right time of the day for radio communications. Somehow I have an idea we couldn't get in contact with either Meekatharra or Kalgoorlie on the low frequency so we used either 6890 and we got in contact with Port Augusta or it might've been 6950 and we got on to Alice Springs. I can't remember which.

Anyway, they said, 'Where's the nearest airstrip?'

It was probably mid-afternoon by then, so we had to make a decision as to whether we'd go up to Neale Junction and north to Warburton or down south to Rawlinna, which is on the east-west railway line. Well, we had a bit of a think and we decided that if Lionel was really crook, then Rawlinna was at least heading on our way home.

Now, seeing that the radio conditions where we were at that time were not really good because of the bad weather and the lightning and so forth we arranged with the RFDS that we'd phone them when we got to Rawlinna. And so we set out toward Rawlinna and, I tell you, the rain just got heavier and heavier.

Lionel: The weather had come in by then and we had to go through some pretty heavy downpours and, with so much rain, it formed huge waterholes all along the track. But, fortunately, it was solid underneath. I was pretty crook by then and so I was lying down in the back of the vehicle, a Nissan Patrol, and, oh, it was very rocky. In fact, one of the blokes likened it to driving over an everlasting cemetery because it seemed as if we were going over rocks the size of tombstones.

So, yes, it was terribly rough, particularly for me in my condition, and also, of course, you couldn't see what was ahead of you, on the track, because there was so much water. Not only that, but another problem was that there were other tracks branching off the one we were on which confused the issue. Anyhow, luckily, Rex had brought his GPS—Global Positioning System—along and so we tracked ourselves with that, just in case we got lost. So we'd be going along and Rex would say, 'Take the track on the right.'

And sometimes Bill would say, 'Are you sure?'

And Rex would say, 'Yes, I think so.'

So it was a good job that Rex had that GPS because even though by now it was at night, we couldn't have navigated by the stars anyway, you see, because it was so overcast with all the rain.

Bill: Believe me, it was quite an eventful trip, in extremely difficult conditions, driving at night, through water, while trying to follow the track. To keep ourselves alert Rex and I took it in turns, driving two hours each. As for the state of the track, well, in the sandhill country it was alright but once we got out onto the actual Nullarbor Plain it got worse from the point of view that any shallow depression was covered with water. So where there was water racing across the track, before we attempted to drive through it, we had to get out and wade across to see how deep it was. And believe me, in the early hours of the morning it was freezing cold. What's more, you didn't know whether you were going to drop into a washaway or what.

Then we came across a huge stretch of water. It must've been at least a kilometre wide. So we tackled that and I can remember, at one stage, the headlights and the driving lights of the Nissan were completely under the water and we had just this dull brown glow in front of us. Anyway, when we finally came out the other side, we decided we'd call it quits for a while and have a bit of a spell. All this time, of course, Lionel had been trying to lie down in the back and, believe me, he was really crook. Anyhow he agreed and he said, 'Yeah, have a spell and try and get some sleep.'

So we did try to get some sleep, but we were under strict instructions that if Lionel got, you know, really, really bad, he'd better just wake us up and we'd get going again. And that's exactly what happened because we were in our swags for not less than an hour when he said, 'Look, I really don't like to do this, but we've gotta get a move on.'

Anyway, we got going again and the track was still difficult to locate because there were sheets of water everywhere. But we pushed on under very, very adverse conditions and the only way we could really navigate was to use a bit of a line with Rex's GPS.

So I can tell you, it was a pretty welcoming sight when we first saw the lights of Rawlinna, from about 25 kilometres out, because, until then, basically, we didn't know exactly where we were.

Lionel: I suppose the rain had finished by the time we got near Rawlinna, but there was still a fair amount of surface water about. We arrived in town about an hour before daylight and it was in the middle of winter, so it was a bit chilly. I remember there being a lot of light at Rawlinna. There was quite a large building, like a cafeteria or something, and that was still lit up. Then there was another building near the railway line that looked like people might be in, and another house further down. But there wasn't a soul in sight. Really, at that time of the morning it looked to be more or less like a ghost town.

Bill: We got into Rawlinna in the wee hours of the morning. It was just sort of that twilight time before sunrise and, at a rough guess, I'd say the temperature was about minus 3° or 4°, at least. It hadn't rained for about two or three hours and all the puddles were frozen over.

Anyhow, because I'd been to Rawlinna before, I knew where the telephone box was. So I got on the phone and that's where I made the biggest mistake ever. I didn't actually have the RFDS phone number so I thought, 'Well, the logical thing to do is to ring 000.'

Now, I don't know exactly where 000 rang, but I imagine it was Perth. And to use a very common expression, that's where the shit hit the fan—absolutely—because I just couldn't get on to anybody with any sense. The first bloke thought it was a hoax call. Well I took that as an insult and I gave him a serve over that one. Boy-o-boy, did I see red. Next I got on to somebody who told me that he didn't know where Rawlinna was because he couldn't find it on his computer screen. So I tried to tell him where it was. I mean, I could've easily lost my cool but I realised the urgency of the situation. Then eventually, that person put me onto the ambulance people at Kalgoorlie. God knows why he put me onto the ambulance people, but he did, and the bloke that was on duty there, in Kalgoorlie, was an English feller who'd only been in Australia for a fortnight, so the whole procedure started again.

'Where the hell's this Rawlinna?' he asked.

So I tried to explain to him where Rawlinna was then I said, 'Look, we're here, there's an airstrip here and we really need the Flying Doctor urgently.'

'Oh, no,' he said, 'I'll send out an ambulance. How far from Kalgoorlie is this place called Rawlinna?'

I said, 'It's probably 500 or 600 kilometres.'

'Oh, we could be there in a couple of hours.'

'More like half a day, mate,' I said. 'It's at least five hours and possibly more.'

'That'll be okay,' he said, 'we can get an ambulance straight out to him.'

Anyhow, I finally convinced him that it was a waste of time coming out in an ambulance. So then he put me onto the police station and the police realised that, yeah, well, this was quite an urgent problem and they'd better do something about it. So they told me to hold the line and the next thing I was talking to the RFDS and, boy-o-boy, what a relief that was because, by this stage, I'd say it would've taken at least an hour, or possibly more, just to get on to them. And I can assure you, by then, my feet were frozen up to the knees because you know how much protection you've got from the weather in one of those telephone boxes. To use another common expression, bugger-all!

Lionel: The telephone box was right beside the railway line, at the railway station, and Bill seemed to be taking forever in the telephone box, so it was well and truly daylight by then. He seemed to be having some sort of trouble or other but then, apparently, once he got in touch with the Flying Doctor Service, things really started to happen then. After the call we didn't spend much more time in the town because we went straight out to check the airstrip, to make sure it was safe for the plane to land.

Bill: Anyway, we had to do a check on the airstrip and that got a little bit confused as well because the RFDS told me that if I could drive up and down the airstrip at 85 kilometres an hour, in complete safety, that it'd be okay for them to land.

So I said, 'Righto, I'll do that and, if I can't do the safety drive, I'll give you a ring back and let you know.'

Well, we drove up and down the strip and there was no problem so I didn't bother to ring them back. But, what they should've said, or what I should've said was that I'd ring them back and advise them one way or the other as to the safety of the airstrip. But anyway that didn't happen so then there was another hold-up because they were waiting for me to ring back.

Then eventually, the RFDS must've rang a woman in at Rawlinna because she came out and she did the same as we did and she drove up and down the strip to check it. Then she disappeared and she must've rang them again because, the next thing, she came back out and she said, 'The Flying Doctor's on its way.'

Anyway, we lit a fire at the end of the airstrip so that they could get an idea as to which way the wind was blowing and then we sat there and waited in the cold around the fire until we heard an aircraft. By then, I'd say it was probably about half-past eight or nine o'clock and, oh, you should've seen the look of relief on Lionel's face when he heard that sound in the sky.

Lionel: It was a gravelly sort of an airstrip but quite good, apparently. You know, the plane came down and it sailed along fairly well. Then I had to wait until it had slowed down enough to turn around to come back and stop near where we were. It was quite a big plane;

a two-engine job. I've forgotten what type it was but it was quite an impressive sort of aircraft and it was all decked out like a hospital. There was a couch there to lay on and every nook and cranny had something in it, so I guess that they had everything they needed. Of course, they'd get some pretty awful cases to deal with at times so they've got to have enough room to airlift, at least, a couple of passengers back to hospital.

But when they saw me, they realised that I would've been in a lot of pain and, really, to be honest, I was feeling absolutely, terribly sick. So when I got inside the plane they put a catheter straight in, right up my penis. I don't remember the pain being that bad. Perhaps I was already in so much pain that I didn't really care any more. Anyhow, after they put the catheter in I started to get relief almost immediately. But the catheter was quite an ingenious affair; it was just a long tube that went from up in my penis, out into a bag, which had a tap on the end of it, and you just kept emptying the bag.

Actually, I thought I might've been sick for quite some time afterwards because they told Bill that, by then, the urine would've been starting to bank back from my kidneys and so forth. But I was fine, really. In fact, I was feeling pretty good by then.

Bill: Anyway, the RFDS aircraft landed and I could see Lionel struggling up the steps into the plane. The doctor was an English doctor who hadn't been out here all that long. I think he was sort of getting experience through the Flying Doctor Service. But anyway, he must've done a good job because within ten minutes Lionel came back out of the plane with a huge smile on his face. Oh, in fact, he just about ran down the steps. It was just absolutely unreal. So as soon as they, you know, put the catheter in and drained his bladder he was feeling 100 per cent.

Another thing—and this hasn't anything to do with Lionel and his problem—in the meantime, while all this was going on, Rex and I had been talking to the pilot, whose name was one you'd never forget: Robert E Lee. And, I tell you, he reckoned he'd had plenty of comments about that. But it turned out that he knew my next-door neighbour, back home in Nhill. She'd been a Nursing Sister with the RFDS in Kalgoorlie. So it's a small world, isn't it?

Lionel: The Flying Doctor hung around until it was obvious I was getting relief and then they took off and Bill, Rex and I, we just continued on our trip. Actually, I think we might've even gained a bit of time because Bill and Rex had been, virtually, driving both day and night, though you wouldn't want to do that if you didn't really have to. So we didn't alter our plans much other than we went south to the Cocklebiddy Caves and camped there that night and I was well enough to go down into the caves by the following day. So it's pretty amazing what they can do. Then we just carried on home.

Bill: So yeah, the whole show sort of finished there. Anyway, after they put the catheter in, the RFDS people shot through, then. And so Lionel had the catheter and away we went, heading for home. But we popped in to do a bit of caving on the way at a place called Cocklebiddy. And I can tell you, that's another nightmare trip from Rawlinna across to Cocklebiddy.

Anyway, we met a bloke just north of Cocklebiddy. He was the owner or manager or something of a station there called Arubiddy and, because it was getting late in the day and we couldn't find anywhere to camp, we sort of hoped that he might say, 'Oh, come up and camp at the homestead.'

But he didn't. All he said was, 'There's a reserve down by the caves where you can camp. You might be lucky because there's a South Australian caving expedition down there; a cave group, diving.'

So we went down there and camped in the scrub with the caving expedition and the next morning they invited us to use their ladder and their line, down to the water level in the caves. And so we went down there for about an hour and a half, and Lionel was real impressed with that. In fact, he reckoned it was the highlight of the trip, really.

But that was just typical of Lionel's sense of humour. And believe me, he has got a sense of humour. Because on the way home, across the Nullarbor— needless to say we had our swags so we'd just camp in them alongside the road—but Lionel reckoned that he had one over Rex and I because when we'd had too much to drink, Rex and I would be up and down out of our swags all night going for a leak. But, with the catheter in, Lionel didn't have to worry about that because he could just roll over and have a leak while he was still in his swag. And he thought that was great. He reckoned he was going to get one of those catheters put in as a permanent fixture.

Well Prepared

Both my husband, Peter, and I are members of the Q3 District of Lions, up here in Queensland. Lions is a service club that raises money for various charities and helps out wherever it can. It's a great organisation. You'll find them all throughout Australia.

Anyway, several years ago it was the habit of the District Governor of Q3 to get us all together and we'd do what we called A Lion's Safari. See, any of us who wanted to take some time, we'd all pile into a bus and off we'd go and visit the Western Region of Lions Clubs. And it was on one of these—an eight-day trip—that this particular incident happened.

They're a real social event these Lion's Safaris, they are. It's a very friendly atmosphere. We go around to many of the western towns and meet some really lovely people and, of course, we're always shown the various sites of all the places we visit. So we set off from Brisbane, on this eight-day trip, and we hit Charleville and, of course, we were taken out and shown the sights of the district. I remember we visited the Distance Education facilities there, and that was fascinating.

Then, of course, we went off to the Royal Flying Doctor base and we were shown around there, which was also extremely interesting. Oh, they showed us everything. We were even taken out to the aircraft hangar. Anyhow, there we were, strolling around the Flying Doctor hangar, when we noticed the plane they used. And one particular member of our Lions Club—we'll call him Charlie—well, he was particularly interested in aeroplanes and things.

He's really a lovely man, that's why I didn't want to mention his real name. But this Charlie, as I've called him, he wanted to know everything about the Flying Doctor's aeroplane and its operations, so he started asking lots and lots of questions. You know, you get those sorts of people on these tours, don't you?

Anyway, Charlie was asking about this and that, and that and this and, really, by that stage, as I said to my husband, Peter, 'Peter,' I said, 'I'm getting quite hungry.' And it looked like the others were getting quite peckish as well. But that didn't seem to register on Charlie because he kept on firing questions like, 'What altitude does it fly at?' and 'How fast does it go?', 'What's it's flying range?' and all those technical sorts of things.

So after he asked a lot of questions about the aircraft he then walked around it, for a closer inspection. 'Heavens it's small,' Charlie remarked, which it was. Then, at Charlie's request, they let us look inside the plane, and that really got his interest going. He asked about all the nobs and dials, and he examined this and that. 'Dear me,' he remarked, 'there's not much room inside, is there?'

'No, not really,' said the person who was showing us around. 'There's only enough room for the pilot, the doctor, the nurse and the stretcher for the patient.'

'Very interesting,' answered Charlie before he fired off another volley of questions.

Anyway, the visit to the Flying Doctor base finally ended, which, as I said, was very interesting, and we went to lunch. From memory, lunch was at the Lions Den. Of course, as with wherever we went, we were well catered for, so it was a beautiful meal, actually, and greatly anticipated by this stage, I can tell you.

So, there we were, enjoying our lunch, when Charlie got up for some reason or other and he suddenly collapsed over the table and, well, he couldn't move. Now, you always expect the worst in a situation like that, don't you? And in actual fact, it did look quite serious because nobody knew what the problem was.

'No, no, I'm alright,' Charlie kept saying. 'It's just the hip.'

But the thing was, he couldn't move. So we called the ambulance and the next thing we know an ambulance is screaming down and they come into the Lions Den to see to Charlie.

'Yes,' the ambulance people said, 'it's certainly his hip.'

Apparently, he'd previously had a hip operation, but it had a habit of popping out of its socket without any warning. And, well, if you're on a bus trip and you can't walk, well, you just can't carry on, can you? But of course, Charlie had to get home somehow, and we're 1000-odd kilometres, or whatever it is, from Charleville back to Brisbane, aren't we?

So, the ambulance loaded Charlie up and took him to hospital. And it was only a matter of getting the hip back in but the particular surgery, or whatever it was, to get the hip back into the socket could only be done in a Brisbane hospital. So the next day—and here's the irony of this story—the next day the Flying Doctor Service flew him back to Brisbane in the very same aeroplane that he'd taken so much interest in the day before.

As my husband, Peter, said, 'After asking all those questions about the plane and so forth, he was certainly well prepared to experience just what the Flying Doctor does, wasn't he?'

And, oh yes, they fixed him up in Brisbane. In actual fact, a nice end to the story is that a couple of days later we got the message that he was being sent home from hospital.

Where are You?

No matter how experienced you are as a pilot, sometimes you can get a bit caught out. The first time happened, back a few years ago, when I was flying for Aero-medical. That's before it was absorbed into the Royal Flying Doctor Service. Anyhow, Air Ambulance used to fly into a place called Kadina, which is a little town over on the Yorke Peninsula, in South Australia. But, with Kadina being located where it was and having a dirt strip, it was always very difficult to distinguish the actual airstrip from the land around it; you know, with the colour of the earth and everything.

This wasn't an emergency or anything, but, anyhow, the volunteer ambulance crew were on the ground at the Kadina airstrip with the patient, waiting for me to arrive. We were in radio contact so they could hear the aircraft coming in, but I was having difficulty finding the strip and I just needed a little time to get my bearings. What happens in a case like that is, us pilots would tell the ground crew that we were doing 'one zero minute's air work' in the area. Of course, all the other pilots had been in the same situation, so when they'd hear that someone was doing air work they'd have a great laugh. But the ambulance crew, nor the general public, weren't to know that air work was just an excuse to stall for time while you located the strip, because the last thing you want to admit to, as a pilot, is that you're lost.

So I'd just started trying to locate the strip and the woman from the volunteer ambulance crew must've seen the plane up in the air and so she came back over the radio and said, 'Air Ambulance. Air Ambulance, are you lost?'

Well, I mean, when something like that is broadcast over the radio network then every Tom, Dick, Harry and Mary knows that you're lost. So I came back and, in a very embarrassed manner, I replied with, 'Oh, I'm just having a little bit of difficulty in finding this strip.'

Then the ever-helpful woman from the ambulance crew comes back on again and she says, 'Air Ambulance, Air Ambulance, we're just over here.'

Which wasn't much help at all because, if you're in an aircraft and you're hundreds of feet or so above the ground and you can't even find the airstrip, how in the hell are you going to see someone waving at you to let you know that they're 'just over here'? Where's over here? So yes, that was a little embarrassing for me and it also made me realise that while these ambulance volunteers really do try their best, sometimes they just don't get it.

Another one, I suppose, that could cause confusion is the term to 'hold position'. I was coming down from Port Pirie to Adelaide one time and a similar sort of confusion over terminology happened en route. Now, when you're out and about, you often get diversions, and I was probably about 100 kilometres north of Adelaide—just a bit north of Port Wakefield—and I got a call that I had a Code One out of Renmark, which is over near the Victorian border, in the Riverland area of South Australia. A Code One's an urgent response.

Anyhow, I was just about to call up Traffic Control to alter my flight plan and request a diversion to Renmark, when a second phone call came into the RFDS base saying that they had another Code One out at Wudinna. Wudinna's west of Adelaide, over on the Eyre Peninsula. That meant we now had two Code Ones, but they were in opposite directions. Of course, this caused a real dilemma back at base and so, until they decided who was to go where, they called me back and said, 'Please hold your position over Port Wakefield while we decide which place we're going to send you to.'

And of course, being in an aircraft, the flight nurse just started laughing, because by saying, 'Please hold your position'—it almost came across like they wanted us to stop the aeroplane, dead still, in midair and hold it there until they'd decided where to send us. In reality, of course, what we were doing was holding our position by flying around in circles which, I may add, then had Air Traffic Control wondering what the hell was going on with this plane going around and around, circling over Port Wakefield.

Now, I'll tell you this last one, though we'd better not mention any names. But this particular pilot had just moved from Port Augusta down to Adelaide. He was an excellent pilot and was always very efficient. You know, he was one of those guys whose motto may've been along the lines of: let's get the job done as quickly and efficiently as possible so that the patient can receive treatment as soon as possible.

Anyhow, this pilot was in the King Air and he was asked to go to Keith, in the south-east of South Australia, to pick up a patient. Again, I must stress that it wasn't an urgent flight. But from the air, a lot of these small towns look very much the same and they also have very similar-looking airstrips.

So the pilot flew down to Keith but, actually, he mistakenly landed a few miles short at another place called Tintinara. So he landed at Tintinara instead of Keith. And I suppose you'd have to say that, because of his efficient manner, this particular pilot could get a little bit impatient at times. So when he landed at Tintinara and there's no ambulance in sight, he gets on the radio and says, 'Where's this bloody ambulance? We're here and you're not.'

And the ambulance crew comes back and they say, 'Where are you? We're at the airstrip, waiting.'

So he came back and said, 'Well, I'm here and you're not.'

'Well, we're here and you're not,' they replied.

Then he thought he'd better take a pause and have a bit of a think about things. And that's when he worked out that he'd landed at Tintinara instead of Keith.

'Won't be long,' he said.

Wouldn't be Alive

My name is Alex Hargans and I had my ninety-third birthday two weeks ago. These days I'm aching a bit with osteoporosis but I'm still going to have a new hip put in in a few months' time and the doctor told me that I'll be the oldest person he's ever performed that sort of operation on. So there you go.

But what I want to talk about is that, in the previous Flying Doctors book, there was a story titled 'A Piece o' Piss'. It was all about a big head-on accident, involving an elderly couple, out on the dirt road between Halls Creek and Fitzroy Crossing, up in the Kimberley region of Western Australia. I believe it was told by a friend of Penny Ende's, who's the nursing wife of the Flying Doctor pilot who attended that accident. The pilot's name was Jan Ende. Well, that story was about me and my wife, Edna, and I'd like to tell my side of things because, to this day, I truly believe that if it hadn't been for the flying skills of Jan Ende, the RFDS pilot, I wouldn't be alive.

Okay then, here we go. Well, back in 1973, the wife, Edna, and I decided that we'd like to go on a big outback trip in my fairly new V8 Fairmont. So we left our home, here in Bathurst, which is in the central east of New South Wales, and we headed up into south-western Queensland, to Charleville, then on to the Stockman's Hall of Fame at Longreach, before getting on to the Barkly Highway, which came out just above

Tennant Creek. That's where you'll find the memorial to John Flynn, these days.

From there we headed north along the Stuart Highway to Darwin. We fossicked around there for a while then we drove back down to Katherine and took the Victoria Highway across into northern Western Australia before heading south, down the Great Northern Highway to Halls Creek.

Mind you, I don't know why they call them highways because they're not up to scratch as far as highways go. Back then, most of them weren't much more than poorly graded, corrugated, gravel roads, with lots of potholes which were overflowing with that very fine dusty dirt they describe as bulldust. I might add that they're not too wide either so when you come across one of those huge cattle tucks, or road trains as they're known, you've got to be extremely careful, as I was to find out.

Anyhow, our aim was to go and have a look at the tourist resort place of Broome, over on the west coast, then return to Halls Creek and go across the Tanami Track to Alice Springs, then back home again to Bathurst.

Well, we were on our way to Broome and we'd pulled up for petrol at Halls Creek and I was talking to the owner of the place there and he said, 'Do you mind if I give you a bit of free advice?'

'I don't mind at all,' I said. 'I'm always interested in a bit of free advice.'

'Well,' he said, 'from here on a lot of road trains use this road and there's also a lot of bulldust and these fellers know the track like the back of their hand so they don't slow down in the bulldust and there's been a few accidents lately involving people from the east coast who stop and wait for the dust to clear before they move on. And while they've stopped they've been hit by someone coming up from behind them. So my advice to you is,' he said, 'whatever you do, don't stop. If you come across one of these road trains just slow down a bit, but don't stop.'

'Okay,' I said. 'Thanks for that.'

And so we headed off towards Fitzroy Crossing. Then along the way we saw one of the big road trains coming toward us and it was drafting up a huge cloud of bulldust. So I switched on my headlights and I slowed down and kept well over to my left, off near the edge of the road.

Well, the bloke at the petrol station had been right because the bulldust that the road train kicked up was so thick I could only see about two car lengths in front of me.

Anyway, just as the prime mover had almost passed us, I caught this flash of a nickel-plated bumper bar coming straight at me, overtaking the road train in all the dust. It turned out to be a feller driving an old Holden and we found out later that he was towing a great big trailer with no brakes on. He also didn't have his headlights on. My estimate would be that he must've been doing at least 100 kilometres per hour and we were probably doing about 40. So the closing time was pretty brief.

Even so, I think I managed to get my foot on the brake. Though that didn't do much good because, when we collided, the engine of the Fairmont got knocked back under the seat and my right hip got displaced about 6 inches. Most of the damage was done to the driver's side of my vehicle, so I was pinned in the car. I couldn't move at all. I had the dash up under my chin, with one knee threaded up through the steering wheel. Still, I managed to say to Edna, 'Could you get out and undo the bolts underneath the seat so that I can get the seat back?'

And even though, due to the impact of the seatbelt, Edna had a number of broken ribs, she still managed to get out of the car on her side, the passenger's side. Anyway, she went and had a bit of a look around, then she came back and said, 'Look, the back of the car's broken and the tyres are flat, and it's on the ground.'

Now, because his truck had kicked up so much bulldust, the first driver hadn't seen a thing and so he'd kept on driving. So there I was, stuck there, out on this pretty lonely stretch of road and, I can assure you, it was very painful.

Another thing that really, really frightened me was that I always carried my spare petrol on the roof-rack of the Fairmont, in a couple of those spitfire wind tanks. And when the collision occurred, the roof-rack kept going and petrol went everywhere. So all the while I was trapped inside the car, and I couldn't move, there was this strong smell of petrol around the place. And my immediate thought was that: 'If somebody decides to light a fag to steady their nerves, then I'm well and truly done for.'

So I said to Edna, 'Go and see the people in the other car and tell them not to strike a match.'

And Edna went over to speak to them, but I think the driver of the old Holden had a fractured skull and a ruptured spleen or something so he wasn't too interested in lighting up a fag at that stage. And the two women that were with him, they both had broken arms, so even if they wanted a fag—they couldn't light a match because they couldn't use their arms.

Then after a little while a drilling rig team came along. I forget how many vehicles they were travelling in but they were in a bit of a convoy and they stopped and chucked a big hook through where the windscreen used to be and they pulled the dash away from me. Then finally, they got my knee out from under the steering wheel and dragged me out through the back window of the Fairmont.

The next thing, a PMG (Postmaster-General) bloke came along and he had a two-way radio, so he got on to that and he sent out a call. Now, I may be a little bit wrong here but I think that the manager of Christmas Creek Station heard this call and then he came out with a tall antenna on the back of his utility and it was he that actually called the Flying Doctor base in Derby. And naturally the RFDS said they'd fly out as soon as humanly possible.

And the rest of the story is pretty much as it was written up in 'A Piece o' Piss'. You know, about how the drilling rig people and the PMG bloke, along with the Manager from Christmas Creek Station, they blocked off a section of the road and everyone who stopped got out of their vehicles and helped knock down the ant hills and clear the stones and stuff off a straight section of the road so that the RFDS plane could land.

Then Jan Ende flew out with the doctor and a flight nurse and he managed to put down the Queen Air aeroplane on that rough bit of straight road. And then came the other real scary bit with our dodgy escape out of there. Because, in reality, the bit of road Jan had to take off along was far too short for the type of aeroplane he was flying, particularly with its increased passenger weight. So he really had to gun the Queen Air to get it back in the air again and he just made it because, in doing so, the propellers shredded the shrubbery as he inched the plane off the ground.

Both the vehicles were written off, of course, and I never saw my fairly new V8 Fairmont again. Anyhow, Jan and I have kept in touch ever since the accident. Incidentally, he's coming over in August, so I'll probably see him again then.

I've since lost my mate, Edna. I lost her about three years ago now and had she lived for another couple of months, we would've been married for sixty-nine years. And, you know, life's pretty lonely without Edna—real lonely, in fact. And we never had a row, not over all that time. Never a row, and we did everything together, everything that is, apart from the five years and sixty-five days I was serving in the Air Force during the war.

But there's a little bit of a twist to the story about that accident and it's one that I haven't really mentioned too much before. It's got to do with the generosity of humanity. Because, see, Edna and I, we were married back in 1934, in the Depression era. We had a very basic wedding, at the Methodist Manse in Bathurst, with just a couple of witnesses. There were no bridal bouquets or any of that sort of stuff, just a vow and a kiss and that sealed it for life. We were married, and that was it.

As you might know, things were very bad in 1934, you know, with the Depression going on.

Unemployment was rife and so times were tough. Actually, I remember when Edna used to go shopping with just sixpence in her purse—yes, just sixpence— and she'd buy threepence worth of soup bones and threepence worth of soup vegetables, and she'd make up a huge pot of soup and we'd try and string that out.

Anyhow, the way the dole worked in those days was that if you weren't resident in a town, you could only get the dole once. So the people that were on the dole had to line up outside the police station and get interrogated by the cops. You know, they'd ask, 'Why did you lose your last job?' and 'Where was your last job?' All that sort of stuff, and some of them were quite strict about it. And so, about lunchtime, fellers who were down and out would come around and they'd say to Edna, 'Missus, I'll cut you a barrow load of wood in exchange fer a feed.'

And Edna, being Edna, would always reply with, 'Oh, there's no need for you to cut wood for us, but you're welcome to stay for a feed.'

'Oh, thank you, Missus,' they'd say. 'Thank you very much.'

When that happened, Edna would just add an extra cup of water into the soup pot so there was enough to go around.

So that was away back, during the Depression era, in the 1930s. Then in 1973, after we had the accident out on the Halls Creek to Fitzroy Crossing road, whilst Edna and I were recovering in the Derby Hospital— and I must say that they treated us extremely well up there—I got a letter from one of the down-and-out blokes that'd visited us a few times during the Depression. And in the letter he wrote, 'I don't know how you're fixed for money, but I read about your accident. I remember your kindness to me, the meals that I had at your place and I'm enclosing $20, just in case you're a bit short.'

So, wasn't that fantastic? And he was a Scotchman, too.

Final Flight

There's one really memorable trip that sticks in my mind. That was back on 9 February 1981 and I guess it turned out to be one of the main reasons why I gave flying up, in the end.

Of course, I'd been flying for a long time before then. Actually, I first joined the RFDS as a flight nurse back in 1976. That was up here, in Derby. Then after two years of constant flying, I just wanted a break and go overseas for three months with some friends. I already had six weeks' holiday due to me, then I wanted to add to that another six weeks' leave without pay. Anyhow, the Health Department, in Perth, who administered all those sorts of things— and from a long, long way down south, I may add— well, they just said, 'You can't do that. We won't give you leave without pay.'

So, then I resigned and I decided to take a whole year off. And when I was finishing up, the lady down in Perth who did the interviewing and the hiring of people for the Health Department, she said, 'Don't worry, when you come back, just give me a call and I'm sure we can do something for you.'

'Okay, thanks,' I said and off I went and had a wonderful year of travel.

Then when I returned from overseas I went to stay in my parents' house at Mareeba, in far north Queensland, and it was a desperate case of, 'Well, seeing I've got no money left, I'd better get a job.'

So, I wrote to the lady in Perth telling her that I was back in Australia and was enquiring about another position. I also explained that I wasn't available for about three or four weeks because my parents had gone on holidays and I'd promised to look after their house and garden. Next thing I know, a telegram arrives from Perth saying, 'Come immediately. We've got a position available at the Port Hedland RFDS base.'

Then I had to telegram back to say, 'Look, as I stated in my letter, I'm not available. I can't do anything for another three weeks.'

Anyhow, so then I thought they'd naturally go ahead and give the position to someone else. But when my parents returned home, the position was still available so I went to Port Hedland. But I didn't like it that much because Hedland was all emergency stuff. They didn't fly clinics out of Hedland whereas they did out of Derby and it was the clinic work—the people-contact— that I used to enjoy so much. I mean, you know, the emergency stuff was also in Derby and you had to do it, but I didn't thrive on it, if you understand what I mean. Anyhow, I did four months in Port Hedland and then, when a position came vacant up at Derby, I jumped at it. So yeah, in all I'd done my first two years with the RFDS in Derby, took a year off, and then I started up there again in 1979. And I was very pleased about that.

But the constant flying does tend to wear you down after a while, and it was a couple of years later, on 9 February 1981, when we got the call from Balgo Aboriginal Community. By then we'd increased our RFDS fleet in Derby. We now had two pilots and two aeroplanes—a Queen Air and a Beechcraft Baron—though, mind you, we still had just the two flight nurses. But that's the way it went in those days, and so I was one of the flight nurses.

Anyway, the other flight nurse plus a doctor and one of the pilots had already been down at Balgo in the Queen Air aeroplane earlier that day, running a clinic. And while they were there the doctor had attended to a young Aboriginal girl—a nine-year-old—who'd apparently shown some tablets to her mother and said, 'I've just eaten some of these.'

The little girl was a bit slow, you know, retarded. I guess that these days they'd say she was 'disabled'. So the doctor gave the girl some medicine to make her vomit, which she did and, sure enough, the tablets came out. She was still a little bit drowsy, but the doctor thought, 'Well, at least she's got it all out of her system. She should be okay, now.'

Then after they'd finished the clinic at Balgo, they jumped back into the Queen Air and headed back to Derby. But unbeknown to everybody, the little girl had also fed some of the tablets to a four-year-old boy. I forget now, but I think it might've been her baby brother. Now, the four-year-old had gone to bed earlier that afternoon and when his mum had tried to wake him around five o'clock, he wouldn't stir. He was right out of it, and that's when we got the call in at our Derby base.

By this stage, the Queen Air that had been out at Balgo was about due back in Derby. So, with the Queen Air being faster than our second aircraft, the Beechcraft Baron, they said, 'Well, as soon as the Queen Air arrives we'll refuel it and send it straight back out there again to pick up this deeply unconscious little boy.'

So the pilot, myself and a doctor—a paediatrician—arrived at the Derby airstrip ready to go to Balgo. The Queen Air landed and, while they were refuelling it, the two pilots exchanged conversation about the weather. Being February it was wet season so, you know, there was a lot of lightning about and storms and it was pretty blowy and very wet. But from all reports, apparently, at that stage, Balgo, itself, was okay.

Anyway, we took off into this driving rain. It was horizontal rain. Very bad weather. Terrible. We were being buffeted all around the place. But we kept on going and going, and after a while, to me, it seemed that we were taking much longer than expected. Normally, it used to take us around two and a half hours to get out to Balgo in the Beechcraft Baron and here we were in the Queen Air, a faster aircraft, and we'd already been in the air for that long.

Now the pilot we had with us was one of our older pilots. Mind you, he was also a very excellent pilot. He'd flown in Vietnam and places like that, so he'd had a lot of experience. Anyway, we kept flying and flying and I was thinking, 'Gosh, it's taking a long time.'

So in the end, I went up front and I said to the pilot, 'Where are we? Surely we should nearly be there by now.'

'I know we should. It's out there somewhere,' he said, 'but I can't see the lights.' Normally, when Balgo knew we were coming at night, they'd put on their big basketball court lights. 'Perhaps we can't see them because the rain's so heavy between us and them,' the pilot added.

'Oh, okay,' I said and I went and sat back down.

Then, sure enough, much to my relief the lights of Balgo finally came into view. And oddly enough, while it was still raining where we were, when we got over Balgo, there was no rain at all. None at all. Though, mind you, there was still a savage wind.

Anyway, the pilot managed that alright and we landed safely and were met at the airstrip. Then the doctor and I, we were taken straight into the Balgo Clinic to stabilise the child, the little boy. First thing was to put up a drip in case we needed to give him IV (intravenous) drugs. I think the doctor's main concern was that, because the boy was unconscious, he might fit—you know, have a seizure—and the doctor just wanted to have a line in, just in case.

So we sorted out the little four-year-old boy. Then the doctor took a look at the nine-year-old girl and because she was still very drowsy he decided that it'd be better if we took both the children back to Derby with us. We had two stretchers so we laid the children down on those in the Queen Air. We placed the little boy—who was our main concern—with his head to the door of the aeroplane just in case the doctor needed to intubate him; you know, to breathe for him if he should stop breathing, which is always a danger when you've had an overdose of drugs. But the little boy seemed to be alright. We had the drip up and he was breathing by himself, though he was still right out to it. So the paediatrician's sitting over there. I'm here, the baby boy's just over there and then the older one, the girl, she was right behind me on her stretcher, and she was alright. You could rouse her but she was still very dopey.

By the time we'd got them both settled in the Queen Air the rain had started to come in again and there was also still a very strong wind blowing. But we took off alright, it was about nine o'clock at night, and I'm busy down the back, you know, taking obs and everything on the children.

Then we were only about fifteen or twenty minutes out of Balgo, on our way back to Derby, and, you know, when you've flown a lot you tend to get accustomed to the monotonous drone of the engine. Well we'd levelled out at about 6000 feet and I heard this funny noise in one of the engines. I don't know how to describe it except that it was, like, it just wasn't normal. Anyhow I'm still busy with the children but when I hear this odd noise I look up at the pilot and there he is, he's sitting there in the cockpit, with these little half glasses on and he's peering over them at his controls.

So I said to the paediatrician, 'I think there's something wrong with that engine. Can you hear it?'

'No,' he said, 'I can't.'

But you know, as I said, when you fly a lot, you just know these things. Anyhow, because I wasn't backward in coming forward, and I wanted to know what was happening, I went up to the pilot and I tapped him on the shoulder and I said, 'What's wrong?'

And he was a really slow talker. 'Oh,' he drawled, 'I'm having trouble with the port engine.' He said, 'It's running a bit hot.'

Still and all, he didn't really seem all that worried so I just said something like, 'Oh, okay,' then I went back and sat down.

'What's up?' the doctor asked.

'The pilot's having trouble with one of the engines.'

And just as I said it, I was gripped by that fleeting fear of, 'Hey, we could be in big, big trouble here. Someone's got to know about this because if we go down away out here in the Kimberley, nobody will even know what's happened.'

Anyhow there was a radio at the back of the co-pilot's seat, which the nurse could use, so I used that to try and get in touch with Balgo. But there was no answer there. Then there's the red button—the emergency button—it's the same one the station people use in an emergency to get in contact with their nearest RFDS base. By this stage the pilot was talking to someone over his radio, but with all the racket going on with the wind and the rain and everything—I wasn't sure whether he was alerting anyone or not. But we were really limping, so I thought, 'Well, this is an emergency.'

So I pressed the emergency button and the wife of the Base Manager at Derby come over the radio and I said, 'You know how we just had to go to Balgo and pick up these two children?'

'Yes.'

'Well,' I said, 'we're on our way back to Derby and we've run into difficulty. We're having trouble with one of the engines in the Queen Air and I just think you ought to know.'

And the wife of the Base Manager said, 'Thanks very much for that information. We'll stand by if you need us.'

Then just as I'd replaced the radio, the pilot turned around to me and said, 'I'm going to have to close the port engine down.'

Well, from then on we were just so worried that something very serious was about to happen. And it was so dark outside the Queen Air that I couldn't see a thing, and I'm thinking, 'Here we are in this big plane, which is now about to start flying on just the one engine, it's pitch black outside, it's raining, it's extremely windy, and if we're only travelling on one engine then it'll take at least two hours to get back to Derby.'

We were still flying at 6000 feet at that stage, but when the pilot shut the engine down I took a look over his shoulder and I could see the altimeter in free-fall. From 6000 feet it dropped down to 5000 feet and there he was, the pilot, trying to steady the thing. Then it fell from 5000 feet down to 4000 feet, down to 3000 feet, and we eventually pulled up at 2000 feet. From experience, I knew that the lowest safe flying level was 1000 feet and that was because of the mountains that were around us—the 'jump-ups', as they were known.

Then it suddenly hit me, 'How will we ever make it?'

So I'm desperately trying to work out just how long it was going to take us to get back to Derby, on one engine and in these horrific conditions. Now, my maths was never that good but whatever way I tried to figure it out, the result always ended up as being an extremely frightening prospect, indeed. An impossible equation. And, you know, it was one of those times when your whole life sort of flashes before you and I came to the conclusion, well, like, I'm not quite ready to go just yet.

And it was about then that the pilot turned around and said, 'I think we'll try and get back to Balgo. It's not as far.'

'Oh,' I replied, 'what a good idea.'

So he turned the Queen Air around and we started to head back to Balgo. But by that stage we were already twenty minutes out and I knew that they only left the basketball court lights and the airstrip lights on for twenty minutes after a plane left. And that meant, by the time we got back there, all the lights would be out and we wouldn't be able to find the place. So I tried to raise Balgo again on the radio to tell them, you know, 'Hey, switch the lights back on. We're in big trouble here and we have to come back.'

But again, there wasn't an answer. So I continued trying and trying to get on to Balgo and still, nothing, nothing, nothing. Then I realised that the staff in the clinic there would've probably been so pleased to have seen the two children fly out that they would've said, 'Oh well, they're safe now so, with it being such a rotten night, we may as well just pack up and go home and go to bed.'

Then, for the first time that night, luck was with us because as we got closer to Balgo we could just make out the lights from the basketball court. Thankfully, someone must've forgotten to switch them off. What's more, when we got closer, the airstrip lights were still on. And, well, I just couldn't believe it.

Still, there remained the huge problem of trying to land the Queen Air on just the one engine, and in these terrible conditions. It was sheeting rain and you know how, when the pilots prepare to land, they fly across the airstrip then go around to line up so that the airstrip's right there in front of them. Well our pilot went around once, then twice, then three times and so on until he reached his eighth attempt and he still couldn't line up the airstrip to his satisfaction. He'd either lose sight of the airstrip lights in the pelting rain or the driving wind would blow the plane too far this way or too far that way, and by now I'm thinking, We're never going to make it.

But the people from Balgo must've heard our plane flying around because, as we passed over again, we saw some cars coming out to the airport. They hadn't got our message. No message at all. Nobody knew. They just heard the drone of our Queen Air so they thought they'd better come and see what was going on. You know, when the RFDS plane has been your lifeline for so long, it's such a distinctive sound. You never forget it.

Now, back in those days, Balgo used to own Kingfisher Air and they had a plane sitting on the airstrip. So their pilot got in his aircraft and he was able to speak to our pilot. 'What's your problem?' he asked.

'Well,' replied our pilot, 'we've only got one engine. We're being blown around all over the place and I can't see the approach to the airstrip because of the driving rain.'

Then our pilot asked if they could park two cars with their headlights on at the approach to the airstrip so at least he could see where he was supposed to come down. So they did that and we were eventually able to land. And, oh, we were just so grateful when we finally touched down, just so relieved. Actually, we were all in a heap—a complete mess—absolutely spent.

But, you know, the wind was so bad that the windsock on their strip was blowing horizontal. So you really had to give it to our pilot. I mean, to keep his cool through all that and to make the right decisions, and get us all there in one piece. Well, as I said, you really had to give it to him.

So, we then unloaded the two little kids and the Balgo Hospital staff had to get up out of their beds and look after them overnight. We also stayed at Balgo that night, of course. Then the next day the RFDS sent out the little Beechcraft Baron and we brought the little boy back to Derby with us, in that. From memory, I think he'd started to regain consciousness by then. But we didn't take the older girl. She was okay by then. So yeah, they survived, no problem.

But something really scary: first thing on that following morning, before the Beechcraft Baron arrived to take us back to Derby, our pilot went out to try and start up the Queen Air and—you wouldn't believe it— but neither of the two engines would start. Not even the one that we flew in on would work. They'd both gone. And afterwards, when they had the investigation about it, apparently they found out that the driving rain had somehow gone in under the cowl—you know, the hooding around the engine—and it ended up wetting the magnetos, which put the engines out. And so that was the cause. That's what they said.

So, you know, if we would've continued on towards Derby, well, who knows what might've happened. And that's the experience that made me think, 'Well, it must be about time to hang up your wings. You've been at it for a fair while now and I think somebody's trying to tell you something.'

And not long after that I finished up with the RFDS. Actually, what also helped make the decision easier was that I got married. 'Well,' I said, 'I've also got someone else to consider now.'

So that was it for me. There was no more flying.

NEW GREAT AUSTRALIAN FLYING DOCTOR STORIES

Contributors

New Great Australian Flying Doctor Stories is based
on stories told to Bill 'Swampy' Marsh by:

Rhonda Anstee
Bob Balmain
Rod Bishop
Paul Brady
Chris Carter
Donna Cattanach
Jane Clemson
Ruth Cook
Dave Crommelin
Heather Curtin
Phil and Sue Darby
Sarah Fenton
Richard Fewster and
   Ann Ruston
Norton Gill
Jack Goldsmith
David Hansford
Wal 'Dusty' Harkness
David and Christine Harris
Robina Jeffs
Ruth Ko
Margaret Loveday
John Lynch
Susan Markwell

Bill 'Swampy' Marsh
David McInnes
Ian 'Mac' McKechnie
Barbara Meredith
Kevin Murphy
Shirley Norris
Stephen Penberthy
Peter Phillips
Bill Rawson
Cheryl Russ
Chris Smith
Howard William Steer
Kim Tyrie
Esther Veldstra
Nick Watling
Margaret Wheatley
Margaret Worth

To Howard William Steer
—with many thanks for all your help and great spirit
www.howardsteerart.com.au

A Brief History

On a number of occasions people have mentioned that while they've greatly enjoyed the collected stories of the Royal Flying Doctor Service (RFDS), there's never been the one story that gives a brief overview as to just how the RFDS came into being. For me, history isn't just a list of dates that relate to a sequence of events. I had enough of that back in school. But since then I've developed a great interest in the many and varied characters who have been involved in the making of our history: people like the shearers and the drovers, those who have worked and travelled on our railways, those who live and work in little outback towns and pubs.

The RFDS has been, and still is, full of people who are prepared to take on the huge challenges that working our outback regions presents, and for the betterment of all. As one person I interviewed for *More Great Flying Doctor Stories* said, those who are involved in the Flying Doctor Service, 'on a daily basis ... put their lives on the line for people who are complete strangers to them. They don't care who these people are or what their nationality is, or what religion they are. And it doesn't matter [that] those very same people probably wouldn't take a similar risk for them. In fact, they wouldn't even realise the risk. What's more, the RFDS do it for free.'

So where did this amazing organisation have its origins? Who were the driving forces behind its conception? What sort of characters were they? Well, to begin at the beginning, the Reverend John Flynn was the person who had the dream of creating a spiritual and medical 'Mantle of Safety' for all remote and outback people, regardless of colour, race or creed. And what a large dream it was. As Hudson Fysh, the co-founder of Qantas, once wrote of John Flynn: 'Flynn the Dreamer ... who saw a vision of a Flying Doctor well before the days of practical flying, but kept it firmly fixed in his mind'.

John Flynn was born in the late 1880s, at a place called Moliagul in central-western Victoria. He went to a few primary schools, one of which had the rather uninviting name of Snake Valley. In 1898 he matriculated from high school; then, to help pay his way through his further education, he became what was called a 'pupil-teacher' with the Victorian Education Department. Following that he began training for the ministry. His time at theological college was broken up by two important events that ignited his passion for the bush and its people; the first being the couple of periods he spent on a shearers' mission and stemming from those experiences was the publication of his *Bushman's Companion*.

After being ordained in 1911 John Flynn volunteered to go to the Smith of Dunesk Mission, at Beltana, in the remote northern Flinders Ranges of South Australia. Dunesk had been established by the Presbyterian Church and was located in a parish that covered a vast area of the South Australian inland that extended over to the railhead at Oodnadatta. Oodnadatta was situated along the original old Ghan railway line and at that time it had a floating population of around a hundred or so.

Many were Aboriginal, plus there were the Afghan traders—hence the term 'the Ghan'. Oodnadatta also happens to be one of the hottest places in Australia, with temperatures of over 50° celsius having been recorded.

Anyway, that's where the mission had placed a nursing sister and where it had also planned to build a nursing hostel, and it was under Flynn's guidance that the Oodnadatta Nursing Hostel was opened in late 1911. The following year the Church asked Flynn to survey the Northern Territory region and after he handed in a couple of reports—one on the needs of Aborigines and the other on the needs of white settlers—the Presbyterian General Assembly appointed him as superintendent of what was to be named the Australian Inland Mission (AIM). In doing so the South Australian, Western Australian and Queensland Assemblies transferred their remote areas into Flynn's care. So the AIM was officially established and it commenced operations out of Oodnadatta with just the one hostel, the one nursing sister, the one Padre and a 'fleet' of five camels. It began, as it has continued, 'without preference for nationality or creed', and was based on the idea of a remote areas network of nursing hostels and hospitals, all working in conjunction with a Patrol Padre.

By 1918, and despite World War I, John Flynn had managed to establish Patrol Padres out of Port Hedland and Broome in Western Australia, Pine Creek in the Northern Territory and Cloncurry in Queensland. He'd also appointed nursing sisters to Port Hedland and Halls Creek in Western Australia, and to Maranboy and Alice Springs in the Northern Territory.

Flynn's commitment to the AIM was absolute. He even involved himself in the design of the nursing hostels, along with the architects, engineers and the local people. His aim was to make sure that each building suited its own particular regional climatic conditions and the availability of local building material. The large stone building of the Alice Springs Hostel is such an example. He helped design it in such a way that it was cooled via a tunnel under the ground floor, where wet bags filtered the dust, and then the cooled air was drawn, by convection, through the hostel wards. Then as the air heated up it rose to the lantern roof from where it was expelled. Wide verandahs also provided extra cooling.

Another of Flynn's passions was his magazine, *The Inlander*. *The Inlander* was used to spread the word to a wider Australian public. This was where he first mentioned his idea of a 'Mantle of Safety'. The magazine also promoted his fight for a 'brighter bush' with his photographs, documents, statistics, maps and articles telling of the needs of the outback people. He also wrote about inland Australia's potential for development and about how it could only reach its full potential by providing for the women and children. He didn't overlook the Aborigines either. And, mind you, there weren't too many people around back then who were as outspoken or knowledgeable as Flynn was on the subject. In fact, one particular issue of a 1915 *Inlander* was pretty much entirely devoted to the plight of the 'fringe-dwellers' and described how their situation was 'a blot on Australia'. He went on to say, 'We who so cheerfully sent a cheque for £100000 to Belgium to help a people pushed out of their own inheritance by foreigners ... surely we must just as cheerfully do something for those whom we clean-handed people have dispossessed in the interests of superior culture.'

The next part of Flynn's overall strategy of a Mantle of Safety was focused on the possibility of radio communications between doctor and patient and the idea of a 'Flying Doctor'. In Flynn's mind the two had to work hand-in-hand. Even as early as 1925 he said that 'the practicability of the Flying Doctor proposal depends almost entirely on the widespread adoption of wireless by bush residents'.

To that end, in late May 1925, Flynn and a returned soldier and radio technician by the name of George Towns took delivery of a specially designed Dodge Buckboard that was to be used for the first inland experiments in radio transmission. They picked the vehicle up in Adelaide and drove to Alice Springs via Beltana, Innamincka, Birdsville, Marree and Oodnadatta, doing test transmissions as they went. Interestingly enough, they used a pulley drive from the jacked-up back wheel of the Dodge to generate electricity for radio transmission.

The following year the ever-persuasive Flynn talked a man called Alfred Traeger into going to Alice Springs to conduct further experiments. Alf Traeger was to become another vital link in the development of the Flying Doctor Service. Alf was born near Dimboola, Victoria, back in the late 1800s. I guess if he lived today Alf Traeger might be considered a bit of a geek. He was once described as 'a curious, patient, precise child, who, at twelve, made a telephone receiver and transmitted between the toolshed and his house'. So it seems his pathway in life was set very early on.

After his parents had moved to South Australia, Alf attended Balaklava Public School and the Martin Luther School before going to a technical high school. He then studied mechanical and electrical engineering before being employed by the Metropolitan Tramways Trust and the Postmaster-General's Department. When World War I started he tried to enlist but was refused on the grounds of his Germanic heritage, this is even though his grandparents had been naturalised. For Alf, not to be able to serve his country was one of his bitter disappointments.

Instead, Alf threw himself into his work and it wasn't long after he'd obtained an amateur operator's licence and built his first pedal transmitter-receiver that he formed Traeger Transceivers Pty Ltd. That's when John Flynn arrived on the scene and employed Alf to help him out. After a brief outback tour where it's said that despite the severe heat Alf always wore a dark suit and braces, he returned to Adelaide to start developing a transceiver for the Flying Doctor network.

Flynn's basic outline to Traeger was simple: these radio sets had to be cheap, durable, small and easy to operate. So by using bicycle pedals to drive the generator, Alf found that a person could comfortably achieve 20 watts at a pressure of about 300 volts. He then enclosed the generator's fly-wheel and gears in a metal housing, with the pedals outside, and added a cast base so that the whole contraption could be screwed to the floor beneath a table. Traeger built the transceiver into a box, and set up a master switch to separate the crystal controller transmitter from the receiver. To put it more simply, Traeger's wireless was basically a pedal-operated generator, which provided power for a transceiver. But as simple as it seems, once the first pedal sets came on the market in the late 1920s they created a communications revolution, especially throughout the remote inland.

While Traeger was working on his pedal wireless, Flynn had been busy on the second part of his overall strategy, and that was to try to set up an aerial medical service. Some say that Flynn's original vision of a 'Flying Doctor' had been inspired by a letter from a Lieutenant John Clifford Peel—or just Clifford Peel, as he preferred to be known. Now, going back to around 1912, a then eighteen-year-old Clifford Peel had read a book John Flynn had written, titled *Northern Territory and Central Australia: A Call to the Church*. Apparently the book captured Peel's interest in the work Flynn was doing and the problems he faced of being able to cover the huge distances he needed to, to create his Mantle of Safety. The book got Peel thinking about the logistics of how aerial care could be provided to the people in the remote areas of Australia.

Then, later on, after World War I began, Peel trained as a pilot at Laverton in Victoria. The story goes that he wrote to Flynn with some of the thoughts he had on the practicalities of using aeroplanes within the AIM. Now, keep it in mind that, back then, aeroplanes were a relatively new invention and, to the vast majority of people, it would seem bonkers to jump into a basic wooden frame with a bit of canvas stretched over it and go flying into the vast unknown of outback Australia. But the idea excited Flynn. He wanted more information, which in turn produced Peel's much recorded reply of November 1917. At the time the letter was written, Peel was sailing from Melbourne to the

United Kingdom, on his way to begin his life as a wartime airman. In part, it read:

> Aviation is still new, but it has set some of us thinking, and thinking hard. Perhaps others want to be thinking too. Hence these few notes.
>
> Safety.
>
> The first question to be asked is sure to be 'Is it safe?'
>
> To the Australian lay mind the thought of flying is accompanied by many weird ideas of its danger. True there are dangers, which in the Inland will be accompanied by the possibility of being stranded in the desert without food or water. Yet even with this disadvantage the only reply to such a query is a decided affirmative. Practically all the flying for the last three years has been military flying ... and if we study the records available ... we will find that the number of miles flown per misadventure is very large, while the number of accidents per aerodrome per annum is very small.
>
> Difficulties.
>
> As in every new adventure there are initial difficulties ... The first and greatest of these is cost ... With aeroplanes I venture to say that, given proper care, the upkeep is relatively light while the cost of installing compares very favourably if we realise that to run a train, motor car, lorry, or other vehicle, roads must first be made and then kept in repair, whilst the air needs no such preparation.

The problem of overhauls and major repairs presents another great difficulty ... The question of ways and means remains to be solved. Landing grounds may present some difficulties in certain regions, but these will be found where needed. Machines for Inland work will need to have a large radius of action, say a non-stop run of at least 700 miles, so that the fuel carrying capacity will be large.

Many of these and other difficulties loom very large, as we view them from the distance, but with the progress of aviation, and the more universal use of the motor car, many of them will automatically disappear.

Advantages.

The advantage of an air service will be quickly appreciated ... With a machine doing 90 miles an hour, Darwin is brought within twelve and a half hours of Oodnadatta (excluding stops). It takes little imagination to see the advantage of this to the mail service, government officials, and business men while to the frontier settlers it will be an undreamt of boon as regards household supplies, medical attention, and business.

A Scheme.

Just by way of a suggestive scheme, I propose to consider that portion of A.I.M. territory east of the Western Australian boundary. In this large tract of land, consisting of one-third of the Australian continent, I am assuming that the bases are situated at Oodnadatta in South Australia, Cloncurry in Queensland and

Katherine in the Northern Territory. At the present time these are railheads, hence supplies can be brought up with comparative regularity and minimum cost. From each of these centres the A.I.M. workers can work a district of say 300 miles radius, or an area of 270000 square miles.

In the not very distant future, if our church folk only realise the need, I can see a missionary doctor administering to the needs of men and women scattered between Wyndham and Cloncurry, Darwin and Hergott [now named Marree]. If the nation can do so much in the days of war surely it will do its 'bit' in the coming days of peace—and here is its chance.

The credit side of the ledger I leave for those interested in the development of our hinterland to compute. Sufficient to say that the heroes of the Inland are laying the foundation stones of our Australian nation.

J.CLIFFORD PEEL, LIEUT
Australian Flying Corps, A.I.F.
At Sea, 20/11/17.

Unfortunately, Peel didn't live to see just how successful his idea became because only thirteen months later—and only seven weeks before the end of the war—his aircraft disappeared during a routine patrol in France. The mystery of Peel's fate has never been solved. But the seeds had been sown.

How those seeds grew to fruition came about through Flynn's friendship with two men: Sir W Hudson Fysh and Hugh Victor McKay.

Hudson Fysh was born in the mid-1890s at Launceston, Tasmania. It doesn't appear that he was the most dedicated of students because, after attending various schools, he went out working as a jackeroo and wool classer. When World War I started he enlisted in the Australian Light Horse Brigade and served at Gallipoli and in Egypt and Palestine. He was commissioned lieutenant in 1916. Following that he transferred to the Australian Flying Corps where he won the Distinguished Flying Cross.

After the war Fysh and another ex-serviceman, Pat McGinness, along with Arthur Baird, an engineer, decided to enter the Australian Government's £10000-prize contest for a flight from England to Australia. But because of the death of their backer, Sir Samuel McCaughey, that didn't happen. Instead, Fysh and McGinness were paid by the government to survey the Longreach to Darwin section of the contest route. They did this in the first vehicle to go overland to the Gulf of Carpentaria, a Model T Ford.

The next year Fysh and McGinness, along with three Queensland graziers, got together and formed the Queensland and Northern Territory Aerial Services Ltd, or Qantas, as it's known these days. With only an Avro Dyak and an old BE2E war-disposals aircraft, the company moved from Winton to Longreach where the planes were then used as a taxi service, as an ambulance, for stock inspection services and for joy-riding. Around about this time Hudson Fysh and John Flynn struck up a friendship and they talked about the practicalities and possibilities of a Flying Doctor Service. In doing so, Fysh told Flynn that he'd be willing to support him in any way he could.

Hugh Victor McKay was another person who helped John Flynn create a Flying Doctor Service. Hugh McKay was born at Raywood, Victoria, in the mid-1860s. He was the fifth of twelve children and he had very little education other than his parents' devotion to the Bible. By the age of thirteen he was working on the farm.

Back in those days harvesting was done with a horse-drawn stripper and manual winnower. But when the government offered prizes for producing a single harvester that would combine stripping, threshing, winnowing and bagging, Hugh, his father and one of his brothers built a prototype stripper-harvester from bits and pieces of farm machinery. By the early 1890s they'd built an improved model which they marketed as the Sunshine harvester. The Sunshine was an instant success.

Then, when Hugh Victor McKay died in the mid-1920s, he left £2000 to help Flynn's Aerial Medical Service experiment. The bequest was made on the proviso that the Presbyterian Church doubled that amount. The Church okayed the idea and Flynn raised a further £5000. With the money raised, Hudson Fysh honoured his promise of help and Qantas leased to Flynn—on extremely favourable terms—a fabric-covered De Havilland 50 aeroplane, named *Victory*.

On 17 May 1928 *Victory* took off from Cloncurry, Queensland, after the AIM Aerial Medical Service received its first emergency call, no doubt via one of Alf Traeger's famous pedal wirelesses. Arthur Affleck was the pilot and the doctor was St Vincent Welch. And so all the various threads of Flynn's vision of a Flying Doctor Service had now become a reality.

The final part of John Flynn's work began with turning his AIM Aerial Medical Service into a national community service. This vision was far greater than the Church could handle by itself. What Flynn now wanted was an arrangement between state and federal governments and the AIM itself. And so the idea of a National Aerial Medical Service of Australia (NAMS) was set into motion. To get it up and running, Flynn travelled throughout Australia addressing public meetings, talking to politicians and holding press interviews until the NAMS became a reality.

The mid-1930s also saw a different role that the two-way radio was to play for the people in remote areas and the children in particular. Around that time John Flynn was looking to establish a base of the Aerial Medical Service in Alice Springs. In doing so he got help from a long-time educationalist named Adelaide Miethke. At that time Miethke was a member of the Council of the Flying Doctor Service of South Australia. And, on a visit to Alice Springs, she saw the potential of the Flying Doctor two-way radio network, not only as a tool for patient-doctor contact and remote community contact but also for educational purposes.

Adelaide Miethke was born in June 1881 at Manoora, South Australia, the sixth daughter of ten children. Her father was a Prussian schoolmaster. She was educated at various country schools and at Woodville Public School before becoming, as had John Flynn, a pupil-teacher. In the early 1900s she attended the University Training College and her first teaching appointment was at Lefevre Peninsula School

A workaholic by nature, by 1915 she was Founding President of the Women Teachers' League where she fought to place women as headmistresses. The following year she became the first female Vice-President of the South Australian Public School Teachers' Union. She studied part-time to complete her degree and became an Inspector of Schools in late 1924. Miethke applied extremely tough teaching standards. She was a stickler for formality and devoted much of her life to helping improve teachers' industrial conditions and to raising the status of women.

Miethke also believed that 'technically gifted girls should have a chance of developing their bent' and that while 'her home was a woman's place, it need not be her prison'. To that end she also helped set up what were to be known as Central Schools. These were training schools for young women to become housewives of 'skill and taste'. Initially the schools offered pre-vocational training to girls aged thirteen to sixteen. General subjects were studied as well as practical classes in things like laundry work, cookery, household management, first aid, drawing and applied art, needlework and dressmaking. Second-year girls received millinery and secretarial training.

Then after Miethke had become President of the Women's Centenary Council of South Australia, she helped raise money to establish the Alice Springs base of John Flynn's Aerial Medical Service. This was the connection with John Flynn because, by that stage, she'd become the Flying Doctors' state branch's first woman President as well as the editor of the magazine *Air Doctor*. That's when the idea of using the Flying Doctor's two-way radio network to set up a School of the Air came to mind. Some of the teachers at Alice

Springs Primary-High School took radio lessons and trials began after a landline was laid from the base to the school. On 8 June 1951 the first broadcasts of School of the Air were made from the Flying Doctor base in Alice Springs.

But, unfortunately, John Flynn didn't get to see the realisation of this part of his grand vision because only a month before School of the Air was officially opened, he died of cancer in Sydney. At his request his ashes were interred at the foot of Mount Gillen, just west of Alice Springs. It was said at his service that: 'Across the lonely places of the land he planted kindness, and from the hearts of those who call those places home, he gathered love.'

In 1955, the designation of 'Royal' was added to the Flying Doctor Service. As was John Flynn's dream, the Royal Flying Doctor Service is a non-profit organisation that provides free healthcare services to 'all people who live, work or travel in the world's largest medical waiting room': a waiting room that stretches from Christmas Island in the Indian Ocean to Elizabeth Island in the Great Barrier Reef, and all the states and territories in between.

References:

John Behr, 'Traeger, Alfred Hermann (1895–1980)', *Australian Dictionary of Biography*, Volume 12, Melbourne University Press, 1981, pp 251–252.

Graeme Bucknall, 'Flynn, John (1880–1951)', *Australian Dictionary of Biography*, Volume 8, Melbourne University Press, 1981, pp 531–534.

Suzanne Edgar and Helen Jones, 'Adelaide Miethke (1881–1962)', *Australian Dictionary of Biography*, Volume 10, Melbourne University Press, 1981, pp 497–498.

John Lack, 'Hugh Victor McKay (1865–1926)', *Australian Dictionary of Biography*, Volume 10, Melbourne University Press, 1981, pp 291–294.

J. Percival, 'Fysh, Sir Wilmot Hudson (1895–1974)', *Australian Dictionary of Biography*, Volume 8, Melbourne University Press, 1981, pp 603–605.

Neil Smith, 'Lt. John Clifford Peel, Australian Flying Corps', essay published online at www.3squadron.org.au/subpages/peel.htm.

A Short Little Story

Well, I don't talk too much, so it better be just a short little story. I've lived here in Hungerford, now, for about fifty or sixty years or thereabouts. I guess a lot of people mightn't know where Hungerford is, would they? Well, it's right on the Queensland side of the Dog Fence, between Bourke, in New South Wales, and Thargomindah or, if you go the other way, it's between Bourke and Cunnamulla.

As you can see, there's not too much here other than a few houses, the police station and the pub. I live in one of the houses. But if you go back to the old cemeteries around here and you have a good look at the graves, you'd be lucky to find anyone over fifty. I'd say that most of the graves out there are from around the turn of the century and that's when the big sort of flu epidemic came through. And that killed quite a few people.

Anyhow, not that they were about then, but the Flying Doctor Service flies out here about every month and they have a medical clinic, just to keep a check on us all. They usually come out from Broken Hill, or occasionally from Charleville. They were here just last Thursday, actually. Well, you just ring up and say you want to see the doctor about this or that and so, when they arrive, you join the queue. Most times it's just the pilot and a doctor or a nurse; then sometimes there's also one woman comes out, what does the women's health.

I've always supported the Flying Doctor. In fact, they started up an annual field day here a few years back and a big part of it was to raise money for the Royal Flying Doctor Service. They did that out here at the sports ground, and that's been going real well; but then they had to put it on every second year so it didn't run into the one that they had in at Broken Hill. And so now Broken Hill has it one year and we have it the next. It's only a one-day turn-out but, oh, they do lots of things, and at the end of the day they have this big auction and all the dealers and wheelers, they put in different things to be sold. Like, someone might hand in a fish or something and, you mightn't believe this, but it might bring in anything between $300 and $400. Yes, just the one fish. No, there was nothing special about it.

About three or four years ago I think it was, they auctioned a rain gauge, and that brought in around $1000. Just between you and me, I don't know why anyone out here would want a rain gauge because it doesn't ever rain that much. It wasn't even raining then. And there was nothing special about that rain gauge, neither. It was just a normal old rain gauge; I'd say, about thirty odd dollars' worth in the shop. But, see, what would happen was that one bloke would buy it for, say, $200 or $300, and then he'd donate it back in to the Flying Doctor Service and so then they'd go and put it up for auction again and it'd be sold again for another $150 or $200. And it went along like that till it ended up fetching something like $1000, as I said.

So that was a good little earner for the Flying Doctor.

But living out here like, with the Flying Doctor Service, they can have a plane land in Hungerford within the hour, which is fairly fast. And I've seen quite a few emergencies in my time too, and when they get here they stabilise you first. Sometimes they might bring a paramedic or whatever. Actually, my ex-missus would've been dead if it weren't for the Flying Doctor Service. She was having a heart attack out here some years ago and they were here in around the hour, or a bit over. Sometimes it depends if there's a plane available because they fly thousands of kilometres a year. Yes, it's just unbelievable, isn't it? Anyhow, they flew her down to Broken Hill and I went down in the plane with her. This was about ten years ago now. They had the King Airs back then. But I remember when I first came out here, back in the early 1950s, when they had the De Havilland Dragons. You know, the three-engined thing, with the double wing.

A Team Thing

I've got lots of memories of my time with the Flying Doctor Service but some of it's pretty warped medical humour, really—the type of humour that a lot of readers wouldn't understand. But I think probably the main thing I'd like to say is how it's an incredible team thing, not only with the support staff but also when the doctor, the nurse and the pilot go out.

An example of that would be the time we unfortunately bogged the aircraft out at Laura, which is west of Cooktown, on the edge of the Lakefield National Park. I think it might've been the Queen Air or C-90, I'm not exactly sure now, but they had a dirt strip there at Laura and we were flying in for a clinic. So the pilot's coming in to land and there's the local nurse, parked in her car, in a place at the end of the runway, which was making things a bit difficult for our pilot to land. So our pilot's saying, 'What the hell's she parked there for?'

Anyhow, we landed okay and our pilot's taxiing the plane down the strip and he's going on about how dangerous it was for the nurse to park where she had because she could've caused an accident and all that. 'Get outa the bloody way!' he says. Then, after the nurse had moved her car, the pilot went to turn the aeroplane around and he bogged it. So it then became very apparent as to just why the nurse had parked her vehicle over that particular section of the airstrip—to warn him that it was too wet.

Anyhow, we went ahead and we did the clinic that morning. Then once we'd finished the clinic we spent the afternoon digging the aircraft out of the bog. And that turned out to be a real team thing too, because there we all were—the pilot, the doctor and nurse, along with every other able-bodied person in town—all with shovels and so forth, helping get this aeroplane out of the bog.

That's just one incident. Another example was when we had to shut one of the engines down. It was the right-hand engine and because the pilot couldn't leave his seat, he couldn't see out that side of the aeroplane. So he asked me to get up the front, in the cockpit, which I did. Then he got me to look back around the window.

'Can you see the engine?' he asked.

'Yes,' I said.

'Are there any flames?'

Thankfully there weren't.

So not only do we have to work as a team, we've also got to be flexible within that team structure, because there's a lot of times when we might land somewhere and we've got to grab all our gear and get out of the aeroplane and jump into the back of a truck or ute and be driven out along some shockingly rough, slippery, muddy track to where the patient is. And everybody pitches in and helps each other out. Say if there's an accident: usually it's the pilot who's trying to erect a shade over the patient or they're standing there holding the IV (intravenous) drip, or maybe the pilot's running backwards and forwards to the aircraft to 'get the big orange pack' or to 'get the little black pack' or whatever, while the doctor and the nurse are busy attending the injured. Naturally we don't overstep our boundaries and we don't cross disciplines but we all help each other out, under direction, and the best we can.

Then there's other times when we've all had to get in a boat and row across a creek to get a patient out of their humpy and bring them back. That actually happened at Bloomfield, which is up in the Daintree National Park. I wasn't the nurse in that case; another nurse was involved. But with that one, it was wet season and this feller was sick and his mate had radioed for help and warned us that the creek was flooded. So the RFDS crew got the message and they flew up there and when they landed they got a lift out to the flooded creek. Then they jumped in a boat and rowed across the creek, and after they got to the other side, they went off to do the house visit. The feller was pretty crook in bed so they then had to get him out of his house, back to the creek, into the boat, then row him back across the flooded creek, where they got a lift back to the airstrip, loaded the patient in the aeroplane, then flew him out to hospital. I mean, that's service, isn't it?

Also, I guess that a lot of the weather-related stories you've heard have been about dust storms and deserts and that. But because Cairns is one of the wettest places in Australia, we get lots of wet ones up here. So getting bogged is probably our worst problem and also not being able to land because of the poor weather or just having to go round and round and round till you just about throw up. And then you have to call it quits because if you did manage to land, you'd get bogged anyway and you wouldn't be able to take off again, and that doesn't help anybody.

Of course, situations like that can be totally devastating, especially if there's an emergency and you can't land the aeroplane. From that point of view, the worst time I remember was when we were running a clinic in Birdsville, which is in the south-western corner of Queensland, just down near the South Australian border. This was back, very early on in the piece, when I was working out of the Charleville base and a lot of the medical calls were still done by radio. Anyway, we got an emergency call through on the radio from a father who lived about 150 miles east of Birdsville. He was in a shed and he was telling us that his son had been electrocuted. But because the airstrip on his property was so wet, unfortunately there was no possible way we could get out there. In fact, it'd been raining so heavily everywhere east of Birdsville that it was heavy flooding. And having to listen to this call on the radio, over the speakers, it was just very, very ... well, it stayed with me for a very long time, because basically we were trying to talk the father through CPR (cardiopulmonary resuscitation) and when you're very nervous or upset, like the father was, you get the shakes.

Even medical people sometimes get the shakes in emergency situations. That happens because your body's producing adrenaline in an attempt to try and help you cope with the situation. It's exactly like you've had a big fright or something like that. And when people get like that they think they can feel a pulse when, in reality, they can feel the shaking of their own pulse. And this distraught father thought he could still feel a pulse and he was calling out, 'I can still feel a pulse. I can still feel a pulse', and we were trying to explain that there was no possible way we could get out there and land on his strip because of the flooding. So then he's calling out, 'Quick, get a helicopter then. Quick.'

But it's tough to have to say, 'Sorry, it's just not going to help, because even if we could get a helicopter, it'll be at least eight hours before it reaches you.'

What he didn't understand was that the nearest helicopter would've been at Toowoomba, or maybe even Rockhampton, and even if we could've organised a helicopter, it still would've been five or six hours' flying time away. And there's no way anyone could keep doing CPR for that long and have the person survive. Generally, after thirty minutes, that's when you'll make a call. By saying 'make a call', I mean having to make a decision. Usually, if you haven't got any heartbeat back within thirty minutes and you're still doing CPR, well, then you'll 'make a call' and declare the patient dead.

So after being on the radio for at least half an hour and from how the father was describing that his son had turned blue and he was still unresponsive, the doctor was forced to say, 'Look, if you're still having to do CPR and he's not responding, I'm afraid your son's dead.' And the father was still screaming, pleading with us to get a helicopter out there, which, being a parent, you can understand he'd do.

That's probably the saddest story I've got. But we just couldn't get out there because of the wet conditions. Even if it'd been dry it still would've taken, I don't know, maybe an hour or something to fly out there, and that would've also been too late. I mean, we probably would've attempted it because that's the way we are. We never give up. But that was a heartbreaking one, that one was—to hear the father just so, so distressed and there was absolutely nothing we could do about it. Sometimes, logistically, it's a nightmare.

Anyhow, I guess I've got off the track a bit there, because as I said, really the main thing I wanted to get across was that with the doctor, the nurse and the pilot, and even with all the support staff, when you're working for the RFDS, it's an incredible team sort of thing.

Almost but not Quite

I was amazed that in my earlier years as a pilot, with both the Cairns Aerial Ambulance and the Royal Flying Doctor Service, just how we were able to find some of these places, because really we had little to no nav (navigation) aids at all. In fact, I'm certain that somebody up there was looking after us.

Still and all, there were techniques you could use. Like, once you got airborne, if you held the correct heading that you'd flight-planned and you'd allowed for the estimated wind direction and speed, realistically, in the end, you could only be out by as far as the wind forecast was wrong, if you get what I mean. Of course, these weather forecasters, they're human just like the rest of us and while they do their best, at the altitudes we travelled there'd always be the potential for errors in their forecasted winds anyway.

So you'd have to take all that into consideration. For example, if you were flying to a place which is on the coastline, say the Aboriginal Community of Pormpuraaw up in the Gulf, what you'd do was you'd lay off significantly to one side. Then by doing that it'd bring you out 5 or 10 miles north of the community and then, when you came out of the cloud or if it was at night or whatever and you crossed the coast, you knew you had to turn left. But if you didn't allow for that variation and you came across the coast, well, you wouldn't know if you were to the south of Pormpuraaw or the north of Pormpuraaw and you'd then be left with the dilemma of 'Which way do I turn?' So those were the sort of techniques we used to use.

But as time went by and we started getting basic navigational aids at some of the remote locations, then you were pretty much home and hosed. By navigational aids I mean things like a non-directional beacon or VHF omni-ranger. You know, you'd have some sort of electronic guidance to the place via the radio. They call them radio 'nav aids'. Nowadays, of course, a lot of them have been superseded by route navigation based on Global Positioning System (GPS).

In actual fact, I remember the first time we put Global Positioning System in our King Air aircraft. It was after the Gulf War—the first Gulf War, that is—in the early '90s, just when GPS first started becoming available to the aviation community. The end result of this story was actually a bit disappointing but that had nothing to do with the GPS we were trialling. Anyhow, we put a GPS called a Trimble TNL 2000 into our evacuation King Air. There, that's not a bad memory for a bloke who's been out of the game for a fair while, is it? I don't know whether they're still in existence any more, but all of a sudden, with the help of twenty-three satellites or what have you, we were able to go to a geographical point with complete accuracy in all weathers.

Anyhow, a station property along the road up to Musgrave from Laura called us up one afternoon. I think it might've even been Kalinga Station though I'm not 100 per cent sure about that. But it was the middle of the wet season and it was raining and we had a conference here at Cairns that I was involved in. I happened to be on call at the same time so I got dragged away from the conference, with the ever patient nursing sister, and the two of us headed off to this particular property for an 'evac'.

Now, had we not had GPS on board, there was no way in this world—other than by just pure luck—that we would've been able to find the property. But the latitude and longitude of the place were well known and recorded so we were able to enter that into the GPS and it took us straight to the spot.

The only problem was that—and this was the disappointing bit—because it was raining so heavily, visibility was poor. And this is one of the things about visual flying: see, once you come off instrument flying into visual flying, naturally there has to be sufficient visibility for you to conduct a visual approach or what's called a 'circling approach'. That's 'circling', meaning you're making a circuit-type approach rather than straight into a runway. So of course you've got to have sufficient visibility to be able to meet those circling minimum requirements. But on this occasion we didn't have sufficient visibility and each time we tried to make a circuit we'd lose sight of the runway. So it was a case of almost but not quite, and after making three attempts we had to pull out of that one and we never got there.

But, as I said, that had more to do with the prevailing conditions rather than the GPS we were trialling and, as it turned out, three vehicles were already bogged on the airstrip, with the patient, so the odds were that if we'd have landed we wouldn't have been able to help anybody anyway. We'd only have ended up with a stuck aeroplane, which meant that we would've had to tax their fuel by them having to pull us out of the bog, plus taxed their food bill by us having to stay there for a few days until the strip dried out well enough for us to take off again. And so, as I said, all that wouldn't have helped the patient at all.

So, after having found the place with Global Positioning System—and what a tremendous advertisement it was for GPS—we weren't able to finish it off by landing. Anyway, I think it convinced management that the sooner we put GPS into all our aeroplanes the better it'd be for everyone involved. But I must say that it was actually a pretty rare event when a Flying Doctor aeroplane was unable to reach a patient. Anyhow, in the end in that particular case they somehow managed to get a four-wheel-drive vehicle out to the property and they miraculously evacuated the patient to Laura. Then I think he was brought up by helicopter to Cooktown or something, so it was quite a roundabout route to go. But he did survive.

Are You Sure?

Of course, each and every one of us in the Royal Flying Doctor Service always try to present ourselves to the public in the best light possible. That's a given. It's a simple matter of professionalism.

And, anyway, in the greater scheme of things, this was sort of irrelevant, I guess. But we are talking about 'anecdotal' stories, aren't we? I remember when I was working up in Broken Hill. Back in those days I was the administration officer out at the RFDS base up there and we had this doctor who used to ride his push-bike out to work, as opposed to drive. It's about a 5 or 8 kilometre trip, and it can get very hot in the summer. So he'd just wear any old casual clothes he could find laying around his home, and he'd ride his bike out, knowing that, even if an emergency arose, he always kept a set of nice clean clothes there, out at the base, and all he had to do was have a quick shower, jump into his good clothes, and he'd be ready to fly out in no time flat.

Anyway, he and I were what I'd call mates. You know, he'd always come into my office and we'd have a good chat about this, that and the other. The usual sort of stuff that blokes talk about: the weather and that, mixed with a bit of bull. Then one day he was the doctor-on-call and so in the morning he just threw on some old clothes and he rode out to the base, as per usual. But he'd no sooner got to work than he got paged. It was a priority one. An emergency. I think it was a roll over and there were some fatalities. From memory, it was a family with a caravan, out on the Sydney road, the other side of either Cobar or Nyngan, somewhere in that area. And with it being a priority like that there's a lot of organising to be done in a very short time. Other than the medical side of things, there's the assessments for a road landing and things like that. Anyhow, all that's okay; everything's ready. He's been given some details—not all, but some, and they're just about ready to go.

The next thing, he comes rushing into my office. 'I've left my clothes at home,' he says. Apparently he'd taken his good clothes home to be washed or something and he'd forgotten to bring them back out to the RFDS base, as he always did. Well, almost always.

Now, this was back in the good old days when the presentable, and even the fashionable, attire was, you know, the long socks and the good shorts and the open neck shirt. I think it was called the 'Safari era'. So there I was dressed like that and there he was decked out in a dirty old pair of stubby shorts and a tatty old round-neck T-shirt with, I reckon it might've even been a Newcastle Brown beer logo or something of that description, in the middle of it.

Anyway, as it happened he and I were a similar size and so he looked at me and I looked at him and it was basically, 'No option.' So we disrobed in my office. He takes off his stubbies and T-shirt. I take off my shorts and shirt and long socks. I think we might've left our footwear as it was. I'm not sure now, but the thing is, I've now got his dirty old stubbies on and his tatty old T-shirt and he's looking nice and presentable and professional. And so off he flew, out to this high priority along the Broken Hill to Sydney road.

Good, that's all done, and so I go back to work. The next thing, my secretary comes into the office and says, 'There's an official from the Australian Nurses' Federation outside. She's come out to have some discussions with you about our nurses and to see how things are going.'

And there's me, always the one for good presentation and professionalism, and I'm dressed like I've just come in from the garden or somewhere. So this woman comes into the office. She was a good-looking woman: very well presented, very professional looking.

'G'day. I'm John, the admin officer,' I say.

And the shock on her face. You should've seen it. She just stood there, looking me up and down as if to say, 'Are you sure?'

I mean, it was quite embarrassing at the time really, because, as I said, we always try and present ourselves to the public in the best possible light. Still, I guess on that particular occasion, given the circumstances, you could say that I had presented myself in the best available light I could possibly present myself in. But, oh, it was a funny reaction she gave me. I can still remember the look on her face.

Broken

I left school when I was about twelve or thirteen and I got a job out at a place called Ned's Corner Station, which is up there in the top corner of Victoria, near New South Wales and South Australia. I'd say that that was in about 1939. So I got this job with a drover, but what I didn't count on was that I'd be working seven days a week for two and sixpence per week. And not only that—I also had to get up and do a two- or two-and-a-half-hour watch every night of the week and live on damper and corned beef; then, for a change, we'd have corned beef and damper.

But anyhow, I stayed with droving for a good long while and over the time I had a few tangles, mainly with horses. Like, four or five years ago I had some special infra-red ray tests on my lungs and they told me that I've had twenty-two broken ribs. Some might be just cracks, I don't know. So you could say that I've not only broken a few horses in, but also a few horses have broken me in too.

There was one time, back when I was packhorse droving, when a horse kicked my ribs in and I ended up with a big red-blue patch that you could cook a bloody egg on. But anyhow, I kept on working; then ten days later when it was time to come home, I couldn't get up on the horse. So I had to walk all the way back. That one hurt so bad that after a while I went to a doctor and he said that one rib was sitting on top of another and the underneath one was all split. Apparently it'd tried to knit but it kept breaking off and it'd turned into some sort of a big abscess. See, bones have to knit straight; they can't knit crooked. I found that out the hard way.

Then I've also got a few bumps on my foot. See, just there—all those bumps. That happened in '49 or '50 when I broke the bones right across the top, there. It was a Saturday morning, and it'd started to rain, and a couple of mad bullocks had come down from out of the Blue Mountains, so I said, 'I'll just go up and grab these two bullocks.'

So I on the horse flew up a narrow ridge, through wire-grass this high, and the horse went straight into a rabbit warren. He didn't even see the thing. Anyhow, I managed to get clear but when I saw that the horse was trying to get back up, I got back in the saddle. So I got back up but then the horse scrambled in the wet and he slid right down the side of the hill and I went with him.

Now, I don't know exactly what happened but I heard the bones break and I felt my foot crack. I think that the tail of my boot must've hooked against a stone or something and it brought my foot back around like that, twisting it right up, and snap. Then when I looked down, I saw these two bones sticking out of my boot, so I cut the boot off. A good pair of boots, too, they were.

The horse was alright, though. He was better off than me. He was just covered in mud from sliding down the side of the mountain. But then he couldn't get back up to where I was because it was too slippery and there was a fence in his way so I ended up having to crawl for eight hours until I got to help. And I tell you, I was getting a bit worried there for a while because it was still pouring with rain and the gullies were getting fuller and fuller and the water was flowing faster and faster. Anyhow, I eventually made it back.

But a couple of the bones in my foot just wouldn't knit so they had to go and re-break them. That proved to be a bit of a problem too, because it was so hard to get the bones dead straight for them to set and so they had to keep on re-breaking them. In the end I think the foot had to be broken seven or eight times until eventually they set. And then they had to scrape out all the bone chips.

Then there was another droving trip I was on. We hadn't been on the road too long. Anyway, I'd drawn two horses to ride and one of them was pretty flighty, and I knew that if this feller got his head right down he'd do me, so I had to keep his head on his chest. I mean, he was a good horse but he just never wanted to go to work in the morning.

Anyway, one morning just after daylight the bugger threw me and broke my arm. And, oh hell, he done a proper job of it too, because it was all bent around the wrong way. Now this happened somewhere before we got down to Barringun Gate, on the Queensland-New South Wales border. The area was all new to me, but luckily the boss knew his way. So they tucked the arm up there, like that, and they put it in a sling, then the boss and me, we jumped on our horses and off we went for help. Now I reckon we rode for about twenty or thirty mile before we come to a dogger's camp. Doggers are blokes who go out setting dingo traps. Dingoes are a big problem up that way, too. So, anyhow, we got fresh horses there, then we done another 20 mile until we came across a mustering camp. We got fresh horses there again and then we rode another 20 mile to the homestead. I forget the name of the place now, but the Flying Doctor was only an hour or so away and when he come he took me over to the butcher's table.

See, at the homestead there was one of those huge big tables for laying a bullock on to butcher it. The top end was made of wood so that they could cut the beast with knives then the other end was steel so that you could slide half a bullock around. I mean, it was a pretty solid table, bolted down to the floor and all. And it had to be, because you didn't want it to tip over when you dumped a bullock on it. But anyhow, running at an angle from the table to just down the legs, there were these iron stays. Now as I said, my arm was pretty badly broken and for it to have any chance to set, first they had to straighten it out. So they just put my broken arm through one of these stays and the doctor got his feet against the table and he yanked like hell on the arm until he got it back into position. Boy, it hurt. I reckon my eyes just about shot off in different directions, all at the same time.

'There you go,' the doctor said. 'That didn't hurt much, did it?'

Like bloody hell. I mean, it was my arm that was broke, not bloody his.

Anyhow, after the Flying Doctor bloke pulled my arm back together, he plastered it up and I went out and I sat in the sun to let it dry off a bit. Then at about five o'clock that night, after I'd had a cup of tea and a bite to eat, the boss and me, we set out again and we relayed horses all the way back until we got to our camp at daylight, just in time for me to start work again. Anyhow, with my broken arm all plastered up, I picked out a nice quiet horse this time.

But I tell you, that night I was never so pleased to see a dinner camp in my life. Then one of the other blokes, a ringer mate of mine, a black fella, he said, 'Don't worry, Dusty, I'll do yer watch tonight. She'll be alright.'

'Beaut,' I said, and I didn't even wait to have dinner. I just went and curled up in my swag and I slept for hours.

Then about six weeks later I was supposed to go back to the Flying Doctor to get the plaster cut off. But I didn't bother about that. 'Blow it,' I said, and I just got a pair of tin snips and I cut the bugger off myself.

Burns

I worked as a doctor for the Royal Flying Doctor
Service for fifteen years and, while it was a very rich
and rewarding experience, oh, we had some very
harrowing things to deal with. Because unfortunately
not all our retrievals lead to happy endings. But if
you've got a job to do, you just do it and that's all there
is about it. That's the doctor's edict, isn't it? But in my
experience, extremely severe burns cases are probably
the hardest ones to deal with, because if the veins
have been burnt then you can't get the cannula in, to
give them fluids—and they need lots of fluids—plus,
of course, there's the intravenous analgesics to relieve
the pain.

For example, I got a call once on the HF radio that
a feller had gone out on his motor bike to burn off
windrows of scrub on his station property. He was by
himself and he had some sort of fire lighting machine,
or flame thrower, tied around his neck, which ran on
a combination of diesel and petrol. So he was lighting
the windrows of scrub with this machine and whether
he had the wrong fuel combination in it or what I
don't know, but, anyway it exploded while it was still
attached to his neck and he received full thickness
burns and partial thickness burns to over 50 per cent
of his entire body surface area.

As I said, this feller was by himself. What's more,
he had no means of communication with his home
base. So he rolled on the ground to put the flames

out then, with these extensive burns to his body, he got on his motor bike and he rode 18 kilometres back to his home, opening and closing three gates along the way. And that was an amazing act. Because you know how in the bush it's continually drummed into us to 'always leave the gates as you find them?' Of course, you wouldn't expect someone to follow that rule when they have 50 per cent body surface area burns, would you? But he did. This feller, he did it to a tee. He opened and closed three gates along the 18-kilometre journey back to get help. So it's really ingrained in people, isn't it—'always leave gates as you find them.'

Anyway, he finally arrived at the homestead and that's when we got the call. So the pilot flew the nurse and I out there where, first of all, we resuscitated him. Then we prepared him for transport by putting in an indwelling catheter to catch his urine. We then loaded him in the plane and headed off to the Royal Brisbane Hospital. And this feller was in such a bad way that on the flight down to Brisbane his urine was just solid myoglobinuria, from the muscle which had been burnt. So you could say that he was sort of urinating melted muscle.

But he died, the poor feller, four or five days later on, in the Burns Unit at the Royal Brisbane Hospital. But, once again, as distressing as it was, that was a story of just sheer courage in my books. 'Always leave gates as you find them.'

Another extremely distressing event was when we got a call that two fellers had been burnt in an explosion at an oil rig, out on the South Australian border. The most serious of the two had received burns to over 90 per cent of his body surface area. He was still alive but he'd inhaled the flames, which meant that he'd burnt his lungs as well.

Now, the second feller, the one with the least burns, he pulled through eventually so I'll concentrate on the problems we had with the most seriously burnt feller. When we got out there, firstly I had to try and find a vein where there were no burns. With having burns to over 90 per cent of his body, that was difficult. In the end, the only place I could cannulate him was down at his ankle. I then put him to sleep—paralysed him—then I had to put an intratracheal tube into his trachea so that I could ventilate him. This also caused problems as his vocal cords had also been partially burnt and I had to split them before I could get the intratracheal tube into him. I was then faced with a greater problem; perhaps a more ethical one. I had a pretty fair idea that this feller was going to die. But, if at all possible, I wanted him to remain alive at least until his relatives could see him before he did die. And as our destination was the Royal Brisbane Hospital, that meant we'd have to keep him going for a fair number of hours. So we loaded the two fellers into the aeroplane and we called up another RFDS plane and we organised to meet halfway, at Charleville.

At Charleville we performed an escharotomy on the most serious of the two fellers, which entailed the cutting of burnt tissue. See, skin tissue, when it burns, contracts and causes a blockage of the blood flow, which doesn't allow the chest to expand for respiration purposes. So we did an escharotomy on him at Charleville and then we put him in the other plane and they took him down to Brisbane.

And that was that. His family did get to see him while he was still alive. Whether they wanted to or not, I don't know, because he was just a black, black charred mess. But it was very horrible from my point of view having to do these things, and it was also an extremely exhausting and emotional time, because the poor feller of course died, as I figured he would.

Call the Doctor!

By the late 1970s, early '80s, we'd well and truly established our station property, which was about 350 kilometres out from Kalgoorlie, in Western Australia. I was managing the place by this stage and one year we had a team of shearers from New Zealand come through, a large number of whom were Maoris. Anyhow, one morning one of the Maori chaps was shearing away and his handpiece jammed and it flew around and cut him severely on the forearm. With blood gushing everywhere, the first thing his mates did was to grab a towel and wrap it around his arm in an attempt to stem the flow. But this was only a temporary measure because it was obvious that urgent medical help was required.

At the time of the accident, I was working out in the sheep yards and the first thing that I knew about it was when one of the shearers came rushing out from the shed. 'There's been a serious accident,' he called. 'Is there any way we can get in touch with a doctor, and fast?'

Now, I'll just remind you that we were 350 kilometres or so from the nearest hospital. But, as luck would have it, I had the portable radio in the car. So I got straight onto the Flying Doctor base in Kalgoorlie and told them about the problem and how the shearer was in dire need of help.

'Well actually,' the person at the base said, 'at this moment there's a plane on its way back to Kalgoorlie from a clinic run out along the Eyre Highway and Trans-line. We'll divert them. And don't worry,' the person added, 'they should be there in a few minutes.'

So I raced the 4 kilometres or so down to the homestead then I drove on down to the airstrip. The plane arrived not long after and I rushed the doctor back up to the wool shed, where he got straight in and treated the injured shearer.

Now, in this particular case the doctor had arrived on the scene of the accident within an hour. So you can imagine what this team of New Zealand shearers was thinking. They couldn't believe it. Here was one of their mates, having been severely injured, right out on the Nullarbor, which is out in the middle of nowhere, hundreds of kilometres from the nearest town, and help arrived so quickly. Within the hour. To them, it was almost unbelievable, and of course, it brought home the huge importance of the Royal Flying Doctor Service, not only for the shearers themselves but they also realised just how important the RFDS is to everyone living out in these remote areas.

And so appreciative of the service were these New Zealand shearers that, at the end of the shearing, they decided to donate an hour's time in aid of the RFDS. That is, each of the shearers gave one hour's shearing time, the shed hands gave one hour's wages; everyone did, right through to the contractor himself. And for what was an eight-stand team, this ended up making quite a sizable cheque. Then, when the next-door neighbour heard about this, he also cottoned on to the idea. Better still, he had a bigger flock and a bigger shed and of course a bigger team, which in turn translated into an even bigger cheque.

In the end, this giving of time became an annual fundraising event throughout the area. As a follow-on from that, all the shearing contractors in Western Australia ended up establishing a state-wide appeal, with the shearers and such donating an hour of their working time and with all the proceeds going to the RFDS.

Camp Pie

I first started with the RFDS as a flight nurse up in Port Augusta, South Australia, then I went down to Adelaide for a while and now this is my third year up in the Northern Territory, working out of Alice Springs. Initially, I used to get terribly airsick. Oh, for the first three weeks I remember I was as sick as a dog. Then one day I just suddenly got over it, thank goodness, and now I don't have a problem with airsickness, not even when we're going through the roughest of conditions.

Actually, I remember when the turn-about took place. We were flying a young guy back after he'd somehow been blown out of a cherry-picker and had broken just about every bone in his body. This was before we had pressurised aircraft so we had to fly at around the 2000-feet level. I knew it was going to be rough so as we were about to take off my first thought was, 'Here we go again. I'm going to be airsick.'

Anyhow, we took off and as we were flying along, getting bounced around, the doctor wasn't offering a great deal of help and so all of my focus was on this seriously injured patient. Then when I turned around to ask the doctor if he might lend me a hand, there he was with his head stuck in a sick bag, really going for it. Great help, aye. And at that exact moment it struck me: 'Hey, I don't get airsick any more.' And I haven't been airsick since.

But some people just really struggle to adjust to working inside an aircraft while it's in flight. Another time, I remember, we had a paediatrician out with us—he was only a new chap—and we flew from Port Augusta, out to Cooper Pedy, on to Yalata, then back to Port Augusta, and he threw up all the way. Mind you, at the time I was pretty annoyed with him. But then after a while you look back on those sort of things as humorous events, don't you?

One that wasn't so funny was when I first came up here to Alice Springs and we flew out to a community in the Pitjantjatjara Lands for a guy who'd had a heart attack. By the time we arrived it was dark and, so that we could land, the pilot had to activate the lighting on the strip. Then when we walked into the emergency room, this crook bloke, he was very, very sick indeed. Actually, he was grey. After doing ECGs, we decided that we had to give him a couple of doses of a certain medication that helps dissolve the clots in the heart.

Then, just as we were giving him the first dose, a huge thunderstorm hit. Absolutely huge it was, and the lightning struck the power supply and all the lights went out in the community. So we didn't have any lights. Anyhow, the second dose of the medication had to be given thirty minutes after the first dose, that's providing no abnormalities develop in the patient's heart reading. At that stage we were monitoring him with a torch, on the life pack, in an attempt to gauge whether to give him this second dose or not.

In the meantime our pilot's out at the generator, with the essential services officer, trying to see if they can fix the power because the doctor was keen to fax off copies of the ECG to the specialist in Alice Springs. And of course without power, the fax machine wasn't working. The phones weren't working either and we also needed power to light the airstrip so that we could take off. So we waited for half an hour and in the end we just decided to go ahead and give the second dose by torchlight. Then, just as we were doing that, the ambulance drove up and its lights shone straight into the emergency room and we discovered, 'Oh, we've now got light.' So we did the rest by the headlights of the ambulance, and everything went beautifully.

Anyhow, we finished the treatment and we gave the patient pain relief. Finally they got the power back on and the lights sorted out so we prepared the patient and we headed out to the airstrip. Then just as we started getting ready to load the stretcher, the heavens opened again and it just bucketed down. Absolutely bucketed down. There was water everywhere. The only person that was dry was the patient because we'd put a plastic sheet over him.

Of course, now the pilot's on edge because a heavy downpour on a dirt strip can make for an extremely difficult take-off. What's more, the plane was a Pilatus PC 12, which is worth something like $5 or $6 million, all decked out. They're like a flying hospital. Basically, they've got everything you'd need in an ICU (Intensive Care Unit). So they're very expensive things, which was why the pilot was so on edge. The last thing he'd want to do was to drop the thing or bog it or damage it in any way.

Anyhow, there we were, soaked to the bone and freezing cold. Still, we managed to get the patient into the plane and after a careful assessment we took off. But because of the thunderstorm, it was an extremely rough flight and by now I'm going through the possibilities of 'What else could go wrong?' So I made the patient as comfortable as I could and made doubly sure that everything was nice and tight and secure.

'Good,' I said to myself, 'now I can relax a bit.'

No sooner had I said that than the patient started vomiting. And that was the final straw because now there were bits of camp pie being sprayed all over the place. Anyway, we eventually landed back in Alice Springs. The storm was over by then and the next day they flew the patient down to Adelaide, where he had bypass surgery. So it all worked out well for him. But we were left to clean his mess out of the plane and then, of course, my uniform also had chuck all through it. It was just shocking. There was camp pie everywhere.

Captain 'Norty'

Because my name's Norton Gill, everyone out at the base knows me as 'Capt Norty'. So you could say that my wife has a 'Norty' in bed with her every night. I've been a pilot with the RFDS for twenty-four years or so now. And, yes, I still enjoy it. When I get that call at two o'clock in the morning or whenever, I still get out of bed and I just go out there and I do it. But I'm going on sixty years old and I've only got a year and a bit to go before I retire. And when that happens, my wife, Margaret, and I, we'll join the grey nomads and drive around Australia.

But oh, sometimes these aeroplanes can play tricks and, you know, when they do they can really put the wind up you. I can remember going from Cairns over to the Gulf of Carpentaria one time to visit the Kowanyama Aboriginal Community. I was flying a King Air that had just come out of maintenance. Anyhow, it was coming on dark so the sun was just going down. I had the doctor sitting up front with me—a bloke called Gary—when all of a sudden an alarm came on to say that we had a fire in the left-hand side motor or, in flying terms, the port motor.

'What's that?' Gary called out.

'It's the fire alarm,' I said.

Well, he mustn't have comprehended that straight away because he said, 'What, have we got a fire?'

So I had a bit of a look out of my side window and I said, 'No, I don't think so. I can't see anything.'

And that's what you do. If you get a fire warning in these aeroplanes, the first thing you do is have a look and see if there's any smoke coming out anywhere. Then if there is, the first thing you do is close down the motor. It's not really such a big drama. I mean, you've got systems in place. There's fire extinguishers on board and all that to put a fire out. But I've never heard of one ever catching fire.

But the thing that did concern me was that if this King Air had just come out of maintenance, well, it does make you wonder, doesn't it? Anyhow, we continued flying along with Gary, the doctor, breaking out into a sweat while he's sniffing here and there, just in case he can detect smoke. Then, would you believe it, a couple of seconds later the right-hand, or starboard, motor fire alarm comes on. So then we had two fire alarms going. And if poor old Gary wasn't pretty twitchy beforehand, he certainly was now.

'Is there another fire?' he asked.

'Well,' I said, 'look out your side window. Can you see any smoke?'

So he craned his neck as far as it could go. 'No, I don't think so,' he said.

'Well,' I said, 'just you watch this,' and I turned the aircraft about 45° and, when I did, both the fire alarms went out, just like that. So then he started to relax ... just a tiny bit.

But see, what happened in those older model King Airs was that if the sun was at just the right angle it shone, or reflected, through a small gap somewhere and it used to hit these little sensor things inside the motor. That's when you'd get the fire alarm coming on. I mean, you didn't even need sunlight. The same thing used to happen back when I was doing night freight and sometimes you'd start up under normal electric light and a fire alarm would come on. Then, very occasionally, they'd even come on in the rain.

Anyhow, it was quite an interesting thing to have both alarms come on. That was extremely unusual. But it wasn't fire. And in those King Airs they had a turbine motor—the Pratt and Whitney PT6s—and really I've never heard of any of them ever catching fire. It was just that they had these old fire sensors in them, that's all. So yes, poor old Gary, he got quite twitchy about it all. It really put the wind up him. Mind you, I must admit it initially put the wind up me too, especially when both the port and starboard fire alarms came on.

Coen

Yes, well, my husband Col and I weren't rich or anything. We were country people so we just 'made do', if you know what I mean. Anyhow, when Col finished up bee farming—he was a honey man— he wanted to go and see his sister, Jess, who was working up at Coen, almost to the top of Cape York Peninsula in Queensland. After Col retired we still had his work truck so we took the wheels off a little old caravan and we bolted the caravan onto the back of the truck and we went all the way up in that to see Jess. And, oh, what a journey it was. There were times when I was afraid we'd never get home.

Jess was nursing at the Australian Inland Mission Hospital up there. At that time, the last three tribes of full-blood black Aborigines were also living there. The mission had a hostel for them so that they could have their children taught. But, oh, it was very, very primitive. There was no electricity. They did have generators but they didn't run all the time. Then the phone—you could only use it at certain hours; like you could only get through in the evening or something like that.

But Jess had been thoroughly trained in nursing. In her early days she'd been a bush nurse and she'd go around on horseback. She could do anything, just about. And she had to up there too, because there was no doctor up in Coen. The nurse had to do everything. She was three years up there, and that was at the end of her nursing because she was an older woman by then. Her sight was going and she could only manage to do so much for so long.

From memory, the main part of the mission at Coen was all combined in the one building. Then, as far as white people went, there was a lady and her husband running the hostel part. The man was a lay preacher and his wife did the cooking and looked after the children in the hostel part. Jess had a portion of that building as her clinic, and it was a nursing home as well. Now, I don't know how many years the lay preacher and his wife had been working there. I suppose they could've stayed for as long as they wanted to actually, because not too many people would want to go up and live in a place like that.

Now, I'm not exactly sure what the Aboriginal people did because most of them were quite old. The older ones were kept in a separate part. They were living in either brick or cement buildings, which were quite basic. You know, just sort of a building with a room and a stove and a bed. It was just simple. And the government supplied everything for those Aboriginal tribes because they were very primitive and they had all their dogs. They were still walking around with bare feet and they hardly wore any clothes. Really, to be honest, they much preferred to live outside and have a little tiny fire on the ground, like they did in their natural way—like they were used to doing.

With any of the more serious medical problems or injuries, Jess would have to get on the radio and ask the Flying Doctor Service to come up and fly the patients back down to Cairns. Oh, and, of course, she was very well trained as a midwife. So yes, Jess did it all, she even sewed up their wounds, because the Aborigines were on welfare and they were allowed to drink and so there was always trouble. Jess not only had to nurse them, she also had to go around each day and she'd have all their medications ready and everything.

But she did have one couple there, with a little boy, and they were described as Islanders. They weren't the full-blood Aborigines like the three remnant tribes were. I met them and Col and I were taken to where they lived, and they were different altogether because they had a garden and they knew how to farm and grow things like fruit trees and all that.

Then, for the younger black women who had husbands and children, the government had built them cottages. These cottages were designed like our normal houses, but they were all aluminium—the walls, the roof, everything. And the government sent up a lady to supervise that section of it and to keep an eye on things. Anyway, this supervisor lady turned out to be good company for Jess because she helped Jess supervise the young women and their husbands and their children and their babies.

Anyhow, it took Col and I ten days to get from Gosford up to Coen. Also the truck was quite old and so Col didn't want to rush. Well, he couldn't rush really. It was a diesel and you didn't rush diesels in those days. But I tell you, the roads, well, they'd get washed away in the wet season, then they'd fix them up again and they'd get washed away again, and all the crossings were washed away. It was shocking. Luckily we didn't travel in the summer. I think it might've even been autumn. The weather was pretty reasonable anyway, because the creeks were quite dry, though you had to be very careful when you were crossing them, with all the sharp rocks and everything.

I mean, well, Col's a bushman but just the same, he wasn't a bushman for that sort of country. So it was a real struggle to get up there and we did break down a couple of times. The first time, luckily a man came along with his big truck, which was loaded with supplies for the shop in Coen, and he said, 'For heaven's sake, come behind me or you'll never get there.' So that's how we came to travel behind him, and we felt a bit safer then.

Then, when we finally made it to Coen, we broke down again and they said, 'Well, we'll have to send to the coast for the part', and when the part didn't arrive when it was supposed to they said, 'You're in Queensland now, so you'll have to wait until the next load comes because they forgot to put it on the truck.' As I said, that was a long time ago now and so I suppose things would've changed a bit in Queensland by now. I hope so anyway.

But of course my big worry was, 'How on earth are we going to get back home?' I thought we'd be stuck there forever because by that stage the tyres on Col's truck were badly worn and we had to go back through crossings that were full of sharp rocks and logs and things. It was just terrible. It just wasn't suitable for tourists.

But then, coming back from Coen, we hardly had any trouble at all. See, it's when you go out into the unknown, into somewhere different like that, that's when you have all the worries. But once you've done it, then the fear's gone.

Dad

I'm sure you've heard the term 'Mantle of Safety'. That encapsulated John Flynn's dream to cover all aspects of care for those who lived and worked in the outback. So, with Flynn as its driving force, the Australian Inland Mission set up hospitals and sent trained nurses out to those remote areas. Then the Flying Doctor Service more or less supported the services of the AIM, plus the many other outback support organisations.

Another important part of Flynn's 'Mantle of Safety' was to also provide spiritual care and it was to that end that my father, Fred McKay, was recruited by Flynn in 1936 to go out in his International truck and work as a Patrol Padre, throughout western Queensland. Now these Patrol Padres were never heavily evangelical or anything. They tended to be more of a comforting presence to people. I mean, yes, they did weddings. They did baptisms. They did burials. They did all those sorts of things. But they were especially trained to meet outback people on their own level. As Dad used to say, 'I meet people where their greatest need is.' So being the pretty handy sort of feller he was, Dad was always willing to hop in and work in a stockyard or he'd help out doing odd jobs around station homesteads.

Of course, having such a vast area to cover, the truck—the International—was really his home and Dad would sleep out by himself a lot of the time. So the funny thing was that when Dad and Mum married in 1938 and planned to travel together, Mum's parents were so alarmed at what they thought their daughter was getting herself in for, they made sure that Mum at least had something to sleep in, so they bought her a swag. In fact, the bulk of their wedding presents consisted of camping equipment: things like billy cans and tin plates and all that.

Also, by then, Alf Traeger had come up with his pedal-driven radio and for a lot of that earlier time Dad's only communication with the outside world was via the Traeger pedal radio. Really, the pedal radio was the link between the outback people, the Flying Doctor, the AIM hospitals, the Patrol Padres and the other care organisations who had set up missions out in different places as well.

So Dad carried the pedal radio around in the truck and maintained very close contact and ties with the various Flying Doctor bases and so forth. And perhaps I mightn't even be here today if it wasn't for the pedal radio. Because it was in about November 1938, when my mother was pregnant with me, that they were travelling out in south-western Queensland and they broke a king pin in the truck. It was one of those things that Dad had been assured would never happen to an International truck. But it did. And I've still got the broken king pin. It sits in our lounge room. Anyhow, the king pin broke and of course one wheel collapsed. I mean, Dad was a pretty good mechanic and he could do most running repairs but he certainly wasn't able to do anything as major as that. It was a crucial piece of equipment and couldn't be replaced, and certainly not out there.

So Dad and Mum found themselves stuck in a claypan near a place called Cuddapan which was about 50 kilometres, in a direct line, from Tanbar Station. You wouldn't find Cuddapan on a map these days but the closest large place was Windorah, which was about 110 kilometres further on from where they broke down. Anyway, there they were—stuck—and so Dad got on his pedal radio and sent out the message. Then after he'd sent the message he walked back along the track, leaving Mum in the truck. So there was my mother, pregnant with me and worried if she'd ever see Dad again and even whether she was ever going to get out of the situation alive. Anyhow, the feller from Tanbar Station heard the message. Luckily he knew the area quite well so he drove out and he met up with Dad and then they came back and pulled the International out of the claypan, much to Mum's relief.

That's the story I grew up with anyway. But as to other stories, you know, there were stories of Dad's patrol days; stories told by some of these hard-bitten bushmen in the early days of the Flying Doctor Service. One I remember was about an Aboriginal stockman who'd been out mustering and was seriously injured after being thrown from his horse. As luck would have it, Dad was visiting the stockmen's camp on his way through so he threw his aerial up in a tree and got on the radio and called the nearest Flying Doctor base, then he stayed there with the mustering crew until the plane arrived. But of course back in those early days, finding somewhere for the plane to land in many of those remote outback places was a bit of a dicey business too and they often had to chop down scrub to clear a makeshift airstrip. Actually, sometimes it was a bit of a miracle when they did ever somehow land and then take off again.

Anyway, so they cleared a bit of a space and the Flying Doctor's plane landed safely and they picked up this injured Aboriginal stockman. Then, as the plane took off into the sky, one of the old blokes in the camp looked up and when he saw that the shape of the aeroplane, with its wings and body, resembled a cross in the sky, he said to Dad, 'Well, if that isn't the flying Christ, Padre, I don't know what is.'

So that's just another small story. But really, I guess we, as a family, have learnt a lot more about our parents and their early years from reading their diaries rather than hearing a lot of stories. I mean, we used to hear Dad telling other people's stories but they were probably very much embellished and some of them, I recall, were unprintable. But their diaries were different because I think, in retrospect, some of the things they wrote then are more meaningful to me now. There was of course lots about everyday, normal things but then there were the hardships of travelling around the bush in a truck. There were the terrible roads, the extremes of the heat, cold and rain, plus there were all the unexpected events, both good and bad. Then of course there were times of great loneliness, when Dad was out there by himself or, later on, when it was just the two of them.

Though the thing that's most important to me is to read of the sacrifices they made in just trying to be there for other people and it was those sacrifices that made them both realise just why they were meant to be there. Even after Dad died, time and time again it was an absolute revelation to us as a family to read or hear about just how much of a part he'd played in the lives of so many many Australians.

But that was Dad's life's work. Even right up until his last years, when he was in his eighties, people would always be asking him to do something or other and no matter how tired or busy he was he'd always help them out in whatever way he could. Then, when we'd ask him why he continued to work so hard, he'd say, 'Well, it's my calling. This is what I'm meant to be doing. This is why I'm here.'

Difficult Conditions

When I was flying for the RFDS, as far as difficult conditions went, the weather was always the telling factor. It still probably is, though nowadays the aeroplanes are far better equipped to handle most things. I mean, we never had any of these modern 'nav' (navigation) aids or anything so we just had to do the best we could. But things could became scary at times. Thunderstorms are usually the most dangerous, mainly because of the turbulence. To blunder into one of those is not such a good thing. If you try to pull your plane out of the thunderstorm there's the chance that you might rip the wings off and then you end up with a wreckage trail of over 5 kilometres. I saw, just recently up in New South Wales, a plane was torn to pieces in a thunderstorm. So anyone who reckons that thunderstorms aren't scary, well, I'd say they're telling fibs.

Also, up in the higher levels, along with the turbulence you can get hail and that can do terrific damage. Big hail stones can wreck an aeroplane by damaging the front or battering the wings. But of course these days they've got radar and that can pick up the solids that are associated with a thunderstorm, like rain and the hail. And you also have what's called storm-scopes. They can detect the electrical discharge, which gives you a much more accurate picture. Storm-scopes also come in handy when you hit dry thunderstorms. A dry thunderstorm's one that's got no hail or rain in it. Some of them have lightning but mainly it's just severe turbulence. So if you hit a dry thunderstorm, all you can do is to try and hang on until you get spat out the other side of it.

Other than the thunderstorms, there's dust storms. I remember once flying a Navajo out to a station property on the Nullarbor, north of Tarcoola. Someone had had an accident on a motor bike and they needed to be picked up. But on our way out we got stuck in the middle of this hell of a dust storm. And, try as I might, I just could not see a bloody thing. In fact, I never actually found the property that we were supposed to be going out to and in the end I even had quite a job finding my way back home to Port Augusta. That's how crook it was, and rough too.

Fog's another difficulty that we were likely to face. I remember when a call came through that a crop sprayer had had a plane prang down at Naracoorte, in the south-east of South Australia. He happened to be a very good friend of mine, actually. He's okay now, but he was spraying and he flew straight into this great gum tree. Anyhow, we got there at night and there was this fog. Real thick stuff, it was. Now, Naracoorte's notoriously bad for fog, especially at night. So we sort of pushed the limits a bit and we landed in this blooming fog, which would be a definite big 'no-no' these days. You just don't do stuff like that now because of all the rules and regulations they've got in place. But that was a pretty dangerous flight.

So then, let me think: what other sort of difficult conditions were we likely to face? Well, there'd be dirt airstrips, especially after rain. You know, it's as wet as a shag, you land your plane and you get bogged. And believe me, aeroplanes are very easy things to bog and they're terribly hard things to get out once you've bogged them. Usually, before we flew out anywhere we'd check the conditions with the station owners or communities and if there was any doubt at all we'd ask them to go out and drive up and down the strip to see if it was firm enough for the plane to land. If their vehicle left wheel tracks, it was a sign that you could well end up in trouble. Also, of course, by asking them to do that, you'd have to rely on their judgment and most times they'd bias the safety aspect their way and not yours because, especially in an emergency, they'd just be so desperate to get you out there.

As well as that, depending on where you were going, you could ask them to do a run along the airstrip to clear any stock that might be wandering around the place. Then there's always the ongoing problem of the native wildlife like the emus and the roos. You can't do much about them because they'd come out of nowhere and just jump in front of you. And a roo, in particular, can do a terrific amount of damage, because if they hit right on the nose bill, the nose bill could collapse.

Actually, I was pretty lucky with the emus and the roos really, because most of the ones I hit ran through the prop, which basically just chopped them up. I remember at Port Augusta when the RFDS was thinking about buying the Pilatus PC 12 aeroplanes and we had all these guys coming out from Switzerland, picking our brains as to what sort of conditions we were operating in. Basically they were pretty keen to get it right, which they did.

Anyway, this particular time we had a salesman from Pilatus with us and this guy had no idea as to what outback Australia was like and what sort of conditions the Pilatus aeroplane would have to operate in. So we took him for a trip in the King Air, over the Flinders Ranges to Marree then to Nepabunna Aboriginal Community. Nepabunna was a bit of a doozy, actually. It's stuck right in a valley, with high hills all around, and you had to approach it and take off in the one direction—it's what's called a 'one-way strip'—and so we needed a plane with a good climb rate. So we landed there, at Nepabunna, and Nepabunna was a typical example of a stony airstrip. And this guy from Pilatus, well, he'd never seen anything like it. He was so impressed that he even took a handful of stones back to Switzerland to show them just what we were landing on.

I wasn't actually the pilot that time, so when it came time to leave Nepabunna I was sitting in the back and we were just taking off and the next thing, Bang! There's this terrific jolt as we hit this bloody kangaroo fair in the right-hand propeller and we chewed him up into little pieces. Anyhow, we inspected the prop and one blade had a bit of a woof in it. Still, it didn't look too bad so we decided to take off anyway. It wasn't my decision because I wasn't the pilot but you could feel the vibration through the aeroplane as we were flying along. It shook us around a bit. Of course, once again you wouldn't do that these days—you know, take off after an accident like that. That sort of stuff just doesn't go on now.

Then I guess another difficulty we had, especially in the early days, was the night landings. Before we started using flares we used to use cars to light up the strip at night. One time I remember, up at Marla Bore, in the far north of South Australia; this was back when there was only a roadhouse at Marla and it was virtually just about an all-dirt road right the way from Port Augusta up to Alice Springs. Anyhow, this truck missed a bypass around some wet ground and it rolled over with two blokes in it. It was a terrible accident. One of the drivers was crushed in the cabin and it took ages to get the other feller out of the wreck.

But, as I said, they weren't using flares in those days so a heap of vehicles went out and parked each side of the runway, and they sat there with their headlights on so that we could see where to land. The only trouble was that they sort of misjudged it a bit and when we landed there was only a whisker in between our wings and their bull bars. So after a few experiences like that, it then became a gradual process to educate settlements and communities into having night flares. And eventually everyone got those, which saved that mad scramble of trying to get as many cars as you possibly could to come and line up along the airstrip in the dark.

With the flares, the basic ones were either kerosene or diesel in a tin or the battery operated ones. Batteries were a bit of a problem because if you don't use them for a few months the batteries can go flat. Plus, batteries are very expensive. So really, the mix of diesel and sand proved the best. They were cheap and quick and easy to organise because the station people usually had all that stuff lying around the place anyway. You just grab a can or a milk tin or an old oil tin, fill it with sand, stick some rag in it, then you soak the sand with diesel, throw in a match and you've got a good flare that will last a fair while—cheap and easy. What's more, on a good night you could see them from about 30 miles away, no worries. Of course, if somebody mistakenly put in a bit too much diesel they could set fire to the countryside and then you'd get your direction from a hell of a lot further away than 30 miles.

So yes, I guess that's a few of the difficulties us pilots could face. But as the years go by you tend to pick up on what's good and what's bad and so your judgment becomes a little better. Experience has a lot to do with it because you can't be taught about a lot of things. Only experience teaches you.

But one last story—one with a little bit of humour to it—and this has to do with turbulence. I was still at Port Augusta back then and there was this big meeting happening up at Mount Willoughby or one of those places up that way. So there were quite a few 'bigwigs', as I'll call them for the sake of the story, who needed to be flown up to this meeting. I was in the King Air and just as we were on descent into Mount Willoughby we suddenly hit severe turbulence. And as we were going through this turbulence, I heard this sort of commotion going on from down the back of the plane. So I took a quick glance around and, for the life of me, I thought I saw this bloody possum running down the aisle. Then, in the split second while I was trying to work out how on earth a possum had got on board, this woman came chasing after it and she grabbed it in a flash and then she stuck it back on her head. That's what I meant by 'bigwig', and even when we landed it still looked a bit skew-whiff to me. I tell you, I wasn't the only one who was trying very hard not to laugh.

Disappearing Flares

This was an interesting one. It was actually with the same doctor, Gary, I'd put the wind up on a previous occasion when he thought we were about to go up in flames midair. So even before we took off, Gary seemed a bit jittery. We were going up to Cape Flattery. Cape Flattery's a mining place, on the eastern side of Cape York Peninsula north of Cooktown, not far from Lizard Island. It's still operational today as a sand and silicon mine. I think Mitsubishi is the crowd that operates it.

Anyhow, one night we got a call to go up there to Cape Flattery to pick up a lady who was reported to be swimming straight out to sea. And because it's full of crocodiles the local people were naturally getting a bit concerned about her welfare and so for her own safety they wanted her out of the place. Really, I think that basically she was a bit funny in the head, because apparently it was a yearly thing she did in an attempt to try and get the RFDS to give her a free trip down to Cairns 'to do a bit of shopping'.

To explain what I mean by 'to do a bit of shopping' ... Well, I often think a lot of these people are a lot smarter than you and me. So they throw a bit of a 'wobbly' and do something strange or mad, which puts the wind up everyone, and so the community wants them out of the place. Basically, it's all a set-up really. Of course, we don't charge any of our patients so they end up getting a free flight to town. Then after they arrive in Cairns they're taken to hospital where they're fed and watered for a day or two. Then they're released from hospital and away they go, 'off to do some shopping', you see. Well, that's just my take on it, of course.

But anyway, so it's night time and the chap who normally put the flares out for us at Cape Flattery wasn't there on this particular occasion. He was away somewhere, so they organised a replacement feller to do the flare-setting job. When we left Cairns we had a good south-easterly blowing. Now, with Cape Flattery being on the coast and normally blowing a gale, I had it in my head that we'd be landing into a south-easterly. It was only about a twenty-five-minute trip and when we arrived, there was a thin cloud cover at about 1000 feet. Of course, this happened back in the days when we didn't have GPS (Global Positioning System) but the aircraft radar system was able to tell the difference between land and water. So I got myself over water by using that.

Then I let down—lost altitude—over the water, then came down under the cloud and over-flew the airstrip to check on things. Back then they had kerosene flares and I could see that the flares were all set out, ready for my landing. So I came around to position myself with the runway then on the final approach, at about 300 feet, suddenly all the flares went out. It was just like somebody had turned a light switch off. Every flare just disappeared like that—snap.

'God, what's going on here?' I said to Gary.

So straight away I went around. I put the props up and the power up and the undercarriage up and then, as soon as I did that, I got this horn going off ... 'beep, beep, beep. So there's this big red warning light flashing as we went back through the cloud. Of course, Gary the doctor, he's thinking about a previous trip when the fire alarms went off, so he's immediately on edge and saying, 'What's going on here? What's going on here?'

'I've got no idea,' I replied, which didn't inspire him with one iota of confidence, I can tell you.

Now, it wasn't that long before heading out on this trip that I'd been endorsed on this aeroplane. So while I knew the particular aircraft well, I wasn't completely familiar with it, if you understand my meaning. So I rechecked everything and realised that I still had full flaps down. Of course, as soon as I rectified that, the alarms stopped and everything settled down nicely ... except Gary that is. For some strange reason he seemed to be shaking a fair bit.

So then we're back on top of this thin cloud layer again. 'Okay,' I said, 'I'll give it another go.'

As I said, it was night time. So it's back out over the water again, down under the cloud again, came back again, and over-flew the strip again to check the flares and, yes, all was right there. And it was while I was doing that I just happened to notice that about 20 miles away to the north-west of us there was a thunderstorm, and lightning started to flicker.

'Well, that's okay. That should be no problem,' I said. 'Let's attempt another landing.'

I came around again for the second attempt and as I was lining up to come in on final approach, I was getting blown around a bit. At the time I didn't realise it but what was happening was that the thunderstorm was pushing a local wind system in towards the aerodrome. So instead of me coming in against the south-easterly, as I'd assumed we would be doing, by now we were experiencing more of a north-westerly. Of course, I only found all this out later. So down we came again on final. I could see the flares, yes. I lined up, good. I could still see the flares, yes. In we came. Then at 300 feet, exactly the same thing happened again. Bang—all the flares went out. They disappeared.

I thought ... 'Oh, Jesus ...'

Anyhow, we aborted the landing and up we went again. By this stage I sensed that Gary was feeling very uncomfortable about the whole situation.

But I thought, 'That's okay. Third time lucky.'

So I followed the same procedure for the third time and we came back in again. And suddenly the same thing happened. At 300 feet all the flares went out. Now I knew Cape Flattery quite well because I used to fly in and out of there pretty regularly and I knew there was a powerline we had to cross. So then I said to Gary, 'Well, I don't know. This time we're going in further. We've got to investigate this.'

Gary didn't answer me. He just sat there, stony faced and slightly grey. Anyhow, we continued on down and when the landing lights of the aeroplane lit up the powerlines and I still couldn't see any flares on the runway, I said, 'Well, that's it, out we go.'

'Great idea,' Gary said, suddenly sounding a little more enthusiastic. But then, just as we're going back through the cloud his enthusiasm turns to fear and he starts yelling out, 'The right-hand side motor's stopped. The right-hand side motor's stopped.'

'Well,' I said, 'if this aeroplane's climbing so well on one motor, I don't really care.'

Now actually Gary had gotten a bit overly nervous and jittery because what had happened was that we've got the strobe lighting on the end of the wings and, of course, when you go through cloud, visually it looks like the prop (propeller) has stopped. Basically, it's just an optical illusion, with the strobing effect and the cloud. That's all it was. But obviously Gary didn't realise that. He thought the motor had stopped.

'Don't worry about it,' I said. 'Let's just get out of here and go home.'

Then we were halfway back home to Cairns when Townsville calls up and says, 'Oh, the mine at Cape Flattery wants you to go back again.'

And I took one look at Gary and he nodded his head in a very determined manner and replied, 'Nope. Not again tonight. We'll go back at first light tomorrow morning.'

Anyway, we landed back at Cairns and the next morning we were up early and back out there and everything went like clockwork. We sorted out the problem at the mine and we also brought the lady back for her 'shopping trip'. And after that I think that some of Gary's waning faith in me as a pilot was restored ... well, maybe just a little.

But, after thinking about it, I finally worked out what had gone wrong. See, the new feller—the one who'd taken over the flare duties—when he saw the thunderstorm coming he became concerned that the north-westerly wind might blow the flares out. So to protect them from the wind, he placed the flares behind the witches' hats—you know, those conical markers they use on airstrips and roads—and of course that meant when I came in to land and I hit a certain height and angle—which was the 300 feet level—the flares became hidden behind the witches' hats. That's why they all suddenly disappeared on me.

So that solved the case of the disappearing flares.

Down the Lot

About twenty-five years ago my husband, Wayne, was a ranger out at Mootwingee Historic Site. That was before it became a National Park, later named Mutawintji. To give you some idea, Mootwingee is in north-western New South Wales, approximately halfway between Broken Hill and White Cliffs. And, as a ranger, my husband and another ranger looked after the district that went up to White Cliffs. So it was a big area.

But I was a city girl. I was a teacher and I'd come out to live there with our six-week-old baby. There was no television and no telephone and the only way of communication was by the two-way radio. So, as you might imagine, it was a very different life for a city girl, though I must add that it was certainly a very memorable time.

Basically, our only direct communications outside Mootwingee was with the School of the Air and the Royal Flying Doctor Service. The RFDS had medical sessions, mornings and late afternoons. That's when anyone could contact the Flying Doctor base in at Broken Hill and discuss any of their health issues with the doctor. It was exactly like a normal doctor's consultation but conducted over the two-way. So the doctor would listen to their symptoms then tell them what medicines they should self-administer from out of the medical chest that was provided for a small fee to each station property.

Of course, while these consultations were going on everybody else in the area was also tuned in, so everyone got to know all your intimate health problems. It was the same with the telegrams as well, see, because the telegrams were read out over the air every half hour—again, anybody could listen in. So then everyone got to know all your personal business as well as your intimate health problems. Then between the medical calls and the telegrams they used to have what was called the 'Galah Sessions'. That's when the lines were open so that anyone could have a chat to anyone else while, naturally, everybody else was listening in as well. So in such an isolated place, no one got away with anything and everyone out there knew everything about everybody else's business.

Initially, I was unaware of all this. Then when we first arrived at Mootwingee, the other ranger's wife came over and straight away she said to me, 'Oh,' she said, 'if you ever get thrush for God's sake don't call the Flying Doctor Service because everyone's always glued into their two-way radios and they'll have a great chuckle about it.'

Then she told me that, if I ever got thrush, what number the medication was that I should use out of the medical chest we had.

'Oh fine,' I said, 'thanks for telling me.'

But, coming from the city, I still didn't quite believe her. I mean, you wouldn't, would you? That was until our six-week-old got his first cold and, even though it was nothing major, we radioed in to the RFDS doctor at Broken Hill for some medical advice. Then after that, whenever my husband went out on his rounds everyone would say, 'Oh, and how's the baby going? Is he over his cold yet?'

Anyhow, because there wasn't much in the way of other entertainment I must admit that even I started listening in to these sessions. And that brings me to the time I overheard a medical session on the two-way radio with a shearer on an outpost, and this shearer had some sort of a boil. Well, the doctor quizzed him about his diet and suggested that he, the shearer, and the rest of his shearing mates should be eating more vegetables. Then the doctor said that the shearer should take a certain course of antibiotics from out of the medical chest. 'But only take as prescribed,' the doctor warned.

Now, I don't remember the exact name of the antibiotics that the doctor mentioned because, as I said, everything went by numbers. You know, the doctor would just say, 'Get bottle number sixty-five and number twenty-eight out of your medical chest, take one tablet from each twice a day with meals, and that should fix the problem.'

Anyway, soon after the consultation between the shearer and the doctor had finished, the station manager's wife got on to the two-way radio and she called the shearer's cook, the one who was out at the outpost where the shearer with the boil was, and she started going crook on this cook. 'I hear that one of the shearers has got on to the doctor about his boil,' she said.

'Yes,' replied the cook.

Then the station manager's wife said, 'Look, I've told you lots and lots of times that you have to give the shearers vegetables. Feed them lots of vegetables. You can't just give them meat. You really have to cook them vegetables.'

And this is all happening over the two-way radio and, as I said, there I was, a city girl, and as much of an experience as Mootwingee was, entertainment was a bit thin on the ground at times. But I'm just sitting back there listening to all this, with the station manager's wife going on and on, giving the shearer's cook a real ear full. And then in the end she said to the cook, 'Now, I want you to go to the medical chest and get those tablets that the doctor mentioned and you be responsible for giving them out to the shearer. And make sure you only give him the prescribed one tablet at a time because if you give him the whole bottle he'll more than likely down the lot in one go. You know these shearers—they'll try to get high on anything.'

And I just sat there laughing because I just had a vision of this shearer woofing into these antibiotics in an attempt to get high. Then I imagined that now the news was out, everyone in the whole area would be rifling through their medical chests also in search of these particular antibiotics.

Dr Clyde Fenton

Clyde Fenton was one of the first real 'Flying Doctors'.
I say that because not only was he a doctor but he was
also one of the very rare ones that actually flew the
aeroplane. In fact, as a pilot during the war, he had
an outstanding record and he was the Commanding
Officer of Number 6 Communications Unit, out of
Batchelor, which was about 60 kilometres south of
Darwin.

Now, I don't know whether he had a plane when he
first went to Katherine as a doctor or whether he bought
the plane after he'd gone to Katherine. I somehow have
a feeling it was after he'd gone to Katherine that he
bought himself a little plane. This is all second-hand, of
course, but they say that Clyde was a real daredevil in
the air. When he was up in Darwin he wasn't adverse
to doing a few loop-d-loops over the airfield or taking
a low skim over the outdoor picture theatre at night,
to put the wind up the patrons, or even dive bombing
groups who were out having a picnic.

Really, it sounded like he was a bit of a frustrated
adventurer and so he was prepared to take some pretty
huge risks with some of the flights that he did. Now,
don't get me wrong: he was both a very good doctor
and an excellent pilot and he saved many lives. I guess
all those sorts of people took huge risks at some stage
to get out into some of those more remote areas to help
people who were in need. Still, it doesn't help anybody
too much if they crash the plane on the way out or on

the way back, does it? But that's the way it goes and sometimes you can't do too much about it.

Still, I find it interesting that when you look at plane crashes these days, very few people walk away from them, yet back then people did seem to survive more often, didn't they? Perhaps it had something to do with the lesser speeds they travelled at, because the planes back in those early days were made from not much more than wood and canvas so they'd rip apart upon contact with the ground, which was something that Clyde managed to do on a few occasions. I grew up at Humbert River Station, in the central west of the Northern Territory, and I heard about the time when Clyde crashed a plane out on our neighbouring property of Victoria River Downs Station and the wreckage had to be packed up and put on the back of a truck and driven all the way back to Katherine.

It's also well documented that Clyde had a running battle with anything to do with 'the establishment'. In actual fact, he railed against anything to do with authority so, of course, just the mention of the Department of Civil Aviation, or DCA, had him seeing red. At one stage the DCA changed the licensing regulations and naturally Clyde steadfastly refused to go for this new licence. He considered it was just a whole lot of 'red tape, mumbo-jumbo and hog-wash'. Then when they threatened to take away his licence he flew over the house of the boss of the DCA and dropped a few flour bombs on the place. They even tried grounding him on a few occasions. But Clyde never ever took any notice. He simply continued on flying with his old licence. He'd just fly off anyway. I mean, nobody would dob him in if he was going out into the bush to help someone, would they?

So yes, Clyde was a real larrikin, alright. There's even been a couple of books written about him and his exploits. Just an example of one of those was the story about when he received the medal. That was when he was in Katherine; he was decorated with some sort of bravery award or other that came in the form of a medal. Anyway, because it had to do with 'authority' he didn't want anything to do with it. That's how anti-government and anti-establishment he was. But anyway, all these bigwigs still insisted on coming down to Katherine to present him with this special medal. So when they arrived at the Katherine Hospital, Clyde had all the staff lined up to greet them, and that included all the Aboriginal staff. And, much to the bigwigs' surprise and shock, Clyde had made mock tin replicas of the medal he was about to receive and he'd given one to every single member of the staff to wear on their uniform for the big occasion.

Of course, that didn't go over very well. But that was Clyde, and he was tremendously admired up in the Northern Territory, not only for the good he did as a doctor and pilot but also because of his larrikin ways. He was one of those that always tried to buck the system, and we tend to admire people like that in Australia, don't we?

From all Walks of Life

Back in 2000, around the time of the Sydney Olympics, we got a call one night to go on a retrieval up to Oodnadatta, in the far north-east of South Australia. But the thing was, we were getting mixed messages from our local contacts up there about what had actually happened. All they knew was that there'd been an accident somewhere out in the sticks but as yet they didn't have an exact location and they didn't know the extent of the injuries. Now, to my line of thinking, there was no good in us rushing off until we had confirmation as to what the real situation was. But our doctor had the retrieval equipment ready, the nurse ready, and so he wanted to get going as soon as possible.

We all have our areas of expertise in the Royal Flying Doctor Service, and with me being a pilot, basically the care of the aeroplane is my concern, and that includes fuelling. I knew that we could get fuel when we got to Oodnadatta but that meant pumping it out of drums, in the middle of the night, and I wanted to avoid that if possible, especially if it turned out to be an emergency. So I thought, well, I might go via Coober Pedy and take fuel on there, then I can go up to Oodnadatta and come straight back to Adelaide with any of the injured.

But the doctor said, 'No, I want to go straight to Oodnadatta.'

So that's what we did. Off we went to Oodnadatta. We'd found out by then that it was a two-vehicle accident and, being out in that desert area, we assumed it'd probably involve two four-wheel-drive vehicles. Then, when we start the descent into Oodnadatta, I heard the doctor over the intercom saying that as soon as we landed he wanted to get hold of a vehicle and drive straight out to the accident site.

'Oh,' I thought, 'this spells disaster.' Because, what really worried me was that it was a pitch black night and, to make matters worse, they still didn't know the exact whereabouts of the accident.

So I said to the nurse, 'Look, just don't go with them, otherwise we're going to end up with a retrieval team that's lost. Then we're going to have to get a search party to go looking for them and still there's the accident to attend to.'

Anyway, I landed at Oodnadatta and there was no further news. But the doctor remained adamant that he was going to organise transport out to wherever this accident had occurred. By then I'd decided that the safest thing for me to do was to camp out in the aircraft and wait and see what transpired. So they went into Oodnadatta—the nurse as well—and the last I heard was that they were going to try to organise lights— flares—to be moved to an airstrip on a station property, which they believed might be closer to the accident site. Now we didn't normally use the strip on that property at night, so once again I was pretty wary about going there.

Then at about daybreak a chap from the airport came out and when I asked what had happened he said 'Oh, they didn't go out. They're still here in Oodnadatta and they're having breakfast in at the hospital.'

When I got into the hospital I was told that the local people were also concerned about losing the RFDS retrieval team out in the desert and they'd strongly advised the doctor to stay at the hospital while some of the locals went in search of the accident. As luck would have it, they'd come across the two vehicles, away out in the sticks, and they were going to bring the people involved back to Oodnadatta. We were informed that there was one seriously injured person amongst them.

Then while we were having breakfast they told me the exact location where the accident had occurred and I said, 'Look, to save them coming all the way back to Oodnadatta, how about we radio them and say that we'll meet them at Dalhousie Springs.'

And that's what we did and, believe it or not, just as I landed the plane at Dalhousie Springs, they arrived. But while they were loading the patient I spoke to the guy who drove the vehicle out in search of the accident. He was a part-Aborigine who'd grown up in the area and he'd spent some time in the Army. So he was an experienced bushman who knew the area very well, and I said to him, 'How did you go driving out to the accident site then back to Dalhousie?'

'Well,' he said, 'actually I got lost a couple of times but I didn't tell the others, just in case they'd panic.'

So the whole retrieval may well have been a real shemozzle. But thankfully the doctor had taken the expert advice of the locals and stayed put in Oodnadatta. Anyway, we transferred the injured patient to Adelaide. But he was okay. His condition wasn't as bad as was first believed.

But this is the thing: see, you've got various people from all walks of life involved in all our operations. Not only the doctors, nurses and pilots, but there's also all the people on the ground. And it's important that everyone sticks to their area of expertise and be very clear about where they stand. Very clear. The last thing you need is for a pilot to be telling a nurse how to treat a patient or for a doctor to be telling a local how to get to an accident site. It just doesn't work. So essentially I think the organisational side of things within the RFDS is very good. The way it's set up, there's no grey areas.

Anyway, that was quite an unusual one for us really, because that type of accident is normally handled out of Port Augusta. But we're always there to back each other up, just in case of aeroplane or personnel unavailability. And just as well, because with a lot more inexperienced people travelling out into the outback, they're extremely lucky to have an organisation like the RFDS so readily and expertly available.

Gymkhanas

My name's John Lynch. I'm the CEO of the Royal Flying Doctor Service's Central Operations and, if you've got a minute, I've got a few stories to tell. Now, due to the isolation of the outback, the local gymkhanas are a huge social occasion for station people and the like who otherwise would rarely have the chance to get together. And of course, while everyone's in the one place, we usually set up a tent to run a medical clinic so that people can have a health check or whatever. Now I'm particularly talking about the blokes here because, you know, while they're all in town for the gymkhana, it's an opportune time to grab them where there's less focus on them having to make a special appointment and come all the way into town to visit the doctor. You know what blokes are like.

So it'll quite often be, 'Well, mate, if you go across to see the doctor for a health check, I may as well go too.'

'Okay then, let's all go.' That sort of thing.

And also the gymkhanas are usually designed as a fundraiser for the Royal Flying Doctor Service. So I've got a few stories about gymkhanas, and I guess that the first of these stories goes to demonstrate the huge excitement that a gymkhana generates. Now, we had a new doctor who'd never been to a gymkhana and, as I said before, a gymkhana is one of those rare opportunities when everyone gets together. What's more, you must appreciate that some of these young, single fellers and girls might never have had a lot of regular social contact, particularly with the opposite sex. So when they get together they sometimes get pretty—how can I say it?—'frisky'.

Anyway, one of our new doctors went up to this town to run the on-course medical clinic. He arrived on the morning of the gymkhana and the first thing he did was that he went over to the nursing station to introduce himself. 'Hello,' he said, 'I'm Dr so-and-so from the Flying Doctor Service.'

'Yep, no worries,' said the nurse. They all knew his name.

'Oh, I almost forgot,' said the doctor, and he handed over a package to the nurse. 'There you go; I brought along some condoms, just in case they're needed.'

And the nurse looked at him and she said, 'I reckon you might be a bit too late, doctor. The mob got into town last night and they've been having a hell of a good time ever since.'

So the party had already begun.

Then, after he handed over the condoms, this new doctor went off and he set up a little tent to do his medical checks and some of these younger kids, of course they run around all day and they have busters and so forth and so they're always going to the doctor to get their grazes fixed up. Anyhow, one young kid arrives with a grazed knee and the doctor's taking a look at it when a call comes over the loudspeaker: 'Could the Flying Doctor come urgently to the finishing post.'

Instantly of course he thinks, 'Dear me, someone's fallen off a horse and injured themselves badly.'

So the doctor tried to hurry up with this kid but he's interrupted by another call over the loudspeaker:

'The Flying Doctor is very urgently required at the finishing post.'

'Look,' the doctor said to the kid, 'there's an emergency so I'll just stick a band-aid over your graze and if it's still bothering you, come back later and I'll sort it out properly.'

Then he quickly stuck a band-aid on the kid, grabbed his medical bag and he took off like a rocket, out of the tent, through the crowd, under the fence, out onto the track and over to the finishing post, all the while preparing himself for the worst. Then, when he got to the finishing post, he ran up to the bloke with the microphone and he said, 'Yes ... (puff) ... yes ... I'm ... (puff) ... the Flying Doctor. Where's the emergency?'

And the bloke on the microphone said, 'Where the hell have you been? We've been waiting for you to come and draw the bloody raffle.'

So I guess that goes to show the social intricacies of a gymkhana, and what the responsibilities and the expectations sometimes are of the people from the Flying Doctor Service. And we're ever so lucky that those outback people are also just fundamentally open and honest with you. In many ways it's as if we're one big family. It's like that old bloke in one of the original promotional videos, or was it a film? But anyway, I saw this footage of an old weather-beaten bush character. He's right out in the outback and, you know, he's got the typical old battered hat—pushed back with sweat stains all around the brim—that'd been worn for that many years it'd become part of the personality. And even though you don't see it much today because of the health risks, he's got the roll-your-own cigarette, hanging out the side of his mouth, he's wearing the standard checked shirt, with a tin of tobacco stuck in the top pocket, sleeves rolled up, the RM Williams riding boots and the well-worn jeans, and they asked him, 'What does the Flying Doctor mean to you?'

And the old feller, he said, 'The Flying Doctor?' Then he pushed back his hat and scratched his forehead, while he had a bit of a think. Then, with just the slightest glint in his eye, he answered, 'Well,' he said, 'without the Royal Flying Doctor Service I'd reckon there'd be a hell of a lotta dead people livin' out here.'

And, again, that's just so typical of those people. Wonderful people. Wonderful humour.

But while we're talking about gymkhanas and wonderful fellers with wonderful humour, I must mention Johnny Watkins, 'Watto' as he's known. Watto just happens to have found the recipe for that weather-beaten outback look. He's a terrific feller and just one of the greatest supporters of the RFDS. In fact, he's a wonderful supporter of the bush. Watto was the Elders man and auctioneer throughout the north of South Australia so naturally he landed the job as the auctioneer at the William Creek Gymkhana, which is another great fundraising event for the RFDS. It was my first time up at William Creek and a lot of people from Port Augusta got together and formed a syndicate to buy horses for the day in an attempt to try and win some cup or ribbon or other. Of course, much of the money from the buying of horses goes to the Flying Doctor Service.

Anyway, being the CEO of the RFDS in that area, I thought that maybe I should buy a horse as well. Well, the truth be known, Watto very strongly suggested that I should buy a horse. Now I didn't have a clue about horses but Watto stepped in and he told me, in the strictest of confidences, that the next horse to be auctioned was a 'real beauty'. Apparently it had some sort of 'impeccable breeding'. Even the name Bart Cummings may have been mentioned. I forget now but Watto described it as being the 'sleeper' of the entire gymkhana.

'Okay,' I said, 'I'll bid for it.'

'Don't worry,' said Watto, 'I'll make sure you get it at a reasonable price.'

So the bidding begins and Watto calls out, 'Who can start me off with $20?'

Well, I stick my hand up to put in my bid, fully expecting to get the horse for twenty dollars; it sounded like a bargain to me, even being a mug punter. But then Watto said, 'I've got $30. Who can better $30 for this beautifully bred horse? Yes, $40 ... $50 ... Yes, $60 to Johnny Lynch the CEO. $70 ... $80 ... $120 to Johnny Lynch.' And I'm just standing there. I haven't even moved a muscle. I only bid $20 on this nag and the next thing Watto's telling me that I've just bid $120 for it.

Anyway, I finally end up getting this 'beautifully bred horse'—this dead cert—for something like $150 and the only thing I'm dead certain about is that I was the only one to have put in a single bid. No one else even bothered. But anyway, I've got this horse, so I said to Watto, 'What do I do now?'

And he said, 'You need to go over and pay for it.'

So I started to walk across to where I had to pay for the horse and this young Aboriginal feller come up and he said, 'You got a jockey, Boss?'

I said, 'A jockey? No.' I hadn't even thought about a jockey.

'Well,' he said, 'who's ridin' the horse?'

I said, 'I don't know.'

'I'm a jockey,' he said. 'I'm the best.'

'Oh, are you?' I said.

He said, 'You want me to be your jockey?'

I said, 'Well, okay, then.' I said, 'If you want to be my jockey, then you've got the job.'

'Yeah, Boss,' he said, 'I'm the best. You won't regret it.' Then he said, 'Well, we'd better put the horse in the race.'

'Yeah, no worries,' I said. 'What race will we go in?'

He said, 'All of 'em.'

And so the relationship had been struck, and this young Aboriginal feller made it clear that because I was the owner of the horse, I was to be known as the 'Boss', and he was to be called the 'Boy', as, apparently that's what jockeys are called by the owners. And he rode that horse—that dead cert— in every event that was on. There was the peg race. Then they had the distance race. Then there was a 400-metre race. Then there was some bloody race where the horse went around and around in ever decreasing circles. And we never got a prize; never even got a ribbon. Not even a placing. Nothing. In fact, there was one race where the jockey—the 'Boy'— had to go and pick up pegs then put them into a barrel, and I said to him after the race, 'If they have that race again,' I said, 'is there any chance that the horse can ride you because the horse is too bloody slow and you keep missing the barrel.'

But, you know, he was a terrific little feller, this young Aborigine. I think he said he was nineteen, and he rode in every race. And he never missed me because after each disastrous event he always came across to explain to me what had gone wrong with the horse. Then I'd thank him for the explanation and I'd pay him a couple of bob for the ride.

'Thanks, Boss,' he'd say. 'We'll have better luck next time.'

But we never did.

Hats off

Well, I've certainly had a lot more experiences since your first book of *Great Australian Flying Doctor Stories* came out, way back in 1999. So yes, I can give you a few more stories and, mind you, these are from a doctor's point of view, of course. One that knocked me for six was an amazing story of survival stemming from an accident that happened in the Carnarvon National Park, which is in south-eastern Queensland, sort of, north-east of Charleville. It's near a place called Injune.

Okay, it was a week day, about midday, when I got a call on the HF radio from a ranger feller out in the Carnarvon National Park. He said that he'd been driving around the park and he'd come across an accident. A utility vehicle was down in a roadside drain with the male driver slumped over the steering wheel. The driver was unconscious. Because there were no other vehicles about, the feller that reported the accident assumed it'd been a single-vehicle accident. So I advised him what to do until we got up there. I also requested that I be met at the nearest airstrip, at an ETA (estimated time of arrival) to be advised, and for them to be prepared to take us, in one of their vehicles, out to the accident site. The driver chap was still in the car at this time and he still remained slumped over the steering wheel.

So we flew up to the Carnarvon National Park and landed at the Mount Moffatt airstrip, where the Parks people met us in a vehicle. They then took us from there, with all our equipment, up to where they'd found the vehicle. Upon arrival at the scene of the accident my suspicions were immediately aroused because, firstly, there were no skid marks and, secondly, there was no sign of there being any damage to the vehicle. When we got the feller out of his vehicle, my primary assessment suggested that he was in some sort of shock. At that stage I didn't know which sort of shock it was. Anyway, I got a large bore intravenous cannula into him and gave him a couple of litres of fluid fairly quickly, and this improved his situation somewhat. I then did a secondary survey, which is a head-to-toe survey, of his wellbeing. Things did not look good: his face had been badly pushed in; his chest was a bit suspect. I estimated that his belly was full of blood, and he had bilateral mid-shaft of femurs, with both sticking out at right angles. That's his thigh bone. He also had a fractured forearm.

By that stage I'd resuscitated him and he was able to talk to us, just a little, and he managed to inform us as to what had happened. As it turned out, there was just him and his dog and he'd been cutting down a tree for firewood in the National Park, which was illegal—though that was the least of our concerns at that stage. While he was cutting a tree, it had fallen on him, trapping him underneath it. So that's when he had sustained all these injuries I've just described. Then, somehow—and I don't know how—he'd worked his way out from underneath the tree. His ute was parked across the flat and he must've crawled his way over to the ute, a distance of a couple of hundred yards. He then put the dog in the back of his utility vehicle and made sure the dog was safe, then he somehow managed to get himself in the front of the vehicle. How he managed to do this, in his condition, I would not have a clue.

He then drove the vehicle—it was a manual—to a nearby homestead, where he knew there was a telephone. When he arrived at the homestead he couldn't raise anyone. Nobody was at home. So he went back out onto the road where he had obviously at some stage just passed out from the loss of blood. That's when he put his vehicle in the roadside ditch, which was where the ranger feller had come across him, slumped over the steering wheel.

So we stabilised him as best we could. Then we put him onto the back of a vehicle and they took him over a very, very rough road, back to the aeroplane. And, you wouldn't believe this, but the whole way back to the aeroplane he cracked jokes like nobody's business and I'm sure it wasn't just from the happy juice I'd administered to him.

Anyway, we put him in the aeroplane and we took him down to Royal Brisbane Hospital. He had a laparotomy that night—that's opening up his belly—and basically they found that he had a ruptured liver as well as all the other injuries I've previously described.

I'm afraid I didn't follow up on the dog because I had my hands full, assessing and stabilising the patient. But as far as I was concerned I'd have to say 'Hats off' to this feller. Because let's focus on the injuries that he would've sustained when the tree fell on him. As a summary: his face had been quite severely damaged. He had a fractured forearm. He had bilateral mid-shaft of femurs; in other words both sides of his femurs were broken at right angles, which meant that they were sticking out at right angles. He had a belly full of blood, which later on proved to be from a ruptured liver. His chest was suspect at the time, possibly from the blood in the belly pushing up to the diaphragm. I wasn't sure how, at that early stage, but he was still able to maintain his respiratory drive okay, so I didn't have to ventilate him.

Now considering his condition I ask you, with all those injuries, first of all, how did he get out from under the tree? Then how did he manage to crawl the couple of hundred yards across the ground to his ute? Following that, how did he manage to get into the ute and then drive the vehicle to the homestead, keeping in mind that it was a manual drive?

In my time as a doctor, it's one of the greatest survival stories that I have known. And the people at the Royal Brisbane Hospital, they put him back together and he could walk again after all that. In fact, I last saw him walking down the street in Injune.

Heroes of the Outback

What you've got to take into consideration is that it's not just the vast distances we in the Royal Flying Doctor Service have to cover, but also the many, many miles that some of our constituents have to travel to get anywhere. Now this notion of distance may seem inconceivable for someone who is living in a city, where all the amenities are so close. But that's not the way it is out there, in the more isolated areas. For example, take the time we had to cancel a medical clinic—at short notice—from out of our operations at Port Augusta. This was a few years ago now so I can't quite remember where the clinic was originally going to be held and nor can I remember what the exact reason was as to why we had to cancel it. It could've been due to bad weather, which is the most likely reason, or it may have even been aircraft or crew unavailability. Those things happen sometimes. But anyway, the issue was that we were forced to cancel the clinic, and as soon as that decision had been made we let everyone know.

Then shortly after we notified everyone of the cancellation I got a call from a woman who used to attend this particular clinic, whenever the need arose. 'I've just arrived at our front gate and my husband's called to say that you've cancelled the medical clinic,' she said.

'Yes,' I said, 'that's right.'

'Why did you do that?'

'Well,' I said, 'I'm not exactly sure but I can find out and radio you back, if you like.'

'Oh,' she said, 'there's no need for that but I would've liked to have known a little bit earlier.'

Now, if you lived in the city your normal reaction would be to say, 'Well, that shouldn't be too much of a problem; just turn around and go back inside your house.' Because if you do live in the city and you've walked out the door and you've just arrived at your front gate and your husband's called out to tell you that the doctor's now unavailable, then you'd just turn around and go back inside, wouldn't you? It's that easy.

Anyhow, this woman, she said to me, 'Yeah well, I guess that I'll just have to turn around and go back home now, but it seems to be an enormous waste of time.'

'Well,' I said, 'I sincerely apologise but it's still only nine o'clock in the morning.'

'Yes,' she said, 'it may still only be nine o'clock in the morning but I've already travelled well over 60 kilometres, along a dirt track, and that's just from my back door to the front gate of our property.'

And that put it into some sort of perspective. You know, because of the distances that some of these people have to travel—just to reach their own front gate—a cancellation like that is not a simple thing.

So you have to admire people like that, particularly the women. Take our Consumer Network Group. It's a wonderful way of engaging with the actual people we serve. It's made up of predominantly females and we get together every now and then for face-to-face meetings to discuss how the RFDS can better serve its constituents. We're actually reinvigorating it now, which is very exciting, because you get everyone talking about things like the services they're receiving, and the frequency they get them, and the freedom of access and, you know, things like: are we meeting their requirements? Can we do it better? Is there something else we should be looking at?

Now, I'm not saying that we can always rectify all these matters because, as you may be able to imagine, there are huge logistical problems in servicing such vast areas of this continent. Like I said about that woman before—it's not like she could simply just turn around and go back home and get on with her day as if nothing had happened.

And so, when I get to talk to the many people that go to these Consumer Network Group meetings, I'm always reminded of that John Williamson song, 'Woman on the Land'. I don't know whether you've ever heard it or not. It goes something like, 'So I propose a toast to the mothers that we know. Proud to be the better half who really run the show ... To our hero—the woman on the land.' It's a magnificent song. Anyhow, I learned the words for one particular Consumer Network Group meeting because, you know, the last thing we want is for our constituents to reach a point where they're just a recorded number. They're more than that. They're people. They're human beings. And those women, and in actual fact everyone we serve, they are the real heroes of the outback.

Of course, it's not just the Royal Flying Doctor Service who supports them. There are many other organisations involved. And also, of course, the people themselves are also extremely supportive of each other, perhaps sometimes a little too over zealously.

There's one occasion that always tickles me: I remember when I was with one of the doctors during a phone-in medical session. They used to happen over the air, twice daily. The first session was at eight o'clock in the morning, before the School of the Air program started, and the second was at four o'clock in the afternoon, after School of the Air had finished. They were timed that way because the mums were often fairly busy, not just supervising their children during their classes but also helping run the property, as well as attending to the normal 'womanly' chores of washing, cooking, cleaning, plus the multitude of other tasks they take on. Like I said, real heroes of the outback.

Now, what you've got to appreciate is that these medical sessions were open sessions. Anyone could listen in, and they quite often did. It was an easy way for everyone to find out how everyone else was going. So this time the doctor opened the radio and initially he registered who was out there. Then once everyone was registered, he went back to the first person. He gave her call sign and the lady replied with, 'I'm just a bit concerned about little Johnny.'

'Oh yes,' replied the doctor, 'can you tell me his symptoms?'

'Well, Doctor, he's got such and such.' And she described little Johnny's symptoms.

Then before the doctor could even answer, one of the lady's neighbours cut in, over the radio, and said, 'Oh, I can tell you exactly what's wrong with him.'

And I thought that that showed the real essence of the bush: you know, how even if these people are hundreds of miles apart, they're not only comfortable talking about their own personal issues to a doctor, while everyone else was listening in, but they were also willing to put in their sixpence worth if they thought they could help each other out.

I Was the Pilot

I've just been reading your second book of Flying Doctor stories—*More Great Australian Flying Doctor Stories*—and in that book there's one particular story called 'Blown Away'. Now you're not going to believe this but I was the pilot that was mentioned in that story and in actual fact, over my time in the Royal Flying Doctor Service, it's one of my all-time favourite stories as well. So, would you like to hear the story from the pilot's side of the event?

If you don't mind, I've sort of written bits and pieces of it down and I'd like to read it to you more or less as I've written it. So, okay, here goes.

One of my favourite stories happened not long after I started with the Flying Doctor Service. So that must've been about 1990 or thereabouts. Anyway, I was working at Port Hedland at the time and we received a call from a family who were driving along the Canning Stock Route.

Now, I'm presuming here that everyone knows where the Canning Stock Route is. If not, I'd just like to relate a brief overview because it will give the readers a clearer picture of the desolation of the situation. The Canning is an old stock route that runs a distance of 1820 kilometres along a series of wells through the central deserts of Western Australia, from Halls Creek, in the north, right down to near Wiluna, which is just west of Meekatharra. I'm not sure what it's like today, but originally there were supposed to be something like fifty-one wells, or watering points, along the length of the stock route. Then over the stock route's historic period, from when the track was being surveyed and then during the following years when droving was taking place, the records tell us that there were something like ten murders, a number of inflicted woundings and several deaths from internal complications of—and I quote—'unknown origin'. These murders, woundings and deaths from unknown origins involved both white and indigenous people.

Also there were and still are countless sand ridges. And I'll quote again here—'According to Dr J. S. Bard, over one particular section of 470 miles, some 730 sand ridges lay along the stock route, containing enough material to cover the country evenly with sand to a depth of three feet. The biggest sand ridges are between Wells 41 and 42. When formed they are approximately a mile apart, averaging sixty feet in height, with a base of about 320 feet.'

So, if you can calculate that back to the figures we use these days, that might just give you some idea as to what the country out there is like. And while droving no longer takes place along the Canning these days, it's a favourite journey-cum-adventure for many four-wheel drivers.

Anyhow, these people were camped near Well 33, which was right out, oh, it's probably only about 200 kilometres from the Northern Territory border. So it's fairly well east. And they were travelling in convoy with another couple, who were also in a four-wheel-drive vehicle. Anyhow, their young daughter, who was about nine or ten years old, climbed about the only tree that was out in that part of the desert and the branch broke and she fell down and broke what I believe was her arm. In your story, the storyteller thought that she'd fractured one of her thighs. So I stand corrected on that point. Mind you, it was a long time ago.

Now, as luck would have it, they were reasonably close to an old airstrip. The only trouble was that the strip hadn't been used for a very long time. Now, I'm trying to remember just what the name of that particular strip was. No, sorry, I can't remember just offhand. Anyway, it was overgrown with short, low bushes, maybe up to something like a metre high. So, as I said, it hadn't been used for a fair while.

We got the call the night before we went out there and, of course, naturally there were no landing lights on the strip out there or anything so we had to wait until first light to head off. At that point of time, with the airstrip being so overgrown, it was impossible for us to land anyway. But all through the night these people and their other companions worked by their car headlights, clearing the bushes with shovels and spades and what-not.

Then I flew out of our Port Hedland base just before first light in an attempt to arrive at the remote airstrip just on first light. When I arrived, the strip still looked pretty rough but it looked landable so I was willing to give it a try. These people, they'd set up a fire with the smoke to show me the wind direction. Anyhow, I landed the plane on this makeshift strip and we successfully picked up the little girl and her mother and took them back to Port Hedland, where the little girl received further necessary treatment. So that was a very satisfying retrieval.

I think that the people were from Victoria somewhere, and later on we got a lovely letter back from the little girl thanking us for what we did. Then along with her letter the girl's parents sent some lovely photos of, you know, the girl lying in the back of the car and the airstrip before they cleared it and then after they'd cleared it and also of the aeroplane coming in to land. But it must've been a hell of a job to clear the airstrip, which had to be about 1000 metres long. I mean, that's quite a lot of work they did, and, as I said, they worked all night.

But in her letter the little girl also told us how her broken limb had healed and how that everything was now fine, thanks to us. And that really warms your heart. So, there's just another side of that story— 'Blown Away'—that you related in your book *More Great Australian Flying Doctor Stories*, and really, as I said, it is one of my very favourites.

If Only

I can honestly say that the three years I spent in Alice Springs, while I was flying for the Flying Doctor Service, was the most enjoyable and rewarding experience in my life. I had an absolute ball. Though, in saying that, of course everything didn't always go as well as I would have wanted it to go. And unfortunately this was the one particular case that still gets to me because, you know, if only the weather conditions had been different, this patient is one that we could've very possibly saved.

Anyhow, it was three o'clock in the afternoon when I got the call to fly out to Tennant Creek and pick up this little kid. She was a young eleven-year-old girl. The only trouble was that there were storms about everywhere. And, mind you, in Alice Springs you do get some very big storms, especially when it's the wet season up north. Anyway, these storms were a bit too big for my liking. Still and all, the situation sounded very serious so I told them that I'd have another think about it before I made a final call. As you may well know, anything to do with the flying part of the RFDS is up to the pilot, and the pilot not only has to think of the safety aspects of every trip he makes, he's also got to keep in mind that he's responsible for a couple of million dollars worth of aeroplane plus the lives of the doctor and nurse who may be accompanying him on such a trip.

So I did have a good think about it, balancing the safety aspects of such a flight against the desperate need of the child and, based on the fact that it would be in the dead of night when we returned and we had no weather radar, I made my final decision. So I got back in touch with Tennant Creek and said, 'No, I won't go. It's too risky. But I'll definitely be in the air as soon as the storms dissipate.'

Then, the first chance we got, we went. I think we left about one o'clock in the morning—this is up in Tennant Creek—to pick up this young girl.

When we got to Tennant Creek the doctor took one look at the poor little kid and he pulled me aside and said, 'Gee, she's as good as gone. What's more, we can't do anything more for her in Alice Springs than what I can do for her here, in Tennant Creek.' He said, 'There's only two options: one is to take her straight down to Adelaide and the other is to get her to Darwin as soon as humanly possible.'

Darwin was closest, of course, but, as I said, it was the wet season, which was why the storms were so bad in Alice Springs. Anyhow, just in case, I rang up and got the weather report for Darwin and they told me that it was okay for the present.

'Righto,' I said to the doctor. 'Darwin it is.'

So we went helter-skelter to Darwin and because of the restrictive weather conditions and the emergency of the case, I was the only light aircraft to be given permission to land in Darwin that day. Anyway, you wouldn't believe it but the poor little child died just when we got there. We were still on the tarmac. A girl it was—a dear little eleven-year-old girl, just a kid.

And that case still gets to me because if only I'd been able to fly up to Tennant Creek the night before, who knows what might've happened. But the weather was against us. Everything was against us. And the thing is, as I said, as a pilot you're not only responsible for yourself and the aeroplane but there's also the nurses and the doctors that you've got to think about. And each and every one of us has to ensure that we're there to fight another day.

But in the three years I was in Alice Springs that was the only one, you know, that I had any doubt on. Yes, of course, others have died, which was unfortunate, though there was more than a good chance that they would've died anyway. But that little girl was the only one I have any doubt about. And it still gets to me, even to this day.

In Double Quick Time

I've got a story here that has quite an amusing aspect to it. See, from time to time, the Flying Doctor Service used to get the occasional complaint about how long it took us to get out to some of these remote places to pick people up. You know, along the lines of, 'Gees, youse took yer bloody time', sort of thing.

But of course we couldn't be everywhere at the same time and, mind you, we did have vast distances to cover. And then of course we're all human beings so, naturally, when someone's seriously ill or injured or something, well, we all get a bit upset and stressed when help doesn't arrive immediately.

Anyway, this is when I was flying the King Air aeroplanes, so it'd be back in the early 1990s, and on this particular occasion we'd been up to one of the Aboriginal communities—it was either Kowanyama or Pormpuraaw—to pick up someone. So we were on the way back home with this patient. At that stage of the game our base in at Cairns received an emergency call from a certain property—Bolwarra—to say that they had a stockman who'd fallen off his horse and he had a very badly broken ankle. The people from the property had spoken to the doctor in at our Cairns base and the doctor had said, 'Well, we'd better do an "evac" and get the feller out of there as quick as possible.'

Now, unbeknown to the people on the property of Bolwarra, we turned out to be flying virtually right over the top of them when we got the message. So within fifteen minutes of their call I had the King Air landing at their airstrip. And they were amazed. 'For heaven's sake,' they said, 'you wouldn't get a faster service from the road ambulance in the city.'

So we reckoned we'd made up for any perceived 'tardiness' we might've had in the past, just on that one 'evac'. You know, to be able to produce the aeroplane, in front of an anxiously waiting group of people and a seriously injured stockman, within ten or fifteen minutes of them calling Cairns was just about unheard of. It was just pure luck, of course. As I said, we just happened to be returning from picking up another patient and were basically right over the top of the place.

But the poor bloke—the stockman—he was really in a bad way. He had an extremely bad compound fracture, where the bone was actually protruding through the skin of his ankle. It was a shocker. Very distressing, really. But it was just typical of these outback people. I tell you, they're as tough as nails and with an amazing sort of resilience, because when the stockman was asked, 'Is it hurting?' he gave a wince and replied, 'Oh, it itches a bit.'

Anyhow, we got him back to Cairns in pretty quick time and he didn't lose his ankle or his foot. Mind you, I'm not sure he was able to run as fast as he had in the past but they were able to fix his foot up. So he could walk and that was great.

In the ...

When I first went up to Cape York to work with the Australian Inland Mission, there was a story going around that went something like this. Now, you know how cooks have the reputation of being temperamental people. Well, one of the station properties had this rather large cook who, when he got into a 'paddy' about anything, would grab a book and go out and plonk himself down in the outhouse toilet and, depending on the gravity of the paddy he was in, maybe not come out for anything up to a couple of hours.

Of course, back then there weren't any septic systems in those remote areas so the type of toilets they used were the 'long-drop' type. For those of you that may not know, the long-drop toilet is basically, you know, a wooden box type of thing with a hole in the top where the seat goes, and that's all placed over a very deep hole, which is where all the 'waste' goes. For privacy, it's surrounded by a few sheets of corrugated iron, a roof and a wooden door. That particular style of toilet was well suited to Cape York because, being an old mining area, the actual toilet itself was simply plonked down over an old mine shaft, which saved a lot of digging.

Anyway, early one morning this cranky cook got his knickers in a knot about something or other, so he grabbed a book and went out and plonked himself down on the toilet. Unfortunately, the white ants must've been very busy of late because when he sat down the toilet crumbled from under him and he, in turn, disappeared down this old mine shaft. Actually, you could liken it to what happened to Alice in the book *Alice in Wonderland*, except that this cook really landed in the ... well, you can imagine what he landed in, can't you?

Now, seeing that all the ringers and stockmen and that who worked on this station property were well aware of the cook's temperamental nature, when he hadn't come out of the toilet by breakfast time they didn't worry too much, and they just went ahead and helped themselves. Even by morning tea there was still only some semi-mild concern. But by lunchtime, some hours later, these stockmen were starting to get pretty hungry and even though the cook wasn't what you'd call 'a gourmet specialist', at least he dished up a pretty hearty meal.

Anyway, one of the younger ringers drew the short straw and he got landed with the job of going over to the outhouse to check on the situation. So he wandered over to the long-drop, knocked on the wooden door and said, 'Cookie, are yer okay?'

There was no answer so the ringer knocked a little louder, 'Hey, Cookie, we're getting hungry.'

Still no answer. Then, just as the ringer was about to walk away, he thought he heard a very faint voice. 'This's a bit odd,' thought the ringer and he called out for his mates to come over and offer a second opinion. They all gathered around the outhouse. 'Hey, Cookie!' they shouted.

'Help,' came the distant reply.

So they broke down the toilet door and that's when they discovered that the cook had disappeared down the old mine shaft.

'Hey, Cookie, are yer down there?'

'Yes,' came the echo.

Anyway, while someone went over to the homestead to get on the radio and call the Flying Doctor, the stockmen knocked down the outer, corrugated iron, toilet structure and then they got the ropes and all the rest of it and they hooked up a 'windlass'—a winch lift—to haul the cook out.

Even though the cook had been extricated from his predicament by the time the Flying Doctor arrived, the poor chap was still in rather a smelly state. But the doctor, being the professional that he was, checked the cook out to make sure that he was okay and luckily, apart from a very bruised ego, the cook had survived the experience without too many injuries at all. But just to be on the safe side, the doctor decided to give him a course of antibiotics, because of the, you know, the particular situation he'd been in. And as the story went, the cook lost a little of his temperamental sharpness after that event and even when he did throw a paddy, just before he'd storm out of the kitchen he'd announce to all and sundry, 'Won't be long, fellers.'

In the Beginning

I got into flying in quite an odd sort of way, really. Back during World War II, my older brother, Bill, had been a flying officer in the Royal Australian Air Force (RAAF), Number Thirteen Squadron, up in Darwin. He was flying Hudsons. Then on 19 February 1942 he got shot down over the Timor Sea and was listed as missing. And that event changed the course of my life really, because at that stage I'd put my age up and had already enlisted in the Army. But then, after Bill went missing, I resolved to get into the Air Force when I'd reached their required age of eighteen.

Finally, after being accepted into the RAAF, my initial training was held at Victor Harbor, which is south of Adelaide, in South Australia. After that I was posted to Narrandera, in south-western New South Wales, where I was instructed in elementary flying in the Tiger Moths. After eight months there, I returned to South Australia, this time to Mallala, where I built up one hundred and forty flying hours. I was then deemed ready for service with the RAAF.

After the war had ended, I went back on the land and although I maintained my private licence through the Aero Club of South Australia, my flying career basically went on hold. But even then I still continued to explore any possible opportunities towards a flying career. To that end, in 1959 I purchased my own Cessna and started up as a charter pilot, based in the far west of New South Wales, at a place called

Wilcannia. My main work out there came through stock firms like Elders, Goldsbrough Mort and Dalgety's. But then the drought of 1963 put paid to all that and so I adapted my aircraft and began selling pest control products throughout South Australia, Queensland and the Northern Territory. As it turned out, there was an untapped market in those outback areas and flying the Cessna was a great way to reach them, because in those days you could land just about anywhere. So even though I wasn't a salesperson by nature, because of the accessibility I had, I still had great success.

Then in 1965 I sold my aircraft to Ross Aviation and joined their firm in Adelaide. Ross Aviation was a sales and charter company so I had a combination of work, with demonstrating and selling aircraft plus flying charter. That job took me all over Australia, and from Adelaide I was offered a job in Perth, doing charter flying in King Air aeroplanes. By charter work I mean, someone might come along with a group of, say, half a dozen people and they'd want to go to some place that would take them ages to reach by road, like from Perth to Darwin or Perth to Sydney. So they'd charter an aircraft. It was like a taxi service, really. That's all it was, like an air taxi. Prices varied, of course, and the clients were a mix of tourists and business people, and so pretty soon, I'd done 7500 hours, which included a lot of bush flying.

Then one day in 1968 while I was in Perth I was talking to one of the blokes about flying and he mentioned that the Queensland Section of the Royal Flying Doctor Service was advertising for four pilots to replace their previously seconded TAA (Trans-Australia

Airlines) pilots. There must've been some sort of change within the organisation there somewhere, and now the RFDS wanted to employ their own pilots.

But I think that my interview for the job deserves some sort of mention. Now, because the senior pilot of TAA was on a trip to Perth, I had a preliminary interview with him to see if I was a suitable applicant for the job with the Flying Doctor Service. That recommendation was positive and it was relayed back to the RFDS Head Office in Brisbane. Then they, the Flying Doctor Service, got in touch and informed me that my final interview was set for ten o'clock, on such-and-such a date, at their Head Office in Queen Street, Brisbane.

Well, that was good news, and so I just assumed that the interview was to be held at ten o'clock in the morning, as you would. But the thing was, I didn't want my employers in Perth to find out that I was going for another job. That just wasn't done in those days, and also my feeling was that there'd be a lot of excellent applicants going for the four RFDS flying jobs. So even though I'd got over the first hurdle and had been recommended, I wasn't all that confident. Anyway, I made up an excuse as to why I couldn't fly for the Perth company on that particular day—the day of my interview in Brisbane—and a friend of mine, who was also a pilot with the same company, he said he'd sub for me, for just that one day.

So, with everything all organised on the Perth workfront, unbeknown to my current employers I flew off to Brisbane for this interview. It didn't cost me anything. The RFDS saw to all that. Accommodation and flights there and back were all paid for.

When I got to Brisbane, I rang the RFDS Head Office to let them know that I'd arrived. 'I'm here,' I said. 'I'll see you tomorrow morning at ten o'clock.'

'Well, no,' they informed me, 'we have interviews already organised throughout tomorrow, sir, and yours isn't set down until ten o'clock tomorrow night.'

Well, that certainly set the cat among the pigeons because I'd only sorted out things back in Perth for that one day. Anyhow, I stayed for my 10 pm interview and caught a flight back to Perth the following day—a day later than expected. So, in saying that it didn't actually cost me anything, well, in a funny sort of way it did, because by the time I returned to Perth the company I was working for had found out that I'd been to an interview for another job. So it was a case of being welcomed back and being told, 'Well, you're finished with us now.'

So, having realised I'd done my last flight with that mob, there followed an extremely nervous wait to see if I'd got the job with the Queensland RFDS. And even though I had all the requirements, including an endorsement on the Queen Air aeroplane, which I'd been flying in Western Australia, as I said, I still wasn't all that confident of getting one of the pilots' positions because I knew there were a lot of very strong applications.

Anyhow, thankfully they gave me the job. That was in May 1968, and my first appointment was out at Charleville, in south-western Queensland. And during the following six or so years I worked at Charleville, I was on call seven days a week, twenty-four hours a day, except for annual holidays. Back then, I'd say that Charleville was the busiest of the RFDS bases. We ran clinics up to four days a week, with overnights at many a remote station property and also at towns like Jundah, Birdsville, Windorah, Thylungra, Bedourie and Thargomindah. On top of all that we then averaged one evacuation per month, to Brisbane.

Then in 1974 I was appointed to the Cairns base, where I worked until my retirement in 1988. So my flying career for the Royal Flying Doctor Service spanned twenty years and, over that time, I clocked up over 20000 flying hours. But really, because it was my first appointment, the township of Charleville is, and always will remain, very dear to me.

In the Boot

Actually, I got into the Flying Doctor Service in a roundabout sort of way, really. I'd been working out bush as a Remote Area Nurse and the girls from the RFDS knew me and they needed someone to do some relief work for them, so they gave me some relief work and it just followed on from there. I went part-time and finally I went full-time, which was great. That was at our Port Augusta base, which is in South Australia.

Then, as far as stories go, there's one particular accident I still remember quite vividly. It happened to a midwife from Adelaide. At the time she was visiting people on a station property, out along the Transcontinental Railway Line that runs between Port Augusta and Kalgoorlie. I'm not exactly sure how far out the property was just now, but we got an urgent call saying that somehow a brick fence had fallen on this midwife woman and she'd been caught and her lower leg was a mess.

On that occasion we flew out there without a doctor; there was just myself and the pilot. When we landed at the airstrip on the property, there was a ute already waiting for us, so I just grabbed some gear and in we went to see the injured woman. In all, from the time we'd been notified about the accident till the time we arrived, I'd say it took us about an hour and a half to reach her. By then they'd taken the bricks off her and she was lying on the ground, with her foot going in a very odd sort of direction. So I just took one look and I thought, 'What am I going to do here?'

It was a real mess. The pilot even had to walk away from it, that's how horrific it was. Anyhow, the woman was still conscious so I took her pulse and while I was holding her hand I was summing up the situation. 'What am I going to do? How am I going to go about this?'

The wall was a garden wall, and she'd been lying outside on the ground right next to it. Now, I don't know what made it fall over—I didn't actually ever ask that—but when it fell over it pinned her lower leg. It was just like, well, to be absolutely honest, it was a near amputation. Her clothes were even stuck between the broken bones of her leg. Oh, it was sort of all mashed up, mushed up, with the clothes wedged in the break, and I daren't remove them without risking her bleeding more badly than what she already was.

Anyhow, after taking her pulse I thought, 'Well, to start with, I'll cut her shoe off just to see which way her foot's really going.' So that's what I did and when I took a look, I thought, 'There's no way I can reposition this. It's just got to stay in the shape it's in, and I've got to support it the best I can.'

Actually, I was a bit worried about not trying to reposition her foot but, anyhow, I ended up deciding to stabilise the fracture as it was, in that awkward position. I put an IV (intravenous drip) in and gave her some pain relief. All this time the people that she'd been staying with were holding up a blanket to give her some shade. It wasn't that hot. It was quite reasonable weather, you know, not too hot or cold, just reasonable. That was a good thing, and I don't remember there being too many flies about either, which was also a very good thing, too. I just hate it when you go to an accident where there's blood and there's millions of flies about.

So I got her as settled as I possibly could and then, when we went to move her back to the aeroplane, we laid her on a mattress—which would've been more comfortable than a stretcher—then we put her in the back of the ute and we drove her back out to the aircraft. To me, that seemed to take about twenty minutes. Then we returned to Port Augusta and from there she was taken down to Adelaide.

And later on I felt justified in my decision not to try and reposition the foot because actually all the doctors and that, they even decided to leave it the way it was before they did the X-rays and everything. They didn't try to do anything until further down the track. And, luckily, as it turned out, her leg was saved. Mind you, they had a lot of trouble with it. But they managed to save it, so that was a nice ending to a rather challenging accident.

Then, on a lighter note, there's the story about the same pilot I went out there with on that particular day, when the wall had fallen on the midwife. I won't mention the pilot's name but he was just so funny to work with, which, mind you, is exactly what you need in some of those more serious and critical situations. But this pilot just loved his dog. It went everywhere with him.

Anyway, one time we got this Code One out from Port Augusta. A Code One is an emergency. And when the pilot got the call he just grabbed his gear and ran out of his house. Then, just as he was about to get in his car, he noticed that the boot was open, so he slammed it shut, then he jumped into his car and drove flat out to the airport, where he started preparing the aeroplane for take-off.

Then, just as we're about ready to leave Port Augusta, I get this phone call from his wife saying, 'Rhonda, I can't find his dog anywhere. Is it out there with him?'

Now, I'd seen the pilot arrive but I hadn't seen his dog.

'No,' I said, 'I haven't seen his dog.'

'Perhaps it's in his car.'

As it happened, I could see his car from where I was and it didn't look like there was a dog in it, so I said, 'No, the dog isn't in the car.'

'Well, that's strange,' his wife said, 'because it always stays around the house when he's gone. Look,' she said, 'just on the off-chance, would you mind asking him to check to see if his dog's somehow ended up in the boot of his car?'

So I went out and I told the pilot and sure enough, when he unlocked the boot of his car, there's this sheepish looking dog, looking very pleased to see its even more sheepish looking master.

Injections

I've only ever given injections once and, unless it's a life or death situation, as far as I'm concerned it won't happen again. I just hate giving injections. I don't know why. It's just one of those things. I just can't do it unless, of course, it's an absolute life and death situation. I remember one guy who came into Gibb River Station, in the Kimberley area of Western Australia. He was up here working in a Main Roads Maintenance Camp, and afterwards he told me that he just knew it was an accident waiting to happen. They apparently had an urn placed out on a bench, with the tap poking outwards so, of course, when he walked past the urn, the tap hooked onto his short pants, didn't it? Over it went and he ended up with boiling water all down his side.

With Gibb River Station being the closest place to where the Main Roads crew were camped, they drove him in and asked if we'd call the Flying Doctor Service and get them to come out and treat him. In the meanwhile, the guy asked for some morphine to ease the pain. Apparently he'd been badly burnt before with a motor bike accident and so this poor bloke he just knew what he was going to have to go through with all these terrible burns. You could actually tell that he was thinking, 'Oh, not again', if you know what I mean.

Back in those days, the RFDS medical chests contained morphine in both injectable and tablet form; the injections, of course, being the much quicker acting.

I mean, we don't have morphine in the medical chests any more because of the chance of it being abused. But I just couldn't bring myself around to give him an injection, no way, so I gave it to him as a tablet instead. Then, just before the RFDS plane came to pick him up, it came out in discussion that we actually did have morphine in the injectable form. But I just told him that I didn't have the confidence to give him a shot. 'Oh bugger!' he said. 'If I'd known about that I would've given myself the injection!'

Oh, he was a big bikie sort of feller. So it was obvious that it wouldn't have worried him too much to have given himself an injection. But there was no way that I was going to give him one.

Then there was another occasion when I just couldn't give an injection. It's one that really stands out in my mind. It was with a little Aboriginal boy, Devon. He's still around town, here in Derby, but he was only about seven months old when this happened. It was also during the time that my husband and I were out on Gibb River Station.

As usual, these things always seem to happen in the wet season. I don't know why, but the wet's always the worst time for accidents and illness and so forth. Anyhow, Devon's people—his Aboriginal people—came up from Mount Barnett Station and they were all playing cards with our lot at Gibb River Station. Then, as it does quite often in the wet, a huge storm hit us in the afternoon and the house creek just went whoosh and the water level came straight up. We were then flooded in which meant that these Aboriginal people couldn't get back across the house creek to get out to the main road to go home. So they were stranded, and they had this little baby, Devon. He was just there with his grandma and so he wasn't being breastfed or anything. And because they weren't supposed to be staying overnight they hadn't brought along any of the baby formula to feed him with.

Anyhow, they brought this baby, Devon, up to me and asked if I had any baby formula, which we didn't. At that time we didn't even stock baby formula in our store on Gibb River. I tell you, after that we certainly always did. Anyhow, oh, this poor little baby, he was just so sick and I noticed that he had a swollen fontanelle—you know, the little bulging part in his head. Not only that, but he was also very lethargic which to me straight away signified that he could well have had meningitis.

So I got on to the Flying Doctor base in Derby and they suggested that I go to the medical chest and give him an injection. Now, you're supposed to put the injection in the bum, but I just couldn't do it, and especially not to a little baby, no matter how sick he looked. I've seen one of these injections given and, from the reaction, it was really difficult to get the needle into someone, plus it hurt like hell. So you know, I just said to the doctor, 'I'm really, really sorry but no, I can't; not to a little baby like that.' I said, 'I just can't give him an injection. I just can't do it. Is there any other way of treating him?'

Anyhow, we then had to put little Devon on 1000 micrograms of penicillin, as a liquid, which, mind you, is a huge dose of penicillin for a child. But to make matters even worse, with all the rain and the creek having risen so much, the Flying Doctor pilot couldn't land on our strip because it was too wet.

And the Aboriginal people kept saying, 'Why can't they come?'

'They can't come,' I tried to explain, 'because the airstrip needs to dry out before the Flying Doctor aeroplane can land on it.'

'Then why can't they get a chopper (helicopter) to come out for him?'

'They can't,' I said. 'They just can't. It's too overcast for even a chopper to get in.'

Really, there was nothing we could do but sit and wait until the airstrip dried out because, basically, we were stranded. Of course, in the meantime this little fella, Devon, was really struggling. Then I remembered that we had some baby yoghurt in at the clinic and so we fed him with some of this baby yoghurt mixed with water. We also had Sunshine milk but we didn't give him that because it probably would've made him sicker. And dear me, he'd just look at you with this big pair of eyes and your heart just went out to him. He was just so sick, the poor little man.

Then—and my memory's a bit vague here—it was either the next morning or the next afternoon when the RFDS were able to get a plane in. By then the weather had cleared and the house creek had gone down. The house creek does that. It just goes up and down, up and down, like a yo-yo, with each storm, if you know what I mean. But with the Gibb River Station airstrip, it only needs a few hours of sun and it's alright. So they flew in and they got little Devon and they took him into Derby Hospital, with his grandma.

And Hugh Leslie—who was the RFDS doctor at the time—well, he rang me after and he said, 'Cheryl, you did a really, really good job.' He said, 'He has got meningitis but I think he'll be okay.'

So I felt really proud and very relieved about that, and Devon's nanna also told me, 'Oh, Missus,' she said, 'you shoulda seen him. When they bin give him that bottle, he bin like it's all he wanted.'

And that really sticks out in my mind because meningitis is pretty deadly, you know. The poor little fella could've easily died. I really should've given him the needle but you know, again, I just didn't have the confidence. So that's why these days when I see Devon around town I always get a good feeling about that. I guess that he'd probably be about fourteen by now, maybe fifteen.

But there was one old lady who I did give needles to, and that was quite a funny one, in the end really. Old Maggie, it was. She was a beautiful old Aboriginal lady. She used to work in my garden and things like that when we were out on Gibb River Station. And this time she had a terrible dental abscess, so we rang up and we were told that she had to be given one penicillin injection per day, for four straight days.

On the first of the four days, she came into my house and she was nearly as bad as me, so to help her relax I got her to lie down on the bed and I said, 'Wriggle your toes, Maggie. Get ready.'

So she wriggled her toes and I took a deep breath to prepare myself and then one ... two ... three ... and I gave her the first of these daily needles. Anyhow, so that day went okay. We survived it, both Maggie and I. So that was day one. The next day Maggie seemed even more tense, you know, which of course made me feel even worse. So we go through the same procedure:

'Lie down, Maggie. Wriggle your toes,' and I somehow managed to give her the needle. So we both survived day two. Then on the third day Maggie arrives and she's even more tense than the day before and I'm even worse still. She's shaking. I'm shaking. She breaks out in a cold sweat. I'm already in a cold sweat. But we survived the experience ... just. Then come the fourth day she arrives even more tense than the previous three days put together, and by now of course I'm just a complete wreck. Absolute. So I asked her straight out, 'You feel pretty good today, Maggie? You feel okay now?'

And she looked at me with such a look of great relief on her face and she said, 'Yeah, I'm feelin' real good Missus.'

'Good,' I said, 'then how about we won't worry about the needles today, aye, Maggie?'

'Nah, Missus!' she said. 'We don't worry about that no more!'

She didn't want them. I didn't want to give them. And when I told her 'No needles today' she was out of there like a shot. But, oh, they're terrible things to give—just terrible, you know. And that's the only time I've given injections and I don't ever want to give another one again unless, that is, as I said, it's in an absolute life and death situation.

Joe the Rainmaker

Well, it stirs me up a bit just thinking about some of the things I could tell you, especially about the Aboriginal people. But stories like this must be told. They must get out there. Now, don't get me wrong—and I want to make this very clear—this isn't your usual Flying Doctor story. This is not a story like that. In actual fact, the only connection this story has to the RFDS is that it was told to me by two nursing sisters, Brenda Preston and Barbara Struck, who at the time were in charge of the Australian Inland Mission Hospital at Birdsville, up near the South Australian-Queensland border.

Now, I guess you'd know that the Australian Inland Mission [AIM] was the precursor of the Royal Flying Doctor Service in as much as John Flynn was the driving force behind the AIM setting up care facilities and hospitals in remote areas and sending trained nurses out to work in them. Then the Flying Doctor Service was later formed, more or less to support those services of the AIM, plus, of course, any of the other outback support organisations. That's how the RFDS came about.

Anyhow, the AIM Hospital in Birdsville was opened in 1923, and two women by the names of Grace Francis and Catherine Boyd became the first nursing sisters there. It then became their responsibility to provide what was the only community-based health services in that area. And, mind you, it was an area that covered something like 1000 square kilometres. So it was quite vast. What's more, these two women were also responsible for acute first-response emergency care, general outpatients, home and community nursing services, health education and promotion. They also gave advice on public health matters, as well as providing pharmaceutical supplies, basic radiography, administration—the lot—plus they were also, at various times, called upon to provide veterinarian and dental assistance.

Now, my first contact with the actual township of Birdsville didn't happen until much later, in the early 1960s, which by then was when the two nursing sisters, Brenda Preston and Barbara Struck, were in charge of Birdsville's AIM Hospital. At that time I was running the administration for a French mob called the Compagnie Générale de Géophysique, and we were part of a seismic survey party that was constructing a road across the Simpson Desert. That road, or track really, was known as the French Line. Anyhow, Nursing Sisters Preston and Struck became my first port of call for back-up medical support when we were working through that area. So basically I had an office in a caravan out in the desert, and if anybody got sick or was injured I'd take them into the Birdsville Hospital. By that stage, in 1963, the population of Birdsville consisted of eight whites and sixty-three blacks.

Anyhow, I got on very well with these two nursing sisters and they told me some amazing stories, and one of those stories was about an old Aboriginal man called Mintulee, or Joe the Rainmaker as he became known. And I believe that this is a very special story and, like I said, it's one that must be told. But, first, to give you a bit of background. As a young man, Mintulee, as he was originally known, was among just a handful of survivors of an 1888 massacre that was conducted by the Queensland Native Police (QNP). That massacre occurred at a permanent waterhole, at a place called Kaliduwarry, which is on the Eyre Creek. The policeman who organised the massacre was a feller called Sub-Inspector Robert Little and, apparently, what had led to the police attack was the killing of a station cook near Durrie, on the Diamantina River.

Now, that particular massacre by the QNP was timed to wreak the maximum effect on some two hundred to three hundred young Aborigines who were known to be assembling there at Kaliduwarry. As to just why they were there was that on a regular basis great gatherings of Aboriginal youth were held and these gatherings attracted eighteen-, nineteen- and twenty-year-old Aborigines from as far away as St Vincent Gulf to the south, and the Gulf of Carpentaria to the north. These occasions or gatherings were known as 'Warrthampa ceremonies' and they were held to celebrate the sexual maturity of those Aboriginal youths who were sent to represent their hordes or, as we would call them, tribes. To explain a little further: see, the Aborigines lived in quite small communities that consisted of around thirty people and there were up to eight of those smaller communities within the larger horde. That's how it worked.

But of course to get two or three hundred natives congregated all together in the one spot provided the perfect opportunity for the Queensland Native Police, because they could just burst in and kill the lot of them. You know, some pastoralist might've simply got in touch and said, 'Hey, they're all gathering out near our place.' So then the QNP came out and of course they were armed with rifles and so forth and so they just went in and, at Kaliduwarry, they hacked to death something like 200 innocent souls. And like so many of these atrocities—and there's no doubting that there have been a great many throughout white history in Australia—the official description of such an event was of it being merely 'a disturbance'. So then it was a case of, 'Oh, wonderful. Job well done, chaps', and all the records were destroyed.

And I know I'm getting off the track a bit here but to me that's one of the things that us white Australians are really saying 'Sorry' for. It's not simply for just the taking of the Aboriginal children—'the stolen generation', as it's been called. It's also for all the massacres, the murders and the poisonings of the waterholes that have occurred over time. And, believe you me, there are many horrific stories that have been completely blotted out from our history.

Anyhow, that's just some of the background. So this Mintulee, or Joe the Rainmaker as he later became known, and about four or five of his Wangkangurru mates managed to escape the vengeance party at Kaliduwarry that had been led by this Sub-Inspector Robert Little, and they limped back into the desert. The story follows on that a year later Sub-Inspector Robert Little was said to have fallen from his horse in Birdsville and died of a broken neck. He was subsequently buried in the Birdsville Cemetery—and I'll tell you more about that later at the end of this story.

So then more than ten years passed before Mintulee and what remained of his Wangkangurru horde finally emerged from the southern Simpson Desert to make camp by the Diamantina River, within sight of the township of Birdsville. Like so many of the other native refugees they were attracted by the number of white settlers and their promises of 'keep' in return for work. But of all the Lake Eyre hordes, to the best of my knowledge the Wangkangurru were the last of the Aboriginal peoples to have direct contact with Europeans and, in doing so, they were also the last to relax their own ways in favour of white man's culture. So it must've been a pretty big shock that after all those years of living in freedom, no sooner had Mintulee arrived out of the desert and set up camp by the Diamantina River than he was placed in the care of the local Protector of Aborigines and given a number. Henceforth Mintulee was known by his white protectors simply as 'J11'.

Now, how he then got the name of Joe the Rainmaker was that a feller by the name of George Farwell solemnly declared that Joe had told him how he'd once made the Diamantina come down in flood. And with Birdsville's annual rainfall hovering around the 5-inch mark—that's if it was lucky—Joe felt duty-bound to relieve all droughts with his well-prepared rainmaking rituals ... in return, of course, for a few shillings for his successes. In her book *From City to the Sandhills of Birdsville*, Mona Henry, who was herself also a Birdsville AIM nursing sister from around 1950, actually wrote of Joe's rainmaking requirements, and I quote: 'In bygone days it was human blood, but, in these civilised times, he [Joe the Rainmaker] had to be content with animal blood. Emu feathers, if available, built into a mound over the rainstone, helped bring success to the ceremony. When he was ready he would sing the tribal rainsong and, like Gandhi, was fast to bring results. Rainmakers must be good weather prophets, as I have yet to hear of one dying of starvation. When sufficient rain had fallen, Joe would visit the settlers to collect his fees.'

Anyhow, one time during the early 1960s, when I was visiting Birdsville, Nursing Sisters Preston and Struck went on to tell me about the last days of white treatment for Joe the Rainmaker. By that stage he was quite old—well into his nineties—and even though he was dying in at the AIM Hospital, Joe remained adamant that he wanted to return to his people and await his end, in as natural a manner as possible. But as was the way in those days he was strapped down to his hospital bed for his own good and safety. Then, after he'd been held in his bed for three days, he eventually persuaded the two nurses to release him from the hospital. That they did and so Joe the Rainmaker returned to his camp on the banks of the Diamantina and he positioned himself under a tree, where he could have a good view of everything that was going on. You know, he could see the piccaninnies running around and he was able to see the women going out digging and the men going out hunting and when they'd come back in they'd all see him under the tree.

And the two nursing sisters told me that Joe the Rainmaker survived under that tree for six months. He didn't eat much food and he only asked for water, yet being among his adopted horde and seeing them go about their lives, and being visited constantly by anyone coming and going about the camp, he was kept happy and was fulfilled until the day he died. And isn't that such a great lesson for us more modern-day white Australians, where we tend to stick our aging grandparents or whoever in some God-forsaken nursing home and try to forget about them? Anyhow, as it turned out Joe the Rainmaker ended up living to be ninety-five years of age and he died in the September of 1955.

And here's the nice twist to the story: see, what they did was, when Joe the Rainmaker died, Joe was buried only about a foot away from Queensland Native Police Sub-Inspector Robert Little's grave and in doing so, in silent retribution to the perpetrator of the Kaliduwarry massacre, they laid Joe with his feet on a slight incline towards the head of Little's grave. That's how I first saw their site in 1963, then, a few years later, when I went back to Birdsville, I saw, they'd erected a headstone on Joe's grave and the white cross that had been on Sub-Inspector Robert Little's grave was missing. And that's the story, pretty much as it was told to me by the two Australian Inland Mission nursing sisters, Brenda Preston and Barbara Struck.

Laura

What greatly helped me during my time as a pilot with the Royal Flying Doctor Service in Queensland was the fact that already having been a farmer and earth moving contractor, I could actually relate well to the people on the land and had an appreciation of the demands of their lifestyle. Also what came in very handy was my many years of remote area flying, and that gave me the experience and ability to access the roads, paddocks, clay flats and bush strips, with regard to the capabilities of both the aircraft and myself, as a pilot.

That being said, flying still threw up many challenges, especially before the introduction of GPS (Global Positioning System). One such case occurred at Laura, a small remote Cape York location west of Cooktown. Laura held a number of festivals, the two major ones being the Laura Festival, which was a big indigenous dance festival, and then there was the local Laura Races. And of course from time to time there would be a few flare-ups, or altercations, at these festivals, which meant that medical attention or even an evacuation was required.

There was one time I remember being called to Laura on a very wet and foggy night to evacuate a local who was thought to have broken his neck in a horse accident. I flew out there with a female doctor and on our arrival Laura was shrouded in stratus cloud. So, with severely limited visibility, before coming below lowest safe altitude I got in contact with Percy Trezise.

Percy was a local identity and I knew that he'd flown his own aircraft to Laura to attend that particular festival. He was a former TAA captain who by this time had done a lot of flying throughout Cape York. Now, because I knew that Percy had his aircraft at Laura, I wanted to speak to him on the radio and ask him if he'd let me know when I was over the top of the strip.

Anyhow, I got in radio contact with Percy and while I was getting directions I circled for about fifteen minutes without being able to see anything. Not a thing. All the while, the female doctor on board had the headphones on and so she was listening in on our conversation. And because of the tone of Percy's and my discussion, plus our obvious lack of visibility, I think the poor doctor might've started to get a bit concerned about the situation, because at one stage she decided that just maybe the patient didn't have a broken neck after all and perhaps the evacuation could wait until the following morning!

Still, I'd been to Laura hundreds of times before and, knowing the area as well as I did, I assured the doctor not to worry because, with Percy's help, I felt confident of being able to carry out a safe landing. Now, I'm not sure if she was all that convinced about my ability but I went ahead anyway and carried out a let-down safely in heavy cloud. I then advised Percy that when I thought I was on final approach I'd put on my landing lights and he could inform me as to exactly where I was in relation to the airstrip. I then continued descent and, much to the relief of the doctor, all went according to plan. With Percy's help we had no trouble landing and, later on, the take-off to evacuate the injured person also went without a problem.

Now, while we're talking about the festivals out at Laura, another sort of funny thing happened. On an earlier occasion we'd been called out there at night to evacuate Cecil, an Aboriginal employee of Susan and Tom Shepherd. Susan and Tom were from Artemis Station. Cecil had gone off to the festival and had, unfortunately for him, got into a 'blue'—a fight—and his stomach had been cut open quite badly with a broken bottle. We'd been advised that there was—and I quote—'already a doctor on the scene'. Apparently this doctor had been attending the festival and we were assured that he'd look after Cecil until our arrival.

So we flew out there to Laura. The only trouble was that when we arrived it turned out that the doctor who we'd been assured was already on the scene, looking after Cecil, was actually an eye specialist, who I attended regularly. Of course, this injury of Cecil's was a little out of the ordinary to what he usually dealt with on a daily basis. So I think the eye specialist was just as glad as poor old Cecil was to hear the throb of our noisy engines in the distance. And all went well with our landing and take-off on that occasion.

But another time when I had a bit of a mix-up was during an election and, naturally, the people of Cape York Peninsula had to make sure they exercised their right to vote, along with the rest of us. To that end Susan Shepherd loaded up her ute with people from her property to go into Laura for voting day. The trip in went without incident and everyone cast their vote. But then on their return journey an altercation occurred between one of the indigenous women and her bloke. I'm not sure what it was about, whether it was of a personal or political nature, but without thinking of the consequences, mid-altercation, this woman simply picked up her port—suitcase—and stepped off the back of the ute. Now, unfortunately, the ute was travelling along at over 60 kilometres per hour and so the woman suffered quite severe head injuries.

Anyhow, that night I received a call from the RFDS doctor to say we were needed to evacuate this injured woman from Kimba Station—Kimba being the nearest station to where the accident had occurred. So we took off in the Queen Air and headed out to Kimba. Being set among thick scrub as it was, I knew Kimba Station would be difficult to locate, especially at night. But, as was standard practice, I was fully expecting to be guided to the remote property by some car lights lining the strip, awaiting our arrival.

On this occasion, for some reason or other that I've forgotten, that didn't happen. I couldn't see anything at all. But then after flying around for a while in the dark I finally saw some lights on the ground and so I headed in that direction. When I arrived over the property, there were still no car lights to greet me so, by using the Queen Air's landing lights, I picked out the strip near the house and landed there safely. A vehicle soon arrived on the scene and out popped a very surprised family. I looked at them. They looked at me.

'This isn't Kimba Station, is it?' I said.

'No,' came the reply. 'This is Violet Vale Station.'

Anyhow, they were able to give me directions and about half an hour later we landed safely at Kimba Station and the evacuation took place without further confusion.

Lombadina

Back in the 1980s I was working in a voluntary capacity, up in the Kimberley region in the far north of Western Australia. If you know that area, I worked for about four years at Lombadina Aboriginal Mission. I also worked for a year in Derby. Following that I spent a year up at the Kalumburu Aboriginal Mission. Then I worked for another year in what was originally known as Port Keats, which is now known as the Wadeye Aboriginal Community. And with the Royal Flying Doctor Service having a base at Derby, most weeks they used to fly out to all those places to run medical clinics plus, at the drop of a hat and normally at night—and usually in the worst of weather conditions—they'd fly in for emergency 'medi-air-vacs', as we called them.

So yes, you could say I've had some 'interesting' times at some of those Aboriginal communities that have been linked in with the RFDS. Take Lombadina for example; I think there were about two hundred people there in the mid-1980s. Back then, they had a pressed gravel airstrip, made up to a certain standard, which was similar to most of those other places I worked at in the Kimberleys. Lombadina had a generator as well, though from memory, I don't think it had the capacity to be able to light up the airstrip. Anyway, the generator was too far away from the airstrip to run the necessary electrical lines or what-have-you.

So of course when there's a night emergency, first of all there's the having to go out in the middle of the night—and, as I said, it was usually in the most atrocious of weather conditions—and sort out the kerosene lamps to light the strip for the plane to come in and out. The kero lamps were built like a large double cone, with a big reservoir of kero and a wick on the top. They had a good, big light but their only problem was that they lacked any decent wind protection. So if it was too windy or, you know, if it was too wet and stormy to light the kero lamps, which happened a lot up there, you had to con all the blokes into getting out there in their four-wheel drives to line up alongside the airstrip.

For the plane to land safely, you lined the cars up at a good distance apart and they'd be pointing alternately across the airstrip so that their lights weren't aimed at each other. You could say that they were sort of like in a zigzag formation and then you had one or two vehicles right down the very end, on low beam, so that the pilot could gauge where the end of the strip was. And of course there were other things to sort out like always having to clear the cattle off the airstrip. They were a particular danger, especially at Lombadina. We had free range cattle up there and so we had to make sure they didn't get in the way of the plane. So that was all good fun, though I suppose everyone's heard all those type of stories.

With Lombadina, I don't know what the legals were, but away back when the Sacred Heart Nuns and St John of God were the mainstays of the missions, the original people up on the Dampier Peninsula—the Bard Tribe— gave the land to the Church. In those early days the place was just about self-sufficient; you know, for meat, bread, vegetables and so forth. So there wasn't too much they had to bring in, other than fuel and things like that. Then over time the particular religious orders gave the Aborigines the leasing rights to the land, plus the cattle, plus all the windmills and the stockyards that were dotted around the place. We ran the vegetable gardens and the bakeries and the mechanical workshops and all those sort of self-functioning things that were needed to keep the place going. Then over time the Aborigines also took over those functions. Take the bakery, for instance; rather than ship bread up from Broome they had someone baking the mission bread in a nice wood-fired oven and when I ran the store I sold that bread in the store on a commission basis. That's how it worked.

Of course the Aborigines were very itinerant. Sometimes they lived in Broome, sometimes they'd come back out to the mission at Lombadina or they might even go and live more traditionally out on their original beach locations and things like that. And other than the usual weekly clinic duties that the RFDS ran, some of the sort of emergency casualties we'd have were things like childbirths, general accidents and injuries and—you know, I shouldn't say it—but there were the injuries from fights and things like that which was usually the result of some alcohol-related dispute or the like.

But the traditional mourning ceremonies were something very interesting. Different cultures might do it a different way but, with the Bard people, the way they did it up there was that they had what was called a 'smoking ceremony'. Now, I'm not an Aboriginal anthropologist or anything so you'll have to check the facts on this, but it was all to do with smoking the spirits away or as a cleansing process to release the spirits out of the body. And sometimes there were lots of little fires made from gum leaves that were set around the coffin and at other times they carried the coffin past a big fire and the winds blew the smoke across it. Then, you know, because it was a Christian Mission, after the smoking ceremony 90 percent would then have a Catholic Mass in the church followed by a normal Christian burial, which was held in the cemetery just right behind the church.

I remember one extremely moving 'smoking' they held was when they brought back the body of one of the old-time Aborigines to Lombadina. It was one of the old male Elders. They flew in at night for that one and so we had to light up the airstrip. The old man had died and I think the RFDS took the body to Derby for an autopsy, or for some sort of legal thing, then they brought him back for their traditional mourning ceremony, which was this 'smoking'.

So the RFDS plane landed at night and the Aboriginal people came up and they took the body— the coffin—out of the plane and I think they took it back to the house of one of the Elder's relatives. The coffin was still closed, and they had a mourning ceremony with those people and that's when they had the smoking ceremony. Then after that they had the traditional Christian Mass and burial. That was quite a big one, that was. Well, I know I've gone off the track a little but really what I'm trying to get across is that the Royal Flying Doctor Service was a very strong link up there, all throughout the Kimberley region, in so many and varied ways. So yes, they are a great organisation and, personally, for me, the time I spent up there was an unreal yet a really great experience.

Long Days, Great Times

You could just about title this story 'The Longest Day', because to begin with the Royal Flying Doctor Service base in Alice Springs rang me at home at two o'clock in the morning and said, 'We've had an accident case up at Tennant Creek. It's pretty serious so could you fly up there and bring them back down to the Alice?'

In those days, Tennant Creek only had one doctor and a few nurses and I knew that the surgeon was in Alice Springs. So I said, 'Yeah, no problem.'

So we jumped in the De Havilland Dove and I took off at about three o'clock in the morning and we headed off to Tennant Creek. I'd say that it would've taken us about two hours to fly up there, then we spent about half an hour on the ground, then two hours back—which is four hours' flying time—so I guess that would've had us back in the Alice at around 7.30.

We also had a short routine medical visit scheduled for that day. That was supposed to finish at about midday or one o'clock. Now, you don't like to change those if you can help it, because at these remote stations and settlements everyone comes into town especially to see us. So after we got back from Tennant Creek I said, 'Look, let's still do the routine medical visit.'

Okay, so we did the medical visit, then we'd just got back into Alice Springs when the hospital rang up and said, 'Do you feel like flying back to Tennant Creek? We've got a real serious case of peritonitis.'

From memory the appendix had burst and one thing had led to another and things didn't look too good, so I said, 'Yeah. Righto, no problem. I'll go back to Tennant Creek.'

So I flew to Tennant Creek for the second time that day and I'd just arrived home again when the phone rang. It was the surgeon in Alice Springs—I knew him quite well—and he said, 'Neil, they tell me you've already had a bugger of a day. Well, I'm having a bugger of a day, too. I've got this woman here but the longer we keep her on the anaesthetic machine, the more chance she's got of getting brain damage.' He said, 'Look, I've done everything I can possibly do up here and I'd really like to get her down to Adelaide straightaway.'

As it happened, I was the only pilot up in Alice Springs at that time who could do the trip because the De Havilland Dove was an IFR (Instrument Flight Rules) aircraft and I was the only instrument rated pilot around the place. So it had to be me. 'Righto,' I said. 'Yeah, we'll go.'

As soon as that decision had been made, they then had to make enough space in the Dove to fit in the anaesthetic machine. And so, while I was flight planning, the engineer was busy stripping the seats out of the aircraft so that we could fit the anaesthetic machine and everything else in. I'd say that the machine itself must've been about 8 or 9 feet long and about 3 feet wide so it only just barely squeezed in the door. Then I also wanted to scrape every ounce of fuel we could get into the tanks, and so they were filled to the absolute. Actually, in the end we were a little bit overloaded, but I don't think I even bothered with a load sheet.

Anyhow, so then I took off for Adelaide. By that time it was probably about eight or nine o'clock at night. On board with me were the female patient of course, plus a doctor and a nursing sister. But because we didn't have 240-volt power, the doctor and nurse had to work the anaesthetic machine manually. They had to do all the pumping and everything. And on that trip I was in cloud the whole time. I didn't even see a star. Not a single one. It was pitch black. I never even saw a single light on the ground or anything. And normally when you'd go on a long trip like that, the nursing sisters had a big flask of coffee or something to help you keep alert. But that wasn't the case on this occasion. They were so flat out in the back, caring for the patient and doing the pumping and so forth, that they didn't even get the chance to come up and chat with me. So the only thing that kept my sanity was talking on the radio and watching the DME (Distance Measuring Equipment) tick over.

Anyhow, as you might be able to imagine, I was pretty stuffed by the time we finally began our descent into Adelaide. And when we broke out of the cloud, at about 500 feet, it was as clear as a bell. And with seeing the lights of Adelaide and then there ahead, less than a mile in front of me, was the runway, oh gees, I tell you, Adelaide was the most beautiful sight I'd ever seen. And I still reckon it's the prettiest thing I've ever seen because, as I said, for five hours I hadn't seen a thing outside the cockpit, not even a star. Nothing.

Then by the time we landed at Adelaide I worked out that I'd spent eighteen hours in the air and that's not including the time on the ground. But you see back then, there was no one else in Alice Springs who was qualified to fly on instruments apart from me. So that was my longest day: eighteen stick hours in one day. And except for long-distance flights, I'd say that that record would never be broken because these days, first, there's always plenty of properly trained pilots available and second, there's usually plenty of available aircraft around.

Anyway, the woman survived, and I guess that's the most important thing.

So yes, Alice Springs was an extremely fascinating part of my life. Plus it's also what you make it, isn't it? Because, you know, you can go on about the aircraft and one thing and another and, I mean, of course, we didn't have all this fancy stuff they've got today. We even took the auto-pilot out of the aircraft because it weighed too much. The damn thing usually never worked anyway. But, see, originally up in Alice Springs we just had the one doctor, the one sister, the one pilot, the one aircraft and the one engineer. Then over the years the medical side of it built up to such an extent that when I left they replaced me with two pilots and two aircraft. By then I'd flown one thousand, eight hundred and twelve hours in three years. That's six hundred actual flying hours per year, and for that sort of work you'd normally expect to fly a maximum of about four hundred hours a year. But that's what used to happen in those early days and that's why they doubled up the service after I left.

And with us just having the one engineer, the one pilot and the one aircraft, we still kept our aircraft virtually as good as new. I'd write the most minute snags on a piece of paper and stick it on the wall in the engineer's office and he'd fix them up. We had that aircraft in absolutely 'Mickey Mouse' condition.

Actually, the whole time I was there I only ever broke down once, and that had nothing to do with our own engineer. It was because of some sort of a fault in overhaul maintenance while it was in Sydney. What happened was that the aircraft had its usual two-yearly major service in Bankstown and when they put the fuel line on they were supposed to use two spanners on it. But they only used the one spanner and they twisted the fuel line and in doing so they twisted the pipe.

Then after the plane came back from being serviced I went out to a property one day and everything seemed to be going well. But then on our way back home I got up to about 8000 or 9000 feet and the fuel pressure started dropping off and the engine began surging. So I shut the engine down. And that's what they found out afterwards—that the pipe had twisted causing a drop in pressure and, at the high ambient temperature, the fuel vaporised. It was just something as simple as that.

Anyway, after I shut the engine down I said to the doctor, 'Well,' I said. 'Here we are, we're on one engine and it's about 200 miles to Alice Springs. That's a bit too far to go on just the one engine.'

I mean, I could've had a go at it but you don't push your luck in an aeroplane. Never. So then I had to find the closest suitable airstrip to land on the one engine and so we went back to Ernabella Mission. I'm not sure what it's like now but back then Ernabella was a dry mission. Even the merest mention of alcohol there was frowned upon. So we were then stuck at Ernabella Mission for two days without a drink.

Anyway, in those days Alice Springs had a population of only about three or four thousand people, and word gets around. So by the time we got back, everyone knew that we'd been stuck out on a dry settlement at Ernabella. Then the instant we walked into the Memorial Club the barmaid plonked these two huge pots of beer down in front of us. We didn't have to say a thing. And that's what the people were like out there in the Alice. Absolutely great. They knew where we'd been and they reckoned we'd be in need of a big beer so they got the barmaid to pour us one as soon as we walked in the club. So yes, we might've had some long days but, gee, they were great times.

Looked like Hell

My name is now Clemson, though O'Connor was my maiden name when I was working as an Emergency flight nurse for the Royal Flying Doctor Service, out in the west of New South Wales, at both Broken Hill and Dubbo. These days I'm married and we're living on a property just outside Walgett, in the central north of New South Wales. But I was with the Flying Doctor Service for nine years and I enjoyed every moment of it ... well, almost ... because during my time with the RFDS we had to deal with many and varied incidents. Some you could draw humour from. Some were tough to take. So it was not always easy, no.

Now I know that tragic stories don't make for the best of reading but I do remember one time at Moomba, up in the north-eastern corner of South Australia. The Flying Doctor Service had the contract at the Moomba oil and gas fields so we used to go out there and it was absolutely amazing—the harshness of the place and just how unbelievably hot it can get. And this story really brings that sort of thing home to you.

Anyhow, they had a bloke out there who was new to the job so he wasn't acclimatised and so he was unaware of the damage that that sort of scorching heat can do to you. Now, I can't remember what his actual job was but he was working about 100 foot up in the air, doing something on one of those big rigs they've got, and he was out in the sun for about three hours without drinking enough water. So it was purely dehydration that got him because someone just happened to look up and there he was, hanging upside down in a safety harness, swinging in midair and he was fitting (having a fit).

That's when we got the call to fly out and get him. In the meantime, the nurses that were based up at Moomba, they had to somehow get up this big rig and they had to go out to where he was hanging to get the drip into him and then get him down. It was just from him purely being overcooked. And actually he was very lucky to even be alive because his whole body had virtually collapsed. He had muscle meltdown. His kidneys were shutting down. He was bleeding from absolutely every orifice. Everything. Then when we arrived we had to ventilate him, and it was difficult because we couldn't see for all the blood that was pouring out of him from everywhere. In all, it took probably eight hours to stabilise him.

So we flew him down to Adelaide and when we got there we got him into the ambulance and we had an emergency police escort from the airport into Royal Adelaide Hospital. Oh, we had all the lights flashing and all the sirens blaring—everything. They even shut the traffic lights off so that we could get him to the hospital quicker. Then, when we got to the hospital, all the lifts were opened for us, and I think they worked on him for another three or four hours. After that he had to be put on dialysis and then he was on ventilators for a long time.

And now he's back at Moomba. He's just doing light duties, mind you. He might still have a few problems but he's a very lucky man to still be alive, with what he went through. So that was a very difficult one, particularly for the nurses at Moomba who had to get right out of their comfort zone and get up the rig and treat the man while he was hanging upside down and fitting in midair. I mean, you really have to admire people with a commitment like that, don't you?

Then there's another story. This one's also about someone who had to get out of their comfort zone to help a patient, though in a different sort of way. Actually, I'm reminded of this story because just last night we had a storm out here at Walgett. We only had about forty points or something but it was bad enough to cut the power and cut the road. Mind you, the rain's nice and welcome, that's for sure.

But talking about rain reminds me of the time when I was working for the RFDS in Broken Hill and a woman rang us from a property up near the Queensland border. In this case this woman had very little medical knowledge. Apparently they'd had a lot of rain up there and her husband had been out riding his motor bike and it had slipped from underneath him and he'd fallen off, damaging his leg. Unfortunately, they only had a dirt airstrip on their property so we couldn't fly in there at the time, because it was too wet. So we then had to try and instruct the husband's wife, over the telephone, as to what to do and how to go about it.

As I said this woman had very limited medical knowledge but from her description of the injuries her husband had obviously broken the leg, and the break was both the tibia and fibula; yes, both of them. In fact, it was a compound fracture, meaning that bone was sticking out which, as you might be able to imagine, was causing the husband a lot of pain and the woman a lot of anxiety.

So, first we had to treat the pain. For that the woman had to give her husband an injection of pethidine, which was kept in the RFDS medical chest. The only trouble was that she'd never given a needle before. Oh, I think perhaps she might've given a few jabs to some of their cattle or something which, mind you, as it turned out, proved to be a very good training ground. So initially we instructed her how to give the injection for the pain, and she managed that.

The next problem was that, from what she'd told us, it was obvious that the foot wasn't getting enough blood to it. She described the foot as being 'cold and white'. Of course, we didn't want to lose the foot, so after her husband had settled down a bit from the pethidine we had to reduce the fracture in an attempt to keep up the blood flow. Now, to reduce the fracture, the woman had to manually—physically—put the bone back into alignment. And she had to do it all by herself, and unpractised, because there was nobody out there to help her. There was just her and her husband. The only help she had was us, and we were miles away on the end of a telephone.

So we told her how to manipulate the bone back into alignment, which is done by pulling and pulling, as hard as she could, until the bone pops back into place. Naturally, she was a bit apprehensive at first but, with the fate of her husband's foot in the balance, she eventually gathered up the courage and in fact, as it turned out, she managed to do that quite well too. So she got the bone back into alignment and then, because she didn't plaster it or anything like that, she had to keep the leg elevated by putting it on a pillow. Once that was done it was important to keep the husband resting. Then throughout the night she had to keep checking for the pulse, just to make sure that blood was still getting down into the foot. All during this time she was in constant contact with us.

Of course, before we could get the aeroplane in there to pick up her husband and get him back to the Broken Hill Hospital, we had to wait until the airstrip was safe enough for us to land. As it happened, they didn't get any more rain that night and so things looked promising. So the next morning she had to somehow get her husband out of the house and into a vehicle and then drive out and check the condition of the airstrip. She also had to clear the kangaroos from off the strip and check for any holes and twigs or sticks or logs that might get in our way.

Anyhow, after she gave us the all-clear, we flew in there. By then it was about twenty-four hours after the accident. And the woman had done a great job. The leg was looking really good and her husband was relatively pain free. The only trouble was, it'd obviously been a very long and harrowing ordeal for the woman because she looked like absolute hell.

Looking at the Stars

If you like, first of all I've got a story here that's a little bit humorous. It's one that, these days, has almost become part of Flying Doctor Service folklore because you'll hear it, or differing versions of it, being told in just about every pub around western Queensland. What's more, it's a true story. That's what I've been told, anyway.

Now, I haven't got an exact date but at one time the Charleville base of the RFDS received a call from a ringer, and the ringer said, 'Doc, yer gotta come real quick. Me mate's hurt his hand real bad.'

Anyhow, in an attempt to find out how the accident happened, and to get a clearer idea as to just how badly the ringer's mate's hand was damaged, the doctor tried to extract a little bit more information out of the ringer. But, with ringers being ringers and ringers, more often than not, being men of extremely few words, the doctor couldn't get much more information out of him other than his mate had 'hurt his hand real bad' and that the doctor had better 'come real quick'.

So they jumped into the plane and off they went. After they landed at the particular station property where the accident had occurred, they rushed to the scene and there was this ringer, the one with the damaged hand, sitting there looking sad and sorry and forlorn and the other ringers were sort of sheepishly standing around behind him. Anyhow, the doctor walked up to the injured ringer and said, 'Show me your hand, son.'

Which he did. He lifted his hand up and his thumb was totally missing. It was gone.

'Where's your thumb?' the doctor asked.

Well, the injured ringer, who was also a man of few words, didn't say anything but simply motioned towards his mates. So the doctor said to his mates, 'Where's his thumb? What've you done with his thumb?'

'Oh,' one of them said, 'we stuck it over there, on the gatepost, fer safe keepin'.'

And just as doctor turned around to the gatepost, he saw a crow heading skyward, thumb and all. So I don't know how the ringer had actually lost his thumb in the first place, but it had certainly gone missing after the crow had flown off with it.

So that's one story. But I suppose that every time I go out to the bush I come back with another story and this one came about when we were putting together a promotional DVD for the Royal Flying Doctor Service. There was just myself, the director and a cameraman, and we'd based ourselves at Mount Isa and we were filming right up to Bentinck and Sweers Islands. Bentinck and Sweers Islands are just off Burketown, into the Gulf of Carpentaria.

But where this story actually comes from is Burketown itself, and I thought it was rather beautiful. The lady that looks after the Burketown Clinic—if you like, she's the registered nurse there—her name is Glenda. She's an Aborigine, and we fly in there once a week and conduct a clinic. Now Burketown, as you may well know, is a very remote location. Just check it up on your map.

So we were there filming in Burketown and the director happened to ask Glenda, 'Seeing that you're the only one with any form of medical expertise out here in this remoteness, in a situation of an accident of a night time, how do you handle it all on your own?'

And Glenda said to the director, 'Well, first I patch them up as best I can. Next, I call the Flying Doctor and then I go out to the airstrip and I look up at the stars and just wait for one to get bigger.'

Memories of Alice Springs

When John Flynn died in 1951, my father, Fred McKay, took over his position of Superintendent of the Australian Inland Mission. When that happened we moved from Brisbane down to Sydney. Then we'd only been in Sydney for about a year or so and there were some financial problems or other within the organisation of the AIM. I was a bit too young to know all the details about it but it's been well documented. Anyhow, in amongst all that, they were having problems getting staff for the AIM's Bush Mother's Hostel, up in Alice Springs. So my mother, Meg McKay, volunteered her services to be Matron—gratis—and so we all moved up to Alice Springs. By all, I mean it was really just my mother, my elder sister, my brother and myself because Dad still had all his other AIM duties to attend to, so he was coming and going a lot.

The Bush Mother's Hostel was in Adelaide House. That's in Todd Street. It's a National Trust building now, like a museum. And I guess that you know all about how John Flynn actually helped redesign the hostel, with the wide verandahs and the natural sort of air conditioning. That was where the air came up from a tunnel under the building, to cool the place down. I would've only been twelve or so, at that stage, but back then Alice Springs was quite a small town. I'd say that there would've only been about two or three thousand people. They'd just built their first high school, the year before we went up there, and so I was in the first group of students to go to that new high school.

But it was a fascinating place and it just seemed to me that Alice Springs encapsulated a great range of people—people who were all unique, in their own sorts of ways. You know, everyone seemed to be a character who lived their character. And there's books out now about some of these people where they're described as being 'outback heroes and outback identities'.

One lady in particular comes to mind. Her name was Olive Pink. At that time I didn't have a clue as to what Olive did but you'd always see her looking like she was someone out of Edwardian England. Wherever she went, she wore these long white dresses, with a white hat and a white scarf, and gloves. And in a place like Alice Springs that was very much a look that was out of place. But, as I said, while I was there I didn't know what she did and since then I've learnt that she was a quite well known conservationist and environmentalist. Apparently she was very instrumental in opening up and saving a lot of the native vegetation throughout that area. There's even the Olive Pink Memorial Gardens there now and I believe she helped establish a lot of that garden herself. But when you're only in your early teenage years ... well, my memories of her were just of seeing her around town and thinking what a strange lady she was.

Then when they started to build the John Flynn Church, Dad was back a lot more because he was supervising the building. So we watched the John Flynn Church being built. And if you're ever up that way, it's well worth a visit, not only because of its basic structure, but there's also a lot of symbolism in the actual building, which is something that a lot of people don't realise. It's set out like a story of the life of John Flynn and his achievements.

Anyway, I always thought it was just interesting, how some of the things Dad did in Alice Springs seemed to have had far-reaching effects for different people. There was another feller called Ted Smith. Ted didn't have any work but he owned a truck. He was married with two kids. So he was struggling to make a go of things. Then, in the early days of getting the church under way, he sort of turned up one day and offered Dad any help he could give. Of course, back then everything was being shipped up from Adelaide. But just at that point in time there was some sort of big transport problem or other and this Ted Smith arrived just at the right time, with this truck, and saved Dad a momentous problem. And that set Ted Smith up in Alice Springs. He helped Dad out with the building of the church, then he went on to become a very, very highly respected businessman who had this very prolific business, not only in transport but I think he also diversified into other areas.

But us kids, we thought that the whole thing was all just one big adventure because there were times when we'd go out from Alice Springs on different trips with Dad, and we'd camp out on the ground, with the flies and the mosquitoes and everything else, and that was just an accepted part of our lives. And talking about going out camping and some of the people of Alice Springs: something that always amazed me was that while Dad was overseeing the building of the John Flynn Church he was always looking for local materials to build it with. Anyhow, there's quite a bit of a special type of pink marble in the church, and I remember going out in the truck with Dad one time and he'd especially asked these two old Aboriginal fellas to come out and help him find some of this pink marble. So there we were, driving around, away out in the middle of nowhere, north of Alice Springs somewhere, and all of a sudden these old Aborigines told Dad to stop. So he did, and they pointed to a place.

'Over there,' they said.

To me, all the rocks looked exactly the same. But when we took a closer look, there it was. And you would have never known that there was pink marble there until you'd started chipping away at the rock. But somehow ... and don't ask me how ... they just knew it was there.

News Flash

You know, I've been involved in a lot of things up in the gas fields at Moomba and, actually there's not too many funny stories that come out of there. Tragedies aren't good for a book but here's one that has a lighter side to it. It's all hooked into the Flying Doctor Service, and it's probably a case where we did people more of a dis-service than a service, though, it was a sort of humorous dis-service.

I hadn't been at Moomba all that long and what happened was that in about the early 1990s, up in the far north of South Australia, it was one of those very rare times when Lake Eyre was flooded, okay. And when Lake Eyre floods a lot of tourists like to go out there and have a look because it's such an amazing sight, what with all the wildlife and that. Anyhow, all these tourist people, to get a closer look, what they do is they charter aeroplane flights out from places like William Creek or Port Augusta or Leigh Creek and they go out and fly over the lake.

Now, I don't know if you've ever seen Lake Eyre in flood but it's a fantastic experience. And what happens is that when it floods, in most places it's still only got about 2 foot of water in it, and because it's so salty, on a really calm day when you fly over the lake, it's like flying over a mirror. It's like an optical illusion. You could be flying at 100 feet and you look down and it seems like you're at 30 000 feet, and if you've got clouds above you, you'll also get that cloud reflection off Lake Eyre. It's quite phenomenal.

The other thing that's unusual about Lake Eyre is that it's below sea level, right, so when you're flying a plane over it, it's difficult to gauge exactly how high you are. Because in a case like that, when the aeroplane's altimeter tells you that you're at true ground level, you could actually be something like 100 feet off the ground. Add to that the mirror imagery that I was talking about and you'll understand why most pilots are a bit wary about flying too low over Lake Eyre.

So, now to the story. There was one particular charter flight full of oldies—what you'd call 'snow birds'—and the charter pilot took these snow birds over the lake and of course they all wanted to have a real good, close look. The pilot, for whatever reason, mustn't have been paying too much attention as to how high the plane was off the deck and he got a bit low and he ploughed right into the middle of Lake Eyre. Fortunately nobody was hurt, apart from the pilot's ego getting bruised, that is. Anyway, the plane sort of bounced along the water and—chung—it ground to a halt. Then what happened was that the plane's emergency global positioning alert system went off and that's when we were asked to go and do a search and rescue to look for this plane. As soon as we got the story we thought, 'Okay, it's highly likely that it's one of those scenic flights, you know, over Lake Eyre.'

Anyway, we take off in the helicopter and we fly out to Lake Eyre. Now, after the plane had come to a stop, all these snow birds had managed to get themselves out of the plane. As I said, nobody was hurt but they were all very wet, you see, and it was a pretty cold day with a bit of wind, so they were cold and wet and miserable. So these oldies, they came up with an idea to help increase their chances of being found and so they took most of their wet clothes off and they placed them down on the wing of the plane in such a way that they wrote the word 'HELP'. That not only let anyone flying overhead know that they were in trouble but it also helped to dry their clothes out, you see.

So we picked up the signal—the emergency alarm— on the helicopter and we sort of tracked them by the signal until we saw them. They were just this dot in the middle of Lake Eyre. Then the helicopter pilot said, 'Look, I can't land in water.' So he said, 'We'll fly over to reassure them that we know where they are and then we'll head to the nearest station property and sort things out from there.'

'Righto,' I said. 'No worries.'

So we flew in on the helicopter and this's where we did these poor old snow birds a bit of a dis-service, right. We flew in on the helicopter, nice and close until we could see that they were waving at us and they could see that we were waving back. We just wanted to reassure them that they'd been seen. But then, as we pulled away in the helicopter, we created this huge updraft and the updraft just lifted all their clothes up in the air and scattered them back into the water. So their clothes had almost dried but now they're all wet again. And they weren't too happy about it either because they're now shaking their fists at us, the poor buggers.

Anyhow, we contacted the people at the nearest station, which was Muloorina Station, just on the edge of Lake Eyre, and when we arrived there they had some flat bottom boats; they're like punts. So we basically got some four-wheel drives and we got as close to the ditched aeroplane as we could, which was about probably 2 or 3 kilometres. Then we put these flat bottom boats in the water and we sort of walked them out to the aeroplane. Then we piled all these cold, wet and miserable snow birds into these boats and then we walked them back in relays to the shore. From there we got them in the four-wheel drives and took them back to Muloorina Station. Then, the next day, a couple of planes flew in to pick them all up.

But the odd thing about it was, when we first went to Muloorina Station to sort out how we were going to rescue the snow birds, two aeroplanes landed almost simultaneously. One was the RFDS plane from Port Augusta, who'd been asked to come up just in case we needed back-up, and right behind that was the Channel 9 news plane from Adelaide. Now, how on earth they found out about the accident so fast, I would not have a clue.

But anyway, the Channel 9 plane landed and it was really funny because here we are, out on an outback station, you know, and it'd been a bit of a tough day, so everybody's a bit rough around the gills and looking tardy, and the lady from the Channel 9 news crew steps out of their plane, and she's immaculately dressed. Perfect. She looked like she'd just walked right out of a page of a fashion magazine. She'd put her lippy on and changed her dress and everything and then she started running around wanting to interview everybody. And, you know, we're saying, 'Look, excuse me, can't you see that we're a little bit busy trying to coordinate a rescue here?'

But it astounded me just how quickly the news crew flew up from Adelaide, to land at this station in an attempt to get the story. But in the end the news people turned out to be okay, really. You know, we were all still there at last light, and after they'd got their story they stayed on at the station with the rest of us, and we all bunked down in the shearers' quarters together, and then they let their hair down. So a good night was had by all.

Old Ways, New Ways

We were flying from Alice Springs up to the Barkly Tablelands one time, travelling up there to do some routine medical clinics. I was the pilot and, back in those days, they didn't have telephones out on any of these station properties. Their only communication was by radio. Anyway, the people from this particular cattle station called in to the Alice Springs Flying Doctor Service base and said that they had an Aboriginal stockman out there who had a severe toothache. So we were flying along and of course we always listened to these sessions because at times you get diversions and so forth.

Anyway, as luck would have it, we were due to be flying over this particular property within about fifteen minutes and we always carried dental gear on the plane with us, just in case. So the doctor got on our radio and said, 'Look, we're on our way up to the Barkly Tablelands but if you bring him out to the airstrip, we'll drop in there in a few minutes, pull the tooth out real quick, then we'll be on our way again.'

So the station people did that. They came out with the biggest, toughest Aboriginal stockman you would ever see and we just opened the back door of the aeroplane and sat him on the floor of the plane, with his feet hanging outside. That was just about the right height for the doctor to get a good grip on a tooth. Then, after we propped up the stockman, the doctor started to get prepared. He decided not to use a needle because it looked like a pretty straightforward extraction and, anyway, we didn't have the time. As you can imagine, with all this going on, it looked a real sight so I decided to take a photograph of the scene. And I was just taking the photo when it all got a bit too much for the big, tough stockman and he passed out.

'Quick, Neil,' the doctor called out, 'grab his head and I'll pull the tooth out while he's unconscious.'

So I grabbed the stockman's head as firmly as I could and held it while the doctor got stuck into it. The only trouble was that the extraction proved to be more difficult than he'd first thought it might be and so he had to push and pull it this way and that until, finally—pop—and the tooth came out. Then just after the doctor had extracted the tooth, the stockman began to revive and when he fully came around he found that his aching tooth had disappeared. So he was happy. We were happy. Everyone was happy. Then we just said 'Goodbye' and we jumped back into the plane and we continued on our way, up to the Barkly Tablelands.

So that's just one little story. But, I must say, I liked the Aborigines. And out in some of those old mission and community places, like Papunya and Yuendumu, I took to the old blokes in particular. In fact, I even tried to learn a little bit of the local language and I used to try and talk to the old blokes while the doctors and nurses were running their clinics and taking a look at the crookies—the sick ones. So I met some very interesting characters. I remember there was one old Aboriginal bloke at Areyonga, who'd apparently been there with Lasseter, when Lasseter went missing out in the Petermann Ranges area, near the eastern border of central Western Australia. And this old fella told me that it's all just a big myth because Lasseter didn't find any gold. In fact, there was no gold out there at all.

And another old bloke, he took a very keen liking to me, probably because I'd taken an effort to learn the language, and I was talking to him one day and he said, 'Ah, Captain we go for a drive.'

'Oh, right-o,' I said.

So we hopped in a vehicle and we went for this drive, and we go out onto the flat plains. They're dead flat and, anyway, away in the distance there's some rocks sticking up about 20 foot or so, out of the plain. So we drive over there to these rocks, and in amongst them there's this big cave and we go into the cave and, believe me, it's just a mass of native art. It was absolutely amazing. Stunning. And he just took me there as a favour because he liked me. He trusted me.

And that same old fella, he made me a set of boots that the kadaitcha men wear. Now, so that the kadaitcha men can't be tracked, these boots, they're made out of human hair and emu feathers and blood and stuff. You know the kadaitcha man, don't you? He's the spirit man, the magic man, the one that points the bone. Anyway, this old fella made me these kadaitcha boots and he told me that they'd ward away the evil spirits. So I took them home, and my wife—at that time—she said, 'I'm not gonna to have those smelly things in the house.' And she burnt them. And I reckon that's probably one of the reasons why she's now my ex-wife, because things were never the same after that and so maybe ... just maybe ... the evil spirits got to her after she burnt the boots.

But talking about the kadaitcha men and their magic: we flew out to Papunya Aboriginal Community one day and they'd had a lot of babies dying there. The story was that the kadaitcha man was around, trying to pick out who was behind all the bad medicine that was causing the babies to die. Then, of course, once the kadaitcha man decides who the culprit is, the bloke wakes up with a spear through him, and everything gets back to normal.

Anyway, I don't know what had caused the first few deaths of the babies but because all the Aborigines were so fearful of this kadaitcha man, none of them were game enough to come out of their wurlies or huts. So, by the time we arrived, with everyone being too scared to come out of their wurlies, all these kids had by then begun to suffer from dehydration and so forth. And, over time, until the kadaitcha man found out who was causing all the bad medicine, I think we brought something like about seventeen of these dehydrated kids back into Alice Springs where they could be cared for.

But the Aborigines there were fairly primitive back in those days, back in the '50s and early '60s. Mostly, they still lived by their old ways of thinking. For their birth control, they'd 'whistle-cock' the men. Whistle-cocking's when they make an insertion in the penis and that was their form of birth control: to 'whistle-cock' them.

Oh, I could go on forever with the experiences I had when I was flying out of Alice Springs. I've even got photos of initiation ceremonies, because one time I got an old black fella and I lent him the camera. I mean, he was a terrible photographer but he took all these photos for me and, you know, there wouldn't be too many photographs like that in existence. And, anyhow, when they do these initiation ceremonies, part of it is to do the circumcision. And in the old days they used to get two fairly sharp stones and they'd rub them together and cut the foreskin off. By doing it that way, when they removed the foreskin it sort of sealed off the blood vessels, which was supposed to stop the bleeding.

The only trouble was that they didn't necessarily keep these circumcision stones very clean. Now, I didn't actually see this myself but my predecessor was there when it happened. The doctor at that time was a pom, a chap by the name of Edgar Emerson. Even in the middle of summer, when it was as hot as hell, old Edgar still wore his tweeds and his coat, with the patches on and stuff, and he always wore a tie.

Anyway, my predecessor told me that there was this Aboriginal stockman up at Alexandria Downs Station and, see, the male Aborigines can't get married until they've been initiated and circumcised. So this Aboriginal stockman was in his mid to late twenties and he comes in to see old Edgar and he had a shocking infection in his penis from where they circumcised him. My predecessor reckoned that it was an awful sight, because this fella's penis had swollen up to about 3 inches round and it'd gone all purple, with pus running out of it everywhere. Anyway, old Edgar took one look at it and he said, 'Oh, good Lord, he's going to lose it.'

And the Aboriginal fella—the one with the infected penis—said to Edgar, 'Oh, yer should'a seen it when it was real crook, Doc.'

As I said, I didn't witness that one, thankfully. That was told to me by my predecessor. But, of course, that was the old ways because later on they started using razor blades for circumcision. And they were pretty smart about it too, because what they'd do was they'd carry out the circumcisions just before the Flying Doctor was about to come around on a routine medical visit. Then, when the doctor arrived, the first thing he'd be met with was a line-up of young Aboriginal blokes, all waiting to have their penis cleaned up.

One in a Trillion

I first started flying for the Flying Doctor Service in
Alice Springs in the mid-60s, and it was a tremendous
experience. At that time they were bringing the
Aborigines out of the desert and into settlements
because rockets were being launched out of Woomera
and they didn't want to hit some poor unfortunate
Aborigine who happened to be wandering about out
there. When I say 'they', back then I think the ruling
organisation was called the Department of Native
Affairs.

Anyhow, in those days they were very big on
getting the Aborigines vaccinated against everything
because having lived out in the wilderness, so
to speak, they had no immunity to white fellers'
diseases and so forth. So we'd go out to the various
missions and communities and places like that.
Sometimes we'd even land at a remote cattle station
and jump in a vehicle and drive 20 miles or so out
to some little Aboriginal camp or other, where the
doctors and sisters would jab and record them, and
what-have-you.

See, other than the mass vaccination of the
Aborigines, they were also big on recording all their
tribal Aboriginal names and who their father was and
who their mother was, and that sort of business. But
that got a bit confusing after a while because too many
of them seemed to have had too many of the same
fathers and mothers and everyone else seemed to be

known as Auntie Someone-or-other or Uncle Someone-or-other. And that's just the Aboriginal way of family. But it was a real eye-opener because, you know, you'd see all sorts of things; some of the conditions they lived in were indescribable. And the women had legs that were little bigger than broom handles; then sometimes their arms or legs had been broken and had set awkwardly.

But Papunya was probably one of the main places where the Department of Native Affairs brought the Aborigines into. And I'll get a little off the track here and reminisce on a bit and tell you a little story about chance, one that started at Papunya.

We flew into Papunya one time and there was a pregnant nursing sister who worked out there whose name was Marie. Anyway, while the doctor and the nurse were jabbing the Aborigines and recording their names and so forth, I went and had a cup of tea with this Marie. Then a couple of days after I'd flown the doctor and nurse back to Alice Springs, I said to the doctor, 'Gees, I'm itchy.'

'Let's have a look,' he said.

And he just took one look at me and he said, 'You've got German measles. We'll have to go back to Papunya and give an injection of gamma-globulin to all the pregnant women out there, then hope you haven't caused any problems.'

So we went back out to Papunya and, I don't know if you've ever seen it or not, but the gamma-globulin needle is this great, big, long needle which they jab into the rump. It's like a length of number eight fencing wire. Anyway, Marie said to me, 'I'm never having another bloody cup of tea with you ever again.'

Unfortunately, in Marie's case she miscarried. She lost the baby.

Then a few years later I got married and at the wedding I was introduced to the in-laws for the first time and my newly acquired sister-in-law looked vaguely familiar. So I said, 'Haven't I seen you before?'

'Yeah,' she said, 'I know you from somewhere, too.'

I said, 'What's your name?'

'Marie,' she said.

And it turned out that this Marie was the same Marie who was the nursing sister out at Papunya, and I was the bloke who caused her to lose her baby because I had German measles. And I'd just married her husband's sister, which made me her brother-in-law. So what's the chances of that happening? About one in a trillion, I'd say.

Pilatus PC 12

I don't think that by me being a female pilot, it changes the way the plane is being flown. In my case it is more working for the Royal Flying Doctor Service that makes an interesting difference to the way I sometimes fly. For an example, it must've been about four or five months ago we were sent to Cook, out on the Nullarbor Plain, for a patient that got sick on the Indian Pacific train. It was a high priority and when we landed the doctor came along and he said, 'Oh, you will have to taxi into town because the patient is too sick to be transported out to the airport.'

Well, the airport was probably about 500 metres or 600 metres from the town but here you go: safety first. Off the airport I went, onto the track and taxi into town and I park the plane under a shady tree. And that's just one of those things you would never come across anywhere else. It was sort of like a special pick-up and it was because, as I said, it was of a very high priority.

It's the same in Tarcoola, which is also out on the Transcontinental Railway Line. When we go there for medical clinics with the GPs, the first time I came there I asked, 'Where do we go?'

And they said, 'Well, you follow the track and you park the aeroplane behind the hospital.'

So those kinds of experiences, of course, are very different to anywhere else with flying, and also much more so because these are usually all-dirt runways.

Another thing that is different is that we all work as a team in the Flying Doctor Service. We all try to help each other. Like what we had in the bush once at William Creek, in the north of South Australia. There was a car roll over after they'd had a heavy night of partying, I think, and we got called out in the very early hours of the morning. But when we got there, to William Creek, we couldn't get the lights to go on, on the airstrip.

But some of the station crew were already out there, because they knew of the emergency and they switched on, manually, the lights of the strip. So you land the aeroplane on the dirt strip and then you help put a stretcher in the back of the good old 'Aussie' ute, jump in the ute, with the nurse and the doctor, drive to where the person is injured and be of any help you possibly can while they get him stabilised and they assess him and things like that. Then you help get him on the stretcher and put the stretcher again in the back of the ute and you drive back to the strip where we then put him on the aircraft and then you take off. So, you know, those are the real stories of accidents in the bush that you can have happen.

One of the first experiences that I had of a night-time flight was with the flares. For those, the RFDS send out forms to all the different stations to show them how to set the flares out and what the procedure is. They give enough light out, but not a whole lot. And with flares, you don't see them until you are only a few miles out from them. So anyway, this time we had to go to Clifton Hills, which is a station property up on the Birdsville Track. It was a pitch black night. There was no moon out, nothing. I was at about 20 000 feet or something and half an hour out from our destination I could look anywhere and I could just not see a single light outside, anywhere. That's how black it was. And I thought, 'Oh well, this is definitely descending into a black hole.'

Anyhow, they set up the flares and then they have a car with the lights that point to where the wind comes from so that you're flying into the wind when you land. So, yeah, that was quite an experience to do that the first time.

But especially when it is totally moonless and you don't have a horizon or anything to look at, because it's just pitch black, then you've really got to be on the ball to do that, because you are virtually just flying by the instruments. Because sometimes you do often hear of that 'black hole' thing—that is when some people can easily lose their direction and also they lose how high they are off the ground, and even whether they're flying upside down or not. So you've got to trust your instruments, because in a situation like that what the instruments say can be the opposite to what are our own perceptions. For instance, if you accelerate then your body sensation will say, 'Oh, you're accelerating, so you must be going down.'

That is the feeling you get. Your ears will tell you something different than what your instruments do. It is hard but it's something that you just have to learn— to trust your instruments. So, yeah, black holes can be very dangerous.

But we are very lucky with the Pilatus PC 12 aeroplanes. They've got, for instance, the EGPWS. That stands for Enhanced Ground Proximity Warning System, so that if you're going in on a too-steep approach it will give you little things to warn you that you are too steep. Or when the ground comes up towards you, or you don't have your gear down and your flaps out, and there is a runway, it will go off and say, 'Pull up. Pull up. Terrain. Terrain.'

We also have a multi-function display unit which, at night time, we can use to read the ground, so that we can see where any high areas are. You can sort of see outside, but you can't, if you understand what I mean. But all that works on the display unit, with radar and satellite. So all that instrumentation is of an enormous value to us, especially since we are a single pilot operation.

So the Pilatus PC 12 is a most wonderful aeroplane. In fact, the Flying Doctor Service was one of the first major organisations to use the PC 12s. It is a Swiss-built plane that has got a military background. So they're very well built. But also, I believe the PC 12 was a radical move away from normal thinking because while the King Airs have a twin turbo prop (propeller), the PC 12s have a single-engine turbo prop. Of course, with having a single engine, they're a cheaper plane to operate and also they have a shorter landing and take-off length than our King Airs did.

But they are very, very expensive to buy and fit out. I think that I've heard a quote of about $6 million for each aeroplane. That is with all the medical equipment in them, of course. But they've been a great success, and they suit, very much, our type of work. And I think that now the RFDS, especially in the South Australian or Central Section, has got the highest flight time of PC 12s anywhere in the world.

Preordained Destiny

I was reading your last book of Flying Doctor stories—
More Great Australian Flying Doctor Stories—and I
was particularly taken with a story in there called 'In
the Footsteps of Flynn'. In part it describes how Fred
McKay's destiny was set out very early on in his life. If
you recall, that happened when he was a little boy and
he was very ill and he remembered looking up from his
sick bed and seeing his mother saying, in silent prayer,
'Lord, if you make my little boy well, I'll make him a
minister.'

Of course, we all know now that that's what
happened. Fred became a minister and, then, following
John Flynn's death, he took over as Superintendent of
the Australian Inland Mission. So Fred's destiny was
set from a very early age.

Now, I'm not sure if you know but Fred's wife, Meg,
also had a very interesting occurrence of preordained
destiny. As you know, Meg became such an integral
part of Fred's life, not only as his wife but also with
the work they both did within the organisation of the
AIM. And, well, as it's turned out, I've discovered that
that strong connection had its beginnings long before
Fred even came along. But putting it all together from
my memory is a little hard and of course there's been
so much written about both Fred and Meg that it's
probably best if you just read about it in a book. It'd
be more accurate that way. I mean, as in this case,
that's where I came across this particular story about

Meg and her destiny. I found it in a very interesting book that was written by Maisie McKenzie. It's called *Outback Achiever: Fred McKay—Successor to Flynn of the Inland*. And this is where a lot of this information comes from, so my apologies to Maisie, but I just want to get it right.

Now, just a bit of background first. Meg was a Robertson, and her father, Hubert Robertson, had been a Presbyterian minister in Scotland. He and his wife were then invited by the Presbyterian Church to come out to Australia; Hubert as an evangelist. That was in 1913. So they settled in Australia and their first daughter, Betty, ended up attending university at the same time Fred was there. I'm not sure just how good friends they were but they knew each other well enough that Fred got to know the Robertson family through his contact with Betty.

Meg was the second daughter. Her given name was Margaret Mary McLeod Robertson or, as she became more commonly known, Meg. Then, later on, when she was at a Presbyterian-Methodist College for girls, that's when she got to know Fred, through his connection with Betty. Now apparently Meg was quite struck by Fred, even back then. But she wasn't sure about Fred's feelings towards her so it came as a real surprise when Fred asked her to accompany him to an Inter-College Boat Race on the Brisbane River. I believe Fred was at Queensland University at Emmanuel College at that stage, studying Arts and Theology. Now Meg was about eight years younger than Fred so she would've only been, I don't know, about sixteen or seventeen or something. She was still a schoolgirl anyway, and apparently she went off to this boating regatta, along with Fred, all dressed out in the Emmanuel College colours. So she must've been determined to make some sort of an impression.

And that's when they first began to really get to know each other. But at that stage in time they were both so busy, what with Fred and his studies and then, after Meg had finished school, she went to Brisbane to begin her nursing training at the Brisbane Hospital. But her father, Hubert Robertson, had long held a fascination with the work that John Flynn was doing within the AIM, to such an extent that he had then become Chairman of the Queensland Council of the Australian Inland Mission.

Anyway, as the story goes, at one point he had to submit a report to the State Assembly in Brisbane. Meg also attended that State Assembly, along with her family, and she just happened to sit in front of Fred and a group of his college mates. Now, in Maisie McKenzie's book, it says how Fred must've apparently spent more time looking at Meg than he did listening to the Church Fathers, because somewhere during the proceedings he tapped Meg on the shoulder and asked, 'Who's taking you home tonight?'

And, as quick as a flash, Meg replied, 'You are.'

That's when they really first formed their bond because, according to Maisie McKenzie, Fred kissed Meg when they parted that night and I quote: 'that marked the beginning of a life-long commitment to each other—one that was to last through the years and lead them on unexpected paths'.

From then on they sort of developed their relationship over the years. I mean, they went to the boat regatta when Meg was about seventeen and they married when she was twenty-two or something like that so they had a reasonably long courtship. That's if you could call it a courtship because they were apart so often. But apparently the kiss sealed it, and from then on they were committed to each other.

Later on, after Fred had graduated, he was appointed to a Home Mission at Southport, on the Gold Coast. The Gold Coast's about 100 kilometres south of Brisbane. The place suited him well because he liked swimming in the sea and he liked the people. So he was pretty excited about his appointment and he thought he'd settle in there, at Southport, for the next few years. After that his plan was to go overseas to Edinburgh, Scotland, where he wanted to continue with his theological studies.

But while Fred was at Southport, that's when John Flynn came along and asked him to consider becoming a Patrol Padre, with the AIM. As you've said in your book, Flynn had long been eyeing off Fred as a likely candidate to take over the running of the AIM, after his departure. That part of the story is quite well written about in the story 'In the Footsteps of Flynn', from your book of *More Great Australian Flying Doctor Stories*. You know, with Flynn running some sand through his fingers and saying to Fred, 'The sands of Birdsville are far finer than the sands of Southport' then with Fred following Flynn off the beach and walking in his footsteps as they went.

So that was Fred and his destiny. And now, as I said right at the beginning, there's perhaps an even more interesting story of destiny, hidden in there, within the overall story, and it's about Meg and her long-time connection to the Australian Inland Mission; one that

happened long before she met Fred. Now I'd like to quote
directly from Maisie McKenzie's book, if I may, because it
relates that story far better than what I can tell it.

Okay, so this happened soon after John Flynn had
his meeting with Fred on the beach at Southport, with
the proposal of him joining the AIM and becoming a
Patrol Padre, out in western Queensland. And I now
quote:

> And was it in the best interests of the Church
> and of himself to sacrifice the Edinburgh goal?
> And what about Margaret Robertson? How
> would she react? They knew their future was
> bound together, but Margaret was little more
> than half-way through her nursing training. He
> simply had to see her.
>
> He met her at the hospital and they walked in
> the park, while he told her of the extraordinary
> experience with John Flynn, who had asked
> him to be a boundary rider for the Australian
> Inland Mission and to travel throughout western
> Queensland. He half expected her to protest
> that perhaps he was being carried away, or
> some such thing, but, to his utter astonishment,
> Margaret unfolded a remarkable story.
>
> She told him that, when her father, Hubert
> Robertson, had first come out from Scotland as
> an evangelist, in 1913, the Australian Inland
> Mission was in its infancy, having started only
> the year before. But Hubert and his wife read
> about it and this fascinating, adventurous
> work in outback Australia captured their
> imaginations. They found out all they could and,

just before Margaret was born in May 1915, they agreed to dedicate the baby, whatever the sex, to the splendid work being carried out by John Flynn and his Australian Inland Mission.

So, even before she was born, Fred's future wife was invisibly bound to the Australian Inland Mission. Six months after her birth, John Flynn, himself, was staying in their [the Robertsons'] Manse. In his usual style he talked late into the night with the eagerly listening Hubert Robertson, telling of his dreams for the future. In the morning he was holding baby Margaret on his lap. Mr Robertson came up to them and placed a one pound note in the baby's hand. 'Now you are a member of the AIM Inland Legion,' he said.

This [the Inland Legion] was an army of voluntary workers in the capital cities, parcelling up literature for the print-hungry people of the inland. A one pound donation gave membership to the Legion. Years after, when Margaret was a grown woman, Flynn told her he had the utmost difficulty in prising that pound note from her tightly clenched fist. She wanted to keep it.

As she [Meg] spoke, Fred could hardly believe his ears. What an amazing coincidence. Or was it? Margaret's story and her enthusiasm clinched it for him, and that was when he made up his mind that he would offer to be Flynn's boundary rider up there in the North, if the AIM wanted him. He says now that he felt as if "the very Spirit of the Lord was speaking, but that this was no still small voice. Rather it sounded like a hammering in my heart".

"But that would mean coming to Birdsville with me when you finish your training," he said.

Margaret, his Meg, a woman in love, replied, "Yes, Birdsville or Edinburgh or Timbuctoo."

I mean, isn't that amazing? And so later on they were married in December 1938. By then Fred was already 'boundary riding' for John Flynn as one of his Patrol Padres. Then, after they married, Meg started going out on patrol with Fred. Basically, their house was a truck, and they camped out together and stayed at various remote station properties throughout the west of Queensland. And not only did Meg's nursing training come in very handy in that sort of work but she was also given the extra jobs of having to pull teeth out and so forth. Actually, I think she might've even done some sort of a crash course in dentistry because all her old dental instruments have been given to the Fred McKay Museum, there in Alice Springs. So Meg travelled with Fred until their first child, Margaret, was born and so that would've been for another year or year and a half.

But, really, isn't that an amazing coincidence of divine connection? Not only for Fred but for Meg as well, and for both of them to end up becoming life-long partners. I mean, something like that really makes you think about the mysterious ways of preordained destiny, doesn't it?

Razor Blades and Saucepans

Yes now, some of my memories. Well, my flying background goes back to the services. I did my training with the Royal Australian Air Force (RAAF). That was in 1956, and I served with them for fourteen years. Then, when I got out of the RAAF, I came up to Cairns, in far north Queensland, and joined the Aerial Ambulance crowd. Back then the Aerial Ambulance was operated by the Queensland Ambulance Transport Brigade (QATB), which used to run all the ambulance services throughout the state.

So then I flew with the QATB for about ten years, right up until the middle of 1979, which was when the QATB finally decided to get out of the aeroplane side of things. So I was without a job. Anyhow, out of fifty or so other applicants from all around Australia, I was lucky enough to be picked up by the Royal Flying Doctor Service and based here in Cairns. So I was able to stay here, which was a great relief because when I was in the Air Force, typical military, I'd moved twelve times in fourteen years. Actually, my feeling was that if I never moved again it'd be far too soon. But thankfully as it turned out, I didn't have to move anywhere and I started with the RFDS here in Cairns on 1 July 1979.

And I was with the RFDS then from the middle of 1979 right up until I retired in the middle of 1997 and I was basically based in Cairns for the whole of that time. I was their Chief Pilot and also their

Senior Checking and Training Pilot, so that job took me around the ridges a lot, within the confines of the RFDS. You know, I'd find myself out at Charleville and then out at Mount Isa and then down in Brisbane for conferences and all that sort of thing.

Actually, probably the correct sequence should be Training and Checking Pilot, really, but for years and years it's been simpler to just say check and training. And there's a funny little story about that. Years and years ago a crowd called Bush Pilots were operating here in Cairns and they had a feller who was writing stories about them and he couldn't understand what all this 'check and training' was all about. He thought they were saying 'chicken training'.

'What the hell are you pilots training the chickens to do?' he asked, and it had to be explained that it was actually a process of checking and training pilots, which had nothing at all to do with chicken training.

In those earlier days, of course, there were only the three active bases in Queensland—Cairns, Mount Isa and Charleville—and our Head Office was in Queen Street, Brisbane. Of course, it's all changed now. We still have Cairns, Mount Isa and Charleville but now you've also got Townsville, Rockhampton and Bundaberg and the Head Office has moved from its old place in Queen Street out to the Brisbane Airport. So there's been tremendous changes since I retired.

And, with the clinic flying, which was where we took a doctor and a nurse out to virtually provide a GP service, back then the area we covered was inland from Collinsville, which is between Townsville and Mackay, right up to the top of Cape York. In my day we started on a Tuesday and we'd go from Cairns to

Kowanyama, which used to be called Mitchell River. Then from Kowanyama we'd go to Pormpuraaw, which was then known as Edward River. Both Kowanyama and Pormpuraaw are Aboriginal communities. After that we'd go up to Weipa, where we'd overnight, and the next day we'd go down to Aurukun, which is just forty miles south of Weipa. Then we'd fly across to Lockhart River. After Lockhart River we'd go back to Weipa again, to overnight there. Then the following day we might go down to, say, some places like Coen and Musgrave, and then back to Cairns. So it'd be a three-day deal with two nights away from Cairns.

And the aeroplanes we had were the piston-engined Beechcraft Queen Airs. They had those of course before I joined the RFDS in '79. Then, over the years, we progressively phased out the Queen Airs into the turbo prop Beechcraft King Airs. Gorgeous aeroplanes they were. Simply gorgeous. I really enjoyed flying the King Airs. We got our first one, a King Air Super 200, in 1984, then we subsequently got one, two, three, then four King Air C90s. The C90s were a smaller King Air, based on the Queen Air airframe and they had what was called a 'pumped-up fuselage' (pressurised) and, rather than the piston engines, a couple of turbo prop engines came on it.

Actually, one of the air traffic controllers out in Mount Isa—a lady interestingly enough—described them beautifully, I thought. She'd been watching the Queen Airs take off and land for a number of years and when the first of the little turbo prop King Airs turned up in Mount Isa she said it was like a 'Queen Air with balls'. And I still haven't heard it put any better than that.

So then there was sort of a phasing-out period of the Queen Airs, where we went from having four Queen Airs to having three Queen Airs to having two Queen Airs to having one. Actually, I flew the last Queen Air. From memory, I think that was in May 1992 and it finished up as an exhibit in our RFDS Visitors' Centre, here in Cairns.

So the last of our Queen Airs still exists, thank goodness. They were going to chuck it out but I prevailed upon them. I made the very strong suggestion that we really should try and retain some of our own aviation history. To my way of thinking, Australia was far too keen on discarding its older aeroplanes to turn them all into razor blades and saucepans. And of course nowadays everyone's running around trying to find old World War II aeroplanes, you know. And, mind you, that's only just sixty years after the event. But that's another story.

See Yer Later

Now, I've only got just the one Flying Doctor story, so I don't know if it's of use to you.

Okay, well some years ago, after exploring Ningaloo Reef, between Exmouth and Coral Bay, which is up in the northern coastal region of Western Australia, we headed off to Exmouth Airport, with our dive bags and packs, to catch a small plane to Broome. When we arrived at Exmouth, there were only a couple of four-wheel drives in the airport car park. Then, further to that, we discovered that the actual terminal was completely deserted; that is, except for one bloke who was behind a check-in counter.

'G'day,' we said.

'Oh, glad you've turned up,' he beamed. 'You're the only passengers for the day!'

'What? No one else here?' I asked.

'No,' he replied, 'just the bloke in the Control Tower.' Then he gave us the tags to stick on our luggage. 'Here,' he said, 'stick these on your bags and have a good flight.'

Which we did and then, to our surprise, he slipped under the counter and headed out to the car park. So we settled into these terribly bright red seats that were in the waiting lounge. To give you some idea, they were a kind of a cross between a beanbag and a park bench-seat. In actual fact, the whole terminal was done out in probably what some people would call 'post-modern'. But at least the windows were huge, even if the runway and tarmac were totally deserted.

So, anyway, we sat and we waited. And we sat and we waited, and the departure time for our six-seater came and went. Then eventually we heard a plane. As the plane landed and taxied to the terminal, we read 'Royal Flying Doctor Service' on the side of it. Of course, this obviously wasn't our Broome service. Anyhow, the instant the engines died a young woman dressed in uniform jumped out of the plane and she started running towards the terminal. At seeing her urgency and sensing an emergency, I went over to meet her at the gateway.

'I'm sorry,' I said, 'but we're the only people here, except for the bloke in the Control Tower.'

'No worries,' she said, 'I'm just busting for a piss.' And she keep on running, straight towards the toilet.

So I went and sat back down again. Then she emerged a little later, looking far more relaxed, and she walked sedately over to us.

'So where are you going?' she asked.

'Broome,' we said.

'Bad luck,' she said, 'we're heading the other way.'

'Oh,' we said.

Then she said, 'See yer later then,' and rushed back out to the RFDS plane, jumped back in, and they took off.

Speared

Well, I joined the Flying Doctor Service in 1989. That was as a pilot out at Meekatharra, which is in the central west of Western Australia. Then, after about six months at Meekatharra, in early May 1990 I went to work up at their Port Hedland base. I stayed at Port Hedland then for thirteen years, until 2003, and oh, we loved it there. We had a young family and it was such a good, safe place to bring up kids. We also loved camping so there was lots of bush trips and travelling around the Pilbara and the Kimberley. The Gibb River Road's one of my favourite places in Australia. Actually, I think we've done the Gibb River Road about six times and I reckon there's still more to see. Fabulous country up that way. In fact, just about my whole flying career has taken place throughout the tropical areas of Australia. You know, northern Western Australia right across to northern Queensland.

But as far as stories go, you always sort of have your favourites, don't you? One that I think was quite amusing in an odd sort of way—well, both sad and amusing, I guess—happened at Jigalong Aboriginal Community. Jigalong's about 120 kilometres east of the mining town of Newman, in central Western Australia.

Anyhow, once every two or three years the Aborigines conduct what's called Law Ceremonies. Now, these Law Ceremonies happen when all the various communities from within the wider area gather together in a designated community and, along with a lot of celebrations, the Elders review events since the last get-together. So they'd do things like the initiations with the young boys who haven't yet been initiated, and also they'd deal out the tribal punishment for any misdemeanours or whatever that may have occurred over the last couple of years or so. So you could do something wrong and then you might have to wait for a year or more before you got punished, in the appropriate law time.

On this particular occasion there'd been a car roll over and two passengers had been killed and so the driver of the vehicle was brought before the Elders. The Elders listened to what had happened and deemed that it was the driver's fault for causing the deaths of the two others. So he had to be punished and the Elders said that his punishment was to be a stabbing in the thigh, by a spear.

So a few men grabbed hold of the bloke who'd been driving the car and they held him as still as they could, ready to receive the punishment. But apparently the driver bloke was wriggling and turning and writhing around so much that the enforcer of the punishment clean missed his mark and he ended up spearing the driver bloke in the lower abdomen instead of the thigh.

That's when we got an emergency call to go out there to Jigalong Community to pick up the bloke who'd been speared. The only trouble was that, unfortunately, it'd been raining heavily over the area for the past week or so and there was no way we could land the aeroplane on Jigalong airstrip.

But, seeing that it was an emergency, they arranged to charter a helicopter from Karratha. The helicopter was then flown up to Newman and we took the RFDS aeroplane down from Port Hedland, where we all got into the helicopter and we flew out from Newman to Jigalong. Along with the helicopter pilot we took the normal complement of RFDS staff, which was a doctor, the nurse and myself.

And so we went out in the chartered helicopter and landed at the local oval, at Jigalong Community, and they brought out the poor guy who'd been inadvertently speared in the lower abdomen. We quickly laid him on the stretcher, put him onto the helicopter and took him back to Newman. The helicopter then headed back to Karratha and we put the speared bloke into the RFDS aeroplane and flew him back to Port Hedland, where he was going to be treated.

Then we'd only just arrived back in Port Hedland when we got another call asking us to return to Jigalong Community. Apparently, what happened was that the Elders had gone and handed out another punishment and that person had been speared, this time in the thigh. Anyhow, I think that in the end they decided that this new bloke's wounds weren't quite bad enough to warrant us going through the whole procedure again. You know—of chartering another helicopter to fly out there and for us to fly down to Newman, and all that. I mean, the cost was astronomical. I'd estimate that just that one retrieval cost would've been well over $30000.

But the irony of the whole thing was that we later found out that the second call for us to return to Jigalong Community was to pick up the bloke who'd inadvertently stuffed up the first spearing. Apparently the Elders deemed that he should be punished for being such a poor shot.

Stroke

I've got a couple of stories about sort of strokes here, if you like. Well, for a few seasons I worked out at Mulga Downs Station, cooking for the jackeroos and all that. Mulga Downs is just north of Wittenoom, in northern Western Australia. Anyhow, I had a little medical knowledge—not much, but a little—and one time I was out there and the station manager's wife came and woke me up in the middle of the night. 'My husband's having a stroke,' she said.

Well, she thought he was having a stroke, anyway. So I went over to the homestead and the manager was lying on the bed with his legs crossed. To my thinking that didn't really look like he was having a stroke. But he said that he had all these spots in front of his eyes and when he'd tried to get up to go to the toilet he couldn't walk. He was also in terrible pain and was feeling sick in the stomach.

Anyway, I called the Flying Doctor base in at Port Hedland and the doctor there asked if I could give the manager an injection of Stemetil, out of the homestead's RFDS medical chest, and also some pethidine if necessary. Stemetil is what you have for nausea. Pethidine is for the pain. So I gave the manager an injection of Stemetil, which seemed to settle him down a bit. I didn't want to give him the pethidine just then, because I knew it'd mask the cause of whatever his pain was and that'd only make the doctor's diagnosis more difficult. So I kept the pethidine with me in my hand, but only to use if necessary, as I thought it'd be better to try and wait until the doctor came and had a good look at him.

Now, because Mulga Downs only had a small airstrip which could only be used during the day, the Flying Doctor suggested that they meet us out at the Auski Roadhouse. The Auski Roadhouse is on the Great Northern Highway between Newman and Port Hedland. They had an airstrip near the roadhouse there, where the Flying Doctor could land at night. So we rang the Auski Roadhouse to let them know what was going on and asked if they could get somebody to go out and light the lamps along the airstrip. We then loaded the crook manager into the vehicle and drove him the 40 or so kilometres from Mulga Downs to the Auski Roadhouse.

Anyway, the Flying Doctor arrived at Auski and they took him straight back to Port Hedland. But as it turned out, what the manager had was a severe migraine. So it wasn't a stroke, it was a severe migraine. Then the next day, the manager's wife had to go over to Port Hedland and bring him home, and he was okay after that.

Now, to the next story about a stroke, and this was a real stroke. Again I was working out at Mulga Downs Station. The station manager and his wife were going on holiday and they'd organised for their homestead to be painted while they were away. So they asked if I'd come out a little earlier than usual that season and cook for the house painter plus Arthur, the guy who was looking after the windmills, while they went on holidays. That was fine by me and I headed out to Mulga Downs.

For the life of me I can't recall his name just now, but anyhow, there was the painter, Arthur and myself.

That's all. It was stinking hot and the three of us were staying in the one cottage because it was the one that had cooling. Then early one morning, around four o'clock, I got woken up by the painter feller banging on my wall. 'Get Arthur,' he was calling out. 'Get Arthur, I've had a stroke.'

Luckily, he could still talk. So I went in to check on him and there he was, lying on the floor, paralysed down one side. I then went and woke Arthur up and he came in and looked after the painter while I went over to the homestead and called the Flying Doctor. They said that it'd take two hours for them to fly from Port Hedland, out to the small airstrip at Mulga Downs, and pick up this painter feller.

With that done I went back to the cottage to see how the painter was getting on and, oh, he was really worried because he said that he had all his money stashed away in his car. You know how pensioners save up their money; like they put it under the mattress and in odd places like that. Well, this bloke had all his money hidden in his car and he wanted me to go and get it for him, which I did. It was a fair bit of cash too: in the thousands. So it was a lot of money.

When I came back, I gave the money to the painter. 'Thanks,' he said, but, by now, he wasn't looking too well at all; his condition had deteriorated.

Anyhow, I took over looking after him then, while Arthur went and cleaned out the back of a ute so that we could fit the stretcher in. It was just on daylight by now and we knew that the Flying Doctor wouldn't be too far away. So we loaded the painter in the back of the ute and we went down to the airstrip. The kangaroos were particularly bad just on dawn and so the next thing we had to do was to drive up and down the airstrip in an attempt to scare them off. By that stage the painter was going from bad to worse. He kept stopping breathing on me, and even more worrying was that I could see that his hand was clenching. That's a bad sign. So while Arthur was driving up and down the airstrip, I just had to sit there in the back of the ute, continually wiping the painter's face with a wet cloth in an attempt to at least keep him comfortable.

By the time the Flying Doctor arrived it was daylight, and what a welcoming sight that was, I can tell you. The plane landed and the doctor comes down—mind you, he's just dressed in a shirt and shorts, and he also brings the daily paper, for good measure—and the first thing he said was, 'We've been trying to call you on the radio. Why didn't you answer?'

'Well,' I said, 'I couldn't because someone had to stay with the patient.'

Anyway, when the Flying Doctor took the painter's blood pressure it was up around something like 210 over 100 and, you know, normal is somewhere down around 120 or 130. So they quickly loaded him into the plane and flew him back to Port Hedland.

I'm not really sure what happened to the painter after that because I ended up leaving Mulga Downs, though I don't think he ever came back to pick up his car. The station manager later told me that he'd had another stroke and had lost the power of speech. He might've even ended up in Rehab or somewhere. But I've often wondered whatever happened to all that cash of his that I handed over to him, on the night of his first stroke. I'll never know. And so I guess that no one else will ever get to know about it either.

Stuck

One of the worst things that ever happened was when I was driving this very ill lady, Dorethea, in our old ambulance down to Newman, in the central north of Western Australia. Dorethea was one of the great characters of Wittenoom. But then, well, the ambulance broke down, didn't it? Poor old Dorethea, by that stage she'd been projectile vomiting for days and was extremely dehydrated and we only found out later that she had a blocked intestine.

By that stage I'd already called the Flying Doctor Service but they couldn't come out because the RFDS plane was busy, down in Perth. See, there'd been this big accident out on the Newman road where a man and his daughter and, I think, the daughter's friend were all killed. But anyway, someone was also very badly injured in that accident and the RFDS had flown the badly injured person down to Perth. That's why they couldn't get out to us. So, with Dorethea in such a bad state, and with the RFDS plane in Perth, that left us with no other choice than to drive her over to Newman for medical help.

Anyhow, you wouldn't believe it, but about 16 kilometres out of Wittenoom the wheel bearing went on the ambulance. It was almost midnight by then and because it was such an old ambulance, the radio wouldn't work either. So the girl I had along with me, Julie, she decided to walk on the gravel road, in the dark, back to Wittenoom to get help. And that was one of the scariest things because after Julie left I was stuck out there alone, with Dorethea. And, you know, I'm only a volunteer ambulance officer. I'm not qualified, and here's Dorethea vomiting and going into shock, you know. I was giving her sips of water, which she was bringing straight up. They later told me I shouldn't have given her anything but, you know, in a case like that, you don't know what you're supposed to do, do you really?

I remember that it was a warm night and there was no moon, nothing, just really low cloud. So it was really dark. So we were just stuck there and then the lights went out in the ambulance. The battery went flat because I'd had the lights on. That's probably because it was only ever used once in a blue moon and the battery wasn't strong enough. So there I am; I'm there with only the torch light, trying to read the First Aid Manual to see what to do with someone who's in shock and is projectile vomiting at the same time. Oh my God, it was terrible. I really thought she was going to die. I tell you, we both needed all the help we could get so we both decided to pray, together.

Anyhow, I stayed with Dorethea, just hoping and praying for somebody to come along. But they didn't ... well, not for four hours, anyway. By then Julie had walked back to town and woken somebody up. Then, when we eventually got rescued, we took Dorethea back to town. Someone had called the Flying Doctor again and by that time the plane was on its way back from Perth. So then they came up and we sent her by plane to Port Hedland. So the RFDS had a busy night as well.

Then after going to Port Hedland, Dorethea ended up in Perth and eventually she died. And, you know,

I was so worried that I'd done something wrong, especially as I knew her so well. I even ended up calling the Perth Hospital and asking them about it, and they said, 'No, it wasn't from any of your neglect or anything. It was because she had this blocked intestine.'

Mind you, she was also seventy-two by that stage and she'd smoked unfiltered cigarettes all her life and drank wine every day. But it took me a long time to get over that. A very long time. So that was another corker.

Still, I did the best I could and I guess you can't do any more than your best, can you?

That's My Job

I came up to the Kimberley area, in the north of Western Australia, back in 1969 as a lay missionary for the Catholic Church and I worked at St Joseph's Hostel, here in Derby, where we looked after about eighty children. Actually, St Joseph's Hostel burnt down about five or six years or so ago but it used to be up on the corner there. Then I got married to Colin in '73 and we worked out on Mount Barnett Station for the first year of our marriage. After that we went to Gibb River Station, and we stayed there for a total of twenty-six years.

Actually, Colin's family owned Gibb River Station. His father started it in 1922 and we ended up eventually selling it to the Aboriginal people in 1989. Basically, we sold it because, by that time, it had four families to support which naturally made it a bit hard to manage. As you might realise, the pastoral industry's not that strong these days and out there it's marginal country, anyway. I mean, it's quite big because it's something like 1 million acres but you've only got, like, six thousand head of cattle. That's about all it can take.

Anyway, as I said, in 1989 we sold Gibb River Station to the Aboriginal people and they asked Colin and his older brother, Frederick, if they could stay on to help them manage the place. They also wanted help to set up the community in conjunction with the Aboriginal and Torres Strait Islander Commission, or

ATSIC as it's known. So we did that, and Frederick stayed on for three years, I think it was, and then we stayed on for a further eight years after Frederick left. So that was about eleven years in all that we remained there, after selling the property. And over the years we were out there we went from a little 5 KVA generator to the bigger ones like the 3 x 70 KVA generator. And I think something like sixteen houses were built in that time, plus the medical clinic, which the RFDS used to service.

Along with all that, the Catholic Church also became involved. I think they were there for ten years or so before we left. Well, they came in with two nuns from New Zealand and they built a beautiful school there and two houses for the nuns. The school always had about twenty kids in it and it was run very well.

Then we left in 2000. We'd been out there for twenty-six years by then, and we were ready to come into town. Well, it was just circumstances really, and it felt like it was time to leave. We'd already bought a property in Derby five years prior to that, but we'd rented it out. It's one of those 5 acre blocks out on the Gibb River Road. They call them the Gibb River blocks. And it was quite funny really because just the year before we left Gibb River Station, to come into town to live, the base administrator's job here at the Derby RFDS was advertised and the instant I saw it I said to Colin, 'That's my job.'

But, see, we didn't come into town that year. So I was a little bit disappointed about that because I really thought it was a job that I'd like to do and one I was also well suited to do. Of course, by that stage I already had a strong connection with the Flying Doctor

Service because when we were out on Gibb River Station, we used them quite a lot. Well, Gibb River had up to a hundred and twenty people on the property— Aboriginal people, mainly—and I'd helped set up the medical clinic there during our last five or so years. Then we also had the standard RFDS medical chest on the property, which I was responsible for, and we were forever calling them for different things. Oh, well, it was mainly just run-of-the-mill stuff, like accidents, falls off horses, sick kids and all that kind of thing. So, having had to use them so much when we were out on the station, I already had a strong affiliation with the RFDS.

And then, as luck would have it, the next year after we'd moved into town, the same base administrator's job came up. So I applied for the position and got it. And I was really pleased about that because, as I said, when it had originally come up, I felt that it was definitely 'my job'. And now I've worked here at the RFDS in Derby since October 2000. As far as my responsibilities go, we've got fifteen houses for staff, so I look after all the housing. I also combine the three base rosters from the doctors, pilots and nurses and do all the invoicing. I also enter the remote 'consults' (consultations) on the computer data for funding purposes and records. And that's about it really, other than, of course, lots of other little bits and pieces of jobs thrown in. So, basically, what I tell everyone is that, 'I mainly try to keep 'em all happy. That's my job.'

The Normanton Bell

I guess that you've heard about how it was John Flynn who first set up the Australian Inland Mission (AIM) and then the Royal Flying Doctor Service came out of that. But, anyway, the AIM not only sent out nurses and that to remote parts of Australia, there was also a more spiritual side to it and so John Flynn used to send out Padres to various parts of the land and it was their job to 'keep an eye on His flock', so to speak.

So that's a bit of the background to this story and, as I've already told you in my book *Goldie*, I was working up in the Gulf one time, doing a bit of this, that and the other, plus doing a bit of cattle duffing on the side. Right, so I'm back in Normanton, staying out with the Caseys. The Caseys were big cattle duffers up that way. So I was staying with them. They owned a place called Shady Lagoons. Anyhow, I'd come into town from Shady Lagoons and I was drinking with a feller by the name of Jack McNab. Jack was a saddler and he also had a mail run. So me and him, we're up in the top pub—the National Hotel—and we'd been drinking on and off all the afternoon. You know, we weren't downing them one after the other like, we were just drinking nice and steady. Anyhow, by about ten o'clock that night, Jack and me, we're starting to get a bit argumentative with each other and this argument's getting pretty warmed up. I forget what it was about just now, but it was heating up.

Anyhow, Sam Henry, the local sergeant, comes in. Sam's the feller who refereed that fight with me and Ronny Paul. Yeah, so Sam Henry comes in and he's sitting down the other end of the bar and he's thinking, 'Gees, it looks like a blue's on the cards here between Goldie 'n' McNab.' So Sam comes up and he goes through all the change we had on the counter and he hands it over to Ted Kershaw, the publican. 'Ted,' he says, 'give us a dozen beers.' In those days all the beer was in 26 ounce bottles. The big ones. There was no stubbies.

So Ted goes and he gets the beer, see. 'Here yer go,' he says, and he hands it over to Sam Henry.

Then Sam says to me and Jack, 'Righto, youse fellers, come with me', and he puts the carton on his shoulder and he walks out of the pub. So me and Jack, we follow him out. By now, me and Jack, we're just talking and going on. There's no arguing, we're just talking.

So then Sam gets in his vehicle. It's a ute sort of thing and Jack and me, we get in the back and Sam drives us out to the edge of town to an old timber church. Now, this old church was built round the turn of the century, back in the early 1900s. It'd weathered a lot of cyclones so it's leaning over at about a 30° angle. It was one of them old weatherboard ones that's up on stumps; you know, with the white ant caps on top. They didn't even hold services there any more because there wasn't much floorboards left. Like, anybody in town who wanted a bit of timber always went down to the old church to get it. Yeah, that's where they went for their timber.

So Sam drops me and Jack off out there, at this old church, with this dozen beers. Now, outside the front of the church, about 30 feet or something, there was still the original old bell and this old bell had a length of rope hanging off it.

Any rate Sam plonks us there and he says, 'Righto, fellers, go fer yer life. Do what yer like', then he jumps back in his car and he goes back to town.

So me and Jack, we're left sitting there. We'd both long forgot what the argument was about, so now we're bored and we're looking for something to do. And, see, around Normanton there's a lot of goats walking around all the time. So I says to Jack, I says, 'Let's have some fun. We'll catch a goat 'n' tie his back leg ter the rope on the bell, 'n' as he's trying ter get away he'll be ringin' the bell.'

'Okay,' Jack says, and so we tried to catch one of these goats, aye, but we're too drunk to catch a goat. They kept getting away from us.

'This's no good,' I says to Jack. 'We're gettin' nowhere. So how's about we ring the bell ourselves?'

'Yeah,' he says. 'Good idea.'

So I start ringing this bell, aye. By now it's about two o'clock in the morning, and we're ringing away and we can see all these house lights being turned on around town, left, right and centre. Now at that time there was only one minister in Normanton. I forget his name just now, but he was what they called a 'Padre' because he belonged to the Australian Inland Mission. Anyhow, he lived a way over on the other side of Normanton. A way over. So I must've been making a real racket, aye, because next thing this Padre comes flying down in his car.

I says, 'Oh, how yer goin', Padre? Have a drink.'

But he's in no mood for that, aye, because he gives us this big lecture on the evils of drinking. Then he says, 'You shouldn't be ringin' that bell.'

I says, 'Why's that?'

He says, 'Because when a church bell's rung, it's meant to be the call for all sinners to come to church.'

So I says, 'Well, this must be a pretty righteous town, aye, Padre?'

'Why's that?'

I says, 'Because you're the only person who's turned up.'

After that he sort of gave up on us and he got back in his car and he drove back into town. So that's the story of the Normanton bell and the AIM Padre.

The 'Singing'

I'll never forget the first trip I did, from Alice Springs out to Yuendumu Aboriginal Community, as a pilot with the Flying Doctor Service. I remember we pulled up at Yuendumu and the doctor took one look out the plane window and he said, 'Jesus, there's something strange going on here.'

And he was right, too. You wouldn't believe it: all the Aboriginal men were over in one group and all the women and the kids were in another group and they were all wailing. Gees, it was a real eerie, haunting sort of sound, you know, like, 'Woo ... woo ... woma, woma ... woo.' And when you've got a whole mob of people wailing like that, it makes a fair bit of noise.

Anyway, they had two nursing sisters working there and one of the sisters came over and she explained that the Aborigines were 'singing' a young bloke, for pinching the Tjuringa Stones. You know what the Tjuringa Stones are, don't you? They're the sacred stones. They're like how we keep a history book or a diary; well, they actually etch their stories into these stones. If you ever see them, they've got circles and all sorts of patterns etched on them. It could be all about some big meeting or a corroboree or some sort of gathering or anything. And they treasure these Tjuringa Stones and they bury them in a special place, somewhere safe like a cave or somewhere like that.

I've got one, actually. An old Aboriginal fella gave me one and I never worked out why he gave it to me, because he wasn't really a bloke I knew that well. But, with me being a pilot with the Flying Doctor Service, he knew who I was, of course, and one day he just came up and he gave me this string of stones. If I showed it to you I wouldn't be able to tell you what the story's about. But they know. And my wife won't touch them. They scare her. She reckons I should give the thing back to them, and she's probably right.

But anyhow, so this young Aboriginal fella at Yuendumu, Leo his name was, they used to call him 'Useless Leo'. Leo was only about seventeen and what he'd done was, he'd pinched these Tjuringa Stones and he was going to sell them on the open market. See, being a one-off, they'd be worth quite a few bob; perhaps a couple of hundred thousand dollars or maybe more if he sold them to someplace like a museum. Of course, he'd have to have contacts to sell them to a place like that. So someone might've even put him up to it. I don't know.

Anyway, they caught Leo pinching these Tjuringa Stones and so they 'sung' him, which was like putting a death curse on him. It's similar to pointing the bone.

So the doctor said, 'Okay, after we've finished our routine medical visit here, we'd better get this Leo on the plane and take him back to Alice Springs.'

Now, the doctor had a plan. See, it's all psychological, and that plan was to collect some old stones and a bit of wire and things like that, and when he got Leo in the plane he'd put him under anaesthetic to knock him out. Then, while Leo was out to it, the doctor was going to make a superficial cut across his stomach and when Leo woke up he'd simply hand Leo the wire and stones and stuff and say, 'There you go,

Leo. I've just operated on you and I've got all the "bad stuff" out, so now you'll be okay.'

That sort of thing had worked before on a few occasions and when the Aboriginal fellas take a look at the wire and stones, they think, 'Oh, I'm cured now. The doctor's got all the bad stuff out that the witch doctor had done to me.' And then they're fine.

So that's what the doctor was going to do this day. And when Leo walked onto the aircraft he was as fit as a fiddle. He was scared, naturally, but he was medically okay. It was only an hour and a half flight back to Alice Springs and he'd died by the time we were landing in Alice Springs. The doctor told me that he'd been trying to get an adrenaline shot into Leo's veins, but he said it was like trying to put a needle into a piece of string because all Leo's veins had collapsed from the shock of him being 'sung'.

Now, I don't know if you believe in those sorts of things—like pointing the bone and being 'sung'—but Leo certainly must've believed in it. Amazing, isn't it? He walked on the aircraft, unaided, and he was dead within an hour and a half.

The Sweetest Sound

I would like to tell you just the one story. It may be a little bit long-winded but it's a magnificent story I believe, because it was something that personally happened to me. When I first joined the Royal Flying Doctor Service, about ten years ago, I went out on a clinic run and we flew out to a property called the Pinnacles, which is up in the Cape York area of Queensland.

Now, if I could just sort of set the scene for you. As the aircraft landed at the Pinnacles I looked at the four horizons. It was the dry season so it was a pretty dry and unforgiving land that stretched out before me. In fact, there was a cruelty and harshness about it. But, given all that, I suppose the emotions that went through my mind at that particular time were of an overriding beauty. And I suppose that it was my first realisation or understanding of where the great architects of verse—the likes of Banjo Paterson and Henry Lawson and Dorothea Mackellar and so forth—got their inspiration to write about this wonderful land of ours.

But, even apart from that, I felt rather blessed because after we flew in, the original white pioneers of the Pinnacles were there to visit the Flying Doctor. As I said, it was a clinic trip and these two people had long retired. In fact, they were well into their eighties at this time, and they needed to see the doctor on that day. So they were there, waiting, and it was just a marvellous coincidence that I was there to meet them. And while I was looking out at, you know, these barren never-never lands of ours, I happened to say to the old man, 'Just what gave you the fortitude to come out here?'

And without hesitation he simply replied, 'The Flying Doctor.'

And it was at that moment the penny dropped, because I remember many years ago I either read it or heard the words of a speech that Sir Robert Menzies made when he was Prime Minister. And Sir Robert Menzies said something along the lines of, 'The greatest single contribution to the development of inland Australia was Flynn's Flying Doctor Service.' And it hadn't really sunk in until I was standing there with these two old pioneers at the Pinnacles.

But what was to really blow me away was a statement that I'll basically take to the grave with me, because it was just so wonderful. This old man's beautiful old wife, she looked at me and she said, 'Stephen, the sweetest sound in all the world is the sound of the Flying Doctor aircraft overhead.'

When she said that I conjured up a mental image of her as a young lady giving birth to their first child. So I verbalised that to her and she gave me a bit of a wise smile and said, 'Yes, you're right, that certainly was a pretty tough time and the Royal Flying Doctor Service got me through that one okay.' Then she went on to say, 'But, really, it was many years later when our eldest son was about thirteen and he'd fallen from his horse.' And she pointed to the ground, only metres from where we were standing, and she said, 'I sat right over there and I cradled my precious son's unconscious head in my lap and I cried and I prayed and I cried and

I prayed and then I heard the Flying Doctor aircraft overhead. That was the sweetest sound.'

Well, honestly, let me say that when a beautiful old pioneering lady tells a new chum on the block a story like that, well, she truly reached forward and indelibly touched my soul. And, you know, in various fundraising appeals now, for many years, the RFDS has used her statement, because it pretty much depicts, I think, how a lot of people out in those remote lands feel about the Flying Doctor Service.

The Wrong People

Actually, I was up in Whyalla for ten years, working as a pilot with Air Ambulance, before I was transferred to Adelaide. Then I guess I was probably only down here for twelve months or less when they decided it'd be a much better set-up if Aero-medical and the Royal Flying Doctor Service came under the one umbrella. I think it all might've had something to do with the way both the federal and state funding bodies worked. But it wasn't really such a big difference for us because the pilots with Air Ambulance just changed uniforms and became Flying Doctor pilots. It was as simple as that, and that would've been around 1990. So you could say that I'm in about my sixteenth year with the Flying Doctor Service, as such, but I was with Air Ambulance ten years prior to that. So that's twenty-six years in all, which is a fair time.

But it's really a fascinating job. Of course, like any type of employment it has its ups and downs. Probably its biggest drawback is the rotating shift work. That gets you down occasionally, because with the longer shifts we're actually on page (on call) at home for a twelve-hour period and if it is a Code One or a retrieval we've only got forty-five minutes from the time we get paged to 'doors closed' in the aircraft. That means that, virtually, you've got to be in your uniform at all times because when you get paged you have to drive to the airport, get the forecast, check the aircraft and everything and be ready within that forty-five-minute time frame. Of course, if it's just a normal routine-type transfer, you get more time and that's sixty minutes' notice.

A normal type transfer would be, say, taking a patient from somewhere like Port Augusta Hospital to the Royal Adelaide Hospital, as well as transferring people back home. To some it may sound a little bit odd to be using an expensive aircraft for moving people around like that but in reality it's probably more feasible to do it by air than by road. Because, firstly, it's important for the road ambulances and their crews to remain stationed within their community, just in case there's a disaster or something. And, secondly, if an ambulance crew's driving someone from Port Lincoln to Adelaide, they'd have to travel during the day, overnight in Adelaide, then drive back home the next day. So the community would be without an ambulance, effectively, for two whole days. Whereas if you're using an aircraft, in a normal shift we might fit three of those type of transfers in. So really, by using the aeroplane you're saving up to six days work for an entire ambulance crew. What's more, it's less stressful for the patient to travel by air.

But the patients don't know all that. I mean, sometimes they don't even realise they're going to travel with us. They may think they're going by road but the ambulance only takes them as far as the local airstrip where they're loaded onto the aircraft.

Though you do get some mix-ups. Now, I won't mention any names of course, but some years ago one of our pilots flew over to Kingscote, on Kangaroo Island, in South Australia, to pick up a patient. So he gets to Kingscote and he lands and he's greeted by a despondent looking ambulance crew.

'Where's the patient?' the pilot asks.

'Sorry,' they said, 'we haven't got him.'

'What do you mean, you haven't got him?' the pilot asked.

'He escaped from the hospital and we can't find him.'

So the pilot had to turn around and go back to Adelaide without the patient.

And there's another one that I think was extremely funny—and I must stress that this was back before Aero-medical came under the umbrella of the Royal Flying Doctor Service. I just want to make that nice and clear. Anyhow, the chaps from Air Ambulance were asked to fly down to Hamilton, in south-western Victoria, to pick up two patients and bring them back to Adelaide for some minor treatment or other. These two people were 'sitting patients', which means they weren't serious cases so they could make their own way out to the airstrip, without the need for an ambulance. Anyhow, the instruction came through that these patients would be waiting for the plane to arrive.

Now, I don't know if you've ever been to the Hamilton airstrip or not but back in those days there wasn't much there. Anyhow, they'd just landed the Chieftain at Hamilton when these two people walked across to the aircraft and said, 'Have you come to pick us up?'

There was nobody else about so the pilot and the nurse said, 'Yes. Hop in.'

So they loaded the two patients into the plane, where they were made nice and comfortable. 'Thank you. Thank you,' they kept saying. 'You're very kind.'

Then just after they took off, one of the passengers leaned over to the pilot and said, 'So, what's the weather going to be like in Melbourne today?'

'Melbourne?' asked the pilot.

'Yes, we've purchased two tickets to fly over to Melbourne to do some shopping.'

So it was a case of, 'Oops, we've obviously picked up the wrong two people.'

Things that Happened

On 21 August 2001 the Guild of Air Pilots and Air Navigators awarded me a Master Air Pilot Certificate— number 868—which, as it states, is 'awarded in recognition of skill, experience and service in the profession of aviation'. In all, I was a pilot for over forty years, and twenty-one of those were with the Royal Flying Doctor Service. So would you like to hear about some of the things that happened when I was with the RFDS? I've got a few notes already written down here that Bob Rogers, the ex-President of the Royal Flying Doctor Service in Queensland, requested for his book on the organisation. Now, I'm not a great storyteller, as such, so do you mind very much if I pretty much read from what I wrote for Bob's book?

Okay, I suppose there's been many memorable, and not so memorable, incidents that have happened over the twenty-one years I was flying with the Royal Flying Doctor Service. But, as is my way, I've never been one to be totally governed by rules and regulations. That's just not me. So I've been hauled over the coals by the DCA (Department of Civil Aviation) on a few occasions, perhaps the most ironic being one time out at Jundah.

Jundah's in south-western Queensland and we were called out there to pick up a patient who was suffering the DTs (delirium tremens) due to the severe effects of alcohol consumption. Because of this condition, the patient was quite difficult to handle and by the time we talked the person into getting on the aircraft an approaching dust storm had turned things quite dark. So it was a very big dust storm. Anyhow, I wasn't unduly bothered because, as was normal in such situations, I organised for some cars to light up the airstrip and, along with the aircraft lights, we took off safely and the patient was delivered.

Not long after that particular event I received a 'please explain' from the DCA saying that the shire clerk out at Jundah had reported the incident of my taking off in such poor conditions, by using just the headlights of a few cars and those of the aeroplane, as being unsafe. So I fronted up and dealt with that. But the irony of it all was that not long after, we were called back to Jundah at ten o'clock one night to evacuate someone who'd suffered a heart attack. So it was obviously dark. When we arrived there we discovered that the patient was the same shire clerk who'd put in the complaint to the DCA. And I can tell you, he was very pleased to see us arrive, and this time there was certainly no complaint about my taking off in the dark, aided by just the headlights of a few cars and those of the aeroplane.

Another memorable night-time event occurred at Nockatunga Station, in the south-western corner of Queensland. We were urgently required to fly out there for an evacuation. Of course, when landing an aeroplane it's standard procedure to land into the wind. To that end, as I always did before I left base, I checked with Nockatunga as to what the wind direction was and the lady there advised me that the wind was 'an easterly'.

By that stage, people were aware of my requirement of using the lights of three cars in a V shape to assist a night-time landing, so that was organised by the time we got out there. The only trouble was that the lady's understanding of 'an easterly' was that the winds were going to the east and not coming from the east. So an easterly is, in actual fact, a wind that is blowing in from the east. Consequently, on her bad advice I found myself landing downwind and rapidly running out of airstrip. And that really put the wind up the 'light keeper' in the car right at the end of the strip. Because as I was trying to pull up the aeroplane, he came to the rapid conclusion that there was no possible way that I could stop before I hit him, so he bailed out of his vehicle, post haste. Yes, he was out of that car in a flash and he took off.

Anyway, fortunately I was able to pull up without incident. But from then on, whenever I was checking the local conditions I made doubly sure that I phrased my questions in such a way that that type of mistake never occurred again.

But back in the days when cars were used quite extensively to act as runway lights, you really did have some close ones. One of the blokes I really enjoyed flying with was Dr George Ellis. George worked with me in Cairns for a couple of years. And there was one particular night that gave him great cause to worry.

There was a child on Hurricane Station who'd been diagnosed with leukaemia. At that stage the child was able to remain at home, though evacuations were needed from time to time when treatment was required. Anyhow, again it was night, but on this occasion the people helping to light the airstrip proved to be a little too enthusiastic, because as we were coming in to land George exclaimed, 'Gee, Phil, those cars are parked pretty damn close together.'

'Yes,' I replied, trying to gauge if I could land between them without losing our wings.

Then, just as we were about to land, an extremely nervous George asked, 'Do you reckon we'll make it?'

'No,' I said, and we ascended at the rate of knots, weaving our way among the hills, which was a great relief to George.

Now, while I'm on about landing in difficult spots: at one stage in the late '70s, the Cairns *Post* reported how I'd landed my Queen Air aeroplane on a, quote, 'winding mountain road, in the Mount Surprise area'. Well, I'd say to that, 'Don't believe everything you read in the newspapers.'

The true story is as follows: a group of lads were driving over to Karumba, in the lower Gulf area, when they rolled their car about 15 kilometres out of Mount Surprise. It was quite a bad accident and we were told that the boys may well have spinal injuries. Again, George Ellis was the doctor-on-call and he advised the locals not to move the lads until we arrived.

Naturally, George wanted me to land as near to the accident scene as possible. I'd done a number of road landings over the years, and just as long as the distance between the trees on either side of a reasonably straight stretch of road was sufficient to land the plane, I could see no problem in achieving that. I'd already been in radio contact with the police from Mount Surprise about all this and requested that they organise for the white roadside posts to be removed for approximately 2000 feet, which they did. Consequently, while it may have looked like a very close thing to those on board the Queen Air aeroplane, including poor George, I landed, again, without incident.

Then after getting help to manually turn the aircraft around we were able to taxi back, closer to the accident site. There the boys were treated by George and the nursing sister, who were then able to use the appropriate shifting techniques to prevent possible further spinal injuries. Once again that evacuation demonstrated the versatility of the Queen Air as being the ideal aircraft for RFDS operations.

Though not all landings went so well. Around 1976, with big rains and flooding across north Queensland, we were called out to Gunnawarra Station, which is south-west of Mount Garnet. Tom Atkinson, the son of the owners, was seriously ill and the doctor decided that even though the weather was terrible, Tom needed to be evacuated to Cairns Base Hospital. When we took off at about midday, this time in a Beechcraft Baron, we could see the Barron River had broken its banks and spread across the Smithfield floodplain.

Following a routine flight we landed on a rather damp Gunnawarra airstrip and were met by Vern Atkinson, Tom's father. Tom was loaded onto the aircraft but, as we taxied for take-off, the nose wheel bogged and, in doing so, the wheel-strut was badly bent. We then radioed the engineers in Cairns who suggested we somehow weld the strut in a fixed down position.

Tom was then off-loaded and we all spent the night at Gunnawarra discussing how we'd make the repairs. Being surrounded by practical blokes—myself included—the following morning we took two pieces of angle-iron out to the plane and, by applying weight on the tail, we lifted the nose wheel off the ground and were able to weld the angle-iron to brace the strut.

With the job now done, Tom was then reloaded and we made the slow and wet journey back to Cairns, with the landing gear fixed down.

As I half-expected, later in the week the DCA contacted me again. I fully appreciated it was a reportable incident. An investigation was launched with lots of questions being asked. But, in the end, the department decided that, although it was an unusual procedure, under the circumstances they decided not to prosecute. So no further action was taken against me, as pilot in command. And that was another run-in with the DCA.

Another beautiful Atkinson property was the Valley of Lagoons, at the headwaters of the Burdekin River. We conducted regular monthly clinics there so we were well known to the owners. On one occasion we were called there after a mustering accident involving Mark Atkinson, the son of Ivy and Bob, from Glen Eagle. Mark was in a bad way with a broken pelvis and other injuries. This time I was in the King Air and again rain had been falling, which made the airstrip quite a challenge. We landed fine but then, as we taxied, the plane became bogged and we needed to be very practical in solving the problem. So, together with the owner, we used a tractor to tow the aircraft out onto firm land and this second time the take-off went without a hitch. Anyhow, the DCA didn't find out about that one and so there was no further mention of the incident.

Then, no doubt you've heard many stories about having to clear the airstrip of stock such as horses, cattle or sheep, and, of course, there's the ones about kangaroos or emus hopping in front of the aeroplane and being chopped up. But I very much doubt if you've heard of anything like this happening: late one afternoon we took off from the Aboriginal settlement of Kowanyama to go to Pormpuraaw settlement, where we were to run another clinic. Pormpuraaw would only be half an hour's flight from Kowanyama, maybe less. Anyhow, we were up at about 1500 feet, doing the circuit area of Kowanyama, when there came this terrible bang!. Oh, I can tell you, it shook up everyone in the aircraft, me included.

Then, when I looked out the starboard or the right-hand side of the aircraft there, much to my surprise, I saw the backside of an eagle. On further investigation, the rest of his body was embedded in the leading edge of the wing. The poor thing had been happily freewheeling through a beautiful day, not looking where it was going, and the next thing, bang, it'd flown into the wing of the aeroplane, and that's where it stuck. As you might imagine, the wind resistance caused by this body being embedded in the wing disrupted the airflow, which in turn caused the aircraft to veer to the right. There was no hope for the poor bird I'm afraid but, luckily, still being in the circuit area, I decided to land back at Kowanyama, which I did safely and much to the relief of everyone on board. A number of photos were then taken of this magnificent bird, which had a wing-span of over 8 feet.

But of course not all the things that happened were caused by external influences. Some disasters happened on board. Such an event I remember only too well. We were called to Killarney Station, in the centre of Cape York, to evacuate a seventeen-year-old who'd broken his ankle while riding a motor bike. It turned out that the lad was the nephew of the owners and was out there holidaying from town. And this young 'townie' had primed himself to the absolute for his 'bush holiday' by giving his image a complete 'manly' overhaul. Oh, this lad was dressed in all his new, and obviously expensive, gear, which was obviously much prized by the lad; you know, the flash RM Williams riding boots, the moleskin trousers, the checked bush shirt, the lot.

Anyhow, after we arrived the doctor wanted to examine the broken ankle. But because of the swelling they were unable to remove the boot so they had to cut off the expensive RMs. That was the first dent to the lad's new, and expensive, image. Then after his RMs had been cut off, the doctor wanted to get a decent look at the other injuries, so then the precious trousers were cut off. Apart from being in considerable pain the patient was now also severely distressed at realising that this 'manly' image of his was being slowly cut from him and that his 'bush holiday' was coming to a rapid and disastrous end. But more was to follow. Because, amid much screaming, the lad was finally settled onto the stretcher and loaded onto the plane. Then, as we took off for our two-hour flight, the young frightened patient called out, 'I'm gonna shit myself.'

'No, you'll be all right,' replied the extremely patient doctor.

'I won't,' came the loud cry from the lad, as the most shocking smell pervaded the cabin of the aircraft.

'Bush holiday' well and truly over. 'Manly' image completely and utterly destroyed.

Through a Child's Eyes

Now, here's a little ditty for you, and one that's quite cute in its way. It's all to do with how people see things, children in particular. This happened on Killarney Station, which is somewhat north of the Pinnacles, in Queensland, around the Cape York Peninsula region. Now, the people from Killarney Station and the Royal Flying Doctor Service in Queensland had just arranged for the RFDS to begin flying in there on a regular basis to run medical clinics. So, of course, we'd never been to Killarney before. Anyway, we'd arranged that our aircraft was to come into the station, I think it was at something like ten o'clock in the morning, on such-and-such a day.

Anyhow, all during the day before we were due to fly out there, and even more so as it got towards nightfall, the family from Killarney were getting pretty excited about our arrival, especially the daughter, who was a young girl of about eleven years of age. So, as the day progressed into night her excitement about the grand occasion built to such an extent that she was almost beside herself. If you could imagine, it was a bit like the grand anticipation of Father Christmas coming the next day. She was forever asking her parents, 'When's the Flying Doctor coming?' and 'How long will it be before the Flying Doctor gets here?'

Now, how they finally got the girl to bed on the night before our arrival, I don't know. And I don't think she even slept a wink. That's how excited she was at the prospect of seeing the Flying Doctor arrive. Then she was up and dressed at about six o'clock the next morning, and wanting to go down to the airstrip.

'Look,' her mother said, 'just leave it a while.'

Anyway, the young girl left it to about eight o'clock, until she could wait no longer, and so then she wandered down to the airstrip by herself, there to stand gazing up into the skies. At about 9.45 am the mother came down to join her. And the little girl, you know, by this stage she could hardly control herself at the prospect of the Flying Doctor arriving. It was just beyond her.

So the mother and the daughter, there they are, the seconds ticking by and they're looking into the heavens in great anticipation. Then as ten o'clock approached they see this tiny, little speck in the sky and, just at the sight of this speck, this little girl's eyes are becoming the size of saucers. She's just so excited. 'Look, Mummy. Look, Mummy,' she calls, 'it's the Flying Doctor.'

Then as this little speck gradually gets larger and larger and the aeroplane comes more clearly into sight, the little girl's mouth falls open and she looks at her mother in great disgust and disbelief and she grumbles, 'That's not the Flying Doctor, Mummy. It can't be. That's just an ordinary old aeroplane.'

And so, in her childlike imagination, this little girl truly believed that the Flying Doctor was a real doctor, with wings and all, who was going to fly into Killarney Station. And of course Howard William Steer, the great artist of Broken Hill, always paints the Flying Doctor that way: depicting a person, with wings attached, flying through the sky, holding the doctor's bag.

Too Close

I've been with the Flying Doctor Service for nineteen years now and, even still, it's very difficult at times to separate the nurse part of you from the heart and soul person. I guess a good example of that would be when there was a big bus accident out of Coober Pedy, the opal mining place up in the north of South Australia. A group of kids were on a school excursion from Melbourne and about thirty or forty of them were taken to Coober Pedy which, of course, overwhelmed their hospital's resources. Now, I'm not sure just how many injured kids we ended up ferrying out to Adelaide, but we had three aeroplanes working up there. They even flew a plane over from Broken Hill to help out on that one, too. So, it was a big accident.

But in cases like that you always feel for the parents, because no matter how hard you try, sometimes you just can't neglect the mother inside you. And the thing that got to me was that these Melbourne kids were the same age as my own children. And there they were, they'd gone off on a fun school holiday, like most kids do, but, yeah, they ended up in an horrific accident like that. Oh, there were a lot of routine injuries but there were also a few really critically serious ones as well.

So yeah, it took me a long time to come to terms with that. Though an odd thing happened about that accident because some years later, after we'd moved down to Adelaide, I did an interview for a local newspaper and during that interview they asked me, 'What's been the worst thing you've ever been involved in?' So I mentioned that accident, out at Coober Pedy, and I told them why. Then the night after the newspaper article came out there was a knock on my front door and it was the young lady who owned the house across the road from us.

'Guess what?' she said. 'I was one of the kids who were involved in that bus accident.'

So yeah, that was great, because she told me how some of them had got on and what they were doing, further down the track. So you never know, do you? She was a virtual stranger, just someone you'd say 'hello' to in the street or whatever, and she turned out to be one of the kids we helped that particular night out at Coober Pedy.

But no, to be honest, you don't always survive emotionally intact. Sometimes you're just too close to it all and you get very hurt. Really, one of the reasons I left Port Augusta was that I was starting to pick up people I knew. Some I'd even known when they were babies and I'd seen them grow up, and that was devastating because sometimes they'd suffered indescribable injuries and sometimes they were even killed. So, yes, it became hard, very hard.

Another accident that I found quite emotionally difficult started out when we were on our way up to Mintabie one time. Originally that was for a routine pick-up so we didn't have a doctor with us, because on the more straightforward trips like that you don't need one. So there was just the pilot and myself and we were diverted to Oodnadatta, which is north of Coober Pedy. There'd been a vehicle roll over involving eight people and they were being brought into town by locals, just as we landed. Anyhow, it turned out to be a family that both my husband and I knew very well. Some had even been at school with our children.

But what made it even more difficult was that, other than having to deal with the emotions of knowing these people, basically, to start with there was just myself and two other nurses, plus a man and a woman from Oodnadatta, to attend to these eight people. And a number of them were critically injured and one died before any other help arrived.

Anyhow, we worked on these people for three hours before a retrieval team got in Oodnadatta. The retrieval doctor on that occasion was Fred Gilligan. Fred was lovely. He was just wonderful. As it transpires he went on to be a board member of the RFDS. Yeah, he's just a darling. I fell in love with him that night.

But as you might be able to imagine, with only the three of us there to start with, trying to deal with eight critical patients, stuck out in the bush in a small 'cottage-hospital' well, we were under a huge amount of stress and pressure. We had no X-rays, we had nothing, and we were trying to do the very best we possibly could. So you couldn't really expect us to give the same care as a large city hospital would.

But obviously that's what they expected down in Adelaide. Because after we'd got to the Royal Adelaide Hospital and handed our patients over, I walked outside and discovered that some of the paperwork or something was still in my pocket. Of course, you wouldn't do that these days. But anyway, when I went back to hand it in, one of the Adelaide doctors was going on to Fred Gilligan about the level of care that the patients had received, pre-hospital. And, on top of everything else, what with knowing these people and working under almost impossible conditions, that really hurt, you know. Really hurt.

But Fred stuck up for us. He told them straight out, 'You just have no idea what you're talking about. This was an absolutely horrific accident and those people were working in the most unbelievably difficult conditions.'

So I just thought, 'Good on you, Fred. I love you. At least you understand what it's like.'

Watch What You Say

Just off the bat, I tell you what: you've got to be very, very careful what you say when you're around people who are unconscious, because they can recall things. It's like when someone's in a coma. The best thing to do is to just sit there and chat away to them because quite often, on some subconscious level or other, they can hear you. In cases like that, it's beneficial to the patient. Then, of course, within the Flying Doctor Service there's the other side to it where, particularly if there's been an accident or if there's a fatality where a child is involved, you just don't talk about it anywhere around anyone who's unconscious, especially if it happens to be the parents.

But one, which was a bit of a scream, was when a pilot of ours was doing a retrieval out of Peterborough, in central South Australia. It could've been a road accident, though I'm not sure. But it was out of the old Peterborough airstrip and he was flying the Chieftain and by the time they were ready to take off, he had quite a load. You know, on a trip like that there's not only the retrieval team and the patient but they also carry a lot of extra gear.

Anyhow, the patient was unconscious and because the pilot had so much weight on board, even though he'd done all his calculations, he was still just a little concerned that he didn't have quite enough airstrip to take off. Like, he was sure but not quite 110 per cent sure, if you catch my meaning. And so as he was starting to roll down the runway, this pilot turned back to the retrieval team and he remarked, pretty much tongue-in-cheek, 'When I yell out, I want you all to take a deep breath so I can get this thing airborne.'

Anyway, later on in hospital, when the patient gained consciousness, some part of him remembered that remark. And when he made enquiries he was told that, yes, in fact the Peterborough airstrip wasn't the most suitable for a retrieval like that and the Flying Doctor Service had mentioned the situation to the authorities, and his particular case was mentioned. Then, after he recovered, he was so grateful to the RFDS that he was the one who instigated the airstrip being moved to a better location and he was also the one responsible for it getting lengthened. I think the old one used to be north-east of Peterborough, out near the meatworks, and the new one's to the south of Peterborough. So that was one of the rare cases where the spoken word around an unconscious patient actually did do some good.

Then I had an incident with a nurse once. It didn't turn out funny, but I thought it was at the moment, though maybe that's just because of my odd sense of 'pilot's' humour. I went to Kadina one time with a nurse. It was in the Chieftain again. So we took off, then, because I couldn't get the green light to come on to give the okay that all was right with the main undercarriage, I decided to return to Adelaide. Really, in a situation like that, in your mind you're fully convinced that it's simply a micro-switch fault. But of course if the worst came to the worst and we did have undercarriage problems, well, it was best to come back to Adelaide and land, because Adelaide Airport has all the fire facilities and the emergency services and so forth.

Anyhow, as we were coming back to Adelaide, coming in to land on runway one and two, from the Gulf, I briefed the nurse on the evacuation of the aircraft. See, as the pilot, it's your job to calm everyone down so they can deal with the emergency. Then, once they're calm, you can go about briefing yourself so that you're also better able to deal with the situation.

But anyway, this nurse kept on asking me question after question and I was getting to the stage where I could hardly think myself. Then as we were coming in on final landing and we were getting in on short-final landing, she said, 'What's the worst that could possibly happen here?'

By this time I was getting a little bit sick of all these queries so I replied in a more or less flippant manner, 'Well, the worst thing that could happen is that we crash and burn.'

She just fell into complete silence then and I didn't think any more about it because I was concentrating on the job at hand. So we landed and everything went okay and I taxied back to the hangar and went and spoke to the engineers about the problem. After I'd finished doing that, another pilot came up to me and said, 'What did you do, or say, to the nurse? She's down in the back room in tears.'

And I said, 'Oh God, sorry. I know what it is. I told her that we were going to "crash and burn".'

So I had to go down and console her about it. But, you see, I said it straight off the bat. As a pilot, during your training you're taught to focus in an emergency and delete any of those unnecessary peripheral interferences. So it meant nothing to me, you know, but she asked the question and in the worst case scenario that was the worst thing that could possibly happen— that we would 'crash and burn'. I mean, naturally you don't want that to happen. But, anyway, that's what I said and she took it very seriously.

So you do have to be careful what you say around people, even if they are conscious. And, off the top of my head, that's all I can think of at the moment.

West of the Cooper

There was an old grazier; for the sake of the story we'll call him Arthur. Well, old Arthur lived out west of the Cooper, around the border area of south-western Queensland and north-eastern South Australia. The name of the station just escapes me for the moment so we'll just stick with 'west of the Cooper'.

Now, what you've got to realise here is that a lot of these old fellers who live out in those remote parts of this wide brown land of ours have probably never been out of the bush. So you can imagine that some of them are probably not quite as academically educated as some of us. In fact, some of them can't even read or write. Mind you, that doesn't make them any less of a person. It's just the way it is.

But old Arthur had a cardiac condition and he needed to go and see a specialist, so I gave him a referral to go and see a specialist in Brisbane. Brisbane was the town of his choice. It wasn't an emergency or anything, it was just routine, so he got on a commercial flight from Windorah and headed off to Brisbane. It was all a new experience for him because, firstly, I don't think he'd ever been on a commercial aeroplane before and, secondly, to my recollection, he'd never been to Brisbane.

When the specialist saw old Arthur, he reckoned that there wasn't much more to be done other than what I'd already recommended he do. That was reassuring to me. But a few weeks later the specialist sent Arthur an account and on the account you've got the Medicare item number which was, we'll say for argument's sake, 'Item number seventy-six'.

Anyway, when old Arthur looked at this account, he couldn't make head nor tail of it. But he did see this number seventy-six. And you know how all the drugs in the RFDS medical chest are labelled by numbers, well, when old Arthur saw this number seventy-six he thought, 'Well, that specialist feller must want me to take number seventy-six out of the RFDS medical kit.'

Then when I was out there, the next month, I saw old Arthur and he said to me, 'Gees,' doctor,' he said, 'that number seventy-six didn't do me a scrap of good.'

'What do you mean?' I said.

'Well,' he said, 'look here: on my account it's got number seventy-six.'

And that's when I discovered that old Arthur had, in actual fact, mixed up the Medicare number with the item number in the RFDS medical kit and had been taking some sort of anti-fungal medication.

The next story also comes from out west of the Cooper.

I got a call one evening—it was after last light—to go out to South Galway Station. One of the ringers there was in some sort of strife. So, you know, we asked them to put out their flares and one thing and another and I told them that we'd be in touch with an ETA (estimated time of arrival) as soon as we got in the air. There was the pilot, a nurse and myself.

Then, when we called through to South Galway Station with the ETA, they told us that there were severe thunderstorms in the area. Now, thunderstorms are a real hazard to flying. First, they can create incredible turbulence. Second, with these being dirt airstrips, they can turn to mud in an instant.

Anyway, the pilot said, 'Oh well, we'll just continue on and see what happens.'

So we continued on. But then just as we arrived over South Galway Station so did the thunderstorm. Oh, it was blowing a beauty and it was raining like crazy. This, in turn, caused most of the flares, which they'd lit for us along the runway, to be either blown out or doused in the rain—one or the other. But fortunately the pilot knew the strip quite well and he reckoned that by using the flashes of lightning as a guide, he could see just enough of the airstrip to land the aeroplane. And that's what he did: he put the plane down on the strip by using the flashes of lightning, along with the few flares that still remained alight. Some of these pilots do amazing things, and that was just one of them.

Anyhow, luckily for us they'd already brought the injured ringer out to the strip, which saved precious time. But even still, with it now raining cats and dogs and the dirt strip rapidly turning greasy, I quickly assessed the situation and decided that if I didn't open the door, put the injured ringer on board, quickly tie him down, shut the door again and get out of there, we'd end up being stuck on the strip— bogged. All patients in stretchers have to be tied down. It's procedure.

So we did that. We loaded this ringer as quickly as we could. Then we tied him down in the stretcher, shut the door, and I told the pilot to get going, which he did, and we took off safely.

But, of course, with this thunderstorm going on all around us, the turbulence was something incredible.

As I assessed the patient, we were being tossed around like anything. So I thought, Well, the first thing I need to get into him is an intravenous cannula and a drip.

So I put a tourniquet on him and I literally threw the cannula into his arm like a dart, sort of thing, and it happened to hit a vein. Then I looked over at my nurse, fully expecting her to pass me the drip set, only to find that she had her head stuck in a sick bag. Well, it was all too much for me and I then also had to grab a bag. So there I was, being tossed around in the turbulence, while trying to keep a bag over my face, with one hand holding the drip into the ringer's arm and the other hand trying to put the giving-set into the drip.

And that's when the ringer looked up at us and he said, 'I think I'm probably the best of all of yer.'

What If

We used the Flying Doctor Service in 1980 when my daughter, Megan, got bitten by a redback spider. At the time we were caretaking out at Mount Barnett Station, in the Kimberley area of Western Australia, while the owners went away for holidays over the wet season. Megan was about six years old, in Year One. Her dad, Colin, was playing guitar and she was sitting on a cyclone bed. You know those old cyclone beds, the pipe ones with the hollow legs with the wire mesh on top. Well, Megan was sitting on one of those and she said, 'Daddy, something just bit me.'

Then, when Colin looked down the hollow pipe, he saw a redback spider sitting in there. So we called the Flying Doctor. That was at about one o'clock and they said they'd attempt to get there by three o'clock. In the meantime, of course, we had to try and keep Megan calm and also try and keep ourselves calm.

Anyhow, with it being the wet season, the river was in full flood and the airstrip was on the other side of the river from where the homestead was. So then Colin and I, we had to row Megan across the flooded river in a little dinghy. The distance was probably, oh, a couple of hundred yards or so; you know, from about here, where I'm sitting, right over there to the corner of the road. Yes, that'd make it about 200 yards or so, and when we finally got to the airstrip there was a new doctor on the plane. The funny part about that was— and, mind you, it wasn't too funny at the time—when we got on the plane, there he was, this doctor, busily looking up some book or other trying to find out what you're supposed to do with someone who'd been bitten by a redback spider.

And I thought, 'Oh, this looks real good, this does.'

But that was the thing in those days with the RFDS because back in 1980 they didn't have their own doctors. Back then, the Flying Doctor Service was using the local hospital doctors. And you get a lot of turnover up in the Kimberley and the frustration with that was that, when a new doctor arrived, quite often they wouldn't be familiar with RFDS procedure and, for that matter, a lot of them weren't even familiar with the contents of the RFDS medical chest. You know, what number equates to what medicine you're supposed to take for whatever the ailment or problem you have. Worse still, if these doctors had just graduated from Perth or wherever they probably didn't even know that the RFDS medical chest existed, if you know what I mean.

Anyhow, I must say that it was a great relief to have the plane arrive and take us back to Derby. But Megan wasn't given anything until we got into hospital. Even then she had to wait because it wasn't until six o'clock that another doctor came in and said, 'Has she been given the anti-venom yet?'

'What're you talking about?' I asked.

'Oh,' he said, 'if it was my kid, she'd be given the anti-venom straight away.'

'Okay then,' I thought, 'if it's a doctor saying that, surely they'll do it soon.'

But still nothing, and Megan was just left to lie there in the hospital bed. And though she wasn't all that sick, you could see the bite mark and her leg had become quite swollen. But I didn't know anything about spider bites. I didn't know how sick she was supposed to be.

Anyway, this all happened just before the people we were caretaking for at Mount Barnett Station—John and Bronwyn Tiddy—were going to go back out there. So they were in Derby and John Tiddy came into the hospital and I remember the nurse suddenly appearing with the first injection. And Megan, all her life she just hated injections. Oh, she just hated injections.

Then the nurse held up the needle and said, as easy going as anything, 'We're just going to give you this for pain.'

And John Tiddy knew all about Megan's hatred of needles and you could see that he was just about to have a go at the nurse, because, you know, Megan hadn't been given any warnings that she was even going to have a needle. Anyhow, the nurse went ahead and gave Megan the needle for the pain. Then, just when Megan was starting to get over the trauma of that, they came back in and said they had to give her a few more test shots for the anti-venom. In the end, I think they gave her three needles all up. And each time the nurse came back brandishing a needle, Megan was getting more and more upset and John Tiddy's getting madder and madder.

And, well, the reason why John was the only male there with me was because Colin was still out at Mount Barnett. They couldn't take Colin on the plane because they didn't have enough room for him. They only took me and Megan. And that was quite funny too, actually, because I found out later that after we'd flown out, when Colin had started rowing back to the homestead the dinghy got caught in a whirlpool or something and he ended up being taken a fair way down the river before he could get himself onto land again. And when he finally managed to do that, he had to walk all the way back to the homestead. So there was another drama going on.

Anyway, they gave Megan the anti-venom and everything and then of course from that day on she had to wear a Medic-Alert bracelet. See, back in those days the anti-venom was given in a horse serum base and she had to wear the bracelet to alert everyone that if she was bitten again and had to have a second dose of the anti-venom, they had to watch her very carefully because the second dose could well bring on an anaphylactic reaction. An anaphylactic reaction is a full-on, life-threatening allergic reaction where, you know, you start swelling up and you can't breathe and all that sort of stuff. It's like having a heart attack. Of course, these days all the anti-venom's given in synthetic bases so Megan doesn't have to worry about that any more.

So, you know, for all the fuss and worry that it caused later, I really think that Megan would have probably been better off not having the anti-venom. We discovered afterwards that she was most probably bitten by the less venomous male redback because she didn't end up getting the full-blown symptoms of a spider bite, you know, with the vomiting and the heavy sweating and all that sort of stuff. Megan only had a swollen leg and a tiny red area around the bite. So in fact she didn't really need the injections or the anti-venom or anything like that.

Then, of course, after she was injected with the anti-venom in a horse serum base it caused us a lot of anxiety because we were always worried about what would happen if she got bitten by something again and she had to have another anti-venom injection. You know, whether she'd have an anaphylactic reaction and all that. So it was all very scary because living in that country you always think, 'God, what if she's bitten by an extremely venomous snake like a king brown and she has to go through it all again?' So that's the end of that story.

Glory, Glory—
The Flying Doctor Song

Verse 1

A ringer lay dying out in a stock camp
Thrown from his horse and trampled about
In a feverish haze and in sickening pain
He raises his head and then he says

Chorus

Glory, Glory what can it be
There's a sound up on high that only angels can see
Glory, Glory what can it be
The Flying Doctor is coming for me

Verse 2

A child is lost a long way from home
Out in the distance water forms
So she walks and she walks till she stumbles and falls
Then she raises her head ... and she calls

Chorus

Glory, Glory what can it be
There's a sound up on high that only angels can see
Glory, Glory what can it be
The Flying Doctor is coming for me

Bridge

In the footsteps of Flynn these women and men
Give of themselves our faith in their hands
Come every day they're working to spread
A Mantle of Safety across this wide land

Chorus

Glory, Glory what can it be
There's a sound up on high that only angels can see
Glory, Glory what can it be
The Flying Doctor is coming for me

Verse 3

Out from the Alice a lady moans
Heavy with child and on her own
No chance could there be that the baby be saved
So she raises her head and she prays

Chorus

Glory, Glory what can it be
There's a sound up on high that only angels can see
Glory, Glory what can it be
The Flying Doctor is coming for me

The RFDS Today

The Royal Flying Doctor Service of Australia (RFDS) is a not-for-profit charitable organisation that provides free aero-medical emergency and comprehensive healthcare services to people who live, work and travel in regional and remote Australia.

RFDS statistics for the year ended 30 June 2009:
- Service area—7 150 000 km².
- Patients attended—274 237 (daily average—751). That figure includes patients at clinics, patients transported, immunisations and telehealth.
- Aero-medical evacuations—36 832 (daily average 101). That figure includes interhospital transfers.
- Healthcare clinics—14 004 (daily average 38).
- Distance flown—23 923 440 kilometres (daily average 65 544 kilometres).
- Number of landings—71 770 (daily average 197).
- Telehealth—85 290 (daily average 234).
- Number of aircraft—53.
- RFDS bases—21. A RFDS base is a health facility that houses an aircraft and provides health services.
- RFDS Health Facilities—5. A RFDS Health Facility is a health facility that does not have an aircraft but provides health services.

- Other facilities—10.* Other facilities include marketing, fundraising and public relations as well as the National Office.
- Staff—964. That figure includes 297 part-time and casual staff.

*Source—Royal Flying Doctor Service website.

How You Can Help

The RFDS relies on generous contributions from individuals, community groups, business and the corporate sector as well as funding provided by the Commonwealth, state and territory governments to help meet the costs associated with running a twenty-four-hour emergency and comprehensive healthcare service.

The RFDS relies on your help to:

- Buy vital medical equipment
- Purchase and outfit aircraft (at a cost of more than $8 million each)
- Develop a range of outback and rural health initiatives.

There are many ways in which you, your workplace, community group or school can help the Flying Doctor. By raising money and awareness about the work of the RFDS, you are helping to save lives.

To help our service and save lives in the outback you can:

- Donate online at www.flyingdoctor.net
- Become an RFDS supporter
- Leave a bequest
- Fundraise for the RFDS
- Join an RFDS Workplace Giving initiative
- Volunteer your time or expertise
- Organise an RFDS speaker
- Offer corporate support

- Make a purchase through our online shop
- Send a cheque (made payable to the Royal Flying Doctor Service of Australia) to:
    Australian Council of the RFDS
    Level 8, 15–17 Young Street
    Sydney NSW 2000
- Phone the RFDS on 1300 669 569 or 1800 467 435

All donations of $2 and above are tax deductible.